BISON
BOOKS

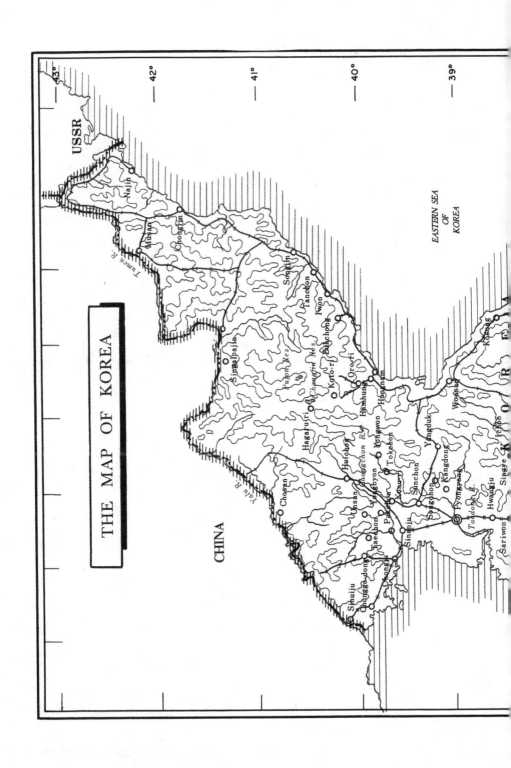

THE MAP OF KOREA

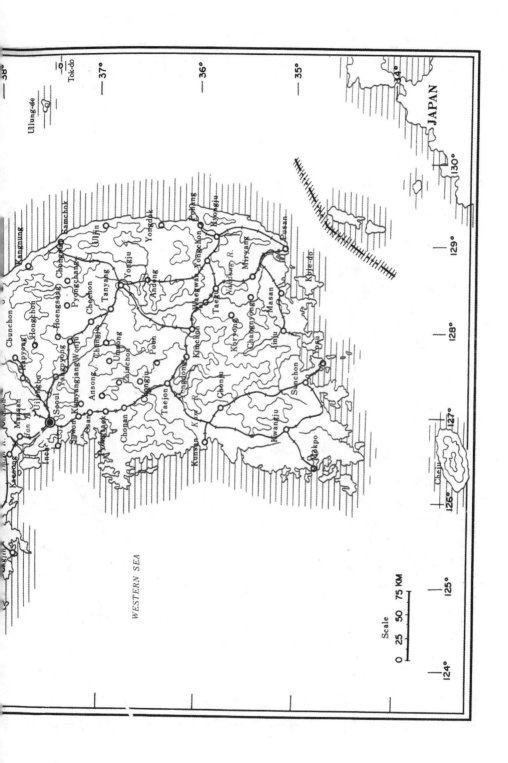

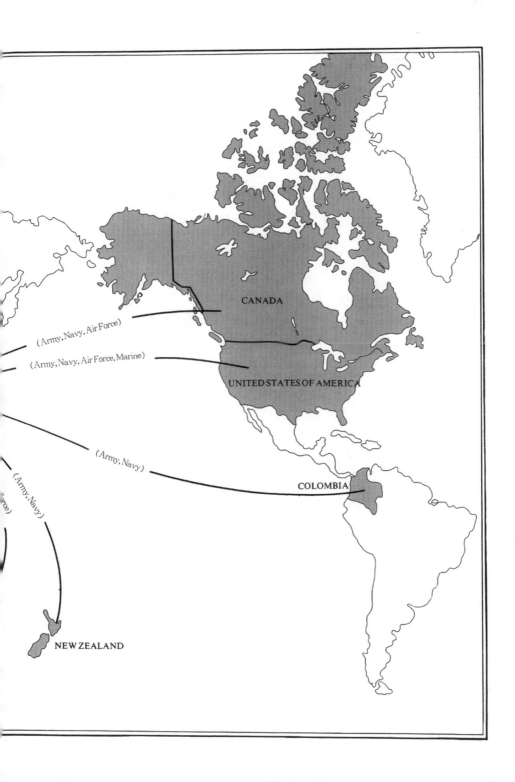

THE KOREAN WAR

VOLUME 1

KOREA INSTITUTE OF MILITARY HISTORY

INTRODUCTION TO THE BISON BOOKS EDITION BY
Allan R. Millett

UNIVERSITY OF NEBRASKA PRESS
LINCOLN AND LONDON

© 1997 by Korea Institute of Military History
Introduction © 2000 by Allan R. Millett
Photographs courtesy of Korea Institute of Military History
All rights reserved
Manufactured in the United States of America

⊗

First Bison Books printing: 2000
Most recent printing indicated by the last digit below:
10   9   8   7   6   5   4   3   2   1

Library of Congress Cataloging-in-Publication Data
The Korean War / Korea Institute of Military History; introduction to the Bison
Books edition by Allan R. Millett—Bison Books ed.
p.   cm.
Originally published: Seoul, Korea: Korea Institute of Military History, 1997.
Includes bibliographical references.
ISBN 0-8032-7794-6 (pbk.: v. 1: alk. paper)
1. Korean War, 1950–1953—Campaigns.   I. Korea Institute of Military History.
DS918 .K5636   2000
951.904'24—dc21
00-056783

Introduction

Allan R. Millett

While it has become fashionable to call the Korean War "forgotten" in the United States, it is far more accurate to call it "misunderstood." If the histories of the Korean War have not exactly made the bookshelves groan as the volume of literature on World War II and the Vietnam War has, a student of the Korean War can still find ample accounts of American participation in the war, especially the thrill of victories and agonies of defeat experienced by the U.S. Eighth Army. However, when soldiers from the Republic of Korea (ROK) ever wander onto the scene, they are usually limited to depictions of ill-trained and confused "Katusas," or conscripts from the Korean Augmentation to the United States Army (KATUSA) program. Filling gaps in infantry battalions for which the U.S. Army apparently could not find replacements, these South Koreans arrive in and disappear from war accounts in anonymity. When the army of the Republic of Korea (Hangukgun) enters the story, it is almost always as a South Korean division fleeing to the rear in panic. Leaving the gallant American GIs to fight desperately to prevent their own extinction at the hands of the vicious North Koreans and the armed "hordes" of "the Chinese Communist forces," the Korean soldiers rally only at rear-area safe havens. Or so the stories go.

The American official histories of the Korean War do scant justice to the South Korean army, let alone the American officers and men of the Korean Military Advisory Group (KMAG). The KMAG advisors helped create an army in the middle of a guerrilla war (1948–50) and then built, trained, rearmed, and supported a South Korean army adequate to defend the Demilitarized Zone (DMZ) after the armistice of July 1953. The experience was not without its moments of despair. One chief of the KMAG said that it was impossible to underestimate a South Korean division. Anyone who later studied the Vietnam War would wonder how the miserable Korean army of the 1950s could have sent two crack divisions and an elite marine brigade to South Vietnam in the 1960s, all together a force so tough and disciplined that *everyone* gave it a clear berth in the field. The eventual success of the KMAG is part of the war story, but it remains to be told in full yet today.

Of course the South Korean army, in terms of longevity and experience, had a history that went back centuries; it simply did not have that history contained between book covers because the Japanese colonial government (ruling from

1905 to 1945) would hardly have permitted the publication of books about a Korean national army. It had exterminated that army in the early twentieth century as part of the Japanese annexation of Korea. After liberation (August–September, 1945), Koreans on both sides of the 38th Parallel—to the north with the rapacious Russians and to the south with the confused Americans—picked up the arms the Japanese left behind. Although the actual weapons have since been replaced many times by more modern arms, weapons are still in the hands of the In Min Gun (the Army of the Democratic People's Republic of Korea) and the Hangukgun, and they are still pointed at one another. As the South Korean army built itself into a modern force during the 1960s, under the patronage of general-turned-president Park Chung Hee, it also wrote about its past to inspire and harden its people and soldiers against an uncertain and dangerous future.

Writing a history of the army's participation in the Korean War seemed essential to the South Korean generals who dominated national security planning and defense policy in the Park Chung Hee era. But the agenda of the Ministry of Defense's War Compilation Committee was more complicated than the writing of official military history in the United States in the 1960s. Neither Korea nor its army had reached a point of self-confidence and security that would have allowed a systematic, frank examination of the Korean army's operations from 1950 to 1953. Personal reputations and professional issues attached to the war still had significant political meaning. (Americans should recall the controversy attached to the compilation of the *War of the Rebellion Records* [1880–1901] in terms of individual and unit reputations, a controversy allayed in part by the commercial publication of *Battles and Leaders of the Civil War* [1884–88], a multivolume account of the Civil War written by the surviving senior commanders of both the Union and Confederate armies and their principal staff officers.) In any event, the War Compilation Committee sponsored an eleven-volume official history of the war, the *Hanguk Chonchaengsa* (*Korean War History*), published from 1967 to 1977. This history was never available in English, thus it seldom influenced American writing on the Korean War because the American scholars most likely to read Korean—and Chinese (also necessary)—were too anti-Park and too anti–Korean War to accept any history written by members of the Korean army and sponsored by the Park regime. Korean scholars, both uniformed and civilian, knew under what circumstances the volumes had been written. They also had often read American documents about their army in the United States archives. They knew that the *Hanguk Chonchaengsa* was uneven and incomplete because of its gentle treatment of Korean and American operational and leadership failures.

The liberalization of South Korean politics and a new openness about Korean military policy in the 1990s made it possible for Korean scholars—most of whom were army officers, either serving or retired, with degrees from American universities or experience in the Korean diplomatic service—to consider a revision of the *Hanguk Chonchaengsa*. The War Compilation Committee had given way to a better organized, stable Korea Institute of Military History (KIMH), sponsored by the Ministry of Defense and located in the War Memorial at Yongsan, Seoul. In 1990, under the sponsorship of Maj. Gen. Um Sop Il, the organization's director, the Institute started a revision (in Korean) of the *Hanguk Chonchaengsa* and then published the finished volumes from 1995 to 1997. The Institute of Military History established a War History Department, a unit roughly analogous to a combination of the U.S. Army Center of Military History and the U.S. Army Military History Institute. The department included a research library and a documentary archive to support research on the Korean War and other aspects of Korean national security policy. The department also included a staff of professional historians headed by Lt. Col. Chae Han Kook (retired), a serious scholar who could translate Korean into English and who was acutely aware of the limitations of the original *Hanguk Chonchaengsa*. Under his direction, his staff historians wrote the revised version of the *Hanguk Chonchaengsa* while a team of translators led by Ambassador Choi Sang Jin (a retired brigadier general and Ph.D.) and Dr. Cho Sung Kyu (professor emeritus, Department of History, Yonsei University) tackled the problem of preparing an English-language version for limited distribution. From start to finish the translation project took six years. The first of three volumes appeared in 1997, the second in 1999, and the third in 2000.

My own involvement in the translation of the second version of the *Hanguk Chonchaengsa* began in 1997 with an invitation from Professor Cho to examine volume 2. He had been an acquaintance of my family for years and my own friend since 1991, the year I served for four months as a Fulbright Distinguished Visiting Professor at the Korean National Defense College. That experience, subsequent trips to Korea, and my relationship with three graduate students who were officers in the Korean army convinced me that I could write a more comprehensive, insightful account of the Korean War than any other that already existed in English. My limitations in the Korean language—verified by my performance as a student at the Yonsei University Korean Language Institute in 1996—made the prospect of a translated *Hanguk Chonchaengsa* a day of jubilee for me in doing research on the Korean War.

I read the chapters avidly and found myself annotating and rewriting them as I read. I found errors in military usage, awkward word choices and sentence structure, and some errors in explaining the decisions of American commanders as well as in the titles and functions of American military units. Apparently my work made some contribution since Ambassador Choi made me an official volunteer member of the ETS, or English Translators, one of the most able and sociable group of eight colleagues with whom I've ever worked. The ETS already had American anglophones working on the book: two were a retired U.S. Army colonel and his wife and another was an English professor at Yonsei University. I assume my attractiveness to the ETS was that I had previously worked well with Korean colleagues; I had seen many of the battlefields in South Korea; I was a retired colonel of infantry in the U.S. Marine Corps Reserve and knew professional military vocabulary; I had a modest but working knowledge of the difficulty of translating Korean into English (and vice versa) in matters of grammar and vocabulary; I had written five books and other scholarly and popular articles, including pieces on the Korean War; and I had an intense personal interest in having the *Hanguk Chonchaengsa* translated into English. I thus became a consulting editor on military matters and English usage for volumes 2 and 3.

I am pleased that the University of Nebraska Press has taken the risk to publish the English-language version of *The Korean War*, the most significant contribution to date to the literature linked to the war's fiftieth anniversary. The only comparable achievements are the books and articles in English on the Chinese participation in the war, written from Chinese sources by Chinese and Chinese-American scholars, and the publication of Chinese, Russian, and North Korean correspondence, obtained from Russian and Chinese sources, by the Cold War International History Project of the Woodrow Wilson Center in Washington DC.

A major strength of *The Korean War* is that the revised version includes material from these newly available Chinese and Russian sources. Another improvement is the wider use of American archival documents collected for the archives of the War History Department, an ongoing project. This revision is not completely current because it does not include, for example, documentation from the Gen. James A. Van Fleet Papers at George C. Marshall Library, but copies of those papers have been sent to Seoul for future use. The current revision also reflects the new cooperation between the War History Department and the office of the historian of the Combined Forces Command/United Nations Command, which maintains a reference file of Korean War materials and manuscripts and employs an able historian, translator, and liaison officer in Lt. Col. Kim In Hwa, ROKA (retired).

For Americans who think that only GIS and their comrades from the United Nations contingent fought effectively from 1950 to 1953, *The Korean War* will be a surprising introduction to the valor and sacrifice of the South Korean army. Recreating the history of a new, ill-organized, and war-ravaged army is no small challenge. Many of the sources are American or Chinese simply because there was no systematically kept, complete archival collection of South Korean operational reports to rely upon. To draw an American parallel, it would be as if the history of the American Revolution depended upon documentation and analysis provided by the French expeditionary army. In South Korea's case, the Chinese accounts help some, but the Chinese have been reluctant to publish actual documents or allow outside scholars to work in the archives of the Central Military Commission and the General Staff and Political Department of the People's Liberation Army. I have personally experienced this reluctance on two trips to Beijing. Although American forces captured some documents in Pyongyang in October 1950, they do not make up a comprehensive collection nor are they even from the central files within the In Min Gun's operational and political structure. And obviously such documents cover only the opening months of the war.

The story of the Korean army then depends to a large degree on personal narratives and interviews, which are always subject to errors of memory and natural self-congratulation and self-deception. To counteract these biases the Korean historians attempted to collect multiple accounts of the same event and sought out the principal commanders of the actions, many of whom were still alive in the 1990s because they had been such young generals and colonels in the early 1950s. Fifty years later one of the wartime chiefs of staff of the South Korean army, Gen. Paik Sun Yup, is not only alive but is the chairman of the Korean War commemoration commission. General Paik also enjoys a place of preference in Western understanding of the war through the publication of *From Pusan to Panmunjom* (1992), his account of the Korean War drawn from his much longer and interesting memoir *Gun Kwa Na* (*The Army and I*) (1980). General Paik's book opened the door to the first serious consideration of the South Korean army's role in the war, a process that began with the publication of his book in the United States and his subsequent appearance at a Korean War history conference at the U.S. Air Force Academy in 1992. With the publication of *The Korean War* in a format appealing to the general reader, the University of Nebraska Press and I hope that the reappraisal of the South Korean army's participation in the war will continue from a much firmer base of evidence.

What can a reader find in these volumes that might reshape one's perceptions of the conduct of the Korean War? First, volume 1 shows that the army that lost Seoul and the Han River valley in June 1950 rallied to play a major role in the desperate defense of the "Pusan Perimeter," the United Nations Command (UNC) bridgehead maintained for the counteroffensive of September 1950. Americans should learn about the battle of Pohang, in which Korean soldiers and student volunteers died by the thousands to hold the northeastern hinge of the UNC position. They might appreciate the Battle of Tabudong, in which General Paik's First Division (a reborn amalgamation of three divisions ruined in the defense of Seoul) rallied in concert with the U.S. Twenty-seventh Infantry Regiment to close the door to Taegu to a North Korean armored force. Although South Korean officers of all ranks made mistakes of catastrophic consequences in many actions, one might see how American corps commanders seldom provided ample fire or logistics support to their Korean divisions, while Korean corps received even less help from the Eighth Army until Gen. James A. Van Fleet became the senior American field commander in April 1951. Few Americans—even soldiers and historians—know that a Korean division during 1950 to 1953 had only one (not four) field artillery battalions. These lone divisional artillery battalions started the war with models of the 75mm and 105mm howitzers designed for airborne operations, and they had a range half that of the standard Russian field guns employed by the North Korean army.

Volumes 2 and 3 will tell the painful story of the Chinese intervention, the seesaw war of November 1950 to October 1951 and the geographically stalemated war of 1952–53. Even Americans reasonably interested in the Korean War know little of the important battles along the Main Line of Resistance (MLR) in the autumn of 1952 and the spring-summer Chinese offensive of 1953, for most of these battles focused upon the South Korean army, selected for destruction by the Chinese high command. The Chinese wanted to split the Korean-American alliance and force the collapse of the government of President Syngman Rhee, which had won few friends with its constitutional legerdemain in the summer of 1952 to keep Rhee as president. It was not President Dwight D. Eisenhower's mild threats of nuclear action that brought an armistice in July 1953 but the ability of the ROK army to rally and hold in the wake of the Kumsong Offensive of the Renmin Zhiyuanjun (Chinese People's Volunteers Force). Americans know about a battle to hold Pork Chop Hill (a company-sized outpost) in 1953, but they know nothing about the massive struggle for White Horse Mountain (October 6–15, 1952), in which the ROK Ninth Division held a nearby hill against the sustained attack of two reinforced Chinese divisions in a battle that rivals Verdun for its intensity and the bloodletting suffered by the engaged Korean and Chinese units. The Battle of Paekmasan, which occurred there, is the Gettysburg of the South Korean army, and today one can ring the Liberation Bell in the DMZ at the spot where the Ninth Division held the MLR. The division patch is a rampant white horse.

Along the massive facade of the War Memorial in Seoul, obsidian plaques— one hundred of them—fill the columns of the Gallery of the Honored War Dead. Each service of the Korean armed forces and the National Police have memorial plaques; the army plaques are further identified by division insignia. For the years 1945 to 1950, a period in which Americans believe there was no Korean War, the plaques honor the 7,235 servicemen and policemen who died in the vicious guerrilla and border war that eventually led to the North Korean army's invasion of June 1950. This attack was a desperate effort to save the insurgency in South Korea and to strike before the South Korean army turned its growing military assistance from the United States into an effective defense along the 38th Parallel. For the "real" war—that is, the war that created the United Nations Command and brought an international expeditionary force of half a million to Korea—the plaques memorialize the 141,113 servicemen and police officers who died between June 25, 1950, and July 27, 1953. Unlike many of the civilians who died on either side of the 38th Parallel in those years of fratricidal slaughter—as victims of Communist political "cleansing" or American air power—the soldiers of the South Korean army died with weapons in their hands and their faces toward the enemy. It was not the first time Korean soldiers had fought each other in civil war nor was it the first time Korean soldiers had faced an army of invaders from China since one of the most honored battles in Korean military history is the victory of General Ilchi Mundok over the Chinese in the battle of Salsu, A.D. 612. *The Korean War* honors the army of the Republic of Korea and restores that army's rightful place in the history of that conflict, as it should be remembered in the United States as well. This three-volume history is a fitting tribute to that beleaguered army and to the American advisors who shared its trials.

Foreword

The Korean War broke out on June 25, 1950, just five years after the liberation of Korea from Japanese colonial rule. The war lasted for three years and a month before the two sides agreed to the cessation of hostilities on July 27, 1953, and the uneasy truce survives to this day.

The Korean War unfolded in the broader context of the Cold War under the US-USSR bipolar system. Triggered by North Korea's southward invasion, the war initially was an intranational conflict between South and North Korea. As the world's two ideologically opposed camps intervened, however, it developed into a full-blown international war involving troops from twenty different nations. Only in a geographical sense was its scope limited to the Korean Peninsula. During the war, the Korean people suffered horrors and tragedies unprecedented in Korea's five-thousand-year history. The Korean War, however, has only replaced the 38th Parallel with what amounts to a cease-fire line, and has failed to provide the Korean people with permanent relief from another fratricidal war.

The War History Compilation Committee of the Ministry of National Defense, forerunner to Korea Institute of Military History, chronicled the history of the Korean War over a ten-year span starting in 1967. The resulting work, in eleven volumes, has made a significant contribution to the study of the Korean War both within the country and abroad. This work, however, was published in limited edition and had such a broad scope that demand for a new, more accessible history of the Korean War has been increasing in recent years.

In response to this interest, Korea Institute of Military History decided to write a new history of the war. While based on the old edition, this work will reflect subsequent findings—in particular, newly declassified documents made available to the public by the countries that participated in the war. The Institute is presently writing a three-volume work with the goal of completing it by the 50th anniversary of the Korean War. Volume 1 examines the background of the war and sketches its development up to the intervention by Communist China. Volume 2 then covers the period up to the opening of the armistice talks, and Volume 3 deals with the conclusion of the war.

The present volume, first in the three-volume series, focuses on the war planning steps taken by North Korea and re-examines our government's early direction of defensive efforts as well as the collective security measures taken by the United Nations. This volume then summarizes by stage and by battle area the subsequent delaying operations, the "stand or die" defense along the Naktong Line, and the full-scale counteroffensive carried out in conjunction with the UN Forces. As for the northward advance into North Korea, this work focuses on the initial decision to advance beyond the 38th parallel, the subsequent occupation of P'yongyang and Wonsan, and the advance up to the Korea-Manchuria border.

I am confident that this new history of the war will contribute to an understanding of the realities of the Korean War. Not only will it demonstrate that "the Korean War was a planned war of aggression by North Korea," but it will also show the will of our people to defend freedom, the direction of the war effort by our government, and the valiant fight by our armed forces. I sincerely hope that this work will offer valuable lessons for national security and defense.

I would take this opportunity, first of all, to pray for those who gave their invaluable lives to the cause of defending freedom and peace of the world, and also to express my deep, profound gratitude to those living soldiers who fought with us side by against Communist aggressors. I also tender my thanks to the nations and their people who came to our aid when we were in trouble.

A number of people have contributed to the development of this work. I am grateful to Professors Yang Hee Wan and Lim Won Hyok at the Korea Military Academy for their immaculate translation of the Korean version into English. I am indebted to US Army(Ret.) Colonel Thomas Lee Sims, his wife Laura Marie Sims and former chief researcher of this Institute, Kim Chong Gu for their revising labour of the English version. The following three people made especially valuable contributions to the development of the book, and I am grateful to them. The Chief of War History Department Chae Han Kook, senior researcher Chung Suk Kyun, and junior researcher Yang Yong Cho collected data, wrote the Korean version, and proofread all or part of the manuscript.

December 31, 1997

Um Sub Il
President
Korea Institute of Military History

Notes

1. Chapters, sections, and subsections are inscribed as the following:
   eg.　Chapter : One, Two, Three⋯
   Section : Roman Numerals(I , II, III, etc.)
   Subsection : Arabic Numerals(1, 2, 3, etc.)

2. Proper names of Korean personalities are inscribed with the family name at the front and the first name at the end.
   eg.　Kim Hong Il
   But there are exceptions for names of established international use.
   eg.　Syngman Rhee

3. Natural features are inscribed with flexibility as follows :
   (1) mountains & hills
   eg.　Pukhan-san or Pukhan Mountain
   P'il-bong or P'il Hill(or Peak)
   But names of established use are exceptions.
   eg. Capitol Hill
   (2) rivers & creeks
   eg.　the Han-gang or the Han River
   the Ian-ch'on or the Ian Creek
   But names of established use are exceptions.
   eg.　the Yalu River
   (3) pass(ryong)
   eg.　Cho-ryong, Cho Pass, or Cho-ryong Pass

4. Administrative units such as 'do', 'shi', 'gun', 'myon', 'ri(ni)', and etc. are not hyphenated.
   eg.　Injegun, Hajinburi
   Ch'ungch'ongnamdo or South Ch'ungch'ong Province

5. Periods after initials are deleted.
   eg.　ROK, UN

Contents

Chapter Three Delaying Action 273

Chapter One   Background of the War

I . Division and Conflict

1. Japanese Invasion and Korean Independence Movement

Before Korea became a target for the colonial powers in the nine-
teenth century, the Korean people had been able to maintain, for over 1,000
years, a single nation-state based on a common linguistic and cultural heritage.
Although the rulers of the "Hermit Kingdom" of Choson (1392-1910) wished to
keep its doors closed to the outside world, they lacked the technological means
to repel foreign powers armed with modern military hardware and capitalist
ideology.

Starting with the Kanghwa-do Treaty with Japan in 1876, Choson had
to switch her foreign policy from a "closed-door" to "open-door" regime and
took its first step toward becoming a full-fledged member of the international
community.

Choson's road to modernization was to be fraught with conflicts both
from within and without, however. Domestically, the proponents of an "open-
door" policy and westernization clashed with the conservatives who wished to
preserve the status quo and keep the borders closed to foreigners. Interna-
tionally, the Ching Dynasty (China) vied with Japan for influence in Choson,
and this Sino-Japanese rivalry shaped the international context of the Mutiny
(Imo Kunran) of 1882 and the Coup d'etat (Kapsin Jongbyun) of 1884 in Choson.
These two critical events consolidated China's position in Choson, and led to

the weakening of Choson's open-door policy and the heightening of nationalistic sentiments among the Korean people.

China thus emerged as the winner in the initial round of the Sino-Japanese conflict which had been unfolding ever since Choson implemented its open-door policy. The regional inter-power conflict over Choson intensified with the passage of time, and the addition of Russia and Britain as powers with some interest in Choson only served to accelerate this trend. While the powers were fighting for the right to control the Korean peninsula, Japan's economic invasion of Choson intensified, and the political situation in Choson grew increasingly chaotic. Staged partly in response to the deepening national crisis, the Tonghak (Eastern learning) Peasant Uprising of 1894 sought to drive out the Japanese and other foreigners and institute a general reform of the Choson society. The Tonghak Uprising was put down by the Ching and Japanese Armies, but it was still a watershed event both in the history of Korea and that of Northeast Asia. By providing the impetus for the Reform of 1894 in Choson, the Tonghak Uprising precipitated the collapse of Choson's feudal system, and by triggering the Sino-Japanese War of 1894, it provided a catalyst for the transformation of the Sino-centric regional order in Northeast Asia.

Emerging victorious from the Sino-Japanese War, Japan increased its influence in Choson, and obtained Liaotung Peninsula from Ching as a territorial concession, only to give it up under pressure from Russia, Germany, and France. After succumbing to the pressure from Western powers, Japan saw the emergence of the pro-Russian faction in the Korean court and a noticeable weakening of its own influence in Korea. Desperate to reverse the political tide in Korea, Japan went so far as to assassinate Queen Min of Korea in 1895. This desperate measure, however, only led to a further weakening of Japanese influence in Korea as King Kojong of Korea escaped to the Russian Legation and formed a new pro-Russian cabinet. Moving out of the Russian Legation in

February 1897, Kojong renamed the country "the Dae Han Empire" and proclaimed to the world that Korea had become an empire, at least in name and
formal structure.

Russia and Japan continued to vie for influence in Korea. The two nations oscillated between confrontation and negotiated settlement, which included, among other solutions, Japan's proposal to partition Korea along the
38th parallel, but their irreconcilable differences eventually led to the outbreak of war. Emerging victorious from the Russo-Japanese War (1904-1905),
Japan, through a series of agreements with Russia, Britain, and the United
States, won recognition of its exclusive rights over Korea. Thus paving the way
to occupy Korea, Japan illegally validated the 1905 Protectorate Treaty over
the protests of the Korean government officials, and completely divested
Korea of its sovereign power to maintain diplomatic relations with foreign
governments. Japan then forced Kojong to relinquish his throne in 1907, and,
on the pretext of a tight budget, dissolved the entire Korean army units.
Japan's plan to occupy Korea came to fruition 3 years later, with the proclamation of the 1910 Annexation Treaty.

As Japan was undermining Choson as a sovereign nation, there were
those who engaged in an armed struggle against Japan by forming "Volunteer
Armies for Justice," or "Righteous Armies." From 1895 on, the Yangban
(Korean literati) class, together with peasants, servants, and ex-soldiers, put up
active resistance against the well-equipped Japanese Army. However, by the
time the Annexation Treaty of 1910 was forced upon the Korean people,
Japan's heavy-handed suppression of the armed struggle had made it virtually
impossible for the Righteous Armies to continue their fight within Korea.
Turning their eyes toward Manchuria and the Russian Maritime Territory
where there were sizable Korean communities, the leaders of these armies
shifted their bases to the north, and dauntlessly continued their armed struggle

against Japan as independence fighters. It was here that Korean independence armies were to be born within a decade.

As the center stage for the anti-Japanese guerrilla warfare moved to the north of the Korean Peninsula, independence struggle within Korea's borders increasingly took the form of the Patriotic Enlightenment Movement. Also, to a limited extent, secret societies such as Doklip [Dong-nip] Uigun Bu (the Righteous Army Command for Independence) took the place of the Righteous Armies.

As the 1910s were drawing to a close, Korea's struggle for independence was intensifying both within and beyond its borders. It was at this time that US President Woodrow Wilson's advocation of the principle of "self-determination" raised the expectations of the Korean people. Proposed as a basis for the establishment of a new order after World War I (1914-1917), the principle of self-determination seemed to provide a rationale for occupied nations to pursue with renewed hope independence from the colonial powers. The Korean people felt that this new trend in international politics provided them with a golden opportunity to seek independence from Japan. It was around this time that the Korean people heard the news of the mysterious poisoning death of Emperor Kojong. Enraged by the probable assassination of Kojong at Japanese hands, the Korean people of all classes and ages participated in a non-violent independence movement which swept across the country in 1919.

The nationwide Samil Undong (March First Movement) was ruthlessly put down by Japan, but it provided the impetus for the leaders of the Korean independence movement to establish the Provisional Government of the Republic of Korea. The establishment of the Provisional Government in Shanghai ushered in a new chapter in Korea's independence movement by enabling the leaders to continue their struggle in a much more systematic and coordinated way.

The situation within Korea's borders looked bleak. Although the June 10 Independence Demonstration of 1926 and the Kwangju Student Movement of 1929 clearly demonstrated that the brutal suppression of the March First Movement had not put an end to the Korean people's desire for national independence, the unarmed demonstrators were no match for the well-equipped Japanese Army.

Thus, it was only natural that the most active component of Korea's struggle for independence during this period would be provided by independence armies operating outside the Korean Peninsula. In particular, many independence army units in Manchuria contributed a great deal to the independence movement by directly engaging the Japanese Army.

Among the most active independence armies were the Northern Route Military Command under the leadership of Kim Choa Jin, the Western Route Military Command under the direction of the Provisional Government, and the Korean Independence Army under the command of Hong Pom Do. Resorting to guerrilla tactics, these independence armies attacked Japanese units and police both in Manchuria and the Korea-Manchuria border areas. Two of their most spectacular victories were achieved in 1920 at the Battles of Pongodong [Feng-wu-tung] and Ch'ongsanri [Ch'ing-shan-li]. In order to get away from the vengeful Japanese Army which massacred many innocent Korean young men in retaliation for these battles, the main elements of the independence armies moved to the Soviet Union, but suffered heavy losses in the Free City Incident of 1921 when the Red Army attacked Korean independence fighters who refused to allow themselves to be disarmed. Thus betrayed by the self-claimed champion of national liberation movement, the much weakened remaining units returned to Manchuria to form the core of the Chung ui (Justice), Cham ui (Participation), and Shinmin (New People's) Armies. These three armies later became the cornerstone of the Korean Independence Army and the Choson Revolutionary Army.

After the Manchurian Incident of 1931, the Korean Independence Army allied with the National Salvation Army delivered a devastating blow against the Japanese and Manchurian Armies in many battles such as the Battle of Shulan.[1]

As Japan consolidated its position in Manchuria, however, the Korean Independence Army began to lose its base, and had to assemble around the Korean Provisional Government and seek time to rebuild. After negotiating with China, the Provisional Government established the Korean Restoration Army on September 17, 1940. The command post was located in Sian. Lee Ch'ong Ch'on assumed the overall command, and Lee Pom Sok took the Chief of Staff post.

While the Korean people were redoubling their efforts to gain independence, Japan, deluded by the grandiose vision of the Asian continent under its domination, started the Sino-Japanese War of 1937, and, as a member of the Axis Powers, launched a surprise air strike on Pearl Harbor in December 1941. Japan's attack against the United States marked the expansion of World War II into the Pacific theater. In order to supply the personnel and materiel for the war, Japan conscripted young Korean men into the Japanese Army and plundered the countryside for rice and other resources. Japan's wartime policy pushed the Korean people to the limits of their endurance, but their struggle for independence continued. The Korean Provisional Government formally declared war against Japan on December 9, 1941, and conducted anti-Japan campaigns in concert with the Allied Forces. In particular, from 1942 on, the Korean Restoration Army conducted combined operations with the Chinese in accordance with an agreement reached with China. Also, after signing a military agreement with Britain in June 1943, the Korean provisional government sent units of the Restoration Army to the Burma-India theater to assist in propaganda campaigns, POW questioning, and reconnaissance missions.

The long reign of the treacherous Japanese colonial regime and the travails of the struggle for independence, however, had produced a sizable pro-Japanese faction in Korea, and the increasing penetration of Communism was leading to a conflict between nationalists and Communists to whom the ideology, rather than the nation, was of paramount importance. These seeds of division unfortunately would later grow into a confrontation which would tear apart the fabric of the nation, and the hope of achieving national harmony upon independence would be dashed.

2. Wartime Allied Conferences and the Liberation of Korea

While the Korean people continued their bloody struggle for independence, the US involvement in World War II had turned the tide of the war against the Axis powers. Realizing its enormous military potential through wartime mobilization, the United States, aided by the other Allied Powers and national liberation armies, achieved a series of victories both in the European and the Pacific theaters. With Italy's unconditional surrender in June 1943 and the Allied Forces now poised to launch a decisive all-out offensive, the Allied Powers began to discuss the final settlement of the war and, as part of their discussion on Japanese occupied territories, they touched on the issue of Korea's independence.

First among the Allied Conferences to discuss the Korean problem in some depth was the Cairo Conference (November 22–25, 1943) attended by President Franklin D. Roosevelt of the United States, Prime Minister Winston S. Churchill of Britain, and Generalissimo Chiang Kai-shek of China. In regard to the Japanese occupied territories, including Korea, the three leaders declared:

> Japan shall be stripped of all the islands in the Pacific which she has
> seized or occupied since the beginning of the first World War in 1914,...
> all the territories Japan has stolen from the Chinese..., [and]... all other
> territories which she has taken by violence and greed. The aforesaid
> three great powers, mindful of the enslavement of the people of Korea,
> are determined that in due course Korea shall become free and inde-
> pendent.[2]

The Cairo Conference was followed by another summit conference in
Teheran (November 28–December 2), this time attended by the leaders of the
United States, Britain, and Soviet Union to focus on a possible Soviet involvement in the Pacific theater and discuss measures to hasten the ending of the
war. At the Conference, the Soviet leader Joseph V. Stalin agreed to the basic
principles laid out in the Cairo Declaration in regard to the Korean problem.
The terms of the Cairo Declaration thus became the basis for the resolution of
the Korean problem after World War II.

The inclusion of the expression "in due course" in the Declaration implied that Korea's independence would be secured after a certain number of
years, and not immediately upon Japanese surrender, and this disappointing
expression led the Korean people to harbor some doubt about the Allied inten-
tions. President Kim Ku of the Provisional Korean Government noted that
there was no justifiable reason for delay and strongly argued: "Korea should
become independent immediately upon Japan's defeat."[3] Against the wishes of
the Korean people, however, this disappointing term increasingly took concrete shape as the Allied postwar plans progressed.

As the year of 1945 dawned and the final defeat of Japan appeared imminent, the leaders of the United States, Britain, and the Soviet Union met at
Yalta (February 4-11, 1945) to discuss among other problems the settlement of

the defeated powers, independence of colonies, and division of "wartime spoils." The Yalta Conference was conducted in secret, and the secret Protocol, made public a year later, only provided territorial and other concessions to the Soviet Union as conditions for Russian entrance into the war against Japan, and made no actual mention of Korea.[4] During the Conference, Roosevelt and Stalin agreed on a tentative plan for a 4-power trusteeship for Korea, to be administered by the US, the USSR, China, and Britain. No foreign troops were to be stationed on Korean soil. As for the duration of the trusteeship, Roosevelt, drawing from the American experience in the Philippines, surmised that such an arrangement might last for 20 or 30 years, but Stalin suggested that the shorter the duration of the trusteeship, the better.[5]

In order to facilitate the implementation of the Yalta Protocol, the US State Department sought cooperation from Syngman Rhee, a prominent Korean politician who was at the time staying in the United States to gather support for Korea's independence. In response to the US request, Rhee suggested that Washington immediately recognize the Korean Provisional Government in Chungking. He harshly criticized the US government for engaging in yet another secret scheme to undermine Korea's position while the memories of the 1905 Taft-Katsura Secret Agreement were still fresh on the minds of the Korean people.[6] Rhee's pointed statement could not change the major powers' policy directions and agreements, however.

Five months after the Yalta Conference, what was to be the last of the Allied Wartime Conferences took place in Potsdam from July 17 to August 2, 1945. By this time Germany had already surrendered, and only Japan was putting up final resistance against the Allied offensive. In order to hasten the ending of the war and minimize further casualties, the Allies at Potsdam discussed postwar settlement policies toward Japan; the timing of the Soviet entrance into the war against Japan and the necessary US-Soviet coordination; and the use of the atomic bomb, whose successful testing had preceded the conference. The Potsdam Declaration, announced on July 26, reaffirmed the principles of the Cairo agreement and demanded Japan's immediate unconditional surrender. The Declaration stipulated that Japan's sovereignty was limited to the main islands of Honshu, Hokkaido, Kyushu, and Shikoku, and minor islands as determined by the Allied Powers.[7]

While discussing the Soviet entry into the war against Japan at the Potsdam Conference, the US and Soviet military representatives developed, to a considerable extent, a plan concerning the partition of Korea, Manchuria, and the East Sea (or, the Sea of Japan) into US and USSR zones. It was at this time that the military planners considered an operational boundary approximating the 38th parallel.[8]

Tokyo immediately refused the Allied ultimatum as laid out in the Potsdam Declaration. To deal a final blow against Japan, the United States dropped atomic bombs on Hiroshima and Nagasaki on August 6 and 9, and between these two dates, on August 8, the Soviet Union declared war against Japan. Coordinating its wartime efforts with Washington, the Korean Provisional Government dispatched a part of the Korean Restoration Army to the OSS training unit, and established an anti-Japan Secret Operations Unit. At the same time in Fuyang and Sian, the advance corps of the Restoration Army was receiving airborne and special training under the support of the US War Department, and was preparing to advance into Korea. No longer able to withstand the combined Allied offensive, Japan offered conditional surrender on August 10, but the Allied Powers refused.

Japan's offer of August 10, however, served as the starting point for the Allies to lay out the procedure for Japan's unconditional surrender. In what was to be called General Order 1, Washington instructed Japanese commanders to surrender to designated Allied officers, and issued a directive to

Koreans give hearty cheers at the liberation

partition Japanese-held territories into occupation zones in order to facilitate the surrender of the Japanese troops.

With regard to Korea, Washington wanted the dividing line to be as far north as possible, but also had to consider the US troops' ability to advance and take the place of the Japanese troops. Balancing these two factors, Washington settled on a plan to divide Korea into two surrender zones along the 38th parallel, which would secure for the United States the two logistically important cities of Seoul and Inch'on. Included in General Order 1 are the following provisions concerning the surrender of the Japanese troops in Korea:

> 1. ...(b) The senior Japanese Commanders and all ground, sea, air and auxiliary forces within Manchuria, Korea North of 38 degrees North latitude, Karafuto [Sakhalin], and the Kurile Islands, shall surrender to the Commander in Chief of Soviet Forces in the Far East... (e) The Imperial General Headquarter, its senior Commanders, and all ground, sea, air and auxiliary forces in the main islands of Japan, minor islands

adjacent thereto, Korea South of 38 degrees North latitude, Ryukyus, and the Philippines shall surrender to the Commander-in-Chief, US Army Forces, Pacific.[9]

Finally, on August 15, 1945, Japan announced its unconditional surrender, and General Order 1, approved by US President Harry Truman, was put into effect with the Soviet, British, and Chinese agreement. World War II thus came to an end, and the Korean people were liberated from Japanese occupation. Freed from the 35 years of Japanese colonial rule and oppression, Koreans entertained high hopes and aspirations for building a new nation. The joys of liberation were, however, to be short-lived as uncertainties over Korea's future posed a new set of challenges to the Korean people.

3. Conflict over the Establishment of the National Government

(1) Military Government and Communist Takeover in Northern Korea

After the Soviet declaration of war against Japan on August 8, the Soviet ground forces advanced across the Tumen River into Korea while the air bombing of Najin, Ch'ongjin, and Unggi was carried out. A division-strong Soviet ground force reached Ch'ongjin on August 13, two days before Japan's surrender.

Finally liberated from Japan's colonial rule, leaders of Korean independence movement began to prepare for the establishment of a new nation. In P'yongyang, Cho Man Shik gathered political leaders, including indigenous communists, to form the South P'yongan Provincial Branch of the Committee for the Preparation of Korean Independence, and other leaders formed similar organizations in other major cities. While Korean nationalists were actively preparing for the establishment of the Korean government, the Soviet forces quickly advanced southward, reaching P'yongyang on August 24 and Kaesong the next day. By August 28, the Soviet forces had advanced to Haeju, Shinmak, Pokgye, Kimwha, Hwach'on, and Yangyang and occupied all areas north of the 38th parallel.[10]

The Soviet forces that occupied northern Korea under the command of Colonel General Ivan M. Chistiakov[11] was the 25th Army[12] of the Soviet 1st Far East Command. With the nucleus of five divisions and one brigade of 120,000, the 25th Army included the naval facilities unit of the Pacific Fleet and other auxiliary forces of 30,000, for a total strength of 150,000.[13]

The 25th Army set up the Soviet Military Command in P'yongyang on August 26, and established a military government regime for all of northern Korea. The General Office for Civil Administration, under the command of Major General Andrei. A. Romanenko, was charged with the responsibility to administer the military government. Under the control of the Military Conference (Political Command), this organization included nine "advisory departments," which covered political, economic, cultural, public health, news and publications, and judiciary areas.

As these military government bodies were being established, the Soviet forces disarmed the surrendering Japanese Army, built up positions along the 38th parallel with guards and machine guns, and strengthened checkpoints. In addition, the Soviets shut down major railways and roads at the 38th parallel, including the Seoul-Sinuiju and Seoul-Wonsan lines, and severed communications links between the South and the North.

After sealing off the border, the Soviets began to organize People's Committees.[14] Soviet Commander General Chistiakov recognized Cho Man Shik's People's Political Committee, and made clear that the future capital of unified Korea need not be located in Seoul.[15]

〈Table 1〉 The Organization of the Soviet Military Government in Northern Korea

This statement partially reflected the Soviet desire to establish a Communist government in Korea. At the same time, the Soviets encouraged the formation of People's Committees in order to give the impression that Koreans were in control of their own destiny. From August 24 to the end of September, these measures led to the disintegration and consolidation of many political organizations into Provincial People's Committees.

Each People's Committee was handed the administrative powers upon the Japanese surrender of government bodies including the police and economic organizations. The Soviet Military Government allowed a Korean to assume the chairmanship of People's Committees, but appointed a Soviet officer as advisor, and placed in key posts Soviet-Koreans who had followed the Soviet Forces into Korea. Although the People's Committees appeared to operate under Korean control, these organizations were actually following the policy directions of the Soviet military command. Consequently, as time passed, an increasing number of nationalists were ousted from these organizations and replaced by the Sovietized Korean Communists.

The Soviet scheme reached its climax on October 14, 1945, when the Military Government sponsored a mass rally to introduce Kim Il Sung, who was then a captain in the Soviet Army.[16] Under the sponsorship of the Soviet military command, Kim began to seize power from this point on. Angered by the Soviet scheme to back Kim Il Sung and eliminate nationalists from positions of power, Cho Man Shik and other nationalist figures formed the North Korean Democratic Party and garnered warm support from the Korean people.

To consolidate their control, however, the Soviet Military Government established on November 18 the Administrative Body for Five Provinces (of northern Korea) which would supervise the operation of the People's Committees, and had Kim Il Sung assume the post of Secretary of the North Korean

Communist Party. Thus designated as the top man of the Party four months after the establishment of the Soviet Military Government, Kim Il Sung began to build a communist system in northern Korea.

(2) Military Government and Turmoil in Southern Korea

Facing an imminent defeat of his home country, the Japanese governor-general of Korea took steps to protect the lives of Japanese residents and their property in Korea, and, as part of this effort, moved forward with plans to transfer some of the administrative powers to respected Korean leaders, who could co-operate with the Japanese authorities to ensure a peaceful transition. Among the leaders contacted by the governor-general on this matter were Song Jin Woo and Yo Woon Hyong. Reasoning that the Korean Provisional Government in China was the only legitimate government for the Korean people, Song Jin Woo refused the Japanese proposal. He supposedly believed that the Allied Forces should transfer power to the Provisional Government. In contrast, Yo Woon Hyong thought that an Independent Government should be established, encompassing all the revolutionary groups both inside and outside Korea. He accepted the Japanese offer, and quickly moved ahead to form the Committee for the Preparation of Korean Independence, setting up local branches across Korea. The Committee was, however, soon infiltrated by Communists, and became a leftist organization under their influence. In the meantime, conservative "Nationalists" formed a political party of their own to check the expansion of Communist organizations, and prepared for the return of the Korean Provisional Government.

While various political factions were actively organizing to fill the power vacuum in liberated Korea, General Douglas MacArthur received General Order 1 from Washington, and designated the US 24th Corps, then in Okinawa under the command of Lt. Gen. John R. Hodge,[17] to carry out the terms of surrender in Korea. On September 4, twenty-two days after the Soviet forces had advanced into the Korean Peninsula, an advance party from the 24th Corps landed at Kimp'o Airfield near Seoul. This advance party was followed by the US 7th Infantry Division, which landed in Inch'on on September 8 and advanced to Seoul, Kaesong, and other areas in the vicinity south of the 38th Parallel. The 7th Division also occupied the Central Provinces of Kyonggi and Ch'ungch'ong. Arriving near the end of September, the US 40th Infantry Division was deployed in the Southeastern Province of Kyongsang, and the 6th Division, landing in Korea on October 16, occupied the Southwestern Province of Cholla. The US occupying forces had a total strength of 77,600, and were organized as shown in ⟨Table 2⟩.

⟨Table 2⟩ The Organization of the US Army Forces in Korea (September 8, 1945)[18]

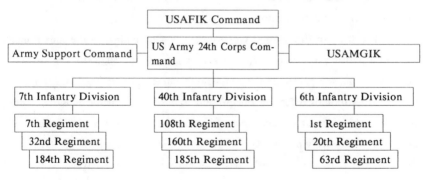

Having received from Washington no specific guidance on the operation of the US Army Military Government in Korea (USAMGIK), Lt. Gen. Hodge decided to hold on to the Japanese government-general system and keep Japanese officials in place for the time being. These Japanese bureaucrats were to be supervised by the USAMGIK until their replacement by Americans, who, in turn, would be gradually replaced by Korean officials. Colonial Japanese bureaucrats thus remained in posts even after the US Military Government received the Governor-General's surrender on September 9.

Incensed by the fact that the USAMGIK was, in effect, prolonging the Japanese colonial rule, the Korean people reacted violently to Hodge's policy and pressed him to dismiss Nobuyuki Abe, wartime governor-general of Korea. On September 12, Hodge appointed Maj. Gen. Archibald V. Arnold, commander of the US 7th Division, Military Governor of Korea. At Hodge's request, Mr. H. Merrell Benninghoff, a Department of State official, was assigned as his Political Advisor, and helped Hodge to establish the Military Government directly controlled by the US Army Forces in Korea (USAFIK).

Hodge decided to duplicate the structure of the Governor-General, and appointed former Japanese officials as advisors to complement American department heads, who clearly lacked the local knowledge necessary to function effectively as administrators.

The Korean Provisional Government in Chungking, in the meantime, had sent a petition on August 17 to President Truman, through the US Ambassador to China, for permission to send representatives to Korea and participate in "all Councils affecting the present and future destiny of Korea and Koreans." This request, however, was not accepted by the US government. A few days after arriving in Korea, General Hodge suggested to General MacArthur that leaders of the Provisional Government be returned to Korea under Allied sponsorship to act as "figureheads" until the political situation stabilized and elections could be held, but no action was taken on this suggestion, either.[19]

In the end, declaring itself the only government south of the 38th parallel, the US Military Government decided not to recognize even the Korean Provisional Government which had led Korea's struggle for independence; however, Washington-Tokyo-Seoul inconsistencies regarding occupation policy produced further confusion.

Hodge complained that the US Military Government would fail with-out clear policy guidance, and his advisor Benninghoff commented that the USAMGIK headquarters had "no information in regard to the future policy of the United States or its allies as to the future of Korea," and added that USAFIK was in small strength and had too few competent military govern-ment and other officers to operate effectively as military government.[20]

The USAMGIK was faced with other urgent problems as well. Indus-try in Korea at the time was virtually at a standstill with the whole economy in crisis. Politically, not only were a large number of newly formed parties at odds with one another over ideological and personal differences, but their so-called leaders had almost no political experience. The Japanese colonial poli-cy of appointing virtually no Koreans to responsible posts either in govern-ment or industry made it nearly impossible for the USAMGIK to find well-qualified Koreans for these posts. General Hodge had received no specific in-structions on ways to resolve these political complexities and to deal with the damaging heritage of the Japanese colonial rule.

Even in the absence of policy guidance and social turmoil, however, the USAMGIK had managed to get on track by early October. On October 5, Military Governor Arnold replaced the Japanese advisors with 11 well-known Korean leaders, including Kim Sung Su. Building on this foundation, the USAMGIK adopted in December a "double-head" policy of hiring Korean de-partment heads alongside the Americans. Thanks to these measures, the num-ber of Koreans working in the USAMGIK had reached 75,000 by the end of 1945. Organizationally, as shown in ⟨Table 3⟩, the USAMGIK consisted of 9 departments and Provincial Branches at the time.

While General Hodge was consolidating the USAMGIK structure in Korea, General MacArthur finally received specific guidance from Washing-

⟨Table 3⟩   The Organization of the US Army Military Government in Korea
(USAMGIK)[21]

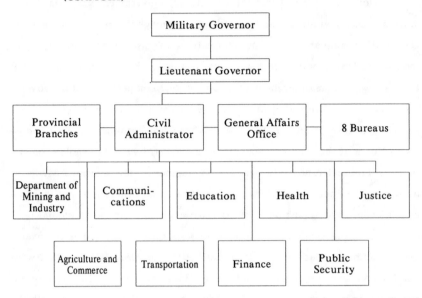

ton on October 17. The basic initial directive defined the USAMGIK's mission
as follows :

> The United States ultimate objective in Korea is to foster conditions
> which will bring about the establishment of a free and independent na-
> tion capable of taking her place as a responsible and peaceful member
> of the family of nations. In all your activities you will bear in mind the
> policy of the United States in regard to Korea, which contemplates a
> progressive development from this initial interim period of civil affairs
> administration by the United States and the USSR, to a period of trus-
> teeship under the United States, the United Kingdom, China, and the
> USSR, and finally to the eventual independence of Korea with member-
> ship in the United Nations organization.[22]

Clearly, the US policy envisioned a progressive three-stage development of military government to trusteeship to full independence for Korea. The issuance of this directive to General MacArthur coincided with the return of some members of the Korean Provisional Government as individual citizens. Syngman Rhee arrived on October 16, and Kim Ku with many other government members returned to Korea on November 23. As the US Military Government refused to recognize the Korean Provisional Government and permitted the freedom of political activity for all parties and social organizations, however, the confrontation between the democratic and communist camps became increasingly serious in the South. This political development was in stark contrast to the consolidation of the Communist system under Kim Il Sung in the North.

(3) Trusteeship Plan and Confrontation Between the Left and the Right

After setting up the military government system in the South, the United States sought to hold a meeting with other powers to discuss the future of Korea within the framework established through a series of Allied wartime conferences. The Soviet Union, however, seemed to be proceeding with a plan to seal off the 38th parallel and turn the North into a satellite under Kim Il Sung. The Soviet response to the US plan to hold a new meeting was lukewarm at best. To break the deadlock, the US Secretary of State James F. Byrnes proposed a meeting of foreign ministers in December, and managed to bring about a meeting in Moscow of Byrnes himself, British Foreign Minister Earnest Bevin, and Soviet Foreign Minister V. M. Molotov.

In regard to the future of Korea, the three foreign ministers agreed to implement the terms of the Cairo Declaration, and set up a US-USSR joint commission to facilitate the creation of a provisional Korean democratic government after a five-year trusteeship period:

① With a view to the re-establishment of Korea as an independent
state..., there shall be set up a provisional Korean democratic government.

② ...there shall be established a Joint Commission consisting of representatives of the United States in southern Korea and the Soviet
command in northern Korea.

③ The proposals of the Joint Commission shall be submitted, following
consultation with the provisional Korean Government for the joint
consideration of the Governments of the United States, Union of Soviet Socialist Republics, United Kingdom and China for the working
out of an agreement concerning a four-power trusteeship of Korea
for a period of up to five years.

④ ...a conference of the representatives of the United States and Soviet
commands in Korea shall be convened within a period of two weeks.[23]

The terms of the Moscow agreement upset the Korean people who had
looked forward to immediate independence, and touched off nationwide anti-
trusteeship demonstrations. The party that spoke for the Korean people's aspirations in the strongest terms was Kim Ku's Provisional Government group,
and all the leftist political parties and organizations, including the Choson
Communist Party, also joined in the demonstrations.

At its December 28 political affairs meeting, Kim Ku's Provisional
Government group defined the anti-trusteeship campaign as the second independence movement, and planned national rallies under the leadership of the
newly formed action committee.

After receiving a directive from the Soviet Communist Party at the beginning of January in 1946, however, Communist groups in the South reversed
their earlier position on the trusteeship proposal and began to support the
Moscow agreement. Their about-face intensified the confrontation between the

Left and the Right as they now clashed over the trusteeship proposal. With their pro-trusteeship position, the Left alienated many Korean people, and began to lose popular support.

Meanwhile, P'yongyang broadcast a Soviet directive on the radio on January 2 and made it clear that the Soviet policy supported the trusteeship proposal, explaining among other things that "the agreement reached at the Moscow Conference does not envision a trusteeship but rather a sponsorship, and Choson retains sovereignty under this arrangement." A January 4 meeting of the Administrative Bodies of the Five Provinces, held under the guidance of the commander of the Soviet Military Government, adopted a resolution supporting the Moscow Conference. When Cho Man Shik objected to this resolution and attempted to organize anti-trusteeship rallies with other nationalists, the Soviet Military Government imprisoned him and removed his supporters from positions of power. With the nationalist groups now purged from the political scene, the Communists increasingly took the initiative to shape the political future of northern Korea.

(4) The Collapse of the US-USSR Joint Commission

As required by the terms of the Moscow Agreement, representatives from the US and Soviet commands in Korea held a meeting in January 1946. Lt. Gen. T. F. Shtykov led the Soviet delegation of more than 70 to Seoul on January 15, and, closed to the public, the first meeting between the two sides began the next day. The US and Soviet representatives clashed over the selection of the main agenda, however, and ended the meeting without much result, except for the agreement to establish the Joint Commission.

The US command designated Maj. Gen. Arnold, and the Soviets, Lt. Gen. Shtykov as their head delegats, and held the first meeting of the US-

USSR Joint Commission in Seoul on March 20, 1946. The Soviet side contended that only those political parties and social organizations in support of the
Moscow Agreement should be included in Korean bodies to be consulted with
respect to the creation of a provisional Korean democratic government. This
course of action would effectively exclude non-Communist groups from the
consultative process and hence from the interim government, and give the Soviets a free hand to establish a pro-Soviet Communist regime in Korea. In
response, the US delegates argued that all political parties and social organizations ought to take part in the consultative process under the democratic principle of freedom of political expression. As the two sides refused to budge from
their respective position, the first round of talks at the Joint Commission was
adjourned indefinitely after the 24th meeting on May 8, less than 50 days from
the opening of the round.

The deadlock at the Joint Commission was followed by the eruption of
diverse opinions on the establishment of the Korean government. As before,
Kim Ku called for the establishment of a single united provisional government
for all of Korea while Kim Kyu Shik, a moderate rightist, attempted to accelerate the unification and independence process by forming a coalition with Yo
Woon Hyong, a moderate leftist. In contrast to these leaders, Syngman Rhee,
after observing postwar international developments, concluded that compro-
mise with the Communists was all but impossible, and began to advocate the
establishment of a separate government in the South. With the support of the
Korean Democratic Party, Rhee organized a General Headquarters for
National Unification and demanded that the United States place the Korean
problem for discussion before the General Assembly of the United Nations.
Rhee visited Washington in January 1947, and sharply criticized the
USAMGIK policy. General Hodge too returned to the United States to discuss
the future of Korea. Rhee's advocacy for the establishment of a separate gov-

ernment drew attention from US policymakers, as it coincided with the intensification of the US-USSR confrontation in the postwar world.

The US Military Government in Korea, however, was committed to the left-right coalition efforts, and had already established in December 1946 the South Korean Interim Legislative Assembly consisting of those Korean leaders favorably disposed toward the coalition efforts. With Kim Kyu Shik as chairman, the Assembly was the first democratic lawmaking body to be established in Korea after her liberation, and was responsible for legislation until the formation of the National Assembly of the Republic of Korea. The US Military Government subsequently created a Korean chief civil administrator position under the Military Governor, and appointed Ahn Jae Hong to the post in February 1947. The USAMGIK thus sought to defuse the political tension in Korea by increasing Korean representation in the Military Government and gradually transferring administrative authority to the South Korean Interim Government established in June 1947.

As Washington began to counter the postwar Soviet expansionism with the Declaration of the Truman Doctrine[24] in March 1947 and the Marshall Plan,[25] however, the US Military Government's effort to build a provisional Korean democratic government under a left-right coalition started losing its momentum. Under the new US policy regime of containment, the four-power trusteeship based on US-USSR agreement noticeably began to lose its rationale and urgency, and so did the effort to form a left-right coalition in Korea. Under these circumstances, it was only natural that calls for the establishment of a separate government would gain support.

Around this time, the Soviets finally agreed to the US request for the resumption of talks, and their delegates attended the second round of the US-USSR Joint Commission meetings on May 21, 1947. Both sides, however, held on to their previous positions, and repeated the deadlock of 1946. In an attempt to break the impasse, the United States proposed on August 26 that the four major powers meet again to decide how the Moscow Agreement could be implemented. Britain and China agreed to the proposal, but the Soviet Union refused, arguing that the existing US-USSR Joint Commission could carry out the Moscow Agreement. On October 21, 1947, the Soviets withdrew their liaison mission from Seoul and broke off the second round of the Joint Commission.

Established in accordance with the Moscow Agreement, the US-USSR Joint Commission thus wasted close to 2 years without making any progress. During this time, efforts to set up a separate Communist government were going ahead in the North while calls for the establishment of a separate government were also gaining support over the left-right coalition program in the South.

4. Establishment of Separate Governments in South and North Korea

(1) Transfer of the Korean Problem to the United Nations

While the US-USSR Joint Commission was discussing the Korean problem, the relations between the two superpowers rapidly deteriorated into a "cold war," and proposals to place the Korean problem before the United Nations began to be put forward in some circles. Disillusioned by the collapse of the two rounds of the Joint Commission meetings and the Soviet rejection of a four-power conference, Washington's policymakers also began to consider transferring to the United Nations the authority to resolve the Korean problem. The transfer of the Korean problem to the UN implied that an independent Korean government could be established without further discussion of the trusteeship question. Such a course of action would not only suit the wishes of the Korean people but also would help the United States to lean on the United Nations to block a possible Soviet attempt to dominate the Korean Peninsula.

Explaining why the United States had decided to bypass the trusteeship process and present the Korean problem to the United Nations, US Secretary of State George C. Marshall made the following statement before the UN General Assembly on September 17, 1947:

> For about two years the United States Government has been trying to reach agreement with the Soviet Government... [But] the independence of Korea is no further advanced than it was two years ago... It appears evident that further attempts to solve the Korean problem by means of bilateral negotiations will only serve to delay the establishment of an independent, united Korea... We do not wish to have the inability of two powers to reach agreement delay any further the urgent and rightful claims of the Korean people to independence.[26]

In spite of strong objections raised by the Soviet Union, the US proposal was adopted as an item on the agenda for discussion, and in a draft resolution on October 16, the United States recommended that "Korea hold general elections not later than March 31, 1948, under the observation and supervision of a UN Temporary Commission and that the occupying powers completely withdraw their armed forces upon the establishment of the united Korean national government."[27]

While the General Assembly was considering the US proposal, the Soviet representative protested that the UN had no jurisdiction over Korea and that foreign troops must be withdrawn before the establishment of a united Korean government. His counterproposal recommended that the occupying powers withdraw their troops at once, but this proposal was not adopted by the General Assembly. On November 14, 1947, the United Nations General

Assembly approved a resolution supporting the US proposal and created the UN Temporary Commission on Korea.[28] Thus, establishment of a united national government under UN supervision replaced creation of a four-power trusteeship as the basic framework for the resolution of the Korean problem.

(2) The Birth of the Republic of Korea

In accordance with the UN resolution, the UN Temporary Commission on Korea was established under the chairmanship of India's K.P.S. Menon. The Soviet Union, however, refused to cooperate with the Commission and barred it from entering northern Korea. Consequently, the Temporary Commission was able to execute its mission only in southern Korea, and discuss the establishment of a national government only with southern leaders. Even the political leaders in the South were divided over this issue, however. Syngman Rhee and his supporters favored the establishment of a separate government in the South, while Kim Ku and Kim Kyu Shik led an uphill battle to create a unified Korean government through South-North negotiation.

Under these trying circumstances, the UN Temporary Commission on Korea submitted four alternative courses of action for consideration before the Interim Committee of the UN General Assembly:

① Hold general elections only in southern Korea
② Hold elections for Korean representatives who could take part in international negotiations
③ Explore other possibilities including a conference between southern and northern leaders to discuss national independence
④ End the mission of the UN Temporary Commission on Korea and resolve the Korean problem at the General Assembly[29]

On February 26, 1948, the UN Interim Committee adopted the first proposal, and the USAMGIK promulgated on March 18 the May 10 Election Act enacted by the South Korean Interim Legislative Assembly.[30] This Act allotted 100 seats to the North based on the principle of proportional representation, and provided the legal foundation for the election of 198 members of the Constitutional Assembly on May 10, 1948. Under UN observation, the election was held only in the South.

The Constitutional Assembly convened on May 31, and elected Syngman Rhee as its chairman. On July 17, the National Assembly promulgated a constitution consisting of 10 preambles and 103 provisions, and produced as its first legislative act the Government Organization Act, which permitted the establishment of 12 administrative ministries. The preamble of the Constitution declared: "We, the people of Korea, possessing a glorious history and tradition from time immemorial, imbued with the sublime spirit of independence as manifested in the declaration to the world of the establishment of the Republic of Korea after the March 1st Movement in the year of Kimi (1919), are now being engaged in the restoration of an independent democratic nation..."[31] The Constitution thus made it clear that the Republic of Korea (ROK) derived its political and historical legitimacy from the Provisional Government's struggle for independence. In accordance with the Constitution, the National Assembly elected Syngman Rhee and Lee Si Yong President and Vice President, respectively, and proclaimed the new Republic of Korea on August 15, 1948. The UN Temporary Commission on Korea reported to the UN General Assembly the birth of the Republic, and on December 12, the General Assembly approved a resolution establishing the UN Commission on Korea, and declared:

> that there has been established a lawful government (the Government of the Republic of Korea) having effective control and jurisdiction

over that part of Korea where the Temporary Commission was able to observe and consult in which the great majority of the people of all Korea reside; that this Government is based on elections which were a valid expression of the free will of the electorate of that part of Korea and which were observed by the Temporary Commission; and that this is the only such Government in Korea...[32]

(3) The Establishment of the Communist Regime in North Korea

The de facto establishment of a Communist government in the North dates back to February 8, 1946, when the North Korean Interim People's Committee was created with Kim Il Sung as its chairman. Building on the foundation of the Provincial People's Committees, pro-Soviet Communists dominated this central government and got rid of nationalists from positions of power.

Now in control of the central government, Kim Il Sung held the first municipal People's Committee elections at the province, city, and county level in November 1946, soon followed by elections at the village level. At this time, the Korean Democratic National Front nominated a single candidate in each district to be elected by black-or-white balloting.[33] Elected People's Committee members formed the North Choson People's Committee on February 17, 1947.

A legislative body to draft a constitution was established in November 1947, and a Soviet-style People's Constitution was adopted in April 1948. In July, the central government resolved "to put the Constitution into effect in northern Korea until all of Korea is united" and "to hold Supreme People's Congress elections in accordance with the Constitution." These elections were held in 212 districts throughout the North by open balloting on August 25, 1948.[34]

Of these elections, the North's Communists declared that secret underground elections were held simultaneous in the South, and proclaimed the new Democratic People's Republic of Korea (DPRK) on September 9, 1948. On the illegitimate nature of the establishment of the North Korean regime, the UN Commission on Korea would later report on July 28, 1949:

> The northern regime is the creature of a military occupant and rules by right of a mere transfer of power from that Government. It has never been willing to give its subjects an unfettered opportunity, under the scrutiny of an impartial international agency, to pass upon its claims to rule.[35]

Though provided with an opportunity to build a unified independent nation at the time of liberation, the Korean people thus could not overcome the initial partition caused by the major powers' wartime decision to draw the 38th parallel. In particular, the Soviet desire to create a satellite in Korea helped to cement the division along the 38th parallel and lead to the establishment of the democratic Republic of Korea in the South and the communist Democratic People's Republic of Korea in the North.

5. Armed Struggle of the Communists

Since the early days of the US Military Government, the Communists in southern Korea had engaged in political struggle. After being caught attempting to circulate counterfeit bank notes in June 1946, the Communists went underground and started agitation campaigns, sabotage, and strikes. When the election under UN observation to establish a separate government in the South became an accomplished fact in early 1948, they initiated the so-called "February 7 National Salvation Struggle," and obstructed the activities of the UN Temporary Commission on Korea to make preparations for the election. They also called for the withdrawal of the US and Soviet forces from Korea.

Once the South Korean Labor Party (SKLP) cells started infiltrating into factories and transportation facilities and agitating for strikes, their "political struggle" rapidly developed into riots involving raids on police stations, arson, vandalism, and destruction of public facilities, including severance of telegraph and telephone lines. The February 7 Riot was followed by sailors' strikes on ships and coal miners' strikes as well as student strikes in Seoul and other cities. The wave of strikes spilled even into weather forecasting stations and meteorological services. The Riot lasted almost two weeks on a nationwide scale, and as a result a total of 8,479 persons were arrested.[36]

At the end of March 1948, Kim Dal Sam, the SKLP cell operative in the Island of Cheju, decided to take over the Cheju region by force, and jointly instigated an armed insurgency with the cell operative of the 9th Regiment of the Republic of Korea Army (ROKA). To obstruct the forthcoming election, the insurgents raided police stations, set fires, and killed police officers and innocent people. As a result, the May 10 election could not be held in two of the districts in North Cheju.[37]

The US Military Government tried to put down the rebellion with police, but only suffered casualties without achieving the desired result. The USAMGIK then ordered in the 9th Regiment, which at the time was responsible for the defense of the Cheju region, and additionally dispatched the 11th Regiment stationed in Suwon. When this counter-insurgency operation destroyed the guerrilla base in Cheju Island, the SKLP retaliated by assassinating Col. Park Chin Kyong, commander of the 11th Regiment. Undaunted by the Communist tactics, Park's successor managed to separate the guerrillas from residents, and did much to stamp out the insurgents.[38]

A large-scale rebellion, however, broke out again in Cheju Island on October 1, and caused many deaths. When the situation worsened with numerous police stations raided, the ROK government declared martial law, and established the Cheju Area Command to eradicate the guerrillas. It took till May 1949, more than 13 months since the beginning of the insurgency, to root out the guerrilla organizations and restore public order in Cheju Island.[39]

Rebellions flared out in other areas as well, usually instigated by communists who had infiltrated into the ROK army. On October 19, 1948, a military rebellion masterminded by SKLP members broke out in the Yosu-stationed 14th Regiment, which at the time was on its way to Cheju Island for counter-insurgency operations. Receiving a directive from the SKLP, the regiment cell operative MSG Chi Ch'ang Su and other party members instigated an armed rebellion. The rebel army attempted to block the sending of the counter-insurgency units to Cheju Island, and hoped that their rebellion would have spillover effects in other regiments.

While the 14th Regiment was preparing for the departure, more than 40 SKLP members and supporters seized armories and ammo dumps, gathered troops on the parade ground, and declared: "...We are opposed to the fratricidal operations in Cheju Island. Let us kill all the officers who are no more than agents of the American imperialists." Killing more than 20 officers and NCOs and taking over the regiment, they led more than 1,000 rebel troops to downtown Yosu that night, and took over the city after a brief engagement with the police. They advanced into Sunch'on the next morning, and committed atrocities there. As the occupation zone under Communist control was expanded, SKLP members in the Yosu area joined the rebellion, and the strength of the rebel army swelled to 3,000. Their main effort headed in the direction of Kwangyang-Namwon-Chonju, while the others attempted to advance in the direction of Polkyo-Kwangju-Iri.[40]

As the rebel army's strength became greater and their occupation zone larger, the ROK government established a Counter-Rebel Combat Command in

Kwangju on October 21, and declared a martial law in the Yosu-Sunch'on areas on October 23. The Counter-Rebel Combat Command recovered Sunch'on, Polkyo, Posung, and Kwangyang on the 25th, and restored order in the Yosu area.[41] Subsequently the rebel army moved into the Chiri-san and conducted guerrilla warfare, and the counter-insurgency operations continued for more than 15 months. It was not until January 15, 1950, that the martial law was lifted.

After the Yosu-Sunch'on Rebellion, another military rebellion broke out in the Taegu-stationed 6th Regiment in November 1948. At the time, the three core battalions of the regiment were in Cheju Island and the Yosu-Sunch'-on area, and only the regiment headquarters unit and some security forces were left behind in Taegu. The dispatching of two companies to Kimch'on, Youngch'-on, and P'ohang had further dispersed the unit. Rebellion in this regiment occurred at three different times. Initially, on November 2, 1948, the regiment cell operative Sergeant Major Kwak Jong Jin took advantage of the absence of the main units, and placed the regiment headquarters on alert. He falsely informed the gathered troops that the Yosu-Sunch'on rebel army had advanced into Taegu. After killing more than 10 soldiers who refused to cooperate, he led the rebel troops into Taegu and attacked police stations. Repelled by military and police units, however, Kwak and his supporters had to flee to the P'algong-san.

When this rebellion broke out, the 1st Battalion in the Yosu-Sunch'on area was ordered to return to Taegu, but when the battalion reached the vicinity of Wolbae in Talsonggun on its way back to the regiment, rebellious leftist elements in the unit killed nine commanding officers and attempted to coerce the troops into joining the rebellion. Their attempt was, however, put down by military and police units, and they too had to flee to P'algong-san (Mt.).

On January 3, 1949, yet another similar incident took place in the 4th Company of the 6th Regiment stationed at Och'on Airfield near P'ohang. This company was scheduled for re-assignment at the time, to purge the unit of leftist elements following the series of rebellions in the regiment. Detecting this plan, the leftists in the company killed platoon leaders and senior NCOs, and attempted to gather troops for rebellion. When the company members refused to cooperate, however, the leftists fled. The series of rebellions in the 6th regiment thus came to an end after producing many casualties and victims.[42]

With the armed struggle of the communists ending in failure in the South, the North Korean regime came to believe that the SKLP Communist takeover of South Korea through violent means was all but impossible, and shifted its top priority to a military build-up in preparation for war.

II. North Korea's War Preparations

1. Establishment of the People's Army

(1) The Origins of the People's Army

Until the Soviet Military Government was firmly established, Jawidae (self-defense forces) organized by the nationalists, and People's Guards formed by the native Communists were responsible for the maintenance of law and order in northern Korea. The Soviet Military Government, however, soon began to impose restrictions on the activities of these organizations, and after Kim Il Sung's return to the North, it established a Red Militia at each provincial capital and built up native armed organizations. Though delegated by the Soviet Military Government to exercise police powers, these armed organizations often clashed with one another and contested for the initiative to shape political events in the North.

Using these clashes as a pretext, the Soviet Military Government disbanded these armed organizations on October 21, 1945, and forced them to turn in their weapons and materiel to the Soviet Army. In their place, the Soviets created in November a new Security Corps consisting of 2,000 selected men who were judged to be faithful followers of the Soviet Military Government and thoroughly equipped with the Communist ideology. The establishment of this constabulary-type unit in Chinnamp'o was followed by the creation of a provincial security force. By early 1946, these forces had assumed the responsibility for the maintenance of law and order and the security of main public facilities. In June of the same year, a training center for Security Corps members was established in Kaech'on, and its branches set up in such places as Sinuiju, Chongju, Kanggye to recruit and train constabulary troops. Together with the People's Army, the Security Corps later became a core element of the North Korean troops.[43]

Arguing that the Security Corps by itself could not ensure public security, in particular the security of railroad lines, the Soviet Military Government and Kim Il Sung established in January 1946 the Railway Security Guards with central headquarters in P'yongyang. Later to be transformed into full-fledged military units, these security forces guarded railroad tracks, tunnels, and stations in northern Korea. Equipped with Japanese model 99 rifles,[44] they underwent military training and grew in size to become the North Choson Railway Security Command in July 1946.

Under the Command, railway security forces were organized into 13 companies[45] and prepared for eventual absorption into the regular army. Training centers for the Railway Security Guards were established in Kaech'on and Nanam to supply personnel.[46]

Through the establishment of the Security Corps and Railway Security Guards under Soviet support, a solid foundation for the creation of a regular army was secured in northern Korea. In addition, on February 8, 1946, Kim Il Sung set up P'yongyang Academy in Tohangni, Chinnamp'o, with the mission to produce military and political cadres for the army.

Kim Il Sung's partisan comrades controlled P'yongyang Academy, and in order to expand their political base, they travelled around the provinces and recruited core members of People's Committees for admission. Korean officers with Soviet army experience instructed military training and political education courses at the academy. Their military training program emphasized physical training, marksmanship, and Soviet military doctrine; whereas, the political education program included political science, Russian language training, history of the Communist Party, and, above all, ideological education to ensure the unity of ideology.[47]

Such education sought to produce core members in each field of expertise, and not just for the army. Kim Il Sung's partisan group sought to consolidate their political position by recruiting young talent, and P'yongyang Academy became the forerunner to various schools and institutions designed to produce such core members.

Starting with a four-month course, the Academy produced the first graduating class in July 1946. A fifteen-month program was soon established, and the first class of 800 matriculated under this program. P'yongyang Academy graduated a total of 2,500 before the Korean War, and these graduates assumed cadre or instructor positions in the Communist Party as well as the security forces.

While P'yongyang Academy was putting out cadres for the Communist regime, the Central Security Officers School was established in Kangsogun, South P'yongan Province, in July 1946 to produce military officers. This school admitted the first class of 300 upon recommendation by the Central Committee of the Communist Party, and assigned them to infantry, armor, and engineer companies for branch education. After producing the first graduating class in October 1947, the school newly established medical, finance, and signal companies. The graduates of the Central Security Officers School later became platoon leaders, company commanders, and instructors in the People's Army.[48]

To integrate these military institutions and to ensure unity of command, the Soviet Union and Kim Il Sung's faction established the Security Officers Training Command in P'yongyang on August 15, 1946. Initially consisting of P'yongyang Academy, Central Security Officers School, constabulary train-

〈Table 4〉　　　The Organization of the Security Officers Training Command in Northern Korea

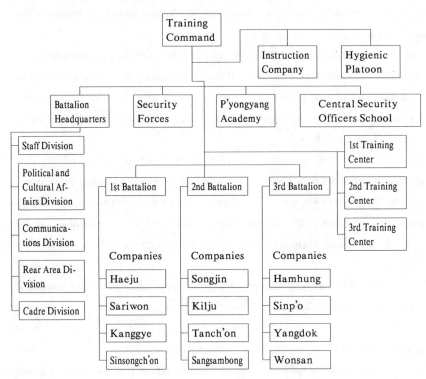

ing centers, and railway security forces, the Security Officers Training Command later underwent a series of reorganizations to form three battalions centered around the 13 companies of the Railway Security Guards and integrated training centers into three places.[49]

The Training Command gradually built up military facilities and personnel, and each training center became the nucleus of a newly formed division. The Training Command recruited young men of ages between 18 and 25, but eventually resorted to conscription and forced the members of the Party and the Democratic Youth League to enlist when an increasing number of youths shunned military service. In the beginning, the troops were equipped with Japanese Model-38 rifles.[50] As Soviet-made rifles and ammunition were furnished and Soviet officers were secured as military advisors,[51] it seemed only a matter of time that the regular North Korean army would be established.[52]

(2) Reorganization into the North Korean People's Army

By May 1947, the confrontation between the US and the USSR had become so serious that the possibility for a negotiated settlement in Korea seemed remote. Believing that conditions were now ripe for the creation of a regular army, P'yongyang reorganized the Security Officers Training Command into the People's Army Group under the command of Gen. Choi Yong Gun. The 1st Security Officers Training Center was reinforced and reorganized as the 1st Infantry Division, the 2nd Training Center became the 2nd Infantry Division, and the 3rd Training Center, the 3rd Independent Mixed Brigade (or, Provisional Division). From this point on, Kim Il Sung expended much effort to build up the armed forces and secure military assistance from abroad, and the Soviet Army furnished these divisions with mortars, howitzers, antitank guns, and various types of machine guns, burp guns, and rifles.

At the time of establishment, the strength of each division in the People's

Army Group was about 14,000, and that of the Third Independent Mixed Brigade, roughly 3,400. Of this total strength of 30,000, approximately 17,000 were
trainees.[53] P'yongyang introduced a system of military ranks at this time, and
began to hold tactical training exercises. On February 8, 1948, P'yongyang declared the establishment of a regular army, named it the North Korean People's
Army (NKPA), and established the General Headquarters for the People's
Army.[54] The formation of the NKPA preceded by 7 months the formal establishment of the North Korean Communist regime. Accordingly, the NKPA, at
least in principle, was little more than an armed organization, not a national
army. Kim Il Sung, however, declared that the NKPA was not just another
armed organization created after the liberation of Korea, and explained that he
established a regular army in response the tumultous political events of late
1947 and early 1948. Adding that revolutionary imperatives necessitated its formation, Kim Il Sung justified the NKPA as the armed organization of a people's

⟨Table 5⟩ Establishment of the North Korean Infantry Divisions(May 17, 1947)[55]

Unit	CP Location	Commanding Officer	Nucleus of the Unit
1st Infantry Division	Kaech'on	Maj. Gen. Chon Sung Hwa	1st Security Officers Training Center in Kaech'on; 1st, 2nd, and 3rd Regiments, with an artillery regiment
2nd Infantry Division	Nanam	Maj. Gen. Kang Kon	2nd Security Officers Training Center in Nanam; 4th, 5th, and 6th Regiments, with an artillery regiment
3rd Independent and Mixed Brigade	P'yongyang	Maj. Gen. Choi Min Chol	3rd Security Officers Training Center in Wonsan; 7th, 8th, and 9th Regiments, with an artillery Regiment

government with a mission to repel provocations by the US occupation forces in the South.

The NKPA's navy and air force were at a relative inferiority to its ground forces. The origin of the NKPA's navy can be traced back to the Marine Security Corps established in July 1946 consisting of units in Wonsan on the east coast and Chinnamp'o on the west. The Marine Security Corps was reorganized into the Coast Guard in December of the same year, and was under the jurisdiction of the Interior Department. At the time of the creation of the NKPA, the Coast Guard's strength was reinforced to more than 6,000. As for educational institutions, the Coast Guard Officers School was established in July 1947, and was renamed the NKPA Naval Officers School with the establishment of the NKPA.[56]

The air force started out as Sinuiju Air Unit in October 1945. Originally little more than a flying school of purely civilian character, the Sinuiju Air Unit was transformed into a flight-strength unit when it became a part of P'yongyang Academy in June 1946. It later became an independent air squadron with the creation of the People's Army Group in 1947.[57]

Upon the establishment of the NKPA, Kim Il Sung declared: "Our People's Army has the noble mission to consolidate the gains from the establishment

⟨Table 6⟩   The Organization of the NKPA General Headquarters(February 2, 1948)

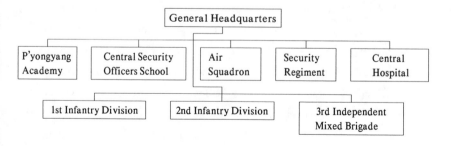

of democratic North Korea, to protect the People's Committee, and to secure complete independence for our nation. We must all be prepared for total mobilization whenever the entire nation calls for the defense of our fatherland."[58] In this speech, Kim Il Sung implied that the NKPA's main objective was the communization of the South through armed invasion. This was an expression of Kim's intent to communize the entire Korean Peninsula now that the task of building a Communist system in the North had been largely completed. His statement was also in line with the Soviet global strategy, and was rewarded with increased military assistance from Moscow.

2. The NKPA's War Preparations

(1) Military Build-Up under the Support of Communist China and the Soviet Union

With the proclamation of the DPRK on September 9, 1948, North Korea reorganized the People's Army General Headquarters as a Ministry of National Defense consisting of 11 administrative divisions.[59] Having thus reorganized the military administrative system, North Korea received equipment from the Soviet occupation forces and rapidly built up its armed forces under the support of the Soviet Union and Communist China.

Not only did the Soviet Union provide materiel and equipment, but it also advised North Korea's top military leadership, units, and training institutions. The Soviets provided a colonel-rank advisor for each division commander, and in all, 150 Russian advisors worked with each division, down to the company level. For armored and air units, the Soviets sent specialized advisors who would supervise equipment replacement and maintenance as well as tactical training. Through this process, the NKPA was moulded according to the Soviet doctrine, reflecting in part the accelerating Sovietization of the whole North Korean society. The number of Soviet advisors in North Korea had increased to 2,000 by the end of 1948, but began to dwindle rapidly with the withdrawal of the Soviet occupation forces. The Soviets pulled their advisors out from the company level, and instead sent special military missions to provide direct supervision of the NKPA's war efforts.[60]

With the equipment furnished by the withdrawing Soviet forces, North Korea upgraded the 3rd Mixed Brigade to a division, and established the 4th Independent Mixed Brigade on September 9, 1948. The NKPA also created the 105th Armored Battalion, and upgraded this unit to a regiment with sixty T-34 tanks, self-propelled guns, sidecars, and trucks furnished by a Soviet armored division.[61] Reinforced with hundred IL-10 attack planes and YAK-9 fighters, North Korea's air squadron under the Ministry of National Defense was also reorganized into a wing.

In mid-December 1948, after the Soviet forces had completed their withdrawal, Soviet Defense Minister Field Marshal N. A. Bulganin hosted a Moscow meeting of five Soviet generals with representatives from Communist China and North Korea to discuss ways to maximize the combat strength of the North Korean People's Army. At this conference, the three countries agreed to build up the strength of the NKPA to a level sufficient for an invasion of South Korea within 18 months. The Soviets also agreed to send a special military delegation to North Korea. Their secret military agreement included the following provisions:

① Six infantry divisions shall be organized as assault divisions.
② To form these assault divisions, Communist China will provide 20,000 to 25,000 Korean-born veterans of the Chinese army as cadres for the NKPA.
③ Besides assault divisions, eight combat and eight reserve divisions

shall be organized.

④ Two armored divisions shall be established with 500 tanks furnished by the Soviet Union.

⑤ In consideration of international repercussions, the formation of air force units shall be put off until the necessary date.[62]

In accordance with this agreement, a Soviet military delegation consisting of five generals, twelve colonels, and twenty or so junior officers left for North Korea at the end of December. General Shtykov, who was appointed the first Soviet ambassador to North Korea, was the chief delegate. The majority of these Soviet generals were armor experts. The delegation first met with Korean and Chinese officials in Harbin to confirm the availability of the Korean-born veterans in the Northeast Volunteer Army, and arrived in P'yongyang in January 1949. At a meeting with the North Korean leaders, the Soviet delegation accommodated P'yongyang's request for more aircraft, and promised to provide additional 150 planes. On the other hand, taking Korea's rough terrain into account, the Soviets halved the number of armored divisions to be created, and made other adjustments suited to the local conditions.[63]

North Korea's war preparations moved rapidly ahead with a Moscow meeting between Kim Il Sung and Stalin on March 5, 1949. At this conference, both leaders agreed to bring about the unification of Korea by force and signed a treaty providing for a Soviet loan of 200 million Roubles ($40 million) from June 1949 to June 1952.[64] With this loan, North Korea imported military equipment.

For the first year, North Korea requested on May 1 a supply of more than 110 different types of military equipment, including rifles, tanks, artillery pieces, ships, airplanes, ammunition, and radio communications equipment. This list of equipment was approved by the Soviets on June 4, as shown in ⟨Table 7⟩.[65]

〈Table 7〉   Soviet Military Assistance to North Korea According to the North
Korea-Soviet Agreement: First Year (approved on June 4, 1949)

Equipment Type		Number/Amount
Airplane and Air Force Equipment	IL-10	30
	IL-10 (for training)	4
	YAK-9	30
	YAK-11	6
	YAK-18	24
	PO-2	4
	Spare engine AM-42	6
	Parachute	250
	Spare Part	350,000 Roubles
Armor Equipment	T-34 Tank	87
	SU-76 Self-Propelled Gun	102
	BA-64 Armored Vehicle	57
	M-72 Sidecar	122
	Spare Part	200,000 Roubles
Small Arm and Artillery Piece	7.62-mm Rifle	10,000
	7.62-mm Sniper Rifle	1,000
	7.62-mm Carbine Rifle	4,000
	45-mm Antitank Gun	48
	76-mm ZIS-3 Gun	73
	122-mm Howitzer	18

Subsequently, North Korea received from the Soviets 15,000 rifles, 139 artillery pieces, 87 T-34 tanks, and 98 airplanes, and secured from Communist China the return of 50,000 Korean veterans from various Chinese army units, including the 166th Division under the command of Pang Ho San, 164th Division under Kim Ch'ang Dok, and Independent 15th Division under Chon Woo. This arrangement had been made at a North Korea-China meeting of April 1949, and the Korean-born veterans returned to North Korea between July 1949 and May 1950.[66] Thanks to the Soviet and Chinese support, North Korea was

NKPA's T-34 tanks penetrating the 38th parallel, 1950

able to upgrade the 4th Independent Mixed Brigade to a full-strength division, activate the 5th and 6th Divisions, and reorganize the 115th Armored Regiment as the 105th Armored Brigade on may 16, 1949. Consisting of three armored regiments with 40 tanks each, a mechanized infantry regiment, instruction regiment, and an SU-76 battalion, the 105th Armor Brigade in effect had a division-level strength.

Moving from the volunteer system to conscription, P'yongyang declared total mobilization at the beginning of 1949, and conducted military training programs for high school and university students. In addition, a Democratic Youth League Training Center established in each province made it possible for the NKPA to secure reinforcements and reserves on a short notice.

The pace of North Korea's war preparations accelerated in 1950. On February 4, Kim Il Sung drafted a plan to increase the strength of ground forces to 10 divisions, and when the Soviets approved the plan, he requested on March 9 that the Soviet loan of 130 million roubles scheduled for 1951 be moved for-

⟨Table 8⟩   The Additional Activation of NKPA Infantry Divisions

Unit	Place of Activation	Date of Activation	Nucleus	Subordinate Units
4th Division	Chinnamp'o	October 1948	three infantry regiments from the 4th Independent Mixed Brigade and six independent units	16th, 17th, and 18th Regiments and an artillery regiment
5th Division	Nanam	August 1949	10,000 troops from the Northeast Volunteer Army, Chinese 164th Division	10th, 11th, and 12th Regiments and an artillery regiment
6th Division	Sinuiju	October 1949	10,000 troops from the Northeast Volunteer Army, Chinese 166th Division	13th, 14th, and 15th Regiments and an artillery regiment
10th Division	Sukch'on	March 1950	2nd Democratic Youth League Training Center in South P'yongan Province	25th, 27th, and 107th Regiment and an armored Regiment
12th Division	Wonsan	May 1950	Northeast Volunteer Army, Chinese 15th Division, and other Korean-born veterans	30th, 31st, and 32nd Regiments
13th Division	Sinuiju	June 1950	1st Democratic Youth League Training Center in North P'yongan Province	19th, 21st, and 23rd Regiments
15th Division	Hwach'on	June 1950	3rd Democratic Youth League Training Center in North Hamgyong Province	45th, 29th, and 50th Regiments

ward by one year. Kim Il Sung sought to equip three additional divisions with this loan, and the Soviets accepted his request.[67]

Kim's secret visit to Moscow in April 1950 facilitated the shipment of Soviet equipment. From April to May, so much Soviet materiel and equipment arrived at the Ch'ongjin Harbor that the shipment exceeded the offload capacity. The shipment included T-34 tanks, SU-76 self-propelled guns, mortars, howitzers, anti-aircraft guns, communications equipment, landing equipment, engineer equipment including a river-crossing gear, and ammunition.[68]

With this Soviet equipment, P'yongyang equipped the 12th Division consisting of the Korean veterans of the Chinese 15th Division, and, in addition, created 3 new divisions the (10th, 13th, and 15th) centered around trainees from three Democratic Youth League Training Centers. P'yongyang thus came to possess 10 combat-ready divisions.[69] Furthermore, by creating an additional independent armored regiment with the newly arrived Soviet tanks, the armor strength of the NKPA increased to a brigade plus a regiment, with a total of 240 T-34 tanks.

Besides the 5th, 6th, and 12th Divisions, NKPA infantry divisions were reinforced with the returnees from the armies of Communist China and the Soviet Union. Consequently, one-third of the NKPA troops were combat-experienced veterans, and their full strength was 11,000. They possessed formidable firepower, equipped as they were with Soviet 61-, 82-, and 120-mm mortars; 76.2- and 122-mm field artillery pieces; 45-mm antitank guns; and SU-76 self-propelled guns.

In addition to building up the People's Army units, P'yongyang strengthened the Security Corps under the jurisdiction of the Ministry of Internal Affairs, and increased border security along the 38th parallel. In July 1947, the 38th Border Security Forces was established in Sariwon. Centered around the Security Corps, this unit was responsible for guarding the 38th parallel. In

⟨Table 9⟩   The Establishment of North Korean Security Brigades

Unit	CP Location	Date Activation	Security Zone: Strength
1st 38th Security Brigade	Kansong	May 1949	Chorwon-Kansong: 5,000
3rd 38th Security Brigade	Chukch'on	September 1949	west of Haeju-Yellow Sea: 4,000
7th 38th Security Brigade	Sibyonri	1949	west of Chorwon-Haeju: 3,000
5th Railway Security Brigade	P'yongyang	January 1949	all railway lines: 3,000
2nd Border Security Brigade		September 1949	Yalu-Tumen River vicinity; battalion each in seven security zones: 2,600

early 1948, this unit was upgraded to the 38th Border Security Brigade, and in 1949 security forces along the 38th parallel were reorganized into three brigades. Deployed in Chukch'on (3rd Brigade), Shibyonni (7th Brigade), and Kansong (1st Brigade), these brigades shared the responsibility for border security. Also, the Railway Security Battalion was upgraded to the 5th Railway Security Brigade, and the 2th Border Security Brigade was created for security along the Yalu and Tumen River border.[70] These security brigades too were equipped with Soviet-made machine guns and mortars, and trained and supervised by Soviet officers with special emphasis on ideological education. In addition to these military units, the 766th Ind. Inf. Unit was established in Hoeryung in April 1949 to operate ranger units, and the 12th Motorcycle Reconnaissance Regiment created in Ch'ongjin in April 1950.

⟨Table 10⟩   The Strength of the North Korean People's Army

Army	10 Divisions	120,880
	Support and Special Units	61,820
	Subtotal	182,680
Navy and Marine Corps	3 Garrison Commands	**4,700**
	Naval Combat Team	9,000
Air Force	1 Air Division	2,000
Total		198,380

The original air squadron of the NKPA was transformed into a wing in January 1949, and was furnished with 30 Soviet propeller-driven aircraft such as IL-10's and YAK-9's. With additional aircraft arriving in December, this wing was upgraded to a division consisting of pursuit and assault wings and an instruction regiment plus an engineer battalion. Then received 60 additional IL-10's and YAK-9's from the Soviets in April 1950, and 60 more IL-10 attack planes just before the invasion. The NKPA thus possessed more than 210 airplanes. It goes without saying that the North Korean Air Force too was "nurtured" by the Soviet advisors. Pilots and maintenance crew received instructions at Soviet air bases and military schools. At the time, the Soviets were operating more than 10 air bases in North Korea, in such places as P'yongyang, Sinuiju, Anju, Ch'ongjin, Yonp'o, P'yonggang, and Shinmak.[71]

The affiliation of the North Korean Navy was changed from the Ministry of Internal Affairs to the Defense Ministry only in December 1949. The NKPA Navy thus had a rather late start. Reinforced to the strength of 15,000, the NKPA Navy established Garrison Commands in Ch'ongjin, Wonsan, and Chinnamp'o, and received more than 30 medium-and large-sized ships from the Soviets. In 1950, the North Korean Navy established a battalion-strength com-

⟨Table 11⟩   The Equipment of the North Korean People's Army

Tank and Armored Vehicle	T-34 (with 85-mm gun)	242
	Armored Vehicle	54
Self-Propelled Gun	SU-76 (76-mm)	176
Howitzer	122-mm	172
	76-mm	380
Mortar	120-mm	226
	82-mm	1,142
	61-mm	360
Antitank Gun	45-mm	550
Anti-Aircraft Artillery	85-mm	12
	37-mm	24
Aircraft	YAK-9 Fighter Plane	
	IL-10 Fighter Plane	
	IL-2 Fighter Plane	
	Training and Reconnaissance Plane	
	Total	211
Naval Vessel	Patrol Ship	30
	Support Vessel	80
	Total	110

bat unit at each Garrison Command, and created the 549th Unit just prior to the invasion, a combat unit to be committed to the landing operation along the eastern seashore.

Organized and trained under Soviet officers and armed with Soviet equipment from 1946 to 1950, the North Korean People's Army thus grew into a formidable force of 10 infantry divisions, 3 naval garrison commands, and 1 air division.

(2) The Infiltration of the People's Guerrilla Forces

In conjunction with the military build-up, North Korea systematically trained and sent guerrilla forces to facilitate the communization of the South. Those who had crossed the 38th parallel to the North were selected as secret agents and sent back to the South. With the establishment of the P'yongyang Academy in 1946, the South Operations Section was created with the mission to train South Korean Labor Party (SKLP) members for infiltration into the South. These operatives worked together with leftist elements and remaining SKLP members in the South to carry out terror and sabotage campaigns and to instigate military rebellions. They played a leading role in subversive activities in the South. In January 1948, P'yongyang established the Kangdong Political Academy and began to produce armed guerrillas in large numbers.[72] Designated the People's Guerrillas, they underwent additional training at the Yangyang People's Guerrilla Training Center. A total of 3,000 guerrillas were produced prior to the outbreak of the war. Before closing the Kangdong Political Academy, North Korea established the Third Military Academy in Hoeryung in April 1949, and specially trained the 766th Unit in unconventional warfare tactics.[73]

With ROK expeditionary units diverted to South Cholla and Kyongsang Provinces to put down the Yosu-Sunch'on Rebellion, the People's Guerrillas began to infiltrate into the South in large numbers. The first wave of guerrillas, numbering 180, infiltrated into Odae-san from Yangyang. Advancing through the mountains, the guerrillas came as far down south as T'aegi-san (Mt.), but most of them were wiped out by ROK expeditionary forces, and the remaining guerrillas had to flee in the direction of Chech'on in North Ch'ungch'ong Province. P'yongyang analyzed the causes of the failed infiltration operation, and sent another guerrilla unit of 400 into the Odae-san area on June 1, 1949. This attempt too ended in failure, however. On July 6, 1949, 200 guerrillas attempted yet another infiltration into the Odae-san area, but were largely anni-hilated by ROK expeditionary forces, and only 30 or so were able to flee to the Chungbong-san (Mt.) area.[74]

When the three infiltration operations all ended in failure, North Korea sent an elite unit of 300 under the command of Kim Dal Sam (instigator of the Cheju Insurgency) to the Ilwol-san area on August 4, 1949. When they were unable to make further advance into that area, the guerrillas reinfiltrated into Chikyungri in Youngilkun. Establishing a stronghold in Pohyun-san in North Kyongsang Province, the guerrillas formed the East Sea Group and engaged in systematic guerrilla warfare. Eventually, however, they too were routed by ROK expeditionary units. North Korea then established a new guerrilla strong-hold in the Ch'olwon area, and sent an advance party of 15 to Yongmoon-san on August 12, 1949-only to end in failure. The main unit of more than 40 infiltrated into Yongmoon-san via Myungji-san on August 15. When ROK expeditionary forces detected the infiltration attempt and subsequently shot to death more than 20 guerrillas, the remaining guerrillas fled away.

When the series of infiltration operations by the unconventional war-fare units ended in failure, P'yongyang sent to the T'aebaek-san area 360 People's Guerrillas under the direct command of Lee Ho Che, who was then the superin-tendent of the Kangdong Political Academy. Most of these guerrillas were wiped out, but approximately 100 of them managed to join the Kim Dal Sam Unit. Together with Kim's troops, the guerrillas were routed by the ROK expe-ditionary forces.[75]

Infiltration attempts continued even after this date. On September 28, approximately 50 guerrillas infiltrated into Keumokch'iri in Yangyangkun, but were driven back by the ROK troops. On November 6, approximately 100 guer-rillas infiltrated into Chikyungri in Youngilkun by sea, and joined the Kim Dal Sam Unit in Pohyun-san. After a brief lull, roughly 700 guerrillas under the command of Kim Sang Ho and Kim Moo Hyun infiltrated into Odae-san and Pangdae-san from the Yangyang, Inje, and Yanggu areas. They were elite units equipped with strong firepower, but were wiped out by ROK expeditionary forces.[76]

Overall, North Korea attempted a total of 10 infiltrations with roughly 2,400 guerrillas. Apparently, P'yongyang expected these guerrilla units to conduct a large number of harassment operations in rear areas at the time of a fullscale military invasion. Spoiling the North Korean plan, however, the ROK expeditionary forces killed or captured more than 2,000 of these guerrillas.[77]

Weakened security along the 38th parallel and elsewhere was the cost of this success, as parts of a frontline division and 3 rear divisions were committed against the North's unconventional warfare operations. Expressing its concern over the North Korean infiltrations, the UN Commission on Korea reported before the 4th General Assembly of the United Nations that P'yongyang was sending an increasing number of guerrillas to the South and strengthening its propaganda campaign.[78]

The sending of the People's Guerrilla Forces was a reflection of the North's emphasis on mixed tactics. Combining regular combat with unconventional warfare in the rear area, the mixed tactics sought to create a second front and disrupt the enemy's mobilization and reinforcement efforts. Turning both the front and the rear into battle grounds, mixed tactics sought to neutralize the enemy's will to fight and annihilate the enemy's troops.[79] North Korea's sending of the guerrillas was thus designed to create a second front prior to the invasion by its regular army. Although the failure of the infiltration operations meant that the objective of mixed tactics was not achieved, these operations nevertheless managed to disperse the rear strength of the ROK Army, and made a significant contribution to the initial success of the invasion.

While sending guerrillas to weaken or divert the strength of the ROK

Army and to sow confusion in the South, P'yongyang went on a peace offensive and proposed a North-South dialog to cover up its war preparations.

(3) North Korea's War Preparations and Peace Offensive

The foundation for North Korea's war preparations was provided by the regimentation of the whole society, which had already begun at the end of 1945. Student and youth groups were integrated, intellectuals and artists were mobilized for propaganda efforts, and various mass rallies were held to ensure that no one could exist as an individual outside a social organization. Everyone had to join the Communist Party or its suborganizations, and carry a resident registration card. Those classified as a reactionary or a counter-revolutionary were put under surveillance, and eventually driven out of the society. As a result, organizations opposed to the Communist Party began to disappear from North Korea, and everyone was subjected to control by the Party.[80]

In conjunction with the regimentation of the whole society, Kim Il Sung began to establish the North's military industrial base at the end of 1946 and encouraged weapons production on the belief that domestic production of military equipment and materiel was of crucial importance in building up military strength. By March 1948, the North had begun the domestic production of submachine guns, and set up factories by specific fields to manufacture such firearms as pistols and mortars as well as ammunition, artillery shells, and grenades. In addition, North Korea held a launching ceremony for a domestically produced patrol ship at Wonsan Shipyards in 1949, and produced the same type of patrol ships at Namp'o Shipyards.[81] Thus, prior to launching a purely economic development drive, North Korea mobilized resources to build up its military industry and prepare for war.

In addition, on July 15, 1949, P'yongyang organized the National

Defense Sponsors' Association under the pretext of providing support for NKPA soldiers and their families. This Association established branches down to the *ri* level. All residents between 18 and 45 years of age were obliged to join the Association, and take part in the so-called national defense enterprise. Following Kim Il Sung's instructions, the Association conducted a large-scale donation campaign for the modernization of the NKPA as well as for the support of NKPA families.[82]

While organizing the masses in such a fashion, P'yongyang embarked on a socialist economic reform program. First to be put into effect was the Land Reform of March 1946. Wealthy landowners and capitalists were purged during this reform, which confiscated 1 million chongbo (one chongbo equals 2.451 acres) of land without any compensation to the owners and freely distributed this land to peasants. The Land Reform of March 1946 was followed in August by the nationalization of major industries, which affected approximately a thousand industrial facilities. Subsequently, North Korea's landowners, capitalists, and men of religion fled to the South to seek freedom, and P'yongyang began to consolidate its economic base by instituting an economic planning system. By 1950, North Korea had completed 3 rounds of economic plans.[83]

Thus, by 1949, North Korea's Communist regime, with the assistance of the Soviet Union and Communist China, had largely succeeded in securing sufficient military power and organizing the society according to its design. P'yongyang's next move was to embark on a peace offensive. At the World Conference for Peace in April 1949, the North Korean representative followed the lead of the Soviets to speak out against arms races and military budget increases. Also, establishing the Democratic Front for National Unification (DFNU) on June 29, P'yongyang proposed its plan for peaceful unification the next day. At this time, P'yongyang estimated that the Left could gather approximately 80% of the vote in the North and 65-70% in the South.[84] P'yongyang believed that

Seoul naturally would refuse to accept this proposal. The South's refusal would allow North Korea to score a political victory. At the Peace Conference in Stockholm in March 1950, North Korea expressed full support for the ban on the use of nuclear weapons and arms reduction proposals, and went on to organize a peace commission and embark on a nationwide signature-collecting campaign back home.

On June 7, 1950, the DFNU proposed to hold an election throughout Korea in August based on the principle of self-determination rather than under UN observation. When Seoul rejected this proposal, P'yongyang once again proposed this same plan for peaceful unification, this time in the form of a resolution. North Korea also proposed to exchange the imprisoned nationalist leader Cho Man Shik with high-level spies who had been arrested in South Korea. On June 19, just six days prior to the outbreak of war, North Korea declared that it was willing to discuss plans to achieve unification through inter-parliamentary agreement. P'yongyang's peace offensive and proposal for inter-Korean talks was, however, merely a ploy to score a political victory and to cover up its war preparations.[65] As if to prove this point, the NKPA provoked a series of clashes across the 38th parallel to test the strength of the South Korean army and to secure favorable terrain.

(4) Provocations Across the 38th Parallel

By July 1947, the NKPA 38th Security Forces had already replaced the Soviet guards and established favorable positions along the 38th parallel. When the ROK Army took over the border patrol responsibilities from the US occupation forces and began to build up defensive positions in early 1949, the NKPA guards disrupted the work by firing at the ROK soldiers. After the 38th Security Forces was expanded to three brigades, the NKPA began to resort to more provocative measures to intimidate the ROK Army, going as far as to send its troops to strike across the 38th parallel.

The NKPA frequently launched simultaneous attacks across the 38th parallel in the Kaesong, Ongjin, P'och'on, Ch'unch'on, and Kangnung areas. Prior to the outbreak of the Korean War, there were a total of 847 illegal firing incidents and attacks by the People's Army. This total translates to an average of approximately once every three days since the day of Korea's liberation, or more than once a day since the establishment of the North Korean regime.[86] The NKPA, however, always blamed the skirmishes on the ROK Forces in its propaganda campaigns. A brief list of major provocations by the NKPA are as follows:

Kaesong Area: In November 1948, the 11th Regiment of the ROK Army took over the border security responsibility for the sector between Ch'ongdan and Korangp'o, and was building up its positions. At the time, the enemy had occupied Songak-san (altitude: 488m), which borders the 38th parallel on the north. Friendly forces were building up defensive positions on Hill 475 and Hill 292, which extend southward from Songak-san. On May 3, 1949, a battalion-strength NKPA unit moved southward along the ridgeline of the highest peak of Songak-san, and attacked to seize Hill 292 as well as Hill UN and Hill Dove in the vicinity. This NKPA unit consisted mainly of troops from the 3rd Regiment, 1st Division. Lt. Col. Ch'oi Kyung Rok, commander of the ROK 11th Regiment, responded by organizing a battalion-strength attack with fire support from 105-mm howitzers and 57-mm anti-tank guns. The commander of the 2nd Battalion led the ROK troops including the regiment NCO training unit, but could not overwhelm the enemy, who fired from their totschkas [A totschka (from Russian) is a bunker with concrete-enforced walls from which machine gun and small arms fire can be delivered] After suffering many casualties, the ROK troops decided to carry out a suicide attack and selected 9 soldiers for the special mission. Departing from the valley of Hill Dove, each member of this suicide unit attacked and destroyed his assigned totschka on the enemy hill. In recovering the lost hills, 39 ROK soldiers lost their lives, including the 2nd Battalion commander, NCO training unit commander, and 10 members of the suicide attack unit.[87]

After the Songak-san battle, the NKPA initiated a series of small-scale clashes, and sought to advance into the Paech'on area. On May 17, 1949, a battalion-strength NKPA unit crossed the 38th parallel and attacked Paech'on. The 7th Company of the ROK 11th Regiment requested reinforcements, and was able to push back the invaders with support from the 5th Company.

The confrontation between the ROKA and NKPA units continued over the strategically located Songak-san area. Having secured Hill 488, the highest peak of Songak-san, the NKPA in effect had a covering terrain to look down upon downtown Kaesong and frequently intimidated the city with surprise small-arms fire. On July 25, the NKPA pushed the limit and fired mortar shells on Kaesong. In response, Gen. Kim Sok Won, commander of the ROK 1st Division, ordered the 1st Battalion of the 11th Regiment to attack to seize Hill 488. The skirmishes over Songak-san continued until August 3, but the 11th Regiment eventually overcame the initial disadvantages of terrain to secure Hill Lighthouse (475m), Hill 292, and Hill Dove.[88]

Ongjin Area: On the Ongjin Peninsula, a company of the ROK 12th Regiment and three companies of the Mobile Police Unit in Kyonggi Province were responsible for security along the 38th parallel, which ran along a chain of hills and mountains: Turak-san-Kuksa-bong-Hill Ch'ungmoo-Eunp'a-san and Kach'i-san. On May 21, 1949, concurrently with their provocations in the Kaesong area, NKPA units launched a surprise attack against a southern hill of

Kuksa-bong, and penetrated deep into the ROK defensive area on May 26. Consisting of more than 200 troops from the 3rd Brigade of the 38 Security Forces, the NKPA units also occupied Chak-san to the east of Turak-san far below of 38th Parallel. In response, the ROK 12th Regiment stationed in Inch'on launched a counterattack and drove back the invaders, but had to retreat when the NKPA units resumed their attack on June 7 with reinforcements. In response to the intensified NKPA offensive, the ROKA established the Ongjin Area Command and carried out a major counterattack to throw back the enemy.[89]

Having lost the First Battle of Ongjin, the NKPA sent the 3rd Brigade Commander Ch'oi Hyun to the area and prepared for another invasion. On August 4, the NKPA units attempted to penetrate through the Kuksa-bong and Hill Ch'ungmu area to seize the Ongjin Peninsula. Holding their ground against the initial enemy attack, the ROK 18th and 2nd Regiments under the Ongjin Area Command carried out an audacious counterattack and retained Hill Ch'ungmu.

After the failure of the second invasion, the NKPA sent two battalions of the 3rd Brigade on October 14 to recover Eunp'a-san which they had lost during the first invasion. To recover Chak-san, the ROK Army had first seized Eunp'a-san to its north during the First Battle of Ongjin. Although the ROK 2nd Regiment fought hard to hold Eunp'asan, it could not match the enemy's firepower and eventually had to retreat from the mountain. The 2nd Regiment subsequently launched a series of retaliatory strikes against the enemy, but returned to its position each time.[90]

P'och'on Area: Having failed in the Kaesong and Ongjin areas, the NKPA attempted an open attack in the P'och'on area. On June 12, 1949, the NKPA sent roughly 200 troops to attack Sajikri. Having secured intelligence regarding this attack, however, the ROK 1st Regiment concealed its two companies in ambush and annihilated the invaders.

Ch'unch'on Area: On August 6, 1949, a battalion-strength unit of NKPA troops from the 1st Brigade of the 38 Security Forces advanced southward from Inje to Kwandaeri. Firing mortar shells, they crossed the Soyang River and attacked Hill 682, Hill 704, and Hill 600. In response, the Ch'unch'on-based ROK 7th Regiment sent the 1st Battalion from Hongch'on to carry out a counterattack, and recaptured Hill 682 and Hill 704. The regiment, however, failed to secure Hill 600 to the east, even after 7 successive attempts. Aware of the significance and symbolic value of the operation, the Army Chief of Staff issued a special order to commit the Wonju-based 8th Regiment to the counterattack, and with this support, the 7th Regiment managed to recover Hill 600.[91]

Kangnung Area: The NKPA also carried out a series of provocations along the shores of the East Sea to the north of Kangnung. The 1st Brigade of the 38th Security Forces frequently crossed the 38th parallel to commit indiscriminate crimes against civilians, including kidnapping, looting, and arson, and to strike against the ROKA positions in the area. In February 1949, the ROK 10th Regiment repulsed the enemy who had invaded into the Chankyori area from Sorim and Kit'omuonri. In retaliation for the invasion, the 10th Regiment also delivered 105-mm fire at the enemy Naval Detachment Unit in Kit'omunri. In a similar vein, to strike at the source of the problem, a part of the 10th Regiment attacked the North's guerrilla training center in Yangyang and withdrew.[92]

This series of provocations by P'yongyang seemed to have been carried out with two objectives in mind: to evaluate the combat readiness of the People's Army as well as the defensive strength of the ROK Army units; and to disperse the ROK security forces along the 38th parallel in order to facilitate the infiltration of the People's Guerrillas. As the United States went ahead with its plan to withdraw its troops from Korea in spite of the continuing provocations by the NKPA units, the Republic had to redouble efforts to improve its own ability to defend the nation.

III. The Establishment of the ROK Army and Its Self-Defense Efforts

1. The Establishment of the ROK Army

(1) Establishment Plan

While caught in the turmoil of politics in post-liberation Korea, those returning from Japan, Manchuria, and China with military background began to form various military organizations with an eye to playing a leading role in the establishment of the regular army for the new nation. Even the communists formed private armies on the belief that the possession of armed forces would help them to seize the initiative in the establishment of the national government. The proliferation of small-scale paramilitary organizations, numbering more than 30, made bleak the prospect that any one of them would become the nucleus of the new national army. The indiscriminate expansion of the communist military organizations even brought about social instability.

It was at this treacherous time that Cho Byong Ok, the Korean Chief of Police in the US Military Government, proposed an alternative plan to establish the national army. Heeding the advice of Lee Ung Jun and Won Yong Dok, Cho suggested to Gen. Lawrence E. Schick, Director of the Police Bureau, that a Ministry of National Defense be created to draw up a plan for the establishment of a native defense force in Korea. Within the USAMGIK itself, the issue of or-

ganizing a native defense force was actively discussed. USAFIK Commander Lt.
Gen. Hodge requested that a plan to establish the Korean army be drawn up,[93]
and set up a commission within the USAMGIK to formulate national security
plans for Korea.

On November 13, 1945, the USAMGIK Headquarters issued Ordinance
No. 28[94] and established an Office of the Director of National Defense. This ordinance was based on the premise that all private military organizations would
be disbanded. The US Military Government was concerned that if these military organizations were to join force with an equally confusing array of political
parties, social turmoil could only be amplified. Ordinance No. 28 gave the Office of the Director of National Defense jurisdiction over the Bureau of Police
and over a new Bureau of Armed Forces consisting of Army and Navy Departments.[95]

> Ordinance No. 28:
> In order to prepare for the eventual independence of Korea... to assist civil-
> ian police agencies in the maintenance of civil peace and security and the
> defense of the rights of the people against civil disorder and maintain free-
> dom of religion, freedom of speech and property rights, to inaugurate the
> recruiting, organization, training and equipping of the requisite armed
> forces on land and sea, and to guarantee the evolution of administration of
> nationhood, the office of the Director of National Defense of the Military
> Government of Korea is hereby established.

The USAMGIK regulated the activities of private military organizations in accordance with Provision 3 of Ordinance No. 28, and taking Lee Ung
Jun's national defense plan as its starting point, the Office of the Director of National Defense led the efforts to draw up a plan to establish a Korean national
defense force. The plan made the following list of recommendations:

① A Korean national defense force shall be created and developed to supplement the National Police.

② The national defense force shall have a total strength of 45,000 men and shall consist of the Army and the Air Force. There shall be one corps of three infantry divisions supported by essential service troops for the Army, and one transport and two fighter flights, together with ground components, for the Air Force.

③ The Navy, or Coast Guard, shall be limited to 5,000 men.[96]

Since it was more than likely under the prevailing circumstance that this new national defense force would undergo American-style training, the US Military Government first established the Military English Language School to facilitate communication between US officers and future cadres of the Korean armed forces. Founded on December 5, 1946, the School admitted its first class after oral tests, physical exams, and military background checks. The curriculum emphasized military English, but it also included national history, staff functions, driver's education, and small-arms training. The School was closed after commissioning 110 officers in succession over four months.[97]

After the closing of the Military English Language School, the Office of the Director of National Defense established the Korean National Defense Constabulary Academy on May 1, 1946. Those officer candidates who had not graduated from the Military English Language School were admitted into this Academy. Subsequently renamed the Korean Constabulary Academy and Korea Military Academy, this school produced the cadres for the new national army.

After establishing the Military English Language School in preparation for the establishment of the native defense force, the USAMGIK sent its further plans to Gen. MacArthur. Judging that the plans were outside his jurisdiction, Gen. MacArthur reported them to the State-War-Navy Coordinating Committee (SWNCC). The SWNCC stated that it could not make any decision on the establishment of a native defense force until political issues were resolved by the US-USSR Joint Commission. The Committee, however, added that a native police-type force could be equipped with surplus US arms to ease the security responsibility of the US occupation forces in Korea. In accordance with this decision, Gen. Hodge gave new instructions to Col. Arthur S. Champeny, the newly appointed Director of National Defense of the USAMGIK. Reducing the size of the originally planned native defense force, Col. Champeny drew up a proposal to create a constabulary reserve similar in character to a police force rather than an army.[98] Designated the Bamboo Plan, this proposal envisioned the establishment of a police regiment for each of the eight provinces in southern Korea, for a total strength of 25,000. During the discussion leading to this plan, Lee Ung Joon, then advisor to the Office of the Director of National Defense, suggested that each province maintain a division-strength force, but his advice was not accepted by the US Military Government. The Bamboo Plan included the following provisions:

① One company shall be formed in each of the eight provinces of southern Korea and organized as US-style infantry, less weapons platoons. Each company shall consist of 6 officers and 225 enlisted men, the former to be furnished by a centralized officers' training school.

② In each province, a company shall be formed overstrength by approximately 20 percent. After a short period of training, a second company shall be built around the surplus of the first.

③ The new company shall likewise be recruited overstrength, to provide a cadre for a third. A battalion shall then be formed, and thereafter gradually expanded to one regiment of Constabulary in each province.[99]

According to the Bamboo Plan, a Korean native defense force was established with the title of the Korean Constabulary Reserve or the Korean National Defense Constabulary.[100] In spite of their objections, most private military organizations were disbanded, and their members were absorbed into the Constabulary.

(2) The Establishment and Reinforcement of the Korean Constabulary

Based on the provisions of the Bamboo Plan and USAMGIK Ordinance No. 42(January 14, 1946), the Korean National Defense Constabulary was established with 25,000 constabulary reserves plus a coast guard for inshore patrol.[101] Starting with the establishment of A Company, 1st Battalion, 1st Regiment in T'aenung on January 15, the Constabulary created a light infantry company armed only with rifles for each province. After the establishment of the General Headquarters on February 7, the Constabulary pushed ahead with the task of organization and recruitment. By April 1, 1946, the Constabulary had completed the establishment of the first eight regiments by creating a core company for each of the provincial regiments.[102]

Mostly Military English Language School graduates were placed in responsible posts in the Constabulary. Soldiers were recruited, but since even the former members of leftist private armies were accepted, the Constabulary was later to suffer from ideological conflicts within its ranks. The Korean National Defense Constabulary gradually expanded each provincial unit, from company to battalion to full regiment, and had largely completely this work by March 1947. By that date, a new provincial regiment in Cheju Province plus the originally planned eight regiments, except the one in Taegu, had been upgraded to full strength. Leftist elements in the 6th Regiment had delayed the organization in Taegu.[103]

Each provincial regiment consisted of three battalions, each of which in turn comprised three companies. The rank structure had three main divisions: officer, NCO, and enlisted. Each officer was assigned a 5-digit ID number, and each enlisted man, a 7-digit number. The Constabulary was initially equipped with captured Japanese-model 38 and 99 rifles and dressed in Japanese-style uniform. From September 1946, however, US weapons and US-style uniform gradually replaced these vestiges of the Japanese colonial occupation. Training focused on the maintenance of public security, and emphasized bayonet drills, rifle-handling exercises, and riot control. It had little to do with combat training.[104]

While the groundwork for the establishment of a national army was being laid down, efforts to create a navy as well were being made. First, Sohn Won Il and Chung Keuk Mo formed a private organization called the Naval Service Society. Their group participated in the Committee for the Preparation of Korean Independence for a while, before merging with Patriotic Naval Group of Korea to establish the Choson (Korean) Naval Association. Through subsequent negotiation with the US Military Government, the Choson Naval Association agreed to form a coast guard of 200 men and establish its headquarters in Chinhae. The group formally established the coast guard on November 11, 1945, and named it the Naval Defense Corps.[105]

The Naval Defense Corps was absorbed into the Office of the Director of National Defense on January 14, 1946, and Sohn Won Il became its first commander. From the beginning, the lack of personnel and equipment was a problem for the Naval Defense Corps. To secure personnel and equipment, the Corps established the Naval Defense School on January 17, 1946, and built shipyards. The Navy Personnel School was later renamed as the Choson Coast Guard Academy, and produced the founding members of the Korean Navy. After the establishment of the Republic, this school became the Korean Naval Academy.

While pushing ahead with the establishment of the Korean Constabulary, the Office of the Director of National Defense was upgraded to the Department of National Defense on March 29, 1946, as part of a general restructuring and upgrading of government bodies in the USAMGIK.[106] The Soviet representative at the US-USSR Joint Commission immediately protested, contesting the US use of the term "Department of National Defense," which seemed to imply a government body of a full-fledged nation. Accepting the Soviet protest, the USAMGIK on June 15 changed the name to the Department of Internal Security. Accordingly, the Korean National Defense Constabulary was changed to the Korean Constabulary; the National Defense Constabulary Headquarters, to the Constabulary General Headquarters; and the Naval Defense Corps, to the Korean Coast Guard.[107]

⟨Table 12⟩　　The Organization of the Department of National Security in Southern Korea

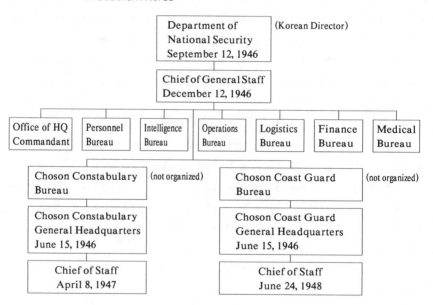

Korean military leaders protested against the name changes, but Gen. Hodge justified the move on grounds of US-Soviet relations. In response, the Korean leaders renamed the Department of Internal Security as the Department of National Security (T'onguibu). In order to preserve the legitimacy of the armed forces and to reaffirm the value of independence, a former Restoration Army commander, Gen. Ryu Dong Yol, was appointed as the first Director of the National Security Department on September 12. Secretary Ryu worked with Lt. Col. Song Ho Sung and Lt. Col. Lee Hyong Kun, Commander of the Constabulary, to purge the armed forces of communist infiltrators, and pushed for the establishment of a regular army.[108]

When Director Ryu took his office on September 12, military command was, in effect, transferred to Korean nationals. US officers played the role of advisors, and Koreans began to assume command at the Constabulary General Headquarters and at the provincial regiments.[109] There were approximately 20 American advisors at the National Security Department, and 10 or fewer at the General Headquarters of the Korean Constabulary. In addition, each field advisor worked with two provincial regiments on recruitment, administration, organization, and training matters.

Another turning point in the establishment of the Korean armed forces came in October 1947, when the Soviet delegation at the US-USSR Joint Commission proposed the withdrawal of the occupation forces from Korea. In response to the Soviet proposal, the US War Department requested Gen. MacArthur and Gen. Hodge to look into the possibility of creating a national army in Korea. After considering Korea's poor economic conditions, lack of training facilities and competent officers, language barriers, and the USAFIK's diminishing capability to provide support, they concluded that it would be premature to establish a national army in Korea. Instead, they decided to expand the Constabulary to 50,000 men and provide heavy infantry weapons, including artillery pieces and armored vehicles.

This measure was taken not only to improve internal security in Korea, but also to prepare for the eventual withdrawal of the US forces. In view of the future national security needs after the establishment of the Korean government, the National Security Department merged the existing nine regiments into three groups of three, and thus created three brigades, on December 1, 1947. Also, in accordance with the Constabulary expansion plan, the Security Department redoubled its efforts to secure recruits, and established three additional regiments and two brigades in April and May of 1948.

⟨Table 13⟩   The Activation of Regiments in Southern Korea

Regiment	Date of Activation	Place of Activation	Founding Commander
1st Regiment	Janaury 15, 1946	T'aenung	Capt. Ch'ae Byong Dok
2nd Regiment	February 28, 1946	Taejon	Capt. Lee Hyong Kun
3rd Regiment	February 26, 1946	Iri	Lt. Kim Paik Il
4th Regiment	February 15, 1946	Kwangsan	Lt. Kim Hong Jun
5th Regiment	Janaury 29, 1946	Pusan	2nd Lt. Park Byong Kwon
6th Regiment	February 18, 1946	Taegu	2nd Lt. Kim Yong Hwan
7th Regiment	February 7, 1946	Ch'ongju	2nd Lt. Min Ki Shik
8th Regiment	April 1, 1946	Ch'unch'on	Lt. Kim Jong Kap
9th Regiment	November 16, 1946	Mosulp'o	Lt. Chang Ch'ang Kuk
10th Regiment	May 1, 1948	Kangnung	Maj. Paik Nam Kwon
11th Regiment	May 4, 1948	Suwon	Lt. Col. Park Jin Kyong
12th Regiment	May 1, 1948	Kunsan	Lt. Col. Paik In Ki
13th Regiment	May 4, 1948	Onyang	Lt. Col. Lee Ch'i Op
14th Regiment	May 4, 1948	Yosu	Maj. Lee Yong Sun
15th Regiment	May 4, 1948	Masan	Lt. Col. Cho Am

〈Table 14〉   The Activation of Brigades in Southern Korea

Brigade	Date of Activation	Place of Activation	First Commander	Organization
1st Brigade	December 1, 1947	Seoul	Col. Song Ho Song	1st, 2nd, 3rd Regiments
2nd Brigade	December 1, 1947	Taejon	Col. Won Yong Dok	2nd, 3rd, 4th Regiments
3rd Brigade	December 1, 1947	Pusan	Col. Lee Ung Jun	5th, 6th, 9th Regiments
4th Brigade	April 29, 1948	Seoul	Col. Ch'ae Byong Dok	7th, 8th, 10th Regiments
*6th Brigade	November 20, 1948	Ch'ongju	Lt. Col. Yu Jae Hung	Renamed 4th Brigade
7th Brigade	April 29, 1948	Kwangju	Col. Kim Sang Kyom	3rd, 4th, 9th Regiments
8th Brigade	January 7, 1949	Yongsan	Col. Lee Jun Shik	1st, 9th, 17th, 19th Regiments

〈Table 15〉   The Activation of Support Units in Southern Korea

Unit	Date of Activation	First Commander	Place of Activation	Nucleus
Supply Unit	July 1, 1946	Maj. Ch'ae Byong Dok	Taebangdong	Supply Company, 1st Regiment
1st Ordnance Battalion	January 1, 1948	Maj. So Byong Ki	Yongdungp'o	Ordnance Company
1st Engineer Battalion	January 1, 1948	Lt. Col. Oh Kyu Bom	Kimp'o	21st Motor Company
1st Quartermaster Battalion	January 1, 1948	Maj. Yu Hung Su	Yongdungp'o	
1st Medical Battalion	May 1, 1948	Capt. Han Wang Yong	Yongdungp'o	
1st Army Hospital	May 1, 1948	Lt. Col. Shin Hak Jin	Yongdungp'o	
51st Signal Battalion	May 1, 1948	Lt. Col. Chong Un Wan	Susaek	Signal Detachment at Each Regiment

Soldiers of National Defense Constabulary at machine gun training

The establishment of combat service support units and provision of supplies kept pace with the creation of regiments and brigades. Ordnance, quartermaster, engineer, medical, and signal units began to be established from July 1946.

As for the Navy, by January 14, 1948, the Korean Coast Guard had received a total of 36 ships from the US Navy, starting with 2 LCIs (landing craft) on September 15, 1946, and including 18 AMSs (mine sweepers), 11 JMSs, and one oil tanker. The Coast Guard moved its General Headquarters from Chinhae to Seoul on October 1, 1946, and successively established naval bases in Inch'on, Mokp'o, Mukho, Kunsan, P'ohang, and Pusan as well as a special base command in Chinhae. With the expansion of its naval defense capability, the Coast Guard took over the naval security responsibility from the US 7th Fleet effective August 30, 1947. By the end of the same year, the Coast Guard organization had developed into two special task fleets.

Concurrent with the establishment of the Korean Constabulary, Korean airmen with overseas experience formed the Association for the Foundation of the Air Force on August 10, 1946. After almost two years of effort, on May 15,

1948, the Association succeeded in establishing an air unit under the direct control of the Defense Department. Based in Susaek, Kyonggi Province, this unit was given liaison responsibilities essential to the successful conduct of Constabulary operations. On June 23, the affiliation of this air unit was changed to the Korean Constabulary, and on July 27, with the changing of its name to "Air Base Unit," this unit was moved to Kimp'o. The unit did not yet possess a single plane, and its strength was limited to only 105 men.

As the Korean Constabulary was gradually transformed into a regular army, the Department of National Security and the Constabulary General Headquarters clarified their jurisdiction, with the former assuming policymaking responsibilities and the latter, operations control.[10]

(3) The Birth of the ROK Armed Forces

With the establishment of the Republic of Korea on August 15, 1948, the Korean Constabulary had its new start as the ROK Army. Article 6 of the Constitution declared: "The Republic of Korea shall renounce all aggressive wars. The National Armed Forces shall carry out the sacred duties of national defense."[11] The first Minister of National Defense was Gen. Lee Pom Sok, former Restoration Army commander. Minister Lee tried to promote the harmony and unity of armed forces by accepting into the ranks soldiers with background in the Japanese Army and the Manchurian Army as well as those from the Restoration Army. Finding inspiration in the independence struggle of the Restoration Army, he established national independence, utmost loyalty, anti-communism, and democratic principles as the founding ideology for the ROK Armed Forces.

With the creation of the Ministry of National Defense (MND), the Korean Constabulary was renamed the ROK Army, and the Korean Coast

Guard the ROK Navy. As the Korean armed forces began to take a concrete shape, its legal foundations became urgently needed. Accordingly, on November 30, the Armed Forces Organization Act, drawn up by Chung Il Kwon and Shin Ung Kyun, was passed by the National Assembly.[112]

This Act designated the president as the supreme commander of the armed forces, which was to consist initially of the army and the navy. The air force was to be organized at first as an Army Aviation unit, and later to become a separate service.[113] Also, the armed forces was to consist of the regular army and the reserves.

Equipped with small arms, the army consisted of five brigades and fif-

⟨Table 16⟩ The Organization of the ROK Armed Forces (November 30, 1948)

⟨Table 17⟩   Estimated Strength Needs of the ROK Armed Forces

Army	Regular Army	100,000
	Reserves	100,000
Navy	Regular Navy	100,000
	Reserves	100,000
Air Force	Strategic unit spun off from the Army: one air division Detached to the Navy and Army: small unit	

teen regiments for a total strength of 50,000. The navy, organized into two special task fleets, had 105 ships and more than 3,000 men. The National Defense Minister had the military administration authority; whereas, the Chief of General Staff, while assisting the Minister, exercised military command over the armed forces. The Chief of Staff for each service received instructions from the Chief of General Staff to command and supervise his service.

In accordance with the subsequently enacted Organization Order, the National Defense Ministry initially consisted of five offices (1st to 4th Office plus the Office of Aviation). To complete the organization of the MND and each service headquarters, the Joint Staff Council was established with the Chief of General Staff as its chairman, and the general and special staff offices were set up at each service headquarters.

According to the MND's calculations, the total defensive strength required to deter threats from North Korea and Manchuria was 230,000, but the available strength did not amount to even a quarter of that level.[114]

It was thus imperative that the ROK Forces secure the required level of strength. The ROK Forces were, however, faced with a set of formidable challenges at the time. Internally, the ROK Forces had to deal with ideological conflicts within the ranks. Recruiting with no regard to ideological background in the nascent stage of the Korean Constabulary had created an extremely volatile situation in the army, as communist sympathizers spread their ideology and instigated armed rebellions with support from the South Korean Labor Party. In the end, the Yosu-Sunch'on Rebellion provided the impetus for the military leadership to embark on a great purge in October 1948 to rid the army of the communist infiltrators and to re-establish the chain of command. Externally, the ROK Forces had to cope with the withdrawal of the US occupation forces, and to take up the heavy burden of national defense with limited resources.

2. ROK Forces' Efforts to Secure Self-Defense Capability

(1) The US Withdrawal and ROK Responses

The withdrawal of the occupation forces from Korea formally became a topic of discussion at the US-USSR Joint Commission on September 26, 1947. At this meeting, the Soviet delegate called for the simultaneous withdrawal of all foreign troops from Korea in early 1948. As the Soviets had already established an effective and powerful pro-Soviet government in northern Korea, they apparently believed that they could achieve their objective of establishing a "democratic" government for all of Korea without the occupation forces.[115]

The United States meanwhile pondered its options. A report prepared by Gen. Albert C. Wedemeyer, President Truman's special envoy to Korea and China, suggested three alternative courses of action: immediate withdrawal, indefinite occupation, and simultaneous withdrawal with the Soviets. In the end, Washington concluded that the US had no strategic interests to justify maintaining troops and bases in Korea and that the USAFIK was needed in other regions. On the condition that Korea would not fall under Soviet domination, Washington began to explore ways to withdraw the US troops "as soon as practicable while minimizing its adverse consequences."

As the Korean problem was transferred to the United Nations in the fall of 1947, the withdrawal of the occupation forces from Korea became a hot point of contention at the General Assembly. In its draft resolution on the creation of the UN Temporary Commission on Korea, the United States proposed that all foreign troops withdraw from Korea after a united government be established. In response, the Soviet representative argued for withdrawal prior to the creation of a united Korean government. Adopting the US proposal on November 14, the United Nations recommended that immediately upon the establishment of a Korean National Government, "that Government should...arrange with the occupying Powers for the complete withdrawal from Korea of their armed forces as early as practicable and if possible within ninety days."[116]

On April 8, 1948, in defining its relationship with the ROK government to be formed, the United States accordingly decided to provide support for the native defense force as a means to facilitate the withdrawal of the US forces from Korea. Washington wanted to have in place all the necessary conditions for a full withdrawal by the end of 1948. The US planned to support the ROK government with economic assistance and expand the Korean Constabulary to defend the nation against external aggression except in the case of a full-scale war. The withdrawal of the US troops was to commence on August 15 and to be completed by December 31.[117]

As the planned withdrawal of the Soviet and US occupation forces became an accomplished fact, the newly formed ROK government sought to enhance the defensive capability of its armed forces. The Republic, however, lacked economic resources to build up military strength on its own. Furthermore, the expansionism of international communism and the threat posed by North Korea seemed to call for a collective security arrangement, in particular a close cooperation with the United Sates. The ROK government thus adopted as the basis of its defense policy "combined national defense" instead of the more ambitious "self-defense." Accordingly, the ROK government tried to persuade the

US to scrap or delay the planned withdrawal of its forces, and sought to secure military assistance to enhance the defensive capability of the ROK forces. For its part, Washington planned to fill the gap created by the withdrawal with greater military assistance. On August 24, 1948, the two sides signed a provisional administrative accord on military security, and agreed to discuss the withdrawal procedure and to maintain the security of the Republic until the withdrawal. Seoul and Washington also agreed to continue to organize, train, and equip the ROK forces.[118] The USAFIK commander was granted a provisional authority to exercise operational control over the ROK forces. The US also established a Provisional Military Advisory Group (PMAG) in Korea.

In September 1948, the Soviet Union announced that it would accept North Korea's request to complete the withdrawal of the Soviet forces by the end of December. Requesting that the United States take corresponding measures, the Soviets began their withdrawal on October 19. As the US troops began to withdraw from Korea, the ROK security environment rapidly deteriorated. North Korea's communist regime was going ahead with its extensive military build-up, and communists in the South, sometimes under P'yongyang's direct instructions, were instigating a series of riots and armed rebellions. The ROK Army was extremely inadequate to deal with these challenges to national security. President Syngman Rhee sent a request to President Truman to withhold the planned US troop withdrawal until the complete loyalty of his troops was secured and until they were ready to deal with any internal or external threats.[119]

On November 20, 1948, National Defense Minister Lee Pom Sok explained to the National Assembly the government's position on the US troop withdrawal as well as its strategic implications. Exposing the Soviets' ulterior motive in calling for a simultaneous withdrawal, Minister Lee asked the Assembly to adopt a resolution for the retention of the US forces in Korea. Accepting his request, the National Assembly declared: "Given the domestic situation, we resolve that a continued stationing of the US forces in Korea is necessary until the security of the Republic of Korea is firmly established."[120] Prior to this resolution, the ROK government had persuaded the UN Temporary Commission on Korea to submit a report recommending that the US troop withdrawal be withheld until South and North Korea agree to a peaceful negotiation. Such a report was presented to the UN General Assembly on October 30. Convinced that the US must not keep pace with the Soviets to pull out all its troops by the end of the year, Washington decided to defer to the United Nations in regard to the troop withdrawal.[121]

On December 12, 1948, the UN General Assembly in Paris adopted a resolution on the establishment of the Republic of Korea and the withdrawal of the occupation forces, and recommended that "the occupying Power should withdraw their occupation forces from Korea as early as practicable."[122] Accordingly, the USAFIK secured some flexibility with regard to the withdrawal date. On December 16, however, the Soviet Union unilaterally declared that its troops had completed the withdrawal from North Korea.

The USAFIK dissolved the XXIV Corps on January 15, 1949, and withdrew from Korea, leaving behind only a single regimental combat team (RCT) of 7,500 and the Provisional Military Advisory Group (PMAG). This RCT pulled out of Korea on June 30. On July 1, the day after the completion of the troop withdrawal, the PMAG formally became the US Military Advisory Group to the Republic of Korea (KMAG). The mission of this advisory group was to give advice on the organization and training of the ROK forces and to ensure the efficient provision of US military assistance.[123]

(2) Efforts to Secure Self-Defense Capability

Entrusted with the critical mission of defending the nation, the newly established ROK forces had to build up strength to deter any outside aggression in the wake of the US troop withdrawal. In order to secure the required level of strength derived from its earlier calculations of personnel needs, the Ministry of National Defense had concentrated on expanding the number of infantry regiments since October 1948. As a result of these efforts, the MND had managed to organize a total of six brigades and twenty regiments by January 1949. The ROK Army then took over security responsibilities along the 38th parallel from the US troops, and began to act as a functioning national defense force. Also, in accordance with the ROK-US provisional administrative accord, the departing USAFIK transferred to the ROK Army small arms and ammunition for 50,000 men, more than 2,000 rocket launchers, more than 40,000 vehicles of all types, and a number of artillery pieces and mortars with over 700,000 rounds of ammunition for them. The transferred military equipment had originally cost the US approximately 56 million dollars.[124]

The transferred US equipment, however, was mostly of inferior quality to the Russian equipment provided to North Korea. For example, the 105-mm howitzer M3, the largest-caliber artillery piece transferred to South Korea, was an outdated piece of equipment with approximately half the range of the NKPA's 122-mm howitzers. Moreover, 57-mm and 37-mm antitank rocket launchers did not have the necessary explosive power to destroy enemy tanks. The low quality of the transferred US equipment was but a reflection of Washington's basic position on military assistance to the Republic of Korea: The ROK Army was to be organized first and foremost as a police-type force to quell domestic unrest and maintain internal security, and later to be developed into a defense force capable of deterring North Korean aggression. It followed that the ROK Forces, equipped with the US armament, would not be able to redress the military imbalance with North Korea.

Moreover, the total quantity of the transferred US equipment, for 50,000 men, was derived from the strength of the Korean Constabulary as of

March 1948. By March 1949, however, the strength of the ROK Forces had already reached 104,000 men (65,000 in the army, 4,000 in the navy, and 35,000 in the police force). The lack of equipment prevented further organization. In order to redress the military imbalance with North Korea, Seoul began to increase efforts to secure greater military aid from the United States. At the end of March 1949, the US agreéd to provide individual organizational equipment for an additional 15,000 men in the ROK Army (for a total of 65,000 men). The US also agreed to provide some equipment and ships for the navy as well as a 6-month stock of spare parts.[125] These equipment and spare parts were shipped to Korea in stages, and was completed by the end of 1949.

When the US Military Advisory Group to Korea (KMAG) began its activities in July 1949, the strength of the ROK standing army had reached 100,000 men. Considering the threat posed by the rapid build-up of the NKPA under the Soviet and Chinese assistance, the Ministry of National Defense determined that the total defensive strength required to deter North Korea's aggression would be 400,000 (100,000 in the standing army, 50,000 in the reserves, 50,000 in the police, and 200,000 reinforcements). Seoul actively engaged in military diplomacy to secure sufficient equipment for the ROK Forces.[126]

In a letter to President Truman dated August 20, 1949, President Syngman Rhee said: "American officers tell me we have sufficient ammunition for two months of combat; my own officers tell me it is only sufficient for two days." He argued that if a war breaks out in Korea, it would be a large-scale and total war, and asked for more equipment and ammunition. Emphasizing that US military aid was absolutely needed, President Rhee requested equipment and ammunition listed in ⟨Table 18⟩.[127]

While redoubling efforts to secure military aid, the Ministry of National Defense also gave priority to increasing the strength of the army and the navy and securing independence for the air force. For the army, the MND organized three additional regiments (for a total of 22 regiments) with equipment received from departing US troops, and on May 12, 1949, reorganized the existing six brigades as divisions. The creation of the 8th Division and the Capital Security Command on June 10 raised the total number of divisions to eight.

Each early-established division was built around three regiments with the following elements: the headquarters and headquarters company, artillery

⟨Table 18⟩   Ordnance Inventory (August 20, 1949)

Equipment	Needs of 100,000 Regular Army			Needs of 300,000 Reserves		
	Needed	Actual	Difference	Needed	Actual	Difference
Howitzer, M-2, 105-mm	12	0	−12	4	0	−4
Howitzer, M-3, 105-mm	192	85	−107	64	0	−64
Mortar, M-1, 81-mm	684	275	−409	228	0	−228
Mortar, M-2, 60-mm	962	373	−589	321	0	−321
57-mm Antitank Gun	204	117	−87	68	0	−68
37-mm Antitank Gun	72	21	−51	24	0	−24
Caliber 50 Heavy Machine Gun (Air-Cooled)	400	443	+43	135	43	−92
Caliber 45 Pistol	6,080	4,199	−1,881	2,027	0	−2,027
Caliber 45 Submachine Gun	752	692	−60	274	0	−274
Caliber 30 Light Machine Gun (Air-Cooled)	618	352	−266	206	0	−206
Caliber 30 Light Machine Gun (Water-Cooled)	791	291	−500	264	0	−264
Caliber 30 M1 Rifle	82,320	40,050	−42,270	17,440	0	−17,440
Caliber 30 Carbine Rifle	33,183	14,746	−18,477	11,061	0	−11,061
Caliber 30 Browning Automatic Rifle	2,333	1,091	−1,242	500	0	−779
Bayonet, M1 Rifle	82,320	27,415	−54,905	17,440	0	−17,440
Bayonet, Carbine Rifle	33,183	14,736	−18,477	11,061	0	−11,061
Binocular	1,500	913	−587	500	0	−500
2.36-inch Rocket Launcher	3,264	1,961	−1,303	1,088	0	−1,088
Launcher, M1 Rifle Grenade	−	−	−	−	−	−
Launcher, Carbine Rifle Grenade	−	−	−	−	−	−
Projector, Pyro, Hand, M9	−	−	−	−	−	−

⟨Table 19⟩   The Additional Activation of ROK Regiments
                        (August 15, 1948-June 20, 1949)

Regiment	Date of Activation	Place of Activation	First Commander	Note
16th Regiment	October 28, 1948	Masan	Lt. Col. Park Shi Ch'ang	
17th Regiment	November 20, 1948	Shihung	Lt. Col. Paik In Yop	The 4th Regiment whi-
18th Regiment	November 20, 1948	P'ohang	Lt. Col. Ch'oi Sok	ch took part in the
19th Regiment	November 20, 1948	Kwangju	Maj. Min Byong Gwon	Yosu-Sunch'on Rebel-
20th Regiment	November 20, 1948	Kwangju	Lt. Col. Lee Song Ga	lion was re-organized
21st Regiment	February 1, 1949	Kwangju	Lt. Col. Park Ki Byong	and re-established as the 20th Regiment.
22nd Regiment	April 15, 1949	Taegu	Lt. Col. Oh Dok Jun	The 6th Regiment whi-
23rd Regiment	April 20, 1949	Masan	Col. Kim Jong P'yong	ch staged the Taegu Re-
25th Regiment	June 20, 1949	Taejon	Lt. Col. Yu Hae Jun	bellion was established anew as the 22nd Regi-
Cavalry Regiment	January 1, 1948	Susaek	Maj. Lee Yong Mun	ment.

⟨Table 20⟩   The Activation of ROK Divisions

Division	Date of Establishment	Commander	Assigned Regiments	Post	Note
1st Division	May 12, 1949	Col. Kim Sok Won	11th, 12th, 13th	Susaek	Upgraded 1st Brigade
2nd Division	May 12, 1949	Col. Yu Sung Ryol	5th, 16th, 25th	Taejon	Upgraded 2nd Brigade
3rd Division	May 12, 1949	Maj. Gen. Lee Ung Jun	22nd, 23rd	Taegu	Upgraded 3rd Brigade
5th Division	May 12, 1949	Br. Gen. Song Ho Song	15th, 20th	Kwangju	Upgraded 5th Brigade
6th Division	May 12, 1949	Col. Yu Jae Hung	2nd, 7th, 9th	Wonju	Upgraded 6th Brigade
7th Division	May 12, 1949	Col. Lee Jun Shik	1st, 19th	Uijongbu	Renamed Capital Division
8th Division	June 20, 1949	Br. Gen. Lee Hyong Kun	10th, 21st	Kangnung	
Capital Security Division	June 20, 1949	Col. Kwon Jun	3rd, 8th Cavalry	Seoul	

battalion, engineer company, signal company, ordnance company, quartermaster company, and medical battalion. Of the eight final divisions, however, only four units consisted of three regiments each; the others had two regiments each. Of these units, the 1st, 7th, 6th, and 8th Divisions plus the 17th Regiment assumed responsibility for security along the 38th parallel; the others defended rear areas and carried out counter-insurgency operations. These infantry divisions expended efforts to elevate the status of support units, and reorganized battalion-strength support units into group-strength branch units such as an artillery group. The lack of equipment, however, placed severe limitations on their functions.

In accordance with the Presidential Decree (issued November 20, 1948) and the Armed Forces Organization Act (issued November 30, 1948), the MND also created the reserves. Establishing the Patriotic Army Command (under Brig. Gen. Song Ho Sung as the first commander) at the Army Headquarters in 1949, the MND established a total of seven reserve brigades and 18 regiments around the country between January and July of the same year. A Patriotic Army member was assigned to a reserve regiment in his residential area, and underwent military training for a specified period. The Patriotic Army, however, met a premature end as the ROK government switched from the volunteer system to conscription on August 6, 1949, requiring mandatory service for every male citizen of the Republic. On August 31, the Patriotic Army was dissolved and was replaced by a Youth Guard under the command of a newly established Youth Guard Bureau at the Army Headquarters. Built around the Korean Youth Organization, the Youth Guard was organized at the provincial, city, gun, myon, dong, ri level, but was totally ineffective due to lack of training.

In addition to these units, the ROK Army established special units composed of young men and soldiers who had escaped from North Korea. Organized as Susaek School (Independent 1st Battalion), Horim Unit (Yongdengp'o

Academy), and Patriotic Battalion (803rd Independent Battalion), the special units conducted expeditionary operations against People's Guerrillas from the North, and stamped out regional insurgents. A part of these units were trained to carry out secret operations against North Korea, but the plan was not put into action.

The ROK Navy gained some operations experience during the Yosu-Sunch'on Rebellion by carrying out a naval blockade against the rebel army and supporting the counter-insurgency troops on the ground. By February 1, 1949, the Navy had increased its strength to four fltillas including one training flotilla, and established a naval defense system by assigning operational areas. The Navy also made efforts to secure warships outfitted with modern naval equipment to replace small and outdated ships (most of these were mine sweeping boats) that had been obtained during its Coast Guard days. The US promised to provide several ships and equipment plus spare parts, but sent a few additional old ships and equipment in the second half of 1949. With the equipment provided by the US, the ROK Navy managed to equip each ship with 37-mm guns and machine guns.

To secure modern warships, the Navy then launched a nationwide funding drive. When the funding drive achieved its target, Admiral Son Won Il and others went to the US to purchase four PC's (Pursuit Craft, or Subchaser). The first PC arrived in Chinhae on April 10, 1950. Equipped with a 3-inch gun and anti-submarine equipment, it became the first modern warship secured by the ROK Navy.[128] In addition to establishing a naval operations system and securing warships, the Navy began to upgrade its bases in order to strengthen its operations support system. On June 25, 1949, the Navy established a control center in Chinhae and upgraded each base to a security center.

The Navy also established a battalion-strength marine corps in Chinhae on April 15, 1949. During the Yosu-Sunch'on Rebellion, the lack of a naval combat team had prevented the Navy from launching a landing operation in support of the counter-insurgency effort. This marine corps unit was soon dispatched to the Chinju area on an expeditionary mission, and was sent to Cheju-do on December 28 also on a counter-insurgency mission. After its establishment, the ROK Marine Corps continued to build up its strength.[129]

In the meantime, the ROK Air Force, which existed as the air base unit of the Army, moved to Kimp'o Airfield on September 1, 1948. After receiving ten L-4 liaison planes from the US Forces on September 4, this air base unit was reorganized as an Army Air Base Command on September 13. The L-4 was a somewhat outdated aircraft with a speed of 160.9km per hour and a range of 483km, but it was the first aircraft secured by the ROK Air Force. The Army Air Base Command immediately sent the L-4's to the Yosu-Sunch'on area to carry out reconnaissance, liaison, and commander transport missions. Learning that an aircraft with a longer range was badly needed for the counter-insurgency operations, the Air Base Command soon obtained an additional ten L-5 liaison planes. Air Base Command officers such as Choi Yong Dok and Kim Jong Yol also made efforts to establish an independent air force, and reorganized the Air Base Command as an Army Aviation Command consisting of specialized elements such as an air base unit, a flight unit, and an air force academy.[130]

In early 1949, the Aviation Command gave a briefing to President Rhee on the status of North Korea's Air Force, and requested that military aid funds be secured to obtain fighter planes. Through US Ambassador John J. Muccio and KMAG Chief William L. Roberts, President Rhee sent Washington a request to provide more equipment including fighter planes. President Rhee also sent Korean Ambassador Chang Myon and Special Envoy Cho Byong Ok to persuade US officials, and on April 10, he made a request for armament to equip 3,000 men, including 75 fighter planes, 12 bombers, 30 liaison and reconnaissance planes, and 5 transport planes.[131]

The United States refused to accept this request, and also objected to the establishment of an independent ROK Air Force. The ROK government, however, separated air force elements from the army on October 1, 1949, and thus established a full-fledged three-service system. At this time, the Army Aviation Command was reorganized as an air force consisting of a flight wing, air base command, women's air unit, air force academy, air force hospital and supply depots. The ROK Air Force then launched a nationwide "Patriot Aircraft Funding Drive," and subsequently purchased 10 Canadian-made AT-6 training planes. Equipped with two 0.5-inch machine guns, each AT-6 was given the name "National Foundation" to promote patriotism. The Air Force also established new bases in Suwon, Kunsan, Kwangju, Taegu, and Cheju Island in addition to the existing bases in Youido (islet) and Kimp'o.

Meanwhile, in order to meet increasing logistic and supply needs of the expanding armed forces, the Ministry of National Defense took first steps to reduce its dependence on military assistance and establish its own system of production and procurement. In November 1948, the MND established a Procurement Center to purchase needed materiel both from overseas and domestic sources. The MND also designated the First and Second Armories on January 15, 1949, and the Third Armory in May, to handle the repair of rifles and artillery pieces and to produce grenades and small arms parts. In addition, the MND began to produce combat uniforms and boots in June 1949, and procured non-durables such as grain from domestic sources only.[132]

While the ROK Forces were consolidating the three-service system and building up the supply system, the United States allocated approximately $10,200,000 in military aid for the Republic of Korea for fiscal year 1950. This amount would only cover the purchase of replacement and repair parts for the old equipment transferred to the Republic, and did not leave any room for additional equipment.

Even the KMAG, which had reacted cooly to Seoul's earlier requests for additional equipment, argued that the proposed size of the military aid to the Republic was inadequate. The KMAG suggested that the military aid for fiscal year 1950 should be at least $20 million, including 105-mm M2 howitzers and 4.2-inch mortars for the army, 3-inch guns for the navy, and F-51, T-6, and C-47 planes for the air force. This list of equipment largely agreed with earlier requests made by the Republic, except for the exclusion of tanks, which the KMAG believed would be ineffective in the rough terrain of Korea. The KMAG Chief himself emphasized that $20 million would be the minimum required level of assistance to enable the ROK Forces to have some means of defense, implying that the military imbalance between South and North Korea had reached a critical level.

The US government, however, appeared to have already written Korea out of its national defense plans. On January 5, 1950, President Truman declared that the US would not intervene in Taiwan (Formosa), and on January 12, State Secretary Dean G. Acheson left Korea and Taiwan out of the US defensive perimeter in the Far East. Although the US and ROK governments signed a mutual security and military assistance agreement on January 26, the finalized figure of $10,970,000 in military aid failed to accommodate the Republic's repeated requests for increased support. Of this amount finalized on March 15, only less then 1,000 dollars' worth of signal wire reached Korea before the outbreak of the war on June 25. [133]

Washington's insufficient military aid to the Republic caused a grave concern regarding the defensive strength of the ROK Forces. The KMAG felt that supplies to the ROK combat troops had reached the minimum required level by June 1950. Having run out of spare parts, the ROK Forces could not operate 15% of their weapons or 35% of the vehicles. The KMAG estimated that the ROK Forces could not hold the line against North Korea's invasion for more than 15 days.[134]

In short, the ROK Forces were at a decidedly inferior position to the well equipped NKPA Forces under the heavy support of the Soviet Union. In particular, the inferiority of the air force stood out. As for ground equipment, the ROK Army was thrown into war without possessing a single tank or a single anti-tank weapon to destroy T-34. ⟨Table 21⟩ and ⟨Table 22⟩ show the strength and equipment of the ROK Forces just prior to the outbreak of the war.

The Korean people had staged a long anti-colonial struggle against the Japanese to recover national sovereignty, but could not win national independence on their own. As Korea had to depend on the Allied Powers to secure its liberation from the Japanese colonial rule, the Korean people's wish to establish an independent nation upon the return of the Korean Provisional Government was subjected to international politics. In accordance with the Allied postwar settlement plans, the United States and the Soviet Union divided Korea at the 38th parallel, and, after receiving surrender from the Japanese Army, they established military governments in the South and the North, respectively.

At the Moscow Conference, the US and the Soviet Union agreed to re-establish Korea as an independent state after a trusteeship period of up to five years, and formed the US-USSR Joint Commission to discuss the establishment

⟨Table 21⟩   The Strength of the ROK Armed Forces

Army	8 Divisions (22 Regiments)	67,416
	Support and Special Branch Units	27,558
	Subtotal	94,974
Navy	3 Flotillas, 7 Security Units	7,715
Marine Corps	2 Battalions	1,166
Air Force	1 Air Wing, 7 Bases	1,897
Total		105,752

⟨Table 22⟩　　　　　The Equipment of the ROK Armed Forces

Tanks and Armored Vehicles	Armored Vehicles	27
Self-Propelled Gun	—	—
Howitzer	105-mm M3	91
Mortar	81-mm 60-mm	384 576
Antitank Gun	57-mm 2.36-inch	140 1,900
Antiaircraft Artillery (AAA)	—	—
Aircraft	L-4 L-5 T-6	8 4 10
	Total	22
Warship	Patrol Ship Support Vessel	28 43
	Total	71

of a provisional Korean democratic government. The clash of interests between the two powers and the ideological division of Korean national leaders, however, prevented the formation of a provisional democratic government. As the Cold War intensified in the international arena, the division of Korea was increasingly transformed into an ideological confrontation between democratic and communist camps.

The deadlock between the two camps eventually led to the transfer of the Korean problem to the United Nations. The UN resolved to establish Korea as an independent state by holding general elections under UN observation, but the Soviets objected to this resolution and blocked the entry of the UN Temporary Commission into the North. Eventually, two separate governments were established in the South and the North. The 38th parallel became a fixed border between the two sides, and the division of Korea became an accomplished fact.

Receiving support and directions from the Soviet Union and Communist China, the North Korean regime subsequently built up its military to prepare for war and for communization of the entire Korean peninsula. In contrast, mainly due to mere lukewarm support extended by the US, South Korea failed to secure its defensive needs and close the widening military gap with the North.

These complex historical factors contributed to the outbreak of the Korean War.

Notes

1) Chae Keun Sik, The Untold History of the *Armed Struggle for Independence* (Seoul: Office of Public Relations, 1978), pp. 171-180.

2) US State Department, *Foreign Relations of the United States,* 1943, China, p. 257.

3) War History Compilation Committee, MND, *History of the Korean War,* vol. 1 (old edition), 1967, p. 40.

4) James F. Schnabel, *Policy and Direction: The First Year* (Washington, D.C.: US Government Printing Office, 1972), p. 7.

5) Ibid., Institute of Foreign Affairs, Ministry of Foreign Affairs *Twenty Years of Korean Diplomacy. Appendix,* 1966, pp. 251-252.

6) War History Compilation Committee, MND, *History of National Defense,* vol. 1, 1984, pp. 106-107.

7) Ibid., pp. 514-516; US State Department FRUS, 1945, vol. 2, p. 1474.

8) Schnabel, *Policy and Direction,* p. 8; Roy E. Appleman, *United States Army in the Korean War: South to the Naktong, North to the Yalu* (Department of the Army, Washington, D.C.: GPO), p. 3.

9) WHCC, *National Defense Treaties,* vol. 1, pp. 573-575.

10) WHCC, *History of the Korean War,* vol. 1 (old edition), pp. 55-56.

11) Born into a peasant's family in 1900, Chistiakov joined the Bolshevik Revolution as a Red Army soldier. He was the commander of the Soviet 6th Army during the war between the USS.R. and Germany, and came to North Korea as the Commander of the Soviet Occupation Force.

12) The Soviet Far East Force consisted of the 1st Far East Army, the 2nd Far East Army, Trans-Baikal army and the Pacific Fleet. As the right flank of the 1st Far East Army, the 25th Army carried out a supporting attack to penetrate the Japanese defensive positions in Manchuria and advanced into Wang Quing, Tumen,

Yanji

13) US War Department Intelligence Division, *Intelligence Review,* June 20, 1946.

14) An administrative body in communist countries. In North Korea, Interim People's Committees, People's Political Committees, and People's Committees were formed under the Soviet military government. These Committees had similar functions and were later merged into People's Committees.

15) WHCC, *History of the Korean War,* vol. 1 (old edition), pp. 51-52; Morita Yoshio, *Records of the Korean War,* Annando Publishers, 1964, pp. 184-185.

16) Schnabel, *Policy and Direction,* p. 24; EUSA, *History of the North Korean Army,* p. 90.

17) Born in Illinois, Arnold Hodge participated in World War I as a battalion commander, and won the Battle of Okinawa during World War II.

18) WHCC, *History of National Defense,* vol 1, 1984, p. 179.

19) Schnabel, *Policy and Direction,* pp. 14-15.

20) Ibid., pp. 17-18.

21) WHCC, *History of National Defense,* vol. 1, p. 181.

22) EUSA, *History of USAFIK,* pt. 2, ch. 4, pp. 57-58; Schnabel, *Policy and Direction,* p. 19.

23) WHCC, *National Defence Treaties,* vol. 1, p. 586; US State Dept. FRUS, 1945, vol. 7, pp. 699-670.

24) On March 12, 1947, US President Truman declared that the US would support all the peoples around the world who were under direct or indirect threats from the communists. This Truman Doctrine became the cornerstone of US foreign policy during the early years of the Cold War, and provided the basis for US military assistance to other countries.

25) In a speech at Harvard University in June 1947, US State Secretary Marshall sketched the outline of a plan for economic reconstruction in Europe. Through the Marshall Plan, the US extended generous economic assistance to Western European countries between 1948 and 1951.

26) Institute of Foreign Affairs, *Twenty Years of Korean Diplomacy: Appendix,* pp. 274-176; WHCC, *History of the Korean War,* vol. 1 (old edition), pp. 90-91; United States

Department of State, *Department of State Bulletin* 17, September 28, 1947, p. 620.

27) US State Department, *The Conflict in Korea* (Washington, D.C.: US GPO, 1951), pp. 7–8.

28) Institute of Foreign Affairs, *Twenty Years of Korean Diplomacy. Appendix,* pp. 285–287.

29) WHCC, *History of the Korean War,* vol. 1 (Seoul: Ministry of National Defense, 1977, p. 67; *UN Official Record, Third Session, Supply No. 9,* 1984, p. 26.

30) The small electoral district system was adopted, and each district was defined by law. The small electoral district system allowed for the election of only one National Assembly member per district. A county with a population of less than 150,000 was allotted one district; 150,000 to less than 250,000, two districts; and 250,000 to less than 350,000, 4 districts. A total of 200 electoral districts were established.

31) ROK Office of Public Relations, *Official News No. 1,* September 1, 1948; MND Judiciary Committee, *Collection of Defense Related Laws & Regulations,* vol. 1 (Seoul: Ministry of National Defense), 1960, pp. 1–4.

32) WHCC, *National Defense Treaties,* vol. 1, pp. 592–595; Institute of Foreign Affairs, *Twenty Years of Korean Diplomacy. Appendix,* pp. 292–294; WHCC, *History of National Defense,* vol. 1, p. 127; United Nations, *Yearbook of the UN, 1948-49,* pp. 288–289.

33) In this balloting method, only a single candidate stands for election. Those who are for the candidate cast their ballot in a white box, and those against cast their ballot in a black box. Obviously secrecy cannot be maintained.

34) Choong Ang T'ong Shin Sa, *Choson Choong Ang Yearbook,* 1949, p. 43.

35) Institute of Foreign Affairs, *Twenty Years of Korean Diplomacy: Appendix,* pp. 301–302.

36) WHCC, MND, *History of Counter-Irregular Warfare* 1988, pp. 17–21.

37) WHCC, MND, *Summary of the Korean War* 1986, p. 88.

38) WHCC, *History of the Korean War,* vol. 1 (old edition), pp. 438–442.

39) WHCC, *History of Counter-Irregular Warfare,* pp. 26–30.

40) WHCC, *Summary of the Korean War,* p. 89.

41) WHCC, *History of Counter-Irregular Warfare,* pp. 31-38.

42) ROK Army Security Command, *30-Year History of Counter-Communism,* 1978, pp. 51-52.

43) WHCC, *History of the Korean War,* vol. 1, pp. 87-88; Kim Ch'ang Soon, *15-Year History of North Korea* (Seoul: Chi Moon Kak, 1961), pp. 49-51. Prior to the Korean War, the NKPA ground forces were built around the People's Army, Constabulary Force, and Security Force.

44) Adopted as the standard rifle for the Japanese Army in 1939, the Model-99 rifle improved upon the firepower of the Model-38 rifle by increasing the caliber. A tangent sight was attached to the rifle for anti-aircraft fire.

45) Railroad security companies were stationed in such places as Kanggye, Yangdok, Wonsan, Hamhung, Shinp'o, Tanch'on, Sungjin, Sungsambong, Sariwon, and Shinsungch'on.

46) WHCC, *History of the Korean War,* vol. 1, pp. 88-89.

47) Ibid., pp. 88-89.

48) WHCC, *History of the Korean War,* vol. 1, p. 90; WHCC, *History of the Korean War,* vol. 1 (old edition), pp. 680-682.

49) WHCC, *History of the Korean War,* vol. 1, pp. 88-89.

50) First produced in 1906 and widely used by the Japanese Army during World War II, the Model-38 rifle was one of Japan's most famous small arms. It was adopted as a standard rifle for the Japanese Army in the 38th year of the Meiji reign — hence the name.

51) A Soviet military advisor group, under Gen. Smirnov, oversaw the organization and training of the NKPA units.

52) WHCC, *History of the Korean War,* vol. 1, p. 90.

53) Kim Woong, Director of the Combat Training Bureau, took the command of the NKPA 1st Division on March 24, 1948. Earlier, in August 1947, Kim Chaek had assumed the command of the 3rd Brigade. FEC, *History of the North Korean Army,* pp. 94-95.

54) WHCC, *History of the Korean War,* vol. 1, pp. 92-93; WHCC, *History of the Korean War,* vol. 1 (old edition), pp. 684-689; ROK Army Headquarters G2, *Analysis of the June 25 Invasion by North Korea,* 1970, pp. 39-41.

55) WHCC, *History of the Korean War,* vol. 1, pp. 92-93; ROK Army HQ, *Analysis of the June 25 Invasion by North Korea,* pp. 39-41.

56) WHCC, *History of the Korean War,* vol. 1, pp. 90-91.

57) Ibid., p. 91.

58) *Selected Writings of Kim Il Sung,* vol. 1 (P'yongyang: Humanities Press, 1961), pp. 481 -486; Chang Joon Ik, *History of the People's Army of North Korea* (Seoul: Somundang, 1991), p. 81.

59) North Korea at this time maintained a dual system with regard to military administration. The Ministry of National Defense had jurisdiction over the People's Army, while the Ministry of Internal Affairs oversaw the Constabulary Force and the border guards. Regardless of formal administrative ties, however, the North Korean units were under the effective control of the Political Command of the Soviet Occupation Force. After the Soviet withdrawal, a Soviet military delegation played an important part in North Korea's military affairs.

60) ROK Army Headquarters, *June 25 War: Army War History,* vol. 1, 1952, pp. 72-74; USAFIK, *G-2 Rept 7,* p. 138.

61) North Korea has had a deep interest in the development of armored units since the organization of People's Army Group in May 1947. P'yongyang selected highly qualified candidates for specialized training, and they rapidly accumulated "know-how" under the guidance of a Soviet armored unit (150 tanks and 300 men) which remained in North Korea after the withdrawal of the Soviet armored division in early 1948. The presence of Korean-Soviets in the unit facilitated the training of North Koreans. Under the command of Lt. Col. Pyodor, this armored unit left behind 60 tanks, 30 self-propelled guns, 60 sidecars, and 40 vehicles when it withdrew from North Korea in November 1948. With this Soviet equipment, North Korea promptly formed the 115th Armored Regiment under the command of Yoo Kyung Soo. Established near P'yongyang in Sadong in December 1948, this

armored regiment consisted of two armored battalions, one self-propelled gun battalion, one engineer company, one reconnaissance company, one transportation company, and one medical dispatch unit. WHCC, *History of the Korean War,* vol. 1, p. 95.

62) WHCC, *History of the Korean War,* vol. 1, p. 108; WHCC, *History of the Korean War,* vol. 1 (old edition), p. 705.

63) *"How Russia Built The North Korea Army,"* *The Reporter,* September 26, 1950. Shtykov served on the military committee of the Far East 1st Army, and later became the Soviet chief delegate at the US-USSR Joint Commission and the first Soviet ambassador to North Korea. On behalf of Stalin, he helped to create the North Korean regime under Kim Il Sung, and played a decisive role in the North's war preparations.

64) Ministry of Foreign Affairs, *Soviet Documents* (3), pp. 6-12. Korea Institute of Military History, *Soviet Source Materials,* of the conference between Kim Il Sung and Bulganin.

65) Ministry of Foreign Affairs, *Soviet Documents* (4), pp. 28-31. This section includes a detailed list of all the items transferred from the Soviet Union to North Korea.

66) WHCC, *History of the Korean War,* vol. 1, pp. 94-95; WHCC, *History of the Korean War,* vol. 1 (old edition), pp. 689-690.

67) Ministry of Foreign Affairs, *Soviet Documents* (2), p. 22; *Soviet Documents* (4), pp. 46-49.

68) Joo yong-bok, *An Invasion and Defeat of Choson People's Army,* pp. 212-232; Appleman, ibid., p. 12.

69) WHCC, *History of the Korean War,* vol. 1, pp. 94-95; Schnabel, *Policy and Direction,* trans. by ROK Army Headquarters, p.59. The CCF 15th Division was reorganized as the 7th division in Wonsan on April 25, 1950, and was renamed as the 12th division prior to the outbreak of the Korean War. A new 7th division was formed afterwards.

70) WHCC, *History of the Korean War,* vol. 1, pp. 98-99.

71) WHCC, *History of the Korean War*, vol. 1 (old edition), pp. 697-702; Ministry of Foreign Affairs, *Soviet Documents* (4), p. 28.

72) WHCC, *History of the Korean War*, vol. 1 (old edition), pp. 498-499; Public Relations Association of Korea, *Korean Conflict*, 1973, pp. 148-149. Kangdong Political Academy trained political agents who were to function as underground operatives in the South; military personnel to be sent as guerrillas; and dual-purpose agents. The curriculum included general studies, including the history of the Soviet Communist Party, guerrilla tactics, and communist takeover tactics.

73) Public Relations Association of Korea, *Korean Conflict*, pp. 148-149.

74) WHCC, *History of Counter-Irregular Warfare*, pp. 44-45.

75) Ibid., pp. 44-45.

76) Ibid., pp. 44-46.

77) Ibid., pp. 146-147.

78) ROK Army Headquarters, *June 25 War: Army War History, vol. 2, Appendix*, 1953, p. 7; WHCC, *History of Counter-Irregular Warfare*, pp. 146-147.

79) Ministry of National Defense, *Military Policy and Strategy of North Korea*, 1979, pp. 105-109.

80) WHCC, *History of the Korean War*, vol. 1, pp. 121-124.

81) Research Institute of History, North Korea, *Comprehensive History of Choson*, vol. 24, pp. 274-278.

82) Ibid., pp. 280-285; Public Relations Association of Korea, *Korean Conflict*, p. 127.

83) WHCC, *History of the Korean War*, vol. 1, p.127.

84) Ministry of Foreign Affairs, *Soviet Documents* (2), p. 8.

85) WHCC, *History of the Korean War*, vol. 1 (old edition), pp. 726-728; Ministry of Foreign Affairs, *Soviet Documents* (2), p. 26.

86) WHCC, *History of the Korean War*, vol. 1, p. 146; WHCC, *History of the Korean War*, vol. 1 (old edition), pp. 520-522.

87) Nine members on this suicide mission, including a sergeant, who attacked a totschka on Hill 292 form the 10 valiant suicide attackers.

88) ROK Army HQ, *History of the Development of the Army*, vol. 1, pp. 279-280.

89) Ibid., p. 282. Established on June 5, 1949, the Ongjin Area Command, under the 6th Division Commander Col. Kim Paik Il, consisted of the 12th Regiment, 2nd Battalion of the 13th Regiment, 1st Battalion of the 8th Regiment, 38 Ranger Unit, and a weapons company with 57-mm guns.

90) WHCC, *History of the Korean War*, vol. 1, pp. 149-152.

91) ROK Army HQ, *History of the Development of the Army*, vol. 1, pp. 283-284; WHCC, *History of the Korean War*, vol. 1, pp. 147-148.

92) WHCC, *History of the Korean War*, vol. 1 (old edition), pp. 535-536; ROK Army HQ, *History of the Development of the Army*, vol. 1, p. 284.

93) Korea Military Academy, *30-Year History of Korea Military Academy*, p. 61; Park Kyung Sok, *Five-Star General Kim Hong Il*, (Seoul: Suh Moon Dang, 1984), pp. 267-268.

94) USAMGIK Ordinance 28 consisted of Clause 1, which established the Office of the Director of National Defense; Clause 2, which created the Bureau of Armed Forces; and Clause 3, which outlawed private police and military organizations.

95) WHCC, *National Defense Treaties*, vol. 1, p. 683.

96) WHCC, *History of National Defense*, vol. 1, p. 292.

97) KMA, *30-Year History of Korea Military Academy*, pp. 63-64.

98) WHCC, *History of National Defense*, vol. 1, p. 294.

99) WHCC, *History of National Defense*, vol. 1, p. 294.

100) The Korean Constabulary Reserve was the formal name for the first Korean native defense force. Koreans, however, preferred to call the unit the Korean Constabulary without the word "Reserve" at the end to suggest that this was to become the nucleus of the Korean Armed Force.

101) USAMGIK, Ordinance 42 (January 14, 1946). Clause 1 stipulated that the Coast Guard responsibility be transferred from the Department of Transportation to the Department of National Defennse. USAMGIK Ordinance 86.

102) ROK Army Headquarters, *Early Days of the ROK Armed Forces, Studies on Military*

Science, vol. 11, 1980, pp. 324-325.

103) ROK Army, Military History Division, *Chronicle of Army History (1):* 1945-1950, pp. 19-29.

104) ROK Army HQ, *History of the Development of the Army,* vol. 1, pp. 111-116.

105) WHCC, *History of the Korean War,* vol. 1 (old edition), pp. 547-560.

106) USAMGIK Ordinance 64 changed the names of the government bodies.

107) USAMGIK Ordinance 86(Choson Constabalary and Choson Coast Guards). Clause 1 stipulates that the Korean Defense Department is heraby renamed the Department of Interior security. It also stipulates that the Bureau of Ammed Forces under the Department of Interior shall be abolished. Clause 2 of the Ordinance 28 is repealed as of November 13, 1945. The Korean Contabulary is hereby activated effective Januery 14, 1946, and act as a reserve police force for the purpose of keeping internal security. The Korean Constabalary is under control of the Department of Interior Security.

108) ROK Army HQ, *Early Days of the ROK Armed Forces, Studies on Military Science,* Vol. 11, 1980, pp. 327-328; Lee Eung Joon, *90-Year Memoir* (1890-1981), pp. 242-245.

109) ROK Army HQ, *June 25 War,* vol. 1, pp. 266-267. The following officers assumed the command of the Constabulary General Headquarters: Col. Won Yong Dok (February 22 - June 24, 1946); Lt. Col. Lee Hyung Keun (September 28 - December 23, 1946); and Col. Song Ho Sung (December 23, 1946 - November 20, 1948). The following officers assumed the general chief of staff position: Col. Kim Sang Kyum (April 8, 1947); Col. Chung Il Kwon (September 12, 1947); Col. Lee Hyung Keun (February 11 - July 25, 1948).

110) ROK Army HQ, *History of the Development of the Army,* vol. 1, p. 127.

111) WHCC, *History of the Ministry of National Defense,* vol. 1, p. 399.

112) ROK Army HQ, *History of the Development of the Army,* Vol. 1, pp. 178-182.

113) Judiciary Committee of MND, *Collection of Defense Related Laws & Regulations* (1), pp. 47-50.

114) Report of Internal Affairs Minister Shin Sung Mo at the time of US Army Secretary Royal's visit to Korea (February 8, 1949).

115) ROK Army Headquarters tr., *Policy and Direction,* pp. 29–30; US JCS History: *Korean War* I, pp. 30–36; Chung Il Hyung, *United Nations and the Korean Problem,* pp. 2–6.

116) Institute of Foreign affairs, *20-Year History of Korean Diplomacy. Appendix,* pp. 279 –285.

117) US JCS History, *Korean War* I, p. 28.

118) WHCC, *National Defence Treaties,* vol. 1, p. 34; Sawyer, *KMAG,* pp. 34–35.

119) ROK Army Headquarters tr., *Policy and Direction,* p. 52.

120) WHCC, *History of the Korean War,* vol. 1 (old edition), p. 223.

121) Ibid., pp. 222–223.

122) Institute of Foreign Affairs, *20-Year History of Korean Diplomacy. Appendix,* pp. 292 –293.

123) ROK Army Headquarters tr., *South to the Naktong, North to the Yalu,* p. 7.

124) WHCC, *National Defense Treaties,* vol. 1, p.34; WHCC, *History of National Defense,* vol. 1, pp. 172–173.

125) WHCC, *History of National Defense,* vol. 1, p. 321.

126) Letter from Ambassador Muccio to US State Secretary Dean Acheson; WHCC, *History of National Defense,* vol. 1, p. 322.

127) WHCC, *History of National Defense,* vol. 1, pp. 527–528.

128) WHCC, *History of the Korean War,* vol. 1, pp. 82–83.

129) Ibid., p. 86.

130) Ibid., pp. 83–84.

131) Ibid., pp. 84–86.

132) WHCC, *History of the Korean War,* vol. 1 (old edition), pp. 393–394; WHCC, *History of National Defense,* vol. 1, p. 226; WHCC, *History of the Ministry of National Defense,* vol. 1, pp. 221–222.

133) Schnabel, *Policy and Direction,* p. 36; Sawyer, *KMAG,* pp. 96–104.

134) National Unification Board, *Analysis of the Background of the Korean War,* p. 139.

Chapter Two   North Korea's Surprise Attack and the South's Response

I . NKPA's Invasion Plan

1. Preparation of the Invasion Plan

(1) North Korea's War Plan

Upon the establishment of the North Korean regime in September 1948, Kim Il Sung began to devise a plan to invade the South under close coordination with Stalin and Mao Tse-tung. The origin of the North's invasion plan could be traced back to a change in the Soviet strategy to communize the entire Korean peninsula. Administering a military government in northern Korea, the Soviets had initially attempted to use this base to incite popular uprisings, riots, and mutinies in the South. The Soviets, however, came to realize that the goal of communizing the entire peninsula could not be achieved through such limited tactics, and decided to resort to more violent means.

As the US troops in the South stood in the way of carrying out this new strategy, the Soviet Union induced their withdrawal by unilaterally pulling its own troops out of North Korea in December 1948. In the same month, the Soviet Minister of Defense invited military representatives from North Korea and Communist China to a Moscow meeting. At this conference, the three countries agreed to build up the strength of the North Korean People's

Army around 6 shock divisions, 8 combat and 8 reserve divisions, and 2 armored divisions, and to complete the war preparations within 18 months (i.e., by June 1950).[1] Given that the NKPA consisted of merely 3 divisions at the time of this conference, the provisions of the secret military agreement were nothing short of audacious. By the outbreak of the Korean War, the actual strength of the NKPA had reached ten infantry divisions, one armored brigade (with enough tanks to form two armored divisions), three special regiments, and five constabulary regiments.

Meanwhile, the Cold War was intensifying in the international arena. In places like Berlin, Turkey, and Greece, the US and USSR, former allies during World War II, were taking a hard stance against each other, and in China, a Communist victory over Kuomintang forces seemed imminent. Under these circumstances, Kim Il Sung visited Moscow to have a meeting with Stalin on March 5, 1949. Their summit included the following agenda: Korean unification, economic cooperation and trade, trade agreement for 1949–50, technical assistance, cooperation in cultural and educational areas, construction of a railway between Aoji in North Korea and Kraskino in the Soviet Union, and war preparations and military build-up. Their discussion specially focused on the issues of Korean unification, economic cooperation, and military build-up.

With regard to the unification issue, Stalin agreed in principle to support Kim's policy of "unification through violent means." Having more extensive experience in political as well as military affairs than Kim Il Sung, Stalin suggested that North Korea consider two options: (1) launching a pre-emptive strike against the South and (2) inducing the South to attack first and striking back. Stalin advised Kim to take the latter course of action.

Stalin emphasized that in order to carry out a pre-emptive strike, North Korea's forces would need an overwhelming superiority over the South's. He reminded Kim that US troops were still stationed in Korea and that the US–

USSR agreement on the 38th parallel remained in effect. Stalin added that North Korea's offensive military action against the South could be justified only in the case of retaliation against the South's provocation.[2] Believing that the North's pre-emptive strike would be premature at that time, Stalin thus advised Kim Il Sung to build up military strength and provoke the South into attacking first.

As for economic cooperation, Stalin agreed to provide $40 million in loans and technical assistance to support North Korea's Economic Renovation and Development Plan. P'yongyang used the lion's share of the Soviet loans to purchase armament and equipment for the NKPA.[3]

While being briefed on the military situation in Korea, Stalin burst into laughter when Kim Il Sung said that the strength of the ROK armed forces was 60,000-as if to express his scorn for its small size. When Stalin asked whether the NKPA used Communist infiltrators to set up cells inside the ROK forces, Kim Il Sung replied that Park Hun Young's SKLP members established Communist cells but had yet to reveal their identities. Stalin approvingly said that there was no need yet to reveal their existence, and advised Kim to be on guard against infiltrators from the South. During his meeting with Kim, Stalin further promised to provide support for the North Korean Navy and Air Force and to train North Korean officers at Soviet military schools.[4]

On March 12, Kim Il Sung and Bulganin agreed that the Soviet Union would provide armament for the newly established or reinforced North Korean ground forces; small vessels and battleships as well as naval advisors for the newly established navy; and training airplanes for the air force. Furthermore, they agreed that the Soviet naval base at Ch'ongjin would be maintained as long as US troops are stationed in South Korea.[5]

On March 17, based on these agreements, a North Korean-Soviet accord was signed, covering "the nature of war support, training of North Korean military personnel in the Soviet Union, development of economic relations, and other issues." At the time, North Korea and the Soviet Union formally announced the signing of "an economic and cultural accord." Newly unclassified Kremlin documents have now confirmed the suspicion that the two countries also signed a secret military accord in 1949. These papers show that the focus of the North Korean-Soviet meetings and accords was on war preparations.[6] The Kim-Stalin meeting was a crucial event in the planning stage of the Korean War, as these two leaders agreed to resort to war to bring about the unification of Korea and the Soviets promised to provide support for North Korea's military build-up.

Kim Il Sung and Stalin also agreed that North Korea and Communist China would have a separate meeting of their own to discuss pressing issues. On April 28, 1949, Kim Il (NKLP Central Committee member and NKPA Chief Political Supervisor) visited China to meet with Kao Gang in Shiemyang and have a series of meetings with Chuv Tek, Chou En-lai, and Mao Tse-tung in Peking. At these meetings, Kim Il informed the Chinese leaders of the North Korean-Soviet agreements, and secured a Chinese approval for the transfer to North Korea of Korean divisions then in the People's Liberation Army.(PLA)

Mao expressed much interest in the Kim-Stalin meeting. As for the establishment of communist intelligence agencies in Asian countries such as Myanmar, Malaysia, and Indochina, Mao argued that such a move would be premature given the ongoing war between China and Indochina and the precarious situation in North Korea, but added that such a possibility could eventually be entertained. On the Korean situation, Mao stated: "A war can break out in Korea at any time, and it can end quickly or drag on for a long time. A war of attrition would be disadvantageous for North Korea, for Japan may intervene to support "the South Korean government." But there is no need for worries as the Soviet Union is right by North Korea and we are in charge of

Manchuria." He added, "Should the Japanese intervene in the war, the Chinese Army will be sent to defeat them." Reminding that the international situation not favorable, Mao advised Kim Il Sung to withhold decisive action until the Chinese Communists completely defeated Ching Kai-shek's Kuomintang forces and take full control of China.

As for the Korean divisions in the PLA, Mao agreed to transfer two divisions stationed in the Mukden and Changch'un areas in Manchuria, and promised to transfer one remaining division in southern China to North Korea when the battle against the Kuomintang forces comes to a conclusion, within one month at the earliest.[7]

This North Korean-Chinese meeting has a special significance as it highlighted the Chinese intention to send its troops in the case of a Japanese intervention in Korea. On May 14 and 17, respectively, Mao Tse-tung and Kim Il Sung informed Stalin of the agreements, and thus the three leaders agreed on the policy of pursuing Korean unification through war. After this series of meetings with the Soviets and the Chinese, P'yongyang received from Moscow mainly war materiel and equipment, and from Peking, Korean-born veterans in the Chinese Communist Army. Under the Soviet and Chinese support, the combat power of the NKPA increased by leaps and bounds.

Encouraged by the drastic improvement in the combat power of the NKPA in 1949, Kim Il Sung told Soviet Ambassador Shtykov on August 12 and 14 that North Korea should be preparing for a preemptive strike against the South. Kim argued that the USAFIK withdrawal turned the 38th parallel into a meaningless dividing line and that the NKPA had proved its superiority through a series of provocations across the 38th parallel. He asserted that Seoul's refusal of the peace proposal put forward by the Democratic Front for National Unification left P'yongyang with no alternative but to invade, and added that the invasion would be followed by popular uprisings in the South.

Kim Il Sung argued that the Korean people would not understand should North Korea fail to strike against the South. Believing that the South Korean government had decided to build up a kind of Maginot Line along the 38th parallel, Kim emphasized that North Korea must launch a preemptive strike before the defensive line was set up.[8]

Expressing his doubts over Kim's proposal, the Soviet Ambassador reminded Kim Il Sung of Stalin's directive from their March meeting. In response to Shtykov's thinly veiled criticism, Kim Il Sung proposed to set up "liberation zones" in Samch'ok, Kangwon Province, in the vicinity of the 38th parallel. When the Soviet Ambassador pointed out that even this plan would require thorough preparation and accurate estimate of the situation, Kim put forward a plan to occupy the Ongjin Peninsula.[9] The seizure of the Ongjin Peninsula would not only provide the North with a favorable base from which to launch a future offensive, but it would also reduce the line of combat by 120km and have a devastating effect on the combat power and morale of the ROK forces.

Moscow, however, felt that a preemptive strike by North Korea would be feasible only if it could lead to a complete occupation of the South in a short period of time, and thought that the strength of the NKPA had yet to reach the required level. The Soviets thus objected to Kim's proposal and put his invasion plan on hold.[10] The Soviets were afraid that a preemptive strike by a less-than-fully-prepared NKPA would lead to a prolonged war and to a military intervention by the United States. Through Ambassador Shtykov, Moscow directed P'yongyang to strengthen guerrilla activities and spread popular uprisings against reactionary forces in the South and to focus all its energies on military build-up efforts.[11] Kim Il Sung and Park Hun Young were disappointed with Moscow's cool response to their proposal to establish "liberation zones" and occupy the Ongjin Peninsula. Agreeing with the Soviet assessment that guerrilla activities in the South must be strengthened, however, they sent reinforcements across the 38th parallel.[12]

When a Communist regime was established in China on October 1, 1949, Kim Il Sung allegedly said: "Now time has come for the liberation of South Korea. Guerrillas can't solve the problem. I can't sleep when I think about liberating South Korea." During a dinner party held at Foreign Minister Park Hun Young's residence on January 17, 1950, Kim Il Sung requested Ambassador Shtykov and Soviet counselors to arrange a meeting with Stalin. Kim wished to secure Stalin's approval for a preemptive strike.

Kim Il Sung explained: "At the March 1949 meeting with Stalin, I secured his approval to strike back if South Korea should attack first, but Syngman Rhee has yet to attempt an invasion. As I haven't had a chance to launch a counterattack, the liberation of the people in the South and national unification is being delayed. I need to meet with Stalin to discuss a preemptive strike and obtain his approval." He added that if a meeting with Stalin can't be arranged, he would try to meet with Mao Tse-tung when he comes back from Moscow. Recalling that Mao had promised to provide support North Korea after the end of the civil war in China, Kim noted that Mao would come back from Moscow with directives on all major issues.[13]

From December 16, 1949, to February 17, 1950, Mao visited Moscow to have a series of meetings with Stalin and other Soviet leaders. He came back to China after signing a China-Soviet Mutual Treaty on Friendship and Alliance, an accord on Changch'un Railway, Lushan, and Tairen, and a loan agreement.[14] As was formally announced, the agenda for the Mao-Stalin meeting appeared on the surface to be limited to issues regarding the relationship between the two countries. Given the rapidly developing postwar situation in East Asia and around the globe, however, it is likely that the two leaders discussed ways to coordinate their actions on various issues, including possible division of roles to promote the communization of the world. Kim Il Sung's statements in recently declassified documents suggests that Mao and Stalin probably discussed in some depth how they could support North Korea's invasion of the South.

On March 30, 1950, Shtykov made an arrangement for Kim Il Sung and Park Hun Young to make a secret visit to Moscow and have a meeting with Stalin to discuss various issues including Korean unification, North Korea's economic prospects, and internal problems within the Communist Party. Noting that the international situation had taken a favorable turn for North Korea, Stalin approved of Kim's plan to launch a pre-emptive strike. Stalin added that the final decision over this matter rested with North Korea and China, and the leaders agreed to postpone the decision if China were negative on Kim's plan. On April 25 Kim Il Sung and Park Hun Young returned to P'yongyang.[15]

In accordance with the Moscow agreement, Kim Il Sung went to Peking to meet with Mao Tse-tung on May 13, 1950. When North Korean leaders relayed Stalin's message to Mao late that evening, Mao requested Stalin's direct explanation.[16]

In response to Mao's request, Stalin replied: "I agree with the Korean leaders that actions to achieve Korean unification should be initiated given the favorable changes in the international situation. However, this is a problem for China and Korea jointly to decide, and if our Chinese comrades should disapprove, the decision should be postponed until it can be re-examined."[17]

Upon receiving this message from Moscow, Mao had extensive discussions with Kim Il Sung and Park Hun Young on May 15. Kim outlined North Korea's three-stage plan as follows: [18]

Stage 1: Build up and increase military strength.

Stage 2: Propose a peaceful unification plan to South Korea.

Stage 3: Start the war when the South rejects the peace proposal.

Stating that the unification of Korea could be achieved only through force, Mao supported Kim's plan, and emphasized the importance of making thorough preparations for the war. He added that it was important to give detailed directives to individual soldiers and commanders, and suggested that the People's Army move quickly and concentrate its strength to annihilate the enemy. Mao stated that although the People's Army might lay siege to major cities, it should not lose precious time just to occupy these cities. As for a possible intervention by Japanese forces, Kim Il Sung thought that they were unlikely to take part in a Korean war, but could not exclude the possibility that the US might decide to send 20,000 to 30,000 Japanese troops to Korea. However, he believed that the Japanese troops would not be able to alter the general course of the war and would only strengthen the resolve of the People's Army to fight. Mao noted that an intervention by 20,000 to 30,000 Japanese troops might prolong the war, but agreed that the possibility of a Japanese intervention was extremely remote under the prevailing circumstances. Moreover, he assured Kim that if the United States should intervene, China would send its troops to support North Korea. Mao had thought that China could first seize Taiwan and then carry out operations against South Korea to support P'yongyang. Mao now agreed, however, that North Korea's war against the South became a priority, and promised Kim to provide necessary assistance for this operation. According to what Chou En-lai later said to Soviet Ambassador N.V. Roschin in July 1950, Mao Tse-tung warned Kim Il Sung about the possibility of a direct intervention by US forces in Korea, but Kim seemed to dismiss such a possibility. On May 16, Kim Il Sung's entourage returned to

P'yongyang, having agreed to wait until after unification to sign a friendship and mutual assistance treaty with China.[19]

After returning from Moscow in April, Kim Il Sung had already ordered the General Staff to draw up a detailed invasion plan. Led by Chief of the General Staff Kang Kun and new Soviet chief military advisor Vassyliev, the NKPA finished up the plan on May 29. Having been completed in stages over a period of one month, this plan envisaged the NKPA to launch the attack at the end of June.[20] P'yongyang approved of the plan, and directed the NKPA to complete the war preparations by June. Kim Il Sung was afraid that information on the attacking date might be leaked if it were set to be a later date. Kim preferred the late June date also because heavy rain in July would restrict the maneuver of armed forces, and Soviet advisors shared the same opinion. This plan was reported to Stalin via Shtykov on June 16, and won the Soviet leader's approval.[21] North Korea's invasion plan was thus thoroughly prepared and finalized under close coordination among Kim, Stalin, and Mao. Finally, the invasion date was set to be Sunday, June 25. This choice for the invasion date was to maximize surprise under the expectation that security would be lax on that day.

According to then-Chief of-NKPA Operations Bureau Maj. Gen. Yoo Sung Chul, this plan was titled "Preemptive Strike Operation Plan," and was originally prepared in Russian. As a matter of fact, copies of this plan later seized during the war were in Russian. This suggests that the invasion plan was drawn up under the guidance of the Soviet military advisors in North Korea at the time. The NKPA General Staff at the time lacked the necessary military background to set up a war plan, but their Soviet advisors were expert strategists. Together with an artillery commander and an engineer bureau chief with prior experience in the Soviet Army, Yoo Sung Chul secretly translated this plan into Korean under the supervision of Chief of the General Staff Kang

Kun.[22] Thus was completed North Korea's Preemptive Strike Operation Plan.

(2) Basic Invasion Strategy

Drawn up under close coordination among Kim Il Sung, Stalin, and Mao Tse-tung, North Korea's invasion plan envisaged an all-out initial attack, rapid exploitation, and quick conclusion. The North's basic strategy proceeded as follows: launch an all-out war at the end of June 1950; quickly occupy Seoul; precipitate popular revolts and overthrow the ROK government; rapidly move the NKPA troops down to the southern shores of Korea to prevent the landing of US troops; and end the war within a month and establish a unified people's government in Seoul by August 15, the fifth anniversary of Korea's liberation.

In finalizing the invasion plan, the item that demanded the greatest attention from Kim and Stalin was the possibility of US intervention in the war. Inferior in military strength to the United States, and, in particular, lagging behind in the development of nuclear weapons, the Soviet Union wished to avoid a direct collision with the United States. Moscow was also well aware that North Korea by itself would not be able to defeat the United States. This understanding of the situation had formed the basis of Moscow's attempts to induce US troop withdrawal from Korea prior to the war. Although US State Secretary Acheson declared in January 1950 that Korea was excluded from the US defensive zone in the Pacific, a US intervention in Korea could not be ruled out, for North Korea's invasion would certainly perturb the East-West balance in the Cold War. Kim and Stalin finally concluded that North Korea should and could move quickly enough to end the war before the arrival of US troops-even if Washington should decide to intervene. In other words, the North's basic invasion strategy was to launch a blitzkrieg-like war to occupy

Seoul and advance rapidly down to the southern shores before the deployment of US troops. *The Comprehensive History of Choson* states as follows:

> Our plan is to annihilate the forces of Syngman Rhee's puppet government and advance US troops before American imperialists mobilize large forces. The People's Army shall rapidly advance southward to the Pusan-Masan-Mokp'o-Yosu-Namhae line and liberate all of our land, and their mobile deployment over all of Korea shall prevent the landing of American imperialists.[23]

In a face-to-face meeting with Stalin, Kim Il Sung said: "The people of South Korea harbor much discontent against the Syngman Rhee regime. He is a puppet of US imperialism, and the people want to take over the country. If we just strike a single blow against the Rhee regime, the people will rise up and people's power will carry the day."[24] According to Yoo Sung Chul's account, Kim Il Sung and North Korean leadership trusted Park Hun Young's assurance that "once Seoul is occupied, 200,000 SKLP members hiding all over the South would rise up and overthrow the South Korean regime." They thus mistakenly thought that the war would come to an end when Seoul was occupied within three days. A similar account is provided on this point by Lee Sang Cho, former Deputy Chief of the NKPA General Staff and Chief of the Reconnaissance Bureau.[25]

Park Hun Young's "guarantee" was one of the main factors that fueled Kim Il Sung's war ambitions, but later it became one of the pretexts under which he was purged. At any rate, in addition to a blitzkrieg attack by the NKPA, another key element in the North's invasion strategy was to precipitate popular uprisings led by SKLP members and bring about the collapse of the ROK government. In accordance with this strategy, in a radio broadcast a day after he started the war, Kim Il Sung called for popular uprisings in the South:

Brothers in the southern half of the Republic should not listen to the
orders and directives issued by the puppet government of Syngman
Rhee ···. Workers should stage strikes and riots all over the South ···.
Peasants should not feed the enemy and should actively take part in
guerrilla activities ···. Artists and intellectuals should thoroughly expose crimes committed by US imperialists and Syngman Rhee's cro-
nies, and should serve as a vanguard in the organization of popular revolts.[26]

No popular uprising actually took place after the North's invasion,
however. Kim Il Sung later said: "Park Hun Young, that long-time spy of
American bastards, claimed there were 200,000 underground SKLP members
in the South, and 60,000 in Seoul alone. Two hundred thousand? There was not
even a single revolt when we reached as far as the Naktong line. If only a few
thousand workers had risen up in Pusan, we would have certainly been able to
liberate Pusan and probably prevented the landing of those damned Americans."[27] This statement clearly demonstrates how much Kim had expected out
of popular revolts in starting the war.

Prior to launching the war, P'yongyang went on a peace offensive. On
June 7, 1950, approximately one week after the completion of the preemptive
strike plan, Kim Il Sung adopted a message to the people of South Korea and
proposed in the name of the Central Committee of the Democratic Front for
National Unification: "to hold a general election throughout Korea from
August 5 to 8 in order to establish a united supreme legislative body; to call a
meeting of this legislative body (National Assembly) on August 15 in commemoration of the fifth anniversary of Korea's liberation; and to hold a conference
from June 15 to 17 in Haeju or Seoul to discuss conditions for peaceful unification and procedural matters for the general election."[28] The proposal excluded "national traitors opposed to peaceful unification"(meaning the Syngman

Rhee regime) from the conference, and ruled out interference by the UN Commission on Korea.

This proposal has long been considered as a part of the North's thinly veiled peace offensive. At the same time, however, this statement also provides an important clue in regard to the deadline set by P'yongyang to achieve its goal of communizing the entire Korean peninsula. According to the statement, Kim Il Sung and his Soviet advisors seem to have expected to complete the occupation of South Korea and hold a Soviet-style election to establish a unified Communist government in Seoul by August 15, 1950, the fifth anniversary of Korea's liberation. In other words, this indicates they anticipated an early victory and defined as their objective the establishment of a unified people's government in Seoul by August 15.[29]

In addition to these various stratagems, the NKPA harassed the rear of the ROK Army defense, and dispatched People's Guerrillas prior to the invasion to facilitate the use of mixed tactics during the war. However, the North's basic strategy remained to be: occupation of Seoul within 3 days, overthrow of the ROK government by popular revolts, seizure of all of Korea before the deployment of US troops, and establishment of a unified people's government by the fifth anniversary of Korea's liberation.

(3) Operation Plan

According to Yoo Sung Chul's account, the North's Preemptive Strike Operation Plan was a comprehensive and thorough offensive plan consisting of a combat order and plans for unit movement, logistics and supply, and deception.[30]

Under Kim Il Sung's directive, the plan envisaged a three-stage operation in which attacking units would concentrate their strength in the Kum ch'on-Kuhwari, Yonch'on-Ch'orwon, and Hwach'on-Yanggu areas; carry out offensive operations to envelop and annihilate the core units of the ROK army in the vicinity of Seoul; and aggressively exploit early successes to advance down to the southern shores.[31]

> Stage 1: Penetrate the ROK defensive line and annihilate the main defensive units. Occupy Seoul within 3 days, and advance to the Seoul (Suwon)-Wonju-Samch'ok line.
>
> Stage 2: Exploit early successes and annihilate the ROK reserve units. Advance to the Kunsan-Taegu-P'ohang line.
>
> Stage 3: Pursue down to the southern coast. Deploy down to the Pusan-Yosu-Mokp'o line.

As shown in ⟨Table 1⟩, an intelligence plan for the NKPA's offensive operation (dated June 20, 1950), seized during the Korean War, contained the following operational stages and corresponding objectives for intelligence planning:[32]

⟨Table 1⟩   Operational Stages and Intelligence Planning Objectives

Operational Stage	Operational Area	Intelligence Planning Objective
1st Stage Penetration of Defense Line Annihilation of Main Effort	38th Parallel ∣ Seoul(Suwon)-Wonju-Samch'ok	Forward Defense Organization Seoul Defense Organization Commitment of Reserves
2nd Stage Exploitation Annihilation of Reserves	Seoul(Suwon)-Wonju-Samch'ok ∣ Kunsan-Taegu-P'ohang (Kyongju)	Rear Defensive Positions Forward Movement of Divisions Reinforcements and Supplies
3rd Stage Mop-Up Operations Pursuit to the Southern Coast	Kunsan-Taegu-P'ohang (Kyongju) ∣ Pusan-Yosu-Mokp'o	Defense along Approaches Harbor Activities Harbor Defense Plans

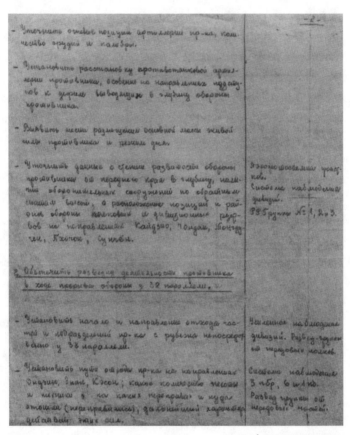

NKPA's Intelligence Plan

* This intelligence annex was captured in Seoul on October 4, 1950, and declassified to be open to the public. It consisted of 7 pages authenticated on June 20, 1950, by the NKPA Chief of General Staff.

In the first stage of the preemptive strike operation, the 10 divisions of the NKPA ground forces were to be organized into two attacking corps. The 1st Corps was to be the main attacking force, and was charged with the mission of applying pressure on Seoul from the north after penetrating the 38th parallel across the Kumch'on-Kuhwari and Yonch'on-Ch'orwon line. The 2nd Corps was to cross the 38th parallel from the Hwach'on-Yanggu area and employ a turning movement to provide a supporting attack from the east of Seoul and Suwon. Under close coordination, the two attacking corps were to envelop and occupy Seoul, and secure the Suwon-Wonju-Samch'ok line.[33]

In accordance with the plan, the NKPA 1st Corps directed the 3rd and 4th Divisions, its main attacking units, to advance along the Ch'orwon-P'och'on-Uijungbu axis under the support of the 105th Armored Brigade (-); the 6th Division(-1) and the 1st Division to attack along the Kumch'on-Kaesong-Munsan and Kuhwari-Korangp'o-Munsan axes; and a part of the 6th Division to attack the Ongjin and Kimp'o peninsulas.

The NKPA 2nd Corps committed the 2nd and 12th Divisions in the direction of Hwach'on-Chunch'on-Kap'yung and Yanggu-Hongch'on-Suwon and Wonju, and ordered the 5th Division to advance from Yangyang to the Kangrung-Samch'ok area. In addition, it directed the 766th and 549th Units to carry out landing operations in Chongdongjin and Imwonjin along the eastern shores and harass the rear area of the ROK army in support of the 2nd Corps.

Since the overall plan itself was based on the premise that there would be popular revolts all around South Korea upon the North's occupation of Seoul, the NKPA expected little organized resistance from the ROK forces after the first stage of the war. Accordingly, in the second stage of the war, the NKPA was to make a rapid transition to the exploitation phase, and overwhelm the ROK reserves to advance to the Kunsan-Taejon-Taegu-P'ohang line. In the third stage, the NKPA was to mop up the remaining ROK troops and secure the Pusan-Masan-Yosu-Mokp'o line.[34]

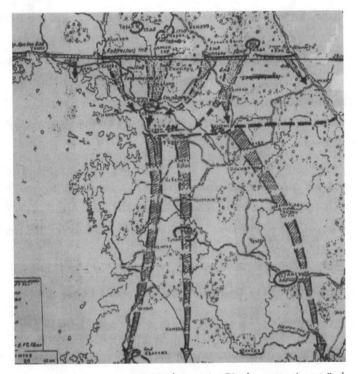

NKPA's Invasion Plan(pre-emptive strike)

* This copy of situatim map for the NKPA'S southward invasion was released by the Yon-hap News Agency, which obtained it from a senior researcher, Dr. Kortkov at the Russia Institute of Military History on August 29, 1992. According to him original copies are kept in Moscow and P'yongyang.

Reorganizing after the occupation of Seoul, the NKPA 1st Corps was to advance along the western and central axes to reach the Mokp'o-Yosu area, and the 2nd Corps was to move along the eastern axis and eastern coastline to advance to the Masan-Pusan area.[35]

Expecting to meet little resistance from the ROK forces and seeking to advance to the southern coast before the deployment of US reinforcements, the North Korean leadership placed a special emphasis on rapid maneuver in the second and third stages of the war. Unlike in the first stage, little synchronization between the corps was built into the second and third stages. The NKPA was to defeat the ROK forces in detail along the 4 axes of advance, and drive swiftly for deep strategic objectives.[36]

During the actual war, the first stage of the operation was carried out as planned, but the execution of the second and third stages diverged a great deal from the plan. This unexpected development of events was due to the non-existence of popular revolts, strong resistance of the ROK forces, and rapid deployment of US troops.

2. Establishment of the Wartime Leadership and Command Structure

After the completion of the operation plan at the end of May 1950, P'yongyang went on a peace offensive in June to cover up its war preparations, and established a wartime leadership and command structure as part of the final-phase preparations to carry out the invasion plan.

On June 10, the North Korean military leadership held a secret meeting at the office of the Chief of the General Staff attended by division and brigade-level commanders. For security reasons, the subject of the meeting ostensibly regarded the maneuver exercise of division-level units, but the meeting really concerned the issuance of directives for troop movement in preparation for the invasion. In accordance with the concept of the preemptive strike operation, troop movement was to be carried out with the objective of forming two attacking corps. P'yongyang decided to establish Corps Commands at this time.[37]

On June 10, P'yongyang organized the 1st Corps Command under Lt.

Gen. Kim Ung (Chief of the Training Bureau, Ministry of National Defense). Two days later, P'yongyang established the 2nd Corps Command under Lt. Gen Kim Kwang Hyop (Commander of the NKPA 3rd Division).[38]

Next P'yongyang established a so-called "Front Line Command," equivalent to a Field Army Command, which would direct the two Corps. Kim Ch'aek (vice premier rank) was appointed as its commander, and Chief of the General Staff Kang Kun was named its Chief of Staff.

Given his rank and place within the North Korean regime, National Defense Minister Choi Yong Gun would have been the natural choice for the post of War Front Commander; however, his opposition both to the invasion itself and to the NKPA's war preparations under Soviet advisors led Kim Il Sung to leave him out of the command post.[39] The Military History of Choson states: "The War Front Command was established to strengthen the command system for the war. Through the establishment of the Command, it became possible to carry out Kim Il Sung's directives with greater accuracy and speed, and to ensure a successful command over the whole front."[40] The Military History of Choson reports that the War Front Command was established on July 5— that is, after the outbreak of the war. According to Yoo Sung Chul's account, however, it is beyond any doubt that the Command was established prior to the start of the war.

Yoo states: "At the outset of the war, the War Front Command was located in a natural cave in Sop'o in the vicinity of P'yongyang. I was receiving situation reports from the front in this cave, which had been used as an ammunition depot by the Japanese during the colonial era. At 0900 on June 25, we were informed that the NKPA had occupied Kaesong. 'Wah …' Cries of joy immediately filled the cave, and we hugged one another and shared the joy of victory."[41]

Having established a field command system for the war, Kim Il Sung seized the power of all three branches of the government and assumed the chairmanship of the military committee in order to take personal command of the armed forces. The Military History of Choson contends that Kim became the military committee chairman according to a special act on the organization of the committee passed by the standing committee of the Supreme People's Conference on June 26. Coming as it did a day after the outbreak of the war, however, this announcement is likely to have been a mere formality. In fact, it may be safely presumed that the military committee was organized prior to June 25.[42]

The special act on the organization of the military committee declared as follows: "A military committee is to be organized for a rapid mobilization of the strength of all people in response to the surprise invasion of the north of the 38th parallel by the ROK forces." The act organized the committee with Kim Il Sung as the chairman and Park Hun Young, Hong Myung Hee, Kim Ch'aek, Choi Yong Gun, Park Il Woo, Chung Joon T'aek as its members. The act concentrated all powers in this committee, and demanded absolute obedience from all people, government bodies, political and social organizations, and military groups. Accordingly, all central and provincial government bodies came to belong to the military committee. As the committee chairman, Kim Il Sung instituted a wartime system for all organizations in political, economic, and cultural areas, and took measures to mobilize all resources for an ultimate victory in the war.[43]

In addition, the Supreme People's Conference announced the appointment of Kim Il Sung to the post of the supreme commander of the NKPA effective July 4. It seems quite clear, however, that this action too was taken prior to the war.[44] As the supreme commander of the armed forces, Kim not only assumed a direct command and supervision of all staff organizations and units under the peacetime command of the National Defense Ministry, but

also exercised command over all quasi-military organizations under the jurisdiction of the Public Security Ministry.

By simultaneously assuming the posts of general secretary of the Communist Party, premier of the cabinet, chairman of the military committee, and
supreme commander of the NKPA, Kim Il Sung exercised absolute power and
started the war with a complete system of wartime leadership and command.
This fact, even by itself, more than adequately demonstrates the thoroughness
with which P'yongyang prepared for the war.

3. Forward Deployment of the Attacking Forces

Upon the establishment of the wartime leadership and command
system, the attacking units of the NKPA moved to the vicinity of the 38th parallel according to the concept of the operation. In order to avoid having their
intent exposed to the South due to the forward deployment of the NKPA, the
North Korean military leadership came up with an ingenious idea: to cover up
the deployment by ostensibly carrying out a large-scale maneuver exercise of
division-level units for two weeks.

During a secret meeting from June 10 to 12 at North Korea's Ministry
of National Defense, the Chief of the General Staff ordered his subordinate
commanders to be fully prepared by June 23 to deter any enemy attack, and
issued the following directive:

> Until now, our People's Army has carried out combat exercises up to
> the division-level, but we are going to mobilize all our combat divisions
> for this maneuver exercise. During this exercise, we will show off all
> our armament and equipment as well as all our basic units ···. This ma-
> neuver exercise may take some time to complete, but two weeks will
> suffice. Since this exercise is being carried out in utmost secrecy, you

must not tell anyone about it, including your family members. Keep
this in mind and maintain the security.[45]

Here, the directive to keep the maneuver plan a secret even from one's
family members is not persuasive at all if the troop movement had indeed been
planned as part of a two-week-long exercise. At any rate, the troop movement
was carried out under the control of the two newly formed NKPA corps.

Up to that point, the NKPA's 1st Security Brigade (Kansong), the 7th
Security Brigade (Shibyunri), and 3rd Security Brigade (Chukch'on) assumed
the responsibility for security along the 38th parallel, and combat divisions
under jurisdiction of the Ministry of National Defense were stationed in each
province in the rear area.

On June 12, the NKPA's attacking units left their garrison and started
moving toward a 10-15km vicinity north of the 38th parallel. Troops stationed

〈Table 2〉　The Forward Deployment of the NKPA Attacking Units[46]

Unit	Garrison	Destination	Unit	Garrison	Destination
1st Corps		Kumch'on	2nd Corps		Hwach'on
6th Division(-1)	Sariwon	Kyejong	2nd Division	Wonsan	Hwach'on
14th Regiment	Sariwon	Haeju, Chukch'on	12th Division	Wonsan	Yanggu
1st Division	Namch'onjom	Kuhwari	5th Division	Nanam	Yangyang
4th Division	Namp'o	Yonch'on	15th Division	Hoeryong	Hwach'on
3rd Division	P'yonggang	Unch'on	Independent		
13th Division	Shinuiju	Kumch'on	Tank Regiment	Nanam	Inje
105th Armored			12th Mtrcl		
Brigade(-1)	P'yongyang	Yonch'on	Regiment	Kilju	Yangyang
203rd Armored	P'yongyang	Namch'on	766th unit	Hoeryong	Wonsan, Kansong
Regiment			549th unit	Kapsan	Songjin

＊ 10th Division : Army Reserve, assembled at Sukch'on.

near the parallel moved on foot, and those far away used trains. In addition, reserve divisions moved to the zone taken up by their respective corps, and supporting units moved to the deployment zone of their supported units. As envisaged in the operation plan, the 766th and the 549th Units prepared for infiltration by sea. According to the directive, the troop movement was completed by June 23. In accordance with the concept of the operation, the NKPA completed the organization of its two corps and entered into the final stage of the preparation for the invasion.

4. Issuance of the Order for the Southward Invasion

At last, coinciding with the troop movement, the NKPA General Headquarters issued top-secret reconnaissance and attack orders for the southward invasion.

First, while the troop deployment was in full progress, the NKPA Staff Headquarters issued Reconnaissance Order No. 1 to attacking units on June 18. This order explained the enemy situation (i.e., deployment of ROK defensive units) in the front of the attacking units, and described in great detail reconnaissance requirements after taking the attacking position prior to the attack and stage-by-stage requirements after launching the attack.

The original copy of the reconnaissance order was handwritten in Russian, and was seized during the war in Seoul on October 4, 1950.[47]

From this reconnaissance order, it is clear that the NKPA 4th Division had Seoul as its objective and the 2nd Division sought to move along the Ch'oonch'on-Seoul road to cross the Han River and advance in the direction of Ich'on and Suwon.

Representative of the reconnaissance orders issued to attacking divisions, the orders issued to the NKPA 4th and 2nd Divisions can be summarized as follows:

NKPA General Headquarters Reconnaissance Order No. 1 (June 18, 1950)

To: Chief of Staff, 4th Division

1. The 1st Regiment of the enemy 1st Infantry Division is defending along the Imjin River to HILL 538. The enemy 13th Regiment, 1st Division, is defending in the right front, and the 9th Regiment, 7th Division, is defending in the left front.

2. Upon occupation of the attack position, the division will carry out observation and reconnaissance missions to find out accurately, by the night before the attack, the main line of enemy resistance, land mines, obstacles, and passage lanes, the location of enemy defensive positions and observation posts, system of fire power, the position of enemy main units, artillery positions and calibers, the deployment of antitank guns. When the attack commences, the division will organize and dispatch an additional reconnaissance unit to find out all defensive positions on avenues of approach along the Uijongbu–Seoul axis and to attack enemy reserves. Upon advancing to the vicinity of Seoul, employ all means to collect information on the concentrated enemy forces in the downtown area and on their street defense measures.[48]

NKPA General Headquarters Reconnaissance Order No. 1 (June 18, 1950)

To: Chief of Staff, 2nd Division

1. The 7th Regiment of the enemy 6th Infantry Division is defending along HILL 590 to HILL 621. To its east, the enemy 19th Regiment is defending abreast. The enemy security positions are set up adjacent to a hill in the vicinity of the 38th parallel. The forward end of the main line of enemy resistance is located 1 to 1.5km in the rear, along the Kajiri line from HILL 590 to HILL 313.

2. Upon occupation of the attack position, the division will carry out observa-

tion and reconnaissance missions to find out accurately, by the night before the attack, the main line of enemy resistance, land mines, obstacles, and passage lanes ⋯. When the attack commences, the division will observe the commitment of enemy reserves and the timing and direction of enemy withdrawal. When the leading units arrive in Saamri, the division will dispatch a reconnaissance unit in ... the direction to watch out for the appearance of enemy units and monitor troop movement along the Seoul-Ch'unch'on railway and roads. When the leading units arrive in Kohyunri and Kangch'onri, the division will send a strong mobile reconnaissance unit to roads leading to Seoul, up to the southern banks of the Han River, and observe the enemy situation there. When the division reaches the Han River, carry out a reconnaissance mission to monitor troop movement along the Seoul-Suwon-Ich'on road and observe the enemy situation in the vicinity of Koksu, Suwon, and Ich'on.[49]

When the NKPA troop maneuver was almost completed, Operation Order No. 1 was issued to the attacking corps and divisions, and they in turn issued orders to their subordinate units.[50] According to Yoo Sung Ch'ul's witness account, the Preemptive Strike Operation Plan included operation orders, and, on June 19, 1950, Park Kil Nam, then Chief of the Engineer Bureau at the NKPA General Staff Headquarters, is said to have ordered Chu Yong Bok, Engineer Major of the NKPA 2nd Corps, to translate into Korean the Engineer Appendix to Operational Order No. 1, written in Russian. This oral testimony suggests that the first operation orders were issued almost a week prior to the war by the NKPA General Staff Headquarters.[51] Although these operation orders have yet to be disclosed, operation orders (handwritten in Korean) issued by the NKPA 4th Division (dated June 22) were seized in the vicinity of Taejon on July 16, 1950. Operation orders issued by the 2nd Division (dated the same day) were also seized during the war, and they together provide unshakable

NKPA's Reconnaissance Order

* This is a photo copy of the NKPA's Reconnaissance Order No.1 issued to the 2nd Division.

evidence on the planned nature of North Korea's southward invasion.

According to its Operation Order No 1, the NKPA 4th Division, was charged with a mission to carry out a main attack on Seoul. It was to complete preparations by June 23, 1950, penetrate the enemy line of defense on order, and advance in the direction of Uijongbu and Seoul. In addition to laying out the basic maneuver plan, the operation order gave detailed missions to supporting units, and defined signal operating instructions for the attack. It could be summarized as follows: [52]

The NKPA 4th Division Operation Order No. 1

1. The enemy (Rok) 1st Regiment, 7th Division, is defending in the front.
2. The division will penetrate the enemy line of defense from the Kwangdong-Ajangdong direction, the most important in the attacking front of the corps. The division will first occupy Majiri and HILL 535, and after occupying P'yong Village and Naehoiam, the division will advance in the direction of Uijongbu and Seoul.
3. The 1st Infantry Division will attack on the right, and the 3rd Infantry Division will attack on the left.
9. Preparatory artillery fires will be delivered for 30 minutes ···.
10. The air wing will destroy enemy military facilities and roads, and deny the assembly of enemy reserves.
11. Anti-air measures ···. When enemy planes come to attack, the division will mobilized 30% of infantry weapons.
12. Anti-tank weapons will be used against enemy tanks.
13. The command post will be deployed from June 23, and its axis of movement will be along the direction of the road that leads to Uijongbu.
16. Basic Signals: Start of Attack-Storm (telephone), 244 (radio)
     Start of Assault-Green tracer, 224 (radio)

Although no operation orders issued by other divisions under the NKPA Corps have been discovered, items 2 and 3 above make it clear that as the main attacking unit of the corps, the NKPA 4th Division was to attack abreast with the adjacent 1st and 3rd Divisions.

Handwritten in Korean, Operation Order No. 1 issued by the NKPA 2nd Division charged the division with a mission to complete preparations by June 22, move to the line of departure on order, and penetrate the enemy line of defense. Within the same day, the division was to occupy Ch'unch'on and advance in the direction of Kap'yung. The operation order could be summarized as follows: [53]

The NKPA 2nd Division Operation Order No. 1

1. The enemy 7th Regiment, 6th Division, is defending in the front.
2. The division will penetrate the enemy line of defense between HILL 882, Songamri, Mojin Bridge, and Map'yungri. As its immediate mission, the division will occupy Shindangri ···. Tojagol, and as its ultimate mission, the division will occupy Ch'unch'on within the same day and advance in the direction of Kap'yung and Kangch'on.
3. The 3rd Infantry Division will attack on the right in the direction of Seoul, and the 12th Infantry Division will attack on the left in the direction of Hongch'on-Wonju and Hoingsong-Yoju.
4. The 6th Regiment will carry out a main attack from the right and the 4th Regiment will attack abreast on the left. The 17th Regiment will follow the main attack.
8. The artillery unit will complete preparations by 2400 hrs, June 22, 1950. Preparatory fire will be delivered for 30 minutes.
9. The engineer unit will secure the Mojin Bridge and guarantee the river crossing of infantry units.

Gen. Lee Ch'ong Song
Commander
2nd Infantry Division

Operation Order No. 1., NKPA's 2nd Divion

* This photo copy forms the 1st page of the NKPA 2nd Division's Combat(attack) order. The Korea Institute of Military History secured this copy from the US National Archives.

This operation order makes it clear that the NKPA 3rd and 12th Infantry Divisions were to attack abreast on the right and left of the 2th Division, respectively. The captured operation orders thus prove that North Korea planned an all-out offensive across the 38th parallel. These orders also confirm the authenticity of the Preemptive Strike Operation Plan as the maneuver plans established for the division level are in agreement of the overall concept of the operation.

It is perhaps no longer necessary to list further evidence on North Korea's preemptive strike to prove the planned nature of the North's southward invasion in June 1950. In official publications, however, P'yongyang continues to engage in a deceptive and preposterous campaign:

> American imperialists and Syngman Rhee's puppet regime at last launched an invasion against the northern half of the Republic and started a war against the Korean people …. As the Korean People's Army set out for a fight to repel the invasion of American imperialists and their lackeys and to defend the nation's freedom and independence, a just war for national liberation had begun.[54]

This is a blatant fabrication of history. P'yongyang's own war plans and documents demonstrate that it was the North's southward invasion which brought about the nation's tragedy.

II. The Defensive Posture of the ROK Forces

1. Estimate of the Enemy Situation

After consaltation with Mao Tse-Tung, Kim Il-Sung & Stalin formulated the strategy for their invasion by the end of 1948; they conclusively fixed the inasion plan in April 1950 and even drew up the plan for the preemptive strike in May.

In order to accomplish the tasks, they began remakably to strengthen the NKPA'S combat capability from 1949; they harassed the rear area of the ROK by sending 2,400 querillas in then separate sorties and at the same time intensified provocations along the 38th parallel. In order to meet the manpower shortage caused by rapid expansim of troops, North Korea adopted a compulsong military jeruice system starting from the summer of 1949. On July 15, 1949, it organized a Suppoters' Association for Defense, thus to help its nationwide war efforts.

Prior to the outbreak of the war, the ROK government made various efforts to secure self-defense capability in response to North Korea's military threats. In March 1949, Seoul began the negotiations for greater military assistance in the wake of the US troop withdrawal from Korea. Washington, however, did not accommodate Seoul's requests. Moreover, in a speech on January 12, 1950, US State Secretary Acheson declared that Korea and Taiwan lay outside the US defensive line in the Pacific, calling into doubt the US determination to provide military assistance to Korea.

Around this time, the ROK government had to mobilize all internal security resources to destroy SKLP cells which had deeply infiltrated into various sections of the society, and to arrest the spread of leftist ideologies. In the political arena, however, the ruling party and the opposition engaged in a bitter fight over constitutional amendments, and did little to promote the unity of the nation.

In this security environment, frontline ROK units took defensive measures against the enemy's armed provocations across the 38th parallel, and rear units carried out counter-insurgency operations against the People's Guerrillas and remaining communist infiltrators. At the same time, the ROK forces also had to purge military units of leftist sympathizers organized by communist cell operatives. These security challenges, combined with the ROK forces' numerical inferiority to the NKPA, made it extremely difficult for the South Korean military to maximize its combat strength and to concentrate its strength in times of crisis. The security of the nation was in danger.

At the end of 1949 (December 27), as if to reflect this precarious national security situation, a comprehensive intelligence report prepared by the ROK Army Headquarters estimated the enemy strength and equipment as shown in ⟨Table 3⟩, and stated that "the enemy would carry out a full-scale offensive campaign in the spring of 1950."

Based on this estimate, the ROK government issued a warning to P'yongyang against its southward invasion, and made diplomatic efforts to secure military assistance from the United States only to be in vain. In order to strengthen defense along the 38th parallel, Col. Kang Moon Bong, ROK Army Headquarters Operations Bureau Chief, included an item in the national defense budget for fiscal year 1950, for building up positions and obstacles along the 38th parallel but this item was cut by the National Assembly.[56]

In January 1950, ROK Army Chief of Staff, Maj. Gen. Shin T'ae Young pointed out to the UN Commission on Korea that the NKPA held a decisive edge in strength and equipment over the ROK forces, and informed the Com-

〈Table 3〉   Rok Estimate of the Enemy Situation (December 27, 1949)

Personmel Strength			
People's Army	91,598	Other	22,000
Constabulary Force	60,424	Total	174,022
Equipment			
Rifle	75,653	Submachine Gun	30,099
Light Machine Gun	5,234	Heavy Machine Gun	2,287
82-mm Mortar	603	120-mm Mortar	126
76-mm Howitzer	218	122-mm Howitzer	73
Vehicle	1,693	Tank	120
Armored Vehicle	60	Airplane	62
Patrol Boat	30	Airfield	17

Conclusion
An overall assessment of the recent enemy situation and general developments suggests that a dramatic change in the enemy situation is expected starting in the spring of next year (1950). Until that time, the enemy will attempt to create conditions favorable to southward invasion by carrying out harrassment operations in rear areas and intensifying subversive activities designed to bring about an implosion within South Korea. Simultaneous with these background operations, the enemy will rapidly build up military strength and prepare for war by mobilizing all resources. The enemy will then launch a full-scale invasion across the 38th parallel and attempt to overthrow the Republic of Korea at a single stroke.[55]

mission, "North Korea has a ripe invasion plan, and it is only a matter of time before they take action."[57]

Estimates by the US Embassy and KMAG were, however, in stark contrast. Americans argued that the ROK forces could defeat the enemy if a war broke out. In fact, they were afraid that the ROK National Forces might invade the North if they grew too strong.

In a press conference with foreign journalists on May 10, 1950, ROK Defense Minister Shin Sung Mo explained, "The North Korean army is moving its troops toward the 38th parallel, and a threat of invasion by the North is imminent."[58] In a press conference with Korean and foreign journalists the next day, President Syngman Rhee said, "It is difficult to predict what will happen in May and June ⋯. Only US assistance can enable us to defend against the North's invasion."[59]

While reports of an imminent North Korean invasion were becoming frequent, ROK Army Deputy Chief of Staff Col. Kim Paik Il and Intelligence Bureau Chief Col. Chang Toh Young gave a briefing on the military situation of North Korea during Foreign Minister's May 12 meeting with the UN Commission on Korean Unification. Among the known documents on the Korean War, this briefing is of great value as it shows the South's intelligence estimate of the North's military strength just prior to the outbreak of the war. ⟨Table 4⟩ summarizes this estimate.[60]

Compared with the December 1949 estimate, the May 1950 intelligence estimate shows that the NKPA's strength and equipment had greatly increased over the previous 6 months due to its feverish build-up prior to the war.

The May 1950 estimate came very close to the NKPA's actual strength and equipment at the outbreak of the war a month and a half afterwards, which shows that the ROK military leadership had a fairly accurate reading of the enemy situation.

As part of the MND's effort to secure sufficient defensive strength in response to this critical situation, Col. Kang Moon Bong submitted an emergency recommendation to the National Assembly in May 1950. Comparing the enemy strength and equipment with that of the ROK Armed Forces, the recommendation called for consolidation of defensive positions approximately

〈Table 4〉   Intelligence Estimate (May 12, 1950)

Personnel Strength			
6 NKPA Divisions	93,500	Constabulary Forces Brigades	24,000
		1 Armored Division	10,000
1 Air Force Division	1,800	Other	37,000
2 Navy Divisions	15,000		
		Total	182,400

Equipment			
85-mm AAA'	24	37-mm AAA'	24
82-mm Mortar	1,223	45-mm Antitank Gun	586
76-mm Howitzer	464	120-mm Mortar	172
Tank	173	122-mm Howitzer	120
Self-Propelled Gun	176	Armored Vehicle	60
Patrol Boat	30	Airplane	190

Enemy Troop Deployment Along the 38th Parallel

Three Constabulary Brigades are deployed along the 38th Parallel. Behind these units, the enemy 6th, 1st, and 3rd Divisions are in position at Sariwon, Yonch'on, and Ch'orwon, respectively. There is an armored regiment in Chorwon, and another armored regiment is deployed in Sariwon and Yonch'on in support of the infantry divisions.

Noticeable Enemy Activities in Recent Weeks

Since March 4, 1950, an enemy security unit of 3,300 men has assembled in the vicinity of the 38th parallel and carried out infiltration attempts into friendly positions. Through these repeated attempts, the enemy troops are trying to keep our National Forces off balance and probe our security strength. On the other side of these probes stands North Korea's regular army, ready to go to war at any time.

300km along the 38th parallel to compensate for the lack of combat strength. Due to a parliamentary election on May 30, however, the National Assembly at the time was not in session, and was unable to debate the recommendation. In the end, the South was thrown into a war without adequate preparation.[61]

2. The ROK Defense Plan

Based on the 1949 year-end comprehensive intelligence report which forecasted a full-scale enemy invasion in the spring of 1950, the Ministry of National Defense quickly established a defense plan on March 25, 1950, and issued this plan in the form of Army Headquarters Operation Plan No. 38.[62]

Under the assumption that the enemy's main attack would be directed along the Ch'orwon-Uijongbu-Seoul axis, this plan established main defensive efforts in the Uijongbu area, and was aimed at driving back the enemy in front of the defensive positions to secure the 38th parallel.

The ROK Army had assumed the responsibility for defense along the 38th parallel since January 1949 in the wake of the US troop withdrawal from Korea. Although the establishment of the National Armed Forces had coincided with the birth of the ROK government, a full-fledged national defense began at this point.

When the defense plan was established in March 1950 in response to increasing threats of southward invasion, the ROK National Armed Forces consisted of the Army, the Navy, and the Air Force. The Army was composed of eight divisions. Frontline units included the 1st Division, which was stationed in the Kaesong area (Ch'ongdan-Choksong); the 7th Division in the Ch'orwon area (Choksong-Chokmokri); the 6th Division in the Ch'unch'on area (Chokmokri-Chinhukdong); the 8th Division in the Kangnung area (Chinhukdong-East Sea shoreline); and the 17th Regiment, which assumed security responsibility along the 38th parallel in the Ongjin Peninsula. Rear area units included the Capital Security Command in Seoul; the 2nd Division, with its headquarters in Taejon;

the 3rd Division, in Taegu; and the 5th Division, in Kwangju.

Operation Plan No. 38 and the ROK Army Defense Plan can be summarized as follows: "With the main defensive efforts deployed in the Uijongbu area, establish three primary defensive positions along the first line of defense (forward defense area). Organize a two-echelon defense with first line units and reserves, and carry out forward defensive operations in stages to deter and repel the enemy attack. Organize rear security units with quasi-military elements such as the police and Youth Security Organizations, and conduct rear area operations under coordination with the Navy and the Air Force.

(1) The Concept of the First Line Operations (Forward Defense)

Initial-Stage Operations (Combat at the Security area): Delay the enemy advance at the line of security positions established along the 38th parallel. Destroying bridges and roads forward of the main battle area, delay the enemy advance up to the main line of defense. Upon the assembly of the 2nd, 3rd, and 5th Divisions, the Ongjin area regiment and the 8th Division pin down the enemy defense in support of the main effort, and use guerrilla tactics to threaten the enemy left and right flanks.

Second-Stage Operations (Combat at the Main Line of Resistance) : Delivering concentrated fire and carrying out massive counterattacks at the main line of resistance, destroy the enemy in front of the defensive positions. Even if the enemy infiltrates into our defensive positions, employ all available means to fix the enemy at this line. If the line is so overstretched as to make it difficult to coordinate defensive efforts, conduct delay operations and gradually move to the line of alternate defensive positions.

Third-Stage Operations (Combat at the Final Line of Resistance) : Concentrate all available fires and carry out counterattacks at the line of alternate positions, and thoroughly disrupt and destroy enemy forces to secure this line to the last.

(2) The Organization and Mission of Defensive Units

First Line of Defense (Forward Defense) Units

1st Division: Direct main efforts toward the Munsan front, and thoroughly rout the enemy attack with infantry and artillery resistance to destroy the enemy forces in front of the defensive positions. In particular, direct fire to the front of the left flank of the 7th Division to support the main battle efforts forward of that unit.

7th Division: Direct main efforts toward the Uijongbu front, destroy the enemy main attack, especially the armored units, in front of the defensive positions with closely coordinated infantry and artillery resistance.

6th Division: Exploiting the rough mountainous terrain, conduct guerilla operations and defensive battles, and contain the expected enemy threat to the right flank of our main defensive efforts. Provide fire support to the right front of the 7th Division to facilitate friendly operations in the main battle area.

8th Division: Exploiting the rough mountainous terrain, conduct guerilla operations and defensive battles, and destroy at the sea shore line enemy units attempting landing operations from the East Sea.

17th Regiment: To facilitate friendly operations in the main battle area, carry out defensive battles and guerrilla operations in the front of the Ongjin area and threaten the enemy left flank. Prepare for a rapid occupation of the Haeju area if necessary.

Reserves

Capital Security Command: Prepare for the defense of the metropolitan capital area including the Kimp'o and Inch'on areas. When necessary, support the 1st and 7th Divisions.

2nd, 3rd, and 5th Divisions: Rapidly assemble in Seoul and establish defensive positions in the periphery of Seoul to prevent enemy infiltration. At the same time, the 2nd, 3rd, and 5th Divisions establish plans to support defensive efforts in the vicinity of the Ch'unch'on-Uijongbu area, Uijongbu-Munsan area, and Munsan-Uijongbu area, respectively. Prepare a plan for counteroffensive if necessary.

Independent Cavalry Regiment: Focusing on the area to the south of Ch'orwon along the Kyungwon (Seoul-Wonsan) Railway, prepare for reconnaissance missions. In addition, establish a reconnaissance plan for the area to the southeast of Seoul within a radius of 32km.

Artillery School Instruction Regiment: Consider the defense of the capital city, and if necessary, prepare plans to provide fire support to the front of the main line of resistance established by the 7th and 1st Divisions.

1st Engineer Corps: Cooperate with the capital defense plan, and if necessary, prepare to support the defensive efforts of the 1st and 7th Divisions.

Rear Security Forces

Rear Security: In principle, the police shall be responsible for the cleaning up of the communist insurgents. Twenty-two military police battalions shall be organized to be deployed. In principle, the police, Youth Security Organizations, Korean Youth Corps shall be responsible for the security of important public facilities.

Coastal Security: According to the Navy Headquarters coastal defense plan, a special police unit and coastal youth security organizations shall establish strong coastal security positions with emphasis on Han River Estuary area, Kunsan, and P'ohang.

Anti-Air Security: According to the Air Force Headquarters anti-air plan, anti-air surveillance units shall be organized. Army units shall organize anti-air elements to defend key locations.

Titled as the basic defensive plan of the ROK National Armed Forces and Army operation plan, prepared in the name of the Army Chief of Staff, this was a very comprehensive operation plan which included appendixes for relevant sections. Furthermore, the phrase such as "according to the Navy and Air Force plan ⋯" suggests that the Navy and the Air Force also had their own operation plans in conjunction with the Army's.

By early May 1950, each division had established an operation plan based on this Army plan. These division-level plans, however, centered on basic plans to secure the line of defense, and had yet to complete supplementary plans in regard to fire support, obstacles, and counterattacks. The following picture shows the defensive deployment of the ROK forces at the time.

3. Combat Readiness of the ROK Forces

Through its intelligence analysis, the ROK Ministry of Defense had a fairly accurate estimate of the enemy situation. It established a defensive plan in March 1950 and warned in May that an enemy attack was only a matter of time. In spite of these estimates and warnings, however, national security at the time was fraught with serious problems due to lack of preparedness.

(1) Preparation of Defensive Lines and Positions

When the ROK forces took over security responsibilities from the withdrawing US troops in early 1949, the only "defensive positions" transferred were road checkpoints established to control the South-North flow of human and vehicle traffic across the 38th parallel. There were no defensive positions for tacti-

Defensive Deployment of the ROK National Forces

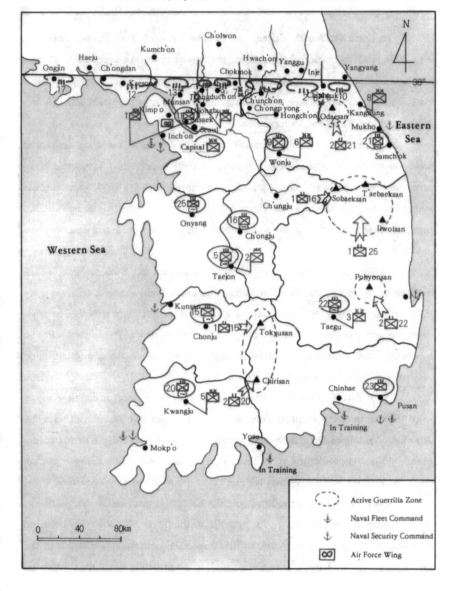

cal purposes, and even the checkpoint facilities consisted only of makeshift installations.[63]

In contrast, North Korea's 38 Border Constabalary Forces began to take over security responsibilities from the Soviet troops as early as July 1947, and underwent a major expansion to become three brigades strong in early 1949. These troops occupied strategically critical points and established formidable positions along the 38th parallel.

Under these circumstances, ROK forces began to build up defensive positions along the 38th parallel. Having already established favorable positions, however, the North Korean troops interfered with the ROK construction work. The North's provocations eventually led to armed clashes along the 38th parallel, further hampering the South's construction work to build up defensive positions.

In addition to the enemy's harassment tactics, the ROK security along the 38th parallel suffered from the lack of separate units charged with security in this area. As the ROK regiments were reorganized into new brigades or divisions, the unit changed with the securty of the front line was frequently relieved by another unit. This also worked as an impediment against the strengthening of security and defense along the 38th parallel.

As the ROK Army was reorganized into division-level units, however, a solid foundation for a sound defensive system was put into place, and with the establishment of the basic defensive plan in March 1950 and division operation plans in May, organization of defense and establishment of positions got on track. As a result, defensive lines began to take shape in the forward areas.

Even up to this time, however, the building up of defensive positions was still behind schedule due to the intensification of the NKPA's provocations, diversion of troops caused by the infiltration of communist guerrillas into the rear areas, and, as before, lack of construction materials. Volunteer work by local residents, students, and patriotic citizen organizations such as the Korean Youth Corps did manage to reduce the work load of the troops.[64] By June of 1950, much progress was made.

With minor differences among divisions, security positions along the 38th parallel were built as follows: In critical areas, open trenches, made of concrete or logs, were connected by communication lines; double concertina, with antipersonnel mines buried between, were placed in front of defensive positions; for main lines of defense and alternate positions, entrance passages leading to connecting passages and open individual foxholes were established, but in most cases, no mines and concertina were set up; and some observation posts and crew-served weapons emplacements consisted of open trenches lined with logs.[65] No obstacles were set up against enemy tanks. In particular, the ROK Army did not have any antitank mines, and thus was vulnerable to armored attack.[66]

Army engineers supported infantry units with their construction works and setting up of obstacles, and prepared demolition plans for important bridges such as the Imjin Bridge and the Soyang Bridge. The engineering corps also established denial plans.[67] ROK artillery, for its part, surveyed the terrain and established observation posts. A battalion-size unit in each infantry division, each artillery unit had completed the selection of deployment positions for supporting forward regiments.[68]

On the whole, however, forward defensive positions established prior to the war had no facilities to protect friendly troops and equipment from enemy indirect fire. Moreover, these positions lacked depth as they were set up under the concept of line defense, and the absence of antitank measures left them extremely vulnerable to armored attack.

(2) Inferiority in Troop Strength and Equipment

The troop strength and equipment of the ROK National Forces were decidedly inferior to the NKPA's, and this military imbalance posed fundamental threats to ROK defense. NKPA's strength continued to rise, and reached a total of 198,380 just prior to its southward invasion, holding a 2-to-1 advantage over ROK forces with its total of 105,752. The friendly-to-enemy strength ratio in forward areas was as high as 1 to 4.4 along the Ch'orwon-Uijongbu-Seoul axis and 1 to 2.2 along the Kaesong-Munsan-Seoul axis, both in the direction of enemy main attack; and 1 to 4.1 in Hwach'on-Ch'unch'on and Inje-Hongch'on axis and 1 to 2.5 in the Yangyang-Kangnung axis, both in the direction of enemy supporting attack. These ratios simply compare ROK defensive unit strength with that of forward-deployed enemy troops, and do not take into account the differences in equipment.

The drastic difference in troop strength in the enemy direction of main attack, as reflected in the lopsided ratio of 1 to 4.4, was primarily due to the ROK Army Headquarters' orders to change unit assignments and attachments just prior to the outbreak of the Korean War. Effective on June 15, 1950, the ROK Army Headquarters assigned to the Capital Security Command the 3rd Regiment, which was the reserve regiment in the 7th Division charged with the frontal defense of the Ch'orwon area. The 3rd Regiment was to be replaced by the 25th Regiment, 2nd Division, stationed in the rear area of Onyang. The 3rd Regiment moved to a rear area as ordered, but the 25th Regiment was not able to move up to the front due to a lack of barracks facilities.[69] Given that warnings had been issued of an imminent enemy invasion, it was obviously against the most basic principle of unit rotation to send forward units to rear areas first. Moreover, given that approximately one-third of ROK troops were on leave on June 25, a Sunday, the actual troop strength ratio was even more lopsided than

〈Table 5〉　　　Strength Comparison Along Avenues of Approach[70]

Avenue of Approach	ROK Defensive Unit	NKPA Attacking Unit		ROKA : NKPA
Kaesong-Munsan-Seoul	1st Division　　9,715 (5,000)	1st Division	11,000	1 : 2.2 (1 : 4.2)
		6th Division (-1)	8,000	
		203rd Armored	2,000	
		Total	21,000	
Ch'orwon-Uijongbu-Seoul	7th Division (-) 7,211 (4,500)	3rd Division	11,000	1 : 4.4 (1 : 7.1)
		4th Division	11,000	
		13th Division	6,000	
		105th Armored (-1)	4,000	
		Total	32,000	
Hwach'on-Ch'unch'on Inje-Hongch'on	6th Division　　9,112 (unknown)	2nd Division	10,838	1 : 4.1
		12th Division	12,000	
		15th Division	11,000	
		Independent Armored	1,100	
		12th MTSP	2,000	
		Total	36,938	
Yangyang-Kangnung	8th Division　　6,866 (unknown)	5th Division	11,000	1 : 2.5
		766th Detachment	3,000	
		549th Detachment	3,000	
		Total	17,000	

＊ The figure in parentheses represent "real strength," excluding personnel on leave.

what appeared on paper. For example, the actual ratio was 1 to 7 and 1 to 4 against in the case of the ROK 7th Division and 1st Division, respectively.

As for equipment, the imbalance between South and North Korea was even more pronounced. Whereas the NKPA possessed 242 T-34 tanks and 211 airplanes, consisting mainly of combat aircraft, the ROK National Forces had zero tanks and possessed a total of 22 airplanes, basically of liaison and training varieties. Moreover, the ROK forces had no effective antitank weapons against armored attack and no anti-aircraft guns for air defense purposes. Though listed in the table of organization and equipment, 57-mm antitank guns and 2.36-inch rocket launchers did not have enough firepower to destroy T-34 tanks under normal circumstances.

While the enemy possessed a total of 552 howitzers including the new 122-mm piece with a range of 11,710 meters, the ROK forces had only 91 105-mm M3 howitzers with a range of 6,525 meters. While the enemy had a total of 1,728 mortars including the 120-mm piece with a range of 5,700 meters, the ROK forces had a total of only 960 mortars consisting of 81-mm pieces (with a range of 3,600 meters) and 60-mm mortars.

The military equipment imbalance between the South and the North was so serious as to make it virtually impossible to have a meaningful comparison between the two sides. In addition to the simple numerical inferiority in equipment, the ROK forces suffered decisive disadvantages in the quality and effectiveness of equipment.

At a Defense Minister's press conference on May 10, ROKA Headquarters Chief of Staff, Kim Paik Il said, "The North Korean puppet army's equipment is two to three times superior to ours, and we must keep in mind that they have a far greater number of airplanes, tanks, artillery pieces, and machine guns. Simple courage by itself will not do against this overwhelming superiority."[71] He thus pointed out that it will be difficult to overcome the inferiority in equipment with the fighting will alone.

It must also be noted that most of the North's equipment was of a new type, imported from the Soviet Union expressly for the southward invasion. P'yongyang even stockpiled equipment reserves for the war. In contrast, most of the South's equipment transferred from the United States was of World War II vintage. Due to this old vintage as well as cool US response to requests for parts, the ROK forces had to scrap 15% of their equipment. Furthermore, a significant fraction of ROK equipment was waiting for repair and maintenance work. In the case of vehicles, the eight infantry divisions possessed only 52% of what was listed on the T/E. Even these vehicles in possession had a operating rate of less than 40%.[72]

As a result, the ROK National Forces had neither the troop strength nor the equipment to deter or repel an enemy attack. Realistically, launching an offensive—namely, a northward invasion—could not be seriously entertained.

(3) Level of Military Education and Training

From the day of establishment, the ROK National Forces were mobilized to conduct operations against communist infiltrators in rear areas, respond to enemy provocations across the 38th parallel, and to carry out counter-unconventional warfare operations against People's Guerrillas. As a result, there was little room to provide systematic unit-by-unit education and training along the chain of command. In fact, it was only in January 1950 that the ROKA Headquarters issued its first education directive. According to the directive, all units in the eight ROK divisions were to complete squad-tactics through battalion-tactics training by March. To conduct training as ordered, forward divisions rotated units deployed along the 38th parallel with units in the rear. Rearward divisions carried out simple training in counter-guerrilla operations areas, but training took a back seat to operations and became a mere formality.[73]

On March 14, the ROKA Headquarters issued Education Directive No. 2, ordering the completion of battalion training by June 1 and regiment tactics training by the end of September. In accordance with these directives, as of June 15, six battalions of the 7th Division, one battalion of the 8th Division, and nine battalions of the Capital Security Command completed battalion-level training. 30 battalions were conducting company-level training, and 17 battalions had yet to complete even platoon-level training. As for two other battalions, 75% of their units had completed platoon-level training, and 50% were in the middle of company-level training.

In addition, 17 battalions and 5 regiment staffs completed command post training, 14 battalions conducted an 8-day maneuver exercise, and 6 battalions underwent antitank combat training.

Thus, only 16 battalions, or 25% of the total of 65 battalions, completed battalion-level training within the specified period. As a result, the ROKA Headquarters took actions to prolong the training period and put pressure on units to finish battalion training by the end of July and regiment training by the end of October.[74]

In contrast, the NKPA conducted systematic training in conjunction with its military build-up under a meticulous invasion plan, and completed division-level self-training by the first half of 1949. From the end of this year, under the control of the Training Bureau in the Ministry of National Defense, division-level comprehensive tactics training was carried out, and offensive operations capability was evaluated and reinforced.[75]

Prior to this division-level training, the NKPA conducted its first command post training in early July 1949, which was titled "Field Training Exercise for Commanders and Staff regarding Infantry Division Attack with Armor and Artillery Units."

This was a maneuver exercise for a corps-level command post that would command and control division operations. In this exercise, Chief of the General Staff Kang Kon played the role of the corps commander, and Training Bureau Chief Kim Kwang Hyop was the corps chief of staff. More than 100 high-ranking military officers participated in this exercise, including more than 10 advisors from various bureaus of the Defense Ministry, Director of the Operations Bureau, Commandant of the Artillery Corps, and Commandant of the Cultural Corps. According to a scenario envisioning division-level offensive operations, these high-ranking officers operated command posts at each echelon and dealt with various situations during the exercise.[76]

After the exercise, the North Korean Defense Ministry organized a training evaluation group consisting of 50 members under the guidance of the Director of the Training Bureau, and began to hold division-level field maneuver exercises. In December 1949, newly organized 5th and 6th Divisions were successively mobilized to carry out infantry division offensive exercises. The 2nd Division was evaluated on air defense and reconnaissance along the coastline and individual and battalion-level combat training, whereas the 1st Division received training that focused on road demolition and reconnaissance.[77]

In February 1950, the engineer corps conducted special training for breakthrough and river-crossing operations. Breaking through enemy positions required engineer special task units to remove obstacles and land mines placed in the front of enemy positions and to detonate permanent positions. For this special training, one engineer platoon detailed from each division (1st, 2nd, 3rd, 5th, and 6th) received instructions and returned to its parent unit to train the rest of the engineer corps.[78] In addition, the Defense Ministry conducted a joint exercise at the end of February. Titled "Assault into Enemy Positions and Infiltration into Enemy Rear," this exercise involved two infantry divisions and armored units and was deemed highly successful.

The NKPA completed large-unit maneuver exercise training by March, and from April, it instructed troops on how to operate new equipment imported from the Soviet Union, and carried out "remedial training" to fix problems discovered during large-unit exercises.[79]

A program of particular importance was a series of lectures and discussions held by "a study group on special military issues," which consisted of 40 high-ranking officers in the General Staff. Formed in 1950, this study group analyzed various aspects of South Korea including: terrain, transportation systems such as roads and railways, organization, equipment, and deployment of the ROK Armed Forces as well as its origins and history, and general political and economic situation.[80] As D-Day approached and with maneuver exercises out of the way, these high-ranking officers in the NKPA General Staff were secretly conducting intensive studies on South Korea and its armed forces so as to provide necessary leadership in wartime.

(4) Security Posture

As the fateful year of 1950 unfolded, there were repeated announcements of an imminent invasion by North Korea along the following line: "North Korea has completed its preparations for war, and a southward invasion is only a matter of time." President Syngman Rhee said: "Something may happen in May or June." In his secret intelligence report sent to Washington on March 10, Gen. Douglas MacArthur called to attention to a recently acquired intelligence which predicted that North Korea would invade the South in June.[81]

While talk of "a May or June crisis" was legion, Maj. Gen. Ch'ae Byong Dok was reappointed as the Army Chief of Staff on April 10, 1950. On April 22 and June 10, Gen. Ch'ae carried out high-level personnel changes, which affected commanders at all eight divisions as well as the posts of Deputy Chief of Staff and Directors of the Operations and Personnel Bureaus. Also, taking into consideration the enemy movement and the domestic situation, he took actions to strengthen the security posture at three separate times.

First, on April 21, feeling that the NKPA and communist guerrillas might attempt to launch an invasion and incite riots around May Day, Gen. Ch'ae ordered each division to carry out a thorough patrol of its given area under close coordination with the police. Next, on May 8, thinking that the enemy might attempt an invasion and riots around the May 30 election, the Army Chief of Staff ordered each unit to be prepared for emergency muster and marshalling of troops and to strengthen security. Finally, on June 11, Gen. Ch'ae put the Army on emergency alert, believing that the North's June 7 proposal for an all-Korea election and June 10 proposal for an exchange of important persons were merely a smoke screen to cover up its intention to launch an invasion. Finding no tangible signs of an imminent invasion, however, the Army Chief of Staff lifted the alert effective 24:00 on June 23.

June 11 to June 23—this was a period in which the NKPA moved troops to attack position. According to their plan, there were all but 2 days left till D-Day. Gen. Ch'ae's order was a truly preposterous command measure. As the enemy had entered the final stage of their preparations and completed troop movement to attack position, it would hardly have been adequate even had the entire ROK forces been ordered to be ready for combat, but, instead, Gen. Ch'ae lifted the emergency alert. When emergency security posture that had been maintained for 45 days was called off on June 24 (Saturday), units gave soldiers a day or night leave, and also put some soldiers on vacation to help with farming during the busy summer season. Having been liberated from a long, tension-

⟨Table 6⟩   Security Posture by Type and Duration

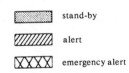

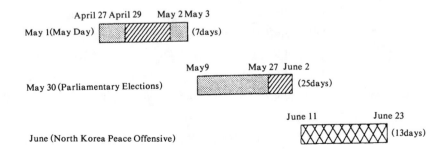

filled period, soldiers wanted to enjoy a day off without any care. Fully one-third of the total strength of the ROK Armed Forces left their post.[82]

While the third emergency alert was in effect, US State Department Advisor John F. Dulles, on a trip to Korea, had an observation tour of the front on June 17. On the next day, he addressed the National Assembly of the Republic of Korea during its opening ceremony. He gave the lawmakers an assurance that the United States would provide both material and moral support to Korea in case of any external invasion. President Rhee, for his part, requested to Dulles that the Republic of Korea be included in the defensive plan of the United States.[83] Neither was to be realized, however. Little time was now left before the North's planned invasion. As a matter of fact, Dulles' inspection tour of the front was even used by North Korea as a piece of "evidence" for the South's northward invasion.

As tension built along the 38th parallel, a local monitor group of the UN Commission on Korea carried out an inspection throughout the 38th parallel zone from Kangnung to Ongjin between June 9 and June 24. Upon returning to Seoul on June 24, the monitor group prepared a report to the UN Security Council. With regard to the general situation along the 38th parallel, the report stated that the South Korean Army was organized solely for defensive purposes and was in no way ready to launch a large-scale offensive against the North Korean Army.[84] On the situation north of the 38th parallel, the monitor group did note a recent evacuation of all civilians north of the parallel for 4 to 8 km and an increased military activity north of Ongjin.[85] The group, however, failed to detect any other sign of irregular activity on the part of the NKPA suggestive of an imminent invasion. Nevertheless, it is significant for the "Who invaded first?" debate that according to this U.N. official report, the ROK Armed Forces were organized solely for defensive purposes.

In the meantime, on June 22 and 23, the ROKA Headquarters situation room received intelligence reporting suspiciously active enemy movement. On June 24, after receiving a report from the 7th Division that what was believed to be a group of NKPA officers seemed to be conducting a ground reconnaissance, the situation room staff concluded upon further analysis: "A full-scale offensive by North Korea seems imminent and this may come today or tomorrow."[86]

Based on this estimate by intelligence staff, Army Chief of Staff Ch'ae held an emergency meeting with the general staff at 15:00 that day to analyze the situation. At this meeting, Lt. Kim Jong P'il and Lt. Lee Yong Kun recommended an immediate suspension of the order to lift the emergency alert and an immediate cancellation of vacation and leave. If these measures could not be taken, they suggested that at least two-thirds of troop strength stand by on post. Gen. Ch'ae, however, did not accept their recommendations, and instead ordered to send an intelligence unit to P'och'on, Tongduch'on, and Kaesong to observe the enemy situation and report the result by 08:00 on the next day.[87]

That night, the Army HeadHead quarters held a party to celebrate the completion of the Army Officers' Club building. Gen. Ch'ae and ROKA Headquarters staff officers, staff college instructors and students, and commanders of various units joined in the festivities. The party continued late into the night.[88]

They thus squandered the final chance to avoid the enemy's surprise attack. While high-ranking officers, from the Army Chief of Staff down, were intoxicated and the security posture of the ROK Armed Forces was at its worst, that fateful dawn was fast approaching.

III. North Korea's Invasion and Early Battles

1. Surprise Attack and Shock

At 04:00 on June 25, 1950, while soft drizzle was falling and valleys were covered with heavy fog, a series of thunderous sounds and blinding light shattered the peaceful silence of the dawn.

Without any warning, the North Korean People's Army struck all across the 38th parallel with synchronized preparatory field artillery and mortar fire. From the Ongjin Peninsula to the west through Kaesong, Tongduch'on, P'och'on, Ch'unch'on, and Chumunjin to the east, Communist units achieved complete tactical surprise as they launched closely coordinated ground operations across the parallel. At the same time, a combat team and guerrilla units also landed at Chongdongjin and Imwonjin in the southern vicinity of Kangnung on the east coast.[89]

With Seoul as its objective, the NKPA 1st Corps (main attack) concentrated its strength along the Yonch'on-Unch'on-Uijongbu axis and the avenue of approach leading from Kaesong to Munsan. The NKPA 2nd Corps (supporting attack) moved along planned avenues of approach toward Ch'unch'on and Kangnung, primarily using the Hwach'on-Ch'unch'on axis. Led by Soviet-made T-34 tanks, the NKPA swiftly penetrated ROK defensive positions along the 38th parallel and continued their southward movement.

Throughout the night before the invasion, the ROKA Headquarters Situation Room had sporadically received intelligence reports showing signs of an imminent enemy attack. By dawn, the Headquarters began to receive a series of situation reports from ROK forward divisions informing of contact with the enemy. At 01:00, the 17th Regiment cabled an emergency telegram. It said: "An unknown number of NKPA troops are approaching from the north of Kuksabong." At 03:00, the 1st Division reported: "The enemy is moving a vessel from Towhari to the front. The vessel seems to be for river-crossing." At 03:30, the 7th Division reported: "Tank noises can be heard in the vicinity of Mansegyo bridge north of Yangmunri." This message was soon followed by a frantic situation report: "Enemy artillery shells are falling on the front of friendly defensive positions." From this moment on, the ROKA Headquarters received a flood of situation reports from forward divisions informing that a large-scale enemy offensive had begun.[90]

On duty at the time in the situation room, Capt. Cho Byong Un, G-3 (Bureau of Operations), and 1st Lt. Kim Jong P'il, G-2, reported the situation to the duty officer and bureau directors, and recommended that emergency measures be taken in response.[91]

Army Chief of Staff, Maj. Gen. Ch'ae Byong Dok had returned to his residence from the Officers' Club party around 02:00, and was asleep when he received the shocking report from the ROKA Headquarters. After summoning Lt. Kim to check the details of the situation, Gen. Ch'ae gave an oral directive to put the entire Army on alert effective 06:00 and to call a meeting of bureau directors.[92]

Gen. Ch'ae then telephoned Defense Minister Shin Song Mo, but could not establish connection. Riding in his jeep, Gen. Ch'ae went to the Minister's residence in person, and reported the enemy invasion at 07:00. According to his secretary's recollection, Minister Shin expressed "shock and dismay—he seemed to have expected an enemy invasion, but he did not seem to have thought that it would come on a Sunday."[93]

The news of the enemy invasion was disseminated to all units, and emergency muster was called. As many commanders and soldiers were enjoying their first vacation or leave in a long time, however, their return to post was delayed in spite of the use of telephones, messengers, radio broadcasts, and other means of communication. After completing his report to the Minister of National Defense, the Army Chief of Staff went immediately to the ROKA Headquarters, and ordered the Director of the Troop Information and Education (TIE) Bureau to employ all means to put the entire Army on alert and to have personnel swiftly return to post.[94]

By Defense Ministry's request, KBS (Korean Broadcasting System) broadcast the first report of the North Korean invasion at 07:00. According to TIE Bureau Chief, Col. Lee Son Kun's recollection, although the ROK forward security positions had already been overrun by NKPA units by this time, KBS tried to reassure the public with this misleadingly optimistic phrase in its report: "There is little cause for concern as 100,000-strong ROK Armed Forces are sound and intact." In Col. Lee's view, "the broadcast was intended not only to inform the general public of the North's invasion but also to have military personnel swiftly return to post from their vacation or leave. It was deemed unnecessary to shake public confidence."[95] The TIE Bureau also organized street broadcast groups, and urged soldiers in downtown Seoul to return to post.

These radio and street broadcasts came as a great shock to the public, who were just getting out of bed. Having experienced many wars and hardships, the Korean people braced themselves for yet another ordeal.

At 08:00, having taken the initial emergency measures, Army Chief of Staff Ch'ae, in consultation with the Assistant chief of staff G-1 Kim Paik Il (concurrently Operations Staff Chief as well), ordered reserve divisions (2nd, 3rd, and 5th Divisions) to move to Seoul. In addition, at 11:00, Gen. Ch'ae ordered the 3rd Regiment, Capital Security Command, to be attached to the 7th Division. He then ordered the training instruction units of the Infantry School and Korea

Newspaper reports on NKPA's Southward Invasion
(Chosun Daily News on 26 June 1950)

Military Academy to assemble in Yongsan and to form a temporary reserve called Seoul Special Unit (under the command of Lt. Col. Yu Hae Jun).[96] To gain a firsthand knowledge of the situation on the front, Gen. Ch'ae also made a personal visit to the 1st Division Headquarters in Munsan and the 7th Division Headquarters in Uijongbu.

As it became clear that its southward invasion had achieved surprise, P'yongyang made a radio broadcast around 11:00, and claimed: "As an act of self-defense, the North Korean People's Army launched a counteroffensive and started a just war." This was P'yongyang's declaration of war on the Republic of Korea. Later, during a 13:35 broadcast, Kim Il Song declared: "South Korea rejected all of the North's proposals for peaceful unification, and this morning invaded Haeju from the Ongjin Peninsula. This act of aggression brought about an important consequence as it led to North Korea's counteroffensive." To cover up the southward invasion, Kim thus fabricated a totally unsubstantiated excuse. The Comprehensive History of Choson follows a similar line[97]:

> US imperialists and Syngman Rhee rejected rational plans for peaceful unification proposed by the government of the republic, and, finally on June 25, they started a war of aggression by launching an armed invasion against the northern half of the republic.
>
> Kim Il Sung ordered the constabulary forces and People's Army of the republic to block the enemy invasion and to make a transition to counteroffensive.
>
> As the People's Army stepped forward to carry out a struggle to repel the invasion of US imperialists and their lackeys and to preserve the freedom and independence of our fatherland, the Korean people's war of justice and national liberation began.

North Koreans have thus fabricated the history of the tragic fratricidal war, which was meticulously planned and launched on their own initiative, and laid the blame on the Republic of Korea, glorifying this war of aggression as a war of national liberation.

By 10:00 on June 25, enemy airplanes were seen carrying out reconnaissance missions over Kimp'o and Youido air bases. Around noon, four NKPA YAK fighters flew over Seoul and delivered machine-gun fire on the Yongsan Railway Station, Seoul Armory, communication centers, and the Office of Land Transportation Bureau. Bombs were also dropped to raise citizens' fears.[98] Around the same time, however, the ROK Defense Ministry released a misleading report that the 17th Regiment in Ongjin had advanced into Haeju. City newspapers carried this encouraging news, giving hope for a moment to hard-pressed troops and worried citizens alike. This comedy of errors was triggered

by a firsthand report by Ch'oi Ki Dok of Yonhap News Agency, who, upon returning from Ongjin, informed the TIE bureau that "the morale of the 17th Regiment soldiers was so high that they could more than attack Haeju." This hopeful report was exaggerated and transformed into a news of a ROK counterattack. This piece of misinformation produced an important unintended result: It
was later cited by North Korea as a piece of evidence to support that the Korean War was initiated by the South.[99]

Amid confusion over the situation on the front, including wild misjudg-
ment based on misinformation, the ROK Defense Ministry at last issued an official statement at 13:00. Quickly disseminated across the country via newspaper
extras, this statement threw the whole country into shock and dismay.

Between 04:00 and 08:00 today, North Korea initiated an illegal invasion
of the South all across the 38th parallel. The North almost simultaneously launched a southward offensive across a wide front, including
such areas as Ongjin, Kaesong, Changdan, Uijongbu, Tongduch'on,
Ch'unch'on, and Kangnung. The North also conducted landing operations along the eastern shoreline. In order to intercept North Korean
troops across the front, ROK Armed Forces are conducting urgently
needed and appropriate operations. In front of Tongduch'on, enemy
tanks were destroyed by our antitank guns ···. Our armed forces have
assumed the posture to punish the enemy relentlessly, and are carrying
on valiant combat in each battle area. We hope that the Korean people
will trust our military and, without being unsettled in the least, carry on
with their daily work and actively support military operations.[100]

President Syngman Rhee, Supreme Commander of the armed forces,
heard the news of "North Korea's massive southward invasion" around 10:00
from Police Superintendent Kim Chang Hung, who was responsible for the security of Kyungmudae, presidential residence. President was fishing at Pandoji

(Peninsula Pond) in Piwon (Secret Garden) at the time. Upon returning to Kyungmudae, President Rhee received a report from Defense Minister Shin Sung Mo (serving also as Prime Minister) that Kaesong had already fallen to the enemy, and Communist units, led by tanks, had arrived in the vicinity of Ch'unch'on. Immediately after receiving this initial briefing on the war situation, the President called an emergency meeting of the cabinet.[101] This emergency meeting was held at 11 o'clock under Acting Prime Minister Shin Sung Mo. Based on intelligence reports up to that point, however, Prime Minister Shin's briefing did not make it clear whether the North's action was a limited border raid (locally contained provocation) or an all-out invasion. The cabinet decided to adjourn the meeting until Army Chief of Staff Ch'ae returned from his visit to the front.[102]

The cabinet meeting resumed at 14:00. President Rhee himself presided over the meeting. At this meeting, Gen. Ch'ae reported: "All across the 38th parallel, North Korean units of 40,000 to 50,000 in strength, led by 94 tanks, launched an illegal invasion of the South. But in every battle area, ROK Armed Forces are destroying enemy tanks with antitank weapons, and taking appropriate measures against the invasion ···. I think we can surely repulse the enemy if we mobilize rear divisions and carry out a counteroffen-sive."[103]

President Rhee issued Presidential Order No. 377 (regarding promulgation of ordinances under national emergency) and Emergency Decree No 1. (special ordinance on punishment of crime committed under national emergency), and imposed severe penalties on those committing a crime against the nation and against humanity in wartime. This action was based on Article 57 of the Constitution regarding presidential powers to declare emergency decrees. Up to this point, however, the ROK government had yet to declare martial law provided under Article 64 of the Constitution. Nor had it taken any measures to make a transition to a wartime regime.[104]

At 11:35, President Rhee received US Ambassador Muccio's visit, and made an urgent request for ammunition supplies. Foreign Minister Lim Byong Jik directed Korean Ambassador Chang Myon in Washington to make diplomatic efforts toward the United Nations and the US. He also made a request to the US State Department, Defense Department, and Far East Command for emergency assistance, and maintained contact with Ambassador Muccio and the UN Commission on Korea. Primarily responsible for monitoring and reporting all events that might lead to armed conflict, the UN Commission began to discuss, from 14:00, measures to deal with North Korea's invasion.[105]

At this time, ROK Armed Forces on the front could take few effective actions against the onslaught of enemy tanks. ROK antitank weapons did not have sufficient firepower to destroy enemy tanks. To delay the enemy's advance, courageous souls had no choice but to resort to a desperate suicidal attack, jumping on an enemy tank to open the hatch and drop in a hand-grenade.

In the meantime, upon receiving the news of the enemy invasion, the ROK Navy issued Naval Headquarters Operations Order Kap [Emergency] No. 18 at 09:00, June 25, and ordered subordinate units to take emergency security posture and be ready for combat. The 1st Fleet in the West Sea [Yellow Sea] and the 2nd Fleet in the East, as well as each Security Command, strengthened maritime security and prepared against enemy landing operations.[106]

The Air Force established its Operations Command at Youido air base at 10:00, June 25, the same time that enemy planes started flying on reconnaissance missions. The ROK Air Force analyzed the war situation and quickly prepared for a combat, deciding to use T-6 and L-model planes to block the enemy advance as much as possible. As the enemy had secured air superiority, however, only around sunset could the T-6's form squadrons and carry out reconnaissance missions along the enemy avenues of approach.[107]

Despite ROK responses, however, the whole country was soon soaked in blood. Obsessed with the dream of communizing the entire Korean peninsula, Kim Il Sung had launched a premeditated invasion and thrown the whole country into a fratricidal war. Outnumbered in troop strength, firepower, and equipment, ROK Armed Forces could only retreat and retreat again on all fronts.

2. Operations in the Capital City Region

(1) Early Battles

The North Korean People's Army placed the focus of its offensive on occupying the capital city of Seoul, mindful of the historical experience that the seizure of the capital had a decisive influence on the course of a war. In addition to being the political center of Korea, Seoul was also the economic, social, and cultural center of the country, and North Koreans believed that the occupation of the capital would have a significant psychological effect on the populace. Setting Seoul as the objective, two NKPA corps directed their main efforts toward the capital. The NKPA 1st Corps placed its main efforts along the Yonch'on-Unch'on-Uijongbu-Seoul axis, and committed supporting forces along the Kaesong-Munsan-Seoul axis. The 2nd Corps committed its main efforts along the Ch'unch'on-Kap'yong-Seoul axis and the Ch'unch'on-Hongch'on-Suwon axis. In accordance with their plan, the NKPA units sought to occupy Seoul by employing a double envelopment.

1) Tongduch'on-P'och'on Area Battle
In front of the ROK 7th Division, north of Uijongbu, the NKPA 3rd Division and 4th Division were rapidly moving southward from Unch'on to P'och'on and Yonch'on to Tongduch'on, respectively, in coordination with the 109th and 107th Armored Regiments.

In the north of Uijongbu, toward which enemy main efforts were directed, the ROK 7th Division was defending a stretch of 47km from Choksong to
Sajikri. Its 1st Regiment and 9th Regiment were responsible for the Tongduch-
on front and the P'och'on front, respectively. One battalion from each regiment
was conducting guard and screening operations along the 38th parallel, and
main units were undergoing training. The assignment of the 3rd Regiment was
changed from the 7th Division to the Capital Security Command. The ROK
25th Regiment, 2nd Division, in Onyang was ordered to take its place, but had
yet to arrive. Consequently, the 7th Division was left without a division reserve.

When the NKPA offensive began, the ROK 7th Division called an
emergency summons to the colors, and ordered forward-deployed security forces to block the enemy advance. The division also hurried to deploy the 1st Regiment (under Col. Ham Jun Ho) and 9th Regiment (under Col. Yun Ch'un Kun) into
defensive positions on the enemy avenue of approach. As the main units of
these forward regiments were undergoing training in Uijongbu at the time, however, it took a considerable amount of time to assemble and commit the troops
along the main line of resistance connecting the mountains of Kamak-san,
Mach'a-san, Soyo-san, Karang-san, and Ch'onju-san.

In front of the ROK 1st Regiment, north of Tongduch'on, the NKPA
4th Division (under Maj. Gen. Lee Kwon Mu) committed along the Chonkok-
Ch'osongri-Tongduch'on axis the 16th Infantry Regiment reinforced with two
armored battalions. Along the Chokam-Bongamri axis to the west of this main
attack, the 18th Regiment was committed as a supporting attack. With the two
regiments attacking abreast, the NKPA 4th Division crossed the Hantan River
at Chonkok, and penetrated the ROK security positions of the 2nd Battalion,
1st Regiment. After occupying Ch'osongri, the NKPA 16th Regiment advanced
toward Tongduch'on behind columns of tanks.

The 2nd Battalion of the ROK 1st Regiment withdrew to main defensive positions in the vicinity of Soyo-san, north of Tongduch'on, and fought a fierce seesaw battle with the NKPA forces. While the 2nd Battalion was blocking the advance of the enemy joint infantry-armor units, the regiment commander committed the 1st Battalion to Mach'a-san, west of the 2nd Battalion, and positioned the 3rd Battalion at Bongamri, south of Mach'a-san. However, when the 1st Battalion occupied defensive positions in the vicinity of Mach'a-san, the enemy had already bypassed to the west of the mountain and had begun to move south toward Tokjong. Accordingly, the 1st Battalion could not make contact with the enemy, and could not support the 2nd Battalion as it was too far removed from Road 3.

The enemy also avoided contact with the 3rd Battalion, and employed a westerly turning movement to advance southward. Consequently, under pressing conditions in the opening hours of the war, while one battalion of the ROK 1st Regiment was conducting an uphill battle against NKPA forces, the other two battalions-strangely enough-failed to make contact with the enemy altogether.

In the meantime, while displacing forward to prepared positions in Bosanri in the vicinity of Tongduch'on, the 2nd Battery of the 5th Field Artillery Battalion, in direct support of the ROK 1st Regiment, delivered concentrated fire and annihilated an enemy battalion which was marching along the road in close formation in front of the 2nd Battalion. When the enemy resumed attack a few hours later with two tanks in front, the 57-mm antitank rocket launcher company of the ROK 1st Regiment fired at the sides of the leading tanks and destroyed both of them. The enemy follow-on forces withdrew to Ch'osongri as a result.

Around this time, the 2nd Battalion and supporting units ran out of ammunition. Although they anxiously waited for resupply, no immediate measures could be taken. Finally, led by tens of tanks belonging to the 107th Armored

Regiment, the enemy 4th Division went on an all-out offensive around 15:00, and began to penetrate the ROK main line of resistance in the vicinity of Soyo-san. Having fought a bloody battle for 10 hours armed with almost nothing but fighting spirit, the 2nd Battalion had to withdraw in the end. The enemy rode this momentum to advance into downtown Tongduch'on by sunset.

ROK units carried out a street fight in the dark, but could not block the enemy advance and had to withdraw and reassemble in Tokjong. Due to both wire and radio communications breakdown, however, the retreat order could not be relayed to the 1st Battalion in Mach'a-san.

The early battle in the P'och'on area unfolded in a slightly different way from that in Tongduch'on thanks to security measures that had been taken prior to the outbreak of the war. Unlike most other commanding officers who allowed their troops to take a leave or vacation just before the war, the com-mander of the ROK 9th Regiment kept all his troops on post. Suspicious move-ment by the enemy's 3rd Division had prompted him to take this command measure.

Mainly targeting ROK security posts and strongholds, the enemy 3rd Division began to deliver preparatory fire at 03:40, twenty minutes earlier than its counterparts in other areas. Led by more than 40 tanks, the 3rd Division committed its main efforts along Road 43 running from Yangmunri (where the 38-Rest Area is currently located) to P'och'on.

The enemy supporting attack, committed along the axis from Yong-p'yongri (west of Yangmunri) to Karang-san (north of P'och'on), advanced along narrow roads toward ROK security positions in close formation in column of four's. Only after ROK units fired at them did they deploy into combat forma-tion.

The 6th Company of the ROK 9th Regiment, the outpost unit deployed in this area, resisted enemy forces tooth and nail and repulsed a series of enemy attacks, effectively delaying the enemy advance. The enemy had intended to strike at the flanks and rear of ROK forces via the Yangp'yongri-Kayangri avenue of approach and accomplish early seizure of P'och'on, thus blocking the line of retreat of the main units of the 9th Regiment. The 6th Company's successful delay spoiled the enemy plan.

In the meantime, the 9th Regiment Commander forward-deployed the 1st Battalion along the main line of resistance in the vicinity of Ch'onju-san, and moved the 3rd Battalion from its assembly area in Uijongbu to Karang-san, including the Shinbukgyo bridge on the left.

The 2nd Battalion, security unit of the 9th Regiment, regrouped and engaged the enemy at HILL 160, south of the Mansegyo. Running short of ammunition, however, the battalion was forced to withdraw to T'oigyewon viar P'yongch'on.

By 09:00, the main units of the enemy 3rd Division advanced to the ROK main line of resistance north of P'och'on through infantry-armor joint operations. Two NKPA tanks, believed to be the enemy vanguard, advanced to the forward edge of ROK defensive positions and destroyed four 57-mm antitank rocket launchers. An hour later, pushing aside the ROK antitank unit, an enemy armored unit crashed in like a furious wave. The enemy unit consisted of more than 80 pieces, including tanks, self-propelled guns, and armored vehicles.

The enemy armored unit quickly overwhelmed the main positions of the 3rd Battalion, and seized P'och'on around 11:00. Riding the momentum, the enemy unit squashed the ROK 5th Field Artillery Battalion stationed south of P'och'on.

It was only then that an oral directive from the ROK 7th Division reached the 9th Regiment via a liaison officer. The order stipulated: "The 3rd Regiment is currently moving toward P'och'on. Coordinate with this unit to block and repulse the enemy along the T'anjang line. If it is impossible to block the enemy advance at the present positions, repulse the enemy at alternate positions."

By this time, however, the enemy had already seized even the alternate positions, and the regiment communications with the division had broken down. On his own judgment, the 9th Regiment Commander decided to join reinforcements at Ch'uksokryong and ordered his unit to withdraw to Kwangnung. Under the cover of dark clouds and rain, the regiment began to withdraw in the direction of Sop'a around 17:00. Due to a breakdown in the regiment chain of command, however, the 3rd Battalion did not receive the withdrawal order and missed the timing. When the battalion did try to withdraw to the vicinity of Tokjong under the jurisdiction of the 1st Regiment on the left, it suffered heavy losses.[108]

Under these trying circumstances, some units were attached to the 7th Division to shore up the defense. After receiving an attachment order, the 3rd Regiment (under Lt. Col. Lee Sang Kun) of the Capital Security Command in Seoul formed two battalions out of more than 600 men. As the regiment commander did not arrive quickly enough, the regiment left the garrison in Sobinggo for P'och'on under the command of Maj. Kim Bong Sang, commander of the 3rd Battalion.

Charged with a mission to reinforce the 9th Regiment on the eastern sector of the 7th Division, the 3rd Regiment reached Songwoori, south of P'och'on, around 15:00, and saw P'och'on engulfed in fire. The 7th Division Headquarters was uncertain of the enemy situation, but the sight unfolding right before their eyes was more than sufficient information. Quickly estimating the overall situation, the regiment commander, who had belatedly joined the unit, decided to organize hasty defensive positions in Songwoori and deployed the two battalions at T'aebong-san and to its south. Before the 3rd Regiment completed the organization of defensive positions, however, a large enemy armored unit began to move toward them. Spearheaded by 7 or 8 tanks, the enemy unit consisted of more than 150 pieces, including self-propelled guns and armored and regular vehicles.

Faced with an enemy unit vastly superior in equipment, the 3rd Regiment massed all its firepower, including 81-mm mortars, and attacked the enemy tanks with 57-mm and 2.36-inch antitank rocket launchers. The regiment, however, could only manage to dump one enemy tank into a drainageway by the road. Overwhelmed by enemy artillery and machine gun firem, the 3rd Regiment almost gave up resistance, and the regiment commander was nowhere to be seen. Judging that it was no longer possible to hold positions, the 3rd Battalion commander had no choice but to order withdrawal in the absence of the regiment commander.[109]

As the ROK 7th Division lost Tongduch'on, P'och'on, and even Songwoori on the very first day of the war, the security of Uijongbu became increasingly precarious.

2) Kaesong-Munsan Area Battle

Along the Kaesong-Munsan-Seoul axis, which is a northwesterly avenue of approach to the capital, the ROK 1st Division (under Col. Paik Sun Yup) was defending a very wide front stretching for 94km from Ch'ongdan to Korangp'o.

The 1st Division forward-deployed the 12th Regiment (Ch'ongdan-Taewonri) and the 13th Regiment (Taewonri-Korangp'o), and retained the 11th Regiment in Susaek as a reserve. Vulnerable as it was due to the wide front, the 1st Division was to maintain security along the 38th parallel, and upon enemy attack, it was to withdraw to prepared forward defensive positions between Munsan and Choksong. If the division could not hold these positions, it was to move to alternate positions in the south of P'aju and block the enemy advance there.

Across from the ROK 1st Division stood two NKPA divisions: the NKPA 1st Division, reinforced with the 203rd Armored Regiment, and the 6th Division(−). The NKPA 1st and 6th Divisions committed main efforts southward along the Kuhwari-Korangp'o-Munsan axis and Kaesong-Munsan axis, respectively.

Without any warning, the NKPA forces struck a devastating blow upon the ROK 1st Division, and defeated in detail its 12th Regiment and the 3rd Battalion of its 13th Regiment in the vicinity of the 38th parallel. The enemy occupied Kaesong around 09:30. While the NKPA 13th Regiment, 6th Division, was attacking the security positions of the 2nd Battalion, ROK 12th Regiment, the enemy 15th Regiment used Seoul-Shinuiju Railway trains to reach Kaesong Station. After quickly occupying the city of Kaesong, the enemy bisected the ROK security positions and began to threaten the rear of the ROK forces.[110]

Having suffered heavy losses in the early battle, the ROK 12th Regiment withdrew in the direction of Changdan-Munsan and Yongjongp'o-Kimp'o Peninsula. Some troops were cut off and had to make their way to the West Sea. The 3rd Battalion, ROK 13th Regiment, also had its forward company penetrated by the enemy, but was able to delay the enemy advance and withdraw to the south of the Imjin River, taking full advantage of more favorable terrain than that enjoyed by the 12th Regiment. In the meantime, in accordance with the division operations plan, the ROK 13th Regiment(−) occupied the main defensive positions in P'ap'yong-san on the right flank of the division, and the 11th Regiment occupied the main line of resistance on the left flank. The 1st Battalion, 13th Regiment, could quickly occupy the positions as it was undergoing training in the vicinity of the main defensive positions at the time.

The enemy continued to advance southward toward the Imjin railway bridge and Kayoul fording (north of Choksong), seeking to secure a bridgehead for a river-crossing. Located forward of the main defensive line of the ROK 1st Division, the Imjin River has a width of 300-1000m, and holds a great volume of water. At high water, the depth of the lower Imjin increases so much as to affect as far as Chuwolri. Moreover, precipices are formed on either bank of the river, except across from Kayoul, which is on the sector boundary with the adjacent ROK 7th Division. It was thus virtually impossible to wade across the river. As these terrain conditions restricted troop maneuver, especially the river-crossing of armored units, the enemy was forced to use the Imjin railway bridge or the Kayoul Ford.

When deploying troops along the main line of resistance to the south of the Imjin railway bridge, Col. Choi Kyung Rok, the commander of the ROK 11th Regiment, took these terrain factors into consideration. He deployed the 1st Battalion on both sides of Road 1 in the vicinity of Majongri, and positioned the regiment 57-mm recoilless rifle company here and reinforced it with another 57-mm recoilless rifle company, which was attached to the regiment from the Capital Security Command via the 1st Division. Col. Choi also established a platoon-strength combat outpost on an unnamed hill on the opposite bank. On the right flank of the regiment, he deployed the 2nd Battalion in the vicinity of Whasokdong, south of the Imjin Ferry Terminal, and retained the 3rd Battalion as a reserve at Chokjonri, where the regiment command post was located.

Around this time, wounded Col. Chon Song Ho, commander of the ROK 12th Regiment, came across over the Imjin railway bridge. Some of his troops withdrew with him, and the enemy was chasing after them. After confirming that the 12th Regiment had safely withdrawn, Col. Choi recommended to the division commander the demolition of the railway bridge. Charged with the responsibility for blowing up the bridge on order, the commander of the division engineer battalion had already assigned this mission to Capt. Kim Dong Il, the commander of the 3rd Engineer Company. But Capt. Kim was nowhere to

Operations in the Capital Region

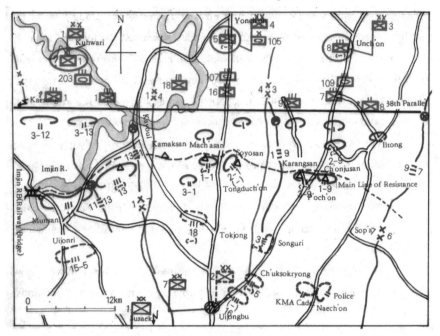

be found when it was time to blow up the bridge. Pressed for time, the engineer battalion commander ordered Capt. Chong Kuk So, battalion operations officer, to carry out the mission. Coordinating with the 11th Regiment commander, Capt. Chung loaded explosives onto the bridge and attempted to set them off, but they misfired and did not detonate.

When Capt. Chung with two soldiers tried to reconnect the detonating cord and the detonator, NKPA troops delivered concentrated fire from the other side of the river. In the end, Capt. Chung could not blow up the bridge and had to withdraw. The Imjin railway bridge thus remained intact, allowing NKPA units access to a high-velocity avenue of approach along the Seoul–Shinuiju Railway.

Around this time, the ROK combat outpost on the other side of the river noticed a large-scale NKPA unit advancing southward along Road 1 in tactical march formation. When the NKPA forces reached the forward area of the combat outpost positions, the ROK unit delivered concentrated fire at them with fire support from the artillery. When their repeated attempts to secure the Imjin railway bridge ended in failure, NKPA forces suspended the attack and concentrated on preventing ROK troops from blowing up the bridge.

Around the same time, the ROK 13th Regiment in P'ap'yong-san was strengthening its defensive posture in anticipation of an enemy advance along the Kayoul-Choksong-Munsan axis. When a battalion-strength NKPA unit did come toward Korangp'o-Chahari late in the day, the regiment delivered concentrated fire in accordance with the division plan and annihilated the enemy in the kill zone.

In short, although its 12th Regiment suffered heavy losses and withdrew on the first day, the ROK 1st Division was able to secure defensive positions along the Imjin River.

3) Ongjin Area Battle

On the Ongjin Peninsula located west of Kaesong, the ROK 17th Independent Regiment (under Col. Paik In Yup) had been carrying out security missions along a 45km stretch of the 38th parallel.

Having detected suspicious enemy movements, the regiment commander ordered the 1st and 3rd Battalions to occupy all prepared positions and beef up security, and had the 2nd Battalion take a marshalling posture on what was to be the day before the outbreak of the war. These measures were taken on suspicion of an enemy attack on Ongjin, and certainly not in anticipation of a full-scale enemy invasion.[111] In the case of a limited enemy attack, the regiment was to hold security positions or conduct delaying action. In the case of a full-scale conflict, the regiment was to withdraw from Ongjin.

The enemy forces confronting the 17th Regiment consisted of the NKPA 14th Regiment, 6th Division, and the 3rd Security Brigade. Led by tanks, the NKPA 14th Regiment carried out a frontal attack on the ROK 3rd Battalion toward Yangwon and Kangryong. Spearheaded by a cavalry unit, the 3rd Security Brigade attacked from Okdong, in front of the ROK 1st Battalion, toward Ongjin.

Faced with the enemy surprise attack, the ROK 17th Regiment fought an uphill battle from the start, and the 1st Battalion's main line of resistance (under Maj. Kim Hee T'ae) on the left front collapsed around 06:00. Regiment Commander Baek immediately committed the 2nd Battalion (under Maj. Song Ho Rim), the regiment reserve, into action, and successfully carried out a counterattack. This time, however, the 3rd Battalion on the right came under a formidable infantry-armor joint attack, and had no choice but to withdraw. Allowing no time for the ROK units to reorganize, the enemy pushed the action (maintained the offensive) and seized Ongjin and Kangryong around 17:00. The enemy thus bisected the regiment defensive positions into eastern and western halves.

No longer able to defend the Ongjin Peninsula, the ROK 17th Regiment Commander carried out a delaying action with the regiment's headquarters units and the 3rd Battalion. On the next morning, they assembled at the port of Bup'o and boarded a naval ship to withdraw. The 2nd Battalion, which had successfully carried out a counterattack in the Ongjin area, also had to withdraw. The battalion boarded a civilian ship for withdrawal after gathering stragglers from the 1st Battalion and the regimental headquarters company.

(2) Forward Deployment of Reserves

In response to these developments, Army Chief of Staff Ch'ae Byong Dok took measures to strengthen the forward defense by committing units stationed in Seoul to forward divisions primarily in the Uijongbu area. These measures were in accordance with orders that had been already issued. Effective 11:00, the 3rd Regiment, Capital Security Command, was attached to the 7th Di-

⟨Table 7⟩   Forward Deployment of Seoul-Stationed Units (June 25-26)[112]

Supporting Unit	Supported Unit	Departure	Deployment
Capital Division		date, hours(place)	date, hours(place)
3rd Regiment	7th Division	25, 11:00(Seoul)	25, 20:00(Uijongbu)
8th Regiment(−1)	6th Division	25, Afternoon(Seoul)	25, Dusk(Kap'yong)
18th Regiment	7th Division	25, 19:00(Seoul)	25, 21:00(Uijongbu)
Seoul Special Regiment			
KMA Instruction Battalion	1st Division	25, Afternoon(Seoul)	25, Dusk(Munsan)
Infantry School Instruction Battalion	1st Division	25, Afternoon(Seoul)	25, Dusk(Munsan)
Korea Military Academy			
Cadet Battalion	7th Division	25, 16:00(Seoul)	25, 19:00(Naech'on)
Police Battalion	7th Division	25, 16:00(Seoul)	25, 19:00(Naech'on)
Army Artillery School			
1st Instruction Battalion(57-mm)	1st, 7th, 6th Divisions	25, 16:00(Yongdungp'o)	25, Afternoon(Divisions)
2nd Instruction Battalion(105-mm)	7th Division	26, 01:00(Seoul)	26, Morning(Kumori)
Independent Cavalry Regiment			
1st Battalion(Armored Vehicles)	1st, 7th, 6th, 8th Divisions Kimp'o Command	25, 15:00(Seoul)	25, Afternoon- 26, Morning (Corresponding Units)
ROKA HQ Officer Regiment	Uijongbu Command	26, 19:00(Seoul)	26, 21:00(Ch'angdong)

vision, and in the afternoon, the 18th Regiment (−1) was additionally attached to it. The 8th Regiment was attached to the 6th Division and committed to the Kap'yong area. In addition, the Seoul Special Regiment was attached to the 1st Division, and the cadet battalion of Korea Military Academy (with one riot police battalion attached) was committed to Naech'on, in case that part of the enemy units in P'och'on might employ a turning movement toward the east of Seoul. As shown in ⟨Table 7⟩, the training instruction battalions of the Artillery School and the cavalry battalion of the Independent cavalry Regiment were also deployed into forward division areas.

As the security of Uijongbu was increasingly threatened by the afternoon despite the earlier defensive measures, the ROKA Headquarters began to commit rear divisions to the front as soon as they arrived in Seoul, with priority given to the Uijongbu area.

Rear divisions had received a mobilization order at 08:00. As these divisions were separately conducting operations by regiment or by battalion and many troops were on a leave or vacation, however, it was virtually impossible for a regiment or a division to assemble and muster all its personnel in time for troop movement to Seoul. As a result, instead of waiting to secure full strength, each division moved battalion by battalion, starting with those battalions that were full strength. In Seoul, Maj. Gen. Ch'ae also felt that the situation on the front was too urgent for the ROKA Headquarters to wait until all rear units arrived, and conducted operations at the division level.

First troops to arrive at Yongsan, Seoul, were the 2nd Division Command and the 5th Regiment (−1). The Army Chief of Staff gave these units an oral directive to "go to Uijongbu right away and block the enemy advance." In response, Brig. Gen. Lee Hyong Kun, commander of the 2nd Division, recommended: "The main units of our division will not be assembled until tomorrow morning. As it is already dark and we are unfamiliar with the terrain, it would be better to make preparations for defense along the Han River line rather than make the mistake of committing forces in a piecemeal fashion." Gen. Ch'ae, however, did not accept this recommendation.

In accordance with Gen. Ch'ae's order, the 5th Regiment (−1) boarded freight trains at Yongsan Station and arrived in Kumori, Uijongbu, at 20:00. The other regiments of the 2nd Division, 16th (−1) and 25th (−1), were committed to Uijongbu by the next morning. In addition, the 22nd Regiment, 3rd Division, and the 15th and 20th Regiments, 5th Division, were also committed by regiment or by battalion to Kimp'o, Munsan, and Uijongbu.

Thanks to these emergency measures, reinforcements committed to the Uijongbu area amounted to 5 regiments, or 15 battalions (including Artillery School, Korea Military Academy, and riot police battalions). However, as these units were hastily organized in a makeshift fashion on a "first-come, first-committed" basis and lacked a communications network, they were unable to achieve not only horizontal but vertical coordination. Operating with neither

⟨Table 8⟩   Forward Deployment of Rear Divisions (June 25-27)[113]

Supporting Unit	Supported Unit and Area	Departure	Deployment
2nd Division		date, hours (place)	date, hours (place)
5th Regiment (−1)	Uijongbu	25, 19:00 (Taejon)	25, 20:00 (Kumori)
16th Regiment (−1)	Uijongbu	25, 19:00 (Ch'ongju)	26, 07:00 (Uijongbu)
25th Regiment (−1)	Uijongbu	25, 21:00 (Onyang)	26, 11:00 (Ch'angdong)
3rd Division			
3rd Battalion, 22nd Regiment	Kimp'o Command	25, 11:00 (Taegu)	25, Afternoon (Kimp'o)
22nd Regiment (−1)	1st Division	25, 11:00 (Taegu)	26, Afternoon (Pyokje)
5th Division			
3rd Battalion, 15th Regiment	1st Division	25, Afternnon (Chonju)	26, Afternoon (Pongil Cr.)
3rd Battalion, 20th Regiment	1st Division	25, Night (Kwangju)	26, Night (Pongil Cr.)
2nd Battalion, 15th Regiment	Miari Command	26, 03:00 (Chonju)	27, 08:00 (Miari)
1st Battalion, 20th Regiment	Miari Command	26, Morning (Kwangju)	27, 08:00 (Miari)

※ Cr=Creeek

sufficient combat preparations nor an established chain of command, these units were almost totally ineffective.[114]

In short, coming under the NKPA surprise attack on June 25, ROK Armed Forces withdrew from the 38th parallel and were staging an uphill battle against the formidable enemy. The ROK 7th Division, stationed forward of the capital region, was rolled back to the Tongduch'on-Songwoori line, with the security of Uijongbu in danger. The 1st Division was confronting the enemy along the Imjin River line, and the 17th Regiment in the Ongjin Peninsula had to withdraw by sea. Consequently, the defense of Seoul hinged on how to block the enemy advance from the north of Uijongbu.

(3) Uijongbu Counteroffensive

ROK Army Chief of Staff Maj. Gen. Ch'ae Byong Dok had hardened his resolve to "hold Uijongbu under any circumstance," and committed to the area not only the Seoul-stationed units but also the urgently mobilized rear divisions immediately upon their arrival in Seoul. Making a personal visit to the 7th Division Headquarters in Uijongbu at 01:00, June 26, Gen. Ch'ae ordered a counteroffensive to the commanders of the 7th and 2nd Divisions.[115] Although he was dissatisfied with the order, the 7th Division commander, Brig. Gen. Yu Jae Hung, accepted it as it was directly issued by the Army Chief of Staff himself. In contrast, the 2nd Division commander, Brig. Gen. Lee Hyong Kun, pointed out that it was not yet time to carry out a counteroffensive, and recommended that combat strength be employed in mass after the arrival of all division troops the next morning. In addition, he once again argued for defense along the Han River line, terrain which favors defense.[116]

Gen. Ch'ae had a cool response to this recommendation. In a strong tone, he told the division commanders to conduct operations as ordered. Furthermore, as a defensive measure against tanks, he strongly ordered troops to assault enemy tanks with hand-grenades and Molotov cocktails.

In accordance with Gen. Ch'ae's order, the 7th Division set out for a counteroffensive in the morning of June 26, with Tongduch'on as its objective, and the 2nd Division planned to advance into P'och'on via the mountain pass of Ch'uksok-ryong.

Troops available to the 7th Division amounted to a total of only five battalions: two battalions of the 1st Regiment, which also had operational control over the 2nd Battalion, 3rd Regiment, and two battalions of the 18th Regiment, attached to the division on the previous day. The actual troop strength thus amounted to a little more than a reinforced regiment.

In the meantime, the NKPA 4th Division had completed reorganization in Tongduch'on, and was waiting for the resumption of the attack, with main efforts directed toward a road that led to Bongamri-Tokjong on the west. Although Road 3 from Tongduch'on was in better condition, they chose not to use it as their axis of advance because they felt that they would meet a formidable ROK resistance there.

For the counteroffensive, the ROK 1st Regiment reorganized withdrawing troops in Tokjong and formed a mixed battalion (under Lt. Col. Han T'ae Won). With this battalion and the 3rd Battalion as the forward attack echelon and with the 2nd Battalion, 3rd Regiment, as reserve, the ROK forces went on the offensive at 08:00 on the 26th.

At the same time, Defense Minister Shin Sung Mo went on the air at the Korean Broadcasting System (KBS): "The enemy is retreating under the counteroffensive of the ROK Armed Forces. Accordingly, our troops went on an all-out counteroffensive. Soon, they will advance all the way to the Yalu River, and realize our people's dream of national unification." This live broadcast was repeatedly aired on the radio, leading the general public to have an optimistic view on the eventual outcome of the war.

Having conducted only defensive operations since the beginning of the war, consisting of withdrawal, defense, and yet another withdrawal, ROK troops welcomed the counteroffensive and advanced northward in high spirits. The mixed battalion on the right encountered unexpectedly few enemy troops along Road 3, and recovered Tongduch'on and reached as far as Soyo-san.

The 3rd Battalion on the left suffered a different fate. Advancing from Yongamri toward Bongamri, the battalion encountered a NKPA armored unit in the vicinity of Habiri. The actual troop strength of the 3rd Battalion amounted to a little more than 150 men, lower than a full-strength company. Though thoroughly outnumbered, the battalion carried out an audacious attack — only to be dispersed 30 minutes after engagement.

Regrouping part of his troops, the 3rd Battalion commander withdrew to Uidong, and occupied Obong-san on the order from the regiment commander. However, part of the battalion led by the deputy commander withdrew to Surak-san and Taerung via Ch'onbo-san, and the unit cohesion of the 3rd Battalion completely collapsed.

In the meantime, although the 1st Regiment Command Post located at Tokjong was initially encouraged by the recovery of Tongduch'on, it soon had to issue a withdrawal order to the mixed battalion. The reason was that the main efforts of the NKPA 4th Division had enveloped Tokjong from an unexpected direction, forsaking Road 3 for a roundabout road on the west.

As for the ROK 2nd Division, the counteroffensive was actually carried out by a single battalion. At the time, the division had only two battalions belonging to the 5th Regiment, and the 16th Regiment from Ch'ongju was not to arrive at Ch'angdong until an hour later. The division commander felt that it was impossible to seize the division objective P'och'on with only these troops, and decided to observe the turn of events from Ch'uksok-ryong before advancing to P'och'on. He thought that the 3rd Regiment had been committed on the previous day to defend Ch'uksok-ryong.[117] By then, however, the 3rd Regiment had already abandoned Ch'uksok-ryong and was withdrawing to Kumori.

The 5th Regiment had no proper commanding officer at the time. The regiment commander, Col. Paik Nam Kwon, had been dispatched to a US unit in Japan, and the deputy commander, Lt. Col. Park Ki Sung, was on leave in Pusan at the time of the enemy invasion. In the absence of these commanding officers, the division chief of staff, Lt. Col. Ch'oi Ch'ang On, took over the regiment, and led the troops to Kumori, located to the northeast of Uijongbu. Before departing to carry out the counteroffensive, the regiment had to request ammunition supply. The regiment had so pressed for time before leaving Taejon on the previous day that it was given less than 50% of what was needed. However, the division too had moved in such haste that it did not have any extra ammunition. In the end, the regiment arranged for a forward-supply with the 7th Division, and set out for the front.

As the leading unit of the 5th Regiment, the 2nd Battalion left Kumori at 03:00 on the 26th and arrived at the top of Ch'uksok-ryong (hill pass) at dawn, but it could not find any trace of the 3rd Regiment aside from a few stragglers. Together with stragglers from the 9th Regiment, they were just standing around by the road, completely lost. Amid all the confusion, one could clearly hear the sound of tanks approaching from the north of Ch'uksok-ryong.

The situation was now taking on ominous proportions. Realizing that he did not have much time, the 2nd Battalion commander (Maj. Ch'a Kap Jun) hastily organized defensive positions on the right and left sides of the Ch'uksok-ryong pass. As the early morning fog cleared, he could see a long column of NKPA tanks climbing up the pass.

The 5th Regiment troops were undaunted by the sight of the enemy tanks. They had some real combat experience through anti-guerrilla operations, but knew nothing about the mighty power of T-34 tanks. It was only natural that these seasoned soldiers would think lightly of NKPA armored units.

The enemy tanks were slowly approaching. Taking into account that the battalion did not have much ammunition, Maj. Ch'a controlled fire until the leading tanks came within 200-300m of the defensive positions. The battalion concentrated all its fire at the tanks. 60-mm and 81-mm mortars as well as 2.36-inch rocket launchers were utilized. Like an invincible monster, however, the enemy tanks shook off all that the battalion had to throw at them, and continued to advance toward the defensive positions. The battalion troops gradually became fearful of these monstrous machines. After using up all their ammunition, they began to flee from their positions. In less than 10 minutes after the beginning of the engagement, the critical Ch'uksok-ryong defensive positions completely collapsed, endangering the security of Uijongbu. Moreover, the 1st Battalion, the follow-on unit, did not even have a chance to occupy Ch'uksok-ryong, and was pushed back by the enemy tanks to T'oegewon.

As the 5th Regiment of the ROK 2nd Division was simply overwhelmed by the enemy, the planned counteroffensive came to naught, and blocking the enemy advance toward Uijongbu became the top priority. The division deployed the 16th Regiment (under Col. Moon Yong Ch'ae) on a commanding ground in the vicinity of Sangkumori, northeast of Uijongbu. About an hour after the troop deployment, NKPA units began to close in, spearheaded by 20 tanks.

A special antitank unit under the command of Capt. Kim Jin Dong (deputy commander of the 1st Battalion) delivered concentrated fire at the enemy leading tank with 2.36-inch rocket launchers, and managed to dump it into a roadside drainage ditch. At least for a moment, the enemy advance was delayed. In this precarious situation, two battalions of the 16th Regiment engaged an enemy infantry unit that had advanced along a ridgeline toward the ROK positions. Outnumbered by the NKPA troops, however, they had to withdraw to Taerung and Howondong. By 12:00 on the 26th, the NKPA 3rd Division penetrated the defensive positions of the ROK 16th Regiment on the northeast of Uijongbu, and the NKPA 4th Division was pressing Uijongbu from the northwest, from Tokjong.

Under this dire situation, Maj. Kim P'ung Ik, together with 2nd Battery Commander Chang Se P'ung, destroyed the track of a leading enemy tank with a 105-mm howitzer. As the commander of the 2nd Instruction Battalion, Army Artillery School, Maj. Kim had established a position in Kumori, directly north of Uijongbu. When he was about to load the second round, however, he was killed by fire from a follow-on tank.[118] Facing little resistance from that point on, the enemy armored units occupied Uijongbu around 13:00 on the 26th. An entrance to Seoul and a transportation center, Uijongbu was deluged with withdrawing ROK troops and wounded personnel and evacuating civilians, but there was nothing that could be done.

In the meantime, the ROK Ministry of National Defense that morning held a serious discussion over the confusing situation in Uijongbu. Upon President Syngman Rhee's directive to consult with military experts to seek a way out of the crisis, Defense Minister Shin Sung Mo invited active-duty and retired senior military experts over to the Ministry at 10:00 and discussed alternative courses of action.

In attendance at this meeting were: the Chief of Staff for each service, Maj. Gen. Kim Hong Il (Superintendent of the Staff College), Brig. Gen. Song Ho Sung (former Commander-in-Chief of the Constabulary), Mr. Yu Dong Yol (former Security Minister), Mr. Lee Bom Sok (former Defense Minister), Mr. Lee Ch'ong Ch'on (former Commander-in-Chief of the Restoration Army), and Mr. Kim Sok Won (former Commander of the 1st Division).

At the outset of the meeting, Minister Shin and Army Chief of Staff

Ch'ae, reported: "Our troops are carrying out a counteroffensive against the NKPA forces in the Uijongbu area, and the situation is developing in our favor." Maj. Gen. Kim Hong Il first argued for the establishment of a sound course of action for future operations. Noting that it was risky to launch a counteroffensive in front of Uijongbu, he spoke in favor of seeking decision south of the Han River. Although Kim Sok Won and Lee Bom Sok agreed with Maj. Gen. Kim, Minister Shin and Army Chief of Staff Ch'ae insisted that Seoul not be abandoned under any circumstance, and the meeting came to an end without reaching a consensus.

Col. Lee Jong Ch'an, who was attending at this meeting, would later re-collect: "At the meeting of military experts, the elders argued that our units should be regrouped and assume a new posture along the Han River line, while Army Chief of Staff Ch'ae and I argued for the defense of Seoul until the end."

Col. Lee added: "At the time, we had to choose between two courses of action: defend Seoul to the end or withdraw to the Han River line. But, withdrawing to the Han River line would amount to abandoning the citizens of Seoul, and, moreover, its effectiveness would clearly be limited due to lack of transport. So, it might be an unjustifiably harsh judgment on Gen. Ch'ae to say, 'Army Chief of Staff Ch'ae's idea of defending Seoul to the end stemmed from his desire to save political face, and was a decisive blunder which ignored such elementary factors as the troop strength ratio and potential and violated the most basic principles of military strategy.' This harsh judgment is nothing more than a criticism based on the result with no understanding of the confusing situation at the time."[119]

After the meeting of military experts, Minister Shin and Army Chief of Staff Ch'ae were requested to attend an emergency session of the National Assembly at the Capitol Building from 11:00, and to brief on the war situation. During the briefing, Minister Shin said, "Our troops are thoroughly prepared to occupy as far as P'yongyang within three to five days." Gen. Ch'ae added an optimistic remark, saying, "We repulsed the enemy out of Uijongbu. We will occupy P'yongyang in three days."[120]

Returning to the ROKA Headquarters after his testimony at the National Assembly, Gen. Ch'ae anxiously waited to hear that the Uijongbu counteroffensive was successful, but the situation report from the front was pessimistic. He ordered Deputy Chief of Staff Kim Paik Il to commit rear divisions into the Uijongbu area as soon as they arrived in Seoul, and headed for Uijongbu himself. By then, however, Uijongbu had fallen into enemy hands.

Gen. Ch'ae regrouped withdrawing troops at the Paeksok Creek and on the spot, he removed Brig. Gen. Lee Hyong Kun from command of the 2nd Division for the failure of operations. Gen. Ch'ae gave the commander of the 7th Division command of the 2nd Division as well, and ordered withdrawal to Ch'angdong. To provide cover for the withdrawing units, he ordered the 25th Regiment (−), 2nd Division, to be deployed at Paeksok-ch'on from their assembly position in Ch'angdong.

Around this time, the mixed battalion of the ROK 1st Regiment in Tongduch'on established a plan to make contact with the 1st Battalion, which was isolated in Mach'a-san. The mixed battalion, however, could not risk having its line of retreat getting cut off by the enemy, and had to abandon the plan and withdraw, on order from the regiment. Assembling at Tokjong Primary School around 17:00, the battalion reached Ch'onbo-san around 21:00 on the northeast of Uijongbu. Downtown Uijongbu was engulfed in flames, lighting up the night skies in red.

Until a few hours previous, a critically important headquarters had been located in Uijongbu. ROK troops were distraught over the loss of Uijongbu, but there was little that they could do. The mixed battalion commander again led his troops via Songch'u-Baekundae and arrived at the regiment headquarters in Uidong the next morning.

As for the ROK 18th Regiment, Capital Security Command, which was to be the left forward echelon of the Uijongbu counteroffensive, the result was much the same. The regiment set out for Bongamri around 10:00, but, when it was about to pass Unhyon Primary School around 12:00, the 7th Division Headquarters ordered the regiment to convert to defensive operations from that position. This action was taken because the 2nd Division had withdrawn from Ch'uksok-ryong and Uijongbu was about to fall into enemy hands.

While the 18th Regiment was establishing positions on hills in the vicinity of Eunhyon, an enemy armored unit appeared from an unnamed road connecting Bongamri and Tokjong. A special antitank unit led by Deputy Commander Lt. Col. Han Shin scored a direct hit on a leading tank with a 2.36-inch rocket launcher, but the tank was not destroyed and returned fire. Judging that the regiment had no chance against the armored unit, Regiment Commander Col. Lim Ch'ung Sik let enemy tanks pass and waited for the follow-on infantry units. Although two hours passed, no enemy infantry units came in sight. Instead, an enemy supply and transportation unit appeared right in front of the regiment, with 12 cow-driven carriages loaded with artillery shells. The 18th Regiment destroyed this unit, and captured 11 NKPA soldiers, including a senior captain. According to the captain's situation overlay board, the sector boundary between the NKPA 4th and 3rd Divisions stretched all the way to Yongdungp'o, and the NKPA units were to advance down to Suwon by July 3.[121]

As the darkness fell, the 18th Regiment was no longer able to maintain radio communications with the ROK 7th Division and receive additional instructions. Not willing to take any more risks, the regiment commander ordered withdrawal around 02:00 the next day, and had his troops move by battalion to Samsongri.

The KMA cadet battalion and the riot police battalion, for their part, defended the right flank of the 7th Division from a commanding ground in the vicinity of Naech'on, midway point between Ildong and T'oegewon. They were deployed there on an order from the ROKA Headquarters around 19:00 on the 25th. The next day, these two battalions fought a fierce battle against NKPA units advancing southward from P'och'on and Ildong, and withdrew to Taerung in the evening and committed into new defensive positions.[122]

(4) Munsan Vicinity Battle

While the Uijongbu Area Battle was unfolding, the ROK 1st Division established a main line of resistance in the vicinity of Munsan, using the natural obstacle offered by the Imjin River. With a resolve to repulse the enemy, the division confronted NKPA units. On the 26th, an enemy armored unit made its first appearance in front of the 13th Regiment on the eastern sector of the division. Moving along the road on the north of P'ap'yong-san, five leading tanks closed in toward the northeast of the mountain. The regiment responded with 2.36-inch rocket launchers, but could not destroy a single tank.

The 1st Battalion commander (Maj. Kim Jin Wi) selected 18 men from his troops and organized two special attack teams. Holding makeshift explosives made up of mortar shells bundled with hand-grenades, the special attack troops dived on to the enemy tanks without any regard for their own lives. As if scared by the suicidal tactics, the five enemy tanks halted their advance and stopped near a thatched-roof house by the road. Seizing upon the opportunity, the ROK troops fired a tracer to set the house ablaze. The fire from the house quickly caught on to the tanks. Observing this scene, the enemy follow-on tanks withdrew to Choksong.

Soon afterwards, a regiment-strength enemy unit came to attack again, but after a fierce close combat, the 13th Regiment was able to hold position.

In the meantime, upon receiving supporting units from the ROKA Headquarters, the ROK 1st Division divided the Seoul Special Regiment and reattached the instruction battalins of the Infantry School and Korea Military Academy to the 11th Regiment and the 13th Regiment, respectively. In addition, to increase the depth of defense, the 15th Regiment was deployed at Wijonri on the final line of resistance, and the 3rd Battalion, 20th Regiment, was attached there. While giving priority of defense to the avenue of approach along Road 1, the division commander wanted to insure cover for the withdrawal of the forward regiments and to secure ground for a counterattack if the main line of resistance should collapse.

Encouraged by the reinforcements from the rear, the ROK 1st Division was shoring up the main line of defense, and planning to launch a counteroffensive if the situation permitted.

However, as the adjacent ROK 7th Division on the right had withdrawn to the Tokjong-Ch'uksok-ryong line, the right flank of the 1st Division was completely exposed. Thus, the NKPA 1st Division was able to attack the eastern flank of the ROK 1st Division without encountering any resistance along the way from Kayoul-Choksong.

Moreover, on the left flank, the NKPA 6th Division committed tanks into the Munsan bulge at night, after confirming that the Imjin railway bridge remained intact. Spearheaded by five tanks in the early morning of the 26th, the NKPA 6th Division launched a full-scale infantry-armor-artillery joint operation via the railway bridge. The ROK 11th Regiment stubbornly resisted the enemy attack, from the south of the railway bridge to deep defensive positions. Lacking appropriate means to deal with enemy tanks, however, the regiment at last had to withdraw to hill mass in South Munsan. Although the situation was turning against the ROK units, the NKPA forces halted the attack in North Munsan and were waiting for follow-on units. Judging that this was the time to launch a counterattack, the 11th Regiment commander simultaneously committed 3 battalions, including the attached Infantry School unit, and was able to drive back the enemy to the north of the Imjin River and recover the main line of resistance on the left flank.

On the exposed right flank, however, the ROK 13th Regiment was unable to block the enemy advance toward the defensive positions in P'ap'yongsan. As the ROK main line of resistance collapsed, the main efforts of the NKPA 1st Division were able to advance westward along Road 320 and threaten Munsanri.

Faced with the dire situation, Division Commander Paik Sun Yup decided to withdraw to the final line of resistance along Wijonri-Tonaeri north of Bongilch'on, and seek decision there. Hoping to bide time for a counterattack, Col. Paik issued the withdrawal order effective 19:00. Accordingly, the division headquarters was moved to Bongil-ch'on Primary School, and the 11th and 13th Regiments took advantage of darkness to withdraw to defensive positions in Kumch'on under the cover from the 15th Regiment deployed in the vicinity of Wijonri.

In short, by the second day of the war, the NKPA main efforts had penetrated the ROK main line of resistance north of Seoul and advanced to the Munsan-Uijongbu line. The ROK forces had to organize a hasty defense along the Bongil-ch'on-Ch'angdong line on June 27, and, committing all available reserves, had to prepare for final resistance in defense of Seoul. Moreover, as the NKPA 14th Regiment, 6th Division in Ongjin began to attempt crossing from Yongjongp'o toward Kangwha-do and Kimp'o Peninsula, ROK forces also had to devise a plan to defend Kimp'o.

3. Ch'unch'on-Hongch'on Battle

Responsible for the central front, the ROK 6th Division deployed the 7th and 2nd Regiments in Ch'unch'on and northeast of Hongch'on, respectively, and retained the 19th Regiment as a reserve in Wonju. The division was defending a wide front stretching for 84km from Chokmokri to Chinhukdong. With the Soyang River flowing from east to west along the front of the division sector, the left, boundary of the sector was marked by the North Han River. Taking advantage of the Soyang River, the 7th and 2nd Regiments established defensive positions along its northern and southern banks, respectively. Assigned to the 6th Division only on June 20, however, the 2nd Regiment, the forward echelon on the right, barely completed its relief in place of the previously stationed 8th Regiment by the outbreak of the war. Combat readiness was little better for the 19th Regiment, the division reserve. Having been assigned to the division on May 1, it had yet to prepare combat readiness.

Just as in the case of other ROK divisions on the western and eastern front, one-third of division troops were on leave just prior to the outbreak of the war. However, based on information given by captured North Korean soldiers on June 19 and confirmed by reconnaissance units sent to Hwach'on and Yanggu, the ROK 6th Division anticipated an enemy attack and took security measures on its own.

Deployed in front of the 6th Division was the NKPA 2nd Corps. As a supporting attack of the NKPA forces, the 2nd Corps was responsible for offensive operations on the central and eastern front. Planning to occupy Ch'unch'on on the first day of the war, the NKPA 2nd Corps committed the 2nd Division as its main effort along the Hwach'on-Ch'unch'on axis, and along the Inje-Hongch'on axis, it employed the 12th Division reinforced with a separate armored regiment. The corps planned to occupy Ch'unch'on and Hongch'on in the early stages of the war, and employ a turning movement toward Ich'on and Suwon to envelop Seoul.

Enemy artillery fire began in the early morning of the 25th throughout the central front. Enemy preparatory fire was concentrated at the south of the Mojin Bridge located on the Hwach'on-Ch'unch'on road. Appreciating the strategic importance of this area, NKPA forces felt that this road would provide their main avenue of approach.

Concentrated artillery fire continued on for almost 30 minutes, leaving ROK soldiers flabbergasted by the scale of the attack for a while. Having closed in under the cover of heavy fog, enemy troops caught ROK soldiers completely off balance, and precipitated much confusion in the ROK camps.

After receiving an urgent report of full-scale enemy invasion, the ROK 6th Division commander in Wonju issued a marshalling order to the 19th Regiment, and headed for Ch'unch'on with his operations staff.

Meanwhile, observing that the enemy artillery fire was massed at the vicinity of the Mojin Bridge, the ROK 7th Regiment commander, Lt. Col. Lim Bu T'aek, realized intuitively that the enemy main efforts were directed toward the Hwach'on-Shinp'o-Ch'unch'on axis. In response to this threat, he deployed the regiment reserve, 1st Battalion (under Maj. Kim Yong Bae), in prepared defensive positions (HILL 164) north of the Soyang Bridge.

Intent on securing a bridgehead by occupying a commanding ground in the southern vicinity of the Mojin Bridge, the enemy delivered heavy artillery fire at the 3rd Battalion, which was deployed in the vicinity of Kot'anri. While artillery fire continued, enemy infantry units in tactical-march columns closed in on the defensive positions, headed by the DPRK flag.

Spearheaded by SU-76 self-propelled guns, NKPA troops were zealously attempting to cross the bridge and secure a bridgehead.

Located 300m south of the 38th parallel, the 250-meter-long Mojin Bridge served as an entrance to the Hwach'on-Ch'unch'on axis. A mechanized unit could not cross the North Han River and advance into Ch'unch'on without using this tactically important bridge. The ROK 7th Regiment, however, had no plans to blow up the bridge, allegedly because this bridge was in such clear view of the enemy that it was impossible to load explosives without being detected.

Approximately 4 meters in width, Mojin Bridge might seem like an unimpressive little bridge, but because the 7th Regiment did not blow up this bridge, the 47km-wide regiment front completely collapsed at a single stroke. Moreover, as there were virtually no friendly units between Kot'anri-Inramri near the 38th parallel and the Ch'unch'on suburbs, the enemy troops were able to advance unimpeded toward Ch'unch'on. Due to the rapid maneuver of the enemy units, ROK troops did not even have a chance to set up a road crater at a defile between Sowon and Yokgol. Blazing across the no-man's land, NKPA troops stopped their advance around 09:00 in Chinaeri, Yokgol, with Ch'unch'on in sight.

Meanwhile, having failed to block the advance of the enemy main attack at the Mojin Bridge, the forward unit of the ROK 7th Regiment withdrew to the planned main line of resistance and occupied prepared defensive positions.

Although the regiment had failed in its initial task, it quickly re-established combat readiness in an orderly manner. Regiment commander Lt. Col. Lim Bu T'aek consolidated the defensive line along the Soyang River, and conscripted civilian vechicles in the operations area to enhance troop maneuverability. Taking all necessary measures, he also secured rice and ammunition for his troops, and organized a new reserve with the regiment's headquarters company.

While these measures were being taken, 2nd Lt. Shim Il, 2nd Platoon,

57-mm antitank gun company, destroyed two enemy SU-76 self-propelled guns in a pine forest by the Oksanp'o road. This was a remarkable feat, as Lt. Shim possessed little more than antitank guns of mediocre quality. Combining antitank gun fire with "human bullet" attack, he was able to destroy the SU-76's.[123] Watching this scene from the nearby HILL 164, friendly troops let out a cry of joy over the destruction of the enemy self-propelled guns. Encouraged by Lt. Shim's heroics, the 7th Regiment troops began to have confidence that they could destroy tanks and overcome their initial "armor-phobia." These soldiers did not exactly know the difference between self-propelled guns and tanks.

Right at that moment, the enemy suddenly opened massed artillery fire at HILL 164 and downtown Ch'unch'on area. Having burst across the 38th parallel with ease, the enemy apparently underestimated our strength and seemed to have jumped to the conclusion that they could seize Ch'unch'on at a stroke. In close formation, they closed in on an open area stretching for 6 km between Yokgol and the Soyang Bridge.

At the time, the 16th Field Artillery Battalion of the ROK 6th Division was positioned south of Oksanp'o, on the north of the Soyang Bridge. However, its closest friendly infantry unit was deployed on a hill 1.5km to east, and was too far away to provide cover for the artillery battalion. This breakdown in coordination was caused by the early collapse of forward security forces. Faced with this precarious situation, the artillery battalion fought off the enemy by massing direct fire. Three 57-mm antitank guns were soon added to the fierce defensive effort. The enemy attacked in waves, repeatedly replacing leading echelons with follow-on units. Though completely exposed in an open field without a single tree to provide cover, the enemy insisted on frontal attack, and heavy losses did not stop them from continuing with the offensive. It was as if they were staking their lives to secure a bridgehead for the crossing of the Soyang River in order to carry out the order to occupy Ch'unch'on on the first day of the war.

The enemy also attacked the eastern front of the ROK 6th Division. As the ROK 2nd Regiment on the right had not relieved the 8th Regiment until the 24th, ROK troops had not even had the time to learn about the terrain in the operations area when the enemy dealt a surprise blow on the 25th. The 2nd Regiment deployed the 1st Battalion on the left in the vicinity of Kwandaeri and positioned the 3rd Battalion on the right in the vicinity of Hyonri. The 2nd Battalion was retained as reserve in Kyolunri north of Hongch'on, but arriving in Hongch'on only on the 24th, the battalion had not even had the time to unpack their equipment.

The NKPA 12th Division launched a frontal attack on the ROK 2nd Regiment, with its armor-reinforced main attack directed along the Yanggu–Shinnam-Hongch'on axis and supporting attack committed to the Inje-Hyonri approach. As there was a heavy rainfall on the previous day, however, the swollen waters of the Soyang River presented a formidable obstacle to the enemy's advance. The enemy had much difficulty wading across the river in the vicinity of the Manojin ferry terminal, which was to be the first main battle area of the day.

Deployed on a hill in a cross compartment of terrain in the vicinity of Ch'ongguri, south of the ferry terminal, the security forces of the 1st Battalion detected two enemy river-crossing attempts in the early morning and seized the momentum by annihilating these enemy troops. Thus twice stalled, the enemy delivered heavy artillery fire on friendly positions, and committed an attacking echelon for the third time under the close fire support of two 45-mm antitank guns forward-deployed in the vicinity of Manojin.

Coming under the enemy artillery fire, our troops deployed in Ch'ongguri lost two-thirds of strength and ran out of ammunition. A few more than 20 soldiers carried out a hand-to-hand combat in order to hold position,

Ch'unch'on-Hongch'on Battle

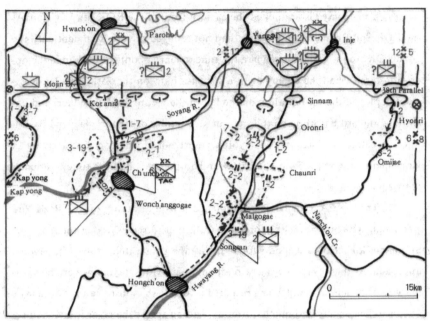

but had to disperse and withdraw in the end.

While the security forces of the 1st Battalion were putting up a fierce battle in the vicinity of the Manojin ferry terminal, the ROK 2nd Regiment commander Col. Ham Byong Son deployed the 2nd Battalion, regiment reserve, on the left side of Oronri, and redeployed the withdrawing 1st Battalion on its right. Having been committed to the front without a sufficient knowledge of the terrain, however, many regiment troops lost a sense of direction on their withdrawal and wandered around in the mountains.

Meanwhile, in the Hyonri area, the 3rd Battalion (under Maj. Lee Un San) had a fierce battle in the vicinity of Hukgogae-Chindari near the 38th parallel, and established resistance positions in Omijae via Maewhagogae (mountain pass) south of Hyonri.

A gap was thus created along the middle of the ROK 2nd Regiment, bisecting its defensive sector into eastern and western halves. The regiment headquarters lost all communications link with the 3rd Battalion in the Hyonri area and could not even locate its position. Moreover, the 9th Company, which had been deployed as the right forward unit of the 3rd Battalion, was now isolated in the enemy area. Unable to withdraw in the direction of Omijae, the comany had to pursue an independent course of action.

Restoring some sense of stability in the Oronri area, the 2nd Regiment sought ways to destroy enemy tanks, but lacking the necessary antitank weapons, it could not come up with any brilliant idea. In the end, the regiment commander issued an order to form a special antitank attack team.

Accordingly, a special attack unit of 20 men was organized under the leadership of 2nd Lt. Kang Sung Ho, 1st Platoon, 5th Company. While ambushing by a road in the vicinity of Tamuri Pass north of Oronri, they saw an enemy tank advancing southward with its hatch open. Seizing upon the opportunity, the special attack unit destroyed the leading enemy tank by combining hand-grenade attack with 2.36-inch antitank rocket fire from 30 meters away. It was then that the enemy gave the 2nd Battalion a golden opportunity. While attempting to push this leading tank aside by the side of the road, a second enemy tank fell into the road side ditch. Massing all its fire on the enemy formation, the battalion separated the enemy tanks from the infantrymen and carried out an audacious counterattack to annihilate the foot soldiers. Having lost the two leading tanks and the infantrymen, the six follow-on tanks fled north.

Gaining confidence from this battle, the ROK 2nd Regiment commander established a plan to launch a counterattack with two battalions early next morning and recover Hills 402 and 488 north of Oronri. His ultimate aim was to recover the 38th parallel using these hills as base. Given that the 2nd Regiment still did not have artillery support, however, this operational design was some what of a gamble.

In the meantime, on the morning of June 26, the 2nd Battalion, ROK 19th Regiment, was deployed from Wonju to Udu-san, north of the Soyang Bridge. Soon afterwards, the enemy began to assemble in the vicinity of Yokgol-Oksanp'o. Deployed on Hill 164 forward of Udu-san, the 1st Battalion, ROK 7th Regiment, detected enemy activity at a spot 2km to its west and decided to launch a spoiling attack in order to seize the initiative before the enemy was further reinforced. Striking a surprise blow, the 1st Battalion advanced all the way to Shindongri and prepared for an enemy counterattack. After being pushed back to Chinaeri, the rear slope of Yokgol, the enemy 2nd Division committed the reserve 6th Regiment to pass the lines of forward regiments and resume the offensive.

Using heavy artillery fire to pin down two ROK battalions on Hill 164 and Udu-san, the enemy planned to advance to Oksanp'o-Majonri (a.k.a. Karaemok Ford, presently an area buried under water near the 2nd Soyang Bridge) and cross the Soyang River at a stroke.

Separately from this unit, five enemy self-propelled guns approached via the eastern passage and avoided defensive artillery fire to advance to the river bank in the vicinity of the Soyang Bridge (presently, the 1st Soyang Bridge). As they passed a thatched-roof house by the road, however, they were ambushed by flank fire from ROK 57-mm antitank guns. Upon seeing that the two leading self-propelled guns had been destroyed, the three follow-on guns changed direction and fled north.

Around this time, an enemy echelon that had advanced to a sandy lot in the vicinity of the Karaemok Ford was nearly annihilated in the kill zone. The Soyang River turned red with blood. The enemy committed a second and a third wave of attack into the same avenue of approach, but suffered further losses under accurate and intense ROK artillery fire. No NKPA soldier made it across the Soyang River.

Observing this scene from Bongui-san in the rear of Ch'unch'on, the ROK 6th Division commander became confident that he could defend Ch'unch-on from enemy attack. Aware that the 2nd Regiment in Hongch'on was fighting an uphill battle due to inferiority in firepower, the division commander dispatched an artillery company to Hongch'on. At the same time, judging that it was time to narrow the defensive front, he repositioned all units deployed north of the Soyang River to the final line of resistance on the south bank on the night of the 26th.

Accordingly, with respect to the Soyang Bridge, the 7th Regiment was deployed on the east and the 19th Regiment on the west. Upon troop redeployment to the south of the Soyang Bridge, the division engineer battalion commander (Maj. Park Jong Chae) recommended that the bridge be demolished to delay enemy advance. Thinking that the bridge would help to faciliate the ROK counterattack, however, the division commander suspended the demolition of the bridge, and, instead, ordered his men to place more obstacles on the bridge as well as at the bridge entrance.[124]

As the enemy pressure was building up in the north of Ch'unch'on that day, the ROKA Headquarters dispatched to Kap'yong the 8th Regiment (−1), Capital Division, and the 8th Company, 3rd Foot Reconnaissance Battalion, Independent Cavalry Regiment. These units were sent to fill the gap between the 7th Division and the 6th Division, but, as the situation in the Seoul area became more urgent, they had to return to Seoul early the next morning. As a result, in the vulnerable area around the gap, only the 3rd Battalion (−), 7th Regiment, was blocking the avenue of approach that led from Whaak-san to Kap'yong.

On the morning of the 26th, the 2nd Regiment on the east launched a counteroffensive from Oronri as planned. Facing an immediate counterattack

from the enemy, however, the ROK unit had to fight a tough battle from the outset and gradually took a beating under heavy pressure from the enemy joint infantry-armor unit. In the end, the ROK 2nd Regiment had to withdraw to
Chaunri, south of Oronri. The 1st Company, 16th Field Artillery Battalion, was
hastily dispatched from Ch'unch'on to establish a position south of Chaunri and
provide cover for the withdrawing 2nd Regiment. The enemy, however, gave no
time for the ROK unit to reorganize, and relentlessly pursued the ROK troops.
Under the enemy attack, the ROK chain of command collapsed and in the state
of total disorganization, the 2nd Regiment suffered many casualties. In the end,
the regiment had to withdraw again, this time from Chaunri to Ch'oljongri.

When the 2nd Regiment gathered troops in Ch'oljongri in the late
afternoon, the regiment strength had dwindled to that of a battalion. While
reorganization was underway at Hangye Primary School in Ch'oljongri, the
regiment commander decided to move the regiment tactical command post to
south of Mal-gogae (hill pass), and establish new defensive positions at Mal-
gogae. The terrain in the vicinity has the following characteristics: The High
and Low Mal-gogae offer a commanding view of the lower ground in the vicinity. The Whayang River, which joins the Naech'on Creek south of Ch'oljongri,
flows around the Low Mal-gogae and provides protection to the flank. Moreover, as the Inje-Hongch'on Road meets another road stretching from Hyonri at
Ch'oljongri and extends to the Low Mal-gogae, it is impossible to advance to
Hongch'on without going through this pass. Last but not the least, this pass is
narrow and extremely crooked, and is ideally suited to antitank defense.

The 2nd Regiment commander deployed the 1st Battalion (under Maj.
Kim Ju Hyong) at the Low Mal-gogae, and deployed the 2nd Battalion (under
Maj. Moon Jong Sik) at the High Mal-gogae, with an order to establish a deep
tank trap / kill zone and operate a special antitank attack unit at each company. He established a kill zone at a steep road bend in the vicinity of Ch'oljongri

Hangye Village. The 3rd Battalion, in the meantime, was withdrawing from Omijae that afternoon. As the enemy temporarily halted its advance at Chaunri, the battle went into a lull.

Around this time, the enemy instituted a drastic change in its plans. The main objective of the NKPA 2nd Corps was to occupy Ch'unch'on on the opening day of the war, and advance in the direction of Suwon to support the 1st Corps' Seoul Offensive. Its 2nd Division, however, failed to occupy Ch'unch'on and instead suffered heavy losses. Pressing for time the enemy 2nd Corps commander redirected two regiments (with one armored company attached) of the 12th Division from Hongch'on toward Inje-Ch'unch'on and strengthened the offensive pressure on Ch'unch'on. The two regiments arrived in the northern vicinity of Ch'unch'on in the evening of 26th, and joined the NKPA 2nd Division.[125]

As the day broke on the 27th, the NKPA 2nd and 12th Divisions carried out a massive attack on Ch'unch'on.[126] From early morning, artillery shells fell like a downpour on the south bank of the Soyang River and the vicinity of Bongui-san. Enemy artillery shells also hit downtown Ch'unch'on and engulfed the city in flames. From around 10:00, the NKPA forces, spearheaded by T-34s and Su-76s, launched a massive attack at Bongui-san, and attempted wading across the River at Karaemogi with a regiment-strength unit. The ROK 7th Regiment prevented the enemy crossing with 57-mm antitank guns and 105-mm howitzers, and buried the enemy attack waves into water. The Soyang River turned blood-red.

Prior to the enemy attack, the ROK 6th Division commander had visited the 2nd Regiment and had made an important decision. Receiving a briefing that the 2nd Regiment was under heavy pressure from an armor-led enemy unit, the division commander got the impression that the situation at Mal-gogae was more urgent than in Ch'unch'on. He feared that if Mal-gogae and hence Hongch'on should fall into enemy hands, the division line of retreat would be blocked.

Deciding to commit the division reserve to Hongch'on and reinforce the 2nd Regiment, he returned to Bongui-san. The ROK 6th Division did not know that the main efforts of the enemy 12th Division had already moved to Ch'unch'on.[127]

The 6th Division reestablished connections with the ROKA Headquarters. The Headquarters Chief of Staff (Col. Kim Paik Il) issued a directive along the following line: "The western front has completely collapsed. The ROKA Headquarters is withdrawing to Shihung. The 6th Division commander shall use his own judgment and carry out delaying action on the central front centered around the Central Railway." The communications broke down again soon afterwards.[128] Having thus finally become aware of the war situation on all fronts, the 6th Division commander thought that if the enemy should seize Seoul, it was highly likely that they would advance in the direction of Yoju and envelop the central front from the rear. However, he believed that no matter how dire the situation, he should secure at least 24 hours for the evacuation of Ch'unch'on citizens and administrative bodies.

In accordance with this belief, the division commander ordered the 7th and 2nd Regiments to hold present positions, and immediately moved the 19th Regiment to Hongch'on to establish a second defensive line and provide cover for the withdrawal of the two forward regiments. He also ordered the 16th Field Artillery Battalion (−) to support the 2nd Regiment.[129]

The 7th Regiment temporarily organized the headquarters battalion into a new reserve, and deployed it in the area which had hitherto been defended by the 19th Regiment. That afternoon, the 19th Regiment and the 16th Field Artillery Battalion (−) left Chunchon in march formation and headed toward Hongchon.

While the 7th Regiment was establishing defensive positions after the 19th Regiment had left, the enemy resumed its offensive. Having failed to cross the Soyang River in the morning, NKPA forces this time committed tanks to the

Soyang Bridge. Two enemy regiments attempted to wade across the river from Karaemogi, and another regiment crossed the river from the Wonjin ferry terminal, northeast of Chunchon, and advanced in the direction of Kubong-san. Enemy tanks at last made it across the Soyang Bridge, and broke through the defensive line of the ROK 7th Regiment. As the gap was exploited by the enemy, blocking of the rear from the right flank became an increasing concern. After Bongui-san fell into enemy hands, the ROK 7th Regiment abandoned Ch'unch'on around 17:30 and withdrew in the direction of Wonch'ang Pass. The NKPA troops finally entered downtown Ch'unch'on.[130] However, they were 48 hours behind the schedule, and, moreover, their 12th Division was off the original planned axis of advance, thus greatly upsetting enemy plans. After withdrawing from Chunchon, the ROK 7th Regiment delayed the enemy southward advance along the Kuksa-bong-Anma-san-Taeryong-san line and established new defensive positions at Wonch'ang Pass by noon of June 28.

While the battle was raging in Chunchon on the 27th, enemy units in front of the ROK 2nd Regiment on the east showed few signs of offensive action, aside from committing a small joint infantry-armor unit to Mal-gogae to carry out reconnaissance in force and sporadic harrassment fires. The 2nd Regiment deployed the 3rd Company, 16th Field Artillery Battalion, with the 1st Company in the south of Mal-gogae in order to strengthen the defensive posture of Mal-gogae. Also, arriving in Hongchon that evening, the 19th Regiment ordered the 3rd Battalion to organize a special antitank attack unit, and deployed this battalion in the southwestern rear of Mal-gogae. The regiment (−1), for its part, strengthened the Hongch'on defense line by moving to Mangryong-san, from which it is possible to suppress the two roads into Hongch'on from Ch'unch'on and Yanggu-Inje.

On the early morning of the 28th, the 2nd Regiment ordered the 1st Battalion (under Maj. Kim Ju Hyong) to carry out a spoiling attack to interfere with expected enemy preparations for an offensive. Conducted under the cover of heavy fog, this attack achieved surprise and overran what was believed to be a command post in the vicinity of Bokgol. According to those who took part in the attack, the battalion killed more than 200 enemy troops and destroyed five truckfuls of supplies before returning to position.[131]

When the fog cleared around 09:00, the NKPA 12th Division $(-)$ launched a well-prepared attack, led by more than ten tanks and self-propelled guns and a mechanized unit organized around tens of trucks. As if they were ready to overrun ROK defensive positions at once, the enemy troops quickly advanced to Hangye Village, north of Mal-gogae. This area formed a half-moon-shaped basin, and ROK troops had set up a kill zone here.

At last, when all of the enemy main efforts had advanced into the kill zone and leading tank column had begun to climb up the Low Mal-gogae, all defensive fire was massed on the kill zone.

Encountering unexpectedly formidable firepower, the enemy was completely thrown off balance and their tanks were separated from the infantrymen. In spite of the hellish confusion, however, part of the enemy troops deployed into attack formation and began to assault the Low Mal-gogae. At that moment, a ROK machine-gun duo opened rapid fire from their ambush position in a road culvert the middle of the kill zone. Displacing positions, they fired at enemy troops from close range. After cutting down many enemy soldiers, they themselves were killed in their third position. Thanks to the heroics of these unknown soldiers, the enemy infantry unit was prevented from joining the armored unit.[132]

Separated from the infantry unit, the enemy tank column began to inch up the pass. A SU-76 led more than 10 T-34s and self-propelled guns delivering tank-gun and machine-gun fire. A ROK 57-mm antitank gun, which was deployed at the first S-shaped bend on the pass, opened fire and scored a direct hit. The enemy tank, however, shook that off, and subsequently the antitank gun team was wiped out and the gun was destroyed by a shell fired by a follow-on tank. Watching this scene by the side of the road, the ROK troops began to have a fear of tanks and became hesitant about launching a "human bullet" attack.

The enemy tank column soon reached the second S-shaped bend near the middle of the pass, the most crooked spot on the pass. When the self-propelled gun at the head of the column exposed its flank, SFC Kim Hak Du, the 1st Squad leader, 2nd Platoon, 57-mm Antitank Gun Company, loaded ironclad ammunition and direct-fired at the flank of the self-propelled gun. From 30m away, he continued to fire at the enemy gun. Hit by the first shell, the enemy gun stopped after advancing 2–3m farther, and was rear-ended by a follow-on tank. Encouraged by this sight, the squad leader now directed fire at the second tank.

At that moment, PFC Cho Dal Jin of the special antitank attack unit, 19th Regiment, got on the first tank, opened the hatch, and threw in a grenade. Moments later, flames erupted with a deafening sound.[133] As the two leading tanks were destroyed, the enemy follow-on tanks had to halt. Seizing upon the opportunity, the ROK special antitank attack unit assaulted the enemy tanks with grenades and gasoline bombs. Taken aback by the assault, the fourth tank fell into the Whayang River while trying to turn north. The tank crew were shot to death while trying to escape. When the tank column halted, the tank commander in the rearmost tank opened the hatch and began to watch the rear. At that moment, the special antitank attack unit fired a 2.36-inch antitank rocket from a ridge 10m away on the left. The rocket went into the hatch and completely destroyed the tank.[134] More than 10 enemy tanks were thus annihilated at a narrow, crooked spot on the Low Mal-gogae.

This was the largest destruction of tanks since the beginning of the war. Although the ROK troops lacked the equipment to destroy tanks through normal methods, they took maximum advantage of the terrain to fire at the vulnerable parts of tanks and to carry out "human bullet" attack. This shining moment in the history of the Korean War boosted the morale of the ROK Armed Forces and raised their confidence in combat. The enemy, on the other hand, was further frustrated as the troops were unable to penetrate Mal-gogae even with tanks.

Meanwhile, the ROK 7th Regiment withdrew to Wonch'ang Pass, and its 2nd Battalion established defensive positions on the top of the pass. Concerned with the possibility that the enemy might block off the line of retreat, the regiment's main efforts withdrew to Sahyon, north of Hongch'on. Approximately 600m above sea level located on cross-compartment ridge crossing the Ch'unch'on-Hongch'on road, Wonch'ang Pass commanded this avenue of approach 10 km south of the Soyang River.

The enemy began to attack the pass on the night of the 28th. On the next morning, receiving continuous artillery support, an enemy force of two regiments in strength appeared in the front of the 2nd Battalion. Exploiting the favorable terrain, the 2nd Battalion was able to repulse the enemy's repeated attack. Around 11:00, a battalion-strength enemy unit appeared, this time waving a white flag. Thinking that the enemy was finally about to surrender, the 2nd Battalion prepared to accept these troops, when, suddenly, the enemy took out burp guns and opened fire from 20m away. Although the 2nd Battalion troops engaged in close combat, they could not repulse this surprise attack and had to give up the strategically important pass.

While the ROK 7th Regiment was coming under enemy attack at Wonch'ang Pass, the 2nd Regiment at Mal-gogae too was faced with a new threat from the enemy. This time, the enemy employed an outflanking maneuver toward the two flanks, while carrying out a diversionary attack along the road from the front. They occupied Ch'ongbyok-san (HILL 451) on the east of Mal-gogae and advanced in the direction of Yangjimal north of Hongch'on, threatening to block the ROK line of retreat.

As these prominent hills forward of Hongch'on fell into enemy hands on the 29th,[135] the ROK 6th Division commander ordered the withdrawal of the 2nd and 7th Regiments to the south of Hongch'on. The 6th Division thus completed the five-day-long battle to defend forward areas and began to withdraw in stages in the direction of Hongch'on-Wonju.

A day before this withdrawal, Col. Chang Ch'ang Kuk, director of operations, ROKA Headquarters, had arrived in an L-5 liaison plane at the 6th Division Headquarters to give the following operations order: "Establish a new line of defense in Wonju to cover the withdrawal of the 8th Division from the East Coast Front. At the same time, deploy a regiment in Ich'on to secure the exposed flank."

Judging that it would take at least 48 hours for the 8th Division to move to Wonju, the 6th Division commander decided to delay the enemy between Hongch'on and Hoengsong for as long as possible.

In short, although the NKPA 2nd Corps was able to occupy Ch'unch'on and put pressure on Hongch'on during the Ch'unch'on-Hongch'on Battle, and although its 2nd Division hurried toward Seoul after the occupation of Ch'unch'on, its advance was so delayed that it was unable to make any contribution to the NKPA 1st Corps' Seoul Offensive. Moreover, the NKPA 2nd Corps not only suffered heavy losses in personnel and equipment, including tanks, in early phases of the battle, but also faced such stiff resistance from the ROK 6th Division in stages that its plan to advance rapidly into Wonju-Ich'on was running against a major snag.

The NKPA Director of Operations Yu Song Ch'ol later recollected: "The 2nd Corps was scheduled to pass through Ch'unch'on, Hongch'on, and Ich'on to arrive in Suwon by the 28th and envelop Seoul. Facing stiff resistance from the ROK Armed Forces, however, its advance was stalled in the vicinity of

Hongch'on." He added: "To press the fight, I myself went to forward areas in the 12th Division commander's jeep. But the jeep was hit by an enemy mortar, and the commander, Col. Ch'oi Ch'ung Kuk, suffered a serious wound. He died while being evacuated."[136]

4. Kangnung Battle

The ROK 8th Division (under Col. Lee Song Ga), responsible for the defense of the eastern coastal area, was an under-strength unit consisting of only two regiments at the time of the Korean War. The division deployed the 10th Regiment along the 38th parallel, and retained the 21st Regiment as a reserve in Samch'ok.

The division sector stretched for 26km from Chinhukdong, coordination point with the 6th Division, to Kitomunri on the eastern seashore. In case of enemy attack, the division planned to commit the reserve 21st Regiment to the left front, and use the two regiments to repulse the enemy at the 38th parallel and defend Kangnung under any circumstance. Accordingly, the division organized security positions on a hill mass south of the 38th parallel, and established main resistance positions along the Kwangwonri-Odae-san-Yongok-ch'on line. To its south, the division secured the Undu-ryong-Sa-ch'on line as alternate positions.[137]

The ROK 8th Division, however, had to commit a battalion from each regiment for expeditionary operations against the enemy unconventional warfare unit, which had infiltrated in the middle of June. As these two regiments were diverted to the Odae-san-Kyebang-san area,[138] the division was left with only four available battalions when the enemy launched their full-scale invasion. In particular, the 10th Regiment was in the middle of replacing its 1st Battalion on the left front with the 3rd Battalion, as the 1st Battalion had to be diverted for counter-guerrilla operations.

Deployed in front of the ROK 8th Division was the NKPA 5th Division. By committing the main effort along the coastal road from Yangyang to Kangnung, the NKPA 5th Division planned to launch a frontal attack on the ROK 10th Regiment from the north. In addition, by landing the 766th Unit and the 549 Naval Combat Team at Chongdongjin and Imwonjin on the south of Kangnung, the division planned to interdict reinforcement to the ROK 21st Regiment. Thus defeating the two ROK regiments in detail, the NKPA 5th Division planned a pincer attack on Kangnung from the north and the south. The division then intended to join with the remaining guerrilla units in T'aebaek Mountains and facilitate the operations of the NKPA 2nd Corps.

At 04:00, June 25, the NKPA 5th Division opened preparatory fire and broke through the 38h parallel as planned. While the main attack advanced toward Chumunjin, the supporting attack began to move southward following an avenue of approach along the Yangyang-Sorimri-Woniljonri Valley.

The forward units of the ROK 10th Regiment, which had established security positions by platoon or by squad, were completely overwhelmed by the formidable firepower of the enemy. The security area quickly turned into shambles, and, without even having a chance to fight, the ROK troops had to withdraw toward prepared resistance positions south of the demarcation line. Unable to occupy even the resistance positions, however, the 2nd Battalion (under Maj. Cho Won Yong) on the axis along Road 7 retreated to Chumunjin, and the 1st Battalion (under Maj. Park Ch'i Ok) on the left front carried out a series of delaying actions at Kuryong-ryong and withdrew toward Kwangwonri.

Meanwhile, around 04:00 that day, numerous NKPA troops made a landing by the seaside village of Tungmyongdong, Chongdongjinri, south of Kangnung. They coerced village residents to move ammunition and supplies from a cargo ship to a hill in the back of the village.[139] By this time, some NKPA

soldiers had already prepared individual foxholes midway up the hill for security purposes. The leading enemy unit had apparently landed before 04:00, and
crossed the 38th parallel much earlier than this time.

Early that morning, the enemy killed a policeman on duty at a seaside
security post in Tungmyong-dong, and achieved complete surprise. When village residents saw the NKPA troops, the leading unit had already occupied a
landing spot. A member of the Korean Youth Corps in the village reported the
appearance of the NKPA troops to Aninjin police station 4km away, and this
information was quickly disseminated to other police and military units. The
ROK 8th Division commander received this information from the Chief of the
Kangnung Police Department around 05:40, and the 21st Regiment commander,
from the Chief of the Samch'ok Police Department around 06:00.[140]

Having secured the landing area, the enemy combat team used motor
boats as well as sail boats to land its main troops. One regiment in strength,
these troops landed in stages. In order to block the Samch'ok-Kangnung Road,
the enemy main effort occupied Bamjae, and sent a battalion north toward
Kangnung and another battalion south toward Okgye. In addition, around 07:00,
the 766th Ranger Unit landed at Imwonjin. One group infiltrated into the T'aebaek Mountains and another group advanced north toward Samch'ok.[141]

Meanwhile, at the ROK 8th Division Headquarters located on the
Kangnung Air Field, the division commander called an operations meeting at
06:00 upon receiving the reports of the collapse of forward security positions
and the massive landing of enemy troops in rear coastal areas. At this meeting,
he ordered the 10th Regiment to delay the enemy for as long as possible, and decided to move the 21st Regiment to Kangnung and repulse the enemy at the
Yongok-ch'on-Sa-ch'on line. Thus resolved to defend Kangnung until the end,
he organized the division engineer battalion into a reserve, and made an urgent
request to the ROKA Headquarters for a regiment-strength reinforcement. The

ROKA Headquarters replied: "The division commander shall do his best within his own disposal. As the defense of Seoul is more urgent, your request for a regiment-strength reinforcement is denied." After this message, all communications broke down.

Upon receiving the message from the ROKA Headquarters, the division commander estimated that the war would be prolonged. Effective 10:00, June 25, he declared martial law throughout the operations area and devised plans to disperse all materiel to Jinburi over Taegwan-ryong and evacuate administrative bodies and dependents of military and police personnel to rear areas. He also impounded civilian vehicles to secure maneuverability.

Accordingly, the division provided military dependents with six-months' pay and food, appointed a civilian affairs director to administer martial law, and established an evacuation plan for residents as well. No other ROK divisions took such actions to prepare for a prolonged war. Through these actions, the ROK 8th Division won the trust and active support of residents. More than 1,400 students in the Kangnung Students' National Defense Corps even volunteered to carry ammunition and supplies, aid patients, and do liaison work.

In order to deal with the enemy landing in the rear area of Tungmyong-dong, the 10th Regiment commander (Lt. Col. Ko Kun Hong) hastily dispatched the 4th Company and the 57-mm Antitank Gun Company to Anmok-Aninjin on the south of Kangnung. Around this time, part of the enemy landing unit was advancing southward along the coastal line, and some of this team were trying to approach the pier of Aninjin. It was right at this moment that the ROK Antitank Gun Company opened fire on the fleet of enemy vessels. Massing its fire, the ROK company was able to repel the enemy. Meanwhile, as it was feared that the enemy combat team might advance northward along the mountain range into Kangnung, the 4th Company hastily established defensive positions at Taep'odong, west of Aninjin, which provided the most favorable terrain for defense. Upon locating a company-strength enemy unit, the 4th Company annihilated it and removed the threat.

After a comprehensive analysis of the situation in Aninjin and Taep'odong, the division commander concluded that the defense of Kangnung made it imperative to prepare for the enemy threat not only from the north but from the south as well. He accordingly decided to establish defensive positions along the Kunson River, 12km south of Kangnung. He quickly found out, however, that he had no available troops other than the Division Engineer Battalion. In the end, the division commander ordered the 10th Regiment commander to assume the defense of the Kunson River in addition to its forward defense responsibilities, at least until a reinforcement from the 21st Regiment arrived. For this, the division commander ordered the attachment of an engineer company to the 10th Regiment, and had one battery of the 18th Field Artillery Battalion provide direct support to these units.[142] He also deployed the engineer battalion along the main line of resistance in Yongok-ch'on, and moved up the division tactical command post to Sach'on Primary School. In accordance with the order from the 10th Regiment commander, the reserve 3rd Battalion hastily established defensive positions along the Kunson River with the attached 10th Company, 21st Regiment, and the engineer company.

In the meantime, after receiving a report of the enemy landing, the ROK 21st Regiment commander in Samch'ok ordered the 1st Battalion in Bukp'yong to verify this information. While conducting reconnaissance operations in the vicinity of Okgye, the battalion reconnaissance unit and the 1st Company saw a company-strength enemy unit advancing southward. Carrying out a surprise attack with support from the police and Korea Youth Organization members, the ROK unit inflicted a devastating blow on the enemy. The ROK unit also confirmed that the enemy main effort was to block Bamjae.[143] At the time, the 21st Regiment commander (Lt. Col. Kim Yong Bae) was preparing to move to Kangnung as had been ordered, impounding civilian vehicles in the area. Upon receiving a report that a battalion-strength enemy unit was blocking the road at Bamjae, the regiment commander, after much deliberation, decided to employ a turning movement along Bukp'yong-Bakbong-ryong-Sapdang-ryong-Kusanri. The 21st Regiment accordingly organized two march echelons. The main effort left Samchok at 19:00 on the 25th and, via Kangnung, took over the defensive positions along the Kunson River around 10:30 the next day. The 3rd Battalion first assembled in Samchok its two companies deployed in Changsong and Imgyeri, and joined the main unit in Kangnung.

Under the order from the division commander to deploy along the main line of resistance, the Engineer Battalion (under Maj. Kim Muk) completed organization for combat and was attached to the 10th Regiment to occupy main resistance positions at Yongok-ch'on. This battalion was the first engineer unit to conduct infantry combat. At the same time, the 1st and 2nd Batteries of the 18th Field Artillery Battalion were respectively deployed at Sokgyori and Sach'-on Primary School, in the rear of the main line of resistance.

Having thus secured the main line of resistance, these units were able to provide effective cover for the withdrawal of the 2nd Battalion, 10th Regiment. As the 21st Regiment completed its deployment along the Kunson River and an antitank gun company was reinforced on the morning of the 26th, the division was able to adjust defensive deployment at Yongok-ch'on and to look for counterattack opportunities.

While the 10th Regiment was reorganizing defensive positions along the main line of resistance, the Korea Youth Organization Corps in Sach'onmyon provided 40 committed members as volunteers to collect information on the enemy situation. The resident women's organization and the youth group also made a great contribution to operations by establishing a field mess and providing military and police personnel with rice balls.

The main defensive sector of the 8th Division extended for 4 kilometers from Yongok-ch'on to Songrimri and went 3 kilometers deep from the 38th parallel to Sa-ch'on. Yongok-ch'on was only 200–250m wide, but was so deep that it was impossible to wade across the stream except at the fords at Kyodong and Songrimri. Also, although there was a wooden bridge where Road 7 meets Yongok-ch'on, this bridge was not sturdy enough to allow the passage of heavy equipment, including self-propelled guns. Instead of demolishing this wooden bridge, the 8th Division planned to set up a kill zone in its vicinity and lure the enemy into this zone.

After attempting an assault river-crossing right in front of the ROK engineer battalion at 04:00, June 26, the enemy sporadically sought engagement but launched no large-scale attack. Taking advantage of this lull, the 2nd Battalion, ROK 10th Regiment, that night attacked and seized Ch'onma-bong, a commanding ground forward of the main line of resistance. Upon securing this bridgehead for launching an attack on Chumunjin, the division issued an order to attack Chumunjin. Around this time, however, the enemy had completed preparations for attack, and was only waiting for an order to commence attack. Unfortunately, the ROK division was not aware of such a situation.

Around 04:00 the next day, one hour earlier than the ROK division's H-hour, the enemy opened fire first. The enemy massed preparatory fire on Ch'onma-bong, where the 2nd Battalion was forward-deployed. More intense than ever before, the enemy fire soon forced the dispersion and withdrawal of the 2nd Battalion from Ch'onma-bong. The ROK units in the main defensive positions, however, did not receive any situation report on this development, and made a mistake of taking enemy troops for friendly units. This blunder led to a partial collapse of the defensive line, and enemy follow-on units soon overran the main defensive positions.

While the main defensive positions were collapsing and the crisis was reaching its peak, the reinforced 3rd Battalion, ROK 21st Regiment, was committed to the Sa-ch'on line to cover the withdrawing troops and to block the enemy. A crisis was thus narrowly averted.

Meanwhile, after the enemy had reached the main line of resistance, the ROK 18th Field Artillery Battalion (under Maj. Chang Kyong Sok), deployed at Sachon Primary School and at the chestnut tree forest across from the road to the west, no longer had any time to coordinate and synchronize its fire. In desperation, the Battalion continued to fire its guns individually. This resistance by the artillery battalion played a decisive role in delaying the enemy's advance beyond the main line of resistance, and gave time for the withdrawing ROK troops to organize resistance positions along the Sa-ch'on line.

Eventually, however, the attacking enemy units crashed in on the field artillery position. With no infantry protection available, the artillerymen initially responded to the enemy threat with direct fire. When the enemy penetrated the artillery position, the artillerymen engaged the enemy in a desperate hand-to-hand combat, with rifles, entrenching shovels, pickaxes, or whatever they could grab. In the end, these exceptional artillerymen were able to repulse the enemy. The 18th Field Artillery Battalion then withdrew to the vicinity of Ojukhon under the cover of the 3rd Battalion, 21st Regiment, and continued to provide fire support.

Due to the total breakdown in communications, the ROK 8th Division commander had little idea about the situation on all fronts and was having much difficulty in commanding his unit. Taking into consideration the enemy situation, available strength, and terrain, the division commander, after much deliberation, decided to avoid reckless combat and withdraw to the Taegwanryong pass before the situation became irreversible. He thought he could launch a counteroffensive from there, depending on the situation.

Around this time, the enemy unit that had occupied the ROK main defensive positions in the vicinity of Yongok-ch'on was undergoing reorganization, and along the Kunson River line in the rear area, the ROK troops were repulsing the enemy's sporadic attack and holding position. Under this circumstance, the ROK 8th Division commenced withdrawal at 14:00 on the 27th. Crossing Taegwan-ryong, the division headquarters and the 10th Regiment assembled in Yuch'onri that night, and the 21st Regiment assembled at Hoenggyeri. Around 21:50, the enemy advanced into Kangnung.

Upon checking the condition of the reorganized two regiments, the ROK 8th Division commander confirmed that the strength and morale of the division remained intact. Encouraged by the condition of his troops, the division commander decided to launch a counterattack with the objective of recovering Kangnung. On the morning of the 28th, the 21st Regiment commenced attack. The 1st Battalion, 10th Regiment, was forward-deployed at Ch'ilbong-san on the east of Kusanri to cover the flank of the attacking echelons, and two 105-mm artillery pieces were forwarded to the entrance of Bogwangri on the east of the Taegwan-ryong to provide fire support.

When the attacking echelons were about to advance into the suburbs of Kangnung, 8th Divison Headquarters were able to make a dramatic radio contact with the 6th Division Headquarters in Wonju. The 6th Division relayed to the 8th Division units the ROKA Headquarters' order to withdraw to Wonju. Halting the planned attack, the attacking echelons returned to Taekwanryong.

Assembling in Yuch'onri and Hajinburi on the evening of the 28th, the 8th Division completed preparations for march, and the next day moved toward Wonju by vehicle. Learning that Hoengsong had fallen into enemy hands from a refugee in Daewha, however, the division commander changed the destination to Jech'on. He feared that the enemy might arrive in Wonju first.

Battle in the Vicinity of Kangnung

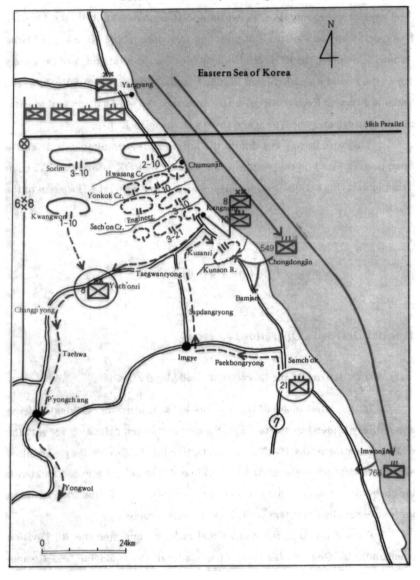

In short, the ROK Armed Forces on the eastern front put up a spirited fight against the enemy. In Ch'unch'on and Hongch'on, the ROK 6th Division blocked the advance of the 2nd and 12th Divisions of the NKPA 2nd Corps. Around Kangnung, the ROK 8th Division blocked the joint attack of the enemy 5th Division and a combat team that had landed ashore. Eventually, however, under a directive from the ROKA Headquarters, the 6th Division had to withdraw in the direction of Wonju and the 8th Division, to Jech'on.

This withdrawal was due to the failure of the simultaneous defensive operations in Seoul on the western front. Part of the ROK efforts to make transition to delaying action, this maneuver was due to a general adjustment of the frontline.

Ⅳ. The Fall of Seoul

1. Seoul Defensive Operations

(1) War Directives by the Government and Military Leaders

In the initial phase of the war, the ROK Ministry of National Defense and military leadership was faced with a choice between defending Seoul to the end or retreating to the Han River line. Opting for the former, they committed all reserve strength to the north of Seoul in order to defend Munsan and block the enemy at Uijongbu and move on to a counteroffensive. By the 26th, however, these strategically important cities were in enemy hands.

Pressed for time, the Army Chief of Staff appointed the 7th Division commander Br. Gen. Yu Jae Hung Commander of the Uijongbu Area Combat

Command effective 17:00 on the same day. Taking command of all forces committed to this area, Gen. Yu was given an urgent oral order to block the enemy at the Changdong-Uidong line, and carry out a counteroffensive with the 3rd and 5th Divisions to recover lost areas.[144]

Around this time in the Munsan area, the ROK 1st Division was withdrawing to Bongil-ch'on, and in the Kimpo Peninsula, a hastily formed Kimpo Area Command was organizing defense in response to the enemy's crossing attempts to the estuary of the Han River. This rapid development of the situation put into question the feasibility of "defending Seoul to the end," and began to threaten the basic ROK plans for the conduct of the war.

To discuss emergency measures, the ROK Defense Minister called a joint meeting of high-level military leadership attended by the Chief of Staff of each service on the late night of the 26th. In the end, they agreed on the following basic guiding principle for the war efforts: "In case that the Army has to withdraw repeatedly, it shall in the end put up guerrilla resistance until the end, and the Navy and Air Force shall cooperate with ground operations, and finally assume the responsibility for the transport of key members of the government-in-exile."[145]

At 01:00 on the 27th, an emergency cabinet meeting was convened at the Capitol Building. At the meeting, former Prime Minister Lee Bom Sok proposed to make a decision on the basic national strategy, and argued: "We must quickly decide whether we will continue our resistance at the outskirts of Seoul and conduct a delaying action, defend Seoul until the end, or withdraw from Seoul. If we must withdraw under the present circumstance, we should first take measures for the safety of the citizens of Seoul and deal with the problem of blowing up the Han River Bridge." In attendance with the Army Chief of Staff after concluding the high-level military leadership meeting, Defense Minister Shin contradicted an optimistic briefing by the Army Chief of Staff, and proposed that the capital be moved to Suwon. Cabinet members agreed, and the relocation of the capital was decided. As for the citizens of Seoul, there was no evacuation plan from the beginning, and this meeting did not produce any.

Afterwards, both the Defense Minister and the Army Chief of Staff attended a special late-night session of the National Assembly. As he had done at the cabinet meeting, Gen. Ch'ae maintained: "We will defend Seoul to the end, and move on to a counteroffensive. And we will put up our national flag at the top of Mt. Paekdu." [Translator's Note: Located on the Korean-Chinese border, Mt. Paekdu is the highest and most sacred mountain in Korea.] Speaking in his capacity as the acting Prime Minister, Defense Minister Shin implied: "Given the war situation, it is inevitable that the government be relocated." After an acrimonious debate, the members of the National Assembly resolved to "defend the capital to the end with the one million citizens of Seoul."

After the late-night session of the National Assembly, Minister Shin convened a high-level national defense leadership meeting around 05:00 in order to discuss the withdrawal of the ROK Armed Forces upon relocation of the government. Those in attendance included Vice Minister of National Defense Chang Kyong Kun, Chiefs of the 1st, 2nd, and 3rd Bureaus, Chief of Staff of each service, and Deputy Chiefs of Staff, and Intelligence, Personnel, and Logistics Chiefs from the ROKA Headquarters. Almost in tears, Minister Shin explained that Seoul would have to be abandoned due to the critical war situation. Everyone seemed distressed by the news. At that moment, MND 2nd Bureau Chief Col. Lee Son Kun slammed on the desk and got up to speak. He asserted: "Let us defend Seoul to the end even if we have to mobilize the million students. We can't just leave the citizens behind and withdraw."[146]

In the end, the meeting came to a close with Army Chief of Staff Ch'ae declaring that the armed forces would defend Seoul to the end even if the government moves to the south. Immediately after the meeting, however, Gen.

Ch'ae received a gloomy report on the war situation estimating that it would be difficult to check the enemy advance past that night.

While this series of emergency meetings decided to relocate the government and was debating on the withdrawal of the armed forces, President Syngman Rhee, the supreme commander of the armed forces, left the Kyongmudae around 03:00 and evacuated from Seoul.

When a nation is facing an external invasion and its capital is about to fall, the conduct of the president is of utmost importance for the fate of that nation. Under these circumstances, of crucial importance is when and how he leaves the capital-in other words, his decision on the timing of evacuation and actions taken as the supreme commander of the armed forces. On this point, then-First Lady Mrs. Francesca Rhee has given the following account :

Defense Minister Shin arrived at the Kyongmudae around 02:00 on the 27th, and the Mayor of Seoul and Mr. Cho Byong Ok followed him into the residence. Minister Shin earnestly suggested: "Your Excellency, it is prudent that you leave Seoul." The president said: "No! Defend Seoul to the end! I can't leave!" Those around him were, however, concerned that if something unfortunate should happen to the president, a much greater turmoil would result. In the end, the president decided to follow their advice and move to the south.[147]

At 06:00 on the 27th, the government announced its relocation to Suwon, and at last the citizens of Seoul became aware that the capital was under an imminent threat. From the northern suburbs of Seoul, refugees were continuing to stream into downtown, and some citizens were hurrying to evacuate; whereas, trucks carrying ROK reinforcements were coming up from the south. Downtown Seoul was thrown into a chaos. The mayhem reached its peak especially in the vicinity of the Han Pedestrian Bridge and the Seoul Station.

When the Ch'angdong line collapsed from around 10:00, Gen. Ch'ae at last did an about-face on his decision to defend the capital to the end. After obtaining Minister Shin's permission to withdraw from Seoul, he held a meeting of the ROKA Headquarters and capital region commanders at 11:00. At this meeting, it was declared that the Navy and Air Force Headquarters would be moved to Suwon while the Army Headquarters would relocate to the Army Infantry School in Shihung. As for the withdrawal of frontline troops, no mention was made, however.

Chief of the Engineer Corps Col. Ch'oe Ch'ang Shik then gave a briefing that the bridges over the Han River (Great Han Bridge, 3 railway bridges, and Kwangjin Bridge) would be blown up 2 hours prior to the enemy advance into downtown Seoul, and added that given the current situation, the estimated time of demolition was 16:00. He further informed that the engineer corps would have 18 engineer boats to handle the river-crossing of withdrawing troops from the front after the demolition of the bridges.

Col. Lee Jong Ch'an of the Capital Security Command strongly argued that there could be no withdrawal of the armed forces without taking evacuation measures for the citizens of Seoul, but his opinion was not reflected in the final decision. Even under these dire circumstances, the radio stations continued to broadcast encouraging reports on the war situation, and aired a pre-recorded reassuring message from President Rhee. Citizens, however, no longer trusted the government.

Gen. Ch'ae ordered that utmost security be maintained about the withdrawal of the armed forces. The withdrawal commenced at 12:30. The ROKA Headquarters moved to the Army Infantry School in Shihung, and upon learning this, the US Military Advisor Group also relocated to Shihung.

At this moment, a news of impending US assistance arrived. Immediately after crossing the Han River, Col. W. H. S. Wright, acting chief of KMAG, received a cable from Gen. MacArthur informing that the US Joint Chiefs of Staff had given him operational control over the military activities of the US armed forces in Korea, including the military advisor group and that he was planning to send a survey party[148] soon. After arriving in Shihung, Col. Wright received another message: "An important decision is imminent. Cheer up." The acting chief of KMAG interpreted these messages as meaning that the military advisor group ought to stay in Korea. Canceling an earlier withdrawal plan, he decided to return to Seoul with other military advisors who had stayed with him.[149] Col. Wright also explained the content of the messages to Gen. Ch'ae and recommended the return of the ROKA Headquarters to Yongsan.

Meanwhile, in Suwon, Minister Shin heard of the impending US assistance from a US embassy employee, and immediately relayed the message to Gen. Ch'ae. "Since the United States is coming in to support us with its naval and air forces, conduct delaying action until their arrival while minimizing our losses," he said.[150]

Encouraged by the news of US assistance, Gen. Ch'ae decided to cross the Han again and return to Yongsan instead of conducting delaying action at the Han River line. Since the outbreak of the war, defending Seoul to the end had been his consistent policy. Although his decision was not in agreement with Minister Shin's directions, Gen. Ch'ae's military command authority was second only to that of the president.[151] Moreover, the president had declared his determination to defend Seoul to the end, and the ROK Armed Forces were fighting a close battle along the Ch'angdong-Miari line at the time.

Gen. Ch'ae's decision has received two diametrically opposite assessments. One group holds that his decision was forced upon him by the situation prevailing at the time, whereas judging from the result, the other group argues that it would have been better to switch earlier to defense along the Han Line.

In accordance with Gen. Ch'ae's decision, the ROKA Headquarters returned to Yongsan around 18:00. Around this time, newspapers widely reported the establishment of the Advance Command and Liaison Group (ADCOM) by the US Far East Command as the top news. In order to boost the morale of soldiers, the Military Education and Information Bureau, for its part, operated street propaganda squads.

(2) The Ch'angdong-Miari Battle

While the national leadership and military command structure were debating over the direction of war efforts after the fall of Uijongbu, Br. Gen. Yu Jae Hung, doubling up as the commander of the 7th Division and Uijongbu Area Command, was planning to establish a defensive line centering around Ch'angdong. Assembling the forces committed to this area, he sought to set up new defensive positions in a hill mass along the Tobong-san (Uidong)-Surak-san (Sanggyedong) line.

Originally deployed as a covering force in the vicinity of Paeksok-ch'on, south of Uijongbu, the ROK 25th Regiment (−), 2nd Division, was following the withdrawing ROK units to the south around this time. When this regiment came under attack from the NKPA 3rd Division from around 17:00 on the 26th, it became doubtful whether the ROK forces would be able to secure sufficient time to establish the planned defensive line. The 25th Regiment, however, held its own against the enemy. The leader of a 2.36-inch rocket launcher section ambushed and destroyed an enemy tank near the Paeksok Bridge, and that night a special antitank attack unit formed by the 11th Company commander assaulted and destroyed two stationary tanks. Perhaps surprised by the unexpected loss of these tanks, the enemy halted attack that night, and resumed the offensive early next day. In the meantime, the ROK covering force was able to disperse and withdraw.

Meanwhile, the ROK Uijongbu Area Command gathered the withdrawing forces and was able to deploy a total of 6-battalion-strength units in the

Uidong-Ch'angdong hills, consisting of the 1st, 3rd, and 9th Regiments of the 1st Division; the 5th, 16th, and 25th Regiments of the 2nd Divisions; as well as remaining troops from the 22nd Regiment of 3rd Divison. The withdrawing units of the 9th Regiment (−) were deployed in the Pulam-san area on the right flank, whereas the KMA Cadet Battalion, under the command of Superintendent Br. Gen. Lee Jun Shik, from Naech'on was deployed on a hill near KMA. Although the Officer Regiment of the ROKA Headquarters tried to organize troops in the vicinity of Ch'angdong, they were not very effective. They were disbanded by the Headquarters and ordered to carry out liaison missions at various regiments.

The wide corridor between Tobong-san and Surak-san provided a very favorable terrain for the maneuver of the enemy's mechanized units. Around 10:00 on the 27th, the NKPA forces, reinforced by more than 40 tanks and self-propelled guns, struck the ROK forces before they had time to establish defensive positions. Under the fire support of six 105-mm howitzers provided by the 2nd Instruction Battalion, ROK Artillery School, the defensive units put up spirited resistance until they ran out of ammunition. In the end, they were unable to block the advance of enemy tanks, and had to disperse and withdraw to the vicinity of Miari and Taenung. Col. Ham Jun Ho, the 1st Regiment commander, was hit by an enemy bullet in Suyuri and died a heroic death.

Meanwhile, along the Miari-Hoegidong line, Maj. Gen. Lee Ung Jun, Miari Area commander as well as 5th Division commander, was gathering withdrawing units under an order from the ROKA Headquarters to defend Seoul. He established defensive organizations with his own 2nd Battalion, 15th Regiment, and 1st Battalion, 20th Regiment, as well as the 2nd Battalion, 8th Regiment, Capital Division. As the enemy halted its advance after occupying Ch'angdong, there was a brief lull in the battle. The 9th Regiment (−) and the KMA Cadet Battalion were maintaining contact with the enemy in the vicinity of Taenung.

Lt. Gen. Lee and Br. Gen Yu decided to organize a so-called Miari line connecting Chungrung (Hill 171)-Miari-Ch'ongrayngri (Hill 106). To defend Seoul, Lt. Gen. Lee assumed the responsibility for the western sector, including Road 3, and Br. Gen Yu took up the eastern sector.

Since the cross compartment of the terrain along the defensive line was advantageous to the defender, they hoped that they would be able to defend against the enemy's tanks just by blocking the road at Miari, and channeled all their energy into building up defensive positions.

Lt. Gen. Lee deployed the 1st Battalion, 20th Regiment, on the east of Hill 171; the 1st Regiment (battalion-strength) at a public cemetery, north of the Kirum Bridge; and the 2nd Battalion, 15th Regiment, on Hill 132, mear Miari pass. Br. Gen. Yu deployed a mixed regiment[152] on the northeast of Hill 164; the 2nd Battalion, 8th Regiment, on Hill 143 in Hoegidong and on Hill 106, south of the Chungnang Bridge; and the 16th Regiment (battalion-strength) at Tonam Primary School as a reserve. For fire support, six 105-mm howitzers were emplaced in Tonamdong, and six 57-mm antitank guns were deployed forward of Hill Miari and two at the Chungnang Bridge. Even troops from support branches such as quartermaster, finance, and ordnance were committed.[153]

By the afternoon of the 27th, approximately more than 3,000 troops were deployed along the Miari-Hoegidong line. With a heroic and solemn resolve to defend Seoul to the end, the ROK leadership, starting from the Chief of Staff down, was trying to boost the morale of the mixed units at the Miari line.

An engineer battalion mobilized civilians to establish foxholes in the vicinity of Miari. Col. Kang Mun Bong of the ROKA Headquarters forward command post, conscripted tens of vehicles in Miari and set up road obstacles on the avenue of approach. He made preparations to blow up the Kirum Bridge when the enemy's tanks close in, while, on the right flank, the Engineer Battalion of the ROK 3rd Division demolished the Chungnang Bridge on the Seoul-Ch'unch'on Highway.

Meanwhile, in accordance with their pre-emptive strike plan, NKPA forces were busily carrying out the operation to "strike from the front, the flanks, and the rear to envelop and annihilate ROK forces in the vicinity of Seoul."[154] In front of Seoul, the enemy 4th and 3rd Divisions avoided infantry engagement in order to maintain a rapid pace, and employed armored units to establish avenues of approach. From the northeast of Seoul, the enemy 1st Division and the 6th Division(−) applied pressure, and on the western flank, the 14th Regiment, 6th Division, was preparing to advance to the front of Kimp'o. Enemy forces in the Ch'unch'on area were, however, falling behind their schedule due to the fierce resistance of the ROK 6th Division.

On the night of the 27th, the enemy resumed the offensive under heavy rain. Around 19:00, an enemy cavalry reconnaissance unit, together with about 10 tanks, attacked Miari from the direction of Suyuri. The forward-deployed 1st Battalion, ROK 20th Regiment, channeled all its energy and put up spirited resistance, but failed to block the advance of the enemy tanks. Engineers buried explosives under the road to block the tanks, but they also failed.

Soon afterwards, however, three 105-mm howitzers, three antitank guns, four 81-mm mortars, and 2.36-inch rocket launchers concentrated their fire at the enemy tanks, and finally succeeded in destroying the leading tank. Some citizens, encouraged by the news of an imminent participation by the United States, provided soldiers with food and moral support.

Contact with the enemy along the Miari line briefly discontinued when the night fell. This situation, however, was suddenly transformed when several enemy tanks, led by an infantry reconnaissance unit, advanced to Miari from Suyuri again under pouring rain around 24:00. Coming under the enemy's surprise armor attack in extremely poor visibility conditions, ROK units deployed

Defensive Operations in Seoul

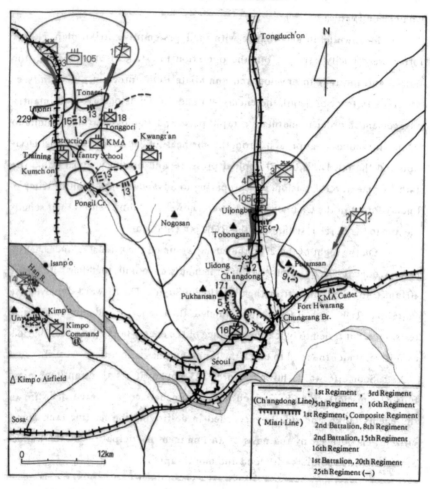

by the side of the road near the Miari cemetery began to disperse in detail.

Pushing aside obstacles set up at the Miari junction with ease, the enemy tanks advanced toward the Kirum Bridge. At this time, to demoralize ROK troops, an enemy plain-clothed infiltration unit shot up tracers from everywhere in downtown Seoul.

Deployed on a hill on the left of the Kirum Bridge, the 2nd Battalion, ROK 15th Regiment, concentrated fire at the bridge when the enemy tanks closed in. The battalion commander led a "human bullet" assault and resisted the enemy's advance until running out of ammunition, but in the end, allowed the advance of two enemy tanks to the hill. Thus, around 01:00 on the 28th, Seoul's final line of resistance collapsed. The 2nd Battalion, 8th Regiment, engaged the enemy in the vicinity of Hoegidong, but had to withdraw after running out of ammunition. The 9th Regiment (−) and KMA Cadet Battalion in Taenung also withdrew after maintaining contact with the enemy until the morning of the 28th.

Unaware that enemy tanks had advanced into downtown Seoul, the remaining ROK units on the Miari line held their positions until the early morning hours. Only after they came under an attack of enemy infantry forces, did they begin to disperse and withdraw.

(3) Battle in the Vicinity of Pongil-ch'on

While the enemy 3rd and 4th Divisions were massing their offensive strength along Road 3 in Uijongbu-Miari on the north of Seoul, the enemy 6th Division (−) and the 1st Division were advancing toward Pongil-ch'on from Munsan-Pobwonri on the northwest of Seoul. Deploying along Road 1 and Road 307, the enemy forces had their sights set on Seoul.

In Pongilch'on, the ROK 1st Division from the Imjin River had deployed the 15th Regiment (with the 3rd Battalion, 20th Regiment, attached) at Wijonri on Road 1, and placed the 13th Regiment at Donaeri on Road 307. Retaining the 11th Regiment as a reserve, the division thus established a final line of resistance, and was making final preparations for a decisive showdown with the enemy. Having dispersed to withdraw in the initial phase of the battle, the 12th Regiment was reorganizing at Kumch'on.[155]

Spearheaded by tanks, the main effort of the NKPA 6th Division launched a frontal attack on the ROK 15th Regiment around 10:00 on June 27. Having established a deep antitank defense zone on Road 1, Maj. Choi Byong Sun (3rd Battalion commander, 15th Regiment) realized that 57mm recoilless rifles and 2.36-inch antitank weapons were ineffective against the enemy tanks, and decided to carry out a "human bullet" assault. He ordered the 11th Company commander to attack the leading tank, and himself led a special hand-grenade attack unit to close in on the rear tank. There were a total of 6 tanks in front of the 15th Regiment, and all tank commanders had their torso out of the tanks. Although the special attack unit launched an assault at once, they suffered heavy losses by tank machine-gun fire, and the 11th Company commander(Capt. Lee Son Doh) lost his life while trying jump onto a tank. In this mayhem, 2nd Lt. Park Jong Sun, leader of the 2nd Platoon, 11th Company blew up the leading tank with a hand-grenade. Losing the six tanks, the enemy halted the offensive and withdrew to Munsanri. Having repulsed the enemy attack, the ROK 15th Regiment troops overcame their armor-phobia, and became confident that they could defeat the enemy.

While the 15th Regiment on the left front was putting up a fierce battle, the 13th Regiment on the right had a relative lull. Around 19:00, however, the 13th Regiment came under a joint infantry-armor attack from the NKPA 1st Division, which threatened to split the ROK defensive positions. A 2.36-inch rocket launcher section led by 1st Lt. Shin Hyon Cho of the 2nd Company narrowly averted the crisis by destroying the track of the enemy's leading tank. Encouraged by a temporary halt in the enemy attack, the regiment was able to recover its position.

When heavy rain fell that night in the vicinity of Pongil-ch'on, however,

the enemy took advantage of the bad weather conditions and launched a surprise nighttime attack. The ROK final line of resistance collapsed, and the 1st
Division had to withdraw to Pongil-ch'on over night.

Prior to this withdrawal, a ROKA Headquarters operational guidance
team (under Maj. Gen. Kim Hong Il) had visited the 1st Division Tactical Command Post. After briefing on the war situation along the Miari line, Maj. Gen.
Kim recommended that the 1st Division establish a contingency plan and prepare to withdraw across the Han River. The division commander, however,
noted that his unit could not withdraw without an express order from the Army
Chief of Staff, and requested that some immediate measures be taken in this regard. Since communications had broken down between the 1st Division and the
ROKA Headquarters, Maj. Gen. Kim, who had no independent command authority, could only promise that the request would be forward to the Army
Chief of Staff.[156]

On the next morning (28th), an L-5 liaison plane dropped a message at
the tactical command post. The message only contained a ROKA Headquarters
instruction for the division to "defend present positions to the end," and made
no mention of withdrawing to the south of the Han River.

Issuing an already prepared order for a counterattack, the division
commander launched the attack on the morning of the 28th. Having become the
left forward element due to the withdrawal of the 15th regiment, the 11th Regiment repulsed the enemy 6th Division without heavy engagement. Occupying
an intermediate objective along the Wijonri-Donaeri line, the regiment partially recovered the left side of the final line of resistance. The 13th Regiment, on
the other hand, fought a seesaw battle against the enemy 1st Division, and could
not launch a counterattack. Without hesitation, the division commander committed the attached Seoul Special Regiment and the 3rd Battalion of the 20th
Regiment to fill the gap between the 13th and 15th Regiments and connect the

line of defense.

The enemy did not display determined resistance on that day. Having thus recovered a part of the final line of resistance without much difficulty, the ROK 1st Division Tactical Command Post began to harbor expectations for the recovery of the main line of resistance.

(4) Battle in the Vicinity of Kimp'o

While the Uijongbu and Pongil-ch'on areas on the north of Seoul were under formidable enemy attack, another enemy unit was threatening the left flank of Seoul from the Kimp'o area, at the mouth of the Han River. Since the estuary at the northern tip of the Kimp'o Peninsula was 2-3km in width and was influenced by sea tides, it was very difficult to conduct river-crossing operations in the vicinity. Assured by these terrain conditions, the ROKA Headquarters did not even have a defensive plan for this area.

As if it had detected such vulnerabilities in the ROK defense, the NKPA 6th Division had already transferred the jurisdiction of the occupied Ongjin Peninsula to the 3rd Brigade, 38 Security Forces, and assembled at Yongjongp'o by the morning of the 26th. Patroling for a suitable river-crossing point, the 6th Division was making preparations to move in the direction of Kanghwa Island (Kanghwado) and Kimp'o Peninsula.

Informed of these signs for an imminent enemy river-crossing attempt, the ROKA Headquarters hastily appointed Namsan Academy Superintendent Col. Kye In Ju as commander of the Kimp'o Area Command, and ordered him to organize a defense in response. Units under his command included officer candidates at Namsan Academy, Infantry School, and Engineer School; troops from the Patriotic Battalion; part of the Independent Cavalry Regiment; and the 2nd Battalion, 12th Regiment, which had crossed the river to reach the area.[157]

Col. Kye planned to defend the Kimp'o Peninsula from the mouth of the Han and Yomha (creek) centering around T'ongjin. He deployed the Patriotic Battalion and the 1st Battalion, Cavalry Regiment, on the left side of the Kanghwado-Tongjin Road. On the right, he positioned the 3rd Battalion, Cavalry Regiment (Foot). In addition, he deployed the 2nd Battalion (mixed), 12th Regiment, and the platoon-strength unit of Namsan Academy on the northern tip of the Kimp'o Peninsula, and retained as reserve the officer candidate battalion from the Infantry School.[158]

Around 16:00 on the 26th, just when these units were about to complete the organization of defensive positions, the enemy's reconnaissance activity became pronounced. Two hours later, several enemy vessels began to approach Kangryongp'o on the northern tip of the peninsula. Just as the enemy's two-company-strength unit began to disembark, the 5th Company, 2nd Battalion, ROK 12th Regiment, delivered synchronized fire and annihilated them. Also, a ROK armored platoon deployed on the bank of Chogangri detected an enemy freight ship and fired a 37-mm gun to sink it.

Under the cover of darkness that night, however, the enemy stealthily infiltrated a small unit to a hill in the vicinity of Kangryongp'o and secured a bridgehead for river-crossing. In addition, a company-strength unit which had landed in Kangwha crossed the Yomha from Kapgot, and attempted to block the ROK forward element's line of retreat by striking the Patriotic Battalion from the rear.

At dawn on the 27th, the enemy 14th Regiment made a full-scale river-crossing attempt with fire support from the opposite bank. The ROK defensive units, including the 2nd Battalion, 12th Regiment, fought a desperate battle, and when they realized that their line of retreat was blocked, the defensive line began to collapse.

Fully aware of the magnitude of the crisis in the Kimp'o area, the

ROKA Headquarters attached to the Kimp'o Area Command the 3rd Battalion, 22nd Regiment, 3rd Division; the 3rd Battalion, 8th Regiment, Capital Security Command; and the 8th Company, Foot Reconnaissance battalion, Cavalry Regiment.

By that evening, the Kimp'o Area Command gathered withdrawing units and deployed newly committed units to establish a new defensive line without gaps between units. Deployed along the Unyu-san-Hill 37 line, the final line of resistance, were the officer candidate battalion of the Infantry School; the 3rd Battalion (−), 8th Regiment; the 3rd (−) and 2nd Battalions of the Cavalry Regiment; and the 3rd Battalion, 22nd Regiment. Retained as reserve in Kimp'o was the 2nd Battalion, 12th Regiment. Having seized the vicinity of Changrim, the enemy's main effort temporarily halted pursuit and reorganized.

At dawn on the 28th, the enemy resumed the attack from two directions. Moving up the Han River, several enemy fishing boats carried troops to full capacity and landed troops on the river bank north of Taech'on. Almost at the same time, the enemy's main effort, spearheaded by two tanks, launched a frontal attack against the 3rd Battalion, 22nd Regiment through the avenue of approach that heads into Kimp'o.

ROK troops in the Kimp'o area put up a stubborn resistance with 2.36-inch rocket launchers and 37-mm direct guns. Although they fought until they ran out of ammunition, they could not block the advance of the enemy tanks. When a part of the defensive line collapsed, the reserve was immediately committed, but they too could not overcome the enemy. In the end, the defensive units had to withdraw to Kimp'o, where the enemy's artillery shells had already begun to fall.

2. Seoul Withdrawal Operation

(1) Demolition of the Bridges over the Han River

The pressure on Seoul exerted by the NKPA 1st Corps from the direction of Kimp'o, Kumch'on, and Miari began to take its toll on the ROK defense by June 28. Around 01:00 that day, the enemy tanks supporting the NKPA 4th Division went over the Miari Pass and overran the ROK defensive positions. No longer able to sustain organized resistance, some ROK units began to withdraw. The final line of resistance for Seoul had thus collapsed.

Around 01:45, upon receiving a report that the enemy tanks had entered downtown Seoul, Army Chief of Staff Chae immediately ordered Engineer Corps Chief Col. Choi to blow up the bridges over the Han River.

Delegating the authority to command forward troops to the field commanders and to Deputy Chief of Staff Kim Paik Il, Gen. Chae crossed the Han River and headed for Shihung.

The preparations for blowing up the Han River bridges had already started on the evening of the 26th. After the fall of Uijongbu and the withdrawal of the ROK units to Ch'angdong, Gen. Chae reminded the Engineer Chief of the prior failure to blow up the Imjin Bridge, and ordered him to make thorough preparations for a successful demolition of the bridges over the Han River.

At 09:00 on the 27th, the Engineer Chief ordered Lt. Col. Uhm Hong Sop, Engineer School Superintendent, to prepare for the demolition. Superintendent Uhm set up a command post at the South Han River Police Station, and charged 1st Lt. Hwang Won Hoe and 1st Lt. Lee Ch'ang Bok with the mission to blow up the bridges. By 15:30, they finished loading explosives onto the five bridges over the Han.[159]

Having been ordered by Gen. Chae to blow up the bridges two hours prior to the enemy's advance into downtown Seoul, Engineer Chief Choi had initially set the estimated time of demolition at 16:00 on the 27th.

Upon the return of the ROKA Headquarters from Shihung to Yongsan around that time, however, the demolition crew had to remove the demolition equipment for the time being in order to facilitate the passage of vehicles and trains. As the situation on the front rapidly deteriorated, however, around 23:30 the crew was ordered again to prepare for a demolition. Under the pouring rain, the demolition crew reloaded the explosives.

After learning that an order to blow up the bridges had been issued, Maj. Gen. Lee Ung Jun, Brig. Gen. Yu Jae Hung, and Brig. Gen. Lee Hyong Kun all requested that the demolition be put off until the forward troops safely withdrew across the Han. Just coming from the Miari Line, these commanding generals pointed out that the forward troops had yet to receive a withdrawal order from the ROKA Headquarters. Col. Kim Paik Il accepted their request, and ordered Operations Bureau Chief Col. Chang Chang Kuk to postpone the demolition.

Col. Chang immediately headed for the South Han River Police Station, where the demolition command post was located, but the roads were jammed with cars and people. Although President Syngman Rhee had issued a "stay home" order to the citizens from June 26, now almost no one took the order seriously. The massive influx of people and cars from the north of the Han created a major havoc and almost completely blocked the passage of military vehicles and equipment.

Meanwhile, at the demolition command post, Engineer Chief Col. Choi was carrying out the Army Chief of Staff's order to blow up the bridges. Around 02:00 on the 28th, Col. Choi relayed the demolition order to Lt. Col. Uhm, who in turn ordered 1st Lt. Hwang to set off the explosives. At the time, the situation on the Pedestrian Bridge was beyond control. Both the Military and Civilian Police tried to block the vehicles withdrawing without an order or permission-but in vain. Lt. Hwang first signalled the engineer security squad to block the passage of vehicles, but Vice President Lee Shi Young's car passed at that very moment. More than 10 cars quickly followed the way.

When the signal for ignition was given, thunderous noises and flames engulfed the Pedestrian Bridge and the three railway bridges. Due to a dud charge, however, the Seoul-Pusan double-track railway bridge and the west-bound Seoul-Inchon single-track railway bridge were not completely demolished. This failure was to allow the river-crossing of the enemy's tanks and to have a significant influence on later operations. Unable to relay the stop order in time, Col. Chang heard the blasting sound when he was on a hill in the vicinity of the demolition command post. The time was around 02:30.[60] The Kwangjin Bridge was blown up an hour and a half later.

Since the Pedestrian Bridge was blown up while people and cars were still on it, approximately 500-800 refugees are estimated to have lost their lives.[61] In addition, more than 40 to 50 vehicles in the vicinity of the North Han Police Station were destroyed by the blast and shrapnel, injuring many people. Part of the withdrawing ROK troops were able to use locomotives to cross the Han River via the undestroyed railway bridges.

In short, the demolition of the Han River bridges was conducted without taking any prior evacuation and withdrawal measures for citizens and troops alike. Consequently, most of the 1.5 million Seoul citizens had to live under the enemy rule. In addition, the line of retreat for the ROK main efforts were cut off, and vehicles, equipment, and supplies sufficient in quantity to support several divisions were taken by the enemy.

Seoul civilians evacuating, 1951

(2) Street Fighting in Seoul

The Miari Line collapsed around the same time that Army Chief of Staff Maj. Gen. Chae Byong Dok decided to leave the ROKA Headquarters in Yongsan for Shihung. His determination to defend Seoul to the end had obviously evaporated, and as the enemy tanks advanced into the lightly defended downtown area, the fall of the capital became only a matter of time. The ROKA Headquarters devised such emergency measures as setting up obstacles with conscripted vehicles, but because no systematic plan had been established, it was impossible to make a transition to organized combat in built-up areas. As a result, the Capital Security Command, part of the 1st Engineer Corps, and some withdrawing troops from the front had to conduct combat with little coordination.

Organized by the Engineer Chief, a special antitank attack team of the 1st Engineer Corps advanced to the Hyehwadong area, and set up road barricades across from the Ch'anggyung Palace; however, they failed to block the advance of the enemy tanks. As a result, the enemy tanks were able to advance in separate directions toward Ch'ongryangri, Tongdaemun, Chungangch'ong (Capitol Building), Chongro, Map'o, and the Bank of Korea. By 08:00 on the 28th, three enemy tanks passed by the Seoul Railway Station and were moving toward Samgakji.

Around this time, the 1st Battalion, 18th Regiment, Capital Security Command, was defending the Samgakji and Map'o areas. It was also operating an anti-aircraft team (with cal.50 machine gun) at Chungangch'ong, Nam-san, and Map'o. The unit deployed in Samgakji fired a 57mm recoilless rifle at an enemy tank, but the tank was not destroyed and escaped in the direction of the Han River. The ROK battalion, however, was able to destroy the enemy's follow-on vehicles and killed more than 30 enemy troops. An hour later, seven follow-on enemy tanks approached. The battalion delivered concentrated fire from the nearby buildings, and carried out "a human bullet attack" on the tanks. After halting for a moment, however, the enemy tanks advanced toward the Han River, and the ROK troops moved to Map'o to prepare for withdrawal. The only saving grace was the shooting down of an enemy YAK plane by the machine-gun fire of 2nd Lt. Park Myong Ung's anti-aircraft section at Nam-san.

In the meantime, while withdrawing from the Miari Line, part of the 3rd Battalion, ROK 5th Regiment, saw 12 enemy tanks and some infantrymen advancing into downtown Seoul from Chongryangri. MSG Paik Bok Song quickly organized a special antitank attack team of 10 men, and dropped a hand-grenade into a tank. It was, however, impossible to confirm whether the tank was destroyed as only three members of the attack team made it to the assembly area.

In Nam-san, Col. Lee Yong Mun of the Staff School gathered troops (company-strength) and organized the "White Tiger" unit. The troops resisted until the end and died heroic deaths, and some surviving members carried out guerrilla warfare.[162]

At Seoul National University Hospital, the entire security platoon died heroic deaths while resisting the enemy. More than 80 out of approximately 100 patients died while putting up resistance from a rear hill. After seizing the hospital, the enemy committed such atrocities as shooting wounded soldiers at random.

The determined resistance of ROK troops in downtown Seoul delayed the enemy's advance, and the enemy was able to reach the Han River Line more than 10 hours after the collapse of the Miari Line.[163]

While the fighting in downtown Seoul continued, the ROK troops at the Miari Line began to disperse and withdraw. After learning that the Han River bridges had been demolished, these units went to the outskirts of Seoul and assembled at such ferries as Kwangnaru, Map'o, Haengju, and Isanp'o. How desperate they must have felt when they saw the wide and blue Han without any river-crossing equipment and with the enemy on their heels. At the crossroad between life and death, the troops just had to cross the river by any means, hoping that some day they would repulse the enemy and recover Seoul.

Civilian vessels were the only means available to them. Racking their brains, they had to come up with various floating devices and cross the river.

(3) The Fall of Seoul and Its Repercussions

It was around 11:30, June 28, that the NKPA troops entered the central part of Seoul. By that night, they completely seized the capital city. Seoul turned into a world of reds, and its streets were dominated by the enemy tanks. Upon seizing the city, the enemy went to the Map'o and Sodaemun Jails and police stations to free all prisoners, including political prisoners. Calling these prisoners the heroes of the people, the North Koreans put them at the forefront of the welcoming party for the People's Army, and of the search party for the so-called anti-nationalists. They also spread a rumor that the NKPA troops had already seized Taejon, Kimch'on, Kunsan, and Wonju and were continuing to advance southward. Deceived by this disinformation campaign, many refugees returned home.

Citizens showed various responses to the enemy's occupation of Seoul. Some welcomed the People's Army with a red banner in their hands. This group included those who had been attracted by, or sympathized with, the communist cause from the past, as well as those who chose to collaborate with the enemy now that Seoul had fallen into the enemy hands. This group included more than a few National Assembly members and high-level politicians.

On the other hand, some citizens only pretended to welcome the enemy. They had initially tried to hide away in their house or run away into the mountains, but could not bear the risk of getting caught. The ROK stragglers or police officers left behind in Seoul had to hide away for the whole duration of the enemy occupation. Some even fought against the NKPA troops in the initial phase of the occupation. For someone like Col. Ahn Byong Bom, advisor to the Youth Defense Organization, the thought of military withdrawal without the prior evacuation of civilians was too humiliating and upsetting that he cut his belly open and committed suicide in Inwang-san near Segomjong on the 29th.

The NKPA carried out the planned occupation policy from day one. On the 28th, Kim Il Sung broadcast a speech in commemoration of the occupation of Seoul, and announced the establishment of a People's Committee in Seoul. Minister of Justice Lee Sung Yop was appointed chairman of the committee.

The North Koreans then seized various public institutions such as the Capitol, the City Hall, UNKRA (United Nations Korean Reconstruction Agency), various embassies, newspaper publishers, broadcasting stations, and transportation and communications facilities. They also mobilized by coercion the representatives of various political and social organizations, and confiscated the private property of the ROK government officials and capitalists.

The North Korean Military Committee issued a decree that both the North and South Korean currencies would be jointly circulated. The exchange rate was set at one North Korean won for eight South Korean won, the South-North trade in goods was banned, and the deposits made prior to June 27 were frozen. Subsequently, the South Korean won was printed in massive quantities, debasing the currency and triggering serious inflation.

Although the North Koreans announced that basic foods would be equally distributed through a comprehensive registration system, no household except for the officials and bereaved families of the so-called Volunteer Army received its food allotment.

In addition, the North Koreans shut down all existing newspapers, and replaced them with communist papers such as the Liberation Daily and Choson People's News. Although these new papers as well as other mass media repeatedly launched disinformation campaigns, they had little effect on the ordinary citizens, who were getting fed up with the North Koreans' plundering and deception.

The People's Committee labelled the former leading citizens as the enemies of the people, and asked them to turn themselves in. Those who turned themselves in were then used to persuade and convert other citizens through radio broadcasts and speeches.

In sum, Seoul was occupied the NKPA 1st Corps. In coordination with the 105th Armor Brigade (−), the NKPA 3rd and 4th Divisions from Ch'orwon penetrated the ROK defensive lines in Uijongbu, Miari, and Ch'angdong, and advanced into Seoul.

Around this time, the NKPA 1st and 6th (−) Divisions from Munsan were putting pressure on Seoul from the Bongilchon line, but had yet to penetrate the defensive line of the ROK 1st Division. A regiment from the NKPA 6th Division, on the other hand, advanced southward across the length of the Kimp'o Peninsula and was approaching the vicinity of the Kimp'o Airfield. Meanwhile, the advance of the supporting attack, the NKPA 2nd Corps, was being blocked by the ROK 6th Division. The NKPA 2nd and 12th Divisions were unable to occupy Ch'unch'on on time, and were stalled north of Hongch'on.

At the time of the fall of Seoul, the front line was formed along Kimp'o, Bongil-chon, Seoul, Hongch'on, Taegwan-ryong Pass, and Kangnung. Although the NKPA troops were able to occupy Seoul in three days as had been planned, they failed to envelop the ROK units. Moreover, they were faced with stiff resistance from the ROK troops and the people of South Korea-not popular uprisings as they had hoped. In addition to the UN sanctions, these hostile and formidable responses from the South forced major adjustments in the North's strategy and plans.

The ROK Armed Forces, for its part, were caught off balance by the North's surprise attack and, in confusion over war policy, initially resisted the enemy's advance with a plan to defend Seoul to the end. With the collapse of the forward defensive lines, however, Seoul did fall into enemy hands. The ROK military leadership committed unit by unit the Seoul-stationed troops and reserve divisions to the north of Seoul, and resisted until the end at each successive defensive line. When the Miari Line collapsed, however, the ROK military leaders demolished the bridges over the Han River lest these bridges be seized by the enemy. As there was no evacuation plan based on the worst-case scenario, most of the Seoul citizens were doomed to live under the enemy rule when the bridges were blown up. Also, although the ROK troops managed to avoid being enveloped by the enemy, they were unable to carry out organized withdrawal and the ground forces and supporting units collapsed as a result. Around this time, however, US forces, as part of the United Nations forces, began to take part in the Korean War. Consequently, the ROK government and military leaders had to formulate a new war policy and make adjustments in their strategy. The fall of Seoul was the greatest tragedy of the Korean War, and provides many political and military lessons for the current and future generations.

V. US Assistance and UN Resolutions

1. UN Resolution Calls for the Withdrawal of NKPA Forces

The armed aggression by the North Korean People's Army destroyed the fragile peace that had precariously been maintained on the Korean Peninsula. In response to this provocation, the US and the UN applied sanctions against North Korea and took measures, in stages, to restore the status quo ante bellum in Korea.

The news of the North Korean invasion was disseminated all around the world via correspondents and diplomats in Korea. In the American case, the US Embassy and military attache in Korea and the KMAG, as well as foreign journalists, relayed the news to Washington within five hours of the invasion (by 09:30, local time, on June 25 or by 20:30, June 24, Washington time). US Ambassador John J. Muccio's telegram reached the State Department at 21:26, June 24 (Washington time). The telegram informed Washington that the city of Kaesong had been reportedly captured by North Korea at 09:00, June 25, local time, and concluded: "It would appear from the nature of the attack and the manner in which it was launched that it constitutes an all-out offensive against the Republic of Korea."[164]

After consulting with the Defense Department officials, the US State

Department decided to present this crisis to the United Nations, and informed UN General Decretary Trygve Lie of the situation in Korea. Meanwhile, State Secretary Dean G. Acheson called President Harry S. Truman at 13:20 on June 25 (23:20, June 24, Washington time). The US President was resting at his home at Independence, Missouri, that weekend. After securing Truman's approval, Acheson requested that a special meeting of the United Nations Security Council be held at once.[165]

The North Korean invasion reminded Washington officials of the Japanese surprise attack on the Pearl Harbor. The shock was even greater to the UN General Secretary as it reminded him of the Nazi invasion of his home country Norway during World War II.[166] Returning to the White House without delay, US President Truman recalled the historical lessons that had been learned from the outbreak of World War II, and was resolved to punish the communist aggression by summoning the strength of the free world. He was determined to prevent this aggression from escalating to World War III and to defend the authority of the United Nations. Truman later recollected:[167]

> I felt certain that if South Korea was allowed to fall Communist leaders would be emboldened to override nations closer to our own shores. If the Communists were permitted to force their way into the Republic of Korea without opposition from the free world, no small nation would have the courage to resist threats and aggression by stronger Communist neighbors. If this was allowed to go unchallenged it would mean a third world war, just as similar incidents had brought on the second world war. It was clear to me that the foundations and the principles of the United Nations were at stake unless this unprovoked attack on Korea could be stopped.

Meanwhile, in Seoul, President Syngman Rhee received US Ambassador Muccio's visit at 11:35, June 25, and exchanged opinions on the war situation. President Rhee said: "The ROK National Forces will run out of ammunition within 10 days. The entire Korean people-man or woman, old or young-will rise up and fight the enemy, with sticks and stones if necessary. The morale of the Korean people will be even higher if a sufficient supply of ammunition can be guaranteed."[168] Around 13:00, after the meeting with the US Ambassador, President Rhee telephoned Counsellor Han Pyo Ok and Ambassador Chang Myon at the Korean Embassy in the United States. Concerned that ROK Armed Forces alone would not be able to repel the North Korean invaders, President Rhee ordered them to make a direct request to Washington.[169]

> They invaded us. Our National Forces are putting up a courageous fight, but I'm worried whether we can defeat them with our strength alone. We are determined to fight to the end. You must make every effort so that American assistance can arrive here as soon as possible.

The ROK National Assembly also sent a message to the President and the Congress of the United States. Informing them of the North Korean aggression, the ROK National Assembly requested that the United States "extend effective and timely aid in order to prevent this act of destruction of world peace."[170]

Having received the directive from President Rhee, Ambassador Chang's party visited the US State Department at 15:00, June 25 (01:00, June 25, Washington time), and relayed the ROK government's request for assistance. At this meeting, the party was informed that the United States had requested a meeting of the UN Security Council to discuss the Korean problem.[171]

In Seoul, the United Nations Commission on Korea held a meeting between 14:00 and 18:00. At 21:00, via the Korea Broadcasting System, the commission requested that "the North Korean Forces immediately cease military action and withdraw to the 38th parallel and resolve the crisis through a peace conference." The commission's detailed report on the Korean situation arrived at the UN General Secretary's desk around 24:00 (10:00, June 25, Washington time).[172]

> Government of Republic of Korea states that about 04:00 hrs. 25 June attacks were launched in strength by North Korean forces all along the 38th parallel ···. The latest attacks have occurred along the parallel directly north of Seoul along shortest avenue of approach ···. Commission wishes to draw attention of Secretary-General to serious situation developing which is assuming character of full-scale war and may endanger the maintenance of international peace and security. It suggests that he consider possibility of bringing matter to notice of Security Council.

Meanwhile, Gen. MacArthur, US Commander-in-Chief, Far East (CINCFE), learned of the North Korean invasion at 09:25, June 25, from the military attache and liaison officers in Seoul. At 21:35 (10:35, June 25, Washington time), Gen. MacArthur sent a comprehensive situation report to the US Department of the Army. He informed Washington officials that he was sending a shipment of ammunition to Korea, and recommended that the US 7th Fleet be ordered into the Korean seas as a preliminary measure.[173] At that time, Gen. MacArthur was charged with no mission, and was given no authority, with respect to the conduct of war in Korea—except that of providing logistical supplies to the US Embassy and the KMAG and implementing the evacuation plan for noncombatants in case of emergency. Nevertheless, he took independent actions to provide the Republic of Korea with ammunition, carefully watching the situation unfold in Korea.

At the United Nations, the Security Council was called into emergency session under a formal US request at 04:00, June 26 (14:00, June 25, Washington time).[174] General-Secretary Lie opened the session by citing the report by the UN Commission on Korea. He insisted that the United Nations take measures to restore the peace and security in Korea which was faced with armed aggression. Next, US Deputy Representative Ernest A. Gross explained the situation in Korea based on Ambassador Muccio's report, and read a draft resolution calling upon the North Korean authorities to cease hostilities and withdraw their armed forces to the 38th parallel. He also proposed that the Security Council invite a South Korean representative to hear his pleas. The Yugoslavian representative to the UN suggested that a North Korean representative be also invited, but this motion was overridden. Finally given a chance to speak in front of the Security Council, Korean Ambassador Chang read a prepared statement. He argued: "The North Korean armed aggression is a crime against humanity. The United Nations played an important role in the establishment of the Republic of Korea. It is incumbent upon the Security Council, with its basic responsibility to maintain international peace, take active measures against this unprovoked aggression."[175]

After a few minor revisions, the Security Council adopted the resolution by a vote of nine to zero, with one abstention (Yugoslavia). At that time, the Security Council consisted of 11 member nations, including 5 permanent members with veto power (United States, Soviet Union, Nationalist China, Britain, and France). The resolution was adopted partly because the Soviet representative was not present at the Security Council to exercise a veto at the time. He had begun a boycott of the Council in January 1950 in protest of the UN's refusal to replace Nationalist China with the Communist China.

This resolution has a great significance as the first of UN resolutions during the Korean War to deter aggression and restore peace through collective security measures. The resolution called upon the North Korean authorities to cease their aggression and withdraw their armed forces to the 38th parallel.[176]

Resolution of the UN Security Council Calling for the Cessation of Hostilities in Korea, June 25, 1950:

The Security Council recalling the finding of the General Assembly in its resolution of 21 October 1949 that the Government of the Republic of Korea is a lawfully established government "… and that this is the only such Government in Korea" …; noting with grave concern the armed attack upon the Republic of Korea by forces from North Korea, determines that this action constitutes a breach of the peace,

1. Calls for the immediate cessation of hostilities; and Calls upon the authorities of North Korea to withdraw forthwith their armed forces to the thirty-eighth parallel;

2. Requests the United Nations Commission on Korea

   (a) To communicate its fully considered recommendations on the situation with the least possible delay;

   (b) To observe the withdrawal of the North Korean forces to the thirty-eighth parallel; and

   (c) To keep the Security Council informed on the execution of this resolution;

3. Calls upon all Members to render every assistance to the United Nations in the execution of this resolution and to refrain from giving assistance to the North Korean authorities.

The US Ambassador to the Soviet Union relayed a message from Washington requesting that Moscow use its influence to have P'yongyang comply with the UN resolution. This request was denied, however.

2. The United States Takes Limited Military Measures

While presenting the Korean problem for discussion at the UN Security Council, the United States also took actions on its own. After arriving in Washington, US President Truman held a National Security Council meeting at the Blair House around noon, June 26, Seoul time (19:45–23:00, June 25, local time).

This dinner conference was attended by the State, Defense, and Service Secretaries as well as the Chairman of the Joint Chiefs of Staff and the Service Chiefs. Truman approved the limited military measures that had been issued by the JCS as preliminary measures to the CINCFE—namely, "to send a survey party to Korea to assess the situation and to use air and naval cover to assure the delivery of ammunition as well as to protect the American dependents being evacuated from Korea." This was soon issued as a formal directive:[177]

1. Send a survey party to Korea for the purposes briefed during the prior teletype conference.

2. Provide appropriate naval and air cover to assure the delivery of ammunition and equipment deemed necessary to prevent the loss of the Seoul-Kimp'o-Inch'on area.

3. Commit necessary naval and air forces to protect the Seoul-Kimp'o-Inch'on area to assure the safe evacuation of the American dependents and other American noncombatants designated by the US Embassy in Korea.

4. The Seventh Fleet is to move immediately to Sasebo and be placed under the operational control of Gen. MacArthur.

Before receiving this directive from Washington, Gen. MacArthur received a telephone call from President Syngman Rhee at 03:00 on the 26th. Rhee simultaneously made a protest and a request: "Who is responsible for today's crisis? If your country had expressed a little more interest and concert, things would not have gone this far. Didn't we give you repeated warnings? Now you get us out of this mess."[178]

Prompted by Rhee's request for assistance and directed by the JCS, MacArthur began to take military measures. Under Ambassador Muccio's decision, US noncombatants began to evacuate from Korea at 01:00, June 26. MacArthur used naval and air forces to transport these civilians to Japan. Together with other foreign nationals in Korea, American noncombatants completed the evacuation by June 29.

Although the US naval and air forces did not provide direct support for ROK Forces, an American fighter plane did engage in open combat and shot down a North Korean YAK during the evacuation operation. As a result, the North Korean attempt to secure air superiority was denied from the early stages of the war.

In order to assess the situation in Korea and to obtain information essential to command measures, Gen. MacArthur organized a survey party under Maj. Gen. John H. Church on June 27. Newly authorized to assume operational control of all US military activities in Korea, MacArthur designated this party Advance Command and Liaison Group in Korea (ADCOM), and dispatched it to Suwon. Gen. Church established a temporary command post at the Suwon Agricultural Experiment Station, and met with Gen. Chae Byong Dok the next day to advise him on defensive operations. American military assistance thus started in earnest.[179]

Meanwhile, most of KMAG members evacuated to Japan from June 27 to 29. Only the KMAG leadership, including Col. Wright, and a few others remained in Korea. Placed under MacArthur's operational control from the 27th, KMAG crossed the Han River the next day to move to Suwon and brief ADCOM on the war situation. Those who had evacuated to Japan were recommitted when US ground forces were deployed in Korea.[180]

In short, the first military measures taken by the United States included: safeguarding the evacuation of American noncombatants from Korea, supporting ROK Forces with ammunition, and giving the CINCFE operational control of US Forces in Korea in preparation for future operations lest the UN resolution not be implemented.

3. The United States Provides Naval and Air Support

In spite of the June 26 UN resolution, the North Korean People's Army continued to advance southward, and reached the outskirts of Seoul by the 27th. The evacuation of foreign nationals and military advisors were underway.

Faced with the rapidly deteriorating situation, President Syngman Rhee telephoned Counsellor Han at the Korean Embassy in Washington around 02:00, June 27 (12:00, June 26, Washington time). President Rhee said: "Things are getting out of control. Although our Armed Forces putting up a courageous fight, we have too many shortcomings. Pay a visit to the White House at once with Ambassador Chang. Explain to President Truman that military assistance is urgently needed, and request cooperation."[181]

Ambassador Chang met with President Truman, and relayed the resolution adopted by the ROK National Assembly requesting "effective and timely aid" in order to repulse the North Korean invasion. He also brought President Rhee's vehement appeal to Truman's attention.[182]

Truman reminded Chang of the French support for the American War of Independence and the US assistance for those European countries under the German attack in 1917. Alluding to these historical examples, Truman made it clear that American support would be forthcoming.[183]

On the same day (June 26, local time), grim and shocking situation reports from Korea were pouring into Washington, including MacArthur's report which noted that Seoul was under the enemy threat and estimated that a complete collapse was imminent. Concluding that North Korea had no intention to comply with the June 26 UN resolution, Truman held a second National Security Council meeting at the Blair House at 21:00, June 26, local time.[184]

The Council decided to lift restrictions on US naval and air operations against North Korean military units, tanks, and artillery below the 38th Parallel, and to offer ROK Forces as much support as possible. Soon afterwards, the following directive was issued to Gen. MacArthur:[185]

> All restrictions on the Far East naval and air forces are removed. Maximum support is to be provided in order that ROK Forces can be reorganized. The measures above are designed to support ROK Forces in accordance with the resolution adopted by the United Nations on June 25. [June 26, Korean time] In addition, the Seventh Fleet is to be so positioned as to protect Formosa from the Communist China's attack as well as to prevent an attack from Formosa on the mainland.

In regard to naval and air operations, detailed directives were as follows:

> In supporting and aiding the defense of the Korean territory, all prior restrictions on the operation of the air forces in the Far East are removed with respect to operations south of the 38th Parallel. Air attacks on all North Korean tanks, artillery, troops, military targets below the 38th Parallel are approved. The objective is to remove North Korean military strength from South Korea. Likewise, naval operations against those units attacking South Korea on the coast or the sea below the 38th Parallel are to proceed without restriction.

Next day, US President Truman issued a statement announcing American military assistance to the ROK Forces. President Truman declared: "I have ordered United States air and sea forces to give the Korean Government troops cover and support," as North Korea had defied the UN Security Council resolution calling for the cessation of hostilities.

Following the June 26 UN Resolution, the United States thus proceeded with a second round of military measures in the form of naval and air operations against North Korea. These measures were immediately put into effect by the CINCFE.

4. The UN Adopts a Resolution to Apply Military Sanctions Against North Korea

On June 27, the ROK government and National Assembly sent a request to the UN General Assembly for assistance, and the UN Commission on Korea called upon the General-Secretary to take additional measures against North Korea. The commission pointed out that its effort to contact North Korea had met only with negative response in the past, and observed that North Korea had yet to cease hostilities and withdraw its troops. Arguing that the June 26 UN resolution was unrealistic given North Korea's past and present behavior, the commission sent a report recommending additional measures.[186]

Meanwhile, at Blair House, the National Security Council decided that it would be best for the United States to act under the UN auspices if possible. Although it had decided to extend naval and air support to the Republic of Korea and these military measures were consistent with the spirit of the June 26 UN resolution, the council felt that it would be best to secure an international approval for these actions. Accordingly, the council decided to present to the UN Security Council a draft resolution recommending that other members provide South Korea with necessary assistance to repulse the North Korean attack.[187]

The UN Security Council was reconvened at 04:00, June 28 (14:00, June 27, local time). Warren R. Austin, US Representative to the UN, opened the meeting by briefing on the Korean situation and explaining the military measures taken by the United States. Noting that the North Korean troops were continuing to advance southward in defiance of the UN resolution, he requested that the Security Council take adopt a stronger resolution and apply military sanctions against North Korea. Korean Ambassador Chang Myon also demanded that the United Nations take effective measures.[188] The Yugoslavian representative again put forward an alternative requesting that an invitation be extended to a North Korean representative, but was denied again.

At 13:45, June 28 (11:45, June 27, local time), after an 8-hour marathon session, the Security Council voted 7 to 1 (Yugoslavia) for the resolution, with two abstentions (India and Egypt). The Soviet representative was still absent. The resolution was as follows: [189]

Resolution of the UN Security Council Recommending Assistance to the Republic of Korea

The Security Council

> Having determined that the armed attack upon the Republic of Korea by forces from North Korea constitutes a breach of the peace ⋯ ;
> Having called upon the authorities of North Korea to withdraw forthwith their armed forces to the 38th parallel; and
> Having noted from the report of the United Nations Commission for Korea that the authorities in North Korea have neither ceased hostilities nor withdrawn their armed forces to the 38th parallel, and that urgent military measures are required to restore international peace and security; and
> Having noted the appeal from the Republic of Korea to the United Nations for immediate and effective steps to secure peace and security,
> Recommends that the Members of the United Nations furnish such assistance to the Republic of Korea as may be necessary to repel the armed attack and to restore international peace and security in the area.

The June 28 UN resolution thus called upon the members of the United Nations to provide the Republic of Korea with necessary military assistance to repulse the North Korean attack. The US Ambassador in the Soviet Union once again relayed a message from Washington requesting that Moscow use its influence to have P'yongyang cease hostilities in compliance with the UN resolution. The request was again denied, as had been expected.

The June 28 UN resolution, together with the June 26 resolution, has a great significance as the first collective security measures taken by the UN since its foundation to restore peace by applying military sanctions against a destruction of international peace. The resolution also marked an important turning point in the Korean War, as the participation of UN member nations transformed the nature of the conflict into one pitting the North Korean Forces against the ROK and UN Forces.

Based on this resolution, the United States expanded the scope of naval and air operations to the entire Korean Peninsula on June 29 and 30, and later sent ground forces to Korea with other UN member nations.

In summary, under Stalin's guidance and support, North Korea's Kim Il Sung secretly pushed ahead with a plan for southward invasion, which had been his goal since the establishment of his regime. In close consultation with Mao Tse-tung, Kim completed his plan to communize the entire Korean Peninsula by force, and secured a final approval from Stalin and an agreement from Mao.

The final plan envisaged a quick seizure of Seoul and an overthrow of the ROK government by a popular uprising triggered by the outbreak of the war. The invasion plan called on the North Korean People's Army to advance rapidly to the southern seashores before the US troops could land in Pusan. With the objective of finishing the war within a month and establishing a unified people's government in Seoul on August 15, fifth anniversary of Korea's liberation, North Korean Forces burst across the 38th Parallel on June 25, 1950.

Through a number of intelligence estimates, South Korea had read the North's intent, and belatedly established defense plans. The South's inferiority in troop strength and equipment, lack of training, and lax security, however, allowed the North to launch a surprise attack.

In order to "envelop and annihilate ROK main forces on the north of the Han River and occupy Seoul within three days," as laid out in its pre-emptive strike plan, the NKPA committed main efforts toward the Seoul area and applied pressure along the entire frontline in the initial phase of the war. In response, while the military leaders in Seoul were debating the merits of "defending Seoul to the end" vs. "withdrawing to the south of the Han," the ROK Armed Forces put in their best effort to defend Seoul, but, in three days, Seoul and the forward defense areas fell into the enemy hands. On the same day, however, the United Nations, urged by the United States, adopted a resolution calling for military assistance to the Republic of Korea. Following its earlier resolution requesting the withdrawal of North Korean troops, this UN resolution opened a way for member nations to take collective security measures against the North Korean armed aggression.

Thus, although North Korea occupied Seoul as had been planned, its troops failed to envelop ROK Forces and, instead of a popular uprising in support of the North, they encountered a stiff resistance. UN military sanctions further disrupted their basic strategy. South Korea, on the other hand, suffered the fall of Seoul and severe losses in the strength of its forces, but was hopeful that the UN support would turn the tide of the war.

Notes

1) War History Compilation Committee, *History of the Korean War*, vol. 1 (old edition) (Seoul: Ministry of National Defense, 1967), p. 705.

2) Ministry of Foreign Affairs, *Soviet Documents* (2), p. 4.

3) Ministry of Foreign Affairs, *Soviet Documents* (2), p. 2; *Soviet Documents* (3), p. 2, p. 8.

4) Ministry of Foreign Affairs, *Soviet Documents*, (3), pp. 9-10; *Soviet Documents* (4), pp. 28-31.

5) Korea Institute of Military History, Soviet Documents, April 1993.

6) WHCC, *History of the Korean War*, vol. 1, 1977, p. 130; *Dmitri Volkogonov, Stalin*, p.369; Ministry of Foreign Affairs, *Soviet Documents* (3), pp. 8-11.

7) Ministry of Foreign Affairs, *Soviet Documents* (2), pp. 6-7; *Soviet Documents* (3), pp. 19-22.

8) Ministry of Foreign Affairs, *Soviet Documents* (2), pp. 10-11.

9) Ministry of Foreign Affairs, *Soviet Documents* (2), p. 11; *Soviet Documents* (3), p. 31.

10) Ministry of Foreign Affairs, *Soviet Documents* (2), p. 12; *Soviet Documents* (3), p. 32.

11) Ministry of Foreign Affairs, *Soviet Documents* (3), pp. 51-53; *Soviet Documents* (2), p. 17.

12) Ministry of Foreign Affairs, *Soviet Documents* (3), p. 53; *Soviet Documents* (2), p. 18.

13) Ministry of Foreign Affairs, *Soviet Documents* (2), p. 20.

14) Korea Institute of Military History, *Red China's Army in the Korean War*, 1994, p. 93.

15) Ministry of Foreign Affairs, *Soviet Documents* (2), p. 9 and pp. 23-24.

16) Ministry of Foreign Affairs, *Soviet Documents* (2), p. 25.

17) Ministry of Foreign Affairs, *Soviet Documents* (2), p. 25; *Soviet Documents* (3), p. 72.

18) Ministry of Foreign Affairs, *Soviet Documents* (2), p. 26.

19) Ministry of Foreign Affairs, *Soviet Documents* (2), pp. 24-27.

20) Ministry of Foreign Affairs, *Soviet Documents* (2), p. 26.

21) Ministry of Foreign Affairs, *Soviet Documents* (2), pp. 27-28; *Dimitri Volkogonov, Stalin* (Seoul: Segyong Press, 1993), pp. 372-373; Yu Song Chol, "My Testimony" (8)-(9), (Seoul: Hankook Ilbo, 1990), p. 119.

22) Yu, Song Chol, "*My Testimony*", Hankook Ilbo, November 9, 1990.

23) Research Institute of History, *North Korea, Comprehensive History of Choson*, vol. 25 (Pyongyang: Social Science Academy, 1981), p. 85.

24) Jerrdd L. Schecter, *Khrushchev Remembers* (Little Brown, 1990), p. 145; Chung Hong Chin, tr., *Khrushchev Remembers* (Seoul: Halim Publishing Co., 1971), p. 352.

25) Yu Song Chol, "*My Testimony*"(10), Hankook Ilbo, November 13, 1990; "*My Testimony*" (2), Hankook Ilbo, June 18, 1990; Kim, Chang Sun, *15-Year History of North Korea* (Seoul: Chimungak, 1961), p. 145; Park, Gap Dong, *The Korean War and Kim Il Sung* (Seoul: Winds and Waves Press, 1990), pp. 80-84.

26) Research Institute of History, North Korea, *Comprehensive History of Choson*, vol. 25, p. 83.

27) WHCC, *History of the Korean War*, vol. 1, p. 145; ROKA Headquarters, *Analysis of the June 25 Invasion by North Korea*, 1970, p. 318; Yu Song Chol, "*My Testimony*"(10), Hankook Ilbo, November 13, 1990.

28) WHCC, *History of the Korean War*, vol. 1, p. 167; Appleman, *South to the Naktong, North to the Yalu*, p. 19; *Comprehensive History of Choson*, vol. 25, p. 66.

29) Appleman, *South to the Naktong, North to the Yalu*, p. 19; FEC, *History of the North Korean Army*, p. 4.

30) Yu Song Chol, "*My Testimony*" (8), Hankook Ilbo, November 9, 1990.

31) *Comprehensive History of Choson*, vol. 25, p. 107; Yu Song Chol, "*My Testimony*" (8), Hankook Ilbo, November 9, 1990; NKPA General Headquarters, *Reconnaissance Plan for the Offensive Operation*, June 20, 1950 (Collection of Documents, Korea In-

stitute of Military History)

32) The original copy of this document is in Russian. The Korea Institute of Military History has a duplicate copy of this document as well as a copy of its English translation. NKPA General Headquarters, *Reconnaissance Plan for the Offensive Operation,* June 20, 1950

33) *Addendum to the NKPA Reconnaissance Order*; "*Operation Order* No. 1 of the *NKPA* 2nd and 4th Divisions", June 22, 1950; NKPA "*Operation Map for the Pre-emptive Strike Plan*" (duplicate): Yu Song Chol, "*My Testimony*" (9), Hankook Ilbo, November 11, 1990; *Analysis of the June 25 Invasion by North Korea*, p. 131.

34) NKPA General Headquarters, *Intellegence Plan for the Pre-emptive Strike Plan* (duplicate), June 20, 1950; *Comprehensive History of Choson*, vol. 25, pp. 85-86.

35) NKPA "*Operation Map for the Pre-emptive Strike Plan*" (duplicate) (Seoul: Yonhap Press Documents, August 29, 1992). The Yonhap Press obtained this duplicate copy of the actual operation map from Dr. Kortkov, a senior researcher at the Russia Institute of Military History. According to this researcher, Moscow and Pyongyang each has an original copy of the map.

36) NKPA "*Operation Map for the Pre-emptive Strike Plan*" (duplicate). The first-stage plan for the operation as indicated on the map is consistent with the seized operation order for the NKPA 2nd and 4th Divisions. Given this consistency, it is likely that the indicated maneuver plans for the subsequent stages are also credible. After a comparative analysis with the Soviet documents and the Intelligence Plan, the subsequent phase of the operation were divided into two stages.

37) WHCC, *History of the Korean War*, vol. 1, p. 180.

38) Appleman, *South to the Naktong, North to the Yalu*, p. 180; *History of the North Korean Army*, pp. 41-43.

39) *History of the North Korean Army*, p. 91; Yu Song Chol, "*My Testimony*" (9), Hankook Ilbo, November 11, 1990.

40) *Comprehensive History of Choson*, vol. 25, p. 162.

41) Yu Song Chol, "*My Testimony*" (9), Hankook Ilbo, November 11, 1990.

42) Institute of Communist Bloc Issue Research, *Overview of North Korea*, 45–68, 1968, p. 524.

43) Ibid., p. 524; *Comprehensive History of Choson*, vol. 25, pp. 98–99.

44) *History of the North Korean Army*, p. 91; Institute of Historical Research, *History of the War for National Liberation*, vol. 1(Pyongyang: DPRK Science Academy, 1961). It is stated in this book that the NKPA Supreme Command established a southward invasion plan in accordance with strategic guidance provided by Kim Il Sung, and that the People's Army was thus able to make a rapid transition to the counteroffensive. The peacetime command structure of the NKPA includes no such organization as "the NKPA Supreme Command."

45) *History of the Korean War*, vol. 1, p. 190. It is stated in this book that Operations Chief Kim Kwang Hyop issued this directive. Yu Song Chol, however, claims that he was the Operations Chief at the time, and that the Chief of the General Staff was the one who issued the directive. Ministry of Foreign Affairs, *Soviet Documents* (2), p. 28.

46) *Analysis of the June 25 Invasion by North Korea*, pp. 108–109; WHCC, *History of the Korean War*, vol. 1, pp. 180–181; *History of the Korean War*, Map No. 4. The 10th Division was positioned in Sukch'on as a reserve.

47) *Enemy Documents*, GHQ, FEC, "Allied Translator & Interpreter Section", Issue No. 6, Copy No. 11, Item 2 200564. A seized enemy document, this was classified as "Confidential" and was stored at the US National Archives. On April 28, 1987, it was downgraded to unclassified status. This document contains the English translation of the Reconnaissance Order issued to each division by the NKPA General Headquarters.

48) General Staff of the North Korean Army to the Chief of the 4th Division, "*Reconnaissance Order* No. 1", June 18, 1950.

49) General Staff of the North Korean Army to the Chief of the 2nd Division, "*Recon-*

naissance Order No. 1", June 18, 1950.

50) This order is titled "Battle Order" in Korean; whereas, the English translation says "Operation Order." Whether designated Battle Order or Operation Order, it is clearly an attack order.

51) General Staff of the North Korean Army, *"Intelligence Plan for the Pre-emptive Strike Plan"*, June 20, 1950; Yu Song Chol, *"My Testimony"* (8), Hankook Ilbo ; Chu Yong Bok, *Southward Invasion and Defeat of the North Korean People's Army,* pp. 244-245. The author was a Russian translator, and was the Deputy Chief of the Engineer Section, NKPA 2nd Corps, at the time of the invasion.

52) Staff of the 4th Infantry Division, *"Operation Order* No. 1", Okgyeri, June 22, 1950.

53) 2nd Division Headquarters, *"Operation Order* No. 10001", narrow valley, northeast of HILL 214, June 22, 1950.

54) *Comprehensive History of Choson,* vol. 25, p. 69 and p. 72.

55) WHCC, *History of the Korean War,* vol. 1, p. 567.

56) Ibid., p. 752.

57) *"Report of the United Nations Commission on Korea"*, 1949-1950, in Reference Materials for Legislation, vol. 35, 1965, p. 304.

58) Ibid., p. 306.

59) WHCC, *History of the Korean War,* vol. 1, p. 567.

60) Ibid., p. 568; *"Report of the United Nations Commission on Korea"*, 1949-1950, pp. 306-307.

61) WHCC, *History of the Korean War,* vol. 1, p. 17.

62) "ROKA Headquarters *Operation Plan* No. 38" (March 25, 1950). The Korea Institute of Military History has the ROK Basic Defense Plan(ROK Operation Order No. 38) and the following appendixes: "Army Organization"(Appendix 1), "ROK Operation Order"(Appendix 4), and "Signal Plan"(Appendix 6).

63) ROKA Headquarters, *History of the Development of the Army,* vol. 1, 1969, pp. 278-279.

64) Ibid., p. 279; WHCC, *History of the Korean War*, vol. 1, p. 247, p. 319, and p. 397.

65) WHCC, *History of the Korean War*, vol. 1, p. 247, p. 319, and p. 397.

66) Ibid., p. 247.

67) Ibid., p. 285 and p. 396.

68) Ibid., pp. 198-217 and pp. 396-398.

69) "ROKA Headquarters *General Order* No. 43"(June 1, 1950), WHCC, *History of the Korean War*, vol. 1, p. 318.

70) The strength comparison is based on the figures from Appleman, *South to the Naktong, North to the Yalu*, p. 11 and 15, but see *History of the Korean War*, vol. 1, p. 245 for the figure on the strength of the Separate Armor Regiment in the Inje Area. As no precise data were available on the strength of the 549th Detachment, it was estimated as one-third that of a naval combat team. Figures in the blanks represent the strength and the ratio excluding those ROK troops on leave.

71) WHCC, *History of the Korean War*, vol. 1, p. 569.

72) Sawyer, *KMAG in Peace and War*, p. 104.

73) ROKA HQ, *History of the Development of the Army*, vol. 1, p. 215.

74) Sawyer, *KMAG*, p. 78. The book gives the impression that the US military advisors changed the training schedule. Since the rescheduling was effected via the ROKA Headquarters, however, the phrasing here has been changed accordingly. War History Compilation Committee, *History of National Defense*, vol. 1(Seoul: Ministry of National Defense, 1984), pp. 356-357.

75) WHCC, *History of the Korean War*, vol. 1, 1977, p. 172; *Analysis of the June 25 Invasion by North Korea*, p. 49; ibid, p. 199.

76) Chu Yong Bok, *Southward Invasion and Defeat of the North Korean People's Army*, pp. 170-171.

77) WHCC, *History of the Korean War*, vol. 1, p. 171; *Analysis of the June 25 Invasion by North Korea*, p. 49.

78) Chu Yong Bok, *Southward Invasion and Defeat of the North Korean People's Army*, pp.

203-205.

79) *History of the Korean War*, vol. 1, p. 173; *Analysis of the June 25 Invasion by North Korea*, p. 50.

80) Chu Yong Bok, *Southward Invasion and Defeat of the North Korean People's Army*, pp. 207-208.

81) WHCC, *History of the Korean War*, vol. 1, p. 758.

82) Ibid., p. 573.

83) Schnabel, *Policy and Direction*, p. 40.

84) *"Report of the United Nations Commission on Korea"*, 1949-1950, pp. 332-335.

85) Ibid., p. 335.

86) WHCC, *History of the Korean War*, vol. 1, p. 575.

87) Ibid., p. 575.

88) Ibid., p. 575.

89) *Comprehensive History of Choson*, vol. 25, pp. 115-116.

90) WHCC, *History of the Korean War*, vol. 1, p. 577.

94) Ibid., p. 578.

95) Ibid., p. 608.

96) ROKA HQ, *"Operation Order No. 84"*(June 25, 1950); ROKA HQ, *"Operation Order No. 85"*(June 25, 1950)

97) *History of the US JCS: Korean War*, vol. 1(Seoul: Ministry of Defense, 1990), p. 56; Appleman, *South to the Nakkong North to the yalu*, pp. 21-22; *Comprehensive History of Choson*, vol. 25, pp. 69-72.

98) ROK JCS: *Korean War*, p. 787.

99) WHCC, *History of the Korean War*, vol. 1, 1977, p. 495; Appleman, op. cit., p. 21.

100) WHCC, Ibid., p. 580. None of the antitank weapons in the ROK Army's arsenal at that time could destroy T-34 tanks. The only saving grace was that a direct hit on the tank's vulnerable spots might incapacitate it-i.e., force the tank out of action without destroying it.

101) WHCC, Ibid., p. 610; JoongAng Ilbo, *Testimony of the Nation, vol. 1*, 1973, p. 18; Francesca Rhee, Memoirs: *June 25 War and President Syngman Rhee* (1), June 25, 1983.

102) WHCC, Ibid., p. 611.

103) Ibid., p. 611.

104) Ibid., p. 611.

105) Ibid., p. 614.

106) WHCC, *History of the Korean War*, vol. 1, pp. 770-771.

107) Ibid., pp. 804-805; US JCS: *Korean War*, p. 788.

108) WHCC, *History of the Korean War*, vol. 1, pp. 336-338.

109) WHCC, *Early Battles Along the 38 th Parallel (Western Front)*, 1985, pp. 74-75.

110) *Analysis of the June 25 Invasion by North Korea*, p. 122; Appleman, p. 23.

111) WHCC, *History of the Korean War*, vol. 1, p. 465.

112) WHCC, *History of the Korean War*, vol. 1, pp. 358, 370, 380, 381, 429-431, 505, 582, 664. The ROKA HQ Officer Regiment consisted of approximately 100 officers, and was under the command of Lt. Col. Kong Guk Jin. ROKA HQ, *"Operation Order* No. 84"(08:00, June 25, 1950); ROKA HQ, *"Operation Order* No. 85"(11:00, June 25, 1950); ROKA HQ, *"Operation Order* No. 87"(16:00, June 25, 1950); ROKA HQ *"Operation Order* No. 90"(12:00, June 25, 1950); ROKA HQ, *"Operation Order* No. 94"(12:00, June 25, 1950); ROKA HQ, *"Operation Order* No. 96"(17:00, June 25, 1950).

113) WHCC, *History of the Korean War*, vol. 1, pp. 356, 429-431, 517, 519, 534, 589, 591, 592, 675, 676; ROKA HQ, *"Operation Order* No. 84"(08:00, June 25, 1950); ROKA HQ, *"Operation Order* No. 97"(10:00, June 27, 1950). (1) Together with the Instruction Battalion of the Infantry School, the 3rd Battalion, 5th Regiment, 2nd Division, was committed to the Munsan area. The 3rd Regiment, 16th Regiment, arrived in Seoul on the night of the 26th, and was committed to Ch'angdong. The 1st Battalion, 16th Regiment, and 1st Battalion, 25th Regiment, continued to

carry out counter-guerrilla operations. (2) Of the two regiments of the 3rd Division, the 23rd Regiment was later committed to Uljin along the East Coast from Pusan. (3) First to arrive among the 5th Division units, the 3rd Battalion, 15th Regiment, and the 3rd Battalion, 20th Regiment, were committed to the 1st Division area under the command of Col. Choi Yong Hui, 15th Regiment commander. The 2nd Battalion, 15th Regiment, and the 1st Battalion, 20th Regiment, arrived later, and were deployed in the Miari area under the command of Col. Park Ki Byong, 20th Regiment commander. The 1st Battalion, 15th Regiment, and 2nd Battalion, 20th Regiment, continued to carry out counter-guerrilla operations.

114) WHCC, *Early Battles Along the 38 th Parallel* (Western Front), pp. 77-78.

115) ROKA HQ, *"Operation Order* No. 91"(08:00, June 26, 1950).

116) WHCC, *History of the Korean War*, vol. 1, p. 359.

117) Up to that point, the ROKA Headquarters as well as the 2nd and 7th Divisions did not know that the 3rd Regiment, committed to Songwuri in the afternoon of the 25th, had already been defeated and dispersed.

118) WHCC, *Early Battles Along the 38 th Parallel (Western Front)*, p. 92.

119) WHCC, *History of the Korean War,* vol. 1, pp. 587-588.

120) Ibid., p. 588.

121) WHCC, *Early Battles Along the 38 th Parallel (Western Front)*, p. 84.

122) At the time, the Cadet Corps consisted of the first two graduating classes in the history of Korea Military Academy. When the Korean War broke out, 263 members of Class #1 were to be commissioned in two weeks, and 334 members of Class #2 had entered the Academy only 25 days before. The Riot Police Battalion belonged to the Capital Police Department, and had a strength of 300.

123) Lt. Shim Il was killed in action on the central front on January 26, 1951. On September 17, 1951, he was posthumously awarded the Taeguk Order of Military Merit for his heroics in the Ch'unch'on Battle.

124) *Testimony of Park Jong Chae* (April 14, 1977), Document Files, Korea Institute of

Military History.

125) Appleman, op. cit., pp. 26-27; ROKA HQ, *Analysis of the June 25 Invasion by North Korea*, p. 126; Chu Yong Bok, *Southward Invasion and Defeat of the North Korean People's Army*, p. 283; FEC, *History of the North Korean Army*, p. 70. The NKPA 12th Division burst across the 38th Parallel on the 25th and collided with the ROK 6th Division in the vicinity of Naep'yongri. Changing its initial attack plan, the 12th Division moved toward Inje-Ch'unch'on, and attacked Ch'unch'on on the 27th in coordination with the 2nd Division. This supports the theory that the NKPA 12th Division troops arrived in Ch'unch'on on the 26th. The Independent Armor Regiment committed to Inje had about 30 tanks, but only 9 tanks(or, a single company strength) advanced into Ch'unch'on on the 27th.

126) FEC, *History of the North Korean Army*, p. 70.

127) WHCC, *History of the Korean War*, vol. 1, pp. 262-263.

128) Ibid., pp. 537-538.

129) ROK 6th Division, "*Operation Order* No. 32"(June 27, 1950)

130) WHCC, *History of the Korean War*, vol. 1, p. 289; ROKA HQ, "*Historical Documents of the Korean War: Detailed Battle Reports*"(53), p. 26; ROK MND, *First Year of the Korean War: A Chronicle, War Situation*, June 27; FEC, *History of the North Korean Army*, p. 47; *Testimony of the Nation*, vol. 1, p. 117; "*Testimony of Kim Jong Su*"(then-Commander of the 2nd Battalion, 7th Regiment), October 26, 1993 (Korea Institute of Military History Collections). As to when the enemy advanced into Ch'unch'on, minor differences exist among documents. The detailed battle report of the ROK 6th Division records that the 7th Regiment abandoned Ch'unch'on at 17:30, June 27, and *History of the Korean War*, vol. 1, states that the enemy occupied Ch'unch'on at 18:00. Maj. Kim Jong Su remembers receiving a withdrawal order around sunset on June 27, when his battalion was positioned on a hill midway between Chunchon and the Wonch'ang Pass.. His regiment commander ordered Maj. Kim's battalion to withdraw to the Wonch'ang Pass.

131) WHCC, *History of the Korean War*, vol. 1, pp. 264-266.

132) *Testimony of Shin Man Jin and Won Sung Jin* (residents of Hangye Village, Ch'-oljongri, Hwach'onmyon, Hongchon). Having been unable to evacuate to the rear area, they were hiding in the mountains when they witnessed the heroics of the machine gunner and his assistant. After the battle, the residents buried these two unknown soldiers, who had repulsed the enemy infantry troops. Their graves were, however, bulldozed away when the Engineer troops, expanded the Mal-gogae road in February 1959.

133) WHCC, *Early Battles Along the 38th parallel (Middle·Eastern Front)*, p. 167; Chong Ch'un Ok, 2nd Lt., Hongch'on Corps, Korean Youth Organization, stated that he saw a destroyed enemy tank on Mal-gogae while he was transporting ammunition. (May 25, 1980)

134) *Testimony of Kim Song,* commander of the 16th Artillery Battalion (July 1, 1977), Korea Institute of Military History Collections.

135) ROKA HQ, *Historical Documents of the Korean War* (53), "*Detailed Battle Reports of the ROK 6th Division*", p. 28. The 10th and 11th Companies, 3rd Battalion, 7th Regiment, put up a spirited fight at Mokdong-Kap'yong, but withdrew in the direction of Wonju on the 28th upon ROKA HQ's directive. They later joined the parent unit.

136) Yu Song Chol, "*My Testimony*"(1), Hankook Ilbo, November 13, 1990.

137) WHCC, *History of the Korean War*, vol. 1, pp. 197-199.

138) WHCC, *History of Counter-Irreaular Warfare Operations*, p. 138.

139) *Testimony of Shin Chae Ran* (resident of Tungmyongdong, Chongdongjinri), May 25, 1990. Visit to the Battlefields on the Eastern Front(Album), Korea Institute of Military History Collections. No village resident witnessed the landing of the enemy itself. Residents did see the enemy troops showing up in the village, however, and that time is recorded here.

140) WHCC, *History of the Korean War*, vol. 1, p. 199 and p. 209; WHCC, *Early Battles*

Along the 38th Parallel(Middle·Eastern Front), p. 203; Public Security Bureau, *History of the ROK Police* (Seoul: Ministry of Internal Affairs, 1973), p. 254.

141) WHCC, *History of the Korean War*, vol. 1, pp. 207-208; WHCC, *Early Battles Along the 38th Parallel(Middle·Eastern Front)*, pp. 214-216.

142) WHCC, *Early Battles Along the 38th Parallel(Middle·Eastern Front)*, p. 218.

143) WHCC, *History of the Korean War*, vol. 1, p. 207; WHCC, *Early Battles Along the 38th Parallel(Middle·Eastern Front)*, p. 233.

144) WHCC, *History of the Korean War*, vol. 1, p. 591.

145) JoongAng Ilbo, *Testimony of the Nation*, vol. 1, p. 154.

146) WHCC, *History of the Korean War*, vol. 1, pp. 594-595.

147) Francesca Rhee, *Memoirs*(1), Jun 25 1950.

148) The group was initially named "Survey Party," but was soon re-designated GHQ Advance Command and Liaison Group (ADCOM & LG), or simply ADCOM.

149) Sawyer, *KMAG*, pp. 125-126. According to its evacuation plan, KMAG evacuated from Suwon on June 27, leaving only 33 members behind in Korea. The US Embassy in Korea moved to Suwon at 09:00 the same day.

150) JoongAng Ilbo, *Testimony of the Nation*, vol. 1, p. 158. Lt. Col. Shin Dong Woo, chief secretary of Defense Minister Shin, states that he memorized Minister Shin's directive and relayed it to Gen. Chae.

151) *Testimony of Air Force Chief Kim Jong Yol* (February 10, 1977). Although the Defense Minister was second in command to the President, he had only military administration powers, and the Army, Navy, and Air Force Chiefs exercised separate military command authority over their respective service. Thus, when the war broke out, a person who could exercise military command powers over the three services and coordinate their operations was urgently needed. Air Force Chief Kim states that he advised Army Chief Chae to assume the overall command of the Army, Navy, and Air Force. Thereafter, public notices and statements as well as radio broadcasts were issued in the name of the Chief of the

General Staff..

152) The mixed "regiment" consisted of stragglers from the 3rd, 5th, 16th, and 25th Regiments, but had only a battalion strength.

153) Brig. Gen. Yu Jae Hung (7th Division commander) and Maj. Gen. Lee Ung Jun (2nd Division commander) were designated the Commander of the Uijongbu Area and Miari Area, respectively.

154) Research Institute of History, North Korea, *Comprehensive History of Choson,* vol. 25, p. 108.

155) Assigned to the 5th Division, this 15th Regiment consisted of the 3rd Battalion from the original 15th Regiment and the 3rd Battalion from the 20th Regiment. Under the command of Col. Ch'oi Yong Hi, this mixed unit was attached to the 1st Division.

156) WHCC, *History of the Korean War,* vol. 1, pp. 213-214.

157) *Oral Directive,* Morning, June 26, ROKA HQ "*Operation Order* No. 97"(10:00, June 27, 1950).

158) The Kimp'o Area Command grew to a five-battalion strength, but was unable to maintain the organization and establish a chain of command due to the lack of a communications network. Among the units, the Patriotic Battalion consisted of 174 NKPA defectors, who had carried out pacification activities and psychological warfare prior to the outbreak of the war. The Officer Candidate Battalion of the Infantry School had not even undergone rifle training. The 2nd Battalion(-), 12th Regiment, assembled in Yongjongp'o south of Kaesong, and withdrew to Kangryongp'o on the Kimp'o Peninsula. WHCC, *Early Battles Along the 38th Parallel (Western Front)* (Seoul: Ministry of National Defense), pp. 260-262.

159) As of June 1950, there were five bridges over the Han River: the Great Han Bridge (pedestrian bridge) connecting Noryangjin and Yongsan; the double-track railway bridge on the Seoul-Pusan line; single-track railway bridge on the Seoul-Inch'on line; and the Kwangjin Bridge (pedestrian bridge) across from the

Kwangnaru (ferry terminal). [Translator's Note: The term "pedestrian bridge" here in effect means that the bridge was not a railway bridge and allowed the passage of both pedestrians and vehicles.]

160) As to the demolition time of the bridges over the Han, minor differences exists among documents. At the court marshall of Col. Choi Chang Shik on September 15, 1950, the verdict officially pronounced 02:30, June 28, as the time of demolition based on various witness accounts, and this is cited here. WHCC, *History of the Korean War*, vol. 2, pp. 558-559. See the verdict.

161) WHCC, *History of the Korean War*, vol. 1, p. 547; Appleman, op. cit., p. 33.

162) Appleman, op. cit., p. 34; WHCC, *History of the Korean War*, vol. 1, p. 550.

163) The official US history of the Korean War notes that had the demolition of the bridges been delayed until the enemy actually reached the Han River line, ROK Forces would have had about 6 to 8 hours to move troops and heavy equipment across the Han. Appleman, op. cit., p. 34.

164) WHCC, tr., *US JCS: Korean War*, vol. 1, pp. 58-59. Here, Korean time is used as the standard throughout. EDT(Eastern Daylight Savings Time) or EST(Eastern Standard Time) is used to indicate local time in Washington or New York. Korean time is 13 hours ahead of EDT, and 14 hours ahead of EST.

165) Ibid., p.61; WHCC, *History of the Korean War*, vol. 1, p.870.

166) Barros, James, *Trygve Lie and the Cold War*, 1989, p.274.

167) WHCC, tr., *US JCS: Korean War*, vol. 1, p. 60.

168) WHCC, *History of the Korean War*, vol. 1, p. 614.

169) Han Pyo Uk, *ROK-US Diplomacy: Cradle Period*, (Seoul: JoongAng Ilbo), pp. 76-78.

170) WHCC, *History of the Korean War*, vol. 1, p. 948.

171) Han Pyo Uk, *ROK-US Diplomacy*, pp. 76-78.

172) WHCC, *History of the Korean War*, vol. 1, p. 875; Han Pyo Uk, *ROK-US Diplomacy*, p. 81.

173) WHCC, tr., *US JCS: Korean War*, vol. 1, p. 62.

174) Han Pyo Uk, *ROK–US Diplomacy,* p. 81.

175) Ibid., pp. 80–84.

176) WHCC, *History of the Korean War,* vol. 1, pp. 942–945.

177) WHCC, tr., *US JCS: Korean War,* vol. 1, pp. 70–72.

178) Francesca Rhee, *Memoirs,* vol. 1, *JoongAng Ilbo,* June 27, 1984.

179) Appleman, op. cit., p. 43.

180) Ibid., pp. 42–43.

181) Han Pyo Uk, *ROK–US Diplomacy,* p. 86.

182) Ibid., pp. 86–87.

183) Ibid., p. 87.

184) WHCC, tr., *US JCS: Korean War,* vol. 1, p. 78.

185) Ibid., pp. 80–81.

186) WHCC, *History of the Korean War,* vol. 1, p. 950.

187) WHCC, tr., *US JCS: Korean War,* vol. 1, p. 79.

188) Han Pyo Uk, *ROK–US Diplomacy,* pp. 89–90.

189) WHCC, *History of the Korean War,* vol. 1, p. 954.

Chapter Three   Delaying Action

Ⅰ. Defense Along the Han River Line

1. ROK Forces Organize the Han River Defense Line

(1) NKPA's Operational Intent

In the early morning of June 28, the fourth day of the war, the North Korean People's Army went on a total offensive with an intent to envelop and annihilate ROK main forces in the vicinity of Seoul. The Han River bridges had already been blown up by ROK forces, and the Miari line, final line of defense for Seoul, had collapsed. The enemy 1st Corps (under Lt. Gen. Kim Ung), in coordination with the 105th Armor Brigade (under Maj. Gen. Ryu Kyong Su), sealed off river-crossing sites and seized crucial institutions in Seoul, the NKPA's strategic objective. These institutions included: the ROK Capitol, Ministry of National Defense, Army HQ, broadcasting stations, central telegraph station, and Map'o as well as Sodaemun Prisons.

In spite of its occupation of Seoul, however, the North Korean Supreme Command encountered continuing ROK resistance after the moving of the ROK government to Taejon[1] and faced the unexpected prospect of intervention by UN naval and air forces. Aware of the possibility of eventual intervention by UN ground forces, the North Korean Supreme Command hastily issued a preplanned advance order so as to seize the entire Korean Peninsula before such intervention. Accordingly, the NKPA decided "to carry out an assault-crossing of the Han; annihilate and mop up ROK main forces; and occupy the area along P'yongt'aek-Ch'ungju-Uljin line prior to US intervention; and to direct the main attack along Yongdungp'o-Suwon-P'yongt'aek and have a supporting attack along several other directions in order to achieve this objective."[2]

The NKPA 1st Corps directed its main attack, the 4th Division (under Maj. Gen. Lee Kwon Mu), from vicinity Shinch'on toward Yongdungp'o, and directed its supporting attack, 3rd Division (under Maj. Gen. Lee Yong Ho), from Yongsan-Hannamdong toward Maljukgori. These NKPA troops busily prepared for river-crossing operations. Meanwhile, joining the 1st Corps from the direction of Munsan, the 6th Division (under Maj. Gen. Bang Ho San) assembled in the vicinity of Susaek and prepared to support the 14th Regiment, which had already advanced to the vicinity of the Kimp'o Air Field. Also, the main effort of the 1st Division (under Maj. Gen. Choi Kwang) entered Seoul from the direction of Sodaemun, and became a follow-on echelon for the 3rd and 4th Divisions. Maintaining security in downtown Seoul and providing support for the river-crossing of infantry units, the 105th Armored Brigade was looking for crossing opportunities of its own.[3]

Upon occupying Seoul, the NKPA 1st Corps hastened to cross the Han River as the North Korean Air Force lost air superiority and intervention by US ground forces loomed on the horizon. Assigned the mission of leading the penetration of the Han River line, the 3rd and 4th Divisions deployed their artillery regiments at the bottom of Nam-san and in the vicinity of Sinch'on to provide fire support.

In addition to making preparations to cross the Han, however, P'yongyang had to face many difficult choices connected with the estimate of the situation after the occupation of Seoul and establishment of contingency plans.

Accordingly, the NKPA needed some time to explore various solutions to these problems.[4]

Meanwhile, in the NKPA 2nd Corps zone on the central eastern front, the 2nd Division was advancing toward Yongin via Kap'yong, while the 12th Division (under Maj. Gen. Choi Chung Guk) was moving southward along the central axis keeping pace with NKPA troops on the western front. As a corps reserve, the 15th Division (under Maj. Gen. Park Song Chol) was following on, intent on advancing toward Yoju-Changhowon in the future. Along the eastern seashores, the enemy 5th Division (under Maj. Gen. Ma Sang Chol) occupied Samch'ok without encountering much resistance due to the earlier withdrawal of the ROK 8th Division, and was advancing southward along the East Seashore Road. After landing at Chongdongjin and Imwonjin, the 766th Independent Regiment (under Sr. Col. Oh Jin U)[5] and the 549th Naval Combat Team blocked the Kangnung-Samch'ok Road, and was supporting the southward advance of the 2nd Corps from the central front while attempting to infiltrate into the inland areas.

(2) The River-Crossing and Withdrawal of the ROK Armed Forces

Having neither foreseen the need for withdrawal nor established any withdrawal plan, the ROK government and military could not systematically control the withdrawal from Seoul. The capital city was covered with fear and confusion under the enemy's pressure, and refugees from the north only aggravated the situation.

As the ROK military and police were also unable to control the flow of refugees along the Seoul-Suwon National Road, all military transport operations on the road were disrupted. Moreover, prior to the outbreak of the war, the Han River had only been mentioned as a possible delaying defense line in case of an enemy attack, as the river seemed to provide a good, natural obstacle against the enemy advance; there was no concrete plan to implement this concept.[6] The worsening of the situation due to these various factors prevented the rapid disengagement of ROK Forces following its tactical withdrawal, and complicated its reorganization efforts after crossing the river.

Under these extremely confusing circumstances, ROK Forces began to cross the Han on the morning of June 28. Unable to use bridges, however, ROK troops could not transport heavy equipment (field artillery pieces, vehicles, mortars, etc.) across the river. Carrying only rifles, the withdrawing troops used rafts or ferries to cross the river individually or in small units.

After trying to block the enemy's advance mostly in the front of Miari, mixed units withdrew from ferry terminals and crossing sites at Map'o, Hajungri (Sogang), Sobinggo, Hannamdong, Ttuksom, and Kwangnaru. ROK units committed to the Munsan front crossed the Han from Haengju and Isanp'o. Among these units, those who came from Kwangnaru immediately assembled in Suwon; the troops from Sobinggo, Hannamdong, and Ttuksom assembled in Shihung and Suwon; and the troops from Haengju, Hajungri, and Map'o mostly assembled in Shihung.[7] Between the night of the 28th and morning of the 29th, the withdrawing troops finished assembling.

The soldiers were fatigued from repeated combat and withdrawal, and the gathered troops of a regiment would amount to only battalion strength. ROK Forces faced even tougher challenges in the area of logistics. The demolition of the Han bridges trapped all 1,318 vehicles loaded with ROK division supplies on the north of the river. On the south, the lack of appropriate transport and communication control centers aggravated the supply problem to rear units, and communication breakdowns made it difficult to maintain contact with adjacent units, to say nothing of higher and subordinate units. The command and control system broke down as a result.[8]

ROK Forces had no time to formulate a systematic plan for defense, and could do little but to proceed on an assumption that the enemy's main attack would penetrate the Noryangjin front and advance along Shihung–Anyang–Suwon on the Seoul–Pusan National Road. Troops were committed in this direction as soon as they were gathered. The Han River defense line now emerged as a lifeline on whose defense the nation's survival depended.

(3) The Formation of Han River Defense Line

The Han River in the vicinity of Seoul has a width of 700 to 1,500 meters and an average depth of 3 meters. To ROK Forces who had lost Seoul, the Han River provided a good terrain for defense. At the same time, however, several ferry terminals on the river bank were large enough to serve as assembly points for vehicles and could be used as good river-crossing points.

Also, a couple of bridges over the Han River still could be used as river-crossing routes. Although the Pedestrian Bridge, the westbound track on the Seoul–Inch'on Railway Bridge, and the Kwangjin Bridge were successfully severed by the ROK demolition team, the eastbound track on the Seoul–Inch'on Railway Bridge and the Seoul–Pusan Railway Bridge were not completely destroyed and still could be used. As the enemy did not possess river-crossing equipment for tanks, it seemed certain that the enemy would attempt to seize these bridges. The securing of the bridges thus emerged as a pressing problem for both sides.[9]

Just before the fall of Seoul, the Chief of the General Staff Maj. Gen. Chae had decided to block the NKPA along the Han River defense line. After moving the ROKA HQ to the Suwon Agricultural Experiment Station, Gen. Chae had Maj. Gen. Kim Hong Il, Superintendent of the Army Staff College, take over the Shihung Area Command and take up defense along the Han River line. Brig. Gen. John H. Church of ADCOM[10] also advised Gen. Chae to defend along the Han River line.

Maj. Gen. Kim Hong Il had a remarkable career. To seek political asylum, he went to Shanghai in 1918, and after graduating from Kangmu Academy in China, he joined the Korean Independence Army, eventually serving as the commander of the Korean Volunteer Army. In 1925, he joined the Chinese Nationalist Army and later served as a division commander. He was the Chief of Staff of the Korean Restoration Army when Korea was liberated from Japan. He returned to Korea, and was serving as the superintendent of the Army Staff College when the war broke out. At that time, among ROK military leaders, Gen. Kim was the only man with any experience in commanding a division-or-above unit.[1]

After establishing the command and organizing the staff in Shihung, he named Brig. Gen. Yu Jae Hung commander of the Mixed 7th Division, Col. Lee Jong Ch'an commander of the Mixed Capital Division, and Col. Lim Son Ha commander of the Mixed 2nd Division. Gen. Kim then began to organize frontal defense for the 24-km-long stretch on the southern bank from Anyangch'on to the Kwangjin Bridge.

The operational concept of the ROK troops was to defend the Han River line to the end. Anticipating that US ground forces would soon be committed, the Shihung Area Command sought to defend the Han River line so that these forces could be deployed as far north as possible. The Han River line defense order issued by the command included the following key points:

1. The command intends to defend the Han River line.
2. The Mixed 2nd Division will hold the line along Sinsari–Tongjakri.
3. The Mixed 7th Division will hold the line along Tongjakri–Taebangri.
4. The Mixed Capital Division will hold the line along Singilri–Yangp'yongri (Anyang-ch'on).

Defense Along the Han River Line(June 30~July 4, 1950)

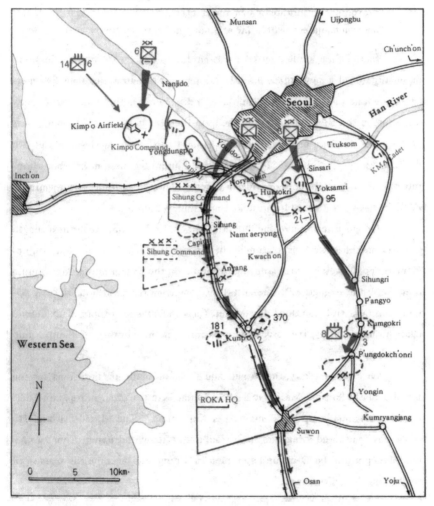

5. The Kimp'o Area Command will block the enemy at the present position (Kimp'o).

6. Each division will spoil the enemy's river-crossing attempts.

7. Each division will thoroughly check the identity of refugees so as to prevent the infiltration of communist agents.

8. The command post will locate at Sihung (Infantry School).[12]

Establishing collecting points to gather stragglers in Sihung, the command organized a new mixed battalion whenever the total reached 500 men. The command also encouraged each mixed division to gather troops after they had crossed the Han and redeploy them on the river bank. As the enemy was likely to use the Han bridges, Gen. Kim Hong Il gave priority to the Mixed 7th Division in the vicinity of Noryangjin and committed new mixed battalions into this area. Hastening to organize a defense centered around ferry terminals, ROK Forces were able to form the defense line by June 29.

On the afternoon of the 29th, the Mixed 7th Division, with the strength of seven mixed battalions, channeled its energy into securing the Noryangjin-Yongdungp'o riverside area and high grounds in the Tongjakdong-Noryangjin area. With the strength of three battalions, one armored battalion, and two 57-mm recoilless rifle platoons, the Mixed Capital Division prepared to defend against the enemy's river-crossing operations in the vicinity of Kimp'o and Yongdungp'o.[13]

On the same day, the Mixed 2nd Division made preparations for the defense of the Sinsari-Maljukgori area. In the Kimp'o area, more than 2,000 mixed troops made up the Kimp'o Area Command.[14] The Mixed 3rd and 5th Divisions[15] gathered stragglers in Suwon, and, after withdrawing from Isanp'o and Haengju, the 1st Division assembled in Sihung and became the reserve of the Sihung Area Command.

In addition, the 6th Division on the central front was withdrawing to Ch'ungju after striking a big blow against the enemy's plans by carrying out effective defensive operations in Ch'unch'on-Hongch'on. On the eastern front, the 8th Division was withdrawing from Taegwan-ryong toward Jech'on on the

〈Table 1〉 Comparison of ROK and NKPA Forces at the Han River Line(Jun 29, 1950)

ROK Sihung Area Command (Maj. Gen. Kim Hong Il)	
Mixed Capital Division (Col. Lee Jong Ch'an)	8th(−) and 18th(−2) Regiments and 1st Armored Battalion of the Cavalry Regiment
Mixed 7th Division (Br. Gen. Yu Jae Hung)	1st(−), 9th(−), 15th(−), 20th(−2), 25th (−2) Regiments
Mixed 2nd Division (Col. Lim Son Ha)	3rd(−), 5th(−), 16th(−)Regiments, Mixed Regiment of Infantry School, and 2nd Cavalry battalion of the Cavalry Regiment
Mixed 3rd Division (Br. Gen. Lee Jun Shik)	22nd and 25th(−) Regiments and KMA Cadet Battalion
1st Division (Col. Paik Sun Yup)	11th, 12th, 13th Regiments
Kimp'o Command (Lt. Col. Lim Ch'ung Shik)	18th Regiment(−) and parts of the 8th, Cavalry, 12th, and 22nd Regiments
NKPA 1st Corps (Lt. Gen. Kim Ung)	
3rd Division (Maj. Gen. Lee Yong Ho)	7th, 8th, 9th Regiments and an artillery regiment
4th Division (Maj. Gen. Lee Kwon Mu)	5th, 16th, 18th Regiments and an artillery regiment
1st Division (Maj. Gen. Ch'oi Kwang)	14th, 2nd, 3rd Regiments and an artillery regiment
6th Division (Maj. Gen. Pang Ho San)	1st, 13th, 15th Regiments and an artillery regiment
2nd Division (Maj. Gen. Lee Ch'ong Song)	4th, 6th, 17th Regiments and an artillery regiment
105th Armored Brigade (Maj. Gen. Ryu Kyong Su)	107th, 109th, 203rd Armored Regiments

order from the ROKA Headquarters. The axis along the eastern seashores was in effect open, and almost without any defense.

Although mixed divisions under the Sihung Area Command completed deployment by the 29th, each mixed division really amounted to only a regiment strength. Moreover, the only crew—served weapons in each mixed regiment were 2 or 3 mortars and 5 or 6 machine guns, and only added up to the firepower of a small rifle unit.[16] 〈Table 1〉 compares the strength of both sides as of June 29.

Initially, the Sihung Command was charged with command responsibility for all ROK units along the Han River line. Due to poor communications, however, it primarily commanded the Mixed 7th and Capital Divisions, and concentrated on the defense of Noryangjin-Yongdungp'o. As Kwanak Mountain disrupted communications with the Sihung Command, the Mixed 2nd Division was really under the direct operational control of the ROKA Headquarters. Also, as of June 29, the Kimp'o Area Command was almost independently conducting defensive operations with its six battalions. As a result, ROK Forces along the Han River line did not have the unity of command.

Feeling that it was difficult to carry out a systematic counterattack or surprise attack with this disorganized potpourri of troops, commanders decided to deploy forces along the river bank and repulse the approaching enemy from the front.[17]

2. US Expands the Scope of Its Support

(1) Decision to Send US Ground Forces

Before moving to Taejon, the ROK government and National Assembly formally requested the United Nations and the US to extend "immediate and effective" support so as to repulse the NKPA attack. When North Korea continued hostilities in defiance of its June 26 resolution, the UN Security Council recommended that the members of the United Nations furnish military assistance to the Republic of Korea. Prior to the commitment of US ground forces (July 1) in the Korean War, the US President decided to send naval and air forces to Korea and ordered the Seventh Fleet into the Formosa Strait.

While the ROK Armed Forces were focusing all their effort on forming the Han River defense line, Brig. Gen. Church of ADCOM met with Chief of the General Staff Chae Byong Dok, and insisted that the Han River defense line be maintained at all costs. After observing the general war situation, Gen. Church came to the conclusion that if the 38th Parallel were to be restored, US ground forces would have to be committed. He radioed this opinion to Gen. MacArthur in Japan.[18]

Sensing that the war situation had reached a critical point, MacArthur decided to make a personal visit to Korea. In spite of bad weather and the threat of enemy air attack, he made a flight and landed at Suwon Airfield on June 29. On the flight to Korea, he ordered bombing operations north of the 38th Parallel.[19] When MacArthur's party landed at the airfield, the end of the runway was still covered in black smoke from an earlier enemy bombing attack. Gen. MacArthur was greeted by President Rhee, Ambassador Muccio, and Gen. Church. After listening to a briefing on the war situation given by the head of ADCOM, MacArthur's party drove north past refugees and soldiers to reach the Han River defense line, where the 1st Battalion, 8th Regiment, Mixed Capital Division was deployed. They could see Seoul across the river. After personally witnessing sporadic enemy artillery fire from the city, MacArthur returned to Tokyo.[20]

Around this time in Washington, as the possibility of a limited, indirect engagement by the US became more remote by the hour, the Joint Chiefs of Staff established a plan to strengthen the authority of the Far East Command (FEC). After securing President Truman's approval, the Joint Chiefs of Staff sent additional instructions to FEC.

Received by Tokyo on June 30, these instructions included: 1. operation of Army service troops to attend to crucial tasks such as communications; 2. operation of Army units, both combat and service troops, to secure the port and the air facilities in the Pusan—Chinhae area; 3. commitment of naval and air forces to attack military targets in North Korea, while staying well clear of the frontiers of Manchuria and the Soviet Union; 4. giving MacArthur operational control of the Seventh Fleet.[21]

These measures were taken with a view to achieving the following effects: First, although the United States decided to send ground forces to Korea, the commitment was to be limited to the strength of a regimental combat team, conducting rear security instead of front operations. Second, the naval and air operation area was to be expanded to the entire Korean Peninsula. (On his flight to Suwon, MacArthur had already expanded the scope of naval and air operations by ordering bombing operations north of the 38th Parallel.) Third, the US naval presence around Korea was to be greatly strengthened.

A few hours after receiving the additional instructions, MacArthur sent to Washington a report of his personal visit to Korea. Arriving in Washington around 03:00, June 30, the report informed the Joint Chiefs of Staff :

> ···The ROK Army is entirely incapable of counter-action and there is grave danger of a further breakthrough··· The only assurance for the holding of the present line, and the ability to regain later the lost ground, is through the introduction of US ground combat forces into the Korean battle area If authorized, it is my intention to immediately move a United States regimental combat team to the reinforcement of

the vital area discussed ⟨the Han River defense line⟩ and to provide for a possible build-up to a two-division strength from the troops in Japan for an early counter-offensive.[22]

After receiving a report from the Joint Chiefs of Staff, President Truman immediately approved dispatching one regimental combat team (RCT) to the battle area. At a subsequent meeting of the State, Defense, and Service Secretaries, the US President approved orders to dispatch two divisions from Japan to Korea and to conduct a naval blockade of North Korea.[23] Thus, the decision to send US ground forces to Korea was made on June 30.

In short, the United States took the following steps in expanding its support to the Republic of Korea : 1. naval and air operations south of the 38th Parallel ; 2. naval and air operations extended north of the 38th Parallel ; 3. commitment of ground forces. This was made possible through extensive and rapid exchange of information among ADCOM in Korea, FEC in Tokyo, and the JCS and national security apparatus in Washington.

(2) Deployment of US Ground Forces

As soon as the decision to commit US ground forces was made on June 30, Gen. MacArthur ordered the Eighth US Army (EUSA) commander to dispatch the 24th Division in Kyushu. As time was of the essence, this division, stationed closest to Korea among US Forces in Japan, received the first call.

Lt. Gen. Walton H. Walker, commander of the EUSA issued the following deployment directives to Maj. Gen. William F. Dean, commander of the 24th Division : 1. A battalion commander will organize a task force to conduct a delaying action with two rifle companies, two 4.2-inch mortar platoons, and a 75-mm recoilless rifle platoon. The task force will be transported by air to Pusan, and upon reporting to Gen. Church, it will follow his directives; 2. The rest of the division will follow by sea ; 3. The division will secure a bridgehead for an early counter-offensive; 4. Upon arriving in Korea, the division commander will assume the command of all US Forces in Korea.[24]

Designated to command the leading detachment, Lt. Col. Charles B. Smith, commander of the 1st Battalion, 21st Infantry Regiment, stayed up all night to organize Task Force Smith cented around the battalion's B and C Companies. At Itatsuke Airfield, Gen. Dean told Lt. Col. Smith: "When you arrive in Pusan, head to Taejon. We are trying to delay the enemy as far north from Pusan as possible. Go as far north as possible and block the main roads. Meet Gen. Church first." At 08:45, July 1, Task Force Smith arrived in Pusan to a warm welcome of the citizens.[25]

The task force departed from Pusan by rail at 20 : 00, and arrived in Taejon at 08 : 00, July 2. Lt. Col. Smith went to ADCOM to report to Gen. Church and listened to a resume of the war situation. After conducting a ground reconnaissance all the way to Chukmi-ryong on the north of Osan, he returned to Taejon. Ordered to occupy P'yongt'aek and Osan, Smith moved the troops again by rail and deployed a company each in the two towns. The command post was located in P'yongt'aek. On July 4, Lt. Col. Millero Perry, commander of the 52nd Artillery Battalion, brought the battalion's A Battery to join the task force.

Among the main effort of the US 24th Division which departed from the Port of Sasebo, the 34th Regiment arrived in Pusan on July 2, and began to move north on the 4th. The 21st Regiment(−) and the 19th Regiment arrived in Pusan on July 4.

On that day, Gen. Dean established the United States Army Forces in Korea (USAFIK) with Gen. Church as deputy commander and ADCOM personnel as staff. On the same day, Brig. Gen. Crump Garvin established the Pusan Base Command of the 8th Army, and began to provide logistical support.[26]

Thus, while ROK Forces were engaging the enemy along the Han River defense line, US Forces completed the deployment of the 24th Division in Korea only four days after the decision to commit ground troops had been made. Other US divisions were making preparations for deployment.

In Japan, there was a total of four US divisions serving as occupation forces at the time. However, due to defense cutbacks after World War II, the US Army had removed the third battalion from infantry regiments, and had similarly reduced artillery and armor units.[27]

3. ROK Forces Defend the Han River-Suwon Line

After occupying Seoul, the NKPA 1st Corps probed the ROK defense line on the other side of the Han River on June 28 and 29, and sporadically delivered artillery fires At the same time, the enemy completed preparations for a river-crossing operation. The 4th Division, the enemy's main attack, was directed toward Youido while the 3rd Division, its supporting attack, was directed toward Huksokdong and Sinsari.

Under the support of concentrated tank gun and artillery fires on the night of the 29th, the NKPA 3rd and 4th Divisions dispatched reconnaissance units to probe the Youido, Huksokdong, and Shinsari areas. In response, the ROK Mixed Capital Division in the vicinity of Huksokdong forwarded a 57-mm recoilless rifle platoon to Youido to attack the enemy units. The platoon, however, came under concentrated fire from the enemy artillery positions, and all its members died heroic deaths.[28] By the end of that night, the enemy managed to secure a bridgehead with a company strength on Bamsom (islet) and on the southern bank in the Huksokdong area.

From the dawn of June 30, the ROK Mixed Capital Division engaged in a series of bloody battles with the enemy 4th Division which sought to advance to Youido Airfield from Bamsom. Eventually repulsed by the ROK troops, the NKPA 4th Division committed a part of its strength to the northern bank in the Noryangjin area, and attempted to restore the eastbound track of the Seoul-Inch'on Railway Bridge, which had yet to be severed. This attempt was, however, spoiled by the 3rd Bombing Squadron of the 5th US Air Force, which at the time happened to be interdicting transportation networks in the vicinity of Seoul. The squadron completely destroyed the railway bridge.

Meanwhile, taking advantage of the bridgehead which had been secured the night before, the NKPA 3rd Division began to carry out a large-scale river-crossing operation at dawn, June 30. Some attempted to swim across the Han, while others used rafts and ferries carrying 20 to 30 troops.[29] Under the support of the 19th Bombing Squadron of the US Air Force, however, the 9th Regiment of the ROK Mixed 7th Division on the southern bank was able to deliver concentrated fire and block the enemy's river-crossing attempt. While the Han restricted the maneuver of the enemy tanks, ROK Forces put up a fierce fight to block the enemy's advance under the close air support of the 5th US Air Force.

Meanwhile, ROK Forces in the vulnerable Sinsari area allowed part of the enemy 3rd Division to cross the Han that afternoon. Under artillery support, the NKPA troops broke through the defense of the ROK 2nd Cavalry Battalion, and threatened the security of the 3rd Regiment (−), a supporting unit. The commander of the ROK Mixed 2nd Division at last decided to take advantage of the terrain in the vicinity of Maljukgori and block the enemy's advance from there. He deployed the 5th and 16th Regiments in the vicinity of HILL 95, and retained the 3rd Regiment (−) as a reserve in Kwach'on to form a defense line along Namt'ae-ryong−Umyon-san−Hill 95.[30]

On June 30, the first day of the river-crossing operation, the North Korean People's Army intended to seize a chain of hills in the Noryangjin area. Using cover provided from these hills, the enemy intended to move tanks across the Han via the eastbound track of the Seoul-Inch'on Bridge. The NKPA's river-crossing operation was, however, frustrated by ROK Forces.

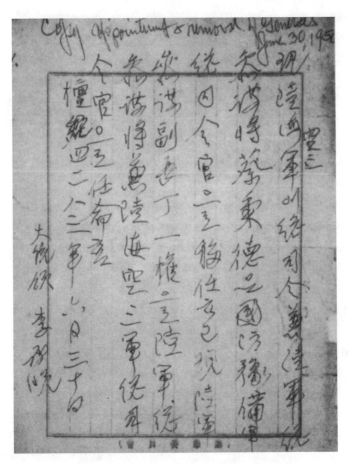

President Syngman Rhee's handwritten order to appoint
Maj. Gen. Chung Il-Kwon to the post of the Chief of the General Staff

At dawn of July 1, the NKPA 4th Division launched a full-fledged river-crossing attempt from the northern bank in the Yongdungp'o area. With a view to securing the Seoul-Pusan Railway Bridge, the only bridge not completely destroyed, the NKPA 4th Division first sent an infiltration unit of platoon strength in ROK uniform to harass the ROK troops in the Noryangjin area. Spearheaded by the 5th Regiment, the division reserve, the NKPA troops then carried out a large-scale river-crossing operation from Map'o and Hajungri Ferry site. After securing a stronghold in Youido, the enemy closed in on the 8th Regiment, ROK Mixed Capital Division, and threatened to break through the ROK defense line at one time. Taking maximum advantage of the terrain, however, the 8th Regiment troops in trenches delivered concentrated small-arms fire and threw hand-grenades at the enemy, and were able to repulse the threat.

As if determined to seize the Yongdungp'o area by July 1, the enemy 4th Division carried out a relentless attack throughout that day, but was eventually repulsed by the fierce resistance of the Mixed Capital Division. With their crossing attempt to Youido running into a wall, the North Korean Army seems to have concluded that the success of the operation depended on obtaining armor support. That night, the NKPA 4th Division mobilized railway workers and ordinary citizens, and stealthily began restoration work on the Seoul-Pusan Railway Bridge.[31]

Meanwhile, in the Maljukgori area, the ROK Mixed 2nd Division learned that part of the enemy troops hit the gap between the 5th and 16th Regiments to infiltrate into the P'angyo area in the rear, but kept its main effort on Hill 95 and Namt'ae-ryong in anticipation of a follow-on attack by the enemy's main attack. Instead, the 2nd Division committed the 25th Regiment to carry out rear operations.

Newly appointed to the post of Army Chief of Staff and the Chief of the General Staff of ROK Armed Forces on July 1, Maj. Gen. Chung Il Kwon[32] analyzed the overall situation of the Han River defense line that day, and insisted that the Maljukgori-Suwon line be maintained at all cost. Otherwise, the line of retreat for the Mixed Capital and 7th Divisions would be blocked, he noted. Following Gen. Chung's directive, the 22nd Regiment of the Mixed 3rd Division organized a second line of defense in the Kumgokri area on the south of P'angyo.

The fierce battle continued into July 2. The NKPA 3rd Division troops who had seized the bridgehead on the bank opposite Noryangjin lacked the numbers to carry out a daring offensive; whereas the NKPA 4th Division on the bank opposite Youido seized the airfield again and attempted to break through the position of the 8th Regiment, ROK Mixed Capital Division. Just like the day before, however, the 8th Regiment repulsed the enemy after a series of bloody engagements, and the battle in the Youido area went into a lull.

On the same day, the situation turned critical in the Maljukgori area. In order to follow the North Korean troops that had already infiltrated into P'angyo, the 8th Regiment of the enemy 3rd Division broke through the position of the ROK 5th Regiment and advanced toward Hill 95. Subjected to bombardment by US planes that happened to appear at that moment, however, the enemy 8th Regiment withheld its advance, and went into troop maintenance. Around this time in the vicinity of Sihungri, the ROK Infantry School Regiment detected more than 30 enemy supply trucks advancing toward P'angyo. This reserve regiment carried out a surprise attack, and denied the supplies to the enemy troops in P'angyo, significantly slowing down the pace of the enemy's southward advance.

With an enemy regiment already in Maljukgori, the ROK Sihung Command directed the Mixed 2nd Division to secure the Kwach'on-Kunp'o Road in order to provide cover for the withdrawal of the main effort along

National Road 1 on July 2. As the Mixed 2nd Division withdrew from the Maljukgori area to carry out this mission, the Mixed 3rd Regiment in Kumgo-kri became solely responsible for the defense of the Maljukgori-P'angyo axis.[33] Meanwhile, with the supplies cut off and US planes continuing to carry out air raids, the enemy troops in P'angyo had to halt their advance and wait for the main attack to arrive.

On July 3, the fourth day of the enemy's river-crossing operation, the situation began to deteriorate as the enemy's main attack broke through the ROK defense line. Having started the renovation work on the Seoul-Pusan Railway Bridge on July 1, the NKPA 4th Division at last began to send tanks across the bridge on July 3. At 04:00, four enemy tanks successfully crossed the Han. Follow-on forces crossed the bridge and turned right toward Yongdung-p'o. Soon afterwards, 13 more tanks and troops advanced to the southern bank by rail, and began to overrun the Noryangjin and Yongdungp'o area.

Part of the NKPA 3rd Division crossed the Han to reach Noryangjin and began to threaten the rear of Yongdungp'o. At the same time, part of the 14th Regiment, NKPA 6th Division, broke through Oryudong and advanced to Yongdungp'o under the cover of two tanks. Exposed to the enemy threat from the rear, the defensive position of the 8th Regiment, ROK Mixed Capital Division, began to collapse. Seizing this opportunity, the enemy troops in front of Youido crossed the Han and began to advance toward Yongdungpo.

A transportation hub on the southern bank of the Han, the Yongdu-ngp'o area was crucial to the maintenance of the Han River defense line as a whole. In spite of the enemy's envelopment, the ROK Capital Division troops put up a desperate street-to-street fight, taking advantage of such favorable terrain features as factories and other buildings in the area.[34] The situation, however, had already taken a decisive turn in favor of the enemy, and the fall of Yongdungp'o seemed imminent.

With Yongdungp'o about to fall into the enemy hands, Maj. Gen. Kim Hong Il decided that it was time for withdrawal. According to a prepared withdrawal plan, the ROK main effort along the Han River defense line once again dispersed by unit. Some units assembled in Anyang while the others went to Kwach'on. The enemy in the Yongdungp'o area went into troop maintenance; whereas, the enemy 8th Regiment in Maljukgori advanced toward P'angyo. Meanwhile, the NKPA 6th Division in Kimp'o maneuvered toward Inch'on in the evening, spearheaded by six tanks.[35]

Informed of the collapse of the Han defense line on the morning of July 3, Army Chief of Staff Chung Il Kwon noted that the lead detachment of the US ground forces had already advanced to the P'yongt'aek-Ansong line, and decided to delay the enemy's advance at the present position in order to give the US troops time to prepare for combat. Accordingly, he issued an operation order to conduct a delaying action in stages between Yongdungp'o and Suwon.[36] ROKA HQ Op. Order No. 18 (oral order dated July 2, written order dated July 3) stipulated: "ROK Forces conduct a delaying action at the present line in order to buy time for supporting foreign troops." To block the enemy's attack in the Kumgokri area, Gen. Chung committed the 1st Division there. When the 19th Regiment, ROK 6th Division, in Ich'on reported that the leading unit of the enemy 2nd Division was advancing toward Kumryangjang, Yongingun, Gen. Chung dispatched from Suwon the 2nd Battalion of the 8th Regiment as a reinforcement.

Maj. Gen. Kim Hong Il deployed the Mixed Capital Division along the first line of resistance in the Sihung area, and positioned the Mixed 7th Division along the second line of resistance in the Anyang area. In addition, the 15th and 18th Regiments were respectively attached and returned to the Mixed Capital Division after the break-up of the Kimp'o Command. Meanwhile, the Mixed 2nd Division (under Col. Lee Han Lim) was assigned the mission to cover the withdrawal of the Sihung Command in the vicinity of Kunp'ojang. In short, three ROK divisions were deployed along the lines of resistance across the Seoul-Pusan National Road, along which the enemy's main attack was likely to be directed. Each division organized special antitank attack units and committed them in the vicinity of various bridges and defiles.

In the meantime, a line of resistance was formed on the Kumgokri-Suwon axis, and the ROK Mixed 3rd Division was blocking the advance of the enemy 8th Regiment in the vicinity of Kumgokri. The ROK 1st Division advanced to P'ungdok-ch'on in the rear of Kumgokri, and was hastily organizing a second line of resistance.

At dawn, July 4, the enemy 4th Division assembled tanks assigned to the 105th Armored Brigade in the vicinity of Yongdungp'o. Advancing southward along the Seoul-Suwon Road, the NKPA division began to attack the ROK defense positions. The ROK Capital Division on the first line of resistance was attacked from both flanks by the enemy's leading tanks and infantry units under the cover of three YAK fighter planes. Dispersed in detail, the ROK division had to withdraw in the direction of Suwon. Around noon, the ROK 7th Division position on the second line of resistance was also penetrated by the enemy tanks. The appearance of a US air squad at this time temporarily slowed down the pace of the enemy's advance, but the overwhelming shock power of the enemy tanks eventually broke through the ROK 2nd Division position on the third line of resistance.[37]

Synchronizing with the 4th Division, the 8th Regiment of the NKPA 3rd Division launched an attack at dawn, July 4. Brushing aside the ROK 3rd Division, the enemy division advanced southward along the P'ungdok-ch'on-Suwon Road. The ROK 1st Division in P'ungdok-ch'on temporarily repulsed the enemy's two leading battalion with concentrated fires, but its defense eventually collapsed when the enemy broke through the middle of the defense line.[38]

Judging that it was difficult to block the enemy's advance any longer, Army Chief of Staff Chung ordered the Sihung Command to withdraw to P'yongt'aek at 14:00, July 4. Accordingly, the ROK troops assembled in Suwon were to move to P'yongt'aek after the ROKA Headquarters moved. Late in the afternoon that day, when the enemy tanks and troops of the 5th Regiment, 4th Division, advanced into downtown Suwon, the remaining ROK cover troops withdrew at last.

Though eventually forced to withdraw by the enemy's armor units, the Sihung Command, using mixed units, held the Han defense line for no less than a week, and significantly delayed the enemy's advance after the fall of Seoul. The Sihung Command not only bought time for the deployment of US ground forces, but also laid out the groundwork for ROK and US forces to conduct a Combined delaying action. It thus complicated the enemy's strategy and created new opportunities for ROK Forces.

II. Transition to a Delaying Operation

1. Reorganized ROK Armed Forces and US Forces Form a Combined Front

July 4, 1950, marked a critical turning point in the Korean War as the ROK-US combined front was formed on that day. US Forces, deployed along the P'yongtaek-Ansong line, were assigned the western front centered around the Seoul-Pusan National Road, while ROK Forces became responsible for the central and eastern front.

This combined operation was based on an agreement between Army Chief of Staff Chung Il Kwon and Brig. Gen. Church of ADCOM in Taejon on July 1, the day when Task Force Smith landed in Pusan as the leading unit of US ground forces to be committed in Korea. After holding a talk on strengthening US air support, reorganizing ROK Forces, and providing urgent ammunition and equipment replenishment on the first day, the two generals the next day exchanged opinions and reached an agreement on wide-ranging issues related to ROK-US cooperation and combined operations, including the transport and deployment of Task Force Smith, division of operation areas, and planning of future operations.

1. ROK Forces will hold the Han River line for as long as possible.
2. ROK Forces will block the enemy along the sides of the Seoul-Pusan National Road and cover the advance of the US 24th Division.
3. The US 24th Division will take up the western area centered around the Seoul-Pusan National Road, and ROK Forces will take up the area to the east thereof.
4. The initial ROK-US line of resistance will be the P'yongt'aek-Ansong-Ch'ungju-Uljin line, the narrowest east-to-west cross-section of South Korea.[39]

As Task Force Smith was deployed along the P'yongt'aek-Ansong line on July 4, ROK troops under the Sihung Command withdrew from Suwon and assembled to the south of P'yongt'aek. The ROK Ministry of Defense reorganized these units and established the 1st Corps, and pushed ahead with further reorganization and redeployment of ROK Forces so as to carry out the ROK-US combined operation agreement.

The reorganization effort demanded that the Sihung Command discontinue contact with the enemy and disengage, and carried the risk of hasty re-

Establishment of the ROK-US Combined Front (July 4-6)

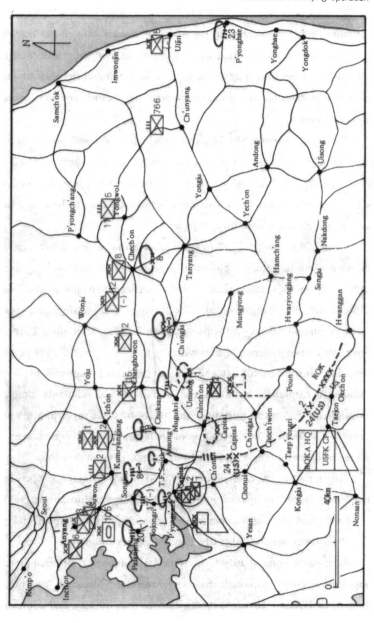

commitment after reorganizing in the none-too-distant rear of the battlefield. As these units had sustained huge losses in men and equipment and their cohesion had severely declined during the defense of Seoul and the Han River line, however, reorganization was a necessary first step before any new operation could be attempted.

The ROK Defense Ministry's plan called for the reorganization of the Sihung Command into the 1st Corps Command effective July 5. The Mixed Capital, 1st, 2nd, 3rd, 5th, and 7th Divisions were to be reorganized into three divisions (Capital, 1st, and 2nd). The ROK Army was thus to be comprised of one corps, five divisions, and three regiments.[40]

Army Chief of Staff Chung directed withdrawing units under the Sihung Command to deploy a covering force along the Osan–Ansong line and ordered units on its east to occupy the Chuksan–Changhowon–and Jech'on line.[41] Regarding the reorganization of ROK units, Gen. Chung later recollected: "The command of the 1st Corps was given to Gen. Kim Hong Il, the only man to have had experience in commanding a division-level or above unit at the time. Part of the Capital, 1st, and 2nd Divisions had dispersed, but as their command structure at the battalion level and above was relatively intact, they were designated reconstruction divisions. In contrast, as the 3rd, 5th, and 7th Division had suffered a complete loss of their command structure, they were disbanded and their strength was added to the reorganized divisions."[42]

Appointed as the commander of the 1st Corps, Maj. Gen. Kim Hong Il at once orally issued an operation order and a reorganization directive. From July 4, he formed the corps command as soon as units assembled in P'yongt'aek, and pushed ahead with the division reorganization plan.

In the afternoon of July 5, the ROKA Headquarters ordered Gen. Kim to redeploy his corps. Although the reorganization of divisions had not been completed, Gen. Kim recognized the urgency of the situation and deployed his

⟨Table 2⟩ ROK Army Reorganization Plan (July 5, 1950; oral directive issued July 4)

Unit	Commanding Officer	Subordinate Units	Incorporated Units
ROKA Headquarters	Maj. Gen. Chung Il Kwon		
1st Corps	Maj. Gen. Kim Hong Il		
Capital Division	Br. Gen. Lee Jun Shik (Br. Gen. Kim Sok Won effective July 7)	1st, 8th, 18th Regiments	3rd, 9th Regiments
1st Division	Col. Paik Sun Yup	11th, 12th, 13th Regiments	15th, 22nd Regiments
2nd Division	Col. Lee Han Lim	5th, 16th, 20th Regiments	25th Regiment
6th Division	Col. Kim Jong O	2nd, 7th, 19th Regiments	
8th Division	Col. Lee Song Ga	10th, 21st Regiments	
17th Regiment	Lt. Col. Kim Hui Jun		
23rd Regiment	Lt. Col. Kim Jong Won		
Cavalry Regiment	Col. Yu Hung Su		

troops. Early morning the next day, Gen. Kim deployed the Capital and 1st Divisions in Chinch'on and Umsong, respectively, and gave the division commanders operational control over the 19th and 7th Regiments of the 6th Division, which were carrying out security operations in the front area. Gen. Kim also moved the 2nd Division to Chungp'yong as a reserve, and established the corps command in Ch'ongju to direct defense on the central front.

Between the time of reorganization and redeployment, the strength of each division was rapidly increased and almost reached the level before the

⟨Table 3⟩   Increase in the Strength of the 1st Corps after Redeployment
(July 6, 1950)[43]

Division	Before Redeployment	After Redeployment
Capital Division	2,500	7,855
1st Division	4,000	5,063
2nd Division	1,600	6,845

outbreak of the war. Troops which had dispersed returned to their parent unit, and stragglers gathered up as well as volunteers from the Korean Youth Group and students provided reinforcements.

Commenting on the rapid reorganization of ROK Forces, NKPA Supreme Commander Kim Il Sung later acknowledged: "Our greatest mistake was failing to encircle and annihilate the enemy and giving them enough time to reorganize and reinforce their units while withdrawing."[44]

Although the ROK Army made a rapid recovery in the area of troop strength, it was continuously plagued by the lack of equipment. The ROKA Headquarters began to establish a rear logistics supply system and set up a supply plan for each unit on July 5, but more time was needed to establish a total war system through wartime mobilization and conscription.[45]

By July 3, the ROK 1st Corps had received twelve 105-mm howitzers, 990 M1 rifles, and ammunition from US Forces. However, as US logistics supply units had only begun deployment and US Forces had the priority of support, US military assistance to ROK Forces was extremely limited at the time of the its reorganization.[46]

Along the ROK-US combined front, the ROK 6th Division was responsible for the area from Songjon to Ch'ungju: the 19th Regiment was on the eastern flank of Ansong, occupying Songjon-Chuksan; the 7th Regiment was to its east, along Mugukri-Tongnakri ; and the 2nd Regiment was deployed in Ch'ungju. The 8th Division was in Chech'on, and the 23rd Regiment was conducting operations in the vicinity of Uljin on the east coast. Except in the vicinity of Chech'on, only battalion- or regiment-strength units were defending the enemy's expected main avenues of approach along the combined front. In addition to the small size of the defending units, wide gaps between them created noticeably vulnerable spots in the combined defense.

Around this time, the NKPA Front Line Command[47] committed follow-on divisions to the front, and reorganized three border security brigades (under the Ministry of Internal Affairs) into the 7th, 8th, and 9th Combat Divisions. It also issued a wartime mobilization decree to support the southward invasion effort. On the western front, the NKPA 4th Division following the 105th Armored Division (upgraded from brigade effective July 5) was leading the offensive, with the 3rd and 6th Divisions as follow-on units. On the central front, the NKPA 2nd and 15th Divisions were advancing southward from Ich'on and Changhowon, respectively. The 12th and 1st Divisions were massing toward Ch'ungju while the 8th Division was advancing in the direction of Chech'on.[48] On the east coast, the NKPA 5th Division was advancing southward.

Under such pressing circumstances, the 34th Regiment of the US 24th Division was deployed in P'yongt'aek-Ansong on July 5, and the three divisions of the ROK 1st Corps were committed to Chinch'on, Umsong, Chung-p'yong on the next day. Thus, the combined front had taken a concrete form by this time.

The ROK Navy and Air Force also began to reinforce their units and coordinate with ground forces and UN naval and air forces for joint and combined operations. The ROK Air Force obtained ten F-51 fighter planes on July 2, and established a combat wing and a reconnaissance wing. The Air Force provided reconnaissance for the ROK 1st Corps and carried out combined close air support missions with the US Air Force. While blocking the advance of the enemy's tanks in Anyang on July 4, Col. Lee Kun Sok, commander of the combat wing, died a heroic death. The US Air Force established an air-land joint operation headquarters in Taejon on July 5, and began to operate six tactical air control parties (TACPs). By strengthening coordination, air forces were able to increase the effectiveness of air-land operations and reduce friendly bombardments.[49]

The ROK Navy began combined operations with US naval and air forces on June 27, and carried out sea operations and support missions for ground forces from both the east and west coast. In carrying out a naval blockade from June 30, US and ROK naval forces took up the north and south of the 37th parallel, respectively. As no NGLOs (Naval Gunfire Liaison Officers) had yet to be dispatched, however, naval support had a limited effectiveness. Military advisors temporarily filled in for NGLOs.[50]

Meanwhile, in order to facilitate war efforts, the ROK government declared martial law in all of Korea except Cholla Province on July 8.[51] Also, following UN Resolution of the establishment of the Unified Command on July 7, the ROK Ministry of National Defense formed a UN Liaison Officers Corps on July 10 to act as liaison between the ROK Armed Forces and the UN Forces as well as the UN Commission on Korea (excluding diplomatic matters).[52]

Under changed circumstances with the involvement of UN and US Forces, reorganization of the ROK Forces, and formation of the combined front, the ROK Defense Ministry eagerly sought opportunities to make an early transition to a counteroffensive. Due to the earlier losses, however, the ROK Forces had little choice but to conduct a delaying action with the US Forces. The NKPA's main attack, the 1st Corps, was pressuring from the Seoul-Pusan Axis and the central western as well as the west coast axis, while the NKPA 2nd Corps, was advancing southward along the central and central eastern axes as well as the east coast road. In response, the ROK and UN Forces established delay lines in stages, along the Ch'a-ryong Mountain Range and the Kum-Sobaek Mountain Range. Their task at hand was to inflict losses on the enemy and yield the minimum space in order to gain the maximum time necessary for a rapid recovery of friendly strength.

2. Delaying Action along the Seoul-Pusan Axis

(1) Battle in the Vicinity of Osan

When the Sihung Command withdrew from Suwon to P'yongt'aek on July 4, Task Force Smith became the forward unit on the western front and began to prepare for an expected enemy attack from Suwon. Charged with a mission to block the enemy as far north as possible, Task Force Smith twice conducted reconnaissance around Osan and arrived at Chukmi-ryong at 03:00 on a rainy July 5.

Chukmi-ryong is a low pass on a cross-compartment ridge along the Seoul-Pusan axis, about 5 km. north of Osan. It comprises a chain of three hills: Panwol-bong (Hill 117), the main hill in the middle; Hill 90 on the west; and Hill 92 on the east. The Seoul-Pusan National Road runs between Hill 90 and Hill 117, and the Seoul-Pusan Railway is on the east of Hill 92.

Across the Seoul-Pusan National Road, B Company of Task Force Smith occupied Hill 90 and Hill 117, while C Company was deployed on Hill 92. The 105-mm Company (with 1,200 artillery shells) was emplaced in Suchongri in the rear of Chukmi-ryong; the number-five howitzer, with six high explosive antitank shells (HEATs), was forward emplaced at the midway point toward Chukmi-ryong. The ROK 17th Regiment[53] deployed its 2nd Battalion on Hill 88 on the right of the US artillery battery.

Braving the dark and the rain, Task Force Smith immediately began to establish positions, but was unable to finish the work by the sunrise. It only was able to complete registering by that time. The combat organization of Task Force Smith was as follows :

⟨Table 4⟩　　　The Combat Organization of Task Force Smith

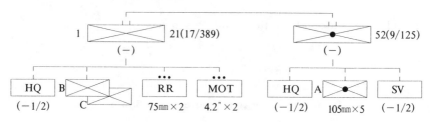

Around 07:00, the NKPA 4th Division, in a long march formation, was observed to be advancing southward from Suwon along the Seoul-Pusan National Road, spearheaded by the 107th Armored Regiment. When eight of the enemy's tanks came within 1.8km of the Chukmi-ryong Pass, Task Force Smith carried out a pre-emptive strike with 105-mm howitzers. In spite of the concentrated artillery fire, however, the enemy tanks continued to advance toward Chukmi-ryong. When the tanks closed within 630m of the infantry position, US troops fired 75-mm recoilless rifles but the NKPA tanks suffered no damages and began to climb up the pass while firing 85-mm self-propelled and 7.62-mm machine guns. When the tanks arrived at the infantry position, a 2.36-inch rocket launcher section fired at the track and rear vulnerable spots from a little more than a 10m distance, but this too failed to make any difference.

When the tanks passed through the infantry position and arrived at the top of Chukmi-ryong, the number-five howitzer fired HEAT ammunition and the two lead tanks were stopped. Very likely these artillery shells from the 105-mm howitzer stopped the two tanks, although the barrage of 2.36-inch rockets might have damaged their tracks. The two damaged tanks pulled off to the side of the road to clear the way, and avoiding engagement with the infantry, a total of 33 follow-on tanks, usually in groups of 4, passed through Chukmi-ryong toward the US artillery position.[54]

The artillerymen did not expect that the enemy tanks could reach the artillery position so soon. They thought that the enemy would turn around and go back upon discovering US ground troops or, at the least, the infantrymen would deal with them before they could reach the artillery position. The artillerymen directed their artillery pieces toward the road and delivered direct fire, and 2.36-inch bazooka teams also joined in on the antitank barrage, but they could not block the enemy's advance. About ten minutes after the first wave of tanks had passed through toward Osan, a larger second group followed. When the second wave of tanks came into view, some of the artillerymen started to panic and disengage momentarily, but returned to their positions under the good example and strong leadership of their commanders. Many of the enemy tanks did not fire on the artillery at all. The second wave of the enemy tanks advanced toward Osan, leaving behind two tanks damaged in their tracks on the side of the road.

After the last of the tank column had passed through, Task Force Smith improved their positions in anticipation of an enemy infantry attack by deepening their foxholes and taking other measures in the steady rain that continued throughout the morning. A little past 11:00, a long column of NKPA trucks and foot soldiers came within 900 meters of the US infantry position. There were three tanks in front, followed by a long line of trucks and several kilometers of marching infantry. With battle against a vastly superior number of enemy troops fast approaching, the arrogant pride of the US troops gave way to apprehension and fear.

Upon battalion commander Lt. Col. Smith's order to fire, Task Force Smith threw all that they had at the enemy—field artillery pieces, mortars, machine guns, and small arms. Enemy infantrymen started to deploy, and the three lead tanks moved to within 200m of the US positions and delivered cannon and machine gun fire. In the meantime, while part of the enemy infantry occupied the ridge running northward from Panwol-bong and provided supporting fire, the enemy main attack fanned out to either side of Chukmi-ryong.

Within an hour, when the enemy began to threaten the western flank of B Company, Lt. Col. Smith switched to all-around defense centered around Panwol-bong and continued to put up resistance. In a few minutes, however, C Company's position on the eastern flank began to be threatened by the enemy. Lt. Col. Smith decided that the time to withdraw was at hand. His unit was about to be enveloped by a large contingent of enemy troops. Due to a breakdown in the infantry-artillery communications inflicted by the enemy tanks, he had no artillery support. In addition, the bad weather precluded the possibility of friendly air support, and there was no hope of obtaining reinforcements.[55]

After holding the position for almost 12 hours, Task Force Smith started to withdraw from Chukmi-ryong around 14:30. Under the cover of B Company, the battalion withdrew in order toward Osan via Hill 92. When B Company was ready to withdraw, Lt. Col. Smith left the hill and withdrew with the artillery unit to Osan. The ROK 17th Regiment withdrew via Pyongtaek.[56]

While withdrawing, Task Force Smith was dispersed by an enemy attack from the eastern flank. One platoon, in particular, had to abandon all crew-served weapons and suffered heavy losses in personnel and equipment. When Task Force Smith assembled in Ch'onan via Ansong, there were about 150 men killed, wounded, or missing. The enemy lost approximately 42 killed and 85 wounded plus 4 destroyed tanks.[57]

The Chukmi-ryong Battle was the first battle between the US Forces and the North Korean People's Army. For the NKPA troops, it confirmed that US ground forces had been committed to Korea. Sr. Col. Lee Hak Ku, operations officer of the NKPA 2nd Corp later captured during the Battle of the

Naktong Line, recollected : "I had no idea that the United States would intervene in the war. I had heard nothing about possible U.S. intervention, and it
came as as a shock to discover US troops in Osan."[58] The US troops, on the
other hand, realized that they had underestimated the enemy strength, and
made a more accurate assessment of the enemy after the Chukmiryong Battle.

(2) Battle in the Vicinity of P'yongt'aek and Ch'onan

While the battle in the Osan area was unfolding, the 34th Regiment of
the US 24th Division formed a second line of resistance along P'yongt'aek-
Ansong behind Osan. The 1st Battalion established a position centered around
the Seoul-Pusan National Road on the north of P'yongt'aek, with the 3rd Battalion (-1) covering the highway in Ansong on the south. Together with L
Company from the 3rd Battalion, the Regiment Headquarters located in
Songhwan. The regiment was deployed without artillery and armor units, and
it had a total strength of 1,981 men.

The P'yongt'aek-Ansong area was on the western part of the ROK-US
combined front, and was bounded by the Asan Bay on the west and by mountains on the east. A critical corridor on the western front, the P'yongt'aek-
Ansong area contained two main roads including the Seoul-Pusan Highway.
The US 24th Division commander hoped that the 34th Regiment would successfully defend the area.

Forward deploying 2.36-inch rocket launcher teams primarily along
the Seoul-Pusan National Road, the regiment prepared for an enemy armor attack. In the vicinity of Sojongri on the afternoon of July 5, 2.36-inch bazooka
teams exchanged fire with the enemy's tanks which had already reached that
point via Osan. After this brief contact with the enemy, there was no further
engagement into the night. As there was still no word from Task Force Smith,

the 34th Regiment began to harbor serious misgivings about its safety.

A little past midnight, however, withdrawing troops and stragglers from Task Force Smith passed through Songhwan via Ansong and P'yongt'aek, and reported what had happened to their unit. Responsible for the enemy's main avenue of approach, the 1st Battalion blew the bridge just north of its position and otherwise improved its antitank defense throughout the night.[59]

As dawn broke on rainy July 6, the 1st Battalion observed through the fog the enemy infantrymen marching in a column of twos behind 13 tanks. They were the 16th and 18th Regiments of the NKPA 4th Division, supported by the 105th Armored Division. The Battle of P'yongt'aek began when the US battalion fired its 4.2-inch mortars. The mortar fire, however, was ineffective against the enemy tank attack, and the enemy infantry began fanning out on either flank to attack the battalion's position. Having been instructed by Br. Gen. George B. Barth "to hold as long as he could but to withdraw if his battalion was in danger of being outflanked and cut off," the battalion commander started to withdraw his unit to P'yongt'aek.[60]

The S-3 of the 34th Regiment confirmed Gen. Barth's earlier instructions, and the 1st Battalion continued to withdraw and reached a point 3.2km south of Ch'onan by the early evening. Upon withdrawal, the battalion abandoned much of its equipment and suffered a breakdown in unit cohesion and the chain of command.[61] On the south of Ch'onan, the 1st Battalion (−1), US 21st Regiment, had arrived in the morning and was establishing a defensive position. Under no contact with the enemy, the 3rd Battalion in Ansong withdrew by rail and vehicles to arrive in Ch'onan late in the evening.

On the same evening, the US 24th Division commander started for Chonan and presided over a meeting at the regiment headquarters. Maj. Gen. Dean angrily demanded to know who had authorized the withdrawal from Pyongtaek. Due to a communications breakdown at the time of the withdrawal, no one had reported the situation to the division commander. The authorization for the withdrawal, in effect, had come from Brig. Gen. Barth who had overseen the forward operation in lieu of Gen. Dean. Gen. Barth had thought that it would be more effective to assemble the regiment in Ch'onan rather than separately deploying its forces in P'yongt'aek and Ansong. His independent judgment, however, was directly contrary to the division commander's intent.

According to Gen. Dean's instructions, the regiment commander the next morning forward-deployed the 3rd Battalion toward P'yongt'aek to maintain contact with the enemy. Led by the regiment patrol and reconnaissance platoons, the battalion went back north along the road jammed with withdrawing ROK troops. When the regiment came within 6 to 8km north of Ch'onan, it came under the enemy small arms and mortar fire. By this time, the US 24th Division had obtained through air reconnaissance signs of an outflanking maneuver by a large enemy unit. A great number of enemy troops had appeared on the east of the 3rd Battalion, and 40 to 50 enemy tanks were assembling in Ansong. Through a message relayed by a liaison plane, Gen. Dean ordered the regiment to proceed with greatest caution.[62]

Later in the afternoon, Col. Jay B. Lovless was relieved of command of the US 34th Regiment, and was replaced by Col. Robert R. Martin, who had served together with Gen. Dean in World War II. While the change of command was taking place, the leading company of the 3rd Battalion engaged with the enemy. Soon the battalion itself came under the enemy's flank attack, and abandoned its position without any authorization. The new regiment commander ordered the 3rd Battalion to return to position at once. While the operations officers of the regiment and the battalion were trying to relay this order to the battalion, they were fired on by an enemy reconnaissance unit. The former was captured and held as a prisoner of war, and the latter apparently died that night. In the end, abandoning some of its equipment, the 3rd Battalion dispersed and withdrew to the south of Ch'onan.[63]

Gathering up their troops, the 3rd Battalion organized a defensive position around the Ch'onan Railway Station, and buried antitank mines in preparation for an enemy attack.[64] The enemy resumed the attack at night. Requesting fire support from the newly arrived 63rd Field Artillery Battalion, the US 34th Regiment concentrated high explosive and white phosphorus shells against the enemy. The NKPA troops, however, broke through the defensive line just before midnight and advanced into downtown Ch'onan.[65]

Before the dawn broke, another wave of enemy tanks rolled into downtown along the mined road. For some reason, however, the antitank mines did not go off. The street fighting continued through the night. When a group of 5 to 6 tanks closed in, the 3rd Battalion responded with hand grenades and 2.36-inch bazooka fire. Regiment commander Col. Martin himself obtained a 2.36-inch rocket launcher and fired at the enemy tanks, but was killed by a tank cannon fire. Col. Martin was posthumously awarded the first Distinguished Service Cross of the Korean War. As the strength of the enemy armor and infantry units swelled after the dawn, the 3rd Battalion was no longer able to hold Ch'onan and had to withdraw from downtown under the cover of white phosphorus shells. The battalion withdrew toward the 1st Battalion on the south of Ch'onan.

Around this time, US 8th Army commander Gen. Walker and Gen. Dean came up to the south of Ch'onan to observe the withdrawal of the battalion. Under a new plan to defend along the Kum River, the division commander ordered the 21st Regiment to defend the Seoul-Pusan Highway and withdrew the 34th Regiment toward Kongju. The P'yongt'aek-Ch'onan Battle of the 34th Regiment thus came to an end.

The US 34th Regiment suffered heavy losses in the Battle of Ch'onan.

In particular, only 175 men from the 3rd Battalion managed to withdraw to the south of Ch'onan. Two-thirds of the battalion were dead or missing. The battalion also lost many individual weapons as well as crew—served weapons such as mortars.[66]

After this battle, Gen. MacArthur of the US Far East Command realized that he could no longer underestimate the enemy and made strong requests to Washington for reinforcement on July 5 and July 7. Gen. Dean also reassessed the situation and made an urgent request for 105-mm HEAT shells and 3.5-inch anti-tank rockets.[67]

(3) Battle in the Vicinity of Chonui and Choch'iwon

After the US 34th Regiment withdrew, the 21st Regiment on July 8 took up the mission of delaying the enemy's advance along the Seoul-Pusan Highway between Chonui and Choch'iwon. Chonui was a small village 20km south of Ch'onan. Located about 16km from the Kum River, Choch'iwon was a transportation center where the Seoul-Pusan and Ch'ungbuk Railways came together.

Having already deployed the 3rd Battalion at Migokri on the north of Choch'iwon on the previous day, the 21st Regiment commander ordered the 1st Battalion (−)[68] to establish a defensive position on hills east and south of Chonui across the Seoul-Pusan Highway. Having supported the 34th Regiment south of Ch'onan, the 1st Battalion (−) was now placed north of the 3rd Battalion. The 21st Regiment received support from a battery of 155-mm howitzers of the 11th Field Artillery Battalion. Also in support of the regiment were A Company, 78th Heavy Tank Battalion (M24 light tanks) and B Company of the 3rd Engineer Combat Battalion.[69]

Instructions from Gen. Dean to the 21st Regiment commander emphasized that the regiment must hold at Choch'iwon and cover the left flank of the ROK forces on the central front until the latter could fall back, and that he could expect no help for four days. The division commander's intent was to have the 21st and 34th Regiments delay the enemy's approach to the Kum River as much as possible.

On the morning of July 9, the 21st Regiment completed moving into the positions, and the 3rd Battalion finished registering its 81-mm and 4.2-inch mortars. Engineers blew up bridges in front of Chonui. Around noon, the enemy resumed its southward advance toward Chonui, spearheaded by tanks. In midafternoon, 11 tanks and an estimated 200-300 enemy infantrymen closed in on the US forward blocking position. Forward observers immediately requested air strike and artillery fire. The heavy bombardment destroyed five enemy tanks and engulfed Chonui in flames. Also, of about 200 enemy vehicles on the road from Ch'onan to Chonui, approximately 100 were destroyed by the air strike, and the enemy's attack came to a temporary halt.[70]

On the next morning of July 10, when a heavy fog was about to clear, enemy tanks began to maneuver along the road to break through the US position while the enemy infantry units carried out a frontal attack and envelopment from either flank. Under the regiment commander's leadership, the 1st Battalion put up a fierce resistance with support from artillery and air units. The US mortar emplacement was, however, soon overrun by the enemy tanks which had passed through the infantry position under the fog, and infantry-artillery communications were severed by the enemy's artillery fire. The artillerymen apparently thought that enemy troops had overrun the forward infantry position and began to fire on them.

The Bixler Platoon positioned on a hill west of the highway came under the enemy's overwhelming attack. Lt. Ray Bixler radioed the regiment commander and asked permission to withdraw, but was ordered to hold the position until relief arrived. Completely outmanned, all members of the platoon met their ends in their foxholes. As the situation became desperate, the regiment commander withdrew with the battalion. While falling back across rice paddies, they had to survive friendly strafing from American jets.[71]

Having lost one-fifth of its strength, the 1st Battalion (−) withdrew to Choch'iwon, and the 3rd Battalion was ordered to recover the lost position before the enemy's reorganization. Under the support of A Company (−), 78th Heavy Tank Battalion, the 3rd Battalion launched a counterattack and recovered the 1st Battalion position. Concerned with another attack by the enemy, however, the regiment commander returned the 3rd Battalion to its position during the night.

The battle resumed in front of the 3rd Battalion position early next morning, July 11. Having passed forward of the NKPA 4th Division at Chonui, the 3rd Division launched a carefully coordinated attack on the US troops. The enemy cut off the rear and attacked the battalion command post to disorganize the battalion.

Pvt. Paul R. Spear, carrying only an empty pistol, neutralized an enemy machine gun emplacement, and the rest of the battalion put up a desperate resistance.[72] The battalion command structure, however, collapsed as the battalion commander and S-3 commanders were killed and S-1 and S-2 commanders were missing. After losing more than half of the 667 men and much of the equipment, the battalion withdrew to Choch'iwon.

Around this time, the 1st Battalion of the 21st Regiment was preparing for an enemy attack in its position 3.2km north of Choch'iwon. While in Choch'iwon, the 1st Battalion had reorganized with Task Force Smith to form a full-fledged battalion. From the morning of July 12, the battalion engaged the enemy troops which had pursued the 3rd Battalion southward, but was eventually ordered to withdraw by the regiment commander.[73] Having thus concluded the Battle of Chonui-Choch'iwon against the enemy 3rd and 4th Divisions, the 21st Regiment was instructed by the division commander to move to the southern bank of the Kum River, the next blocking line.

Fighting against the elite units of the NKPA 3rd and 4th Divisions, the US 21st Regiment (−) delayed the enemy's advance for three days and made a major contribution to the securing of main supply lines to the ROK 1st Corps on the right flank in Choch'iwon and Ch'ongju.　During the battle, on the afternoon of July 10, the US 5th Air Force mobilized every available plane to P'yongt'aek and carried out a massive air strike to destroy 38 enemy tanks, 7 half-track vehicles, 117 trucks, and a large number of enemy troops. The greatest destruction of enemy armor by a single action in the war, this operation had a major influence on the enemy's troop movement, as the North Korean People's Army began to switch to nighttime maneuver.[74]　Meanwhile, the NKPA switched units at Chonui. The enemy 3rd Division began to follow the 21st Regiment along the Seoul-Pusan axis, and the 4th Division changed its direction toward Kongju.

3. Delaying Action along the Ch'a-ryong Mountains

(1) Chinch'on-Ch'ongju Battle

While US ground forces were defending along the P'yongt'aek-Ansong line and ROK troops were establishing positions along the Charyong Mountain Range, the ROK Capital Division moved to Chinch'on on July 6 and had to make quick preparations to block the advance of the NKPA 2nd Division, which had earlier pushed aside the 19th Regiment of the ROK 6th Division. Although the reorganization of the 1st Regiment had yet to be completed, the Capital Division commander committed the unit to Paekgok-ch'on at the northern end of Chinch'on, and directed the 8th and 18th Regiments to occupy Pongwha-san and Munan-san as soon as they arrived.[73]

Having suffered major losses in the Ch'unch'on Battle, the NKPA 2nd Division was replenished with reinforcements according to the wartime mobilization decree, and had a total strength of 12,000 with ten tanks, twelve self-propelled guns, and twenty-six 122-mm howitzers. With an intent to advance into the Chinch'on-Ch'ongju area, its lead regiment moved to Songrimri on the north of Chinch'on, and the main unit was assembling in Kwanghyewonri on July 7.[76]

A critical avenue of approach in the midwestern region, the Chinch'on-Ch'ongju axis connected to Taejon and Poun. It was expected that operations along this axis would have a significant bearing on the Seoul-Pusan axis to its west.

Brig. Gen. Kim Sok Won,[77] who replaced Brig. Gen. Lee Jun Sik on July 7 as the commander of the ROK Capital Division, insisted that the 1st Regiment hold Chinch'on until the main effort arrived and did not hesitate to lead the unit in person. On the next morning, however, the 1st Regiment came under an overwhelming enemy attack spearheaded by tanks, and had to withdraw to Chat-gogae (pass). Chinch'on thus fell to the enemy 2nd Division.

While the 1st Regiment of the ROK Capital Division was maintaining troops at Chat-gogae, the 8th and 18th Regiments arrived. The combat strength of the division was greatly improved by reinforcements from the 20th Regiment, ROK 2nd Division, the 17th Regiment ($-$), Independent Cavalry Regiment, and a battery (four M-2 howitzers) from the 1st Artillery Group. Gen. Kim committed the 18th Regiment at Munan-san and the 8th Regiment at Pongwha-san, and deployed the Independent Cavalry Regiment in the middle, at Chat-gogae. Having thus established the main line of resistance along

Munan-san-Chat-gogae-Pongwha-san, he retained the 17th Regiment(−) as a reserve at Sanggyeri. Gen. Kim also forward-deployed the attached 20th Regiment of the 2nd Division at the right flank of Pongwha-san.[78]

Before the Capital Division completed regrouping and establishing defensive positions, however, the main effort of the enemy 2nd Division launched a coordinated infantry-armor-artillery attack on the morning of July 9. Though fatigued from long marches, the ROK division put up a spirited resistance under the personal leadership of Gen. Kim. After a series of engagements, however, the enemy at last broke through the main line of resistance and occupied the Munan-san-Pongwha-san area. Having secured an area critical to advancement into Ch'ongju, the enemy put off further pursuit and halted to regroup.

The loss of the Munan-san-Pongwha-san effectively gave the enemy the initiative. Convinced that attack was the best form of defense under the circumstances, Brig. Gen. Kim Sok Won decided to launch a frontal attack from the current position (2-3 kilometers south of the main line of resistance) and recover up to Chinch'on. Gen. Kim committed the 8th Regiment on the left, the 1st Regiment on the right, and the Cavalry Regiment in the middle. Deploying the 17th (−) and 20th Regiments on either flank and retaining the 18th Regiment as a reserve, Gen. Kim went on a counterattack. To cover the right flank of the Capital Division, the 16th Regiment of the ROK 2nd Division attacked in parallel.

Under the personal leadership of Gen. Kim, the attacking units broke through the enemy barrage zone, and caught the enemy units undergoing troop maintenance. The ROK troops eventually recovered the original line of resistance along Pongwha-san and Munan-san. At Pongwha-san, the troops were threatened by an enemy counterattack, but were able to seize the objective through the commitment of the 18th Regiment, the division reserve.

From around midnight, the enemy 2nd Division embarked on a relentless counteroffensive. The ROK 18th Regiment in Pongwha-san repelled an enemy regiment on three separate occasions and maintained its position. The ROK 17th Regiment temporarily lost its position under an enemy surprise attack, but was able to recover it through a nighttime counterattack in conjunction with the reserve 1st Regiment.[79]

The ROK Capital Division commander then began to plan to recover Chinchon. As the front on the east and west of the corps was moving southward, however, Gen. Kim was directed to withdraw to Chongju. Accordingly, on the evening of July 10, he decided to withdraw to the south bank of Mihochon in Chongju under the cover of the attached 17th ($-$) and 20th Regiments.

While the Capital Division was pushing ahead with its withdrawal plans, Maj. Gen. Choi Hyon, the enemy 2nd Division commander, changed tactics and attempted to cut off its line of retreat by employing a turning movement. While part of the enemy troops carried out a feint attack on Munan-san, the enemy main effort began to attack the ROK 16th ($-$) and 20th Regiments in Sinjongri and Ch'angwolri, southeast of Chinch'on. Fortuitously, UN B-29 and B-26 squadrons carried out a massive bombardment for over an hour in this area and disrupted the enemy attack. Moreover, follow-on F-51 fighters dropped napalm bombs on the enemy. Under the cover of the UN air forces, the ROK Capital Division could withdraw safely. By the time the enemy had gathered up troops and resumed the attack toward the Yangch'on-san area, even the covering 17th ($-$) and 20th Regiments had withdrawn.

Centered around the Ogunjang Station on the south of Miho-ch'on, the Capital Division hastily organized new positions. From the left, it deployed the 8th, 1st, and 18th Regiments, and retained the 20th Regiment of the 2nd Division as a reserve in Ch'ongju. As the situation in Choch'iwon became precari-

Chinch'on-Ch'ongju Battle (July 6-12, 1950)

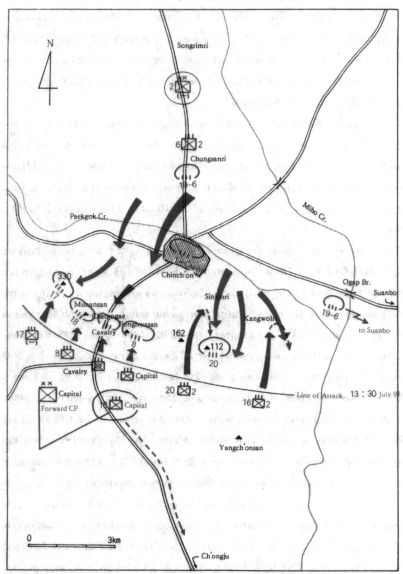

ous that day, however, the 2nd Division troops moved to the left flank of the corps.[80]

The enemy 2nd Division belatedly discovered that the ROK Capital Division had withdrawn, and advanced southward via Yangch'on-san to reach the north of Miho-ch'on by the morning of July 11. Having demolished the Miho-ch'on Bridge and consolidated its position, the Capital Division over-whelmed the enemy leading units with field artillery fire and bombarded the enemy assembly area by securing air support. On the next day, it further spoiled the enemy attack by delivering concentrated fire on the expected ene-my assembly area with support from the corps artillery.[81]

Meanwhile, at the corps command post, an operational conference was held over the issue of holding Chongju. In attendance at this meeting were the commanders of the corps (Maj. Gen. Kim Hong Il), commander of the Capital Division, and G3 of the ROKA HQ (Col. Kim Baek Il) as well as regiment com-manders and their staff. Maj. Gen. Kim in the end decided to withdraw from Chongju and defend along a line to its south. The US forces along the Seoul–Pusan axis had already withdrawn from Choch'iwon and moved to the Kum River line, and although Ch'ongju was a transportation center, street fighting would take a heavy toll on ROK forces. Given these considerations, Gen. Kim intended to block the enemy advance in a terrain more favorable to defense.[82] Accordingly, the Capital Division disengaged from Miho-ch'on on July 13, and withdrew to the south of Ch'ongju.

(2) Umsong–Koesan Battle

Located in a basin near the central part of the Ch'a-ryong Mountain Range, Umsong is a town in the northeastern part of North Ch'ungch'ong Prov-ince. Well-developed transportation networks pass through Umsong, and it was believed that the Changhowon-Umsong, Koesan and Changhowon-Umsong-Chinch'on routes, in particular, were likely to be enemy avenues of approach in the central western part of Korea. As ROK Forces were assigned the defense of the Ch'a-ryong Mountains to the east of Chinch'on, the reorganized ROK 1st Division was charged with the defense of Umsong. Before the arrival of the 1st Division, the 7th Regiment of the ROK 6th Division was maintaining contact with the enemy 15th Division as a covering force.

On July 4, the 7th Regiment was instructed to block the advance of the enemy 15th Division and secure Changhowon. Sent as a leading echelon that night, the 2nd Battalion sighted the enemy in the vicinity of Tongnakri. Upon receiving a report of this encounter, the regiment commander estimated that the enemy had already reached as far south as Mugukri and Saengguk. When the 7th Regiment (−) was about to leave the camp the next morning, however, it was instructed to commit a battalion to Chinch'on right away and support the withdrawal of the 19th Regiment from Ich'on. Accordingly, on July 5, the regiment commander dispatched the 2nd Battalion to Chinch'on, and directed the 1st and 3rd Battalions to attack Mugukri and Saengguk, respectively. Meanwhile, due to a change in the situation, the 2nd Battalion returned to Umsong from Chungp'yong and was retained as a regiment reserve.[83]

Initially used as a reserve of the NKPA 2nd Corps at the beginning of the war, the enemy 15th Division (under Maj. Gen. Park Song Chol) had been first committed into Changhowon from Wonju on July 3. With an intention to break through Umsong, the enemy division deployed the 49th and 48th Regiments in Mugukri and Saengguk, respectively, while retaining the 50th Regiment as a reserve. Although the 15th Division had a total strength of more than 10,000 men, 20 armored vehicles, and various artillery pieces including twelve 122-mm howitzers, it was a relatively poorly trained and in experienced unit.[84]

Umsong-Koesan Battle (July 5-11, 1950)

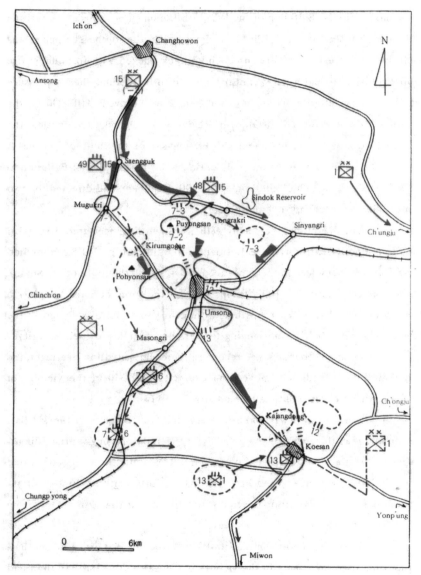

On July 5, the two sides ran into each other at Kirum-gogae [Pass] and Tongnakri. The 1st Battalion of the ROK 7th Regiment occupied Mugukri the next day, but soon had to withdraw to Paegyari to the southeast when it was subjected to a regimental strength enemy attack backed with formidable fire support. The 3rd Battalion was also subjected to increasingly heavy pressure in its engagement with the enemy, and had to withdraw to Hill 290 on the south of Kayop-san. The ROK 7th Regiment commander committed the reserve 2nd Battalion to the vicinity of Puyong-san on the south of Tongnakri to consolidate the defense in the middle. He also instructed the 1st Battalion to support the attached 2nd Battalion of the 19th Regiment, and directed the two units to block the enemy advance abreast.

In the meantime, the enemy 48th Regiment advanced into Tongnakri and found no ROK troops there. Residents reported that the 3rd Battalion had withdrawn by vehicle, and their own reconnaissance to the south of the Sindok Reservoir confirmed that ROK troops had left the town. Perhaps jumping to the conclusion that ROK troops had withdrawn from the town for good, the enemy regiment took up no moving formations and relaxed their security.[85] Upon receiving a reconnaissance report on the enemy situation overnight, the 3rd Battalion immediately moved the troops to Hill 310 in the vicinity of Yongwonri, and prepared to launch an attack at dawn.

When the dawn was about to break, the 9th Company of the 3rd Battalion attacked the enemy leading unit in the vicinity of Yongwonri. Estimating that the attack was carried out by a small ROK unit, the enemy committed only an advance company and had their main efforts wait in vehicles in tight formations. The 3rd Battalion seized this opportunity to attack the enemy from the flanks at once.

Meanwhile, almost simultaneously with the 3rd Battalion, the 2nd Battalion surprised the enemy in the vicinity of Tongakri. The 2nd Battalion had

been charged with the defense of Puyong-san, but upon sighting the enemy vehicles surprised by the 3rd Battalion, the battalion commander immediately
ordered his troops to attack. Finally ordered to carry out an attack after a series of frustrating delay and withdrawal operations, the morale of the battalion
troops reached the heavens.

Thrown into a great confusion by the surprise attack of the 2nd and
3rd Battalions, the enemy abandoned their vehicles and equipment and took
flight. A great number of the enemy troops were killed or captured in pursuit.
The abandoned vehicles were loaded with howitzers, machine guns, and ammunition. When the enemy went on a counterattack around noon, the 2nd and
3rd Battalions withdrew to the south of Tongnakri on order. As a retaliation
for their losses in the battle, the enemy killed a large number of innocent civilians that night.

Through its surprise attack, the ROK 7th Regiment dealt a lethal blow
to the enemy 48th Regiment in the Battle of Tongnakri. The ROK troops captured 132 NKPA soldiers, including the logistics staff officer, and seized much
equipment including 54 artillery pieces and 75 vehicles.[36] This victory earned
the 7th Regiment a presidential citation, and every member of the regiment received the honor of a one−rank promotion. Such honors were a first since the
beginning of the war, and this battle helped to convince ROK troops that they
could defeat the enemy in spite of their inferiority in strength and equipment.

Meanwhile, the ROK 1st Division arrived in Umsong and took over
the front as of 15 : 00, July 8. Division commander Col. Paik Sun Yup deployed the 11th Regiment on the west and 12th Regiment on the east to form a
defensive perimeter centered around Umsong. He then deployed the 13th Regiment along the line of resistance to the south of Umsong and retained the 7th
Regiment as a reserve in the rear.

When the rear unit of the 7th Regiment withdrew in the direction of

Umsong, the enemy's leading unit soon appeared as had been expected. Perhaps judging that all ROK troops had withdrawn, the enemy approached Umsong in a column of two's from Kirum-gogae (pass). When the leading enemy unit was about to enter the sector of the ROK 11th Regiment, another enemy unit followed. When about half of the enemy marching formation had entered the defensive zone, the 11th Regiment delivered concentrated fire under the support of 105-mm howitzers, and disrupted the enemy's advance. The enemy 49th Regiment suffered more than 100 casualties and lost much equipment in this battle.[57]

Delayed by a series of defeats, the enemy 15th Division coordinated with its adjacent units, and resumed its offensive on July 9 from three different directions : along the Mugukri-Umsong and Sinyangri-Umsong roads on the flanks and through the mountains in the middle. At dawn, the enemy concentrated fire at Umsong, and committed a two-regiment strength into the offensive. Under the support of 8 armored vehicles each, the enemy regiments attacked the ROK 11th and 12th Regiments from the front, but were repulsed by the the ROK 1st Division's concentrated fire and counterattack. The enemy, however, again went on the offensive at dawn the next day, and their main efforts began to break through the front of the ROK 11th Regiment.

Around this time, the ROK 1st Division received an instruction from the 1st Corps to "withdraw to Miwon via Koesan" in order to maintain the overall balance along the front. The situation of the adjacent units had deteriorated so much that the front had been pushed back to Ch'ongju on the left and Suanbo on the right. The 1st Division would risk getting cut off by holding on to Umsong. Under the cover of the 13th Regiment on the south of Umsong, Col. Paik began to withdraw his unit in the afternoon of July 10 and established a new defensive position on the north of Koesan. The 7th Regiment returned to the parent unit.

From July 11, the enemy 15th Division closed in on the new ROK position in Koesan. After fighting a fierce battle to delay the enemy's advance on July 12, the 1st Division began to withdraw to Miwon that night.[88]

(3) Battle in the Vicinity of Ch'ungju-Suanbo

When the ROK-US combined front was about to be established along P'yongt'aek-Ch'ungju-Uljin, the 2nd Regiment (−) of the ROK 6th Division was preparing to defend Ch'ungju by itself. Although the whole 6th Division assembled in Ch'ungju on July 3 after withdrawing from Hongch'on, its 19th (+) and 7th Regiments had to be deployed in the direction of Ich'on-Yoju and committed into a covering operation prior to the movement of the 1st Corps.

A transportation hub of the northern part of North Ch'ungch'ung Province, Ch'ungju is surrounded by the South Han River on the north and the Tal-ch'on on the west. Approximately 200 to 250 meters in width, the South Han River is too deep to ford. On the east of Ch'ungju, Kyemyong-san provides a commanding view of Ch'ungju and the South Han. As for transportation networks, the Ch'ungju-Suanbo road was estimated to be the most favorable avenue of approach for the enemy on the central eastern front, and the Ch'ungju-Changhowon and Ch'ungju-Tanyang roads were believed to be critical for horizontal troop movement.

The ROK 2nd Regiment channeled its main effort into the defense of the Wonju-Ch'ungju avenue of approach, and deployed the 1st and 3rd Battalions side by side on the southern bank of the South Han. The regiment utilized the reconnaissance company as a security force on the east of Kyemyong-san. The regiment's defensive position, however, suffered from serious vulnerabilities. Without retaining a reserve, the regiment employed a line defense that which stretched for no less than 21km(2nd Battalion had been attached to 19th

Regiment). The total strength of the regiment amounted to only 2,076, including 1,800 organic troops, 89 artillery men, and 187 police officers. Moreover, the regiment had no adjacent friendly units. In spite of these problems, however, the morale of the troops remained high as they had been able to put up effective resistance against the enemy in the Ch'unch'on-Hongch'on Battle.

On the other side, the NKPA 12th Division (under Maj. Gen. Ch'oi Ch'ung Guk) consisted of three regiments and had a total strength of 9,000 men.[89] While the ROK 2nd Regiment was establishing its defensive position, the enemy 30th Regiment was making preparations to cross the South Han directly in front of the 3rd Battalion. Another enemy regiment was preparing to follow the 30th Regiment, and yet another regiment was carrying out a turning movement toward the eastern flank of the ROK regiment. Meanwhile, the NKPA 1st Division was also moving toward Ch'ungju via Ich'on-Yoju, and an armored regiment, a cavalry battalion, and a sidecar company were also committed into the enemy's Ch'ungju offensive.

On July 7, while conducting a reconnaissance, the ROK 2nd Regiment came into contact with the reconnaissance and leading unit of the enemy 12th Division, and immediately occupied prepared positions. The enemy began to deliver harassing fire at midnight, and abruptly switched to intense preparatory fire. It was primarily aimed at the 3rd Battalion position. The ROK regiment had decided to deliver concentrated fire when the enemy crossed the river, but the enemy's artillery fire inflicted heavy losses and the heavy fog complicated security.[90] All of a sudden, platoon- or company-sized enemy units showed up in front of the 3rd Battalion. The enemy had used boats to cross the river under the cover of the fog.

The ROK 2nd Regiment repulsed the enemy attack with planned fires. As the second and third wave of the enemy unit crossed the river and applied pressure on the 3rd Battalion and the 1st Battalion on the west, however, a left

Ch'ungju-Suanbo Battle (July 6-11, 1950)

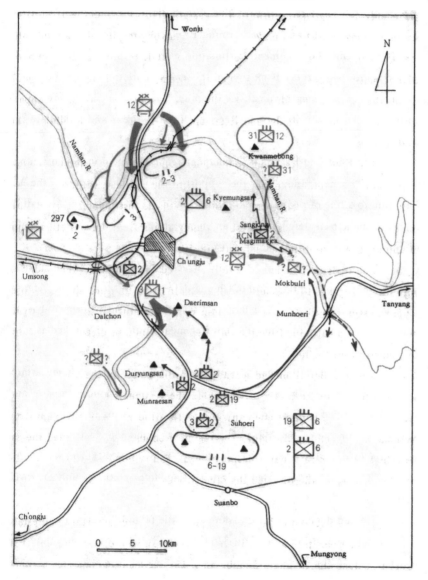

segment of the 3rd Battalion began to collapse in the morning.[91] Meanwhile, the enemy unit bypassing toward the eastern flank crossed the river from Kwanmo-bong (peak) and moved around Kyemyong-san to infiltrate into the rear flank of the ROK regiment. Fortunately, a ROK reconnaissance company advancing to the southern bank sighted this enemy unit and managed to block its advance at Sangjong-Majimak-jae (literally, "Last Pass"). The enemy apparently intended to cut off the 2nd Regiment from the rear and annihilate the ROK troops.

The ROK 2nd Regiment commander requested the division commander for reinforcement, and, under the support of the artillery, withdrew the 3rd Battalion to a line of resistance 2km to the south. He instructed the 1st Battalion to strengthen its defense against an enemy attack from the western avenue of approach, and coordinated defensive positions.

The division commander orally directed the regiment commander to withdraw his troops to the south of Ch'ungju. In order to shore up the defense, he gave assurance that the 2nd Battalion would be returned to the 2nd Regiment and that a battalion from the 19th Regiment would be dispatched as reinforcement within 12 hours.

The 3rd Battalion had already been dispersed by the enemy attack and was forced to withdraw to Ch'ungju. The reconnaissance company and regimental service support company also were withdrawing to Ch'ungju from Majimakjae on the eastern flank. The regiment commander instructed the 1st Battalion to organize a covering position at Tanwoldong-Taerim-san to the south of Ch'ungju, and directed the other troops to assemble in Suhoeri to its rear.

He had decided to take advantage of the favorable terrain and establish a blocking position along Hill 326-Chokpo-san in the rear of Suhoeri in order to defend the Ch'ungju-Suanbo axis. The regiment commander planned to launch a counterattack upon the arrival of the reinforcements. When the 2nd Battalion and a battalion from the 19th Regiment arrived in the evening, he began to make preparations for a counterattack. At 05:00, July 9, the 1st and 2nd Battalions were to carry out a frontal attack toward the north, while the 2nd Battalion of the 19th Regiment bypassed toward Mokbolri.

Around this time, the NKPA 12th Division turned over the operation area to the 1st Division, which had advanced into Ch'ungju from Seoul. With Tanyang as its objective, the 12th Division headed toward Mokbolri via Majimak-jae; whereas, the 1st Division advanced southward under the support of the 190th Armored Regiment.

Unaware of these changes in the enemy situation, the 1st and 2nd Battalions of the ROK 2nd Regiment attacked abreast toward Turyung-san from the west and toward Taerim-san from the east, respectively. Meanwhile, the 2nd Battalion, 19th Regiment, arrived in Mokbolri an hour prior to the time of attack.

The two battalions of the 2nd Regiment ran into the enemy, and engaged the much larger enemy unit. With armored vehicles, the enemy broke through the road between the two battalions and threatened to block their line of retreat. The 1st Battalion managed to withdraw before the enemy's advance, but the 2nd Battalion had its line of retreat cut off by the enemy. The ROK 2nd Regiment commander directed the 1st and 3rd Battalions to strengthen the defense of Suanbo, and instructed the 2nd Battalion to withdraw to Suanbo via the best possible route.

Meanwhile, the 2nd Battalion of the ROK 19th Regiment was having a meal when it was surprised by the enemy 32nd Regiment, 12th Division. The ROK troops had to jump into the South Han River and managed to swim upstream to reach Suanbo.[92]

In Suanbo, the 2nd Regiment was able to turn over the defensive positions to the 19th Regiment. While the 2nd Regiment was undergoing reorganization, a UN air squad flew two sorties within the interval of an hour and heavily bombarded the enemy assembly area. As if to prepare for a new offensive, the enemy disengaged from contact and the battle went into a lull.

(4) Chech'on-Tanyang Battle

When ROK Forces were beginning to carry out delaying actions, the 8th Division from Kangnung was defending the axis along the Central Railway Line in Chech'on. Stretching all the way to Tanyang, this axis was, and still is, the single most important maneuver route in the central front between Wonju and Andong. The railroad track and Road 5 run parallel across the mountains region. A primary obstacle in the vicinity of Tanyang is the South Han River, whose width of 100-150 meters and average depth of 2 meters rules out fording operations. Chech'on is at the intersection between the roads stretching from Wonju and P'yongch'ang, and Tanyang is located 20 kilometers to the south. East-west roads from Ch'ungju and Yongwol merge at Tanyang, which is on the southern bank of the South Han. Judging that the enemy would advance southward via Chech'on-Tanyang, the ROKA Headquarters had instructed the 8th Division to cross the Taegwan-ryong (pass) to Chech'on.

Upon arrival on July 2, the 8th Division commander, Col. Lee Song Ga, initially forward-deployed the 10th Regiment (+) at Sinrim, north of Chech'on, to block the enemy's advance from Wonju. He also positioned the 21st Regiment (−) so as to respond to the enemy threat from P'yongch'ang-Yongwol. In the afternoon of July 4, however, Col. Lee received an abrupt cable from the ROKA Headquarters instructing him to move his division to Ch'ungju.

Col. Lee was suspicious of the order, as it instructed him to abandon the strategically important Central Railway Line axis and move his troops almost 40 kilometers to the west to Ch'ungju, but he had no means of verifying the cable due to the lack of communications facilities. The division commander had no choice but to follow the order. Col. Lee initially wanted to use a route through the mountains, but the enemy had already blocked off this passage. He then decided that it would be better to move his troops by rail via Andong-Taegu rather than have them fight and blaze open a passage.[93]

The troops began to move by rail at 02:00 on July 5. By around 15:00, the leading unit arrived in Taegu, and the rest of the division reached Yongch'on-Andong. When Col. Lee visited the ROKA Headquarters in Taejon to verify the suspicious cable, however, he was informed that no such instructions had been given and was told to go back and secure Chech'on.[94] He immediately returned to Taegu, and went back as far as Tanyang by 18:00 on July 6. By this time, however, the South Han bridge in Tanyang had been blown by ROK engineers,[95] and the leading unit of the enemy 8th Division from Yongwol had advanced to the northern bank of the river.

Col. Lee established the division command post in Tanyang, and deployed the 21st Regiment between Hill 324 and Todamri, retaining the 10th Regiment as a reserve in Tanyang. The total strength of the ROK 8th Division was about 6,000 men, including 500 members of the Youth Defense Organization. The division had about the same level of equipment as at the beginning of the war, including 13 M-3 howitzers.

On the other side, the NKPA 8th Division (under Maj. Gen. Oh Paek Ryong) was organized around the nucleus of the 1st Brigade of the 38 Security Force in early July. It consisted of three infantry regiments (81st, 82nd, 83rd) and an artillery regiment, and had a total strength of 10,000 men. The division possessed a variety of artillery pieces, including ten 122-mm howitzers and twelve 120-mm mortars.[96] For an early occupation of Andong, the enemy division intended to cross the South Han River and annihilate the ROK 8th Division in the vicinity of Chuk-ryong. By July 6, it had established the command post at P'yongdongri, and one of its regiments had set out for the South Han River.

As he led his troops into Tanyang, Col. Lee received instructions to attack Wonju with a regiment and block the enemy's advance with the rest of the division. He felt that this directive had been issued on the premise that the division had arrived in Chech'on, and thought that under the circumstances, it would be prudent to attack Chech'on with a regiment. He decided to postpone the commitment of the other regiment until the situation improved, and began to plan for an attack with the reserve 10th Regiment.

Upon hearing from refugees that the enemy command post was forward-deployed in Maep'ori under loose security, however, Col. Lee decided to attack it first with a battalion.

To attack the enemy command post, the 1st Battalion of the ROK 10th Regiment departed from Tanyang at 23:00 on July 7. Crossing the South Han from Chungbangri, the battalion by 04:00 advanced to Hill 267, immediately south of P'yongdongri. After observing the enemy command post, the battalion confirmed that it was being guarded only by a reinforced company, and launched a three-pronged attack with the 2nd Company as the main attack.

At Maep'o Elementary School, where the enemy command post was located, there were more than 100 horses, 10 small-caliber guns, small armored vehicles, and several trucks loaded with supplies. The fact that they were more than 12 kilometers removed from the South Han apparently gave the enemy troops a false sense of security, and most of them were fast asleep when the ROK troops launched their surprise attack. Completely caught off guard, the enemy troops did not even have time to take their gear with them, and suffered heavy losses. Those who took flight toward the hills came under ROK mortar fire.

The ROK battalion, however, was surprised by enemy troops in Yongch'onri. After suffering more than 20 casualties, the battalion dispersed and returned to the parent unit in Tanyang around 21:00. In the battle of Maep'ori, the 1st Battalion was estimated to have killed or wounded more than 100 enemy troops and destroyed 10 artillery pieces and 3 trucks.[97]

Believing that the enemy's river-crossing operation would soon get underway, Col. Lee committed the 3rd Battalion of the 10th Regiment to the south of Tanyang in order to strengthen the defense of the river bank area. After conducting a series of reconnaissance actions on that evening, the enemy intensified artillery fire and began to cross the South Han from Sangjinri and Todamri. Although the enemy troops were crossing the river right in front of the ROK 21st Regiment, heavy night rain reduced visibility to almost zero and enabled the leading NKPA unit to establish a bridgehead on the southern bank.

Taking advantage of the bridgehead, the enemy launched a full-scale river-crossing offensive at dawn the next day. The enemy troops directed their attack across the whole front and to the eastern flank of the ROK regiment. The enemy unit from Sangjinri broke through the position of the 1st Battalion. Using wires and rafts to cross the South Han from Todamri, a battalion-strength enemy unit put relentless pressure on the 2nd Battalion on the right flank of the defensive line.

Faced with this threat, the ROK 21st Regiment commander at last decided to withdraw the two battalions to Pium-san and Hill 664 to block the enemy's advance. Hill 664 on the right, however, soon fell into the enemy's hands, and the regiment had to establish a new line of resistance along Hill 324–Piumsan–Hill 674.

Mindful of the decreased combat strength of the 21st Regiment, the

ROK 8th Division commander decided to relieve it with the reserve 10th Regiment. Under the tight cover of the 18th Artillery Battalion, Col. Lee committed the 10th Regiment at night and secured the 21st Regiment as a reserve in the vicinity of Changrimri. When a part of the enemy troops advanced as far as Kumgokri and threatened to cut off the ROK line of retreat, the division commander deployed about 300 police officers in the vicinity of Sobaek-san.[98]

Upon completion of the unit rotation, the ROK 10th Regiment launched a counterattack to recover Hill 664 in the early morning of July 10. After seizing the hill, the regiment established defensive positions along Hill 324-Pium-san-Hill 664. The enemy 8th Division resumed its offensive in the evening. While its main effort carried out a diversionary frontal attack on the ROK 10th Regiment, its supporting attack occupied Hill 324 and seized Tanyang.

The 3rd Battalion, ROK 10th Regiment, was responsible for the defense of Tanyang while the attached 9th Company of the 21st Regiment was on Hill 324 without relief. The company commander later reported that he withdrew his troops on his own judgment when the enemy broke through the company's position, and that he retreated as far as Yech'on due to a breakdown in communications.[99]

To block the enemy's advance, Col. Lee decided to commit the main effort of the reserve 21st Regiment to Pukha-Puksangri, and instructed the 10th Regiment to cover the western flank and recover Tanyang when the situation permitted. The 21st Regiment dispatched two battalions to the north at night to organize positions at Puksangri.

The battle went into a lull in the afternoon of July 11. In the evening, the 21st Regiment carried out a spoiling attack under the close air support of two US F-51 squadrons. At night, however, the enemy once again began to attack the forward right flank of the ROK 8th Division with a two regimental sized units. Reinforced by a battalion from the 21st Regiment, the ROK 10th Regiment put up a fierce resistance, but eventually had to withdraw to the Changhyunri-Majori line when the enemy troops broke through the defensive line around midnight.[100]

Under the rapidly deteriorating situation, Col. Lee made an emergency request for close air support at night, and instructed the two regiments to hold the present positions. The enemy, however, once again launched a large-scale offensive across the whole front the next day in spite of F-51 air raids, which began in the morning. The enemy combined a diversionary frontal attack on the 21st Regiment with a main attack on the 10th Regiment, and dispatched a battalion to Kumgokri-P'unggi to cut off the ROK line of retreat.

Col. Lee realized that his division could no longer hold the Chang-hyunri-Majori line. The enemy unit on the right flank was already threatening to block off Road 5 at a defile. He finally decided to withdraw his troops to the vicinity of Chuk-ryong pass and put an end to the Tanyang Battle.[101]

During this battle, the ROK 8th Division suffered great confusion due to a breakdown in communications, and conceded much too easily a stretch of 24 kilometers from Chech'on to Tanyang, with possibly grave consequences for the defense of the Central Railway Line axis and that of the eastern front. The division commander quickly overcame this crisis with effective command measures. He carried out a surprise attack on the enemy's field command post, and organized a systematic defense along the river bank to delay the enemy's advance for 6 days.

The North Korean People's Army also attached great strategic value to this axis and sought to make up for the delay. Besides the 8th Division, the enemy committed its 12th Division to Tanyang after the Ch'ungju Battle and fought to regain the initiative along this axis.

4. Delaying Action in Uljin-Yonghae

Effectively cut off from the rest of the inland regions by the rough terrain of the Taebaek Mountains, the eastern coastal region formed a separate
theater during the Korean War. The East Coast Road was the only major maneuver route within the region. From a military point of view, however, even
this road had many vulnerabilities as it was crisscrossed by a number of
creeks and bridges.

Located south of Kangnung, Uljin marked the eastern end of the ROK
-US combined front which stretched from P'yongt'aek. At Uljin, two small
roads to Ch'unyang-Yongju branched out from the East Coast Road. On June
28, the ROKA Headquarters redirected the 8th Division from Kangnung to
Chech'on, and committed the Pusan-stationed 23rd Regiment (under Lt. Col.
Kim Jong Won), 3rd Division, to conduct delaying operations in this area.[102]

Having occupied Kangnung, the NKPA 5th Division (under Maj. Gen.
Ma Sang Ch'ol) was pursuing the ROK 8th Division with its 11th Regiment, and
was advancing southward along the coastal road without encountering any
resistance. The 549th Naval Combat Team had been incorporated into its 10th
and 11th Regiments. Meanwhile, attempting to make contacts with guerrilla
units in the area, the 766th Unit (under Sr. Col. Oh Jin Woo) infiltrated into
Taebaek-san from Uljin and was moving southward in the direction of Ilwol-
san-Yongyang-Ch'ongsong in order to block the line of communications between Taegu and Pusan. They intended to occupy the P'ohang-Kyongju line
quickly and support the maneuver of the NKPA 2nd Corps on their way to
Pusan.[103]

On June 28, the ROK 23rd Regiment received instructions from division commander Col. Yu Sung Ryol to block the enemy at Uljin. Moving by

Uljin-Yonghae Battle (June 29-July 11, 1950)

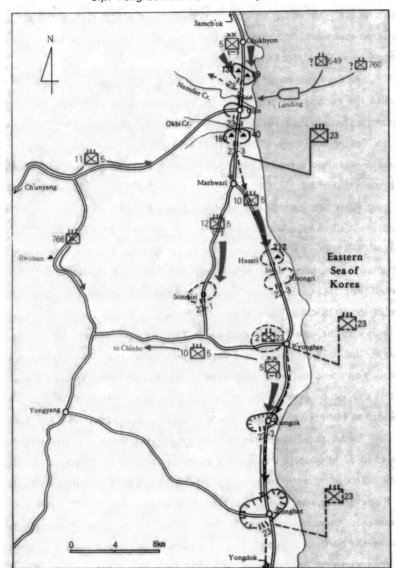

rail from Pusan to P'ohang via Taegu, the regiment advanced as far as Okbi-ch'on on the south of Uljin by the next day. The regiment reconnaissance unit detected that about 250 troops of the 549th Unit were serving as a covering force for the NKPA 5th Division in Uljin.

As the dawn broke on July 1, the ROK 23rd Regiment commander at-tacked the enemy unit with his three battalions. After dispersing the enemy troops, he focused on securing downtown Uljin and the coastal highway to the north. Taking advantage of Namdae-ch'on and Okbi-ch'on, the regiment com-mander organized defensive positions in depth with the 2nd, 1st, and 3rd Bat-talions in that order.

After hearing that the 549th Unit had been attacked, the NKPA 5th Division in Chukbyon launched an attack on the ROK 23rd Regiment. The en-emy 10th Regiment moved along the coastal highway and the 12th Regiment advanced to Namdae-ch'on to carry out a pincer attack. Spearheaded by SU-76 self-propelled guns, the two enemy regiments overwhelmed the 2nd Battal-ion of the ROK 23rd Regiment on the front and forced the ROK troops to withdraw to the south of Namdae-ch'on. Greatly outnumbered by the enemy troops, the ROK regiment commander concluded that Namdae-ch'on and Okbi-ch'on could not be defended. Believing that unit reorganization was ur-gently needed, he gave up the defense of Uljin in the afternoon of July 1 and decided to withdraw to the next line of resistance on the north of P'yonghae.

Under the division commander's approval, the ROK 23rd Regiment marched 31 kilometers through the night and arrived in P'yonghae at 05:00, July 2. Troops from the Independent 1st Battalion and Yongdungp'o Academy in P'ohang were attached to the 23rd Regiment at this time.[104] The regiment commander forward-deployed the Independent 1st Battalion on an unnamed hill on the north of Kisongri, and incorporated the troops from Yongdungpo Academy into the 2nd Battalion.

II. Transition to a Delaying Operation 339

Meanwhile, the enemy 5th Division continued its pursuit. Before the sunrise on July 3rd, the division commander divided the main effort and sent the 10th Regiment along the East Coast Road and directed the 12th Regiment toward the mountains region to the west.[105]

The Independent 1st Battalion in Kisongri proved no match for the enemy 10th Regiment. Having completed the unit reorganization by this time, however, the ROK 23rd Regiment was able to defend the western flank with the 1st Battalion in Sonmiri and cover the Independent 1st Battalion with the 3rd Battalion on the south of Kisongri. The 2nd Battalion was retained as a reserve. The forward-deployed battalions, however, were soon pushed back to P'yonghae under the overwhelming attack of the enemy 10th and 12th Regiments.

When the enemy troops broke through the defensive positions at the north of P'yonghae, the ROK 23rd Regiment commander once again had to conduct a withdrawal operation. On the night of July 3, the regiment, under the cover of the 2nd Battalion, marched 28km south to Yonghae. After a meeting engagement with the enemy lead unit at Kumgokdong, the 2nd Battalion later assembled in Yonghae.[106] By July 4, the 23rd Regiment and the Independent 1st Battalion completed withdrawal to Yonghae and began to undergo unit reorganization.

On the same day, the ROK 3rd Division commander made a request to the ROKA Headquarters for the return of the 22nd Regiment, [107] and attached the Yongdungp'o Academy troops to the Independent 1st Battalion. Meanwhile, the enemy 10th and 12th Regiments continued their pursuit in the direction of Yonghae. The enemy 11th Regiment, which had pursued the ROK 8th Division from Kangnung, moved southward in the direction of P'yongch'ang-Yongwol-Ch'unyang, and followed the main effort from Uljin.[108]

With no support from the division and higher units, the ROK 23rd

Regiment had thus conducted delays for a 60km stretch from Uljin to Yonghae against the enemy's 5th Division and the 766th Unit as well as part of the 549th unit. The main effort of the ROK 3rd Division had already been committed to the Han River line prior to the beginning of the delay operations, and the division was broken up on July 5 as part of the ROK reorganization plan. Nevertheless, the 23rd Regiment speedily moved up north to block the enemy's advance from Uljin, and played a major role in preventing the early fall of P'ohang.

Perhaps unaware of the ROK defensive vulnerabilities along the East Coast Highway, the enemy maneuvered one of its regiments in the mountains from Kangnung and thus failed to strike a concentrated blow against the ROK units. The enemy 11th Regiment maneuvered along narrow mountain passages for 8 days for a total distance of 280 kilometers, but only brought about a reduction in the overall combat strength of the division. The 766th and 549th Units likewise failed to make a major contribution to the main operation.

Moreover, the United Nations naval and air forces began to conduct blocking and interdiction operations against the enemy along the eastern coastline in this period. The UN naval fleet fired on the enemy line of communications and assembly areas, and airplanes bombarded enemy units, main facilities, and bridges to slow down the pace of the enemy's advance. During these air operations, the US military advisor to the ROK 23rd Regiment even directed naval fire and air raids on targets in person.[109] As the enemy 5th Division began to threaten P'ohang, the US CINCFE strengthened the defense of Yongdok and beefed up the security around the Yongil Air Field, providing increased naval and air support.

Under such circumstances, the ROK 23rd Regiment and the NKPA 5th Division once again engaged in a fierce battle at Yonghae along the Kum River-Sobaek Mountains Line on July 13.

In short, from July 5 to 12 the ROK and US forces delayed the enemy's advance along the combined front between P'yongtaek-Ch'ungju-Uljin along the Ch'a-ryong Mountains. After conducting delaying action for a week, the ROK and US troops carried out an operational withdrawal to a line connecting the Kum River and Sobaek Mountains. The US forces took over the Kum Line and ROK forces was responsible for the Sobaek Line, and they continued their delaying operations.

III. The Establishment of the United Nations Command and the Organization of the Military Assistance System

1. The Establishment of the UN Command

In the first week of July 1950, the ROK Armed Forces organized a combined front along the P'yongtaek-Ch'ungju-Uljin line with US Forces sent to Korea under the auspices of the United Nations. ROK-US Forces initially planned to delay the enemy's advance and make an early transition to a counteroffensive, but could not overcome the relative inferiority in troop strength and equipment against the North Korean People's Army. By July 12, US Forces on the western front had withdrawn in stages to the Kum River, and the ROK Armed Forces on the central and eastern fronts had pulled back to the Sobaek Mountains Line.

While conducting a series of delays, ROK and US Forces established the United Nations Command and moved the EUSA Command in order to ensure the unity of command and enhance the effectiveness of operations. As part of this effort, operational control over ROK troops was transferred to the UN Command, and the ROK Armed Forces were reorganized into a two-corps structure.

In the early stage of the war, the ROK government had made a strong request to the UN for support, and many UN member nations had decided to extend military assistance to the Republic in accordance with two UN Security Council resolutions. Following the US entry into the Korean War, Britain and Australia also began to provide naval and air support for the ROK Armed Forces.

On July 3, the UN Secretary General, Trygve Lie, circulated a proposal suggesting that the the United States direct the United Nations Forces in Korea, but with the help of a Committee on Coordination of Assistance for Korea. This committee would coordinate all offers of assistance, promote support by member nations, and receive reports from the field commander in Korea.[110] The United States, however, felt that placing a UN committee between the US government and the field commander would lead to serious operational difficulties, and rejected the projected UN committee.

Instead, the US Joint Chiefs of Staff called for "a command arrangement in which the United States, on behalf of the United Nations, would control the Korean operation, with no positive contact between the field commander and the United Nations." Under such an arrangement, the major policy decisions would not in any way be influenced by the UN commander, but would be made by the US government.[111]

Eventually, a revised resolution drafted by the United States and introduced by Britain and France was adopted by the Security Council on July 7. This resolution (UN Document S/1588) led to the establishment of the United Nations Command overseeing combined operations in Korea. It read :

The Security Council,

Having determined that the armed attack upon the republic of Korea by forces from North Korea constitutes a breach of the peace… ;

3. Recommends that all Members providing military forces and other assistance pursuant to the aforesaid Security Council resolutions make such forces and other assistance available to a unified command under the United States;

4. Requests the United States to designate the commander of such forces;

5. Authorizes the unified command at its discretion to use the United Nations flag in the course of operations against North Korean forces concurrently with the flags of the various nations participating;

6. Requests the United States to provide the Security Council with reports as appropriate on the course of action taken under the unified command.[112]

This resolution thus made US President Truman executive agent for the Security Council in carrying out the United Nations fight against aggressors in Korea. It also recommended that contributing member nations furnish forces to a unified command under the United States.

President Truman designated the Joint Chiefs of Staff his agents for Korea, and General Lawton J. Collins, Army Chief of Staff, assumed the task of serving the JCS as their primary representative in Korean operations. Accordingly, with authority granted by the United Nations, the US Joint Chiefs of Staff became the primary agent for planning and directing the military operations of UN forces in Korea. Offers to send combat or support units advanced by UN member nations were to be reviewed by the JCS via the US State and Defense Departments. The JCS was to make a recommendation on each offer of assistance.[113]

In accordance with the UN Security Council resolution on July 7, the Secretary General presented the UN flag to the US Ambassador to the United

Nations. The US Joint Chiefs of Staff recommended that Gen. MacArthur be placed in command of UN forces in Korea, and obtained President Truman's approval on July 8. Gen. MacArthur was formally notified of his appointment on July 10, and he received detailed instructions from the Depart of the Army on July 12. The directive emphasized : "For world-wide political reasons, it is important to emphasize repeatedly the fact that our operations are in support of the United Nations Security Council." Thus appointed Commander in Chief, United Nations Command (CINCUNC), Gen. MacArthur initially exercised operational control over the UN forces through the US Far East Command before formally establishing the United Nations Command on July 24, 1950. Due to limitations in personnel, however, staff members of the Far East Command, with only few exceptions, were assigned comparable duties on the UNC Staff. In effect, the US Far East Command doubled up as the United Nations Command.[114]

The CINCUNC exercised operational control over UN forces in Korea primarily through the Eighth US Army (ground forces), US Far East Naval Command, and US Far East Air Command— the three service elements of the US Far East Command.

⟨Table 5⟩　　The Command Structure of the United Nations Command[115]

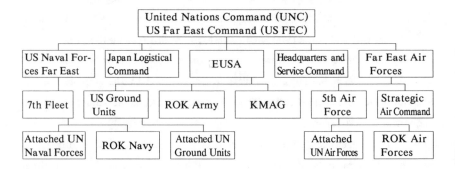

Even after the establishment of the United Nations Command, UN member nations other than the United States had yet to send ground forces to Korea as of mid-July. Compared with naval and air forces, sending of ground forces involved much more time and effort. Besides, the decision to send ground troops carried a much greater risk. Contributions made by many member nations, however, were signifiant not so much in the size of troops provided but rather in the enhanced legitimation of war efforts against North Korea's aggression. For the first time in world history, the free world was united under the UN banner to repel communist aggression in accordance with the spirit of the UN Charter.

On July 6, in order to exercise effective operational control over ground forces, Gen. MacArthur Planned to have Lt. Gen. Walker direct ground operations in Korea. After making a tour of the front, Gen. Walker decided to establish the EUSA Command in Taegu, and sent an advance team as a preparatory measure.

On July 12, Gen. Walker received Gen. MacArthur's oral directive "to assume the operational command of US ground forces in Korea effective July 13." After moving to Taegu from Tokyo on July 13, Gen. Walker opened the command post and began to exercise operational command over US ground forces. On that evening, Br. Gen. Church and his ADCOM staff quit their mission and returned to Tokyo.

As ⟨Table 6⟩ shows, by the end of July, many UN member nations sent ground, naval, and air forces to Korea in support of the Republic.

Meanwhile, the UN flag presented to the US Ambassador to the United Nations was handed over to the CINCUNC in Tokyo by Gen. Collins on July 13, and was relayed to the EUSA commander four days later.[116]

〈Table 6〉　　　Participation of UN Member Nations (July 31, 1950)[117]

Armed Service	Participation by Country
Army	US 24th Division (19th, 21st, 34th Regiment), 25th Division (24th, 27th, 35th Regiment), 1st Cavalry Division (5th, 7th, 8th Regiment)
Navy	US (one combat and supporting fleet), Britain (one aircraft carrier, two destroyers, three small warships), Australia (one destroyer, two small warships), France (one small warship), Netherlands (one destroyer), Canada (three destroyers), New Zealand (two small warships)
Air Force	US (one tactical air wing, two bomber air wings, one air transport unit), Britain (one combat air squadron, one air transport flight), Canada (one air transport squadron), Australia (one combat air squadron, one air transport flight)

2. Transfer of the ROK Armed Forces' Operational Command

With the establishment of the United Nations Command, the US Far East Command in Tokyo began to function also as a general headquarters with unified command authority over UN forces in Korea. In addition, effective July 13, the Eighth US Army Command in Taegu began to exercise directly operational command over UN ground forces. Faced with these developments, the ROK government began to look into the possibility of transferring operational command over the ROK Armed Forces to the UNC. ROK forces had been conducting combined operations with US forces on a service basis for some time, and by July 13, the ROKA Headquarters had moved to the vicinity of the EUSA Command and held combined meetings in Taegu. Thus, by this time, ROK forces in effect had joined the unified command structure of the UN forces.

Taking into account these informal developments in the command structure, President Syngman Rhee decided to place ROK forces formally under the operational command of the UNC, as a policy measure to bring about an eventual victory in the war. After giving the Chief of the General Staff Gen. Chung an oral directive to place himself under the operational command of the UNC, President Rhee sent a letter to Gen. MacArthur and formally transferred the operational command of ROK forces to the UNC during the period of the continuation of the current operational situation:

> In view of the joint military effort of the United Nations on behalf of the Republic of Korea, in which all military forces, land, sea, and air, of all the United Nations fighting in or near Korea have been placed under your operational command, and in which you have been designated Supreme Commander of United Nations Forces, I am happy to assign to you command authority over all land, sea, and air forces of the Republic of Korea during the period of the continuation of the present state of hostilities···.[118]

The operational command of the ROK Armed Forces was thus transferred to Gen. MacArthur effective July 14. Gen. MacArthur, in turn, transferred the operational command of ROK ground forces to the EUSA commander on July 17, and delegated command authority over ROK naval and air forces to the Far East Naval and Air Force commander, respectively. These measures brought about the unity of command for all units fighting against communist aggression in Korea.

In a reply to President Rhee sent through US Ambassador Muccio on July 18, Gen. MacArthur stated that he was proud to have the ROK forces under his command and assured him that "the way be long and hard, but ultimate result cannot fail to be victory." The exchange of letters between President Rhee and Gen. MacArthur became official when it was presented to the UN Secretary-General and brought to the attention of the Security Council on July 25.

Meanwhile, ROK Army Chief of staff Chung summoned a staff meeting at the ROKA Headquarters and emphasized to the 1st and 2nd Corps commanders that the decision to transfer operational command was necessary for effective combined operations with UN forces. His explanations were also relayed to the division commanders.[119]

In actual operations, the operational control of ROK ground forces was normally channelled through the ROKA chain of command. The usual procedure was for the EUSA commander or his chief of staff to request the ROK Army Chief of Staff to take certain actions regarding ROK forces. The ROK Army Chief of Staff then gave the necessary orders or directives to the ROK units. When the ROK unit was attached to US forces, however, it was operationally controlled through the US chain of command. From a purely military point of view, the operational control of the ROK Armed Forces never became an issue during the war; however, when the political interests of the Republic of Korea seemed to diverge from those of the United Nations during certain critical phases of the war, the continued existence of the operational control structure was called into question. Nevertheless, the unified command structure under the UNC was maintained throughout the war.[120]

3. Readjustment of Defensive Lines and Reorganization of the ROK Armed Forces

After its first reorganization in early July had established the ROK 1st Corps and reduced the total number of divisions from eight to five, the ROK Armed Forces conducted delaying operations along the P'yongt'aek-Ch'ungju-Uljin Line with the US 24th Corps. As ROK forces were responsible for the defense of too wide a front, however, the ROKA Headquarters had to commit all five divisions to the front without any reserves. This state of affairs not only limited the ROK ability to respond to contingencies and defend rear areas, but also created serious problems for the reinforcement of frontline troops.

Accordingly, in order to secure a total of eight divisions as at the beginning of the war, ROK Minister of National Defense Shin Song Mo began to study the possibility of re-establishing disbanded divisions and organizing additional units. He officially brought this issue to attention on July 6, the day after the ROKA Headquarters (provisional command post) had moved from P'yongt'aek to Taejon. ROK military leaders discussed the problem with Br. Gen. Church,[121] and decided to re-establish the three divisions and create a new division. In addition, the ROKA Headquarters decided to establish provisional unit organization districts for the defense of the rear area and reinforcement of frontline troops.

On July 7, the Ministry of National Defense issued a general order re-establishing the 3rd Division (under Br. Gen. Lee Jun Shik), the 5th Division (Col. Lee Hyong Sok), and the 7th Division (under Col. Min Ki Shik), and creating the 9th Division (under Col. Lee Jong Ch'an) in Pusan.[122] Available troops and equipment at the time did not even meet the needs of the existing divisions, however, and no additional divisions were created according to the plan.

On July 17, the ROKA Headquarters established the West Coast Command (under Maj. Gen. Shin Tae Yong) to oversee North and South Cholla Prorince unit organization Districts, and reorganized the Kyongsang Province Unit Organization District into North and South Kyongsang Districts. These four District Commands, however, existed only in name and were later disbanded or absorbed into other units.

Meanwhile, the ROK 6th and 8th Divisions on the central eastern front withdrew to the Ihwa-ryong–Cho-ryong–Chuk-ryong Line as delay operations unfolded, making it more difficult for the ROKA Headquarters to exercise operational control over these units. Moreover, the main effort of the enemy 2nd Corps was directed at these divisions, providing an additional impetus for the ROKA Headquarters to consider establishing another corps. On July 12, the ROK Ministry of National Defense established the 2nd Corps in Hamch'ang. Assigning the 6th and 8th Divisions to the corps, the Defense Ministry appointed Br. Gen. Kim Baek Il as the corps commander. Having thus established the two-corps structure, the ROK Army began to conduct defensive operations in the Sobaek Mountains with US forces along the Kum River Line.[123] ⟨Table 7⟩ shows the combat organization of the ROK Army at this point.

As two additional US divisions were committed into the Sangju–Yongdong area centered around Ch'upung-ryong, however, ROK and US forc-

⟨Table 7⟩   The Activatim of the 2nd Corps and Command Structure (July 12, 1950)

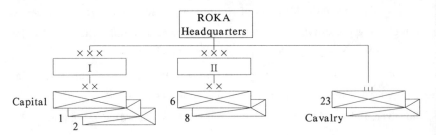

es had to redraw their sectors, and as a result, ROK forces became responsible for the defense of the central-eastern front east of Sangju. As part of the second round of reorganization efforts, the Defense Ministry disbanded the seriously depleted 2nd Division, and newly established a two-corps, five-division structure effective July 20.

Br. Gen. Kim Paik Il returned to the post of chief of staff at the ROKA Headquarters, and Br. Gen. Yu Jae Hung, deputy commander of the I Corps, was appointed as the commander of the II Corps. The 1st and 3rd Divisions were assigned to the I Corps, the 6th and 8th Divisions were assigned to the II Corps, and the Capital Division was retained as a reserve. At the same time, the I Corps handed its sector over to US forces and its headquarters moved to

⟨Table 8⟩　The ROK Armed Forces after the Second Round of Reorganization
(July 24, 1950)

Unit	Subordinate Regiments after Reorganization	Strength
I Corps Headquarters		3,014
Capital Division	1st, 8th (incorporated into 18th), 18th, 17th (attached)	6,644
8th Division	10th, 16th (assigned from 2nd Division), 21st (with 1st Battalion, 25th Regiment, newly assigned)	8,864
II Corps Headquarters		976
1st Division	11th (plus 5th), 12th (plus 20th), 13th	7,601
6th Division	2nd, 7th, 19th	5,727
ROKA Headquarters		3,020
3rd Division	22nd, 23rd, Cavalry	8,829
Headquarters Unit		11,881
Replacement Corps		9,016
Chonju Training Center		8,699
Kwangju Training Center		6,244
Pusan Training Center		5,356
Wounded and Noncombatants		8,699
Total		94,570

Uisong. The Capital Division and the 17th Regiment had to relocate to Andong, and the 1st Division had to move to Ch'unyang. The ROK I and II Corps planned to block the enemy's advance on the eastern and central eastern front, respectively, and make a quick transition to counteroffensive.[124]

Due to unexpected developments on the front, however, the I Corps and its subordinate divisions were unable to move as planned. Moreover, the I Corps was faced with a serious intercommunication problem: that of controlling its two divisions on the opposite sides of the T'aebaek Mountains. Accordingly, the Defense Ministry once again reorganized the command structure on July 24, placing the Capital Division and the 8th Division under the command of the I Corps along the Yongju-Andong axis. The II Corps was to direct the 1st and 6th Divisions in defense of the Munkyong-Hamch'ang-Sangju axis, and the 3rd Division was placed under the direct control of the ROKA Headquarters. ⟨Table 8⟩ shows the final configuration of ROK units after the second round of reorganization.[125]

4. Establishment of the War Support System

As ROK forces had lost enlistment documents and a large volume of supplies amidst chaos in the early phase of the war, it became imperative that the Defense Ministry re-establish a personnel and logistical support system in the rear area at the earliest possible date. As a provisional measure, the Defense Ministry took advantage of Article 58 of the Military Conscription Law and recruited "second-class conscripts" from the street and from various organizations. With the promulgation of the Emergency Decree for Homeland Defense on July 22, the Ministry was able to recruit young males from age 14 up.[126] Recruiting rapidly gained pace from that point on, and personnel administration bodies had to be expanded.

As for the logistical support system, the ROKA Headquarters established the Seoul Area Supply Depot in Kimchon on July 5 in addition to the existing supply Depot in Taejon. In parallel with this, the logistics department at each division was reorganized to facilitate coordination with supply units. As US logistical support increased in the month of July, a great volume of US supplies began to pile up at ROK supply points.[127] Communications equipment began to be supplied, and a wide range of engineer equipment was provided. From July 20, a large quantity of US medical supplies were also shipped into Korea and were sent to the frontline troops.[128]

The procurement system also made a rapid recovery from the initial shock, and a "Special Decree on Requisinion" was promulgated on July 26. As all household goods as well as factory facilities were mobilized for military operations, the Korean War began to take on the aspects of a total war.[129]

In the area of military rations, however, ROK forces still suffered from shortages. Stockpiled rice (including the amount set aside for civilian consumption) outside the Seoul-Inchon area did not meet the absolute minimum requirements.[130] Main and auxiliary foods (equivalent to 20 Hwan (money)per person per day) often did not reach the front in time.

In the area of logistical support, US forces gradually established the necessary support system. Effective July 1, the EUSA began to provide logistical support to ROK and UN forces as well as US forces in Korea. When the EUSA Headquarters was moved to Taegu, the EUSA rear command post remaining in Yokohama carried out logistical support missions for these units via its logistical command in Pusan.[131] As the EUSA served the dual function of commanding combat troops in Korea and providing logistical support from Japan, however, it was unable to focus solely on the former function. This state of affairs continued until the establishment of the separate US Logistical Command in Japan on August 25.

The EUSA primarily resorted to its inventories in Japan, and imported from the United States what was not readily obtained or produced in Japan. Around July 10, the EUSA made preparations to ship 3.5-inch rockets and 4.2-inch mortar shells to Pusan, and on the 18th, it transported to Pusan more than 3,000 antitank mines produced in Japan. In the meantime, the Tokyo Armory transformed old-model tanks into M4A3's and adapted the 105-mm gun carriage and M15A1 semi-track vehicle to the Korean terrain.[132]

It was fortunate for the ROK-US side that Pusan, the largest port in South Korea, was located near the UN logistical base in Japan. Twenty-four ships could be anchored in the inner harbor of Pusan, and 14 LST's could unload their cargoes at the same time. The daily offload capacity was 45,000 tons. Moreover, railways and roads stretching out from Pusan readily served as effective lines of communication. In the month of July, more than 230 ships unloaded a total of 309,314 tons, averaging 10,666 tons per day.[133]

Ⅳ. Delaying Action Along the Kum River-Sobaek Mountains Line

1. Delaying Action Along the Kum River Line

(1) Kongju-Taep'yongri Battle

Having established his command post in Taegu on July 13 to command and control ground operations in Korea, EUSA commander Lt. Gen.

Walker was determined to delay the enemy's advance along the Kum River-Sobaek Mountains line to gain time for UN military assistance prior to making a transition to the counteroffensive.

According to Gen. Walker, the EUSA was to block the enemy's advance and secure the line of defense. While making efforts to stabilize the military situation, the EUSA was to secure reinforcements for the counteroffensive. Under this operational objective, the US 24th Division was to be deployed along the Kum line to block the enemy's advance in the Kongju-Taejon area on the left flank. The 25th Division was directed to occupy a blocking position on a main road in the central mountains region and support ROK forces while defending against the enemy attack. One of its battalions was assigned a mission to secure the Yongil Air Field and P'ohang.[134]

The US 24th Division accordingly completed deployment along the Kum line, and the 25th Division took its positions between July 10 and 15. The US 27th and 24th Regiments were dispatched to Uisong and Sangju, respectively, to provide support to ROK forces. The 35th Regiment was retained as a reserve, and one of its battalions was committed to the Yongil Air Field. Meanwhile, the ROK Ⅰ Corps (Capital Division with the 17th Regiment attached; 1st and 2nd Divisions) was deployed in the Koesan-Miwon area; the Ⅱ Corps (6th and 8th Divisions) was positioned between Ihwa-ryong and Chuk-ryong ; while the 23rd Regiment of the 3rd Division established defensive positions to south of Yonghae.

NKPA, in the meantime, sought to annihilate ROK-US main elements in detail at Taejon and in the southeast of the Sobaek Mountains, and mobilized all its reserves in order to deliver a devastating blow to the ROK-US combined forces.[135] The NKPA Ⅰ Corps (the 2nd, 3rd, 4th, and 6th Divisions with the 105th Armored Division attached) was committed to the Kum line while the Ⅱ Corps (the 1st, 5th, 8th, 12th, 13th, and 15th Divisions) was advancing toward the Sobaek Mountains and eastern seashores.

Originating in the Sobaek Mountains, the Kum River cuts through South Ch'ungch'ong Province before flowing into the Yellow Sea. The river runs a semicircular course around Taejon, providing a natural obstacle for the defense of the most important city in the region. Moreover, with a width of 500 -1,000 meters and an average depth of nearly 2.5 meters, the Kum rules out fording operations.

In the afternoon of July 12, the US 24th Division blew up all ferry terminals and bridges in the Kum River area. The division commander decided to delay the enemy's attack for as long as possible and focus on the defense of Taep'yongri along the Seoul-Pusan Highway. He pinned his hope on the 19th Regiment (under Col. Guy S. Meloy Jr.), which had a rich and distinguished history dating back to the American Civil War. The regiment up to that point in the Korean War had been retained as a reserve. The division commander forward-deployed the 19th Regiment in the vicinity of Taep'yongri and relieved the 21st Regiment. The 19th Regiment was thus directly in front of Taepyongri, the 34th Regiment in front of Kongju, and the 21st Regiment in a reserve defensive position. The division, however, was too thinly stretched over a wide defensive front, and the regiments were understrength, consisting as they were of only two battalions each. Moreover, the units suffered from poor intercommunication.

Meanwhile, the NKPA I Corps set Taejon as its next objective, and its 4th Division was preparing to advance into Kongju and its 3rd Division, into Taepyongri. Under the support of more than 50 tanks, the two divisions began to prepare for river-crossing operations on the night of July 12. However, their morale was on the low side as they had lost 30 to 40% of the troops since the beginning of the war and had been replenished with conscripts.[136]

Until July 13, both the North Korean and the US sides were preparing for a battle along the Kum River line. Anticipating that the enemy would attempt to cross the Kum opposite Kongju, the US 34th Infantry deployed the 3rd Battalion (under Maj. Newton W. Lantron) in front of Kongju and retained the 1st Battalion (Lt. Col. Harold B. Ayres) as a reserve. To support the regiment, the 63rd Artillery Battalion (including a platoon from A Battery, 11th Artillery Battalion) was placed between the 1st and 3rd Battalions. The 3rd Battalion deployed L, I, and K Companies from left to right on the north of Kongju, and used the regimental Reconnaissance Company as a security force on the southwest of Kongju.

As the dawn broke on July 14, the enemy 4th Division shelled the 1st Battalion. The enemy 18th and 5th Regiments attacked from the front while its 16th Regiment attempted to cross the Kum from the flank with a view to block the US line of retreat.[137] Soon, American aerial observation officers of the artillery battalion and L Company of the 3rd Battalion noticed that a part of the enemy 18th Regiment in two small boats had already begun crossing the river and had started moving toward Komsangri. Upon receiving this report from liaison observation planes, the artillery battalion decided not to fire on the boats and wait for larger targets. The battalion briefly fired two of its 155-mm howitzers on the enemy troops, but enemy YAK fighter planes soon drove away the liaison observation planes.

At this time, on the north of Kongju, only L and I Companies of the 3rd Battalion were in position. All personnel of K Company had been evacuated on the previous night due to battle fatigue.[138] Coming under concentrated enemy fire on the morning of July 14, L Company on the left withdrew from their positions without authorization. Completely unaware of this development, I Company alone was left behind.

Although the enemy was unaware of the new situation and made no attempt to cross the river from across Kongju, the enemy troops who bypassed the river line rifle companies threatened American artillery positions in the rear. By the time an outpost of the artillery battalion noticed enemy troops, a full-scale attack was underway. The artillery positions were overrun by the enemy, and the explosion of ammunition trucks added to confusion. In spite of support provided by a ROK Cavalry Company[139] the battalion had to abandon their positions after losing 10 howitzers and from 60 to 80 vehicles.[140]

Until midafternoon that day, Lt. Col. Robert L. Wadlington, acting commander of the US 34th Regiment, was absent from his headquarters, as he was reconnoitering the area to select a site for a possible blocking position. After learning that an enemy force had attacked the 63rd Field Artillery Battalion, Wadlington at once ordered the reserve 1st Battalion to launch a counterattack before sunset. Faced with a stiff enemy resistance and dusk, however, the battalion had to turn back. I Company also withdrew on order.

By the morning of July 15, the US 34th Regiment withdrew to Nonsan and, on the next day, it moved to Taejon. Having occupied Kongju, the enemy was in Nonsan by the evening of July 15. As the assembly of river-crossing boards was delayed, however, the enemy was unable to transport heavy equipment across the Kum as late as the afternoon of July 16.[141]

Meanwhile, in the Taep'yongri area, the enemy 3rd Division began firing on American troops on July 15. Since July 12, the US 19th Regiment had begun deploying the 1st Battalion (under Lt. Col. Otho T. Winstead) near expected crossing sites in the front of Taep'yongri and in the vicinity of Koehwasan. With the 2nd Battalion (under Lt. Col. Thomas M. McGrail) retained as a reserve, the regiment had completed the establishment of positions. E Company was deployed as a security force on high ground west of the Seoul-Pusan Railroad on the eastern flank, and a security force was also dispatched to the western flank adjacent to the 34th Regiment.[142] Artillery support was provided by the 52nd, 11th (−), and 13th Field Artillery Battalions. The 52nd Field Artillery

Battalion was in position in Tumanri, in the rear of the 1st Battalion. The 11th and the 13th Field Artillery Battalions were positioned farther south behind it.

On July 14, Col. Meloy, commander of the 19th Regiment, received information of the attempted enemy crossings from the left flank and the collapse of the 34th Regiment at Kongju. With the left flank thus exposed, Col. Meloy on the next day reinforced the small force there with a special task unit centered around G Company under the command of Lt. Col. McGrail, commanding officer of the 2nd Battalion.[143] As a result, Col. Meloy now had only F Company in reserve.

Taep'yongri Battle

As the evening approached, the enemy 3rd Division began firing on Taep'yongri with field artillery and tank guns. Two UN planes, however, appeared and raided the enemy tank assembly area. That night small enemy groups tested the US defense by attempting to cross the river in front of Taep'yongri and Koehwa-san.

Before the day broke on July 16, with the dropping of a flare from a YAK plane, the enemy began a coordinated attack. Under the cover of intense artillery fire, enemy troops began to cross the river. The US 19th Regiment responded to this attack with support from the field artillery battalions. Abruptly, however, the American howitzer assigned to fire flares over the river position ceased to provide this support. This mishap allowed enemy units to cross the river. Some enemy troops crossed the river in front of Kaehwa-san and moved around the east end of the 1st Battalion position to overrun C Company. Also, enemy units in front of the 1st Battalion surged through the gap between B and A Companies and broke through the US positions in the morning. To counter this threat, Col. Meloy mobilized all available troops from the 1st Battalion Headquarters and the Regimental Headquarters Companies, including all officers, cooks, drivers, mechanics, clerks, and the security platoon. This counterattack force managed to turn back the enemy and defuse the crisis for the time being.[144]

However, simultaneous with its frontal attack on the battalion, the enemy had crossed the river from the left flank and begun applying pressure from there. Pinning down F Company, the regimental reserve, the enemy attacked the 52nd Field Artillery Battalion and occupied an unnamed hill near a sharp road bend to the south before setting up a major roadblock. This North Korean roadblock closed the only exit from the main battle position of the US 19th Regiment in Taep'yongri.[145] Thus, much like the 34th Regiment, the 19th Regiment found itself enveloped by the enemy without putting up an effective fight.

After receiving a report on the North Korean roadblock, Col. Meloy arrived at the site and tried to turn disorganized troops there into an attack unit. While trying to organize this group, he was wounded by an enemy shot and had to give Lt. Col. Winstead command of the regiment. Instructed to withdraw the regiment at once by Gen. Dean, Lt. Col. Winstead ordered his 1st Battalion to withdraw. He was on his way back to the Kum River when he was killed. To break the roadblock, Gen. Dean provided the 2nd Battalion commander with two tanks and six armored vehicles, but in spite of repeated efforts, they failed to clear the roadblock.

Meanwhile, elements of the withdrawing 1st Battalion and the Regimental Headquarters were coming up to the roadblock. At last, several staff officers decided that as a last resort, they would place Col. Meloy in the last tank and run it through the roadblock. The assistant S-3 of the regiment would lead a cross-country movement of personnel. The wounded regiment commander narrowly escaped the enemy fire, and after destroying approximately 100 vehicles, the remaining regimental troops withdrew along the ridges toward Yusong at night. However, wounded personnel who could not make the cross-country movement and a chaplain who remained with them were killed by North Korean soldiers.[146] In the end, the US 19th Regiment lost 481 men out of 1,753 in this battle, and had to withdraw to Taejon for reorganization.

The NKPA 3rd Division, for its part, pinned down the 19th Regiment by frontal attack while carrying out a double envelopment of the flanks. The envelopment of the US troop's left flank resulted in the fatal roadblock which closed the only line of retreat for the American troops. The 19th Regiment was able to repel enemy frontal attacks and major penetrations, but lacked an adequate reserve force to deal with the enemy's flank and rear penetrations. The hot and humid weather at the time also contributed to the deterioration of

US troop effectiveness as well as demoralization.[147]

(2) Taejon Battle

The provincial capital of South Ch'ungch'ong, Taejon's strategic importance derives from its location. Roads radiate outward from Taejon in five main directions, toward Yusong, Nonsan, Kumsan, Okch'on, and Choch'iwon. On the southeast, the Sobaek Mountains screen the city, and to the northwest flow Kap-ch'on, Yudung-ch'on, and Taejon-ch'on, all tributaries of the Kum River. There is an airfield to the southeast of downtown Taejon, and there are two tunnels along the Seoul-Pusan Railway between Taejon and Okch'on.

Taejon Battle

When the Kum River Line collapsed, Gen. Dean, commander of the US 24th Division, decided to delay the enemy's advance at Taejon and assigned this defensive mission to the 34th Regiment. Concerned with a possible turning movement by the NKPA 2nd Division, Gen. Dean deployed the 21st Regiment at Madal-ryong on the eastern flank of Taejon to secure the Seoul-Pusan Road. He also deployed the division reconnaissance company as a security force astride the Kumsan Road, and moved the weakened 19th Regiment to Yongdong.

Col. Charles E. Beauchamp, the new commanding officer of the 34th Regiment, at once deployed the 1st Battalion along the Kap-ch'on Creek opposite Yusong, and secured the 3rd Battalion as a reserve on the eastern edge of the Taejon Airfield. Of the 3rd Battalion, however, a platoon from L Company was forward-deployed along the Kap-ch'on facing Nonsan, and I Company (−) was positioned as a security force along the Seoul-Pusan Railway to the north of Taejon. All remaining elements of the divisional artillery were consolidated into one composite battalion and emplaced at the airfield. By the night of July 17, the US defensive organization was largely completed. However, as the regiment had to defend a wide front and lacked an adequate supply of communications equipment, it suffered from poor intercommunication.

The NKPA I Corps originally planned to commit three divisions in its attack on Taejon. As the advance of the 2nd Division was delayed by the ROK Capital Division in the Chinch'on-Ch'ongju area, however, only the 3rd and 4th Divisions could be used in the attack. Under the new NKPA plan, the 3rd Division was to attack Taejon frontally with tanks to pin down the defenders. The 4th Division was to send a regiment around the southern flank and cut off the Kumsan Road, and then envelop the US troops from the directions of Yusong and Nonsan.[148]

Maj. Gen. Dean initially planned to delay the enemy's advance and evacuate Taejon on July 19 before the NKPA broke through the US positions. His plan, however, had to change on July 18 when Lt. Gen. Walker informed him that the 1st Cavalry Division had started landing at P'ohang and that two days' time was needed to move this unit into position at Yongdong.[149] Gen. Dean now had to defend Taejon until July 20. He placed all American troops in Taejon under the command of the 34th Regimental commander. Also, in order to shore up the defense of Taejon, the 2nd Battalion, 19th Regiment, in Yongdong and the divisional Reconnaissance Company were attached to the 34th regiment.

To deal with the enemy's expected tank attack, 3.5-inch rocket launchers were issued to the regiment. Although this rocket launcher had been under development since the end of World War II, none had been issued to field troops prior to the Korean War. Upon Gen. MacArthur's request, these new-model bazookas were airlifted to Taejon on July 10.[150]

The North Korean attack against Taejon got underway the morning of July 19 with air strikes on the Yongdong Railway Bridge and the Taejon Airfield by 6 YAK planes. Battle on the ground began when a platoon of the divisional Reconnaissance Company engaged the enemy in the vicinity of the Nonsan road. North Korean troops soon overran a platoon of L Company at the Kap-ch'on but Col. Beauchamp narrowly averted a disaster by committing the 2nd Battalion, 19th Regiment (under Lt. Col. McGrail), and recovering the blocking position. The enemy also carried out a coordinated attack from Yusong with intense artillery fire, and forced the 1st Battalion to withdraw its outpost company from the Kap-ch'on.

At night, the US 34th Regiment received reports of enemy tanks appearing in Yusong and a roadblock set up on the Kumsan Road. An enemy sighting in Okch'on was also reported, but the regiment attached no special importance to these reports, apparently judging these enemy actions as part of the NKPA's diversionary effort.

Shortly before dawn the next day, the presence of the roadblock on the Kumsan Road was confirmed and the enemy's attack began in earnest from Yusong. Crossing the Kap-ch'on the enemy carried out a coordinated attack on the 1st Battalion positions on both sides of the Yusong Road. The enemy tanks penetrated the American positions and struck the Battalion Headquarters. Coming under an overwhelming pressure from the enemy, the American positions collapsed within a few hours. The battalion commander managed to send a report of the desperate situation to the regimental headquarters, but due to an ensuing communications breakdown, he had to withdraw his troops south toward the 2nd Battalion, 19th Regiment, without authorization.

The regimental commander went on a patrol toward the airfield to assess the situation. Upon seeing an enemy tank, he led a 3.5-inch bazooka team and set the tank on fire with rockets. The regimental commander thought that the 1st Battalion would still be holding its position at this time and dispatched the reserve 3rd Battalion in support. The lead elements of the reserve unit, however, could not accomplish the mission as it ran into an estimated enemy battalion spearheaded by six tanks on the way.[151]

Having broken through the 1st Battalion position, the enemy tanks with supporting infantry advanced into the downtown Taejon area by 06:30 hours. US troops responded with antitank fire from 3.5-inch rocket launchers. Gen. Dean personally led a bazooka team and destroyed an enemy tank. On this day, 3.5-inch rocket launchers disabled eight enemy tanks and artillery fire destroyed another two. In order to avoid friendly fire, air strikes were primarily targeted at enemy tanks and artillery positions. In the morning of July 20 alone, UN airplanes knocked out five enemy tanks along the Yusong road.[152]

Meanwhile, the 2nd Battalion, 19th Regiment, exchanged fire with

North Korean troops across the Kap-ch'on but it was becoming increasingly difficult to hold the position under the enemy's heavy pressure. When enemy shells began to fall in the vicinity of the command post and the 1st Battalion of the 34th Regiment withdrew past the battalion headquarters, the battalion commander ordered his troops to withdraw. Due to a breakdown of his radio vehicle, the battalion commander had to send a messenger to the regimental headquarters. In the withdrawal, the entire Weapons Platoon of G Company was wiped out by the enemy when it fell behind to expend its mortar ammunition.

The 2nd Battalion planned to withdraw in the direction of downtown Taejon, but upon sighting three enemy tanks at a junction leading to downtown and black smoke filling the skies, the battalion commander concluded that Taejon had fallen into enemy hands. He did not know that these tanks had already been destroyed on the previous night. Accordingly, the battalion followed the 1st Battalion, 34th Regiment, to Pomunsan to the south. Thus, by 1300 hrs. on July 20, the US defensive positions on the outskirts of Taejon had fallen into the enemy's control.[153]

Gen. Dean had yet to receive reports of withdrawal by frontline troops. However, as enemy tanks streamed into the downtown area and as the blocking of the Okch'on and Kumsan Roads exerted pressure from the rear, he decided to withdraw his troops prior to the scheduled time on that evening. Around this time, Col. Beauchamp received reports that enemy columns were approaching from the east of Taejon and that more than 20 enemy vehicles were moving up north from Kumsan. Taking these units for the withdrawing troops of the divisional Reconnaissance Company and the 21st Regiment, however, the regimental commander ordered not to fire on them.

By this time, the US 1st Cavalry Division had arrived at Yongdong. Around 15:30, when the regiment commander's withdrawal order was about to be issued, an armored platoon (5 tanks) of the US 1st Cavalry Division arrived in Taejon to provide cover for the withdrawal. The lead elements of the withdrawing troops, however, were dispersed by an enemy attack near the eastern end of Taejon. Having lost communication with the regimental commander, Gen. Dean instructed the headquarters in Yongdong to send more tanks, and at 17:30, he ordered his troops to withdraw along the Okchon Road.

Meanwhile, around 15:30, Col. Beauchamp directed four tanks from the Reconnaissance Company to secure the Sechon Tunnel and returned to his post under the support of one light tank platoon of the 21st Regiment. By this time, however, the enemy had already seized the tunnel. In order to rescue supply trains at the Taejon Train Station, Gen. Dean requested a locomotive from the Iwon Station, but this effort failed under enemy fire from the Sech'on Tunnel.[154]

In the withdrawal, part of the US troops lost direction and came under the enemy's artillery fire. They abandoned most of their 50 or so vehicles and withdrew in the direction of Okch'on. Some ventured onto the national road blockaded by the enemy and suffered heavy casualties. During this course of events, Pvt. Charles T. Zimmerman and Sgt. George D. Libbey set examples of heroism. Pvt. Zimmerman displayed superhuman courage under enemy small arms fire. While carrying wounded personnel, Sgt. Libbey provided a shield for the driver with his body. After taking wounded men to safety, Sgt. Libbey died from loss of blood.[155]

The 1st Battalion, 34th Regiment, on Pomun-san observed the enemy moving north along the Kumsan Road, but failed to block their advance. The main force of the 2nd Battalion, 19th Regiment, withdrew from Pomun-san to Yongdong via mountain passes. A group from the US troops dispersed by the enemy fire in the downtown area reached Yongdong via Okch'on while another group headed toward Okch'on and Yongdong after breaking through the enemy's blocking position at the Sech'on Tunnel. Even at this point, the 1st Battalion, 21st Regiment, was holding its position on Madal-ryong, barely 2km remote from the enemy.

In the meantime, the deputy division commander gathered the withdrawing troops at Okch'on and Yongdong, and handed over the operational zone to the 1st Cavalry Division, which managed to arrive on July 22. He moved his troops to Taegu for reorganization. The division commander's party, on the other hand, stepped onto the Kumsan Road by mistake, after following the Okch'on Road for withdrawal. Dispersed under fire from the enemy's roadblock position, the group took cover in Pomun-san and was searching for a way out. While looking for water for wounded men at night, Gen. Dean fell down a steep slope and was knocked unconscious. Separated from his party, he wandered in the mountains for the next 36 days, before he was captured by North Korean soldiers.[156]

Later, Gen. Dean noted that his two big mistakes were: not withdrawing the 34th Regiment the night of July 19, as originally planned; and releasing the divisional Reconnaissance Company from its reconnaissance mission along the Kumsan road and attaching the unit to the 34th Regiment.[157] The rest of the division commander's party was spotted by the withdrawing covering force, L Company, 3rd Battalion, 34th Regiment, and they broke through the enemy's roadblock to reach safety.

After occupying Taejon, the enemy 4th Division replenished its units with conscripts,[158] and the enemy Supreme Command bestowed honors upon the 3rd, 4th, and 105th Armored Divisions as well as the 1st Pursuit Fighter Wing.[159] On July 22, the enemy 3rd Division set out for Taegu along the Seoul-Pusan Highway while the 4th Division began to move toward the Muju-Koch'ang area in the western Naktong region on July 23.

(3) Yongdong-Kimch'on Battle

The collapse of the Kum River Line forced Gen. MacArthur to change his plan. He originally had expected that the US 24th and 25th Divisions, together with ROK forces, would be able to block the enemy's advance, and had planned to use the US 1st Cavalry Division for a landing operation. He now decided to commit this cavalry division to the front. Accordingly, he instructed Gen. Walker to move the 25th Division from the central eastern front to the Hwaryongjang-Sangju area and deploy the 1st Cavalry Division along the Yongdong-Kimch'on axis to reinforce the defense of the Hwaryongjang-Ch'up'ung-ryong area. ROK forces were to take over the front to the east of Sangju.

Upon deployment, Maj. Gen. Hobart R. Gay, commanding officer of the 1st Cavalry Division, received Gen. Walker's instructions to defend Yongdong and secure rearward routes as there were no friendly troops in the rear. First among the division troops to land at P'ohang on July 18, the 5th and 8th Regiments reached Yongdong on the 19 and 20th. On the 22nd, they took over the defensive zone from the 24th Division, and provided cover for the withdrawal.

Around the same time, the 27th Regiment of the US 25th Division (under Maj. Gen. William B. Kean) was sent to Hwanggan on the east of Yongdong. The division's 24th Regiment was in support of the ROK 6th Division on the north of Sangju, and the 35th Regiment was retained as a reserve in Sangju.

The 27th Regiment had been supporting the ROK 8th Division in Andong. While moving the regiment to Sangju, its commanding officer, Col. John H. Michaelis, received a revised order to assemble his troops in Hwanggan. This move was designed to block the NKPA 2nd Division's southeastward movement from Poun to Hwanggan and to provide cover for the flank and rear of the 1st Cavalry Division, which was defending the Yongdong-

Kimch'on road at the time. Covering 180km between Andong and Hwanggan in a single day, the 27th Regiment arrived in Hwanggan on July 23. Advancing to Samryongri on the north of Hwanggan, the regiment deployed the 1st Battalion in front of the 2nd Battalion, and relieved the ROK 2nd Division.

Meanwhile, the NKPA Supreme Command was urging its troops to move rapidly and secure the Masan-Taegu-Yongch'on-P'ohang Line after breaking through the Kum River-Sobaek Mountains Line. Accordingly, the NKPA 1st Corps sent the 3rd Division to Yongdong, 4th Division to Koch'ang, 2nd Division to Hwanggan, and 6th Division to Chinju. The NKPA II Corps, for its part, dispatched the 1st Division to Munkyong under the support of the reserve 13th Division, and was preparing to send the 15th Division to Sangju, 12th and 8th Divisions to Andong and Yech'on, and 5th Division to the south of Yongdok.

The US 1st Cavalry (−) positioned the 1st Battalion, 8th Cavalry Regiment (under Col. Raymond D. Palmer), astride the Seoul-Pusan Highway, and deployed the 2nd Battalion at the Muju Road. The division completed its defensive deployment on July 22 by placing the 5th Cavalry Regiment (under Col. Marcel B. Crombez) at an alternate position to the east of Yongdong.

With Yongdong as its objective, the NKPA 3rd Division on the same day began to move its 8th Regiment and some tank units along the Okch'on-Yongdong Road. Simultaneously with this movement, the enemy 7th and 9th Regiments were advancing southward along the Kumsan-Muju axis. On the morning of July 23, the enemy 8th Regiment began to cross the Kum River. Under artillery support, the 1st Battalion of the US 8th Cavalry Regiment destroyed three enemy tanks and repelled the enemy's river-crossing attempts for two days. In the end, however, the US regiment had to withdraw to Yongdong when its rear was threatened by enemy troops who had bypassed to the right flank. On the same day, the 2nd Battalion on the Muju Road also came under an enemy bypassing maneuver and had its escape route cut off by the enemy 7th and 9th Regiments.

The 2nd Battalion was unable to open an escape route on its own. Reinforced by a battalion from the US 5th Cavalry Regiment, however, the unit managed to break through the enemy's blocking line on July 25. Its two rear companies and an armored platoon could escape only after abandoning their crew-served weapons, including seven tanks. The 2nd Battalion of the 5th Cavalry Regiment also tried to provide support for the escape, but one of its companies went into the enemy zone and suffered heavy losses in personnel and equipment. The two cavalry regiments organized defensive positions to the east of Yongdong.

The enemy advanced into Yongdong on the night of the 25th. According to a captured North Korean soldier's account, however, the division had lost 2,000 men due to artillery fire and was only 50% strength at the time.[160] During this battle, enemy soldiers disguised as refugees infiltrated into the rear areas and sought to surprise artillery emplacements and block escape routes. Other enemy infiltrators were caught with radio communications equipment.[161]

At dawn on July 26, the enemy troops coerced hundreds of refugees to walk across minefields set up by the US Cavalry Division. Behind the refugees were four enemy tanks and infantry ready to cut down any escapees. The refugees broke through the mine zone, but the cavalry division blocked the enemy's approach with artillery barrage fire.[162]

In the meantime, on the north of Hwanggan, the reconnaissance unit of the US 27th Regiment began to engage the lead element of the NKPA 2nd Division on the night of July 23. On the next day, under the cover of a morning fog, eight enemy tanks spearheaded the enemy's frontal attack on the 1st Battalion, but the American troops were able to destroy six enemy tanks with 3.5-

inch rocket launchers and close air support. Having held the position, the regiment commander thought that the enemy would attempt envelopment and fur-
tively withdrew the 1st Battalion that night. He then instructed the 2nd Battalion to respond to the expected enemy attack with artillery and tank fire.

The 1st Battalion's position was now vacated. Unaware of the new situation, however, the enemy attempted to cut off the rear of the 1st Battalion's
position with two of its battalions. The US 2nd Battalion delivered concentrated fire with twelve 105-mm. howitzers and nine tank guns and inflicted a major
loss on the enemy troops. Around midnight, the enemy again attempted to envelop both flanks. The US 27th Regiment established new positions at the
northeast of Hwanggan, and reinforced the defensive line with the 1st Battalion
of the 35th Regiment. A resumed enemy attack on the 27th, however, forced
the withdrawal of US troops, and under the cover provided by the 7th Cavalry
Regiment in Hwanggan, the 27th Regiment withdrew to Kimch'on. Due to a typhoon, the US 7th Cavalry Regiment (under Col. Cecil W. Nist) had not landed
at Pohang until July 22. After its 1st Battalion had taken up the security of the
P'ohaugang Airfield, the regiment had advanced to Ch'up'ung-ryong on the
25th and reached to Hwanggan on the 27th.

The US 1st Cavalry Division (−) held its position on the east of
Yongdong. However, the enemy's flanking maneuver toward Chirye on the left
and penetration of the 27th Regiment position on the right raised the possibility that its line of retreat might be blocked. Faced with such a possibility, the
cavalry division withdrew to Kimch'on on the 29th.

In the Yongdong-Hwanggan Battle, the US 1st Cavalry Division and
the 27th Regiment, 25th Division, delayed the advance of two enemy divisions
for a week. They were seeking to move rapidly to the Kimch'on-Sangju area
via Ch'up'ungryong. In particular, although the 27th Regiment lost 323 men in
the battle, it was able to protect the rear of the 1st Cavalry Division and inflict

a loss of more than 3,000 men upon the enemy.[163]

The 1st Cavalry Division made an operational withdrawal to Kimch'on as there was a wide gap between it and the 25th Division on the right and an enemy flanking maneuver was feared on the left. The division deployed the 8th Cavalry Regiment at Namsanri on the Sangju side and positioned its 5th and 7th Regiments at Chirye and at the axis of approach from the Yongdong side, respectively. It thus blocked three roads heading into Kimch'on.

On the morning of July 29, upon receiving a report from the Korean National Police that the enemy had been sighted in Chirye, Gen. Gay immediately committed the division reconnaissance company to assess the enemy situation. He then forward-deployed the attached 3rd Battalion, 21st Regiment, and the 1st Battalion, 5th Cavalry Regiment at Chirye and instructed them to block the enemy under the support of the 99th Field Artillery. Sending follow on elements to join with the 7th Regiment in Chirye, the enemy 3rd Division intended to envelop Kimch'on by employing a flanking maneuver toward the rear of the US 1st Cavalry Division. Simultaneously with the arrival of the enveloping forces in Kimchon on July 31, enemy troops from Yongdong carried out a frontal attack on Kimch'on against the US 7th Cavalry Regiment.

Under artillery and air support, the cavalry regiment destroyed 19 out of 25 enemy tanks and managed to hold its position in Kimch'on, but the risk of being enveloped by the enemy was increasing by the hour. By the 31st, the US 1st Cavalry Division had inflicted nearly 2,000 casualties upon the NKPA 3rd Division and annihilated the 203rd Armored Regiment while suffering 916 battle casualties of its own.[164]

2. Delaying Action Along the Sobaek Mountains Line

(1) Miwon-Sangju Battle

While conducting delays along the Chinch'on-Ch'ongju line, Maj. Gen. Kim Hong Il, commanding officer of the ROK I Corps, was informed that ROK -US forces had decided to delay the enemy at a new defensive line connecting the Kum River and the Sobaek Mountains. When the US 24th Division withdrew to the south bank of the Kum, Gen. Kim decided to pull his troops out in conjunction with this move and establish new blocking positions between Poun and Miwon. Accordingly, the ROK 1st Corps withdrew from the Ch'ongju-Poun area on July 13. The 2nd Division[165] and Capital Division (with the 17th Regiment attached) established defensive positions in the Kounri area while the 1st Division organized blocking positions on the north of Miwon.

The NKPA II Corps, for its part, was planning to break through the Sobaek Mountains Line from Kal-ryong, Hwaryongjang, Ihwa-ryong, Choryong, and Chuk-ryong and move rapidly in the direction of Sangju and Andong. Having occupied Ch'ongju, the enemy 2nd Division was exerting pressure on the ROK Capital Division while the enemy 15th Division in Koesan was moving toward the ROK 1st Division.

After regrouping in Koesan, the enemy 15th Division launched an attack on the north of Miwon before the day broke on July 16. The ROK 1st Division was temporarily in danger as its 13th Regiment in Puhungri was threatened with an enemy envelopment, but it was able to block the enemy's advance at Kori-gogae. Reinforced by three tanks and 12 armored vehicles, the enemy resumed the attack the next day, but was turned back by the ROK troops.

After the battle, all 13 members of a special antitank attack unit received the honor of special promotion for their heroism. In particular, SFC Kim

Miwon-Sangju Battle

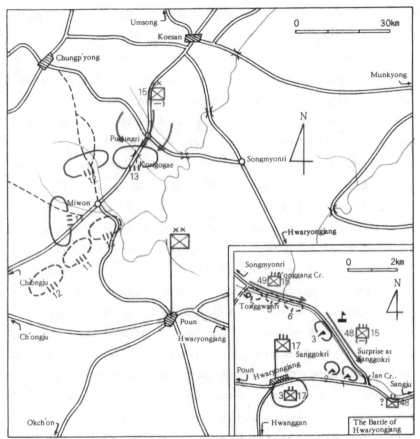

Jae Il was given a two-rank promotion after he had destroyed two enemy tanks in the battle.[166] On July 17, however, the ROK Ⅰ Corps was driven back by the enemy's relentless attack.　The 2nd and Capital Divisions were forced to withdraw from Kounri to Munui and Poun, and the 1st Division had to organize new defensive positions to the south of Miwon.

It was later revealed that there had been a major change in the enemy's strategy around this time. The enemy 2nd Division had originally planned to envelop Taejon from the eastern flank in support of the NKPA I Corps, but changed its course to the Poun-Hwanggan area when its advance to Taejon was delayed. In the meantime, the enemy 48th Regiment, 15th Division, had already infiltrated into the gap between the ROK I and II Corps through mountain trails leading to the Kal-ryong-Hwaryongjang area. In addition, the main effort of the enemy 15th Division in Miwon disengaged and turned eastward on the evening of July 19, and began to follow the 48th Regiment to Hwaryongjang.

By this time, the Ihwa-ryong-Cho-ryong line had collapsed on the right flank, raising the possibility that the enemy might break through the Munkyong Hamch'ang axis and bisect the ROK front into eastern and western halves. Concerned with the possibility of defeat in detail, the ROKA Headquarters decided to shore up the defense of the area. It changed the attachment of the 17th Regiment from the I to II Corps, and dispatched the regiment to Hamch'ang.

The 17th Regiment was assembling in Poun with the Capital Division when it received the new order. Lt. Col. Kim Hui Jun, its commanding officer, sent the 1st Battalion by vehicle at midnight, July 16. Moving along the Poun-Sangju road, the battalion arrived in the Hwaryongjang area the next morning and was informed by village residents that an enemy battalion from Kal-ryong had passed by the area the previous night. The enemy unit was apparently infiltrating into the rear Sangju area. Upon confirming this information, the ROK troops halted the march and began to assess the enemy situation.[167]

This area was the junction at which the Poun-Hwaryongjang-Sangju road and the Koesan-Kal-ryong-Hwaryongjang-Sangju road meet. Up to this point, however, the ROK I Corps was not aware of the strategic importance of the Koesan-Sangju road.[168]

While conducting reconnaissance, the 1st Battalion captured an enemy messenger and seized a written memo to the enemy regiment commander, which stated : "The battalion has occupied Hill 273 which offers a commanding view of Sangju." It was soon learned that "the battalion" in the memo referred to a battalion of the 48th Regiment, NKPA 15th Division.[169] Realizing that the enemy's follow-on forces would soon advance into the area, the ROK battalion commander at once deployed his troops in the vicinity of Sanggokri and prepared for an ambush.

The rest of the 48th Regiment was sighted in the afternoon. In an operation order, the NKPA 2nd Corps commander had warned his troops to strengthen security as ROK forces might be attempting to ambush around mountain passes or narrow valleys,[170] but upon reaching the Sanggokri area, the 48th Regiment halted the march and began to relax. Some North Korean soldiers bathed in the Ian-ch'on right by the road, while others rested on the playground at a primary school. This scene was unfolding right in front of the hidden ROK battalion.[171]

At 1900, upon the battalion commander's order to fire, more than 400 rifles, mortars, and machine guns delivered concentrated fire on the enemy troops, and a fierce battle continued for nearly an hour. Caught completely off guard, the enemy regiment suffered heavy casualties. When the dusk fell, the ROK troops began to focus on preventing the enemy's escape. They had decided to wait for the arrival of the bulk of the regiment before conducting mop-up operations.

By early morning the next day, Lt. Col. Kim, commanding officer of the ROK 17th Regiment, moved his main effort to Hwaryongjang. Upon receiving a report of this situation, the ROKA Headquarters instructed the 17th Regiment to continue operations under the command of the I Corps.

Meanwhile, in the afternoon of July 18, the regiment's Reconnaissance Company captured two enemy messengers carrying an operation order from the enemy division commander. In the operation order, the division commander demanded an interim report from the 48th Regiment commander, and instructed him to prepare to advance to the Kimch'on area with the 49th Regiment.[172] Lt. Col. Kim realized that the enemy division commander had not been informed of the surprise attack on the 48th Regiment. It also became apparent that the enemy 49th Regiment would soon pass through the area as well.

Lt. Col. Kim at once ordered the 2nd Battalion to move forward to Tongkwanri and prepare for a surprise. The battalion deployed its companies along the road and completed the emplacement of machine guns and mortars by that night. In the afternoon of the next day, the battalion sighted and destroyed 10 cow-driven enemy supply carts, but other than this incident, there was no noticeable enemy movement.

To buttress the defensive position, the reserve 3rd Battalion moved forward to the left of the 2nd Battalion that evening. Supplies were forwarded to the troops there, and the regiment maintained high morale as they were able to receive support from local residents.[173]

At last, at 05:30 on July 21, the 2nd Battalion sighted the enemy. Under the cover of heavy fog, these enemy troops were marching in a column of four's along the road without taking any special precautions. They too were ignoring their corps commander's warnings.[174] The 2nd Battalion waited until the enemy troops entered the kill zone, and delivered concentrated fire on order.

Fired upon at a close range, the enemy troops were thrown into confusion. They fled to mountains, rice paddies, and even roadside ditches, but soon the roadside and rice paddies were filled with enemy corpses. An American advisor arriving at the scene with Lt. Col. Kim remarked that he had never seen such a lopsided battle during his 30 years of service.[175]

That afternoon the 2nd Battalion was regrouping after the battle when enemy artillery shells began to fall. The ROK troops at once moved to Ponghwang-san in anticipation of an enemy counterattack. Around this time,

Lt. Col. Kim was informed that the ROK 1st Division would be committed to Hwaryongjang on the 22nd followed by the 24th Regiment, US 25th Division, the next day.

The ROK 1st Division was heading toward Ch'unyang from Poun when it received a revised order on the 21st to move immediately to Hwaryongjang. The US 24th Regiment was forwarded by the 25th Division in Sangju to take over the ROK 1st Division sector.

After its 48th and 49th Regiments had suffered major losses, the enemy 15th Division on July 22 threatened the flank of the ROK 17th Regiment with its remaining troops. The regiment blocked the enemy with support from the artillery battalion of the US 24th Regiment. When the ROK 1st Division arrived at its flanks, the regiment handed its sector over to the division.

After blocking the enemy until the 24th, the ROK 1st Division handed its sector over to the US 24th Regiment when it arrived from Sangju on the next day. The division then moved to Sangju with the 17th Regiment. According to a ROK reorganization plan, the 1st Division was subsequently assigned to the II Corps, and was sent to Hamch'ang to reinforce the 6th Division. The 17th Regiment was committed to Kwonbinri in the vicinity of Hapch'on.

After taking over the operation zone in the Hwaryongjang area on July 25, the US 24th Regiment (under Col. Horton V. White) established defensive positions at Naksori, 16km west of Sangju. This unit, however, lacked a will to fight and frequently took flight to the rear under the enemy's small-scale attack. Moreover, the regiment often failed to make contact with the enemy and retreated without authorization. Subjected to an enemy mortar attack on the 29th, the regiment took leave of its position without authorization and moved back more than 10km. In order to reestablish battle discipline, the division commander on the 30th placed the 1st Battalion, 35th Regiment, in the rear of the 24th Regiment to urge their fellow soldiers to fight. He also court-martialed the deserters. In spite of these strong measures, however, the 24th Regiment once again retreated under enemy pressure the next day. After assembling at the position of the 1st Battalion, 35th Regiment, they withdrew to the south of Sangju.[176]

(2) Ihwa-ryong-Hamch'ang Battle

After delaying the enemy at Suanbo, the ROK 6th Division withdrew to Munkyong and, according to the Kum-Sobaek line plan, took up the defense of Ihwa-ryong and Cho-ryong, two crucial passes in the Sobaek Mountains. Surrounded by mountains between 700–1,000 meters in altitude, the Ch'ungju-Hamch'ang road was the only major route in this area.

Col. Kim Jong Oh, commander of the 6th Division, decided to employ an area defense centered on Ihwa-ryong and Cho-ryong, taking full advantage of the rough terrain around the Ch'ungju-Hamch'ang road. Accordingly, Col. Kim deployed the 2nd and 19th Regiments at Ihwa-ryong and Cho-ryong, respectively, and retained the 7th Regiment as a reserve. He also instructed combat support units such as the 19th Field Artillery Battalion and Engineer Battalion to provide support to the two forward regiments.

The NKPA 1st Division in Suanbo, for its part, was preparing to carry out an attack along the Munkyong-Hamchang-Sangju axis, and the enemy II Corps commander was planning to have the attached 13th Division (−) infiltrate through the western flank.[177] The enemy was having great difficulty maneuvering during the day. Moreover, before passing over the Sobaek Mountains, the enemy could not exploit their tanks.

On July 13, as a result of ROK reconnaissance work, it became known that the lead echelon of the enemy 1st Division had already been making preparations in the Yonp'ung area with two artillery battalions. On the next day, under the cover of early morning fog, the 2nd Regiment of the enemy 1st Divi-

Ihwa-ryong-Hamch'ang Battle

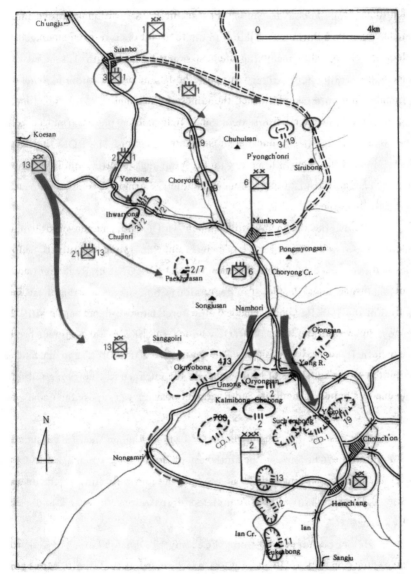

sion launched an attack to break through the position of the ROK 2nd Regiment (under Col. Hahm Byong Son).[178] Part of the ROK position collapsed under the enemy attack, but the 2nd Battalion on the right of Ihwa-ryong managed to block the enemy while occupying successive positions in depth. Taking advantage of the terrain under artillery support, the 1st and 3rd Battalions carried out a timely counterattack and turned the tables on the enemy.[179] With their line of retreat cut off, the enemy troops abandoned field artillery pieces, armored vehicles, and even small arms and fled in separate directions. The ROK 2nd Regiment pursued the enemy all the way to the Yonp'ung Junction, and killed more than 800 men. It also captured 7 enemy soldiers, 3 armored vehicles, 10 trucks and 3 artillery pieces.[180]

Meanwhile, the enemy 3rd Regiment, 1st Division, maneuvered through the mountains with the objective of penetrating Cho-ryong. On July 15, before dawn, it dealt a strong blow to the main force of the ROK 19th Regiment (under Col. Min Byong Kwon). Deployed in depth along Cho-ryong, the 2nd and 1st Battalions of the 19th Regiment engaged in a fierce hand-to-hand battle with the enemy, but within the interval of a few hours, the NKPA 3rd Regiment broke through their successive positions. The main part of the 19th Regiment had to withdrew to the outskirts of Munkyong. As the entrance to Cho-ryong fell into the enemy's hands,[181] the ROK 2nd Regiment position was exposed to enemy attack.

The reserve 7th Regiment (under Lt. Col. Lim Bu Taek) also sighted NKPA troops at Chujinri on the southwest of Ihwa-ryong. It managed to drive back the enemy's leading unit,[182] but by this time the main effort of the enemy 13th(−) Division had already completed preparations to attack and seize Munkyong.

Having occupied Cho-ryong, the enemy 1st Division launched a coordinated attack on July 16. Its main effort was directed at the front of Munkyong while its supporting attack struck the flanks. The ROK 2nd and 19th Regiments engaged in a series of bloody battles with the enemy, but eventually had to withdraw to Namhori to the south of Munkyong. Only the 7th Regiment, after withdrawing to Songju-san and Oknyo-bong, was blocking the enemy at the western flank with support from the artillery battalion.[183]

That afternoon, the UN Air Force flew a couple of sorties and raided the enemy's assembly area, but it also created havoc by attacking the ROK 19th Regiment.[184] While regrouping the 6th Division troops on the south of Munkyong, Col. Kim received an order for a withdrawal from the corps commander. Accordingly, before the day broke on the 17th, he ordered his troops to withdraw to the Yong-gang area on the north of Chomch'on. To provide cover for the withdrawal, the US 35th Regiment in Hamch'ang hastily dispatched a special task force with tanks.

After withdrawing to new positions in the vicinity of the Yong-gang, the ROK 6th Division at once began to make defensive preparations. The enemy 1st Division was closing in from the front of the 6th Division while the enemy 13th Division (−) was threatening to attack from the western flank. The 6th Division deployed its 7th Regiment at Oknyo-bong, 2nd Regiment at Oryong-san, and 19th Regiment at Ojong-san, and concentrated on building up positions. Critical to operations of both sides was the road that stretched from Munkyong to Hamch'ang via Yugok, and the ROK troops made special efforts to secure this road.

Around this time, the NKPA II Corps, for its part, was rapidly moving toward Chomch'on, its next objective. The enemy 1st Division was advancing from Munkyong toward Chomch'on while the 13th Division (−) was moving from Sangoeri to Unsong.

The enemy 13th Division (−), bypassing through Sangoeri, was first to attack. On the 19th, the main force of the enemy 13th Division launched an attack on the ROK 7th Regiment position while its supporting attack broke through the boundary between the ROK 2nd and 7th Regiments. With the enemy troops closing in from the right flank, the 7th Regiment commander committed the reserve 2nd Battalion to block the enemy, but when Oknyo-bong fell into the enemy hands the next day, he had little choice but to withdraw his troops to the south bank of the Yong-gang. That day, Gen. Yu Jae Hung, the corps commander, paid a visit to the division command post and emphasized that the Chomch'on-Hamch'ang axis must be secured given the overall situation along the lines. He added that the 1st Regiment of the Capital Division and 155-mm howitzers from the US 25th Division would soon be provided in support.[85]

On July 21, under the support of artillery and armor units, the NKPA 1st and 13th Divisions launched a full-scale attack on the main line of resistance. The ROK 7th and 19th Regiments each successfully defended against the enemy's regimental-scale attack. In the middle, however, the 2nd Regiment came under attack from two directions, and eventually had to cede Oryong-san to the enemy. Simultaneously with this attack, another group of enemy troops, led by 4 tanks, crossed the Yong-gang via the Munkyong-Yugok road and advanced to the vicinity of the Munkyong coal mines. The main defensive line of the ROK 6th Division was in danger of collapse.

Col. Kim at once made requests for artillery and air support, and the corps commander also asked the US 25th Division commander for armor support. Upon receiving these requests, a US Air Force squadron (F-80's) arrived at the scene of the battle and raided the enemy's assembly area and tanks. Also, six 155-mm howitzers were forwarded and carried out a large-scale bombardment. Under the support of a US armor platoon (five M24), the ROK 2nd Regiment carried out a counterattack and drove the enemy back from Oryong-san.

After fighting a series of fierce battles until the 22nd, each ROK regiment was able to maintain the previous lines. Even a student volunteer unit (180 men) joined the 7th Regiment in its attempt to recover Oknyobong.[186] Urgently in need of regrouping after a series of tough battles, the 7th Regiment was relieved by the 1st Regiment and became the division's reserve.

At dawn on July 23, a regimental-strength unit of the enemy 1st Division launched an assault river crossing operation from the Chinnam Bridge area. Spearheaded by 7 tanks, the enemy troops had moved along the Munkyong-Yugok road. In order to mass fire, the ROK 2nd Regiment mobilized 3 tanks, 155-mm howitzers, and antitank rocket launchers, but part of its defensive line could not withstand the enemy attack and allowed penetration. When four of their tanks passed the Chinnam Bridge, two enemy battalions carried out an attack on the ROK 1st Battalion position at the coal mines in Munkyong. After securing a bridgehead, part of the enemy troops attempted to penetrate farther into ROK positions. When the enemy seized Cho-bong on the western flank, Col. Kim had to withdraw his division to the Yugokri area. In order to provide cover, the 7th Regiment moved up to Yugok, reinforced by an engineer unit and a US armor company.

Col. Kim organized a position around Yugokri in the shape of a half moon, and, believing that it was crucial to recover commanding ground around the area, he launched a counterattack on the next day with the 7th and 2nd Regiments. After 7 hours of relentless attack, the 2nd Regiment managed to recover Cho-bong.[187] The 7th Regiment, however, had to return to position when the enemy's counterattack on the ROK 19th Regiment exposed its western flank. The 19th Regiment was able to drive back the enemy under the support of two UN Air Force squadrons. It was reported that the enemy Suffered more than 500 battle casualties during the engagement with the ROK 6th Division that day.[188]

With the advance of the NKPA 1st Division stalled, the commander of the enemy II Corps moved the 13th Division (−) northeast and launched a frontal attack on the 25th. In response, the ROK 6th Division moved the 1st

Regiment east to Yugok and strengthened the defense of the Yugok-Chomch'on axis. The division mobilized all available fire and received extensive support from the UN Air Force in its defensive effort. Operating an antitank special attack unit, the 19th Regiment defended against the enemy's 4 lead tanks. The 2nd Regiment also managed to hold at Cho-bong. The 1st Regiment, Capital Division, however, lost Yugok after a fierce battle.

The ROK 6th Division was faced with a crisis the next day as the threat from the enemy tanks increased. Enemy shells even reached the division command post in Chomch'on. Fortunately, the ROK 1st Division arrived just in time at Hamch'ang and provided relief.

The 1st Division incorporated the 5th and 20th Regiments, 2nd Division, into its 11th and 12th Regiments, respectively. The two regiments of the 2nd Division had disbanded in Hamch'ang. After reorganization, the 1st Division deployed the 13th Division on the northwest to connect to the left flank of the 6th Division, and prepared to counterattack with the 11th and 12th Regiments.[189] ROK operations in this area thus developed to corps-level from the 26th, and the defensive sector of the 6th Division was limited to the east of Cho-bong.

Before the day broke on the 27th, the 1st Division (under Br. Gen. Paik Sun Yup, promoted on the 25th) launched a counterattack in order to envelop the enemy in front of the 6th Division. The division threatened to block the enemy's line of retreat by recovering the Ojong-san area. The enemy 1st and 13th Divisions began to come apart under this threat. Simultaneously with this, the 6th Division also launched a full-scale counterattack from the south of Yugok. The 19th and 1st Regiments recovered Singiri and Yugok through this counterattack. Also, the 7th and 2nd Regiments completely drove back the enemy from the vicinity of Cho-bong.

The enemy 1st and 13th Divisions suffered heavy losses in personnel and equipment and withdrew to hills north of the Yong-gang. In particular, the 13th Division (−) lost more than 50% of its troops and could no longer function as a full-fledged division. It had to undergo reorganization until the end of July.[190]

In the meantime, while the ROK 6th Division was strengthening positions at Yugok after the counterattack, the 1st Division withdrew to Hamch'ang and took over the defense of northwest Hamch'ang in conjunction with the 6th Division. The 13th Regiment occupied defensive positions centered around the road northwest of Hamch'ang and Ian-ch'on while the 11th and 12th Regiments regrouped in Hamch'ang. The gradual normalization of the logistical support system around this time facilitated the supply of equipment and boosted troop morale.

The NKPA II Corps, for its part, instituted a major change in its plans after the 1st and 13th Divisions, together with the 109th Armored Regiment, had failed to break through the ROK positions at Yugok. From July 28, the NKPA 1st Division began to bypass the ROK defense via the road on the west and advance into the northwest of Hamch'ang. According to analysis of the enemy situation and information provided by residents, an enemy regimental-strength unit was infiltrating into the Nongamri area with armored vehicles.

After confirming the reports, the ROK 1st Division commander at once requested that all fire support be directed to the northwest of Hamch'ang, and committed the 11th and 12th Regiments to strengthen defenses around the road and Ian-ch'on. The 13th Regiment on the right was deployed on a hill on the right side of the road. The 12th Regiment in the middle was deployed on a hill left of the road while the 11th Regiment established a position in the Kuksabong area on the south bank of Ian-ch'on.

Before the day broke on July 29, the enemy 1st Division launched an attack from the front of the 13th Regiment and from the boundary area between the ROK 1st and 6th Divisions. Under the support of the 6th Division artillery, the 1st Battalion of the 13th Regiment blocked the enemy. When an enemy regiment, led by four armored vehicles, approached along the road, the 2nd Battalion delivered concentrated fire as planned and drove them back.[191] The ROK troops learned from North Korean POW's that the enemy in front was the NKPA 1st Division, more than half of which consisted of conscripted, and now demoralized, youths.

After a series of failed attacks, the NKPA 1st Division lost more than half of its troops from air strikes and artillery fire. In the end, following the example of the NKPA 13th Division, the 1st Division disengaged from the battle and went into unit reorganization in the Unch'ok-san area.

Having inflicted major losses on the NKPA 1st and 13th Divisions and blocked their advance to Sangju, the ROK II Corps was instructed by the ROKA Headquarters to withdraw to the Naktong River line on July 31. Accordingly, under the cover of the 1st Division, the 6th Division withdrew to Yonggidong, Songju. The 1st Division subsequently withdrew to Naktongri.[192]

(3) Chuk-ryong-Andong Battle

After the fall of Tanyang, the ROK 8th Division came up with a plan to block the enemy at Chuk-ryong and switch to the counteroffensive.[193] Blocking the enemy in stages, the division arrived at Chuk-ryong on the night of July 12. Faced with enemy troops in pursuit of the ROK division, however, the division commander decided to lure them into P'unggi and annihilate them there. In accordance with this changed plan, he moved his troops to P'unggi.

The Tanyang-Andong national road and the Central Railway ran through P'unggi, which is surrounded by a chain of hills. Col. Lee Sung Ga, commander of the ROK 8th Division, decided to carry out a demonstration as soon as the troops arrived in P'unggi around midnight on July 12. All vehicles had their headlights on and moved as if they were withdrawing to Yongju. While carrying out this diversionary operation, Col. Lee quickly deployed his troops on both sides of the main road that ran parallel to the Central Railway. The 21st Regiment (under Lt. Col. Kim Yong Bae) and 10th Regiment (Lt. Col. Ko Kun Hong) hastily established positions at the hills on the right and left, respectively. The overall troop deployment was in the shape of the letter V.[194]

The commander of the NKPA II Corps noted that ROK troops tended to deploy their main forces on hills on either side of a narrow valley for an ambush and place small units astride a road as a decoy. Accordingly, he warned his troops against a surprise and urged caution.[195] After pursuing ROK troops to Chuk-ryong, the NKPA 8th Division regrouped between the night of the 12th to the morning of the 14th in order to compensate for prior battle casualties.

On the morning of the 14th, a regiment of the enemy 8th Division assembled in the vicinity of Ch'angnakdong north of P'unggi, and dispatched a lead battalion along the road into the V-shaped kill zone. When the enemy troops had moved deep into the kill zone, the ROK 8th Division struck a devastating blow with planned concentrated fire and drove them back.

On the next day, before the morning broke, the enemy again attempted to break through the ROK barrage zone, but the ROK 10th and 21st Regiments delivered massed fire and inflicted more than a battalion-scale loss on the enemy. In the afternoon, the enemy delivered synchronized artillery fire on the whole front, and attacked the left front of the 10th Regiment with a battalion strength unit. This attempt too was thwarted by the ROK defense.

Perhaps due to battle casualties up to that point, the enemy at last disengaged from the battle. Taking advantage of the lull in the battle, the ROK 8th Division regrouped and prepared for subsequent operations. As part of this effort, one artillery battery (new-model M-2's and six 105-mm howitzers) was attached to the division.

The NKPA II Corps, for its part, was instituting a major change in its operation plan. Having suffered heavy casualties in its failed attempt to seize P'unggi, the NKPA 8th Division was ordered to bypass the ROK defense and move along the Tanyang-Yech'on-Andong axis. In its place, the 12th Division in Tanyang was charged with the mission to carry out an attack along the P'unggi-Andong axis.[196]

Placing the artillery regiment of the 8th Division under its operational control to strengthen its firepower, the enemy 12th Division intended to neutralize ROK artillery with concentrated fire and overwhelm the ROK defense with its main attack and advance all the way to Yongju.

At last, before the day broke on July 18, the enemy 12th Division launched an attack on the main defensive line of the ROK 8th Division in the vicinity of Changgun-bong and Noin-bong. The ROK position collapsed under the enemy's massed artillery fire, and the enemy troops broke through the left side of the 21st Regiment in the middle. Under the support of the UN Air Force, however, the ROK troops managed to establish defense in depth by organizing successive positions.

For the first time since the outbreak of the war, civilian workers were deployed in the division. This move was designed to facilitate the supply of food and ammunition to forward units.[197]

Before the day dawned on July 19, the enemy 12th Division massed its main effort in front of the ROK 10th Regiment and launched a full-scale attack. In this battle, the 10th Regiment lost a key chain of hills along the defensive line, and thus yielded a stronghold for the defense of Yongju.

Col. Lee, the ROK 8th Division commander, decided to recover the main line of resistance through an aggressive counterattack. His units, however, made little headway in their attack. In fact, to Col. Lee's dismay, the enemy troops carried out a counterattack of their own on the next day, and seized a chain of hills south of the main defensive line. The ROK 8th Division was now faced with a bleak prospect of withdrawing to the outskirts of Yongju. Fortunately, one UN Air Force squadron raided the enemy troops at that critical moment. Moreover, the 3rd Battalion of the 21st Regiment discovered enemy troops approaching Yongju from Maebong-san, and turned them back with a surprise attack.

Having thus temporarily slowed down the pace of the enemy's attack, the ROK 8th Division hastily organized positions around the P'unggi-Yongju road on the night of July 20. Col. Lee deployed the 10th and 20th Regiments on the western and eastern outskirts of Yongju, respectively. To the 21st Regiment, he also attached the 1st Battalion, 25th Regiment, 2nd Division, which had arrived in Yongju as part of the ROK reorganization. Around midnight, a two-company-strength unit of the 2nd Battalion, 10th Regiment, successfully ambushed an enemy battalion.[198]

The enemy II Corps, for its part, became concerned with the lack of progress made by the 12th Division through the eight days of its operation. It not only reinforced the troops with tanks and self-propelled guns, but also instructed the 8th Division to join in on the attack. As the 8th Division bypassed the ROK defense and advanced to the south of Yongju via Yech'on, the Yongju Battle entered a new stage.

Through pouring rain on July 22, the enemy 12th Division launched a frontal attack with its main effort, and seized a hill on the forward left flank of the 21st Regiment. The loss of Yongju seemed imminent. Attaching an antitank gun company to the 1st Battalion of the 25th Regiment, however, the 21st Regiment commander launched a surprise counterattack and recovered the hill.[199]

Around midnight, led by five tanks and four self-propelled guns, the enemy 12th Division once again launched a full-scale attack. The ROK 8th Division desperately defended Yongju, but an operational withdrawal became all but inevitable.

On the morning of the 23rd, while a UN Air Force squadron was carrying out an air strike, the ROK troops began to withdraw from Yongju. Together with a report on the fall of Yongju, the ROKA Headquarters received an aerial observation report which informed them that the enemy troops north of Yech'on were moving up toward Yongju. The ROKA Headquarters at once committed part of the 18th Regiment, Capital Division, to the 8th Division sector. Under their cover, the 8th Division carried out its withdrawal and organized a defensive position at Naesong-ch'on, north of Ongch'on. Here, with the addition of the newly arrived 16th Regiment (under Lt. Col. Kim Dong Su), 2nd Division, it finally became a full-fledged, three-regimental-strength division.

Together with the Capital Division, the ROK 8th Division was assigned to the I Corps effective July 24. In the meantime, the enemy 12th Division from the western flank was applying pressure in the Uisong-Andong direction, while part of the enemy 5th Division and the 766th Unit were closing in from the eastern flank, in the Chongsong-Andong direction.

A transportation center located along the Chungang(central) Railway axis in the Upper Naktong area, Andong connects to Taegu, Yongch'on, and P'ohang. According to the corps operation plan to defend Andong, the ROK 8th Divisim withdrew from Ongchon on the 29th and organized defensive positions in the outskirts of Andong around the Chungang Railway axis.

Together with the 8th Division, the Capital Division was charged with a mission to defend Andong. After moving from Poun, its 18th Regiment took over the personnel of the 8th Regiment and drove back the enemy troops at Yech'on. Also, after being released from attachment to the 6th Division, the 1st Regiment advanced to P'ungsan located between Yech'on and Andong.

On July 30, the enemy 12th Division launched a full-scale attack from three different directions : Its main effort carried out a frontal attack on the ROK 21st Regiment, and supporting attack was directed against the 10th and 16th Regiments on the left and right. After hours of fierce fighting, the 16th Regiment on the right sustained heavy casualties, and as the enemy troops broke through the 16th Regiment position, the 8th Division no longer was able to hold the line and had to withdraw to its final line of resistance in the Osandong area.

In the afternoon, the division forward-deployed all three regiments and hastily organized defensive positions. The engineer battalion destroyed and sealed off roads in order to block the advance of the enemy's armored units. A sense of crisis heightened, however, as enemy artillery shells began to fall in Andong the division defensive line was only 6km removed from Andong.

As for the Capital Division, the 18th Regiment at Yechon had its line of retreat cut off by the enemy 8th Division. After staging an uphill battle under the enemy's envelopment, the regiment moved to Hamchang and was attached to the II Corps. Having thus lost Yechon, the corps commander dispatched the 1st Regiment from Pungsan to Andong in support of the 8th Division.

At dawn on the 31st, the enemy 12th Division resumed its full-scale attack on the ROK 8th Division. Spearheaded by tanks, the division once again launched a three-pronged attack. Under attack from an enemy regiment led by four tanks, the ROK 21st Regiment temporarily lost its position. After regrouping and under close air support of the UN Air Force, however, the ROK troops managed to recover the position. The 10th Regiment managed to turn back the enemy's armored attack, but five 3.5-inch bazookas, deployed for the first time in the Maekhyon area, failed to turn in a satisfactory performance due to the operators' inexperience with the equipment.[200]

Around this time, the ROKA Headquarters ordered the troops to withdraw from Andong at 24:00, July 31, in accordance with the Naktong River

Line plan. The ROK Ⅰ Corps convened an operation meeting at 20:00 hrs. to discuss plans. The meeting, however, dragged on until 01:00 hrs, August 1, with the decision making: The 8th Division withdraw ahead under cover of the Capital Division. And this delay was to have a devastating effect on the withdrawal operation, which was supposed to have began at 24:00 hrs. Due to a curfew placed on intercommunication, division staffs returning from the meeting had to convene a meeting of their own regimental S-3's. It was already past 04:00 hours when the withdrawal operation began. Some units did not even receive a withdrawal order.[201]

A unit making least contact with the enemy was ordered to withdraw first. The 8th Division commander instructed the 10th and 21st Regiments to withdraw in order, and ordered the 16th Regiment to follow them under cover provided by the 1st Regiment, Capital Division. The 10th Regiment at once disengaged, and between 06:30 and 07:30 hours, they passed the pedestrian bridge. The pedestrian and railway bridges were blown immediately.

Initially, the demolition of the bridges had been scheduled for 06:00 hrs August 1, and Col. Ch'oi Dok Shin, the corps chief of staff, personally directed the operation on the spot. Although the 21st Regiment had not arrived, Col. Ch'oi could not overlook the fact that the enemy division was relentlessly pursuing the ROK troops. Moreover, he recognized that the enemy had a commanding view of the bridges. After assessing the overall situation and consulting with the 8th Division commander, Col. Ch'oi, around 07:30 hours, ordered the bridges to be blown.[202]

When the 21st Regiment arrived at the river bank, they found that the bridges were no longer there. With their backs against the river, they fired rifles on the pursuing enemy troops. As the enemy delivered heavy machine-gun fire, however, the ROK troops realized that they were completely overmatched. After burying their rifles in the sand, they jumped into the river. The enemy's ensuing aimed fire took a heavy toll.[203] With the addition of the withdrawing troops of the 1st Regiment, Capital Division, the situation turned into a total chaos.

But the unit to suffer the heaviest casualties was the 16th Regiment. Because this regiment was in a fierce battle with an enemy regiment, it received its withdrawal order only around 06:00 hrs. As the enemy troops broke through the position of the 1st Regiment, the 16th Regiment was enveloped by the enemy and had to withdraw in detail. While breaking through the enemy envelopment and carrying out a river-crossing operation, the regiment lost 21 officers and 814 men.[204]

After completing the river-crossing operation, the 8th and Capital Divisions began to withdraw to the Naktong River Line along Kumidong-Sangadong.

3. Yonghae-Yongdok Battle

Appointed as the commander of the ROK 3rd Division on July 10, Br. Gen. Lee Jun Shik received orders to defend the Yonghae-Yongdok area with the 23rd Regiment and Independent 1st Battalion.[205] After withdrawing from P'yonghae, the 23rd Regiment was regrouping in Yonghae at the time. Gen. Lee established a plan to block the enemy's advance in stages under the UN naval, aerial, and artillery support, and until July 12, the division channeled its effort into organizing positions between Mokgol-jae and Kamashil-jae south of Yongdok.

Meanwhile, the NKPA 5th Division had lost much of its momentum due to UN naval and aerial bombardment and the stretching of its line of communications. Having reached Yonghae behind the schedule, the division was making preparations to carry out an attack on Yongdok. The enemy 11th and 12th Regiments were to follow the coastal road while the 10th Regiment was to bypass the ROK defense in the Chinbo-Ch'ongsong direction.[206] Having infiltrated into the T'aebaek Mountain, the 766th Unit was already advancing toward Ch'ongsong. Just like the other enemy units, they were conscripting civilians to carry their supplies along the way and generating much ill feeling among the populace.[207]

The coastal road between Yongdok and Kanggu formed an inverse triangle, and the operational zone in this area was favorable for defense. Moreover, the 45-km stretch between Yongdok and P'ohang was well-suited for the ROK troops to conduct delaying operations, by offsetting their inferior numbers with superior naval and aerial support.

After dispatching its 10th Regiment toward Chinbo, the enemy 5th Division launched a full-scale attack on the ROK position with the other two regiments on July 14. The ROK 23rd Regiment and Independent 1st Battalion could not overcome the inferiority in strength and firepower, and after allowing enemy penetration, the troops began to withdraw to successive positions. While withdrawing, the regiment blew up the bridge and tunnel between Yonghae and Yongdok. The naval and aerial bombardment of the enemy assembly area and avenue of approach also helped to delay the enemy's advance.[208]

Despite sustaining heavy losses from the UN bombardment, the enemy division continued to pursue the ROK troops under the cover of the night as if to make up for the previous loss of momentum. The ROK 23rd Regiment did not even have a chance to consolidate its position at the new line of resistance. By midnight, July 16, the enemy troops were threatening to break through the ROK position.

Judging that it would be difficult to hold the present defensive position, Br. Gen. Lee ordered the regiment to withdraw to the south of Yongdok on the morning of the 17th. He planned to carry out a counterattack under naval and aerial support and recover the position after the enemy main effort entered Yongdok.[209] Accordingly, the 23rd Regiment deployed its main effort on Hills 181 and 207 south of Yongdok and positioned the Independent Battalion on Hill 208, and made preparations to launch a counterattack.

That evening, the enemy 5th Division (−) entered Yongdok. Before the morning broke on July 18, an air squadron from Pohang and the UN naval ships began to shell the downtown area of Yongdok upon Gen. Lee's request. The enemy sustained heavy losses, and retreated to the north of Yongdok. The ROK 23rd Regiment was able to recover Yongdok without meeting any resistance,[210] but once again lost the town to the enemy's counterattack the next day.

With the fall of Yongdok, the situation in the eastern coastal region became increasingly critical. In order to assess the overall situation, Lt. Gen. Walker made a personal visit to P'ohang on the 20th. He was accompanied by Maj. Gen. Patridge, commander of the 5th US Air Force, and Maj. Gen. Kean, commander of the US 25th Division. Gen. Walker emphasized that in order to secure Yongdok, naval and aerial support would be indispensable. The aerial and naval strength for the operation was subsequently increased to two air squadrons and six ships. Also, around this time, the 1st Battalion of the US 7th Cavalry Regiment was moved to the south of Yongdok to provide fire support to the ROK 23rd Regiment. The cavalry battalion had been deployed in Pohang as a security force.

On July 21, the ROK-US combined forces resumed the operation to recover Yongdok. The enemy 5th Division (−) suffered heavy losses in personnel and equipment, but at the urging of the corps commander, they resumed their attack on the evening of July 23.

As the enemy applied increasing pressure on Hills 181 and 207, the ROK 23rd Regiment engaged in a series of bloody battles. The two sides contested for the control of Hill 181, as the securing of this hill was critical to the outcome of the battle. During the day, under the UN naval and aerial support, the ROK troops usually went on the offensive while at night the NKPA troops pressed for a close combat. The battle raged on for several days, with a series of bloody engagements each day.

On July 24, after undergoing reorganization in Taegu, the ROK 22nd Regiment (under Lt. Col. Kang T'ae Min)[211] arrived in Kanggu to provide reinforcement. In addition, a naval combat team organized by the P'ohang Security Command arrived in Kanggu as further reinforcement for the 3rd Division.[212] Br. Gen. Lee initially planned to use the 22nd Regiment to recover Yongdok. When Hills 181 and 207 fell into the enemy's hand, however, the division commander changed his plans, and decided to recover these hills with the 22nd Regiment.

Prior to this development, a regrettable incident had taken place in the 23rd Regiment involving its commanding officer, Col. Kim Jong Won—nicknamed "Tiger of Mt. Paekdu." Col. Kim ordered the on-the-spot execution of a platoon leader and an enlisted man of the 3rd Battalion after their unit had allowed enemy penetration on Hill 181. Col. Kim apparently took this severe measure to establish discipline on the battlefield, but he was subsequently removed from command of the regiment and was replaced by the commander of the Independent 1st Battalion.[213]

On the evening of July 25, Br. Gen. Lee made a request for UN naval and aerial support and ordered the 22nd Regiment to attack to recover the hills. Commencing at 12:00 hrs. the next day, intense naval gunfire continued for an hour and forced the withdrawal of the enemy's main effort. The 22nd Regiment pushed aside the enemy's light resistance, and its 3rd and 2nd Battalions recovered Hills 181 and 207, respectively. The regiment drove back a series of enemy attacks that night. In particular, MSG Lee Myong Su, leader of the 2nd Platoon,

12th Company, 3rd Battalion, infiltrated into the enemy position with a 12 man special-attack unit and annihilated an enemy platoon, in addition to destroying enemy self-propelled guns. For his heroism, MSG Lee received a Taeguk Order of Military Merit, the highest such honor in Korea. From Hill 181, a US observation team directed artillery fire on Yongdok and its vicinity.

Having secured the hills, Gen. Lee decided to attack and recover Yongdok as well. Upon his request, the US 7th Fleet and an air squadron, together with a company of the 159th Field Artillery Battalion, began to pound the Yongdok area on July 27. Passing through of the 22nd Regiment, the ROK 23rd Regiment carried out an attack on Yongdok. The enemy 5th Division (−), however, mobilized all its firepower to put up stiff resistance. A fierce battle ensued between the two sides. UN cruisers added their naval gunfire to the battle, and destroyers continued their rear interdiction fire.[214]

Concerned with the situation in Yongdok, Gen. Walker around this time ordered hourly reports sent to his headquarters. The ROK 3rd Division continued its three-pronged attack for several days, and at last, at 18:00, August 2, it recaptured Yongdok and drove the enemy north of the town.[215] Having lost about 40% of its strength in casualties up to that point, the NKPA 5th Division (−) went into mountain valleys north of Yongdok to regroup.

On July 28, while the Yongdok Battle was in full swing, the 10th Regiment of the enemy 5th Division was following the 766th Unit toward Chinbo, on the left flank of Yongdok. In the Chuwang-san area southeast of Chongsong, the 766th Unit had made contact with guerrillas. Located halfway between Andong and Yongdok, Chinbo and Ch'ongsong were two crucial points on the mountain road west of the T'aebaek Mountains. The road stretching from Yongyang to Ch'ongsong through Chinbo offered a favorable avenue of approach for bypassing to Yongdok or advancing to P'ohang and Yongch'on. The enemy supreme commander in Suanbo highlighted the importance of this road, pressing his troops to pick up speed by moving around the mountains.

In order to drive back the enemy from this area, the ROKA Headquarters attached the Independent Cavalry Regiment to the 3rd Division and dispatched the unit to Chinbo on July 26. Col. Yu Hung Su, commander of the Cavalry regiment, deployed his main effort and five armored vehicles on the south bank of the Panbyon-ch'on in Chinbo. He also exercised operational control over a Kangwon Police battalion (under Police Inspector Kim In Ho), and deployed the unit on the easter flank. The police battalion had been fighting guerrillas in the area. Under the cover of armored vehicles, the regiment used a police company to sweep out the enemy 766th Unit and guerrilla forces.

Under the UN air bombardment, the enemy 10th Regiment had halted its attack, but resumed the offensive on the 29th. The enemy regiment massed its main attack on the ROK defensive position at the Panbyon-ch'on while one of its battalions employed a flanking movement to attack the police battalion. The main effort of the ROK regiment managed to turn back the enemy with final protective fire. As the enemy troops broke through the ROK police position before the day broke on August 1, the whole ROK defense was faced with a dire situation.[216]

Under the support of four armored vehicles, the Independent Cavalry Regiment fought an intense battle until the next day. Faced with the threat of being cut off, however, the regiment had to withdraw to the Pibong-san area south of Chinbo. Its four attempts to connect with the 3rd Division in Yongdok failed, and as a result, the regiment had to fight an uphill battle after the fall of Chinbo. Fortunately, the Capital Division moved just in time from the south of Andong to occupy Kiran on the left of the regiment. The regiment changed its attachment to the Capital Division and continued to defend against the enemy attack. This operation blocked the intended turning movement of the enemy 10th Regiment toward Yongdok, and prevented the infiltration of the 766th

Unit. The operation thus prevented the enemy from severing the ROK defense line. The reason that the Yongdok Battle commanded so much attention was that the ROK-UN Forces could no longer be able to retreat if they were to secure the Pohang harbor and Yongil Airfield.

4. Delaying Action in the Southwestern Region

(1) Situation on the Southwestern Front

On July 11, while committing the 3rd and 4th Divisions to the Kongju-Taejon axis, the NKPA I Corps instructed the follow-on 6th Division to employ a turning movement and advance into the Cholla Provinces. Turning westward from Chonan, the NKPA 6th Division in Yesan organized its troops into two echelons on the 13th. Simultaneously with the occupation of Nonsan by the NKPA 4th Division on July 16, the 6th Division crossed the Kum River and seized Kanggyong on the 17th. The division continued to advance to the Iri-Chonju area, with its 13th Regiment turning toward Kunsan. The whole North Cholla Province was thrown into a crisis.

On July 17, the ROK Ministry of National Defense organized the Western Coast Command (under Maj. Gen. Shin Tae Yong) for the defense of the Cholla Provinces. As its subordinates, South and North Cholla Province Unit Organization District Commands, existed only on paper, however, it could not establish a feasible defensive plan. There were only a few real military units in the area. An Independent Battalion (under Maj. Kim Byong Hwa) under the newly organized 7th Division and a 700-strong police unit moved to Kanggyong for the defense of the town, and the Ko Gil Hun Marine Unit moved from Kunsan to Changhang to block the enemy's advance.

The Ko's Unit managed to block the enemy's advance with a preemptive strike, before it eventually withdrew from the battle.[217] The ROK troops that had moved to Kanggyong, however, were completely overmatched. In particular, all 67 officers of the Kanggyong Police (under Police Inspector Chong Song Bong) died heroic deaths.[218] The enemy 13th Regiment, for its part, crossed the Kum River from Changhang and occupied Kunsan on July 19, and on the next day, joined the rest of the division in Chonju.

On July 21, the day after the enemy 6th Division had occupied Chonju, the ROK government decreed martial law in the Cholla Provinces. By the 23rd, the enemy troops had seized the Chongup-Namwon-Kwangju areas. The Western Coast Command and its subordinate commands were disbanded on that day. Its place was taken over by the Min Unit (under Col. Min Ki Shik), which had moved from Namwon to Unbong. After integrating small military units in this area, the Min Unit began to conduct operations under the direct control of the ROKA Headquarters. The small units in the area included detachments led by such officers as Lee Yong Gyu, Kim Song Un, Oh Dok Jun, and Kim Byong Hwa.[219]

In the meantime, the regiments of the enemy 6th Division split in Kwangju and went in separate directions: 13th Regiment, toward Mokpo; 14th, toward Posong ; and 15th, toward Sunch'on. Merging once again in Sunch'on on the 25th, the enemy regiments moved in the direction of Hadong. By this time, the southwestern region had fallen into the enemy's hands, and, as a result, the front line began to shift toward the Kyongsang Provinces. Gen. Pang Ho San, the commander of the enemy 6th Division, declared: "Comrades, the enemy troops are in disarray. The mission imposed on us now is the liberation of Chinju and Masan and the annihilation of the remaining enemy troops···. The liberation of Chinju and Masan will be the decisive blow that will finish off the enemy."[220]

The Eighth US Army, in the meantime, was concerned with the advance of the NKPA 4th Division from Taejon. By this time, the enemy troops had passed Kumsan and were moving toward the valleys of Mt. Chiri. On July 23, aerial reconnaissance confirmed that these troops were moving toward Anui. No UN forces were deployed in this area at the time. The enemy 6th Division was already moving toward Masan, and the 4th Division was maneuvering in the Anui-Kochang direction. These two divisions certainly posed a threat to the EUSA from the rear and the western flank, but even at this point, the US troops had no intelligence report on the movement of the enemy 6th Division.

Finally, when the southwestern front was in danger of collapse, the EUSA committed the reserve US 24th Division to the Chinju-Hamyang-Koch'ang line on July 24. On the next day, the 24th Division deployed the 19th Regiment (with two battalions from the 29th Regiment attached) in the Anui-Chinju area, and dispatched the 34th and 21st Regiments to Koch'ang and Hapch'on, respectively.

On the same day, the ROKA Headquarters appointed Maj. Gen. Chae Byong Dok as the commander of the Kyongsang Province Unit Organization District Command,[221] and instructed him to command the Min Unit as well. At this time, the Min Unit was withdrawing to the Namwon-Unbong-Hamyang area while maintaining contact with the enemy 6th Division. ROK-US forces were now faced with the task of establishing a combined defense along the southwestern front.

(2) Hadong-Chinju Battle

Located on the boundary between Kyongsang and Cholla Provinces, Hadong derived its strategic significance from the fact that it connects to Sach'-on and Chinju. In spite of its strategic importance, however, Hadong was left almost unprotected and exposed to enemy attack. Hadong fell to the enemy 6th Division when a disorganized ROK composite unit was forced to withdraw to

Chinju on the night of July 26.[222] Gen. Chae had received orders to defend Hadong, but he did not have the necessary troops to block the enemy. Upon meeting with the commander of the US 19th Regiment in Chinju, Gen. Chae explained the situation and stressed the importance of Hadong.

Col. Ned D. Moore, the 19th Regiment commander, at once ordered the 3rd Battalion, 29th Regiment, to attack to recover Hadong, and Gen. Chae accompanied the troops. On the morning of the 27th, they encountered a battalion strength unit in ROK uniform at Soe-gogae. When they were about to check the identity of these troops, they were suddenly attacked. The disguised enemy battalion inflicted heavy casualties in this surprise attack. Gen. Chae lost his life, and the US troops had to flee in detail.[223] Later, when Hadong was recovered during the September counteroffensive, ROK-US troops found the corpses of 313 American soldiers at Soe-gogae. According to a North Korean POW's account, the number of American soldiers captured had amounted to nearly 100 as well.

The US 19th Regiment had to defend Chinju with inferior numbers. Col. Moore deployed the 2nd Battalion on a hill near Yusuri along the Hadong–Chinju road, and positioned the 1st Battalion (−) at Kuhori west of the Sach'on Airfield. He also regrouped the remaining troops of the 3rd Battalion, 29th Regiment, and the Min Unit in the vicinity of Chinju. In addition, in the early morning hours of July 29, he deployed three M 26 Pershing Medium Tanks in the downtown area. This was the first time that these tanks were battle-deployed in Korea. According to an aerial observation report, there were two enemy regiments and tanks in Hadong at this time.

On the morning of the 29th, the enemy 6th Division launched a frontal attack by committing the lead unit along the Hadong–Chinju road. The enemy attack that day was thwarted by an ambush by the 2nd Battalion, US 19th Regiment, and a raid by the UN air squadron. On the next day, the enemy carried out a two-pronged attack: The enemy main force frontally attacked the 2nd Battalion, while part of the enemy troops employed a flanking maneuver and attacked the 1st Battalion on the left front.

Moving to the north bank of the Nam River, the 2nd Battalion fought a fierce battle. The 1st Battalion also exploited the terrain and stubbornly resisted the enemy attack, but as the number of casualties rose, it withdrew to the southern boundary of Chinju. The battalion organized a defensive position there with the Kim Song Un marine Unit, which had just arrived.[224]

Before the day broke on July 31, the enemy carried out a three-pronged attack. When a regimental-strength enemy unit broke through the main line of resistance after a fierce battle, the 2nd Battalion withdrew to Chinju. But the enemy was relentless. At last, when the enemy, led by six armored vehicles, carried out an attack on Chinju, Col. Moore ordered his troops to withdraw to Much'onri, southwest of Chinju. As the bridges had already been blown off, the 2nd Battalion had to fight the blazing sun and withdraw along the Uiryong road.

After exchanging rifle fire with the enemy troops that had employed a flanking maneuver, the 1st Battalion and the ROK Marine Unit withdrew along the Masan road. The three Pershings were captured by the enemy after they had provided cover for the withdrawing troops.[225]

After the fall of Chinju, Maj. Gen. Church, the commander of the US 24th Division, at once established a plan to block the two roads connecting to Masan. Accordingly, the US 19th and 29th Regiments, together with the Min Unit, regrouped in the vicinity of Chungamri and blocked the northern avenue of approach; whereas, the newly attached 27th Regiment of the US 25th Division and the Kim Song Un Unit moved to Chindongri and blocked the southern road.

(3) Delaying Action in the Hamyang-Koch'ang Area

While the NKPA 6th Division was maneuvering toward the southwestern region, the enemy 4th Division was charged with the mission to attack Hamyang-Koch'ang after occupying Taejon. The enemy troops conscripted about 2,000 replacements in Taejon and Kumsan, but due to delayed supplies and losses in personnel and equipment, their morale was low. In fact, they could no longer operate their armored regiment. On July 26, the NKPA 4th Division mobilized all available vehicles and headed toward Chinan-Anui via Muju while dispatching part of its troops toward Namwon-Hamyang in a large flanking maneuver.[226]

The 1st Battalion of the US 29th Regiment had reached Anui on July 25 and begun to make defensive preparations. Upon receiving Col. Moore's order, they had hastily moved from Chinju. The battalion forward-deployed B Company in front of Anui and positioned its main force on a hill to the east of the Nam River near Hamyang. The Min Unit, for its part, withdrew to Hamyang while maintaining contact with those enemy troops who had moved to Namwon. In coordination with the US battalion, the ROK troops organized a defensive position to the west of the Nam River.

On July 27, the enemy 4th Division launched an attack with a regimental-strength unit. B Company in Anui was simply overwhelmed by a three-pronged attack from the numerally superior enemy. The American main effort and the Min Unit in Hamyang fought a fierce battle against the enemy, but had to withdraw to Chinju that night. After occupying Anui, the enemy main attack advanced toward Koch'ang.

Koch'ang was the point at which road networks from the northwestern part of South Kyongsang Province converged before radiating out to the western Naktong region. After Anui fell into the enemy hands, the commander of the US 34th Regiment deployed the 3rd and 1st Battalions astride the Anui and Hapch'on roads, respectively. He also deployed a company astride the Kimch'-on road to form a three-sided defense. Having yet to recover from its losses in the Taejon Battle, however, this regiment was understrength and was largely equipped only with individual weapons. In the afternoon of July 28, upon detecting the enemy's approach, the 3rd Battalion directed artillery fire and blocked the road, and moved closer to Koch'ang to buttress its defense.

Before the day broke on the 29th, the enemy 18th Regiment launched a two-pronged attack. Bypassing the US defense, part of the enemy troops cut off the American company at the Kimch'on road while the main attack moved around Koch'ang from the north and broke through to the road on the eastern flank. The US 1st Battalion managed to turn back this attack, but had to move to a supplementary position to the east of Koch'ang. The 3rd Battalion did not even put up a fight and fell back without orders. It had only returned to position on the previous day at the insistence of the division commander. The 34th Regiment subsequently regrouped in the vicinity of Sansuri south of Koch'ang. The engineer troops blew up all the bridges along the way and set off demolition charges in the cliffs overhanging the road.[227]

The fall of Koch'ang had serious repercussions for the defense of Taegu, as the Koch'ang-Taegu axis was now exposed to the enemy's attack. On July 31, as part of ROK-US combined efforts to secure the axis, the ROK 17th Regiment (about 2,400 men) was dispatched to Kwonbinri on the southwest of Koch'ang. The regiment had just concluded its battle at Hwaryongjang.[228] On the next day, when the US 34th Regiment was pushed to the outskirts of Kwonbinri by the enemy 5th Regiment, the ROK 17th Regiment, upon Gen. Church's instructions, moved to the left flank of the 34th Regiment.

Receiving equipment support from the US 24th Division, the ROK 17th Regiment channeled its energy into establishing defensive positions.[229] Upon capturing an enemy sidecar while conducting reconnaissance, the ROK troops realized that the enemy attack was imminent and made thorough defensive preparations.

At 01:00, August 1, when the 5th Regiment of the enemy 4th Division approached the defensive front, the ROK troops surprised them with planned fire. Having failed in their first attempt, the enemy launched a two-pronged attack. While holding the 17th regiment front with a battalion-strength unit, the enemy troops surprised the US 34th Regiment with another battalion and broke through the American position.

With the withdrawal of the 34th Regiment, the ROK 17th Regiment had to fall back to adjust the lines and make preparations for a counterattack. Its 1st and 2nd Battalions subsequently recovered main hills around Kwonbinri through a counterattack. A North Korean war diary described the situation as follows: "Under artillery support, a regimental-strength enemy unit stubbornly defended its position in the vicinity of Kwonbinri, and often launched a counterattack, leading to a bloody battle."[20] The ROK 17th Regiment successfully held the position until that night, when it received an order to withdraw to Hyonp'ung on the Naktong Line. Under the cover of the UN Air Force, the ROK troops began to move toward Hyonp'ung before the morning broke.

In short, the ROK and UN Forces established a combined front in early July and conducted delaying operations by exploiting the terrain of the Charyong Mountains and the Kum River-Sobaek Mountains. After blocking the enemy's advance, they had intended to switch to a counteroffensive and drive back the enemy troops. By the end of July, however, the ROK troops were pushed back to the Hamch'ang-Andong-Yongdok line while the US forces were in danger along the Kimch'on-Sangju line. Moreover, after the enemy troops occupied Koch'ang-Hapch'on-Chinju through a large flanking maneuver, the threat to the vulnerable western Naktong River front was building up.

Thus, although the ROK-UN Forces sacrificed space for time and managed to delay the enemy for 4 weeks, the entire Korean Peninsula northwest of the Naktong River Line was now under the enemy's control. Certainly, with the establishment of the United Nations Command, UN troops were dispatched to Korea in increasing numbers; due to battle casualties, ROK Forces were reduced to five divisions, but were operating on the basis of a two-corps system ; US ground forces were increased to three-division strength, and, moreover, the US 2nd Division, a Marine brigade, and two infantry regiments were scheduled to arrive as additional reinforcement. Still, however, the ROK and the UN had not reached parity with the NKPA troops in ground forces.

In the opposite camp, the NKPA Front Line Command in Suanbo could take little comfort from the fact that its troops had reached the Naktong Line, for they were falling far short of the initial plan to conclude the war within a month. Increasingly concerned with the arrival of UN reinforcement, the North Korean military leaders were demanding their troops to press the fight, although some of the divisions had fallen to 50% strength due to heavy battle casualties.[231]

On the whole, the war situation had reached a decisive stage: The ROK and UN Forces had no more space to yield to gain time; the North Korean People's Army had no more time to lose.

On July 26, Gen. Walker issued preliminary orders for withdrawal to the Naktong Line. [232] By this time, the enemy had seized Yongdong on the Seoul-Pusan axis and was threatening Ch'upung-ryong, entrance to the Sobaek Mountains. After having a meeting with Gen. MacArthur and agreeing that there would be no Korean Dunkirk, Gen. Walker visited the US 25th Division command post in Sangju on July 29. There he issued his order to hold the line—what was to be widely publicized as his "stand or die" order:

··· We are fighting a battle against time. There will be no more retreating, withdrawal, or readjustment of the lines or any other term you choose. There is no line behind us to which we can retreat. Every unit must counterattack to keep the enemy in a state of confusion and off balance. There will be no Dunkirk, there will be no Bataan, a retreat to Pusan would be one of the greatest butcheries in history. We must fight until the end···[233]

In other words, Gen. Walker wanted his troops to overcome their fears and fight till the end, though they might be outnumbered by the enemy. On August 1, in order to defuse the critical situation in the western Naktong region, Gen. Walker hastily dispatched the 25th Division to Masan via Kimch'on-Samrangjin. Simultaneously, he ordered his troops to withdraw to the Naktong River Line. There was to be no more retreat. The delay-and-withdrawal phase of the war thus came to an end.[234]

Notes

1) The ROK government and National Assembly moved to Suwon on June 27 and Taejon on June 29, 1950, and declared martial law throughout the country except for North and South Cholla Provinces. War History Compilation Committee, *The First Year of the Korean War : A Chronicle* (Seoul: Ministry of National Defense, 1951), p. A74.

2) Research Institute of History, North Korea, *Comprehensive History of Choson*, vol. 25: *History of the War of National Liberation I* (Pyongyang: Scientific Encyclopedia Press, 1981), p. 140. The NKPA 2nd Corps' failure to occupy Ch'unch'on at an early date delayed its turning movement toward Suwon and disrupted the NKPA's war plans. WHCC, tr., US JCS, *History of the Korean War*, 1984, p. 346.

3) On July 5, the NKPA Supreme Command, by *Supreme Commander's Order* No. 5, bestowed an honorary title of "Seoul Divisions" on the 3rd and 4th Divisions, as they were the first North Korean units to enter the city of Seoul. The 105th Armored Brigade was promoted to a division and was also given the same honorary title. Research Institute of History, NK, *Comprehensive History of Choson*, vol. 25, p. 128.

4) Ibid., pp.142-143. The North Koreans noted: "It was difficult to restore the Han Pedestrian Bridge in a short time, and the same could be said about the Han Railway Bridge."

5) The NKPA 5th Division was charged with a mission to seize the Yongil Airfield. (ATIS, *Interrogation Rpts*, CPT. Kim Yo Song, N. K. 5th Div, 21 Sept. 50, Korea Institute of Military History Collections). Under the operational control of the NKPA GHQ, the 766th Unit was given a directive to secure a bridgehead along the eastern shoreline and harass the ROK line of communications. FEC G-2, *History of the North Korean Army*, Section 5, 1952, p.60.

6) 8086th AU (AFFE) Military History Detachment, *Evacuation of Refugees and Civilians from Seoul,* Precis, 1956, Korea Institute of Military History, *Historical Document* No. 914, p. 4.

7) In the vicinity of Seoul, there were a total of six ferry terminals along the Han at the time: Hajungri, Mapo, Sobinggo, Hannamdong, Ttuksom, Kwangnaru. There were several small wooden ships at each ferry terminal. *Early Battles Along the 38th Parallel (Western Front),* 1985, p. 299.

8) 8086th AU (AFFE) Military History Detachment, *Evacuation of Refugees and Civilians from Seoul,* Precis, pp.4-5; *Witness Account of Maj. Park Won Kun,* G-3, ROK 7th Divisions (WHCC, *History of the Korean War,* vol. 1, 1967, p. 761.)

9) WHCC, *Early Battles Along the 38th Parallel (Western Front),* p. 299.

10) Roy E. Appleman, *South to the Naktong, North to the Yalu* (Washington: Department of the Army, 1961), p. 43.

11) Park Kyong Sok, *Five-Star General Kim Hong Il* (Seoul: Somundang, 1984), pp. 437-438.

12) WHCC, *History of the Korean War,* vol. 1, p. 710.

13) Ibid., p.760. The Mixed 7th Division was deployed to the right of the Youido Stone Bridge, and the Mixed Capital Division was reponsible for the defense of the zone to its left, all the way to Yanghwa (Anyang Stream). *Witness Account of Col. Lee Jong Chan,* commander of the Mixed Capital Divisions.

14) WHCC, *Early Battles Along the 38th Parallel (Western Front),* pp. 257-296. Anticipating that the enemy would commit units along the Kimpo-Yongdungp'o axis, the ROKA HQ organized the Kimpo Area Battle Command (under Col. Kye In Ju) on the morning of June 26.

15) Appointed as the commander of the Suwon Area Battle Command, Maj. Gen. Lee Ung Jun, 5th Division commander, gathered up stragglers in Suwon. WHCC, tr. *US JCS, History of the Korean War,* p. 346.

16) ROKA HQ, *History of Development of the ROK Army,* vol. 1, 1970, p. 447. Each ROK regiment had only about 300 rifles and 65 light and heavy machine guns at that time. As for anti-tank guns and howitzers, only the 6th and 8th Divisions had a

total of 30 such pieces between them, and the other divisions had none.

17) Dept. of War History, Korea Military Academy, *History of the Korean War* (Seoul: Ilsinsa, 1988), p. 252. *Witness Account of Col. Lee Jong Chan,* commander of the Mixed Capital Divisions (*History of the Korean War,* vol. 1, p.760)

18) James F. Schnabel and Robert J. Watson, *The History of the Joint Chiefs of Staff* (Washington: Joint Chiefs of Staff, 1978); WHCC, tr, *US JCS: History of the Korean War,* vol. 1, 1990, p. 80.

19) MacArthur took such actions 24 hours prior to securing an approval from the US Joint Chiefs of Staff on the morning of June 29, 1950. Ibid, p. 93. Secretary of Defense, *The Test of War: History of the Office of the Secretary of Defense* (Washington : US GPO, 1988), p. 31.

20) Chung Il Kwon, *War and Armistice* (Seoul: Dong-A Daily Press, 1985), pp. 33-34. For security around the Suwon Airfield during MacArthur's visit, Detachment X of the US 507th Antiaircraft Artillery Battalion was deployed. This unit consisted of 33 men had four M55 machine guns. Appleman, op. cit., p. 46; *Secretary of Defense, Test of War, p. 53.*

21) WHCC, tr. *US JCS : History of the Korean War,* vol. 1, p. 96.

22) Ibid., pp. 94-96; James F. Schnabel, *Policy and Direction: The First Year* (Washington: Dep. of the Army, 1972), pp. 77-79.

23) WHCC, tr., *US JCS: History of the Korean War,* vol. 1, p. 101. By JCS 84881, restrictions on the use of the US Army were lifted, and by JCS 56942, it became possible to utilize available Army units.

24) Appleman, *South to the Naktong, North to the Yalu,* p. 59.

25) Ibid., p. 60; Charles E. Heller and William A. Stoff (eds.), *America's First Battle (1776 -1965)*; Roy K. Flint, *T. F. Smith and the 24th Division: Delay and Withdrawal, 5-19 July 1959* (Univ. of Kansas Press, 1988), p. 274.

26) Appleman, *South to the Naktong, North to the Yalu,* pp. 113-116.

27) Roy K. Flint, *T. F. Smith and the 24th Division,* p. 274.

28) The artillery regiments of the enemy 4th and 1st Divisions, as well as an indepen-

dent artillery regiment, provided cover for the river-crossing units. WHCC, *Early Battles Along the 38 th Parallel (Western Front),* p. 312; Japan Land Battle History Research and Dissemination Association, *The Korean War 1,* ROKA HQ, tr., *The Korean War,* vol. 1, 1986, p. 120.

29) NKPA troops primarily used ferries and rafts to cross the Han at that time. There is little evidence that they used other kinds of river-crossing equipment. WHCC, *History of the Korean War,* vol. 1, p. 763.

30) Ibid., p.761. *Witness Account of Maj. Im Baek Jin,* commander of the 1st Battalion, 3rd Regiment, 2nd Division. The 3rd Regiment withdrew from Maljukgori and occupied a position to the south of Kwachon.

31) WHCC, *Early Battles Along the 38 th Parallel (Western Front),* p. 324.

32) Chung Il Kwon, *War and Armistice,* p. 38; WHCC, *Summary of the Korean War* (Seoul: Kyohaksa, 1986), p.203. In order to establish the unity of command and direction, the government appointed newly promoted Maj. Gen. Chung II Kwon as the Army Chief of Staff and the Chief of the General Staff of the ROK Armed Forces as of July 1.

33) WHCC, *History of the Korean War,* vol. 1, p. 762. *Witness Account of Lt. Col. Kim Byung Hui,* 25th Regiment, 3rd Division.

34) Department of War History, Korea Military Academy, *History of the Korean War,* p. 255.

35) ATIS, *Interrogation Rpts.* Pvt. Hong Song Ho, N. K. 6th Div., 11 Aug. 50. The NKPA 6th Division merged with an armored battalion at Yongdungp'o, and had a total of 17 tanks at the time.

36) ROKA HQ, "*Operation Order* No. 18" (oral directive on July 2; written directive on July 3) "ROK forces will conduct delaying actions along the present frontline in order to gain time for the participation of friendly foreign troops."

37) WHCC, *History of the Korean War,* vol. 1, p. 762. *Witness Account of Maj. Im Baek Jin,* commander of the 1st Battalion, 3rd Regiment, ROK 2nd Division. Under pressure from the enemy's tanks which advanced from Anyang and Kunp'ojang, the unit

was dispersed while withdrawing to P'angyo.

38) Ibid., p.762. *Witness Account of Maj. Choi Dae Myong*, S-3, 13th Regiment, ROK 1st Division. "After regrouping in Suwon, we set out for P'ungdokch'on, but we were overmatched and had to withdraw to Pyongtaek."

39) WHCC, *History of the Korean War*, vol. 2, 1979, p. 116.

40) ROKA HQ, "*General Order* No. 2" (July 5, 1950); ROKA HQ "*Special Order* No. 9." The Uijongbu Area Battle Command established on June 26 was, in effect, the first ROK corps to be organized, just prior to the establishment of the Shihung Combat Command on June 29. The ROK 1st Corps amounted to little more than a change in the name of this command.

41) ROKA HQ, "*Operation Order* No. 20" (July 5, 1950); "*1st Corps Operation Order* No. 1" (July 5, 1950).

42) Chung Il Kwon, *War and Armistice*, p. 50.

43) WHCC, *History of the Korean War*, vol. 2, p. 122.

44) Schnabel, *Policy and Direction*, p.114. Order from Supreme Commander, NKPA to All Forces, 15 Oct. 50 in ATIS Enemy Docs. Korean Opns, issue 19. 30 Jan. 51. Item 1. (Policy and Directim, P. 114)

45) ROKA HQ, *History of Development of the Army*, vol. 1, pp. 443-447; Office of the Chief Military Historian, ROKA HQ, *History of the Korean War in Rear Areas (Logistics)* (Seoul: ROKA HQ, 1953), pp. 293-295.

46) ROKA HQ, Ibid pp. 66-67; WHCC, *History of the Ministry of National Defense*, vol. 2, p. 109.

47) The enemy supreme command reorganized the field command according to the changed situation. On July 5, it appointed Kim Chaek and Kang Gon as the commander and chief of staff, respectively. Research Institute of History, N.K, *Comprehensive History of Choson*, vol. 25, p. 166; FEC, *History of the North Korean Army*, Section 5, p. 84.

48) The NKPA 8th Division was formed around the 1st Brigade, 38th Security Force, in early July. WHCC, *History of the Korean War*, vol. 2, p. 160.

49) On the morning of July 3, friendly air strikes by four Australian F-51 planes on ammunition trains at the P'yongtaek Train Station and the ROK 17th Regimentt caused major damage. In the afternoon on the same day, US air planes by mistake raided ROK forces on National Road 1 to the south of the Suwon Airfield and inflicted nearly 200 casualties and damaged more than 30 vehicles. Ibid., pp. 42-43.

50) Ibid., pp. 845-924.

51) ROK Ministry of Natinal Defense, *The First Year of the Korean War: A Chronicle*, p. A74.

52) WHCC, *History of the Ministry of National Defense*, vol. 2, pp. 110-111. A provisional UN Liaision Officers Corps under Col. Im Son Ha was established on July 10 according to MND *General Order* No. 5 (July 7, 1950), and was formally launched on August 6 under MND *General Order* No. 35 (August 2, 1950).

53) ROKA *Order* No. 20 (July 4, 1950). *Account of Col. Paek In Yop*, commanding officer of the 17th Regiment. WHCC, *History of the Korean War*, vol. 2, p. 61.

54) Appleman, *South to the Naktong, North to the Yalu*, pp. 68-70.

55) Ibid., pp. 70-73.

56) *Account of Capt. Yun Sung Kun*, a liaison officer of the 52nd Field Artillery Battalion, WHCC, *History of the Korean War*, vol. 2, p. 63; *Account of Lt. Col. Kim Hui Jun*, succeeding commander of the 17th Regiment. Ibid., p. 62.

57) Appleman, *South to the Naktong, North to the Yalu*, pp. 74-76. The actual casualties were lower than the initial estimate as many of the missing men later returned to Task Force Smith.

58) Ibid., p.70; ROKA HQ, tr., *Korean War*, vol. 1, p. 149.

59) Flint, *T. F. Smith and the 24th Division*, p. 282. Commanding officers did not tell their men about the result of Task Force Smith's operation.

60) Ibid., pp. 282-283; Appleman *South to the Naktong, North to the Yalu*, pp. 79-80.

61) ROKA HQ, tr., *Korean War*, vol. 1, p. 155. Third US general to arrive in Korea after Church and Dean, Brig. Gen. George B. Barth was the acting commander of the division artillery, 24th Division. Gen. Dean instructed him to direct front operations

in his behalf.

62) Appleman, *South to the Naktong, North to the Yalu,* pp. 82–83.

63) Flint, *T. F. Smith and the 24th Division,* p. 285.

64) ROKA HQ, tr., *Korean War,* vol. 1, p. 175. First antitank mines airlifted from Japan were placed underground along the road to the north of Ch'onan.

65) Appleman, *South to the Naktong, North to the Yalu,* pp. 83–86.

66) Ibid., pp. 86–88.

67) War History Department, Korea Military Academy, *History of the Korean War,* p. 265; ROKA HQ, tr., *Korean War,* vol. 1, p. 167.

68) The 1st Battalion (−) was formed around A and D Companies and included the members of B and C Companies who had been excluded from Task Force Smith.

69) Flint, *T. F. Smith and the 24th Division,* p. 286.

70) Appleman, *South to the Naktong, North to the Yalu,* pp. 88–90.

71) Ibid., pp.91–93; Flint, *T. F. Smith and the 24th Division,* p. 288.

72) Appleman, *South to the Naktong, North to the Yalu,* p. 98 (footnote no. 43).

73) Ibid., pp. 96–99.

74) Ibid., p. 95.

75) The total strength of the Capital Division heading toward Chinch'on was 7,855 men. It received 4 new-model 105-mm howitzers from the 1st Artillery Corps which had just been established in Taejon.

76) FEC, *History of the North Korean Army, Section 5,* pp. 54–56; ATIS, *Interrogation Rpts,* N.K. 2nd Div, Maj. Son Dae Gwang, 19 Sept. 50.

77) Around this time, Kim Sok Won was recruiting volunteers in Taejon. Upon receiving a request from the Defense Minister to take command of the Capital Division, he returned to service. WHCC, *Chinch'on-Hwaryongjang Battle* (Seoul: Ministry of National Defense, 1991), p. 36.

78) *Account of Col. Park Ki Byong,* commanding officer of the 20th Regiment. WHCC, *History of the Korean War,* vol. 2, p. 324.

79) Research Institute of History (N. K.), *Comprehensive History of Choson,* vol. 25,

pp. 172–173. It notes ROK counterattacks as follows: "The People's Army occupied the commanding ground of Munan-san-Soul-san to the south of Chinch'on. The enemy repeatedly launched counterattacks for two days from July 9, and there were more than 10 battles on July 10 alone···"

80) WHCC, *Chinch'on-Hwaryongjang Battle,* pp. 85–86.

81) *Account of Maj. Chang Chun Gwon,* commander of the 2nd Battalion, 18th Regiment. WHCC, *History of the Korean War,* vol. 2, p. 324.

82) "Corps *Operation Order* No. 10" (July 12, 1950). Maj. Gen. Kim Hong Il noted: "On this day, Choch'iwon on the left flank fell into enemy hands, and as Ch'ongju was characterized by level terrain on three sides, we risked losing all our troops committed to street fighting if the roads were blocked. Instead of risking such an outcome, we decided to pull back our troops." WHCC, *Chinch'on-Hwaryongjang Battle,* pp. 89–90.

83) WHCC, *Chinchon-Hwaryongjang Battle,* p.131.

84) EFC, *History of the North Korean Army, Section* 5, pp. 74–76. The NKPA 15th Division used South Korean conscripts to move food and ammunition. As the division included many conscripts among its ranks, its overall morale was low. ATIS, *Interrogation Rpts,* N.K. 15th Div, Pvt. Chang Ki Hwa, 20 Sept. 50.

85) WHCC, *Chinch'on-Hwaryongjang Battle,* p. 144. According to S-4, enemy 48th Regiment, 15th Division, when village residents saw the ROK 3rd Battalion withdraw from Tongrakri, they apparently jumped to the conclusion that the ROK troops were taking flight. Informed that the ROK troops had fled from the village, the NKPA unit relaxed security.

86) According to a detailed battle report of the ROK 7th Regiment, the two battalions killed 2,186 and captured 132 enemy soldiers; whereas, the headquarters company of the enemy 48th Regiment gave a figure of about 800 for battle casualties. War History Department, Korea Military Academy, *History of the Korean War,* p. 279.

87) WHCC, *Chinch'on-Hwaryongjang Battle,* p. 149.

88) Ibid., pp. 173–181. Having been attached to the 1st Division up to that point, a bat-

tery of the 16th Artillery was returned to the 6th Division in Mungyong on July 11. The ROK 1st Corps attached another artillery battery (four 105-mm howitzers) to the 1st Division.

89) The NKPA 12th Division was formed around the original 7th Division, which consisted of Korean-national war veterans with the Chinese People's Liberation Army. A new 7th Division (under Maj. Gen. Lee Ik Song) was organized in Haeju on July 3, 1950.

90) WHCC, *History of the Korean War,* vol. 2, p. 231. *Account of Col. Hahm Byong Son,* commander of the 2nd Regiment.

91) Ibid., p. 232. *Account of Capt. Ch'oi Hui Dae,* commander of the 3rd Company, 1st Battalion, 2nd Regiment.

92) Ibid., p. 231. *Account of Maj. Kim Yong Ki,* commander of the 2nd Battalion, 19th Regiment.

93) Appleman, *South to the Naktong, North to the Yalu,* p. 104; War History Department, Korea Military Academy, *History of the Korean War,* pp. 282–283; WHCC, *Tanyang -Uisong Battle* (Seoul: Ministry of National Defense, 1987), pp. 22–23.

94) Apparently, the 8th Division had received a fabricated order by cable. Exactly how this order was issued remains a mystery.

95) WHCC, *History of the Korean War,* vol. 2, p. 201. *Account of 1st Lt. Seo Jong Woo,* S-3, Engineer Battalion, 8th Division.

96) FEC, *History of the North Korean Army,* Section 5, p. 66.

97) WHCC, *Tanyang-Uisong Battle,* pp. 38–43.

98) Ibid., pp.44–50; "8th Division *Operation Order* No. 14" (2000 hrs., July 9, 1950)

99) WHCC, *History of the Korean War,* vol. 2, pp. 183–184. *Account of 1st Lt. Ch'oi Yong Gu,* commander of the 9th Company, 21st Regiment.

100) WHCC, *Tanyang-Uisong Battle,* pp. 53–61.

101) Ibid., pp. 62–66.

102) The ROK 3rd Division was conducting counter-guerrilla operations in Kyong-sang Provinces with its 22nd Regiment (under Lt. Col. Kang T'ae Min) in Taegu

and 23rd Regiment in Pusan. When the war broke out, the 22nd Regiment was dispatched to Seoul, and the 23rd Regiment, to the east coast region.

103) FEC, *History of the North Korean Army, Section 5*, p. 60; ATIS, *Interrogation Rpts,* N.K. 5th Div, Capt. Kim Yo Song, 21 Sept. 50.

104) The Independent 1st Battalion and Yongdungp'o Academy troops were scheduled to be committed to counter-guerrilla operations in southern provinces on June 24, 1950. When the war broke out, however, they were attached to the 3rd Division effective June 28 and assembled in P'ohang.

105) The enemy 5th Division relied mainly on civilians for food. Ammunition was supplied to the division by trucks and cow-driven carts, and was carried forward to the front by conscripted labor in occupied areas. ATIS, *Interrogation Rpts,* N. K. 5th, Pvt. Chong Jong Yop and Pvt. Oh Sang Man, 16 Aug. 50.

106) Research Institute of History, N.K., *Comprehensive History of Choson,* vol. 25, p. 197.

107) The 22nd Regiment was assigned to the 1st Division when the ROK Armed Forces was reorganized on July 5. By a subsequent stay order, however, the unit remained under the control of the 2nd Division. Subsequently, according to *Order* No. 20 (July 21 MND *General Order*) the 22nd Regiment was returned to the 3rd Division and committed into the Yongdok Battle.

108) The enemy 11th Regiment joined the 5th Division around July 10. In its arduous march through the mountains, however, the unit had lost about 1,800 men. Appleman, *South to the Naktong, North to the Yalu,* pp. 105-106.

109) WHCC, tr., *US JCS, History of the Korean War,* pp. 623-625.

110) Schnabel, *Policy and Direction,* pp. 100-101. Committee on Coordination of Assistance for Korea.

111) Ibid., pp. 115-117; WHCC, tr., *US JCS: History of the Korean War,* vol. 1, pp. 109-110.

112) WHCC, tr., *US JCS : Korean War,* vol. 1, p.110 ; Ministry of Foreign Affairs, *30 Years of Korean Diplomacy,* p. 185.

113) Schnabel, *Policy and Direction,* p. 103.

114) WHCC, tr., *US JCS: Korean War,* vol. 1, p. 111; Schnabel, *Policy and Direction,* p. 103.

115) WHCC, *Summary of the Korean War,* p. 206.

116) WHCC, tr., *US JCS : Korean War,* vol. 1, p. 148.

117) WHCC, *History of the Korean War,* vol. 2, pp. 127-128.

118) Seoul Shinmun, *30 Years of USFK,* 1979, p. 169; WHCC, *History of the Korean War,* vol. 2, p. 991. This was the second time that operational command over the ROK Armed Forces was transferred to foreign military leadership. On August 24, 1949, President Rhee had assured Gen. Hodge that US Forces would retain operational command over ROK Forces until the complete withdrawal of the USFK. War History Compilation Committee, *National Defense Treaties,* vol. 1, 1988, pp. 34-38; Robert K. Sawyer and Walter G. Hermes, *Military Advisors in Korea: KMAG in Peace and War* (Washington, D.C.: US Dept. of the Army, 1962), p. 34.

119) Chung Il Kwon, *War and Armistice,* p.78.

120) Applemen, *South to the Naktong, North to the Yalu,* p. 112.

121) ROKA Headquarters, *A Chronicle of the Army History* (July 7, 1950); WHCC, *History of the Korean War,* vol. 2, p. 995.

122) MND Headquarters, "*General Order* No. 3" (July 7, 1950); ROKA Special Order No. 11 (July 7, 1950).

123) Chung Il Kwon *War and Armistice,* pp. 67-68; WHCC, *History of the Korean War,* vol. 2, p. 139.

124) ROKA HQ, "*Operation Order* No. 57" (July 20, 1950).

125) WHCC, *History of the Korean War,* vol. 2, p. 140; Appleman, *South to the Naktong, North to the Yalu,* p. 191; *Urgent Order* No. 8 (July 21, 1950); MND Headquarters *General Order* No. 20 (July 24, 1950).

126) ROKA HO, *History of the Development of the Army,* vol. 1, p. 435.

127) For 3 weeks after the outbreak of the war, US logistical support to ROK forces was provided according to need estimated by KMAG. HQS USAFFE & Eighth Army (Rear), *Logistics in the Korean Operations* (San Francisco, 1954), *Historical Manuscript File,* call No. 8-5, vol. 4, ch. 8, p. 16.

128) ROKA HQ, *History of the Development of the Army,* vol. 1, pp. 450–454. US FEC was taking measures to secure equipment for ROK Forces including artillery pieces and communications equipment. *Logistics in the Korean Operations,* vol. 4, ch. 8, p. 17.

129) ROKA HQ, *History of the Development of the Army,* vol. 1, p. 435.

130) WHCC, *History of National Defense,* vol. 2, p. 288.

131) The Pusan Logistical Command was categorized as a type-B support unit (providing support to 100,000 combat troops) on the US table of organization. *Draft Field Manual,* The Logistical Command, C & GSC, 1950.

132) Appleman, *South to the Naktong, North to the Yalu,* pp. 113–116; James A. Huston, *The Sinews of War: Army Logistics 1775–1953* (Washington, D.C.: Office of the Chief of Military History, 1966), p. 618.

133) WHCC, *History of the Korean War,* vol. 3, 1970, p.38.

134) EUSA *Operation Order* No. 1 (July 13, 1950).

135) Research Institute of History, N.K., *Comprehensive History of Choson,* vol. 2, pp. 169 –170.

136) Appleman, *South to the Naktong, North to the Yalu,* pp. 122–123; ATIS, *Interrogation Rpts,* N.K. 4th, 2nd Lt. Kim Yong Ho, 28 Sep. 50, Maj. Ch'oi Ju Yong, 26 Sep. 50.

137) NKPA *War Diary* (July 13–14, 1950) SN792.

138) The regimental information staff officer (S-3) and signal staff officer of the 34th Regiment and more than 40 members of K Company were evacuated on July 13 due to battle fatigue. Flint, *T. F. Smith and the 24th Division,* pp. 290–293.

139) The 6th Cavalry Company of the ROK Independent Cavalry Regiment was attached to the 34th Regiment on July 9, 1950, and conducted reconnaissance missions before returning to Kongju on the 12th. The company participated in the Kongju Battle. *Account of 1st Lt. Park Ik Gyun,* commander of the 6th Company; *account of 2nd Lt. Cho Don Ch'ol,* a platoon leader. WHCC, *History of the Korean War,* vol. 3, pp. 95–96, pp. 471–472.

140) Applemen, *South to the Naktong, North to the Yalu,* p. 126.

141) NKPA *War Diary* (July 15-16, 1950) SN792.

142) As security forces on the western flank, I and R Platoons of the 2nd Battalion and one platoon of G Company were deployed.

143) Task Force McGrail consisted of commanded G Company(−), 1 machine gun platoon and an 81-mm mortar section from H Company, 2 light tanks, and 2 batteries of the 26th Antiaircraft Artillery Battaliion. Appleman, *South to the Naktong, North to the Yalu,* p. 133.

144) Flint, *T. F. Smith and the 24th Division,* p. 295; War History Dept., Korea Military Academy, *History of the Korean War,* p. 298.

145) Appleman *South to the Naktong, North to the Yalu,* p. 138.

146) Ibid., p. 143.

147) Ibid., p. 145.

148) The enemy 4th Division charged the 18th Regiment with a mission to bypass ROK defense through the mountains and block the Kumsan road. Research Institute of History, N.K., *Comprehensive History of Choson,* vol. 25, p. 192.

149) Appleman, *South to the Naktong, North to the Yalu,* p. 148. Around this time, Lt. Gen. Walker completed the operational concept of blocking the enemy at the Naktong line with the US 24th and 25th Divisions, US 1st Cavalry Division, and ROK Forces. Flint *T. F. Smith and the 24th Division,* p. 296.

150) Applemen, *South to the Naktong, North to the Yalu,* pp. 156-157.

151) Ibid., p. 157.

152) Ibid., pp. 163-164.

153) Ibid., pp. 158-159.

154) Ibid., pp. 168-169.

155) Ibid., p. 173.

156) Ibid., pp. 176-177. Maj. Gen. Dean was returned to Panmunjom as part of POW exchange on September 4, 1953.

157) Ibid., p. 181; WHCC, *History of the Korean War,* vol. 2, p. 534.

158) NKPA *War Diary* (July 23, 1950) SN792. From mid-July, the enemy 4th Division

replenished troops with conscripts from South Korea, and deployed guards to prevent their escape. *Interrogation Rpts,* N.K. 4th, 1st Lt. Kim Yong Ho, 28 Sept. 50.

159) Research Institute of History, N.K., *Comprehensive History of Choson,* vol. 25, p. 192.

160) Appleman, *South to the Naktong, North to the Yalu,* p. 200.

161) Ibid., pp. 197-198.

162) War History Dept., Korea Military Academy, *History of the Korean War,* p. 310; WHCC, *History of the Korean War,* vol. 2, p. 551.

163) Appleman, *South to the Naktong, North to the Yalu,* pp. 200-203.

164) Ibid., pp. 203-205.

165) The ROK 2nd Division was charged with the defense of the gap between the US 24th Division (Kongju) and ROK Capital Division (Chongju). *Periodic Operations Reports, Korean Army,* No. 12, SN 1266.

166) WHCC, *Chinch'on-Hwaryongjang Battle,* pp. 188-189.

167) Some differences exist among sources in regard to the background and dates of the Hwaryongjang Battle. The account provided here is based on the official version. (See WHCC, *History of the Korean War,* vol. 2, p. 454).

168) According to Maj. Gen. Kim Hong Il, commnader of the 1st Corps, ROK troops at the time were using a map that showed all of Korea in carrying out operations. Due to lack of detail on the map, they were unaware that there were mountain roads in the area. An Yong Hyong, *A Secret History of the Korean War,* vol. 2, p. 169.

169) WHCC, *History of the Korean War,* vol. 2, pp. 426-427.

170) NKPA 2nd Corps *Operation Directive* (July 11, 1950) Korea Institute of Military History SN818.

171) *Account of 1st Lt. Kim Hui Je,* operation officer, 1st Battalion, 17th Regiment. WHCC, *History of the Korean War,* vol. 2, pp. 450-451.

172) WHCC, *History of the Korean War,* vol. 2, p. 434.

173) *Account of Maj. Song Ho Rim,* commander of the 2nd Battalion. *Account of Uh Yong Son,* member of the Korean Youth Organization in Hwaryongmyon. WHCC, *His-*

tory of the Korean War, vol. 2, p. 451.

174) NKPA 2nd Corps *Operation Directive* (July 11, 1950) SN818.

175) WHCC, *History of the Korean War,* vol. 2, p.452 ; *Periodic Operations Reports,* Korean Army, No. 16.

176) War History Dept., KMA, *History of the Korean War,* pp. 312-313; WHCC, *Chinch'-on-Hwaryongjang Battle,* pp. 229-230.

177) The NKPA 13th Division (19th, 21st, 23rd Regiments) was organized around the Democratic Youth Federation in Shinuiju in June 1950. Arriving in Seoul in early July, the 23rd Regiment was stationed in Inchon until late July, and the remainder of the division went to Ch'ungju and was charged with the mission to join the 1st Division and attack Mungyong-Yugok. FEC, *History of the North Korean Army,* pp. 72-73.

178) *Periodic Operations Reports,* Korean Army, No. 16.

179) Military History Reserach Institute, *Ch'ungju-Chomch'on Battle,* 1992, pp. 86-87.

180) Ibid., p. 419.

181) Ibid., pp. 97-104. *Account of 1st Lt. Kim Yong Pil,* information officer, 2nd Battalion, 19th Regiment.

182) Ibid., p. 106.

183) Ibid., pp. 116-119.

184) Ibid., p. 116.

185) The 1st Regiment, Capital Division, was in Hwaryongjang on its way to the eastern front from Kounri, south of Ch'ongju, when it received ROKA HQ *Operation Order* No. 55 (July 19, 1950) which attached it to the 2nd Corps. Simultaneously, the corps attached the regiment to the 6th Division in preparation for the Yonggang Battle.

186) *Account of Capt. Ch'oi Hui Dae,* commander of the 3rd Company, 2nd Regiment. WHCC, *History of the Korean War,* vol. 2, p. 704. *Ch'ungju-Chomch'on Battle,* p. 156.

187) WHCC, *History of the Korean War,* vol. 2, p. 168.

188) *Periodic Operations Reports,* Korean Army, No. 31.

189) As part of ROK reorganization efforts, the 5th and 20th Regiments of the 2nd Division were assigned to the 1st Division on July 20. (See Section 3, Chapter 3) The 5th Regiment advanced to Andong from Hamchang on the 24th.

190) FEC, *History of the North Korean Army*, p. 73.

191) *Account of Maj. An Kwang Yong*, commander of the 2nd Battalion, 13th Regiment. WHCC, *History of the Korean War*, vol. 2, p. 721.

192) *Periodic Operations Reports*, Korean Army, No. 49.

193) ROK 8th Division *Operation Order* No. 16 (2300, July 11, 1950)

194) WHCC, *History of the Korean War*, vol. 2, p. 377.

195) NKPA 2nd Corps *Operation Directive* (July 11, 1950) SN818.

196) WHCC, *Tanyang-Uisong Battle*, p. 86.

197) *Account of Maj. Un Hyong Won*, operation officer, 10th Regiment. WHCC, *History of the Korean War*, vol. 2, p. 377; WHCC, *Tanyang-Uisong Battle*, pp. 100-101.

198) WHCC, *Tanyang-Uisong Battle*, p. 112.

199) Ibid., pp. 116-118.

200) Ibid., p. 150.

201) Ibid., p. 153. The withdrawal time as specified in 1st Corps *Operation Order* No. 40 is 2400 hrs, July 31.

202) *Account of Col. Ch'oi Dok Shin*, chief of staff, 1st Corps. WHCC, *History of the Korean War*, vol. 2, p. 662.

203) *Account of 1st Lt. Kim Gwang Ch'ol*, commander of the 8th Company, 21st Regiment. Ibid, p. 662.

204) WHCC, *Tanyang-Uisong Battle*, p.163.

205) The ROKA Headquarters appointed Col. Yu Sung Yol, 3rd Division commander, as the commander of the South Kyongsang Unit Organization District. Br. Gen. Lee Jun Shik, superintendent of KMA, was appointed as the new commander of the 3rd Division. WHCC, *History of the Korean War*, vol. 2, p. 583.

206) FEC, *History of the North Korean Army*, pp. 60-61; Applemen, *South to the Naktong, North to the Yalu*, pp. 107-108. Around this period, the NKPA suffered heavy loss-

es due to heavy daytime air strikes by UN planes. The pace of their attack suffered as well. NKPA 2nd Corps *Operation Directive* (July 11, 1950) SN818.

207) ATIS, *Interrogation Rpts,* N. K. 5th Div, MSG Lee Mun Ok and Pvt. Oh Sang Man (16 Oct. 50), Pvt. Chong Jong Yop (16 Oct. 50).

208) Appleman, *South to the Naktong, North to the Yalu,* p. 184.

209) Ibid., p. 184.

210) The enemy 5th Division lost nearly 400 men due to UN naval gunfire. US Navy, *History of United States Naval Operation* (Korea), translated into Korean by ROKA HQ, 1985, p. 159.

211) The 22nd Regiment was attached to the 1st Corps and was deployed in the outskirts of Poun on July 22. It subsequently returned to the 3rd Division.

212) Appleman, *South to the Naktong, North to the Yalu,* p. 185.

213) Foreign Service of the U.S.A., *Tiger Kim vs. The Press,* 12 May 51, SN328; Applemen *South to the Naktong, North to the Yalu,* p. 186. *Account of Maj. Ho Hyong Sun,* commander of the 3rd Battalion, 23rd Regiment. WHCC, *History of the Korean War,* vol. 2, p. 601. Due to this incident, Lt. Col. Kim Jong Won was removed from his post, and was replaced by Lt. Col. Kim Jong Sun.

214) The enemy 5th Division lost 700-800 men due to UN naval gunfire. Appleman, *South to the Naktong, North to the Yalu,* p. 185; ATIS, *Interrogation Rpts,* N. K. 5th Div, Pvt. Chong Jong Yop (15 Oct. 50).

215) *Periodic Operations Reports,* Korean Army, No. 56 (2400 August 2, 1950).

216) Yu Kwan Jong, *Korean Police in War: A History* (Seoul : Modern Police Books, 1982), pp. 118-119.

217) Marine Corps *Operation Order* No. 1 (15:00 July 14, 1950). During a 7-hour battle, the Ko Gil Hun unit killed nearly 300 enemy troops. Marine Corps Command, *Marine Corps Battles: A History,* vol. 1, 1962, p. 43.

218) Yu Kwang Jong, *Korean Police in War : A History,* p. 97.

219) When the division reconstruction plan was not carried out, Min Unit (under Col. Min Ki Shik), Kim Unit (under Maj. Kim Byong Hwa), Oh Unit (under Col. Oh

Dok Jun), and Lee Unit (under Lt. Col. Lee Yong Gyu) were temporarily organized and took up the defense of Cholla Provinces. Also, one Marine Corps battalion (Ko Gil Hun unit renamed Kim Song Un unit effective July 22) was dispatched to Kunsan by the ROK Naval Headquarters. WHCC, *History of the Korean War,* vol. 2, pp. 726-729.

220) Appleman, *South to the Naktong, North to the Yalu,* p. 211.

221) By ROKA HQ, *"Operation Order* No. 70," Maj. Gen. Ch'ae Byong Dok, former
Army Chief of Staff, was appointed as the commander of the Kyongsang Area
Battle Command. Although he was instructed to block the enemy at the Namwon
-Hadong line, he had almost no actual troops under his command.

222) *Account of Lt. Col. Chong Rae Hyok,* staff of the new 9th Division. WHCC, *History of
the Korean War,* vol. 2, p. 805, p. 841.

223) *Account of Lt. Col. Kim Yong Ju,* commander of the 30th Regiment, Min Unit. Ibid.,
p. 841.

224) Marine Corps HQ, *Marine Corps Battles, vol. 1, p. 55. Account of GS Yom Tae Bok,
7th Company, Marine Corps.* WHCC, *History of the Korean War,* vol. 2, p. 842. They
received equipment from US troops in Chinju.

225) Appleman, *South to the Naktong, North to the Yalu,* p. 232. During the counteroffensive of September, 1950, the 25th Division discovered that 12 US POWs were machine-gunned to death in Chinju with their arms tied behind their back. UN *Operation Report* No. 6, MND, *(First Year of the Korean War : A Chronicle, p. C283).*

226) NKPA War Diary (July 26-27, 1950) SN792.

227) Applemen, *South to the Naktong, North to the Yalu,* p. 226.

228) *Accounts of Col. Yu Hui Jun,* regimental commander, and *Lt. Col. Lee Gwan Su,*
commander of the 1st Battalion, 17th Regiment. WHCC, *History of the Korean War,*
vol. 2, p.818; ibid., pp. 226-227.

229) Ibid., For the first time, the troops received Carbine M2's from US forces after
arriving in Kwonbinri. *Account of Capt. Lee Hyong Ju,* information officer, 2nd Battalion, 17th Regiment. WHCC, *History of the Korean War,* vol. 2, p. 819.

230) NKPA *War Diary* (July 30–August 1, 1950) SN792.

231)Appleman, *South to the Naktong, North to the Yalu*, p. 263.

232) The warning order for a planned withdrawal may be summarized as follows: "In order to stabilize the front line and seize the initiative, withdraw to prepared defensive positions. The time of the movement will be announced later. Maintain contact with the enemy while moving." Ibid., p. 205.

233) Ibid., p. 208.

234) Ibid., p. 250. The ROKA Headquarters instructed the 1st and 2nd Corps to withdraw to the south of the Naktong River under the cover of night on July 31 and August 1. *Periodic Operations Reports*, Korean Army, No. 49.

Chapter Four Defensive Operation Along the Naktong River Line

Ⅰ. The Establishment of the Naktong River Line

1. The Naktong River Defense Line

The Korean War entered a new stage with the conclusion of the delay-and-withdrawal operations at the end of July and subsequent establishment of the Naktong Line from August 1 to 4. The idea of organizing defense along the Naktong River was first discussed on July 17, right after the collapse of the Kum-Sobaek Line. After taking various factors into account, Gen. Walker and his staff selected the Naktong Line as the final line of resistance. From there the ROK-US troops would eventually launch their all-out counteroffensive.[1]

While the ROK and UN Forces were delaying the enemy's advance, Gen. Walker secured the cooperation of residents in the Naktong region to organize defensive positions along the river. On July 26, he issued a preliminary order for withdrawal to his troops. He agreed with Gen. MacArthur that there would be no Korean Dunkirk. On his visit to the US 25th Division on July 29, Gen. Walker issued his "stand or die" order and reminded his troops that any man who gave ground might be "personally responsible for the death of thousands of his comrades." At last, on August 1, he ordered his troops to cross the river to the new Naktong Defense Line, where they would make their last stand.[2]

In organizing defense along the Naktong Line, Gen. Walker attached special significance to counterattack. He urged each unit to counterattack to keep the enemy off balance and disrupt their coordinated attack on friendly positions. Gen. Walker noted that as recent operations in Korea demonstrated, counterattack was highly effective for recovering lost positions and delaying the enemy's advance. He added that counterattack was a decisive element of defense and that its success depended on speed, audacity, and surprise.[3]

The Naktong Line was also known as the Pusan Perimeter, as Pusan was to be the base from which the ROK-UN Forces would launch their full-scale counteroffensive. It was also called the Walker Line after Gen. Walker. This defense line was generally organized along the Naktong River, and was shaped like an inverted L stretching for 80 km east-west and 160 km north-south, connecting Masan-Namji-Waegwan-Nakjongri-Yongdok from the southwest to the northeast.

The Naktong Line consisted of three sections. The first sector used the Naktong as a natural defense line and ran along Nakjongri-Waegwan-Namji. At the time, the Naktong River had a width of 400-800 meters and a depth of 1-1.5 meters. Excluding the river banks, the river water was 200-400 meters wide. The second sector of the Naktong Defense Line stretched from Namji to Chindongri to the west Masan. This sector stretched from the confluence of the Naktong and the Nam all the way to the southern coast. This sector was characterized by rough terrain as it included Chont'u-san (661m, Combat Mountain), P'il-bong (743m), and Sobuk-san (738m). The third sector stretched from Nakjongri to Yongdok, and included the rugged hills of the Taebaek Mountains in the upper Naktong region.

Overall, the defense line mostly ran along the rivers and mountains in the Naktong region, and these natural obstacles facilitated the defense of the exterior line. Moreover, well-developed road networks from Pusan to major towns on the defense line facilitated interior operations within the line as well.

In planning defense along Naktong Line, Gen. Walker carefully considered the strengths and weakness of the North Korean People's Army, and deployed his troops accordingly. He noted that the enemy troops excelled in infiltration into mountain areas, close combat, and flanking maneuver, but showed their vulnerabilities in open-area battle, where the US superiority in firepower and maneuver could be fully exploited. Accordingly, he deployed US troops in open terrain along the Naktong River on the western flank. ROK troops, who had effectively delayed the enemy in mountain areas, were deployed along the chain of hills in the upper Naktong region.

The ROK and UN Forces accordingly established a coordination point at the northern end of Chako-san, north of Waegwan. Three US divisions were to be deployed to the south of this point, down along the Naktong River to the southern coast, whereas five ROK Divisions took up the northern section of the defense line. This troop deployment was to be completed between the night of August 2 and dawn the next day.[4]

Although the lines were not completely connected, the establishment of the Naktong Line had added significance in that it minimized the inter-unit gap, which had been one of the most serious problems for the ROK-US side up to that point.

After reviewing the defense plan along the Naktong Line in early August, Gen. MacArthur ordered the Eighth US Army to establish an alternate defense line in order to secure a landing spot in Pusan even in a contingency situation. Accordingly, Br. Gen. Garrison H. Davidson, engineer chief of the EUSA, designed the so-called "Davidson Line," and built up a 90-km-long alternate position between August 11 and September 1. Established with the assistance of nearby residents, who worked along with the US 25th and 2nd Divisions, the Davidson Line stretched from the northwest of Masan to Sodongri (17km north-

Naktong River Defensive Line (Aug. 1-4, 1950)

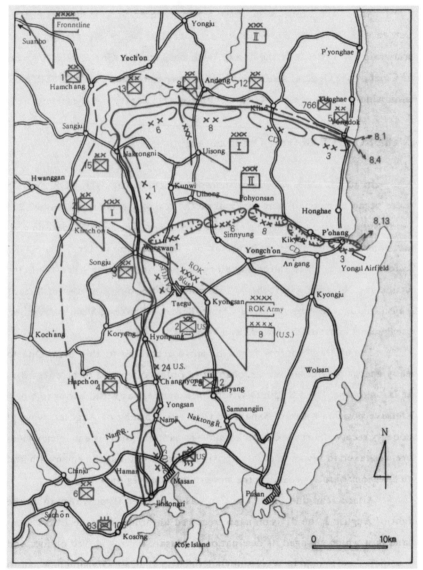

west of Ulsan) via Yuch'on and Muanri, on the north of Miryang.[5]

Around this time, ROK Defense Minister Shin Song Mo issued a statement entitled "Current War Situation and Our Resolve," and expressed his determination to drive back the enemy. And, on August 3, Gen. Chung Il Kwon, the Chief of the General staff of the ROK Armed Forces, circulated a statement nationwide assuring that the ROK-UN Forces were superior to the enemy.[6]

2. The ROK-US Defense Organization

In accordance with the withdrawal order of August 1, ROK and US troops began to move to their positions on the Naktong Line. From August 2 to 3, they were ordered to delay the enemy along the present line (X Line) and conduct reconnaissance along the new Naktong Defense Line (Y Line). The ROK-US forces were to block the enemy along the new line starting August 4. Lying outside the Naktong River, the X Line connected Sobuk-san (west of Masan), Sanjeri (north of Hapch'on), east of Chirye, Kimch'on, Sangju, Yech'on, Andong, Honggudong (north of Ch'ongsong), and Yongdok.[7]

The ROK-US forces began to move according to this plan. Due to heavy enemy pressure, however, changes in orders often had to be effected at the last moment. The US 25th Division, for example, was withdrawing to a new defensive position south of Sangju on the early morning of August 1 when it suddenly received a revised order to move to Samrangjin. This emergency measure was taken in response to late-arriving information that the enemy 4th and 6th Divisions were approaching the western Naktong region.

After a lead unit of the division was dispatched from Waegwan on the night of August 2, the division again received an order from the EUSA command post which changed its destination to Masan. Having moved on foot and by vehicle from Sangju to Waegwan via Kimch'on, the 25th Division now had to move to Masan by rail. On August 3, its 35th and 24th Regiments managed to arrive in Masan at 1000 and 1930, respectively. For successfully carrying out unprecedented maneuver at a critical phase of the war, the US 25th Division received commendation from President Syngman Rhee.[8]

In the meantime, the US 24th Division, deployed along the X Line between Chinju and Masan, was doing its best to defend against the expected approach of the enemy 6th Division. After moving the division command post from Hapch'on to Ch'angnyong on July 31, the commander of the 24th Division decided to conduct reconnaissance in force along the two roads connecting Chinju and Masan to disrupt the expected enemy approach before arrival of the main force of the US 25th Division. In the predawn hours of August 2, the attached 2nd Battalion of the 29th Regiment and the 1st Battalion of the 27th Regiment organized a motorized reconnaissance party with tanks and armored vehicles, and conducted reconnaissance in force toward Chinju from Chungamri and Chindongri, respectively.

The 2nd Battalion, 29th Regiment, was surprised by the enemy and fell back, but the 1st Battalion, 27th Regiment, was able to destroy an enemy supply unit at Chinju pass under aerial support. Although its rear was blocked, the battalion carried out an aggressive withdrawal operation. In the predawn hours the next day, the enemy 14th Regiment counterattacked the US troops at Chindongri Primary School, but the battalion was able to turn them back, killing and wounding 600 enemy soldiers.[9]

Meanwhile, having received an withdrawal order on the morning of August 2, the US 34th Regiment crossed the Naktong and assembled in Yongsan. In the evening the same day, the US 21st and ROK 17th Regiments also withdrew with relative ease and moved to Ch'angnyong via the Koryong-Taegu Bridge. This bridge was blown up by an engineer battalion after the withdrawal. When the 35th Regiment, US 25th Division arrived on the evening of August 3, the 19th

Regiment, US 24 Division, at Chungamri moved to Ch'angnyong the next day.

The US 1st Cavalry Division moved to Waegwan from Chirye-Kimch' on. Although its rear guard 5th Regiment was attacked by the enemy and lost nearly a battalion strength, by August 3, the division was able to withdraw without much trouble. Only the 1st Battalion, 8th Cavalry Regiment, remained as a covering force at the Songju road, southwest of Waegwan. The division was supposed to blow up the bridges that connected to Taegu as soon as the covering force completed its withdrawal. As columns of refugees flooded in after the covering force, however, the demolition of the bridges was delayed to the night of August 4. The US troops tried to keep the refugees on the opposite bank and make a quick withdrawal across the bridge, but they could not control the refugees who were risking their lives to seek safety and freedom. As there was no alternative, however, the bridges were blown up in spite of the refugees. Thus, by August 4, most of the bridges across the Naktong River were blown up.

The ROK forces northeast of Waegwan also began their withdrawal. Through its Operation Order No. 91, the ROKA Headquarters instructed the I and II Corps to move to the south bank of the Naktong Defesive under the cover of the night between July 31 and August 1. Its Operation Order No. 94 ordered the troops to withdraw to the Naktong Defensive Line by the night of August 3.[10]

Accordingly, the 1st Division, ROKA II Corps, in Hamch'ang disengaged from the enemy on the night of August 1 and moved to Naktongri under the cover of the US 25th Division, which was then in Sangju. On the next day, under the cover of the 12th Regiment, the division crossed the river by boat and completed the occupation of new positions by the evening of August 3. To the right of the 1st Division, the ROKA 6th Division was ordered to withdraw from Hamch'ang-Chomch'on to Yonggidong. In the predawn hours of August 2, the division crossed the river under the cover of the 19th Regiment and arrived in the Yonggidong area.

The 8th Division, ROKA I Corps, was ordered to cross the Andong Bridge under the cover of the Capital Division and occupy new positions to the south. However, as this order from the corps was relayed rather late and as the Capital Division did not provide adequate cover, the 8th Division had to cross the river in some confusion and disorder. The Capital Division, for its part, moved to Kiran and organized defensive positions there. The 3rd Division on the east coast concentrated on organizing positions for the defense of Yongdok as it was instructed to carry out the present mission.

Thus, by the night of August 3, the ROK and UN forces mostly completed the occupation of new defensive positions. The ROKA Headquarters and the EUSA command post were located in Taegu, while the ROK I and II Corps directed their units from Uisong and Kunui, respectively.

With its 1st Division, the ROK II Corps took up the defense of a 42-km-long front between Waegwan and Nakjongri. Its 6th Division was responsible for a 26-km-long front from Nakjongri to Sangadong. The ROK II Corps assigned the 8th Division a 20-km-long front between Sangadong and Kumidong, while its Capital Division organized defensive positions along a 24-km-long front between Kumidong and Ch'ongsong. The 3rd Division, under the direct control of the ROKA Headquarters, was responsible for a 16-km-stretch in front of Yongdok.

As for the EUSA, the 1st Cavalry Division organized defensive positions along a 35-km-long front between Waegwan and the north of Hyonp'ung. The US 24th Division, together with the ROK 17th Regiment, was responsible for a 40-km-stretch from Hyonp'ung to Namji. The 25th Division, together with the 5th Regiment Combat Team and Min's unit, defended a 37-km-long front between Namji and Chindongri.

As the movement of the US 25th Division to Masan left the ROK forces with too wide a front, the ROKA Headquarters on August 11 reduced the ROK frontline. By Operation Order No. 119, the ROK forces subsequently moved to a new defense line and established positions along Waegwan-P'onamdong-Suamsan-Yuhak-san-Kunui-Pohyon-san.[11]

3. The Deployment of the North Korean People's Army

On August 1, 1950, the NKPA pushing the ROK Army and the UN troops further down to the south, reached the ROK and UN forces' newly formed defensive line, which extended from the city of chinju to Yongdok, including small cities like Kimch'on, Jomch'on, and Andong in between. At this time, the NKPA's front-line commander Kim Ch'aek, the four-star general, was known to be preparing to move his command post from Suanbo, north Ch'ungch'ung Province, to Kimch'on. And NKPA's Lt. Gen. Kim Ung, the I Corps Commander, and also Lt. Gen. Kim Mu Chong, Commander of the II Corps were maneuvering their attack troops in the suburbs of Kimch'on and Andong, respectively.

In addition, NKPA Gen. Kim Ch'aek deployed 10 infantry divisions reinforced by a tank division alongside the Naktong River and was maneuvering the 10th Division which had been kept in reserve, down toward the Naktong River to resume offensive operations there. He also marshalled the 7th and 9th Divisions in Seoul to get ready for future engagements down south.

So the NKPA's 15th and part of the 13th Divisions of the II Corps responsible for the zone between north of Waegwan and Yongdok, were to prepare for crossing the Naktong just in front of the ROK 1st Division deployed to the north of Waegwan, and eastward, where part of the NKPA's 13th and the 1st Divisions faced the ROK 6th Division. Beyond them, the NKPA 8th Division which had already captured Andong, stood in front of the ROK 8th Division.

Next in line, the NKPA 12th Division confronted the ROK Capital Division.
And finally at this time, on the east coast, the NKPA 5th Division and the 766th
Independent Infantry Regiment engaged the ROK 3rd Division.

〈Table 1〉   Combat Organization & Strength (Early August)

Area of Operation	ROK & US Army Unit	Strength
Yongdok	3d Division, ROK HQs	6,469
Ch'ongsong-Kumidong	Capital Div., ROK I Corps	5,778
Kumidong-Sangadong	8th Div., ROK I Corps	8,154
Sangadong-Nakjongdong	6th Div., ROK II Corps	6,570
Nakjongdong-Waegwan	1st Div., ROK II Corps	7,660
Waegwan-Hyunp'ung	1st Cav. Div., EUSAK	10,276
Hyunp'ung-Namji	24th Div., EUSAK	9,685
	17th Regiment, ROKA	1,762
Namji-Chindongri	5th Regimental Combat Team	
	25th Division, EUSAK	16,928

Area of Operation	NKPA Unit	Strength
Yongdok	5th Div. & 766th Independent	7,500
	Regiment, II Corps	
Ch'ongson-Kumidong	12th Division, II Corps	6,000
Kumidong-Sangadong	8th Division, II Corps	8,000
Sangadong-Nakjongdong	1st Division, II Corps	9,500
Nakjongdong-Waegwan	13th Division, II Corps	9,500
	15th Division, II Corps	5,000
	105th Armored Div., II Corps	3,000
	(with about 40 tanks)	
Waegwana-Hyunp'ung	3rd Division, I Corps	6,000
Hyunp'ung-Namji	4th Division, I Corps	7,000
Namji-Chindongri	6th Division plus 83rd Motorized	5,000
	Rgt. & 104th Security Rgt., I Corps	
	2nd Division in reserve(Kimch'on), I Corps	7,500

In the meantime, the 3rd Division, NKPA I Corps which was in charge of Waegwan-Masan frontal line, confronting the US 1st Cavalry Division, and the 4th Division of enemy I Corps facing the US 24th Division at the Naktong River bulge were preparing for crossing the river, respectively. The NKPA's 6th Division and the 83rd Motorized Regiment of the 105th Armored Division were located west of Masan, standing opposite the US 25th Division. In order to support both the enemy I Corps and II Corps, some 40 tanks of the enemy 105th Armored Division were divided between them. And also the NKPA 2nd Division was assembled in Kimch'on as a reserve unit.

In addition, the North Korean People's Army organized 12 Security Regiments (estimatedly 2,000 men for each regiment) under its Security Command to be used in the occupied areas. These Police Regiments manned their units with civilians recruited from respective local areas, thus 90% of the total unit strength were local civilians and the rest, only a few cadres. As these units were not properly equipped or trained for combat, their main job was limited to providing support to combat units. An exception to this, however, were the 102nd (Chonju), 103rd (Andong), and the 104th (Sach'on) Security Regiments which were given front-line combat missions.[12]

II. NKPA's August Offensive and the Defensive Crisis

1. Operational Goals and Combat Preparedness of Both Sides

(1) The Enemy's Offensive Goal and Its Combat Preparedness

By the end of July 1950 the NKPA, preparing for its river crossing across the Naktong, was planning to capture the city of Pusan as its ultimate goal. For this purpose, the enemy tried to quickly pursue the retreating ROK and UN troops down to the Naktong line thus, keeping them from building a strong defensive position there. In directing the main attack toward Taegu, the enemy simultaneously tried to tie up all available avenues of approach so that in case they succeeded in achieving a breakthrough, they would be able to exploit it rapidly reaching deep down in the rear areas of the remaining South Korea.[13]

The official North Korean history states that, "with successive strikes and daring maneuvers, we [the NKPA] should lay seige to both the US and south Korean troops at Kimch'on-Hamch'ang-Andong line to destroy them totally, and rapidly cross the Naktong to annihilate the enemy [the UN and ROKA troops] core groups in and around the Taegu area. By successfully doing this, we could press hard the Americans to the border line of Masan-Taegu-Yongch'on-P'ohang, creating favorable conditions for us to completely wipe them out. This is our ultimate operational goal of the August offensive."[14]

In line with this operational goal, the NKPA employed half of its front line units in the Taegu area, and developed plans for deploying the 15th and 13th Divisions of II Corps on the the Tabudong-Taegu axis, the 1st Division of the same II Corps in Kunwi-Taegu axis, and finally the 3rd and 10th Divisions of I Corps in Waegwan-Taegu axis in that order. And at the same time, the 6th Division was ordered to make an attack along the Masan-Pusan axis, the 4th Division along the Yongsan-Miryang axis, the 8th Division in the direction of Uisong-Yongch'on, the 12th Division on the Kigye-Kyongju axis, and the 5th Division in the direction of Yongdok-P'ohang, respectively.

As the NKPA's combat divisions were, however, suffering losses in the continuous engagements and battles, and despite commanders of higher echelon's operational directives, so they were unable to peform rapid pursuits against the reatreating the UN and ROK troops. Rather, they had to reequip and replace these losses for further engagements at this critical moment UN and ROK troops started south crossing the Naktong. As a result, they were losing the opportunity for a breakthrough against the UN defensive line.

The combat capability of the NKPA divisions dispersed along the Naktong River front, therefore, was sharply decreased, at this time, by about 50 or 60%, compared to that they had maintained at the early stage of the war. And what made the situation even worse for them was that, deprived of the air superiority by the UN forces, their daylight movement was extremely restricted and the replacements for the losses both in strength and combat equipment were so slow that their combat capability was continually being decimated. However, the enemy managed to maintain its initiative on the battle ground and tried to penetrate the UN defensive positions by increasing the numbers of so-called "Supervising Units" in each front line division.

By early August, 1950, the NKPA's line of communication, with its logistical bases in Manchuria and Vladivostok, was expanded greatly as its front line troops had pushed down to the south. At this time, its main communications routes between North and South Korea passed through Seoul and the enemy front line troops were supplied through dual routes by way of Seoul: one from Manchuria through P'yongyang and Seoul, the other from Vladivostok through the ports Ch'ongjin and Wonsan to Seoul. Accordingly, Seoul was another important logistical base for the enemy's front line units and it was about 300km from Seoul down to Waegwan where they were deployed.[5]

From the outset, the enemy forcibly mobilized tens of thousands of Seoul citizens to repair the damaged Han River bridge, in order to secure smooth ground communication routes. Thus, through those supply routes from Seoul to each local battle ground, they could support 11 combat divisions dispersed on the southern front line. As the U.N. aerial attacks on the enemy supply piles continued during the day, however, they were forced to transport war materiel only at night. So they sent the minimum numbers of equipment such as field guns, mortars, and machine guns needed urgently on the frontline, using motor vehichles and trains during the night. Enemy motorized units were no exception. They had been so severely damaged in the continuous fighting that they no longer had strength compared to that they had had shown in the early stages of the war.[16]

In the meantime, the enemy's strategic bases deep in the rear area of North Korea were almost devastated by the UN strategic aerial bombing with about 50 sorties. As a result of these bombings, not only were the communication routes between North Korea and Siberia blocked, but also the railway switchyard and an arsenal in P'yongyang, the port facilities including an oil factory in Wonsan, the Heungnam Synthesizing Chemical Factory, pier facilities in Najin, the Songjin Iron Works, and an Aluminum mill in Chinnamp'o were all destoyed. The North Korean combat support capability became virtually exhausted.

The first large tank replacement for the NKPA's August offensive operation apparently took place around the 15th of August, when 21 new tanks and 200 tank crews arrived at the front. However, the UN air strikes destroyed many new tanks before they could reach the battle zone.[17] In addition, the enemy's lack of fuel in mid-August also restricted the free movement of their troops.

(2) The Operational Strategy and Readiness for an Armageddon of Friendly Forces

In August, the missions imposed on Gen. Walker, the Commander of the US 8th Army, were to retain, above all, a foothold in Korea and to prepare to launch an attack once the Inchon landing operation plan secretly in progress at the time was implemented. Gen. Walker continually told his key staff officers and to his principal commanders the following :

> You keep your mind on the fact that we will win this thing by attacking. [I want for to] never let an opportunity to attack pass. I want the capability and opportunity to pass to the offensive. Until that time comes I want all commanders to attack—to raid—to capture prisoners and thus keep the enemy off balance. If that is done, more and more opportunities to hurt the enemy will arise and our troops will be better prepared to [convert] to a general offensive when things are ripe.[18]

In order for the UN and ROK troops to get ready for the counteroffensive at the Naktong line, Gen. Waker insisted on the fact that friendly forces continue to throw the enemy troops into confusion through succesive offensive actions and create favorable conditions to pass to the offensive. Even in the defensive positions, he further emphasized that we should not lose any opportunity to pass to the offensive.

In order to accomplish this mission, the ROK and UN troops within the defensive foothold made plans to secure, first of all, the safe communication routes for transporting reinforcements and other supplies to the battle zones, to demoralize all the enemy troops with superior artillery fire and aerial attacks, and finally to stage daring counterattacks against the enemy. Possibly through these efforts, the friendly troops could divert the situation in their favor and start the immediate counter-offensive actions.

At this time, the American ground combat units totaled more than 47,000 men and the principal ROK combat strength was estimated approximately at 45,000 men as of August 4. Thus the United Nations combat forces outnumbered the enemy at the front by approximately 92,000 to 70,000.[19] The relative UN strength compared to the North Koreans in early August was actually much more favorable than commonly represened. However, continued retreat and withdrawal of the UN troops that were being pressed hard by the North Koreans made it appear that the ROK and UN troops were far outnmubered by the enemy. At this time, therefore, it was urgent for the Eighth Army Commander to regroup new reserve units that would be committed at the Naktong line in order to hold it. Gen. Walker's daily concern was to decide how to form a new reserve, and where and when to commit them.

The US Eighth Army's intelligence estimate at that time, collected and analyzed from the aerial reconnaisance, interogation of prisoners and surrenderers, captured enemy documents and the local Korean civilians' statements concluded that the enemy would certainly make general frontal attacks on the Naktong River line with its main efforts on toward Taegu and Masan. And if they successfully made a penetration through the UN defense line, they would rapidly try to exploit it.[20] This estimation turned out to be almost true.

Meanwhile, for the UN troops to secure the opportunity at this time for turning the defensive efforts over to offensive, they should above all have reinforcements, and to meet the need, part of the US ground troops from the US mainland began to arrive. At the same time, th ROK Army itself recruited more soldiers to augment the American troops, and part of other United Nations ground forces, including the British Army, came to Korea's aid.

In line with these efforts for reinforcement in Korea, in the mainland United States, beefing up the armament was in progress so that increased reinforcement troops and supplies could quickly be committed to the Korean battle fronts. Thus, by the early August, the US President Harry S. Truman called in 4 National Guards units for active service duties, thus, getting ready to mobilize as many as 2,500,000 soldiers. In addition, he increased the amount of annual military spending from a once-reduced 13 billion dollars to 35 billion per year.[21] In the meantime, he ordered three civilian rubber factories to produce military supply materiel and made contracts with civilian shipping and airline companies for military transportation, based on his governmment's mobilizing programs of US industries.

From these decisions of the high-ranking American officials, important ground reinforcements from Hawaii and the US mainland began to arrive in Korea, starting from late July. The 5th Regimental Combat Team from Hawaii arrived first on July 31, the 9th and 23rd Infantry Regiments of the 2nd Infantry Division came from the continental United States between July 31 and August 5, and on August 2, the 1st Provisional Marine Brigade also arrived from California. With these reinforcements, the UN troops were able to build up a stronger defensive line.

Meanwhile, in late July, the US Navy carrier, Boxer, crossing the Pacific, arrived in Japan with 145 F-51 Mustangs. In early August, the US Far East Air Forces (FEAF) had 626 F-80 fighter planes and 264 F-51's but only 525 of them were in unit and available and ready for combat. They could carry mission in close support missions, including close interdiction, strategic bombing strikes, reconnaissance and cargo sorties.[22]

One of the most remarkable US troop reinforcements was the replacement of the tank battalions. On August 3, the 89th Medium Tank Battalion, for the first time, arrived in Korea with 50 M4A3 tanks to be attached to the US 25th Division. Other tanks were on the way. Thus the initial imbalance between the UN and NKPA troop equipment began gradually to disappear.

In the meantime, closely related with the reinforcements in strength and equipment, the supply of war materiel was also conspicuously increased. By this time, logistic supplies to the soldiers under the United Nations Command were shipped to Pusan, from nearby Japan at approximately 1 ton per each man. The Eighth US Army, accordingly, planned to increase the resupply rate from the existing 45 days to a minimum of 120 days.[23] And during the month of

July 1950, a total of 309,314 measurement tons of supplies and equipment were offloaded at Pusan, mostly shipped by 230 ships arriving and 214 departing.[24]

At this time, the ROK Government and the US Eighth Army agreed that Korea itself should provide war materiel it could produce, while the US Army, through its logistical system, should provide for other necessary items which the Korean government could not provide.[25] In order to implement this agreement, the Korean government made its own gradational budgets from phases 1 to 4 to cope with the emergency needs. So the ROK defense budget, initially amounted at 27.7% (25 billion won) of the total general expenditure, was raised up to 72 to 75% of the general budget.[26] At the same, for the purpose of the war, the ROK Defense Ministry commandeered civilian properties scattered around South Kyongsang Province and conveyed stored goods in the Chonnam Textile Manufacturing Company to Pusan to use them as substitutes for soldiers' outfit. The government collected for other textile manufacturing factories in and around Taegu and Pusan, trying to meet the war demands.[27]

Armory bases were established in Pusan and on Chejudo island to manufacture ammunition, grenades and parts of small arms, and also to do repair work or maintenance on captured weapons. Volunteers from the Korean Red Cross Society came to the refugees' aid, helped distribute relief supplies, and offered some medical help for the wounded soldiers. That was not all. Members of the Korean National Salvation League at the time volunteered for free labor service for repair and manufacturing work to help the war efforts.[28]

Meanwhile, the ROK Defense Ministry and the US Army made an agreement which reorganized 5 ROK Army combat divisions, activating several infantry divisions, and augmenting parts of Korean enlisted replacements to the US Army units. The ROK Army headquarters, for the first time on August 1, instituted the Korean Army Training Center in Taegu, to systematize the replacement process.

At this time, the number of volunteer students and volunteer service workers was greatly increased. Korean students in groups of ten or more, from all over the country, daily volunteered for the military basic training in the ROK Army units, and successfully acomplished the combat and combat support missions given to them. Beginning from mid. July 1950, considerable numbers of these students joined the ROK Army units stationed in their towns or cities. As one example, the ROK 25th Regiment, one of the replacement training units at the time in Taegu, enlisted about 2,000 students to be trained as army recruits, and among these trainees, some were transfered to Cheju island to be trained to become NCOs, and some others were commissioned as junior ROK Army officers upon graduation from the Officer Candidate Schools.

On July 27, the Korean Student Volunteer Army took an oath for participating in the war, saying that they "swear to save the nation and the people" in Taegu with the approval from the ROK Army headquarters. Separate from this event, the ROK Army Troop Information and Education Office, with an aim to conduct guerilla warfare on the enemy, organized a Student Cadre's Unit comprising 1,500 students. This unit was committed to the front, together with the existing irregular forces stationed in Miryang.

Labor service workers were also helping combat troops on the battle front as well as in the rear areas. They had been recruited by the ROK Army units from among the refugees or citizens in nearby towns and cities, and most of them had volunteered at the time for the job at "the National Service Workers Corps." As these volunteer workers turned out to be effective helping hands, each ROK Army regiment, beginning from early August, recruited additional members. Thus in each ROK Army battalion, an average of 50 to 60 volunteer service workers were on active duty.[29]

Some volunteer workers were organized into the US Army units to provide combat support services, too. Initially these people took charge of the cargo-working jobs at the piers, and transporting war materiel to the battle zones; however, in July of the same year, some of them were recruited by Korean police officials to be augmented to the US Army, being organized into three transportation companies. Their duties involved not only transporting US Army supplies, but also filling aircraft with gas, constructing and maintaining air strips, roads and railways. This was the very beginning of the Korean Service Corps which would officially be activated later, as the ROK Army and the Eighth US Army to Korea (EUSAK) had agreed in early August. Their mission was to provide various services and work to the US Army units.[30]

Meanwhile, some ROK Army and the Korean police personnel were also attached to the US Army to support its combat missions. Gen. Walker initially had made a request for several Korean enlisted cadres at the Taegu replacement training center to be augmented to the US Army through B.G. Francis W. Farrell, the Chief of KMAG. Later, on July 23, Cho Byung Ok, Minister of Home Affairs, and Gen. Walker agreed to allow 15,000 Korean policemen to be attached to the US Army, which would effectively mop up the enemy guerilla forces that had infiltrated into the US Army defensive sectors.[31]

These Korean policemen turned out to be very capable in accomplishing the combat missions given to them. As an example, 133 Korean combat policemen who had joined the 1st Battalion, 7th Cavalry Regiment, US Army suffered a serious loss in the battle, but of the wounded, all refused evacuation except one who could not walk.[32]

In the meantime, the refugee problem was a constant source of trouble and danger to the UN Command in forming defensive positions. During mid-July, it was estimated that about 380,000 refugees had crossed into ROK Army held territory, and that this number was increasing at the rate of 25,000 daily. The refugees were most numerous in the areas of enemy advance. Particularly, the volume of refugees moving through the Seoul-Pusan highway was greater

Refugee Camp on the Naktong River

than at any other time in the war.[33]

In order to alleviate this difficulty, the ROK Government, on July 10, had issued an order to related government officials to the effect that the refugees should be accomodated in dispersion. Accordingly, the ROK Government started to control the refugees by installing refugee camps, stationing combined military and police checkpoints which would give assistance, such as issuing refugee certificates and ration tickets.[34]

Despite these refugee controlling measures, the numerous refugees on the main avenues occasionally hindered the smooth movement of the UN troops and in some cases, the refugees undoubtedly helped the enemy infiltrate the UN troop positions. Disguising themselves as refugees the enemy fifth column frequently infiltrated deep into the rear areas. In the Yongdong area, the enemy trying to make a passage through a minefield, forcing refugees to lead them. And in the vicinity of the Waegwan Bridge, the refugees crowding in succession close on the foot of the retreating UN troops certainly impeded the operations near Waegwan.[35]

In conclusion, the Korean police concentrated then efforts on controlling and protecting these refugees by permitting them to escape from the battle zones as soon as possible. And on August 4, the ROK Government promulgated a provisional law on "Refugee Accomodation" to the effect that it would hike the efficiency of the UN troops' operation, decrease the opportunity for possible refugees' rebellion, and prevent, in advance, epidemic diseases from developing. Based on this law, the refugees took shelters in designated camps.[36]

2. The Crisis in the Northern Taegu Area

Just before the impending Armageddon on the Naktong River front, the NKPA troops were well aware of the fact that their own war support capabilities in the rear had been rapidly declining compared to that of the UN Forces, thus upsetting the existing balance. Time was also running against them. As the enemy might have initially estimated, it could not win a protracted war. Thus facing a crossroad of decision-making, the NKPA Frontline Command, in early August 1950, assembled three divisions, the 15th, 13th, and 1st of the II Corps in an arc around Hamch'ang and Sangju area, and placed two divisions, the 3rd and 10th of the same II Corps, on the west of Waegwan, and prepared for a massive attack on Taegu.

Opposite the five North Korean divisions with their principal axis of attack oriented toward Taegu, was a total of three ROK and US Army divisions dispersed for the defense. Surrounding Taegu, from Hill 328 north of Waegwan to Nakjongri, the ROK Army 1st Division took up the defensive positions, from Hill 303 in Waegwan to Hyunp'ung, the US 1st Cavalry Division, and from Nakjongri to the west of Uisong, the ROK 6th Division took up their defensive sectors, respectively. As the US 25th Division moved to the Masan area, the ROK 1st Division deployed its regiments on the extended defense line of 42km, four times as wide as the regular front, from the estuary of the Wich'on to the north of Waegwan. On the southern banks of the river, from south to north, the ROK 15th, 11th and 12th Regiments in that order took up the positions linking up with the 1st US Cavalry Division to the left. To the right of the ROK 12th Regiment, however, there was a gap of 4 km between this regimental position and those of the ROK 6th Division.

The US 1st Cavalry Division had a great frontage that extended from Waegwan to Hyunp'ung, the west of Taegu. Thus from north to south, the 5th, 8th, and 7th(−) Cavalry Regiments were on line in that order with only a battalion in reserve. The ROK 6th Division put its 19th Regiment in position just in front of Yonggidong, the 2nd Regiment in Changji-bong to its west, and kept the 7th Regiment in reserve. But the divison was separated from other adjacent units. At this time, however, Korean troops recovered their morale and fighting spirit as fresh recruits and student volunteers, including service workers, began to arrive at each division.

Meanwhile, the NKPA 13th and 15th Divisions, after completing reorganization in and around Sangju and Kimch'on area, advanced toward Nakjongri and to its north Kumi, respectively. And across the Naktong, on the banks to the west of Waegwan, was the enemy 3rd Division assembled in Songju area with the aim to attack Taegu. In order to secure close cooperation between these enemy divisions, the 10th Division was moving to the Koryong area.[37] The enemy 1st Division, reformed in the Hamch'ang area was, with parts of its strength, in secret preparation for crossing the Naktong, pressing hard on the ROK 6th Division.

These enemy divisions were superior to the ROK Army units in terms of strength and firepower with many green replacements drafted by the compulsory induction system. The morale of all enemy units, however, was very low because of decreasing supplies and the threatening UN aerial attacks. In such circumstances, the enemy troops sent out reconnaissance teams to locate favorable spots for the crossing of the river.

The depth of the water at the time was only 1 or 1.5 meters due to the long spell of the most severe draught in almost 30 years; so that the enemy troops could wade the river in front of the UN defensive lines. Within the UN defensive sectors, the roads that lead to Taegu from Koryong, Waegwan, Sangju and Andong could provide the penetrating enemy with favorable avenues of approach.

The enemy started crossing the Naktong on August 3. The ROK Army 1st Division, which had taken up positions along the main avenue of approach, immediately attacked the NKPA 13th Division crossing the river at Nakjongri and drove it back several times. On the next day, August 4, when the enemy began to cross the river in full-scale, however, the ROK 1st Division was forced to cut down its frontage as it was impossible to effectively defend the wide frontage with a bulge on the north in its defensive line. At the same time, the division placed its 12th Regiment in reserve. On the next day, August 5, the ROK division came under general attack from the NKPA 13th Division.

Crossing the river through the ROK 12th Regiment sector, one NKPA regiment attacked the ROK 11th Regiment in the high mountains in Naksandong area and captured several hill positions. But the ROK 11th Regiment immediately made a bold counterattack on the enemy troops with the 1st Battalion of the 12th Regiment attached to it and, just in the nick of time, turned them back.

At this time, the enemy troops, dispersed in front of the US 1st Cavalry Division, were still probing for favorable crossing sites, while on its left, the ROK 6th Division engaged the enemy 1st Division that had crossed the river between Hamch'ang and Sangju. Thus from August 5, the UN troops and the enemy led by tanks, were locked in bloody fights pushing and tugging each other.

Crisis in the North of Taegu

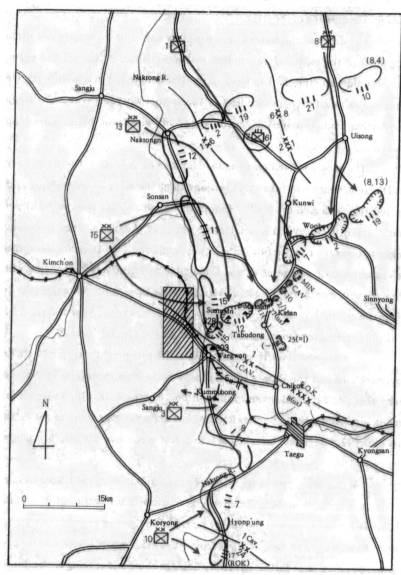

From the dawn of August 8, the ROK 1st Division also came under attack from the enemy 13th and 15th Divisions which attempted crossing of the Naktong. The enemy troops had started wading across the 1.2m deep water between Sonsan and Kumi the day before. On a covertly built underwater bridge at the Majin ferry site, the enemy tanks crossed the river, together with foot soldiers of one enemy regiment, to make a frontal attack on the ROK 15th Regiment. At the same time, another enemy regiment crossed the river at the Kangch'ang ferry to attack the ROK 11th Regiment. The underwater bridge turned out to be an excellent means of river crossing for an enemy deprived of air superiority, as it could not be easily discovered by aerial reconnaissance.[38]

The ROK 11th Regiment immediately knocked down 4 enemy tanks with aid from the UN aeiral attacks and its own firepower; however, resisting the major enemy crossing was beyond its own capacities. Ultimately the Regiment, allowing for the enemy's advance, withdrew to the Haep'yung-ch'on line trying to resist the enemy there. On the next day, the Regiment, monitoring the approaching enemy columns, called in a preregistered barrage of artillery fire on the enemy. At the same time, by committing a special antitank team to destroy five enemy tanks, it could hold out its positions, and thus achieve a great success.[39]

The ROK 15th Regiment[40] faced a serious danger of being penetrated but it narrowly escaped with the support from the ROK 12th Regiment(−) which was kept in division reserve. Rather, the 15th Regiment made an audacious counterattack on the enemy with UN aerial assistance and recaptured those hill positions that had once been occupied by the enemy.[41] The Commander of the ROK 12th Regiment, at that time, committed a 12-man antitank special team led by Lt. Hyun Dok Jin. And this team, comprised of 4 small groups with 3 men in each group, infiltrated into the enemy attack zone to surprise enemy tanks. They launched rocket fire into the turrets and treads of the tanks and succeeded in destroying four enemy tanks.[42] Immediately after this success, the Regiment counterattacked the enemy at dawn of August 10, driving it completely back to the west bank of the river. A UN Air Force flight, in the meantime, conducted saturation bombing of the discovered underwater bridge built at the Majin ferry for two consecutive days.

At about this time, the ROK 6th and the enemy 1st Divisions continued their offensive and defensive battle until part of the ROK 19th Regimental line was broken through. The Division was forced to surrender the Yonggidong area and to withdraw to Wi-ch'on only to hold the enemy in check.[43]

Meanwhile, the US 1st Cavalry Division also came under the enemy attack of the 3rd Division crossing the Naktong about 0300, August 9. The enemy's lead unit launched an assault crossing of the river at a ferry site near the village of Noch'on, 3km south of the Waegwan bridge, holding their weapons above the water.[44] The US 5th Cavalry Regiment, deployed on the opposite bank, immediately directed concentrated fire against the enemy force. However, it was too late to discover all the enemy soldiers and the bulk of the enemy regiment reached the east bank safely.

The regimental commander, in the meantime, estimated that other enemy units would immediately cross the river and issued an order to his subordinates to be well prepared for this. As the commander had expected, the NKPA 7th and 9th Regiments of the 3rd Division started crossing the river near Singi. Having been fully alerted the supporting mortars and artillery on the spot fired flares and star shells brightly illuminating these two NKPA regiments in midstream. American fire from all supporting weapons concentrated on these enemy troops. Instantly, it decimated most of the enemy troops and forced some of them to recross the river.

Later on, however, a UN patrol spotted a battalion sized enemy group which had infiltrated to Kummu-bong hill. The 1st US Cavalry Division Commander, having received the report from the patrol leader, that morning, ordered the Commander of the 1st Battalion, 7th Cavalrey Regiment to eliminate the enemy penetration.[45] After the preparatory artillery fired on the hill, the battalion moved at once, accompanied by five tanks of the Heavy Tank Battalion. As the hill, however, was covered with thick, high brush, and the weather was so hot the battalion could not advance further. The next morning, the battalion resumed the attack against the enemy after heavy air strikes and artillery preparations had blasted the hill. By maneuvering the tanks to the reverse side of the hill, the battalion could attack the enemy troops from both sides, and finally succeed in driving them back.

During the morning fight, however, the assistant division commander, the chief of staff, the G-2, and several military policemen were ambushed and nearly all were wounded on the Waegwan road at Kummu-bong hill. At that moment, the Cavalry Division Commander and his aide stopped near the hill to talk with the 1st Battalion executive officer and a small group of men. An enemy mortar shell made a direct hit on the group, killing or wounding everyone there except the Division Commander and his aide. And when the hill was examined carefully, it was found that the NKPA 7th Regiment of the 3rd Division had been largely destroyed. The 1st Battalion of the 7th Cavalry Regiment counted between 300 and 400 enemy dead in the battle area.

Thus the enemy 3rd Division, which had been the first to enter Seoul at the beginning of the war and had been entitled the "Seoul Division," ended in catastrophe, trying to cross the Naktong south of Waegwan. As the result of this defeat, the once mighty 3rd Division was reduced to a disorganized unit of some 2,500 men and was now temporarily out of the fight for Taegu.[46]

At the same time, the enemy II Corps Commander, committed his 10th Division to the attack against Taegu from the west and southwest. Initially, the 10th Division, which had not been in combat, was to make a coordinated attack with the NKPA 3rd Division to capture Taegu, but it arrived at Waegwan too late, on or about August 8. There it received its combat orders to cross the Naktong River and cut the Taegu-Pusan main supply road. The division assembled in the Koryong area on August 11. The 25th and 29th Regiments of the enemy division advanced to Yongp'o and Hyunp'ung across the Naktong to make the midnight assault crossing with the 27th Regiment in reserve.

One of the enemy battalions of the 29th Regiment was the first unit of the 10th Division to cross the river unopposed near the boundary area between the US 1st Cavalry and 24th Divisions. It immediately captured the high ground near the Hyunp'ung area. This place had initially belonged to the US 24th Division; however, since the ROK 17th Regiment moved into it following the American division, it had remained almost unfortified.

The enemy lead battalion of the 25th Regiment, in the meantime, started crossing the Naktong in the vicinity of the Yongp'o bridge at dawn on August 12 under the cover of dense fog, where the 2nd Battalion, US 7th Cavalry Regiment had been deployed. At that time the 2nd Battalion which had taken up positions about 2km away from the crossing sites learned of the enemy crossing; however, it drove the enemy troops back and dispersed them with the immediate, and powerful assistance of the US air strikes and supporting artillery fire. Still, a more determined enemy tried to cross the Naktong again at the identical sites and the battalion came under attack. But again the air bombing and the pre-registered barrage fire of the US artillery repulsed them. Right after this river-crossing battle, the crippled enemy 10th Division stopped their attack for several days and there was a momentary lull in the fighting.

Meanwhile, the ROK Army leaders were groping for a vital revision in their strategy for maneuvering the ROK troops. Although the US troops were able to repulse the enemy using the Naktong River as an obstacle, the South Korean troops could not, except the 1st Division. In addition, most of the ROK troops had wider frontages than those of the US troops, so that the close coordination between them could not be expected. In such circumstances, the ROK Army's high ranking officials concluded that the South Korean troops could not effectively hold the enemy in check. Therefore, on August 11, the ROK Army issued an order to the 1st Division to move to the north of Waegwan to take up a reduced defensive line that began from Hill 303, through Tabudong and Kunwi, and ended at Pohyun Mountain.[47] To accomplish this misssion, the division, completing its fight in the Naktong River bank sector, withdrew during the night of the next day to new defenssive positions. Likewise, the ROK 6th Division which had been fighting on the left of the ROK 1st Division moved back to the south of Kunwi.

Thus the two South Korean divisions, the 1st and the 6th, were to defend Taegu in the Tabudong and Kunwi area. The Tabudong area which had been held by the 1st Division was a critical terrain feature in control of the road to Taegu. On its left lay Hill 328, and sloping down crosswise ridges of Suam-san and Yuhak Mountain. And on its right, was a hill mass sloping down from Kasan and P'algong-san. On the right side of the 1st Division, the 6th Division took up positions in the southern area of Kunwi and Uisong, which was favorable for the defender with the Wi-ch'on running from east to west in front of the high hill mass of Ungbong-san and Kuktong-san.

On August 13, shortly after the ROK 1st Division had assembled in the Tabudong area, its 15th Regiment advanced to the area of Hill 328, the 12th Regiment to the Suam-san and Yuhak-san area, and the 11th Regiment to the Sinjumak area, respectively. In the meantime, on that day, part of the enemy 3rd Division that had crossed the Naktong at the Yakmok ferry site began to attack Hill 328, while the enemy 15th Division reached Yuhak-san, a step earlier than the ROK troops. The NKPA 13th Division, approaching toward the ROK 11th Regimental front, preoccupied Hill 674 by turning part of its troops around the

ROK Army regiment that had been late in deployment. The result of this action was that the ROK 1st Division faced a serious crisis of being penetrated in the center of its defensive positions and of the fall of Tabudong into enemy's hands. This happened because of the tactical errors made by the ROK troops themselves as they had assembled in the rear area instead of immediately occupying the positions during the period of troop diversions.

The ROK 6th Division, with an idea that they burn the bridges behind them at the high ground of northern Wi-ch'on, placed its 7th Regiment on the Kunwi-Hoyryong road which had been presumed as a possible avenue of approach for the motorized enemy units. And the division also deployed the 2nd Regiment and the 1st Battalion, 19th Regiment at the north of the Wi-ch'on to defend the Uisong-Uihong avenue, while having the 19th(−) Regiment, which had suffered heavy losses in the past, in reserve at the Uihong area. This regiment, in the meantime, was reinforced by about 300 student volunteers.[48] On that day, August 13, the enemy 1st Division assembled in Kunwi, as well as the enemy 8th Division to which the 103rd Police Regiment had been attached, were waiting for the right moment to move down south at Uisong.[49]

The enemy troops which had assembled in front of Taegu resumed their general attack on August 15, the day initially set for "liberating South Korea." The ROK 15th Regiment, 1st Division, engaged this enemy at Hill 328 struggling for the possession of it, and the ROK 12th Regiment made repeated counterattacks against the enemy troops to recapture the Yuhak-san mountain. The ROK 11th Regiment, however, was finally forced to retreat to the Pokgok area by a regimental size enemy unit led by 7 tanks.[50]

The ROK 7th Regiment, 6th Division, was also pushed out of its position by the enemy 1st Division, and the ROK 2nd Regiment of the 6th Division engaged the enemy night patrol team of the 8th Division from the night before.[51] The ROK 7th Regiment, in the meantime, drove the infiltrating enemy troops back several times with audacious counterattacks supported by close air strikes and artillery fire. Particulary, the 2nd Battalion of the regiment on the left held its position fighting to the last ditch.[52] The 2nd and the 19th Regiments of the ROK 6th Division were also hard pressed by the enemy 8th Division from the dawn of August 17, but they successfully held their positions. The most remarkable thing to remember of this battle is that despite the heavy loss, the 1st Battalion of the ROK 19th Regiment repulsed the enemy troops and stubbornly held their position to the end. Almost half of their strength was lost and the commander was seriously injured.[53]

Meanwhile, from August 14, the enemy 10th Division, having once failed at its attempt to cross the Naktong on August 11-12, resumed its attack just in front of the US 1st Cavalry Division positioned in Waegwan area by committing its reserve unit, the 27th Regiment. On that day, part of the enemy troops crossed the river again over the Yongp'o bridge and their main crossing was to follow at Pansong, south of the bridge. The US 7th Cavalry Regiment engaged it with the help of air strikes and supporting artillery fire. The US artillery fired approximately 1,800 rounds into the enemy concentration to repulse it. In this battle, the enemy 10th Division suffered a total 2,500 casualties including 1,000 of the other two regiments and retreated from the battle zone being reduced to a disorganized unit.[54]

About this time on August 14, part of the enemy 3rd Division, menacing the ROK 1st Division on its left, was approching toward Chako-san (Hill 303), north of Waegwan, held by the 2nd Battalion of the the US 5th Cavalry Regiment. This hill was also a critical terrain feature in control of the main Seoul-Pusan railroad and highway crossing of the Naktong, as well as Waegwan itself. Shortly after midnight, an infantry company and mortar platoon on top of the hill came under an attack trying to encircle them.

The 5th Cavalry Regiment Commander committed company-size troops reinforced by tanks several times until August 17, to attack the enemy that had captured Hill 303. But heavy enemy mortar fire stopped them each time. On that day, however, as the airplanes successfully attacked dropping napalm and bombs, firing rockets and strafing, together with artillery preparation, the infantry attacked the Chako-san (Hill 303) unopposed and secured it without suffering any casualties.

Immediately after the battle, they counted approximately 200 enemy bodies that littered the hill, and survivors were presumed to have fled. On the other hand, in regaining the hill, the US 5th Cavalry Regiment came upon a pitiful scene — the bodies of 26 American mortarmen, hands tied in back, sprayed with burp gun bullets. These soldiers, encircled by the enemy, had been informed at dawn on August 15, through radio communication, that a platoon of some 60 ROK soldiers would come to reinforce them. A little later a group of Koreans appeared on the slope and mistaking them for ROK soldiers, they allowed them to approach. But the Koreans turned out to be enemy soldiers and the American mortarmen were taken captive and killed. Because of this incident on Hill 303, the UN Forces Commander issued a strong statement to the NKPA, denouncing the atrocities; however, additional atrocities occurred during this phase of the war.[55]

On the other hand, from 11:58 through 12:24, August 16, when the enemy attack began mounting concern for the safety of Taegu, a massive carpet bombing, unprecedented in Korean war history, was executed. Ninety-eight B-29s, on order by the United Nations Forces Commander who had decided to solve the crisis on the Taegu front, arrived over the target area, a rectangular area 5.6km by 12km of the Naktong River in the northwest area of Waegwan. The bombers dropped approximately 960 tons of bombs. But the damage done to the enemy could not be evaluated because of smoke and dust over the bombed area. Observations from the air and the impact area by the ground patrols were extremely difficult. Accordingly, the second pattern bombing that had been scheduled for August 19 was cancelled. Information obtained later from prisoners indicated that despite heavy damages on enemy artillery, engineer, signal, armor and ammuntion supplies and others dispersed on the west bank of the river, the enemy divisions had already crossed it to be deployed opposite the UN troops.[56] Therefore, it can be concluded that the pattern bombing had not effective in weakening the strength of the river-crossing enemy units, even though it could have had impact on the morale of the attacking troops.

On August 16, in spite of being bombed the day before, the enemy, with an objective to penetrate into the Ka-san area, started attacking Hill 466 on the west side of Tabudong, from their position on Hill 741. The ROK 1st Division, which had been in charge of the area faced a critical situation: to be penetrated by the enemy or to try and hold the hill position to the end. The US Eighth Army, having closely watched this enemy threat, committed, on August 17, the 27th Regiment of the 25th Division which had been kept in army reserve, to the Tabudong defensive line.[57]

At this time, the enemy units which had opposed the US 1st Cavalry Division ceased their activities due to serious losses in the preceding battles, and as a result, days of relative quiet arrived on this front.

However, starting at dawn, August 18, the enemy 8th Division led by 3 tanks resumed its attack southward, and the ROK 2nd Regiment, 6th Division drove it back with the help of the UN fighter-bomber' strikes. The ROK 19th Regiment of the same division also engaged enemy troops, on its defensive positions, and repulsed them. Faced with this strong resistance in this area, the enemy then pressed hard in the Sinjumak-and-Tabudong axis jeopardizing the safety of Taegu.

That morning on August 18 when mortar shells, fired by the enemy troops that had penetrated into Ka-san, landed at Taegu railroad station a crisis developed among the people. The ROK Government during the day ordered the evacuation of Taegu, and the Government itself moved its capital to Pusan. Thus great confusion prevailed in Taegu for a time ; however, the Home Affairs Minister at the time, Cho Byung Ok, accompanied by Korean policemen, personally appeared on the streets to win the hearts of the people, cancelling the evacuation order. Thus, he barely managed to restore order.[58]

In order to find a way out of the difficulties and to regain the defense line that had been penetrated by the enemy, on August 18, the ROK 1st Division commenced an audacious counter-penetration into the enemy positions together with the supporting US 27th Regiment. To win the battle, the American regiment placed its armor battalion on the road on the Taebudong-Tolmori axis, and deployed its two infantry battalions along the lower ridges on both sides of the road. Thus, the regiment coordinating foot soldiers and tank crews led the attacking troops. At the same time, the ROK 1st Division was to attack along high ground on either side of the road maintaining close contact with the US troops.

The enemy, opposing the ROK 1st Division, fiercely countered this coordinated attack with tanks reinforced afresh. It made the frontal attack against the ROK troops during the night, employing coordinated infantry-armor tactics. As a result, a fierce battle between both sides lasted a while. In front of Ch'onp'yong village, the US 27th Regiment destroyed two enemy tanks, with 3.5-inch bazookas. The undaunted enemy column, however, continued its advance, only being interrupted by antitank mines.[59] While the ROK 15th Regiment continued its battle for the possession of Hill 328, using hand-grenades and other weapons, the 12th Regiment suffered heavy losses in the battle at Suam-san. On August 19, the enemy, despite the serious losses, seized the hill positions, and further engaged the ROK 12th Regiment at the Yuhak-san mass. As a result, offensive and defensive battles between enemy and ROK troops were repeated for quite a while; however, the enemy that had tried to exploit its penetration into the ROK defense line could not make it.

Right on that day, the US Eighth Army ordered the 23rd Regiment, 2nd Division to the rear area Tujondong in order to increase the depth of its defensive positions. Meanwhile, the ROK Army headquarters ordered the 10th Regiment, 8th Division to be attached to the ROK 1st Division which had been deployed in the Ka-san area. Still, the general military situation in the vicinity of Tabudong showed that the UN forces, even with the supporting one ROK and two US regiments, felt uneasy.

In order to fill up vacancies that had resulted from an average of 600 or 700 losses in strength every day, the ROK 1st Division recruited students and other civilians. And by that time, an average of 50 or 60 service workers in each battalion helped the combatants, by carrying foodstuff, ammunition and other supply items to the battle fronts and evacuating wounded soldiers on A-frames to the rear areas.[60]

By that time, the ROK 6th Division on the right had, on the whole, held its defense line alongside the Wi-ch'on Stream. However, the enemy 14th Regiment, 1st Division, penetrated into a gap that had developed between the ROK 1st and 6th Divisions and advanced to the Kalmae-Hoyryong line. Having captured the road that led to Kunwi-Tabudong, the enemy further began to threaten the eastern flank of the ROK 6th Division. At this time, the ROK Army Headquarters, after closely examining situations on the whole battle fronts, made a conclusion that the P'ohang front had been settled. Accordingly, it diverted the ROK 5th Regiment (Min's Unit) of the 7th Division and the Independent Cavalry Regiment which had all been deployed in the P'ohang area to the 6th Division line, by means of attaching them to the division.[61] Thus the Commander of the 6th Division, to close the gap between the 1st and his Divisions,

ROKA troops training to fire 105mm artillery

could commit the 5th Regiment to the southern hill mass at Hyoryong, and the Independent Cavalry Regiment to the Kasandong area. With these readjustments, the Commander was able to cope with the possible enemy penetration in the direction of either Hyoryong-Tabudong-Taegu or Hyoryong-Ka-san-Taegu, and further, by using his unit elements, he could strengthen the defensive positions on the Upo-Sinryong avenue of approach.

On the other hand, during the night of August 20, a significant change in the tactics of the enemy was observed. The enemy, possibly making an estimation that it could no longer penetrate into the Tabudong defense line, ordered its 15th Division that had been deployed in the Yuhak-san area to move toward Uisong. This enemy division was given a new attack mission against the ROK 8th Division on the Yongch'on front.[62] However, as part of the enemy 3rd Division took up positions in the Suam-san area, and its 13th Division did on the left of the Yuhak-san, they were no longer menacing to the defender. It was good luck for the ROK troops which had been suffering in the Tabudong front faced with increased pressure from the enemy 1st Division.

From August 21, the progress of the battle for the ROK 1st Division began to improve. What was worthy of notice during the night battle on that day was that a tank-for-tank fight took place in the valley of Tabudong for the first time in the history of the Korean War. On that very night, the enemy troops led by tanks and self-propelled guns ventured a large-scale counterattack directed toward the US 27th Regiment. The enemy 11th Regiment played a supporting role in the attack.

The US 27th Regiment bombarded the enemy with concentrated artillery and mortar fire available at that time, trying to separate the tanks from the infantry. American tanks were called in to hold the enemy. Suddenly, the tank fire from both sides became intense in the valley of Tabudong. Armor-piercing shells fired from the tanks hurtled through the night, and the reverberations of the gun reports appeared to the men of the regiment witnessing the wild scene like bowling balls streaking down an alley toward targets at the other end. So they instantly coined the name "Bowling Alley" battle. In this night battle which had lasted about five hours, the enemy column was destroyed. At dawn, the US troops tabulated 1,300 enemy casualties including 9 tanks, 4 self-propelled guns and several trucks destroyed.[63]

On the morning of August 22, the next day, Lt. Col. Chong Bong Uk, commanding the artillery regiment supporting the NKPA 13th Division, deserted, with a leather map case, to a ROK 1st Division position.

Thus the enemy units appeared to be extremely demoralized.[64] The defected Chong gave precise information on the location of his artillery, and the UN fighter-bombers, based on his statement, immediately attacked seven operable 122-mm howitzers and thirteen 76-mm. guns emplaced and camouflaged in an orchard, and other assembly areas. These bombardments virtually made helpless the artillery fire support for the enemy 13th Division. The ROK 12th Regiment which had attacked the enemy eight times was, for the first time, able to recapture the Yuhak-san area by making a surprise attack that night.[65] During the day, Gen. Collins, the US Army Chief of Staff, accompanied by Lt. Gen. Walker, the Commander of the Eighth US Army and the ROK Army Chief of Staff, Lt. Gen. Chung Il Kwon vistited the US and ROK troops that had fought in the Tabudong area, to encourage them.[66]

Despite the strenthened defensive capability of the ROK troops in the east of the Tabudong area, on August 23, the enemy 1st Regiment, 1st Division, seized nearby Hill 741 which had been held by the ROK 10th Regiment, 8th Division. The enemy further infiltrated part of his troops into the Ka-san area to overrun the command post of the ROK 11th Regiment and to attack the American artillery positions nearby. Undaunted, however, by this enemy surprise attack, the ROK 1st Division, together with the US 27th Regiment, counterattacked from the Bowling Alley toward Sinjumak. The division succeeded in repelling the enemy at Sinjumak. Its 10th and the US 23rd Regiments, in the meantime, closely coordinating with the ROK 15th Regiment and the Independent Cavalry Regiment that had been attached to nearby ROK 6th Division, repulsed the enemy from the Ka-san area. Thus the ROK troops could finally recapture Hill 741 and surmount the crisis that had been created by the NKPA's August offensive in the east of the Tabudong area.

The ROK 1st Division, now having stabilized its last-ditch stand in this front, was able to gain control of the tactical initiative. With the enemy turned back north of Taegu, the US 27th Infantry was relieved from its supporting mission to return to its parent unit, the 25th Division in the Masan area. And at that time, the enemy with notably weakened combat capability virtually terminated his action. The enemy 13th Division could have been helpless, according to the defected enemy artillery unit commander's information, with a total 3,000 losses including 1,500 casualties on the Yuhak-san battle front alone.

On August 26, the ROK 1st Division received orders to relieve the

American troops, and even during the period of the takeover, it did not loosen its own vigilance over the defense line. As if to signal the successful completion of the searching patrol missions, MSgt. Pae Sung Sub, acting leader of the 1st Platoon, Reconnaissance Company of the ROK 12th Regiment, led an eleven-man patrol behind the North Korean lines to the enemy 13th Division command post located in Sangnimdong. There, at dawn of August 27, the next day, his patrol killed several enemy soldiers and captured three prisoners including two officers. For this exploit, the daring sergeant and his men received an award plus a double promotion of rank.[67]

On the next day, August 28, the ROK division took the Suam-san back again, 10 days after it had been seized by the enemy. Initially, the division had planned winning back its defense line including the mountain position by August 12, but the plan was, as it were, postponed to that date. Thus in retrospect, the ROK 1st Division suffered countless losses trying to hold, in vain, the Tabudong front, as Yuhak-san, the most important terrain feature on the defense line, had been preoccupied by the enemy.

In brief, at the beginning of August, the NKPA had committed its five divisions, 10th, 3rd, 15th, 13th and 1st to the Naktong River front that extended from Koryong through Hamch'ang, as its main efforts to seize Taegu. However, the enemy's thrust immediately encountered the stubborn resistance of the US 1st Cavalry, ROK 1st and 6th Divisions deployed along Hyunp'ung-Waegwan-Hill 328-Suam-san and Yuhak-san Sinjumak defense line. Especially, the ROK 1st Division had done its full share in fighting off the three enemy divisions' thrusts at Hill 328-Suam-san and Yuhak-san—Hill 741 front, thus bulwarking the avenue between Tabudong and Taegu.

3. The Battle of the Naktong River Bulge

When they organized the Naktong River front, the US 24th Division held the line that extended from Hyunp'ung on the west of Taegu to Namji, the confluence of the Nam with the Naktong, for a straight distance of 37km or a river front of about 60km. Along this defense line, the Naktong runs 300 or 400 meters wide and 2 or 4 meters deep, with numerous folds and bends resembling a huge snake meandering like a large letter "S." In the vicinities of Ch'angnyong and Yongsan, it runs in a wide semicircular loop forming a bulge toward the west land. So this particular loop of the river and the land it enclosed on three sides became known as the Naktong Bulge in the Korean War history books. The avenue that leads to this bulge from the west of Hapch'on and Chinju had long been disconnected except by way of the only bridge, Namji. Instead, several ferry and ford sites were available. Roads between Pugok and Ch'angnyong, also between Pakjin and Yongsan, however, could be excellent approach avenues for the enemy to reach Miryang by way of Ch'angnyong and Yongsan. Miryang lies on the Taegu–Pusan axis.

Completing its delaying action in the vicinity of Sanjeri, the 24th Division, on August 2 and 3, crossed the Naktong River. Its 34th Regiment was redeployed in and around Yongsan, and the 21st Regiment in Ch'angnyong, respectively. The ROK 17th Regiment that had been attached to the American division moved to the Hyunp'ung area. Thus the division held a few of the hills bordering the Naktong. A serious problem at that time was that, with operable combat capability reduced to 40% and still taking up a wide frontage, they were not able to fill up the gaps between subordinate elements which extended to 4 or 5km. So the division had to intensify patrol and reconnaisance activities on the river bank and the roads.

General Church considered that the North Koreans were more likely to direct their main efforts toward Ch'angnyong because enemy troops had assembled in the Hapch'on area, and many more ford sites were available for them in the vicinity of Ch'angnyong than in Yongsan. For this reason, he decided to reinforce his troops in that part, while having the division reconnaisance company and the 19th Infantry, arrived from Masan on August 3 in reserve in the Ch'angnyong area.[68]

The General ordered all civilians in the 24th Division zone to evacuate and further restricted the Korean refugees' crossing of the river. At that time, the opposing enemy 4th Division assembled to prepare for the river crossing in the Hapch'on area. They had been ordered by the higher echelon to rapidly penetrate into the Naktong Bulge, interdict the rear area of Taegu and to advance toward Pusan along the Seoul-Pusan highway. Completing its search for favorable crossing sites, the enemy division began the crossing at around midnight of August 5. Apart from General Church's anticipation, the major element of the enemy 16th Regiment made a surprise crossing of the river at the Ohang ferry site, just in front of Yongsan, and part of the regiment at the north of the Pugok area, all with red and yellow flares bursting over the river. Most of the men stripped off their clothing, rolling it and their weapons into bundles to be carried on their heads, and stepped into the shoulder-deep water. Others made rafts to float their clothes and equipment across. The enemy force that crossed the river at the Pugok area was machine-gunned and shelled by the American Infantry and artillery and driven back across the river. But other enemy forces that crossed at Ohang penetrated the gap between companies of the 3rd Battalion, 34th Infantry and overran the mortar position, attempting further penetration into the rear area. Aware now of the enemy penetration, the 3rd Battalion headquarters troops there escaped to the rear. After this withdrawl, the artillery positions at Obongri ridge lay completely exposed to the enemy.

On order issued by the regimental commander, the 1st Battalion which had been kept in reserve, immediately counterattacked the enemy that had penetrated into Cloverleaf Hill. However, in its attack, the Battalion had no chance of success: the command post and the leading C Company were surprised by the enemy. A fierce battle developed between the two sides. And during this engagement, part of the American troops managed to reach the bank positions, fighting along the road net that led to them.

Meanwhile, on the morning of August 5, the division commander, aware that the enemy's main attack would direct toward Yongsan, ordered the the 19th Infantry, the division reserve unit, to counter the enemy in the Ohang area. By midmorning, he further ordered the Reconnaisance Company to interdict the Pugok-Ch'angnyong road and together with I Company to fight off the enemy at Pugok. B Company of the 19th Regiment trapped approximately 300 enemy troops in a village east of Ohangdong, and killed most of them. The 1st Battalion, 34th Infantry, also made a continuous counterattack against the enemy and regained part of Cloverleaf Hill. The Reconnaisance Company attacked an enemy force that had by now occupied a hill near Pugokri, but they were repulsed with considerable loss. Enemy reinforcements kept on trying to cross the Naktong at Pakjin, Ohang and Pugokri, but field artillery fire and aircraft prevented them from reaching the east side of the river. Nevertheless, securing attack positions in the vicinity of Ohang and Pugokri, the enemy brought together two more battalions there, that had crossed the river through the darkness.[69]

The continuation of the American counterattack in the bulge, on the morning of August 7, by the 19th Infantry and B Company of the 34th Infantry was a feeble effort. Extreme heat and lack of food and water were contributing factors in the failure to advance. The situation was not helped when friendly aircraft mistakenly strafed the 19th Infantry positions.[70] On their part, the North Koreans occupied Cloverleaf Hill and pressed forward to reach Obongri

Ridge. Both sides had had the greater interests in this hill mass because, from the crests of Cloverleaf and Obongri, the enemy could see the American main supply road stretching back to Yongsan and beyond that town toward Miryang.

At dawn on the same day, part of the enemy troops attempted to cross the river just in front of Hyunp'ung, but they were held back by the grazing fires of the ROK 17th Infantry. Later on that day, the regiment moved to Taegu based on the regrouping program of the ROK Army. And, to take its place, the commanding general of the US 24th Division hastily formed Task Force Hyzer.[71]

This weakening of the line had been partly offset the previous night by the arrival of the 1st Battalion, 9th Infantry, 2nd Infantry Division which had been kept as an Eighth US Army reserve unit, at Ch'angnyong. The battalion was attached to the 24th Division by order of General Walker. The US 9th Regiment(−) also followed it to arrive at Ch'angnyong on August 8.[72]

General Church ordered Col. John G. Hill, commander of the 9th Infantry, to attack at once and drive the North Koreans from the bulge salient.

At 16:00 on August 8, the regiment started forward to counterattack the enemy force, with its 1st Battalion maneuvering toward Cloverleaf and 2nd Battalion toward Obongri Ridge. But the regiment was repulsed with considerable loss because it had been hastily committed to the front with untried green replacements who, being tired after the long foot march, had not been accustomed to the new terrain features.[73] In the meantime, at night on that day, A and L Companies of the 34th Infantry that had held the central front withdrew from their positions, delaying the enemy's advance.

On August 10, the 9th Regiment together with the 2nd Battalion of the 19th Infantry, US 24th Division, resumed their attacks against the enemy. In this fighting, the 2nd Battalion succeeded in capturing a hill mass around Ohang and held it for a brief period, and the 9th Infantry recaptured part of Cloverleaf, but was at once driven back by the enemy. Thus the fighting in these areas

A Seasaw Battle at the Naktong Bulge Area

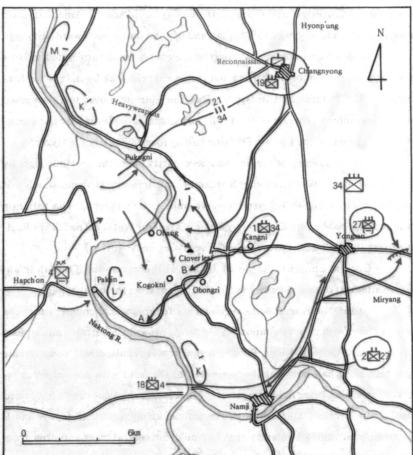

reduced the 2nd Battalion to about 100 effective men in the rifle companies.

That evening, as the attacking troops had not made any progress, the 24th Division Commander, Gen. Church placed Col. Hill, Commander of the 9th Infantry, in command of all troops in the Naktong Bulge. The troops comprised the 9th, 34th, and 19th Infantry Regiments, and the 1st Battalion, 21st Infantry, together with other attached units. This command was now designated Task Force Hill. And Col. Hill was ordered to attack the enemy troops in the bulge and to repulse them. Meanwhile, the enemy 4th Division, completing underwater bridges across the Naktong at Ohang and Pakjin ferry sites during the night of August 10, had moved tanks, mortars and artillery pieces together with large scale foot soldiers to the east side of the river.[74]

On the morning of August 11, when Task Force Hill was at their lines of departure and in their positions, the enemy made a concentrated surprise attack against them. This unexpected enemy attack accompanied by artillery fires crumbled the 1st Battalion, 21st Infantry, that had been waiting in its assembly area, and threw Task Force Hill into confusion. As the plan of attack had failed completely, the division commander changed his order for Task Force Hill from attack to one of dig in and hold.[75]

By that time, the enemy forces, pressing hard against the hill positions with their main elements, let their 18th Regiment move around the hill on the left and thrust into the rear area of Yongsan.[76] On that day, the enemy captured Namji bridge and his artillery fire brought Yongsan under fire for the first time. Shortly afterwards, the Division Reconnaisance Company engaged other enemy troops that had turned around south of Yongsan. In this emergency, General Church dispatched the 14th Engineer Combat Battalion to Youngsan, and General Walker ordered the 2nd Battalion, 27th Infantry, in army reserve, to attack north over the Namji bridge.

Due to an assault from guerillas who had disguised themselves as refugees, the arrival of the 2nd Battalion, 27th Infantry, was delayed until late afternoon in reaching the Namji bridge; however, the battalion was able to fight off the enemy. By that time, Task Force Hill was fighting against heavy odds in a battle of attack and counterattack with the enemy opposing it. In the meantime, east of Yongsan, the main supply line was cut by the enemy who had surprised a supply vehicle.

Col. Hill, on the morning of August 12, the next day, immediately ordered a company from the 9th Infantry together with a platoon of mortars to attack the interdicting enemy troops. But he failed simply because his troops were counterattacked there. On the other hand, 24th Division headquarters assembled from different units about 135 men, including clerks, bakers, military police plus two tanks, under the command of the commanding officer of Headquarters Company. This force hurriedly took up a position at the pass near Simgongri on the Yongsan-Miryang road. Its mission was to block further penetration of the enemy. Armored vehicles came through to them with food, water, and ammunition.[77]

Estimating that about two battalions of the enemy troops might have been positioned in the areas south, and east of Yongsan, General Walker committed the main element of the 27th Infantry in reserve to that front, to clean up the enemy there. The general progress of the battle zones on that day favored the enemy, so it was urgent for the US and the ROK Army to have more reserve units for holding the defense lines. The most critical, weak part in the friendly line turned out to be the Naktong Bulge.

On the day just before the arrival of the main element of the regiment, the 2nd Battalion, with the support of air strikes, had made an attack against the interdicting enemy forces positioned in the east of Yongsan area. And the following day, together with the main forces, it repulsed the enemy. Thus the US 27th Infantry, with the help of the 14th Engineer Combat Battalion which had assembled in Yongsan, and the reinforced 1st Battalion, 23rd Regiment, of the 2nd Division, cleared the enemy from the vicinity of Yongsan.

Having succeeded in denying gains to the enemy in the Yongsan area, on the morning of August 14, General Church again ordered Task Force Hill to launch a general attack against the enemy. Upon receiving the order Task

Force Hill, despite the fact that the preplanned one hundred aircraft support had been cancelled because of the bad weather, forced the enemy's positions. The 9th Infantry, the main attack element of Task Force Hill, reached parts of Cloverleaf Hill. But there the American and North Korean troops locked into a close battle of attack and counterattack that lasted until the following day. In this continuing combat, almost all company officers had been killed or wounded. South of Obongri, the 1st Battalion, 21st Infantry, was virtually surrounded by enemy troops and forced to withdraw with numerous casualties.

Having suffered serious losses in that close combat, Task Force Hill became powerless. In this battle, however, 35 members led by SFC Roy E. Collins on the 2nd Platoon, 1st Battalion, of the 34th Infantry, made a dashing attack on the enemy, launching a grenade fight. The platoon lost 25 men killed or wounded in this savage encounter. While the ten able-bodied men withdrew, while PFC Edward O. Cleaborn, a black soldier, stubbornly stayed behind providing covering fire to the last.[78]

On August 15, General Church and Colonel Hill agreed to discontinue the attack until their combat effectiveness could be restored. General Walker at once came to Miryang to encourage American troops to quickly clean up the situation. For this purpose, Walker decided definitely that he would attach the strongest Marine brigade which had been kept in reserve to the 24th Division. The general situation did not look good for the American forces at this time and friendly forces badly needed reserves almost everywhere. Thus, on this very day, receiving an order that "the 1st Provisional Marine Brigade attack as early as possible on August 17 to destroy the enemy in the bulge east of the Naktong," the brigade started to move from the Masan area to the Miryang–Yongsan area.

On August 16, a day before the general counterattack had been planned, Task Force Hill again came under a full-scale attack from the enemy. The 9th Infantry withdrew from Cloverleaf with considerable loss, and elements of the 19th and 34th Regiments narrowly escaped from Ohang Hill. At about this time, just on the left flank of the division in front of Hyunp'ung, an enemy force estimated at two battalions of the 29th Rement, 10th Division, that had crossed the Naktong the previous day established itself on river hills. This enemy posed a particular danger. General Walker was deeply concerned about their activities; however, comfortingly, they made no effort to leave their positions.[79]

General Church's attack plan placed the 1st Provisional Marine Brigade on the left in front of Obongri Ridge, the 9th Infantry in the center in front of Cloverleaf, and the 34th regiment north of the 9th Infantry. Beyond it 19th Infantry formed extreme right flank of the attack formation. Thus the plan called for the 9th Infantry, after it took Cloverleaf, to be pinched out by either side unit. They were to drive on to the Naktong. The attack was to begin at 08:00, August 17, when the carrier-based Marine Corsairs could participate. The gist of the attack plan, above all, was to seize Obongri Ridge and Cloverleaf Hill with the coordinated attack of Army and Marine troops.

General Church had planned to coordinate a 9th RCT attack against Cloverleaf with the Marine attack against Obongri Ridge. The 5th Marine commander Lt. Col. Murray, however, requested that he be allowed to attack and secure Obongri first before the main attack began. He considered Obongri Ridge as his line of departure of the main attack. General Church granted the 5th Marine commander's request and changed his own plan.[80]

At 07:35, 49 field artillery pieces began to fire the preparation, and 18 Marine Corsairs delivered an air strike on the Obongri Ridge. Immediately after the strike, the marine 2nd Battalion started up the slope. When they reached halfway up the slope, enemy small arms fire began to come from Obongri and Tugok village which was at the southern tip of Cloverleaf.

Among these attack troops, only 2nd Lt. Michael J. Shinka reached the top with 20 marines of his thirty-men platoon. But they were fired on by grazing enemy machine guns and grenades from the right and the reverse slope of the hill, and forced to retreat. Corsairs now returned and worked over the ridge line. After the strike ended, the marines started upward again. Again, only Shinka reached the crest with his 9 men. But they could not stay there any longer, and fell back down the reverse slope. The platoon leader by himself crawled to the top again to see if he could find any marines wounded on top; enemy fire hit him twice, one bullet shattering his chin, the other entering his right arm. By 15:00, in 7 hours the marine 2nd Battalion suffered heavy loss—a casualty rate of almost 60% of the riflemen. The marine brigade commander decided he would have to pass the 1st Battalion through it, and the former completed the relief of the latter, to resume the attack.[81]

After this battle, General Church issued the attack order that he had initially planned for all subordinate elements. Accordingly, artillery preparation was concentrated on Obongri and Cloverleaf hills. Part of the fire was VT fuze air bursts, the flying shell fragments of which could kill or injure entrenched enemy soldiers on the reverse slopes. At 16:00, the 9th Infantry and the marines began their coordinated attack. The 9th Infantry took Cloverleaf without difficulty, and from the hill positions, it now supported with its fire the attack of the marines against Obongri. The marine brigade was able to move to the right, capturing several knobs and hills of the Obongri ridge and finally reach its crest. In this battle, Korean service volunteers helped the American troops by carrying supply items to the ridge and evacuating casualties.

Before dark the enemy 4th Division made its first use of 4 tanks in this battle, and came steadily along the road toward the pass between Obongri and Cloverleaf. The US Marines on the northern knobs of Obongri ridge immediately requested an air strike and placed M26 Pershing tanks in the road in front of their positions. The 75-mm recoilles rifles and 3.5-inch rocket launcher teams were already positioned at the road side and the pass. Three Air Force fighter planes sighted the enemy tanks and made several strafe runs over them but without visible effect. One of the bazooka teams fired the first shot, hitting the leading enemy tank, and then a 75-mm recoilless rifle tore into it. Finally, the American Pershing tank scored a direct hit on the enemy tank. Likewise, two other enemy tanks were knocked out by these weapons, and air action destroyed the fourth tank. When darkness fell, the 19th Infantry, with the help of heavy air attacks and artillery barrages, captured Ohang Hill. In this severe day-long battle, however, the US 19th and 34th Regiments suffered heavy casualties. Finally, cleaning up the battle area until the following day, the US 24th Division and the 1st Marine Brigade troops met at the Naktong.[82]

It was clear by that day, that the enemy unit was decisively defeated and its survivors, in groups of 100, were fleeing westward across the Naktong, being strafed all afternoon by fighter planes. In brief, the North Korean 4th Division never recovered from this battle, losing nearly all its heavy equipment and weapons, and suffering heavy casualties in the battle of the Naktong Bulge. It was never able to come back to any other battle in the Naktong River front. Thus, the battle of the Naktong Bulge was over, the 1st Provisional Marine Brigade, on August 19, moved to the south near Ch'angwon, reverting to the Eighth Army reserve.

4. Counterattack from the West of Masan

The US 25th Division which had hurriedly arrived in the Masan area from Kimch'on took up the Naktong line that extended from Namji on the south of the Naktong Bulge to Masan.[83] General Kean, the division commander, taking over the mission there from the 24th Division, placed, by August 4, the 35th Infantry at Chungamri, the 24th Infantry in the vicinity of Haman, and the

27th Infantry at Chindongri, which had been in action there. With this 27th Regiment,[54] the ROK Task Forces Min, and Kim Sung En under his operational control, and with all elements of his unit, General Kean was to confront the enemy 6th Division. Accordingly, the 19th Infantry of the 24th Division which had delayed the enemy thus far on the axis of Chinju-Chungamri was relieved and returned to its parent unit on that day.

On the previous days, on August 2-3, as the 5th Regimental Combat Team which had arrived from Pusan was attached to the 25th Division, and the 1st Provisional Marine Brigade, the Eighth Army reserve, moved into the Masan area, the combat effectiveness of the American troops was increased remarkably. Despite the intelligence reports that the enemy was massing north of Taegu, the reason for General Walker to concentrate all the reinforcements on the southern front was that he believed the situation was worsening here.

The enemy 6th Division confronting the US 25th Division intended to penetrate into the southern flank of the Eighth US Army and continue to attack in the axis of Chinju-Masan-Pusan. Thus, attempting to quickly seize Pusan, this enemy force concentrated its main efforts on the Masan area. The lead element of this enemy division already had advanced close to Chungamri and Chindongri, and part of the enemy unit had also infiltrated into the rear area of the US 25th Division positioned on Sobuk-san mountain on the south of Haman. As the 83rd Motorized Regiment of the 105th Armored Division had joined the enemy 6th Division, its mobility was increased considerably.[55]

Thus, with this strengthened combat effectiveness on the southwestern front, the Commanding General of the Eighth US Army decided on a counterattack along the axis of Masan-Chinju. The purposes of this counterattack were, first of all, to crush the massed enemy here, and then to help relieve enemy pressure against the perimeter in the Taegu area by forcing some North Korean reserve units southward.[56] This counterattack was significant in that it was to be the first American division level counterattack of the war, breaking from the repeated delaying actions that had been made thus far.

In order to prepare for the attack, General Walker at once requested the Fifth Air Force to use its main strength from August 5 through 6 in an effort to isolate the battle field and to destroy the enemy behind the front lines. He named Task Force Kean as the attack force and gave the hour of attack as 06:30, August 7. The task force was named for its commander, Major Gen. William B. Kean, Commanding General of the 25th Division. General Walker attached the 5th Regimental Combat Team, the 1st Provisional Marine Brigade, and two medium tank battalions of the 89th (M4A3) and the 1st Marine(M26 Pershing) to the 25th Division (less the 27th Infantry Regiment which was in Eighth Army reserve after its relief of the 5th RCT).[87]

Respecting the Eighth Army plan, General Kean broke up the 29th Infantry and attached one battalion each to the regrouped 27th and 35th Regiments. In addition, he had the 87th tank company, the ROK Task Forces Min, and Kim, and one Police Company attached to his command. Thus, altogether, he had about 20,000 men, 100 tanks and 100 field artillery pieces under his command at the beginning of the attack.

The plan for the counterattack required Task Force Kean to attack west along three roads, and seize the Chinju pass. The 35th Infantry would make the attack along the northernmost and main inland road to Much'onri from Chungamri, the 5th RCT along the secondary inland road to Chindongri-Pongamri-Much'onri and whence to the Chinju pass, while the 5th Marines would swing southward through Kosong-Sach'on road to Chinju. At the same time, the 24th Infantry, to which the ROK Task Forces Min and Kim, and Police company had been attached, was to clean out the enemy from the rear, Sobuksan area, and to secure the lateral road running through Haman.[88] Meanwhile, the dispersed enemy 6th Division that had tried to locate weak points on the

Counteroffensive from the western Masan

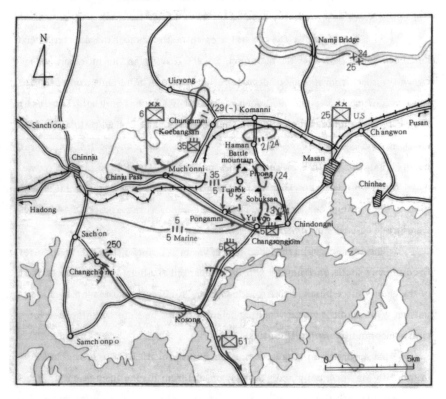

line, launched attacks, at night on August 6, from various directions. It seized a high ground in the vicinity of Chindongri, and succeeded in cutting all friendly supply routes.

Task Force Kean launched the counterattack according to plan.[89] The 35th Infantry rapidly recaptured Kaebang-san knob, and with the help of the air strikes, it repulsed one enemy battalion from the Pugeri area. In this battle, the 35th Infantry inflicted 350 casualties on the enemy, and captured two tanks and five self-propelled guns. Near Pansong, the regiment overran what they thought had been the enemy 6th Division command post and it further advanced to the Much'onri area.

As a heavy fog in the coastal area forced to cancel the air strike that had been scheduled, the 1st Battalion, 5th RCT, early in the morning, led off down the road from its line of departure just west of Chindongri and advanced toward Kosong. However, the 2nd Battalion, 5th RCT, that had held Yaban-san (Fox Hill) came under an enveloping enemy attack. The 2nd Battalion, 5th Marines, moved out to relieve this infantry unit at a spur of the hill, but it ran head-on into the North Koreans. It was a melee, a confused fight in which it was hard to tell who was attacking whom. Despite airdrops of water and other supplies to the soldiers, the furnace hot with the temperature standing at 44 degrees Centigrade caused many heat prostration cases.[90]

The enemy troops that had held a vantage point in the Chindongri area fired mortar shells on friendly supply points and artillery emplacements. Part of the enemy force blocked the road between Chindongri and Masan. In this situation, what made it worse was that friendly tanks had cut up telephone lines causing communication difficulties.

At daybreak on August 8, the 2nd Battalion, 5th RCT, and the 2nd Battalion, 5th Marines, launched attacks from different directions against the enemy positions with the help of an air strike. After hard fighting, they succeeded in driving the enemy back from the Yaban-san area. And the two battalions linked up there. Soon after this battle, the 2nd Battalion, 5th RCT, received an additional order that it would capture a lower hill near Changsongjom, to cover the marine unit that was to attack Kosong. The battalion succeeded in this night attack, and it was the first successful night attack that American troops made in the Korean War.

On the other hand, troops of the 3rd Battalion, 5th Marines, and the 2nd Battalion, 24th Infantry, tried unsuccessfully to dislodge the enemy that had held a vantage point near Chindongri with the help of the air strikes, artillery and tanks. However, the enemy soldiers stubbornly held their positions. Finally, after three days of severe fighting, the two battalions reduced the enemy road-block in the Chindongri area shortly after noon on August 9, inflicting about 600 casualties on the enemy forces.[91]

Thus the way was clear for Task Force Kean to resume its maneuver of the planned attack toward Chinju. The 5th Marines moved rapidly toward Kosong while marine Corsairs flying from aircraft carriers provided close support. Meanwhile the 5th RCT that had been to attack in the center toward Much'onri was delayed because of the increased enemy resistance. Much'onri was its planned junction point with the 35th Infantry.

Although the marine troops advanced without difficulties, the 5th RCT that had, on August 10, reached Pongamni, was surprised by an enemy night attack. On the morning of the 11th, close-in air strikes helped turn the enemy back into the hills. Among the elements of the 5th RCT, the 3rd Battalion had reached Much'onri through the Pongamri pass in the previous afternoon, under the cover of the other battalions. Then, together with the 35th Infantry, it further advanced toward the Chinju pass.

The marine troops chanced to sight the camouflaged 83rd Motorized Regiment column near Kosong and requested for air strikes on them. Immediately, flights of Corsairs and F-51's came over to destroy them. The ground troops found 55 enemy trucks, 45 motorcycles and other equipment destroyed, including 200 enemy soldiers killed.[92]

At about this time, the Eighth US Army urgently needed reserve units everywhere for holding its defense line. On Taegu front, the situation of the Naktong Bulge area deteriorated due to the increased enemy activities, and the northern part of the Taegu area was again under enemy threat. And the ROK 3rd Division that had fought along the east coast was encircled by the enemy forces at Changsadong. Under such circumstances, General Walker sent an operational directive to Major General Kean to the effect that he hoped Kean could secure some mobile reserve units for him. For this purpose, Walker ordered Kean to finish up his actions there by "occupying and defending the Chinju pass line to get ready to release the ROK Min and Kim units to the ROK Army." He further added that "Kean to be ready to release the 1st Provisional Marine Brigade and the 5th RCT on army order."[93]

Accordingly, the commander of the 5th RCT made a plan for passing his unit: the 1st Battalion would secure the north ridge and the pass around Pongamri; the 2nd Battalion, the regimental trains and the artillery in that order would pass through the valley floor of Pongamri; the 1st Battalion was then to disengage and bring up the rear. The division commander, keeping General Walker's order in mind, wanted the regiment to rapidly move forward. But the regimental commander, for fear of possible enemy threats, requested for a delayed movement after dark and it was approved. Right at the moment the 1st Battalion was to secure the Palsan Pass near Pongamri, however, a typed radio order from the commanding general of the 25th Division, General Kean, was handed to the regimental commander. It ordered him "to move the 2nd Battalion and one battery of artillery through the pass at once, but to hold the rest of the troops in place until daylight."[94]

The regimental commander felt that to execute the order would have catastrophic effects, and tried to protest it. But he could not establish communication and therefore implemented the division order. As a result, in the valley floor of Pongamri remained the regimental headquarters, the 555th, 90th, 159th Artillery Battalions, and the Medium Mortars, Service and Medical Companies, all without infantry men to guard them.

Sometime after midnight, sounds of combat were heard from the north ridge of the Palsan Pass. Upon facing the enemy's attack from all around, the commander of the 1st Battalion urged speedy withdrawal. The 3rd Battalion of the 24th Infantry which had been promised by the division had not arrived because the enemy's attack from the southern Sobuk-san prevented it from arriving on time.

Feeling that the nearby pass area had already been surrounded by the enemy troops, the regimental commander decided on speedy movement of his troops toward Much'onri before daylight, and gave the order for the headquarters truck column to move out. They were to be followed by the artillery, and then the 1st Battalion would bring up the rear after it covered the regimental column. When the headquarters column barely rolled over the pass, and the artillery started to move, they were fired on by the enemy from three different sides. The enemy soldiers led by two tanks suddenly appeared from Tundok side nearby and began to fire on the column. The artillery elements were exposed to this fire and suffered a heavy loss. Still, some survivors stood against the enemy with small arms and machine gun fires until Corsairs flew in to strafe and rocket the enemy at daybreak. They managed to escape from the place afterwards.

In the meantime, the 1st Battalion that had held the pass reorganized for the withdrawal and moved toward Much'onri again after the enemy fire subsided. In the case of C Company, however, only 23 men remained to return to the column. When the 2nd Battalion men, on order, reached the scene of the enemy attack at around noon to rescue the artillery crews, the fight was already over.

Upon receiving the report about the extent of the disaster, Major Gen. Kean at once ordered the 3rd Battalion, 5th Marines, to proceed to the scene, Pongamri. The marine battalion, with the assistance of air strikes, crushed the enemy at Koganri, three miles short of Pongamri, and advanced to Pongamri. Before they could attempt to attack into the place itself, however, the battalion received another mission and withdrew from the scene. The 3rd Battalion, 24th Infantry, likewise did not reach the overrun artillery positions.

Thus, on this very day, the US artillery units suffered a disastrous defeat and the name "Bloody Gulch" or "Grave of Artillery" was given to the scene of the successful enemy attack. The 555th Field Artillery lost 180 artillery men including all 8 of its 105-mm. howitzers in the two firing batteries there. The 90th Field Artillery Battalion lost 190 men casualties, all six 155-mm howitzers, and 26 vehicles.[95]

On August 12, when the main element of the 5th Marines reached Sinch'onri, southeast of Sach'on, it came under fire from the remnants of the enemy 83rd Motorized Regiment and the 2nd Battalion of the 15th Regiment. The marine battalion at once launched a counterattack against the enemy with the help of marine Corsairs. In this battle, the Corsairs did accomplish their close support strike mission remarkably in a textbook fashion, as if they were doing routine practice landing operations.

At about this time, the US 24th Infantry was engaging enemy troops in the Sobuksan area with a mission of opening a supply road that had been cut or blocked by enemy mines and small arms fire. It had tried to use tanks and armored cars to open the road for ten successive days, but failed. Meanwhile, the ROK Task Forces Min and Kim plus a police unit that had been attached to the US 24th Division worked together with American soldiers to repulse the infiltrating enemy at a high ground near Chindongri. Securing the supply roads nearby was additional work for them. As of that day, August 12, however, they were released from the 24th Division, and Kim unit moved to Chungamri and Min unit, together with the police unit, moved to Masan.

The Eighth US Army, on August 12, suspended the planned counterattack, reverting Task Force Kean to the area of Sobuksan, and securing the Marine unit as a mobile reserve. At noon, the following day, receiving the withdrawal order from Task Force Kean, the subordinate unit elements moved to the east of Sobuk-san, while the 5th RCT traveled to Masan and the Marine Brigade moved to the Naktong Bulge area. On August 16, following the marine unit's transfer of the previous day, Task Force Kean was dissolved on the Eighth Army order.

Even though Task Force Kean's counterattack during the past 7 days did not accomplish what Eighth Army had hoped for and expected, that is, to recapture Chinju and to divert the enemy's main effort from the Taegu front, it nevertheless did provide certain beneficial results. By chance it met, head-on, the enemy attack against the Masan position. It also gave friendly soldiers a much needed psychological experience of going on the offensive and nearly reaching an assigned objective. Likewise the North Korean 6th Division took heavy losses: thus far 4,000 or 5,000 casualties including 13 tanks destroyed.

Beginning from August 14, the US 25th Division organized its defense line by placing the 35th Infantry Regiment in Namji-Komanri position, the 24th Infantry in the center near Sobuk-san, and the 5th RCT in the south of Chindongri. The 27th Regiment was kept in reserve. At the same time, on the southern ridge of Sobuk-san were 432 ROK policemen to close the gap between the 24th Infantry and the 5th RCT. Meanwhile, some 500 Korean service volunteers carried all supplies to the rugged hill mass front on their backs.

On the other hand, a new enemy reserve unit, the 7th Division (Maj.Gen. Lee Ik Song) arrived at Chinju on August 16, with a mission for protecting the rear area of the 6th Division. Upon arriving there, part of the division continued to move toward Yosu and T'ongyong, the southwestern port cities.[96] In the meantime, the NKPA 6th Division with the newly joined 2,000 replacements, mostly conscripted in the Seoul area, regrouped itself, dividing the unit into battalion size elements. Then, based on their study of the tactics to be used there, the division, with an aim for capturing hills in front of Masan, attempted patrolling the area with special attention on the roadside between Chungamri and Masan.[97]

From August 17, the US 35th Infantry came under attack from the NKPA 13th Regiment of 6th Division which had drawn near to the roadside and Sibidang-san (276m) positions on its right flank. This was the beginning of a day and night battle that lasted for several days between the two sides. The American troops again lost their positions to enemy attack by night and again regained them by counterattack by day, with the help of air strikes and artillery fire. This pattern repeated quite a while, but on August 23, the North Koreans retreated with considerable loss.[98]

The NKPA 15th Regiment's attack against the US 24th Infantry came at daybreak of August 18, from steep mountain positions. The enemy-held Sobuk-san was composed of steep cliffs and gorgelike valleys that limited the mobility of both forces. The bald peak of this mountain mass became known as Combat Mountain, and the enemy which al*ready held this peak could keep the supply road under observation and also see into the rear area of the 24th Infantry. As the enemy forces held this mountain mass making the peaks their stronghold, even the napalm bombs delivered by UN fighter planes were usually ineffective.

For several days, both forces were locked in a fierce battle; the US 24th Infantry, at the early stage of the battle, could not even hold the part of Sobuk-san ridge positions that its 2nd Battalion had occupied, and the northern ridges of Battle Mountain also was in the enemy's hand. But the regiment could recapture Battle Mountain after fighter bombers, in 38 sorties, attacking the crest of the mountain. In this battle, a ROK police patrol had the luck to capture the commanding officer of the enemy 15th Regiment, but unfortuately, he was killed later while trying to escape.[99] On the morning of August 21, the 5th RCT attacked the Sobuk-san again, and the general melee between both forces lasted until noon the next day. Five hours later, the American regiment finally seized the peak.[100]

Generally speaking, however, the fighting in the mountains on the southern front, that is, in the Battle Mountain and Sobuk-san area, was a stalemate. Until the end of August, a usual pattern of fighting was repeated: the enemy would take the mountain crest at night and the American regiments would recapture it the next day with the help of field artillery,tank and mortar fire, and air strikes, in addition to their own machine gun fire and grenades.[101] Thus a record wrote that the Combat Mountain peak changed hands as often as 19 times. In his defense of that part of Sobuk-san south of Battle Mountain, Msgt. Melvin O. Handrich of the 5th RCT distinguished himself as a heroic combat leader. On August 25th, although wounded, Sergeant Handrich returned to his forward position to continue directing artillery fire, and there alone engaged North Koreans until he was killed.[102]

The US 25th Division, by the end of August, greatly contributed to the Eighth Army defense actions, by successfully holding its line against the enemy penetration in the areas of Battle Mountain, Sobuk-san, and in front of Komanri.[103]

However, as the 27th Infantry which had fought as an Eighth Army reserve returned to its parent unit on August 30, and the 5th RCT was diverted to the 24th Division on the same day, the 25th Division had to be prepared for the future actions with only its subordinate elements.

In the meantime, on August 17 when the fierce battle between both forces was going on in the area of mountain mass in front of Masan, one battalion of the enemy 51st Regiment, 7th Division seized the unprotected Kosong without bloodshed. Driving the ROK police company out of T'ongyong, it dominated the town.[104] To counter this enemy force, the ROK Marine Kim's unit which had consolidated itself in Chinhae moved to the scene on board two navy ships. It made a surprise amphibious landing near the town. On the following day, when this unit seized the Wonmun pass that led to T'ongyong, the enemy launched a counterattack against them. The ROK and UN naval forces together with air planes heavily shelled the assembly area and supply cars. At this time, they sank four enemy boats near the Samch'onp'o coast, and one ROK marine company pressed the retreating enemy hard.

On August 19, the ROK marine battalion which took up positions at the Wonmun pass was fired on, on August 19, by another enemy force assembled on the northern part of the pass, and was in jeopardy of being penetrated. However, the close support UN air flights at once flew over to rescue them, and with the help of the air strikes, the marines were able to drive the enemy force out.[105] Afterwards, they repulsed a few more waves of enemy attacks there. According to a prisoner's statement, the enemy soldiers turned out to be students who had been conscripted in South Korea and joined the 21st and 22nd Battalion of the 104th Regiment.[106] After they defeated the enemy there, the marines, fortifying their positions with newly supplied antipersonnel mines, cleaned out the remnants of the enemy troops in the area nearby. They also searched for enemy boats that had been hidden on the coasts of Kosong, T'ongyong and Koje and sank them all.[107]

5. Battle for the Possession of Kigye and P'ohang

The eastern part of the Naktong River defense line was held by the ROK I Corps which had deployed its 8th Division in the area of Uisong, the Capital Division in the vicinity of Kiran. On the eastern flank of the line, near the East Sea shore, the 3rd Division of the same I Corps engaged the North Korean 5th Division for the possession of Yongdok. The ROK Army, estimating that the enemy's main effort would be directed in the Andong-Uisong-Yongch'-

on and Yongdok-P'ohang avenues, placed priority to holding this front. Meanwhile, the NKPA II Corps committed its three infantry divisions, the 1st, 13th, and 15th, to the Taegu front, the 8th Division to the route of Andong-Uisong-Yongch'on, and the 12th Division to the Ch'ongsong-An'gang-Kyongju route. It also committed the 5th Division to the P'ohang area for a continuing drive on Pusan while threatening the safety of eastern Taegu.

The ROK Capital Division of the I Corps took up its defense positions in the area of Kiran, deploying the 1st Regiment at Ch'umokdong, and the 18th Regiment in the hills on the right of the village. The division also placed the Cavalry Regiment attached to it in the Pibong-san area south of Chinbo, together with the Independent Cavalry Regiment and the Kangwon Police Battalion. On the other hand, the ROK 3rd Division put the 22nd and 23rd Regiments in position on Hills 181 and 207 just south of Yongdok, while assigning the flank guard missions to the Independent 1st and 2nd Battalions.

The ROK Capital and 3rd Divisions came under the full-scale enemy attack on August 5. The Capital Division's tactical command post and the 1st Regimental command post were attacked by the enemy troops who had, by surprise, infiltrated into the rear area of the 1st Regiment. As the defense positions had collapsed instantaneously, the regiment, on order from the division commander, withdrew, in dispersion, to the area of Uisong. The 18th and Independent Cavalry Regiments, cut off in their retreat, managed to arrive at Uisong by way of Kusudong the following day.[108]

As a result, the axis of Ch'ongsong-Kigye lay defenseless. The enemy 12th Division at once began to advance, through this defense vacuum, toward Kigye facing almost no resistance. This enemy division, linking up with the 766th Independent Regiment that had already infiltrated in the area of Pohyunsan, committed a regiment of troops reinforced by tanks and supporting artillery, hoping that the main element would follow it.

In the meantime, the ROK 3rd Division was also attacked, at night on August 5, by the enemy 5th Division. It was a large-scale attack, and the ROK troops launched a counterattack with the help of the UN air strikes and naval gunfire for the possession of the southern hill of Yongdok. The ROK and North Korean troops were locked in several close combats. However, part of the ROK 23rd Regimental defense positions were penetrated by the enemy, which led to the beginning of the collapse of the ROK 3rd division defense line. The division commander at once tried to call in the soldiers retreating in dispersion, but he needed considerable time in restoring order and rebuilding his unit.

The following day, the division commander ordered the 22nd Regiment, which had suffered relatively light loss during the withdrawal, to recapture the hill. As had been planned, the UN aerial attack using rockets, napalm, bombs, and naval gunfire concentrated on the assembled enemy in and around Yongdok. After this preparation, the ROK 22nd Regiment moved out in the infantry attack and drove the North Koreans from Hills 181 and 207. It was another bloody, gruesome battle in the Korean War history. Furious barrage fire from various weapons of both forces seemed to transform even the shape of the hills into flat plateaus and inflicted heavy casualties on both sides.

Even an untoward incident occurred at the ROK 3rd Division tactical command post located at Kanggu. When an enemy mortar hit close to the command post and killed several soldiers, the command system was virtually paralyzed with its commander and staff officers went missing for quite a while.[109] Being liable for this incident, the division commander, Brig. Gen. Lee Joon Sik, was relieved, and another Brig. Gen. Kim Suk Won was appointed to succeed him.

The new commander, making his first inspection tour to the foremost front, arrived at Kanggu at sunset to encourage the soldiers. There he decided to place his defense emphasis on the southern hills of Yongdok and to strengthen the defense against a possible enemy's flank attack by positioning the 23rd Regiment in the area of Jikokdong, on the left of Yongdok.

At night on August 8, the enemy 5th Division concentrated its effort on Hill 181 with a series of attacks. The ROK 22nd Regiment that had held the hill was forced to withdraw because of the heavy losses inflicted on its 2nd Battalion, and of the lack of ammunition. And very soon, Hill 207 was also seized by the enemy. Thus the regimental line broke down, and soldiers began to withdraw to the south in dispersion.

In this confused situation, what made it worse was that the commanding officer of the regiment made a serious tactical mistake. At 05:00 on August 9, Lt. Col. Kang Tae Min had ordered the Osi-pch'on bridge at Kanggu blown without securing approval from the division commander. A battalion-sized group of ROK soldiers of the regiment, who had engaged the enemy troops, were still north of the bridge when it dropped. Many of these soldiers drowned in trying to cross the deep estuary flowing into the East Sea.

The Osib-ch'on bridge was built at Kanggu just below Yongdok, and it was impossible for any force to advance from Yongdok toward P'ohang without passing over this bridge. General Walker who had emphasized the importance of the bridge for the successful defense of P'ohang sent a message to a KMAG advisor with the 3rd ROK division, to the effect that the demolition of the bridge should be stopped. However, when the control of the demolitions was passed to Korean troops, the ROK regimental commander committed such a grave blunder that the Yongdok-Kanggu action virtually came to an end with the loss of the bridge.[10]

Learning that enemy forces had been advancing toward Kanggu, the UN naval gunfire began to shell the approaching enemy lead units, and the ROK 23rd Regiment, 3rd Division, took up new defensive positions on the southern bank of the Osip-ch'on. The ROK 22nd Regiment was ordered, at that

Yongdok-Kanggu Battle

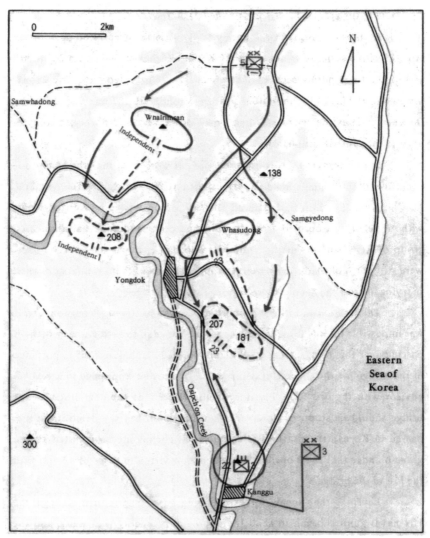

time, to withdraw to Namhodong to be rebuilt up there.[111] However, as one enemy regiment appeared near Naengch'ondong just south of Hunghae, on August
10, moving toward P'ohang, the entire ROK 3rd Division was virtually surrounded.

Despite this critical situation, General Walker instructed the ROK 3rd
Divison to hold in place, resisting the enemy's press southward. Gen. Walker believed that even if P'ohang had fallen to the enemy's hand, the ROK forces
would be able to repulse the enemy there and to protect Yongil Airfield. Earlier
than this, he had ordered the commanding general of the US 2nd Division at
Kyongsan to form a task force for the defense of the airfield. At the same time,
the ROK Army had mobilized Min unit to the P'ohang area to help the American troops in repulsing the enemy force there.

Brigadier General Joseph S. Bradley, Assistant Division Commander,
the US 2nd Division, at once formed Task Force Bradley with the 3rd Battalion
of the US 9th Infantry, except K Company, and late at night on August 10, assumed responsibility for the ground defense of the airstrip. Company K and the
C Battery, 15th Field Artillery Battalion, that had been supposed to join the
main element later, however, were ambushed near a steep mountain valley at
just after midnight, August 11. At this ambush, about 70 were lost and the remaining members withdrew to Kyongju.[112]

While the enemy 5th Division had been pushing forward to Kanggu, the
NKPA 12th Division was attacking against defenseless Kigye. As Kigye is situated at a point where roads to An'gang and P'ohang branch off, the ROK troops
that had lost Kigye came to a crisis in holding their eastern defense line.

It was not until this critical moment that the ROK Army had a correct
understanding of the enemy 12th Division's threat. At once the ROK Army ordered Colonel Lee Song Ga, the Chief of Staff, ROK I Corps, to organize
P'ohang District Command and to hurry to the Kigye front together with the

newly activated ROK 25th Regiment(−). Shortly thereafter, the ROK Army attached the 17th Regiment, Min's Unit and another newly activated 26th Regiment to it.[113]

Meanwhile, the ROK I Corps ordered its Capital Division(−) which
had assembled in Uisong to move to An'gang, and the 18th Regiment, Capital
Division, together with the Independent Cavalry Regiment, to advance to
Hyondong. These ROK troops, in close coordination with the P'ohang District
Command, were to encircle the enemy force from both sides, north and south.

Meanwhile, part of the NKPA 766th Independent Regiment entered
into P'ohang at dawn on August 11, creating a state of alarm.[114] By that time, in
downtown P'ohang were stationed the rearward command post of the ROK 3rd
Division, ROK Naval Guard, and Air Force branch unit. Only a two-platoon-
sized force composed of military, police, volunteer students, and Youth Defense
Guard personnel was guarding against possible enemy infiltration into the
town. They engaged the enemy at P'ohang Girl's Middle School, and both sides
became locked in a small arms fire that lasted until noon on that date. The enemy troops led by 5 armored vehicles continued their attack against the ROK
guard force, inflicting 47 casualties.

With no combat unit, the ROK 3rd Division rear command post evacuated packages of war supplies to Kuryongp'o and tried to collect retreating soldiers at the Hyongsan Bridge. Thus the town of P'ohang which had remained a
no man's land was seized by the enemy. However, UN naval gunfire and aerial
strikes bombarded the enemy troops in and around the town.

Upon receiving the report on the fall of P'ohang, General Walker ordered a tank platoon of the 9th Infantry to proceed to the Yongil Airfield in
order to reinforce Task Force Bradley. He also ordered the ROK 17th Regiment
that had been deployed in the An'gang area to secure Tunnel Hill near the airstrip. Well aware of the situation, Captai Darrigo, KMAG advisor with the ROK

A Seasaw Battle at Kigye-Po'hang

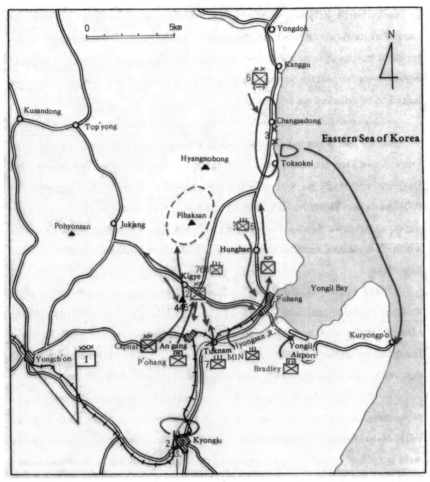

17th Regiment, volunteered to lead the tank platoon. A flight of four F-51 fighter planes delivered a strike on the enemy positions concealed on Tunnel Hill.

Despite every possible effort with which ground troops had tried to secure the safety of the Yongil Airfield, the US 40th Fighter-Interceptor Squadron

(45 aircraft), on August 13, together with air service troops, moved from Yongil to Tsuiki Air Base, Japan, without any prior notice to or coordination with the ground units. At about this time, the surrounded ROK 3rd Division continued a series of battles against the enemy force in the Changsadong area. As another enemy force appeared on the north of Hunghae, the ROK troops were even feared to be attacked on both flanks.

Meanwhile, just before Kigye was seized by the enemy force, the ROK 1st Independent Ranger Battalion (Major Chung Jin) that had advanced to the Pohyun-san area launched an attack against a supply unit of the enemy 12th Division, and made marked military achievements. At night on August 12, the ROK battalion located and surprised the column of enemy supply trucks rolling down southward, with the lights on, at Chukjang. They destroyed 12 trucks with a full load of ammunition, weapons, and other equipment, including two howitzers.[115]

On August 13, the ROK 8th Division, on order by the ROK I Corps, took up defensive positions in the area near Pohyun-san, while the 1st Regiment of the ROK Capital Division proceeded to the An'gang area. The ROK 18th and Independent Cavalry Regiments, in the meantime, began to come down southeastward from Kusandong to counterenvelope the enemy troops.[116]

The ROK 25th Regiment which had advanced to the northern hill mass of An'gang, at this time, took up new defensive positions there together with the ROK Naval Combat Team; however, even before they had dug in trenches, they were surprised by the enemy force. As a result, the ROK forces suffered heavy losses.

By August 13, the ROK 17th, 1st, and 26th Regiments arrived at An'gang in that order, and starting on that day, the ROK Capital Division commander, on order by the ROK Corps commander, took charge of the action there in the An'gang area. The 17th Regiment and the Naval Combat Team had already launched an attack northward the previous day, and the 26th and 1st Regiments joined them immediately after they arrived at An'gang. The latter two regiments advanced to the hills on both flanks of the 17th Regiment, and captured the crests.

Before dark on August 16, the ROK 17th Regiment, with the help of artillery fire and air strikes, eventually recaptured a southern hill near Kigye and proceeded toward Kigye. On the southeastern hill of Kigye, the ROK 1st Regiment dislodged the enemy troops from their positions, and its 3rd Battalion linked up with Min's Unit which had been operating on its right flank, near the P'ohang tunnel. Meanwhile, on the north of Kigye, the 1st Battalion of the ROK 18th Regiment captured a hill near Yonggidong, which was tactically important for both forces, and began to menace the flank of Kigye.[117] The enemy force attempted fragmented counterattacks against the ROK forces; however, facing the threat of being surrounded by the ROK troops, the enemy units began to withdraw northward to the Pihak-san area.

In the meantime, the steadily deteriorating situation in the vicinity of P'ohang caused the Eighth US and the ROK Armies, on August 15, to order the ROK 3rd Division evacuated by sea.[118] US helicopters, first of all, brought medical supplies to the ROK division for the wounded and evacuated them to Pusan.[119] In order to facilitate the evacuation by sea, the ROK division commander deployed the 23rd Regiment in the area of Chikyongdong, and the 22nd Regiment in the vicinity of Toksokri.

At 06:00, August 17, evacuation of the ROK 3rd Division began by four LST's that had been anchored at Toksokri bay, and had completed loading under maximum cover of darkness and naval gunfire. More than 9,000 men of the division, the 1,200 ROK policemen, and about 1,000 laborers successfully escaped to the waiting vessels, and arrived at Kuryongp'ori by 10:30 that morning.[120] The enemy mortar and machine gun fire, from the positions at the reverse hill near

Toksokri threatened the evacuation; however, the UN air strikes and naval gun-fire suppressed them. After the evacuation, the division reorganized itself incorporating replacements until August 20.

In the meantime, the ROK Min's Unit which had been ordered to recapture P'ohang proceeded from the south of P'ohang to the suburbs of the port city. It took up positions in the southern knobs along the Hyongsan River, while on its eastern flank, was Task Force Bradley at Yongil Airfield to protect it from possible enemy attacks.

Min's Unit, aware of the fact that the enemy force had fled to the suburbs of P'ohang with heavy loss inflicted by UN naval gunfire, ordered its 3rd Battalion, at dawn the following day, to enter into downtown streets to clean out the enemy remnants out there.[121] As a US tank platoon had participated in this mop up operation, the ROK soldiers were full of fighting spirit, and completely regained P'ohang. The Min Unit claimed, in this battle, the capture of 180 North Koreans, including 53 artillery and mortar pieces, 160 machine guns, and 940 rifles. Handing over their defensive positions, on August 19, to the ROK 3rd Division, the Min's Unit moved to a position near Taegu.[122]

In the meantime, at dawn on August 18, the ROK troops launched a general attack against the enemy in the vicinity of Kigye. On the north of Kigye, the ROK 18th Regiment struck the enemy force a fatal blow and, in the afternoon on that day, the regiment entered the town of Kigye. At that time, from the south of the town, the 1st Battalion of the ROK 17th Regiment made its way into the downtown streets, mopping up the remnants of the enemy.

Due to the lack of ammunition and food supply, North Korean soldiers became physically so exhausted that they almost lost their will to fight; only part of the survivors fled to the north, leaving numerous casualties behind. The ROK Capital Division, meanwhile, killed 1,245 enemy soldiers and captured a large amount of equipment thus far in the area of Kigye. Upon receiving the reports of winning back Kigye, Shin Song Mo, ROK Defense Minister, visited the ROK Corps command post, on August 19, to encourage the soldiers.[123]

Suffering severely from this battle at Kigye, the enemy 12th Division withdrew to the Pihak-san area. On Pihak-san, due north of Kigye, the enemy division reorganized, on order by its higher echelon unit. In this reorganization, the 766th Independent Regiment lost its identity, its troops being distributed among the three regiments of the division. After incorporating 2,000 replacements and those men of the 766th Regiment, the division reportedly totaled only about 5,000 men.[124]

The ROK Capital Division, having completed its mop-up operation by August 20, took up new defensive positions just north of Kigye. The division placed the 18th Regiment in the Pongwha-bong–Ch'ilgok-san area and the 17th Regiment in the Kajondong area. The 1st Regiment was kept in reserve. This same day, with the emergency in the east temporarily ended, the ROK I Corps ordered the 26th Regiment to be attached to the 3rd Division, the Cavalry Regiment to move to Yongch'on, and the Naval Combat Team to return to its parent unit.

On August 22, the ROK 17th Regiment attacked the enemy positions near Pihak-san area; however, they fell back in face of the stubborn enemy resistance and the rugged mountain terrain. Rather, in order not to expose any weak point in the ROK defense to the enemy, the regiment, on August 25, withdrew to the hill positions north of Kigye, as the 18th Regiment that had flanked the 17th Regiment on the left was pushed back by the enemy to the Inbidong line.[125]

In the meantime, the ROK 3rd Division, to which the 26th Regiment had been attached, reorganized and became a complete combat division with three full regiments under it. On August 21, the division took up positions in the Naengch'ondong–Yangdokdong defense line. During this reorganization period, the enemy troops continued their night attack against Hill 93 on which the 1st Battalion of the ROK 23rd Regiment had been deployed.

Although Hill 93 did not have a great elevation, it was a critical terrain feature in control of a junction of roads that leads to Hunghae and P'ohang, as well as of the surrounding lower hill mass and open field. The ROK 3rd Division, by holding out in this hill position to the last, could annihilate the enemy's attempt to re-infiltrate into this area.[126]

Starting at night on August 26, the enemy force which had reorganized in front of Kigye, resumed the attack against the ROK troops. The ROK 17th Regiment which had not yet taken up defensive positions was at once overrun by the enemy and gave way. At the predawn hours, Kigye fell to the enemy's hands again.[127] At about this time, the ROK 3rd Division, adjacent to the 17th Regiment on the right in the P'ohang area, also came under another enemy attack and fell back.

Upon receiving the reports on this new development on the eastern front, General Walker placed Maj. Gen. John B. Coulter, Deputy Commander, Eighth US Army, in full command of the UN troops in that front to effectively counter the enemy attack there. Gen. Coulter immediately organized Task Force Jackson[128] and visited the ROK I Corps commander at his headquarters at Kyongju, to discuss the problem facing their action there. Task Force Jackson comprised the US 21st Infantry, the 3rd Battalion of the 9th Infantry, and the 73rd Medium Tank Battalion(−).[129] The latter two battalions had been on guard duty at Yongil Airfield.

The ROK Capital Division, on August 27, launched a counterattack against the enemy. It's 17th Regiment recaptured Kigye and stayed there for a while, but the regiment was soon locked in a fierce battle with the enemy troops in the southern hills of Kigye. On the following day, under such circumstances, the 3rd Battalion of the US 21st Infantry, the strongest element of Task Force

Jackson, arrived at An'gang, south of Kigye. At dawn on August 29, the ROK 17th Regiment, with American tank and artillery support, recaptured their position in Kigye. On its right flank, the ROK 1st Regiment advanced to a position northwest of Tangudong. The following night, however, the ROK 17th Regiment lost the Kigye position again and withrew to a new position south of the town.

At about this time, the NKPA was preparing for the final offensive to penetrate into the UN defense line by mobilizing and committing even noncombatants to their front.[130] The enemy 12th Division which had suffered heavy loss in the continued battles thus far incorporated new replacements and part of the NKPA 17th Armored Regiment. Meanwhile, the enemy 15th Division which had proceeded from the Taegu front to the point where the ROK 8th Division had taken up positions got ready to penetrate into the eastern defense line.

By the end of August, a momentary lull in the fighting seemed to be maintained a while in the Kigye-P'ohang front with only skirmishes between patrol forces of both sides taking place. However, UN airplanes and Corsairs frequently flew over to hit the enemy positions there, and American naval cruisers and destroyers continuously delivered their gunfire on the assembled enemy force near Hunghae.

A month earlier, on July 20, North Korean Premier Kim Il Sung once visited the NKPA Front Headquarters at Suanbo to exhort his Communist troops to capture the city of Pusan by August 15, and accordingly, the North Koreans launched a full-scale offensive action against the UN forces, which had lasted about a month; however, the attack virtually ended by August 20. On the western front, the enemy had failed to cross the Naktong, while on the northern and eastern fronts, they had been repelled at the Waegwan-Tabudong-Uihong-Kigye-P'ohang line. As a result, North Koreans fell into an awkward position as their initial objective seemed to be beyond attainment.

III. NKPA's September Offensive and The Diehard Defense

1. Posture of an Armageddon for Opposing Forces

(1) NKPA's Last Offensive and It's Plan of Maneuver

Not to mention Pusan, which had been the August offensive objective of the NKPA, North Korean troops reached a limitation of their operational capacity even before they could seize Taegu. Nevertheless, planning for the September massive attack was underway again for at least the last ten days of August. The objective of this attack was to capture Pusan. The North Koreans' operational directive for this attack called on their subordinate units "to hit hard the enemy concentration in the Naktong River area; the two NKPA assault echelons would attack against the enemy from both flanks, north and west in order to envelope and destroy the combined US and ROK forces at the Taegu–Yongch'on area. The ultimate goal would be to wipe out the enemy's operational bases in Pusan."[131]

In order to implement this order, the enemy I Corps drew up an action plan for breaking up the Naktong defense line first and then for enveloping the disintegrated US and ROK troops there. For this purpose, at 23:00 on August 31, they tried rapidly to cut off the UN supply route between Taegu and Pusan. The NKPA II Corps was to follow the I Corps, to exploit its initial penetration on September 3. Thus the enemy I Corps attempted, first of all, to cross the Naktong River on the west, making it easy for the II Corps to assault against the UN troops and ultimately destroy the core units of friendly forces deployed on the Pusan perimeter.[132]

For the successful September massive attack, the NKPA strengthened its forces by even committing reserve units to the front. Thus the I Corps comprised 6 combat divisions and the II Corps had 7 divisions under its command. These enemy forces were then divided into five major assault groupings to be placed on the attack zone. The enemy's plan for maneuvering these five assault groupings was as follows.

On the NKPA I Corps front, reaching from Waegwan to Masan, were the two assault units. The first assault unit composed of the 6th and 7th Divisions and 104th Security Regiment were to penetrate, first, into the US 25th Division line in front of Masan, and then to capture Kimhae. If they succeeded, they were at once to proceed to Pusan. The enemy 2nd, 4th, 9th, and 10th Divisions, all under assault unit 2, were to break through the US 2nd Division, positioned at the Naktong Bulge, and to advance to Miryang to interdict the Taegu-Pusan highway. Elements of the 105th Armored Division and the 16th Armored Brigade (43 tanks) were to support these troops.

On the other hand, on the NKPA II Corps front, reaching from Waegwan to P'ohang, were the remaining three assault units. The third assault unit comprised the 1st, 3rd, and the 13th Divisions, and was to break through the US 1st Cavalry Division and the ROK 1st Division in the axis of Waegwan-Tabudong to Taegu. The 8th and 15th Divisions under the fourth assault unit were to break through the ROK 8th and 6th Divisions in front of Yongch'on to Taegu or Kyongju. The last assault grouping composed of the 12th and 5th Divisions were to break through the ROK Capital and 3rd Divisions in the area of An'gang-P'ohang to Pusan. The enemy's 105th Armored Division($-$) and the 17th Armored Brigade (about 40 tanks) were to support this corps.

The NKPA Supreme Commander, Premier Kim Il Sung, on August 22, called on his army to do their best, mobilizing all available materiel and manpower, in their preparation for the massive penetration into the UN defense line. Accordingly, the enemy Front Headquarters made an all-out effort in sending reserve troops, equipment and war materiel to the front-line units by the end of August.[133]

Thus the enemy reserve units such as the 10th and 7th Divisions were brought to the front and eventually, in mid-August, the 9th Division was also put into the Yongsan battle zone.[134] These divisions were relatively low in combat effectiveness because 1/3 of their strength were raw recruits, forcibly conscripted in South Korea.

The two enemy armored brigades, the 16th and 17th, which had already been committed to the frontline, were equipped with newly arrived Russian-built T34 tanks. These brigades moved from P'yongyang to the front by rail at night to participate in the massive penetration into the Naktong line.[135] They were the last enemy reinforcements for the enemy troops that had deployed along the Naktong line.

Around late August, North Korean Premier Kim Il Sung ordered Marshal Ch'oi Yong Gun, the North Korean Minister of Defense, to set up a plan for the offensive operations. The Premier also exhorted his Communist troops to fight desperately to the end, and to cut the demands for noncombatants in order to reinforce combat units for enhancing the combat effectiveness.[136]

Faced with severe food shortage, the enemy Front Headquarters, in early August, activated a new supply troop, the 36th Division (Colonel Lee Song Kun) at Kimch'on. This division employed a primitive method of transporting food by mobilizing citizens in the occupied local areas for carrying supplies to the front. Three hundred thousand South Koreans had been conscripted for this sort of work, and many of them underwent hardships because of heavy and constant UN air attacks.[137] Regardless of foul weather or rugged mountain terrain, the mobilized South Koreans were forced to carry about 20kg of supply items to a distance of 20 or 30km per person every night. This work was done in relays;

other towns people would pick up the packages and carry them again to the enemy troops. In this way, a total of about 400 tons of food and other war supplies was carried to the enemy combat divisions, and an individual division secured a minimum amount of about 15 tons of necessary supplies each day.[138]

According to a captured enemy officer, 1st Lt. Kim Yong Ho, of the 4th Division, his unit, as a way of getting replacements, had forced many South Koreans into service since mid-July, and these drafted South Koreans carried food stuffs to the battle zone.[139] As captives in the occupied areas, the local South Korean towns people might have no other choice but to obey the enemy soldiers at gun-point.[140]

However, the NKPA's scheme to live off the country was soon doomed to failure. Despite the North Koreans' increased effort in foraging in the villages through their political organizations called "Peoples' Commitees," the amount of food collected remained trifling, because those mountainous villages where the enemy troops were active had been destitute of food. In addition, most South Korean farmers were recalcitrant.

As a result, the enemy troops had to fight, under the furnace-hot summer weather, almost without food supply. Eventually, to make things more miserable, around the middle of August, they ran short of small arms and ammunition supply. Thus the enemy soldiers were in a state of lowered morale.[141]

Even under such deteriorating circumstances, the enemy troops stubbornly tried to break through the UN defense line. According to the US Eighth Army intelligence estimation, as of September 1, the NKPA brought 13 combat divisions on to the line. Thus the North Korean force numbered a total 97,850 men and distributed variously to each division from 5,000 to 10,000 men.[142] And accordingly, the NKPA's system of logistics was like a rubber band stretched to its uttermost limit that had either to break or rebound. The following tabulation shows a comparision of combat strength of both forces as of September 1.[143]

Armageddon on the Naktong Front (Aug. 31, 1950)

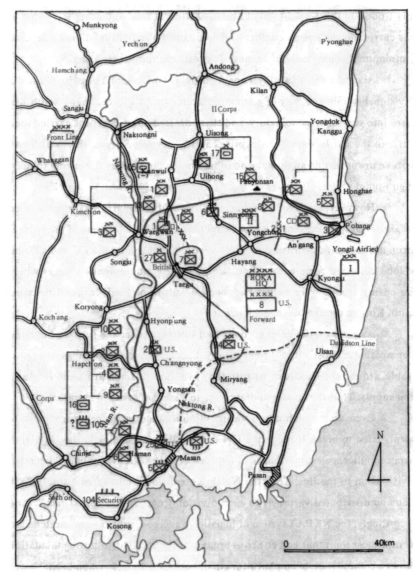

〈Table 2〉   Comparision of Ground Combat Forces(Sept. 1, 1950)

United Nations Forces Total	179,300 men
ROK Army Divisions (Capital, 1st, 3rd, 6th, 7th & 8th)	57,000 men
Supporting Troops	34,700 men
Sub Total	**91,700 men**
US Divisions (2nd, 24th, 25th & 1st Cavalry)	67,800 men
Supporting Troops, US 1st Provisional Marine & British 27th Brigades, US 5th Air Force	19,800 men
Sub Total	**87,600 men**
Number of Tanks	500

North Korean People's Army Total	98,000 men
NKPA Divisions (1st, 2nd, 3rd, 4th, 5th, 6th, 7th, 8th, 9th, 10th, 12th, 13th, 15th & 105th Armored), NKPA Brigades (16th & 17th)	98,000 men
Supporting Troops	Unknown
Number of Tanks	100

(2) The ROK & UN Forces Realignment and Supporting Effort

While the ROK and United Nations troops were driving the enemy forces back during the month of August, a gigantic effort for rebuilding the ground forces was made in the rear areas, anticipating future offensive operations in Korea. During that month, as a part of this build-up, on July 31, the 9th Infantry Regiment of the US 2nd Division arrived in Korea from the United States. It was followed by the 23rd and 38th Regiments of the same division, on August 5, and 19, respectively. The British War Office on 20 August announced that it was dispatching to Korea from Hong Kong two infantry battalions. This force, together with the 27th Infantry Brigade headquaters arrived at Pusan on August 29. Thus Great Britain became the 2nd participant in the Korean War.

Together with these ground forces, supporting elements were also alerted. On August 7, three American medium tank battalions immediately moved to

Korea. The 6th Medium Tank Battalion was attached to the US 24th Division, the 70th joined the US 1st Cavalry Division, and the 73rd on army orders sent its companies to support various ground operations on the UN defense fronts. Still more armor reinforcements, the 72nd Medium Tank Battalion (80 tanks), arrived at Pusan on August 16. During August, therefore, six US medium tank battalions landed in Korea.

The tanks in the battalions were about equally divided between M26 Pershings and M4A3 Shermans, except for one battalion which had M46 Pattons. The tank battalions averaged 69 tanks. Just before the beginning of the September UN massive counterattack, there were about 500 US medium tanks within the Pusan Perimeter. Thus, American tanks outnumbered the enemy's on the battlefield by at least 5 to 1.[144] Meanwhile, on August 30, the US 714th Transportation Railway Operating Battalion arrived in Korea and became responsible for carrying supplies which would be needed for passing defensive to offensive operations.

Near the end of August, General Walker decided on a shift of the boundary eastward between the American and ROK troops as the ROK troops in the eastern sector had withdrawn to be redeployed in other places, and in addition, the new reinforcements had to take up combat positions.

As soon as the last of the US 2nd Division's regiment, the 38th landed at Pusan, the Eighth US Army ordered the 2nd Division to relieve the US 24th Division by August 24, and to assume responsibility for the Naktong River sector. Most of the US 24th Division assembled in the vicinity of Kyongsan, as the Eighth Army reserve, to incorporate new replacements, while its 19th Infantry and the 11th Field Artillery Battalion were attached to the US 2nd Division.

Because it was notably lowered in its combat effectiveness, the US 24th Division, on August 26, reduced the 34th Infantry to paper status, and transferred the remaining personnel and equipment to the 19th and 21st Regiments.

At the same time, the Eighth US Army also reduced to paper status the 63rd Field Artillery Battalion, which had been in support of the 34th Infantry, and transferred its troops and equipment to the 11th, 13th, and 52nd Field Artillery Battalions. Simultaneously, the Eighth Army transferred the 5th Regimental Combat Team to the 24th Division as its third regiment, bringing the division up to full strength with three regiments. The 6th Medium Tank Battalion was also attached to the division.

In the meantime, the US 1st Cavalry Division on 26 August received the Third Battalion for its regimental organization from the United States. Thus, due to battle conditions in the month of August, all US divisions, except the 1st Cavalry, at various times were broken up by this process which resulted in a confused order of battle prevailing throughout the month. However, at the end of August the Eighth Army made an effort to unscramble the disorder. It ordered the 23rd Infantry which had been kept as an army reserve to return to 2nd Division control; it ordered the 27th Infantry from the Tabudong area to rejoin the 25th Division; and it ordered the 5th RCT to join the 24th Division. It kept one division as a reserve unit.

Based on the reinforced American combat strength, the EUSA in late August, shifted the boundary between the ROK and American troops in the eastern sector. It placed American troops in the axis of Sangju–Tabudong–Taegu, which had been an old ROK troops' position and also an objective of the enemy's main effort. This shift of units placed the Tabudong area in the US 1st Cavalry Division zone, and the frontal area of Mt. P'alkong-san in the ROK 1st Division zone. As a result, the ROK 6th Division at Sinnyong took up a reduced frontage.

Meanwhile, as Commander in Chief of the United Nations Command, General MacArthur made organizational changes to simplify part of his command system and clarify his relationship to various supporting service elements. On August 25, he established the Japan Logistical Command as a major organization of the Far East Command. It relieved Eighth Army Rear of all responsibilities in Japan and assumed responsibility as well for the logistical support of all UN forces in Korea. On August 27, the General designated the Far East Air Forces and the US Naval Forces, Far East, officially as part of the United Nations Command. And anticipating future offensive operations in Korea, as he had requested troops for more corps headquaters earlier, he organized, in September, three corps: the I, IX, and X Corps, under the EUSA Command.[145]

On the other hand, as part of its projected expansion program, the ROK Army opened, in August, training schools and centers for replacements. Under the ROK Army Central Training Command (Colonel Lee Jong Ch'an), it opened the 1st and 3rd Replacement Training Centers in August, and the 2nd, 5th, 6th, and 7th by the end of September.[146] The total capacity of these schools was 5,000 or 6,000 and the classes were operated on one or two week schedule. Beginning in September, the ROK Army operated the NCO training centers for selected soldiers, who would specialize in particular weapons and become an expert in each individual field.

At the same time, the ROK Army activated a systematized training center for the army officer replacements. The Korea Military Academy which had temporarily closed at the beginning of the war partially reopened classes, on August 7, at the ROK Army Central Training Command. But it was soon merged into, on August 15, the ROK Army Infantry (Officer Candidates) School. This school was renamed, on August 21, as the ROK Army All Branch School, and then again, on September 7, it was finally renamed as the ROK Army Integrated School. This school was principally a center for training officer candidates and its normal capacity was 250 junior officers a week.

In an effort to increase the strength of the ROK Army, on August 20, it reactivated the ROK 7th Division which had incorporated Min's Unit and the two Independent Anti-guerrilla Battalions, the 1st and 2nd. On August 27, the ROK Army also intended to activate the 11th Division and later, it was in the process of reactivating the 2nd and 5th Divisions. The program for activating the ROK 9th Division and III Corps was also in process. At that time, the American advisors from KMAG gave counsel in such specific fields as operation, organization, troop education and training, and maintenance and use of new equipment.[147]

At that time, the number of volunteer South Korean students was increased. In the vicinity of P'ohang, in mid-August, some of them joined the ROK 3rd Division and took part in the battle. In early September, 153 volunteer students received heavy weapons to take up guard duties on Yongil Airfield, acting like members of the ROK army heavy weapons companies.[148] Standing first on the list, 54 students and 25 patriotic youths from Japan, who had been Korean residents in Japan, volunteered to come to Korea in order to join the US 1st Cavalry Division. After them, 641 more Korean-Japanese youths volunteered and joined the ROK and US Army, and they were committed to the battle front on September 13. Most of these volunteer students, without rank insignias and serial numbers assigned, were attached to each combat or combat support unit. Among them were some girl students.[149]

In the meantime, the ROK Army put the Korean Augmentation to the United States Army (KATUSA) program into operation in close coordination with the US Army. This was to meet the replacement requirement in the depleted American ground forces. The US Eighth Army began planning for it, but it was not until August 15, based on the agreement between President Syngman Rhee and General MacArthur to officially strengthen their forces, that the latter ordered the US Army to increase the strength of the American divisions.[150] The program was, first of all, to provide replacements for the American divi-

Girl students Volunteered to be Enlisted to the ROK Army

sions in Japan, scheduled to come to Korea. As they had to wait quite a while for American replacements from the mainland United States, KATUSA was admittedly a drastic expedient for them to meet their requirements.

For the first time, on August 16, the ROK Army Headquarters shipped 313 recruits to Japan and assigned them to the US 7th Infantry Division. By the 24th the shipment of the ROK augmentation recruits made a total of 8,625 Korean officers and men for the division. Meanwhile, on August 20, the American divisions in Korea received their first augmentation recruits, and the 24th, 25th, 2nd, and 1st Cavalry Divisions, received 250 each. And later, each rifle company and battery of United States troops was assigned 100 Koreans. Near the end of August the plan changed so that every fourth day each division would receive 500 men until it had a total of 8,300 Korean recruits. The Koreans legally would be part of the ROK Army and would be paid and administered by the ROK Government. They would receive only US rations and special service items.[151]

Even though the Far East Command had initially intended to pair Korean augmentation recruits with American soldiers in a "buddy system," this did not work out uniformly in practice in the EUSA. The 1st Cavalry and 2nd Infantry Divisions used the buddy system, with the American responsible for the training of the recruit in use of weapons, drill, personal hygiene, and personal conduct. While one regiment of the 25th Division placed the recruits in separate platoons commanded by American officers and noncommissioned officers, the 24th Division placed all its augmentation recruits in separate squads and platoons commanded by selected Korean officers and NCO's.

Most American units employed the KATUSA soldiers to best advantage as security guards, in scouting and patrolling, and in performing various labor details. The Korean recruits were particularly useful in heavy weapons companies where the hand-carrying of machine guns, mortars, recoilless rifles, and their ammunition over the rugged terrain was a grueling job. They also performed valuable work in support of digging and camouflaging defensive positions.[152]

In the meantime, the number of Korean civilian service workers in the ROK and US army units began to increase. Each ROK Army unit recruited laborers from among refugees or villagers in the nearby towns and villages according to its need. When the Naktong River defense positions were taken up by the friendly forces, the laborers performed magnificient jobs. In order to meet the demand for extensive use of Korean civilians, the US Army Logistical Command at Pusan, in August, set up a new section for obtaining, managing, and controlling the civilian laborer. Soon the American divisions used these laborers at an average of about 500 men to a division. The Korean civilians, with A-frames as cargo carriers, carried war supplies up the mountains to the front lines, on their backs and evacuated wounded soldiers.[153]

At this time, a systematic aid program for the refugees was developed.

Having established about 60 refugee camps in the Pusan-Taegu area under the control of the Central Committee for Refugee Relief Works, the ROK Government, during the month of August set about the work to care for the homeless people. Meanwhile, the Health and Welfare Division under the control of the UN Forces Command took charge of the aid program in Korea, to fulfil the United Nations Security Council's "resolution on the relief for civilians." In addition, individual volunteers and various aid service organizations such as Red Cross societies, domestic and abroad, extended their helping hands to the Korean refugees.[154]

Concurrent with the steps taken to rebuild the armies, the ROK and UN forces planned to be fully prepared for the logistical support of all combat units. About 90% of logistical support of the ROK troops, at that time, came from the US Army as the ROK Government could not provide the proper amount of necessities. In September 1950, US support for ROK Army including police and laborers was raised to a level providing for a strength of 205,000.[155]

During August, the ROK troops began to prepare for future offensive operations by securing the minimum amount of new weapons and supplies. As each combat unit was equipped with the new 3.5-inch rocket launchers, it could now possess an anti-tank capability.[156] The artillery units, the ROK Army's vulnerable point, were reorganized; on August 12, four additional field artillery battalions, which had been equipped with 30 new model 105-mm. howitzers, were activated; they reorganized the six existing battalions which had been in action since the beginning of the war. Thus, by September 10, the ROK Army held a total of 10 reorganized field artillery battalions.[157]

The ROK transportation units also readusted their support service lines by assigning their office in the Taegu area to support the P'ohang-Kyongju -Yongch'on line. The Pusan transportation base office operated a daily average of 60 trains carrying about 700 freight car loads toward the railheads at the

Korean and American soldiers firing at Wae-Gawn, 1950

front. For combat service support, they operated 30 or 50 trains on the railroad between Taegu and Pusan, and 10 toward the P'ohang railhead.

On August 25, General MacArthur established the Japan Logistical Command (JLCOM) so that he could relieve Eighth Army Rear at Yokohama, Japan, of all responsibilities concerning posts, camps, and stations in Japan and assume responsibility for the logistical support of all UN forces in Korea.[158] Meanwhile, the US Logistical Command at Pusan which had been responsible for logistical support of the ROK and UN forces as well as for management of refugees and prisoners thus far in Korea, was deactivated as of September 18, and was reconstituted as the 2nd Logistical Command, still with the unchanged mission. Just before this, on August 20, the 3rd Logistical Command was activated in Japan for the support of the US X Corps.[159]

During the month of August, the UN Forces Command employed skilled Japanese workers in its eight arsenals in Japan to produce ordnance supplies in large quantities for the ROK Army. Nine hundred pieces of the new 3.5-inch rocket were produced to be delivered to Korea, and the total amount of weapons they had produced and delivered to Korea since the beginning of the war was 489,000 small arms, 34,316 pieces of heavy weapons such as machine guns and rockets, 1,418 field artilliery pieces, 743 combat vehicles, and 15,000 general purpose trucks.[160] The daily consumption of mortar and field artillery shells in that month exceeded by far the consumption rate stipulated in the US army field manual. And to fill up the food shortage, the US Army had requested combat rations, and about 20,000 tons of various ration food were shipped from the continental United States to Pusan in the same month.[161]

At that time, the Far East Command carried critically needed items from the United States by airlift, and other large or heavy supply items by surface transportation. In order to reduce the necessity for the large number of airlifts to Korea from Japan, the command organized the so called "Red Ball Express" which had a capacity of 300 tons daily of items and supplies. This Express made the run from Yokohama to Sasebo in a little more than 30 hours, where the cargo was to be transferred directly from train to ship. Then the ship carried the cargo to Pusan in 23 hours, thus making the Red Ball Express to complete its task through rail and water in a total of about 53 hours. Even though the total tonnage delivered to Korea during the month of August by this Express is unknown, the total items and supplies landed at Pusan by September 14 amounted to about 860,000 tons.[162]

Thus, as a result of the efforts and actions during August to bring combat units up to full strength, the ROK and UN forces were well prepared to pass from defensive to offensive operations. They now showed superiority in reserve forces, tanks, and artillery fire, which exceeded those of the enemy force. In brief, the friendly forces secured a strong foothold for future offensive operations.

(3) A Firm Resolution to Hold Taegu

In late August, 1950, the ROK Government and National Assembly were forced to move further down south to Pusan because of the deteriorated situation in the Taegu area. The ROK Ministry of National Defense and the Home Affairs Ministry, however, stayed together with the EUSA at Taegu to help control the ROK Army and Police actions.[163] But, as the enemy force, on August 31, launched its final massive attack against friendly positions near Taegu, General Walker, the Commanding General of Eighth Army, advised Shin Sung Mo, the ROK Defense Minister to move his office from the endangered city of Taegu to Pusan.

Defense Minister Shin suggested the idea to Home Affairs Minister Cho Byong Ok, to move to Pusan, but the latter refused it, insisting he would not budge in that critical situation as most policemen had been attached to the army units for a combat support mission. Rather, he made a visit to General Walker to express his determination that he himself and the police force would hold the city to the last end.[164] He told General Walker that "should Taegu fall to enemy hands, it would jeopardize the Pusan defense perimeter; then the UN forces might face with Korean version of tragedy at Dunkirk or at Ba'atan."

The situation near Taegu during the afternoon of September 4 was tense. Part of the US 1st Cavalry Division and ROK I & II Corps defense sectors in the north of Taegu was nearly penetrated by enemy troops, and everywhere around the perimeter the ROK Army and most of the US divisions appeared to be near the breaking point. Should the existing line be withdrawn to the Davidson Line, what would be the alternate positions? While the Eighth Army headquarters was mulling over that question, the UN Forces Command headquarters were also debating, just before the landing operation would be undertaken, whether or not the existing defensive line could be held successfully.[165]

NKPA 3rd Division entering Tae-Jeon City after penetrating Kum-Gang Line, 1950

General Walker discussed that issue one night with his deputy commander, principal staff officers and most of the division commanders. In that
discussion some officers hoped the Army could stay, pointing out that North
Korean penetrations in the past had waned after 2 or 3 days and that they might
do so again. Others insisted on withdrawal to the Davidson Line for the Army to
be realigned for the counterattack. In order to watch the development of the
matter, General Walker did not make any decision on the issue. Only to prepare
for the possible course of action in the future, he directed Eighth Army G-3 to
draft withdrawal orders for the Army to the Davidson Line. Colonel Dabney,
Eighth Army G-3, and his section at once started working on them all night
long. They were ready for issuing the orders at 05:00, September 5; however, the
order was not given, as at some time during the night General Walker reached
the decision that Eighth Army would not withdraw.

But that morning, General Walker reached the decision to move Eighth
Army headquarters back to the Pusan Fisheries College building for the protec-

tion of the teletype equipment, the Eighth Army's only one heavy signal communication equipment. But General Walker himself and a few staff officers remained in Taegu as an advanced echelon of the army command post, constitut-
ing a tactical headquarters.[166] At this time, Brig. Gen. Garvin, the Commander of
the 2nd Logistical Command at Pusan, ordered his service troops to take defensive positions on the hills in and around the port city if the tactical situation required it.

Eventually, the ROK Defense Ministry, South Korea's supreme national defense organization and the ROK Army headquarters began to move to
Pusan at 24:00, September 5. Upon receiving reports on this withdrawal, President Syngman Rhee at once went back to Taegu, and reprimanded his staff and
officials who had allowed that movement. When he was briefed on the situation
in detail, however, from the ministers of defense and home affairs, and also on
General Walker's determination to hold the existing defense line, President
Rhee admittedly understood the reason for their action. He then instructed the
ministers to give citizens information on the latest development and to ask for
their help in restoring social order by staying home and using prudence in their
conducts

The Defense Minister immediately ordered Colonel Lee Sun Kun, the
Director of Troop Information and Education Bureau to keep the Taegu citizens informed of the situation and tell them not to be agitated over it. However,
it was hard for him to tranquilize their mind under the existing circumstances
that their Government, National Assembly, Defense Ministry and even the
Army headquarters had left Taegu.

At that time, General Walker's unshakable faith was that he would hold
the Naktong line under the premise that an impending landing operation might
be launched in concert with his Army's massive counterattack against the enemy
from the Naktong line. This was why he himself and a few of his staff officers

had remained in tactical headquarters in Taegu even after his main echelon headquarters had moved to Pusan. On one occasion he told his division commanders in effect, "If the enemy gets into Taegu you will find me resisting him in the streets and I'll have some of my trusted people with me and you had better be prepared to do the same. Now get back to your divisions and fight." He added, "I don't want to see you back from the front again unless it is in a coffin."[167]

2. A Showdown on Taegu Front

In its September massive attack against the UN troops, the NKPA had a plan to advance, on September 2, its three combat divisions, the 3rd, 13th, and 1st of the Assault Grouping 3 under the control of II Corps, on the axis of Tabudong-Taegu where the US 1st Cavalry and the ROK 1st Divisions had taken up positions. These enemy divisions had been active during the period of their August offensive operations there. The enemy 3rd Division was to attack in the Waegwan area north of Taegu, the 13th Division down the mountain ridges along and west of the Sangju-Taegu road, and the 1st Division along the high mountain ridges east of the road. Defending Taegu, the US 1st Cavalry and the ROK 1st Divisions, on August 30, set up their respective combat zones. The American division had a front which extended from the confluence of two rivers, the Kumho and the Naktong, to Hill 741, including the Waegwan area inbetween, while the ROK 1st Division took charge of the front between Hill 741 and the northern half of P'algong-san. The 1st Cavalry Division deployed its 5th Cavalry Regiment around southeast of Waegwan, the 7th Cavalry Regiment in the area of Yuhak-san, and the 8th Cavalry Regiment along the road north of Tabudong. Adjacent to this regiment on the right, the ROK 1st Division took up positions due north of P'algong-san.

Prior to this disposition, however, as the Naktong Bulge had been indanger of being penetrated by the enemy I Corps at night on August 31, General Walker, on September 1, ordered the 1st Cavalry Division to attack north or northwest in an effort to divert that enemy strength in the west to other places. Upon receipt of this order, the division commander at once called an operational meeting. Based on the decision made at the meeting, the 7th Cavalry Regiment prepared for an attack to capture Suam-san (Hill 518), while the 8th Cavalry Regiment prepared for diversionary attacks on the 7th Cavalry's right flank. Suam-san, located north of a road between Waegwan and Tabudong, was a critical terrain feature which dominated the only road on the south that led to Taegu. The hill had been considered an enemy assembly area at that time.[168]

This planned attack against Hill 518 chanced to coincide with the defection and surrender, on September 2, of Maj. Kim Song Jun, the S-3 of the enemy 19th Regiment, 13th Division. He reported that the NKPA II Corps was to launch a full-scale attack at 18:00 that day. He said that the enemy 13th Division had just taken in 4,000 replacements, and was now back to a strength of approximately 9,000 men. Prisoner Kim's statement was so well timed that the US Eighth Army could alert all front-line units, in advance, to be prepared for the enemy attack.[169]

As it had been pre-planned, the commander of the US 1st Cavalry Division, that morning, ordered one of his subordinate elements to attack and seize enemy-held Suam-san. It was in effect a spoiling attack against the North Koreans northwest of Taegu. UN Air Force fighter bombers delivered napalm and bombs and the division artillery laid down its concentrations on the hills. Immediately after the final napalm strike, the 1st Battalion of the 7th Cavalry Regiment attacked up the hill. But the attack was doomed to failure because the narrow ridge line forced the attack troops to resolve into a column of companies, and in turn, into a column of platoons and finally into a column of squads. Therefore, the final effect was that of a regimental attack amounting to a one-squad attack against a strongly held position.

That night the US 8th Cavalry Regiment on the right flank came under attack by enemy troops led by tanks, and the 2nd Battalion, 8th Cavalry on Hill 448 west of Tabudong was overrun. On its right, the US 8th Cavalry Intelligence & Reconnaissance Platoon and a detachment of the ROK police on the crest of the Walled City of Ka-san [an ancient fortress and stone wall on the crest of Ka-san] were also pressed hard by the enemy. The ROK 1st Division, adjacent to these friendly troops on the right, was not an exception; however, the ROK division, destroying 3 enemy tanks, could hold its position at P'algong-san as the enemy's fire was light and sporadic. Only light skirmishes between both forces continued for a while.[170]

Considering the tactical importance of the Kasan mountain top (Hill 902) 16km north of Taegu, which could dominate the road between Taegu and Tabudong and give obsevation all the way south into the city of Taegu, General Walker ordered his troops to recapture it immediatley. As the US Cavalry Division had already deployed its three regiments on the front-line positions at that time, the 8th Army Engineer Combat Battalion took charge of the mission.

Perceiving a crisis in the Taegu area casued by the sudden surge of the enemy south toward the city, the commander of the US 1st Cavalry Division immediately ordered Assistant Division Commander Brig. Gen. Frank A. Allen, Jr., to organize Task Force Allen. This task force comprised two provisional battalions formed of division headquarters and technical service troops, the division band, the replacement company, and other miscellaneous troops. It was to be used in combat if the enemy troops broke through to the edge of the city. Being pressed hard, the Eighth Army that day ordered a ROK battalion (Lt. Col. Lee Sang Ch'ol) from the Taegu Replacement Training Center to a position at the rear of the 8th Cavalry Regiment, to counter the enemy penetration into the Tabudong-Taegu front.[171]

Armaggedon in the Vicinity of Taegu

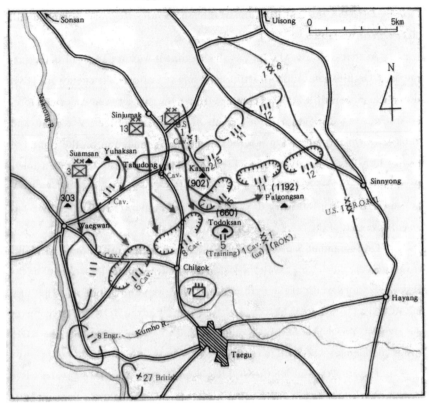

In the meantime, the US 7th Cavalry Regiment again, on September 3, committed its 3rd Battalion to the Suam-san area. The battalion attacked against the hill and continued to fight a bloody battle until the next day; however, as did the 1st Battalion the day before, it wound up in a column of companies that resolved itself into a column of squads, and the 3rd Battalion also failed in its attack. According to a prisoner captured there at that time, 1,200 North Koreans were dug in on the hill, and they had 120-mm guns and 82-mm mortars with ammunition.[172] While these actions were in progress, on the left flank of the Cavalry Division, the 2nd Battalion of the 5th Cavalry Regiment attacked Hill 303 north of Waegwan.

At that time, the US 7th Cavalry Regiment was in danger of being surrounded. Despite continued air strikes and infantry efforts, the enemy 3rd Division on Suam-san (Hill 518) was coming through the gap between American forces and moving down to Hill 464 south of the road between Waegwan and Tabudong. On the left, Waegwan became no man's land, and on the right, the enemy 13th Division advanced to Tabudong. Meanwhile, the US 8th Engineer Battalion which had been pushing forward to the Ka-san area was driven back by September 5 the following day, as a result of desperate resistance by a battalion-size unit of the NKPA 1st Division.

On September 5, upon receiving the report on this crisis, General Walker ordered the American cavalry division to withdraw under the cover of darkness to positions south of the road between Waegwan and Tabudong. That day the ROK 1st Division was also ordered to withdraw as the ROK 8th Division on the right at Yongch'on had been penetrated. This order came from the ROK Corps commander who tried to realign the defense positions.

The 8th, 7th, and 5th Cavalry Regiments of the American cavalry division in that order began their withdrawals starting at night on September 6. However, as they had been engaged with the enemy troops in front of the division line, and as part of the enemy had infiltrated into the southeast of Waegwan and Tabudong area, the disengaging action could not be made rapidly. To make the matters worse, the heavy rainfall that night slowed their withdrawal march.

In addition, in its reverse march, the 7th Cavalry Regiment was to gain possession of an anticipated new defensive position on Hill 465; however, the hill was already in the enemy hands. Be that as it may, the American cavalry division withdrew to new defensive positions during September 6-7. Its 5th(to which the 1st Battalion of the 7th Cavalry Regiment was attached) and 8th Cavalry Regiments took up positions south of the road between Waegwan and Taegu, and the rest of the 7th Cavalry Regiment moved to a point near Taegu in division reserve.[173]

In the meantime, the ROK 1st Division was ordered to move by the evening of September 6 to an area just in front of P'algong-san, and also on order from the ROK corps, it had to reinforce the ROK 8th Division by detaching its 11th Regiment(−) to help save the crisis in the Yongch'on area.[174] The commander of the ROK 1st Divison then attempted to close the gap between his troops and the American cavalry division on the left flank, and also link up with the ROK 6th Division on the right, by placing his 15th Regiment on the left at Namsandong, the 12th Regiment on the right at Taeyuldong, and the 1st Battalion of the 11th Regiment on the division left in the south of the Walled City of Ka-san.[175]

On September 6, now with Ka-san firmly in their possession, the enemy 13th and 1st Divisions established a roadblock below Tabudong and occupied Hill 570 overlooking the road to Taegu. The next day five tanks of the 16th Reconnaissance Company were ordered by the US cavalry division commander to lead an attack against the roadblock and to dispose of the enemy. As US air strikes and artillery kept Ka-san and Hill 570 under heavy attack, the enemy offensive actions there remained passive for two consecutive days. On the morning of the 8th, the 3rd Battalion of the US 8th Cavalry Regiment tried to drive the enemy from Hill 570, but it faced a desperate enemy resistance. According to the US army intelligence, it was estimated that 1,000 enemy soldiers were on that hill. Under such circumstances, General Walker had directed the previous day that the ROK 1st and US 1st Cavalry Divisions select a boundary between them, and consequently, the ROK division on the right flank took charge of the attack mission against the Walled City of Ka-san.[176]

In the meantime, the enemy 3rd Division which had seized Waegwan on the 7th and 8th of September by dislodging the US 5th Cavalry Regiment from Hill 303, attacked the following day against Hill 345, the new defensive position of the 5th Cavalry Regiment, 5km east of Waegwan. Thus, both forces were immediately locked in hard, seesaw fighting.[177] Part of the positions of the 1st Battalion, 5th Cavalry, was penetrated; however, it could finally regain the position after four counterattacks. Until the 14th, the American cavalry regiment and the enemy force repeated the seesaw battle for the possession of Hill 174 which had by now changed hands seven times. Only with such difficulty, could the US 5th Cavalry Regiment hold the hill, suffering heavy losses.[178] That day part of the ROK 1st Division, on division left, had also been pressed hard all day long by other enemy troops, but they successfully held their positions.[179]

At pre-dawn hours on September 10, the NKPA 1st Division resumed its attack in the vicinity of Ka-san. While a part of its strength was moving down south toward Toduk-san (660 metes), another group was approaching the mountain of P'algong-san. Meanwhile, the US 1st Cavalry Division placed at this time the 5th Cavalry Regiment on the hills near Naksandong northwest of Taegu, the 8th Cavalry on the northern hills of Ch'ilgok due north of Taegu, and kept its 7th Cavalry in reserve.

The fighting north of Taegu, on September 11, in the vicinity of high hills was heavy and confused. The positions on the right flank of the 8th Cavalry were penetrated, and even Hill 314 south of those overrun positions was seized by the enemy troops. This defensive failure could cause grave consequences in defending Taegu. Only the ROK 5th Training Battalion, previously hurried into Toduksan on the right flank of the 8th Cavalry prevented the enemy from gaining complete control of this terrain feature. There ROK troops were untested and was poorly equipped.

With a mission to retake the hill, the 3rd Battalion, 7th Cavalry Regiment launched a counterattack the next day. Soon the battalion faced desperately resisting enemy troops; intense machine gun fire, mortar fire and grenades came down on the attacking American troops. But the American soldiers continued the attack, several times engaging North Koreans at close quarters, and finally succeeded in reaching the crest and recaptured the hill. In this battle, however, two American companies lost all their officers and including them, a total of 458 men became casualties. Prisoners said that the enemy also suffered about 700 losses.[180]

After the capture of Hill 314 on September 12, the situation north of Taegu improved; however, the fighting continued unabated. The 2nd Battalion, 8th Cavalry, still fought to gain control of Hill 570 on the east side of the Tabudong highway, while the 3rd Battalion of the same regiment attacked Hill 401, northwest of Ch'ilgok, where an enemy force had penetrated in a gap between American cavalry regiments.

On September 14, the ROK 1st Division also continued its attack northwest and advanced to the edge of the Walled City of Ka-san, in close coordination with the American Cavalry division on the left. The 1st Battalion, ROK 11th Regiment, seized Hill 755 after it had repulsed infiltrating enemy troops, and part of the ROK 15th Regiment reached the stone ramparts of the Walled City of Ka-san. The ROK division had been attached to the US I Corps as of noon on September 13, the previous day, based on the arrangement that had been made to secure a unified command system in defending Taegu. The NKPA 1st Division was the main adversary to this ROK division.[181]

On the other hand, as a part of making preparation for a final close-in defense of Taegu, 14 battalions of South Korean police were brought in and they dug in around the city. Finally, late on September 14, the ROK 1st and US Cavalry Divisions recovered from the crisis and completely defeated the enemy troops at many points about 10km north of Taegu. At this time, the remnants of the enemy 13th and 1st Divisions were withdrawing northward from Tabudong and the Walled City of Ka-san. Eventually the NKPA II Corps' September offensive for capturing Taegu failed.

3. Holding out Ch'angnyong and Yongsan

In the area of Ch'angnyong and Yongsan of the Naktong Bulge area, the US 2nd Division was to confront the 2nd enemy assault grouping under the control of the NKPA I Corps. The American division, which had relieved the 24th Division only a few days before, in late August, placed its 9th Infantry in the Yongsan front reaching from Pugokri to Namji, the 23rd Infantry in the sector just in front of Ch'angnyong, and the 38th Infantry in the hill mass directly in front of Hyonp'ung.

At that time, the enemy assault unit 2 under the command of the NKPA I Corps deployed its 9th Division(−) in the Yongsan area to oppose the US 9th Infantry, and the NKPA 2nd Division which had been rebuilt in the Kimch'on area in the Ch'angnyong front. The NKPA 10th Division assembled along the Naktong River bank just in front of Hyonp'ung.[182] All these enemy troops were prepared for the final offensive, of which the zero hour had been set at 22:00 on August 31.

Upon receiving instructions from Eighth Army for aggressive patrolling, on August 31, the commander of the US 2nd Division, ordered the 9th Infantry Regiment to organize a strong company−sized combat patrol to gain information of enemy plans. The patrol called Task Force Manchu was preparing for crossing of the Naktong just after dusk turned into darkness, when it was surprised by large mass of enemy troops. This meant that three enemy divisions which had assembled along the river bank across the Naktong were making a concerted surprise crossing of the river to begin attacking Yongsan, Ch'an-gnyong, and Hyonp'ung.

The US 9th Infantry was surprised by the enemy 9th Division and instantaneously the enemy broke through the American troops' river line positions, inflicting a heavy loss on the latter. To make the matters worse, the Heavy Mortar Platoon which had been placed at the Pakjin ferry site, as an element of Task Force Manchu, was caught wholly by the enemy. Positions on the left flank was also overrun by the enemy troops which had crossed the Naktong at the Kihang ferry site. In this desperate action, Pfc. Luther H. Story, a weapons squad leader, distinguished himself by engaging the enemy at close range, even though he was badly wounded.[183]

Upon receiving the report of the situation, the American division commander canceled the plan of aggressive patrolling, and his 9th Infantry, in turn, ordered E Company which was to have been the striking force of Task Force Manchu, to take a blocking position at the pass between Cloverleaf Hill and Obongri Ridge. However, the critical terrain features near this hill mass was already under enemy control.

The US 23rd Infantry Regiment which had gone into defensive positions in front of Ch'angnyong also came under enemy attack roughly at about the same time. The NKPA 2nd Division attacked the American regiment, and instantaneously broke through its defense line. Many American soldiers were killed or captured. As the US regiment had been surrounded by the enemy troops, it was unable to withdraw. The Commander of the US 2nd Division at once ordered the 3rd Battalion, the 38th Infantry, to proceed from Ch'angnyong to Mosanri in an effort to rescue them with the help of artillery, tank, and close-support air strikes.

The NKPA 10th Division crossed the Naktong in front of Hyonp'ung and continued to attack against the American troops. The 1st Battalion of the

US 38th Regiment was forced to move back to Hyonp'ung. During this with-drawal, the battalion executed delaying actions, and at night the following day, it moved again southward. At this time, the enemy division caused Eighth Army much concern. In which direction would he attack? But the enemy troops re-mained inactive until the 15th of September, except executing small scale re-connoitering skirmishes in the vicinity of Hyonp'ung. Captured enemy material and statements of prisoners indicated that the enemy division was supposed to remain assembled there until the NKPA II Corps had captured Taegu.[84]

Before the morning of September 1 had passed, North Koreans had pen-etrated everywhere into the US 2nd Division sector and cut the division in two halves: north of Ch'angnyong and southward in the Yongsan area. The divi-sion commander decided that this situation made it advisable to control and di-rect the divided division as two special forces. Accordingly, he placed the divi-sion artillery commander, Brig. Gen. Loyal M. Haynes, in command of the northern group in the area of Ch'angnyong and Hyonp'ung; he placed Brig. Gen. Joseph S. Bradley, Assistant Division Commander, in charge of other units of the division in front of Yongsan in the south. At this time, General Walker pre-sented himself on the 2nd divisional front to watch the development of the situa-tion and to consider the matter of using reserve units.

In the meantime, just in front of Yongsan, the advanced support ele-ments of Task Force Manchu was surrounded by the enemy; in such isolated circumstances, however, the task force, with the help of airdropped supplies, successfully repulsed and checked the advance of the enemy until September 3. But on that day, Lieutenant Edward Schmitt, the commanding officer of the group, was killed in a close quarters battle and only 22 men escaped to friendly lines.[85]

On the morning of September 1, the commander of the US 2nd Division, aware of the fact that the 9th Infantry had virtually no reserve troops to defend

The ROK & U.N. Forces hold out at Ch'angnyong-Youngsan

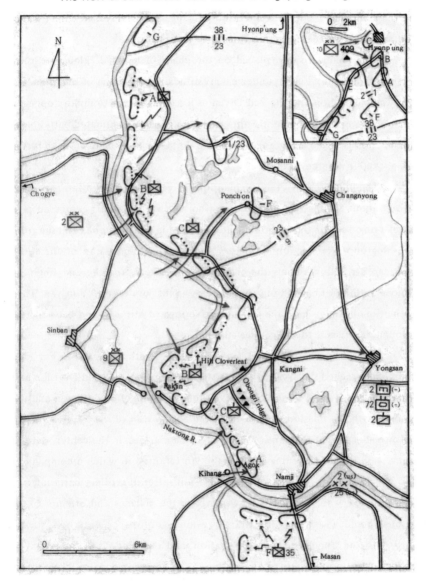

Yongsan, attached an infantry company and an engineer combat battalion to the regiment. The 72nd Tank Battalion and the 2nd Division Reconnaissance Company also were assigned positions close to Yongsan.

The engineers were placed on the chain of low hills along the road north of Yongsan and came under enemy attack. In the south of the town, the 72nd Tank Battalion and the 2nd Division Reconnaissance Company opposed North Koreans in a sharp fight. Four enemy tanks and an estimated battalion of North Koreans seized Yongsan; however, in the suburbs of the town, both forces were locked in a fierce battle.

The following day, the commanding officer of the US 9th Infantry reorganized about 800 men of his regiment who had arrived at his command post east of Yongsan from the overrun positions. In midafternoon tanks and the reorganized group attacked into Yongsan and regained possession of the town. American air action cut off the enemy reinforcement, and the 2nd Engineer Combat Battalion knocked out three enemy tanks just west of Yongsan. Thus for the time being at least, the enemy's drive toward Miryang had been halted, although the crisis in the bulge area still persisted.

At 13:15 on September 2, General Walker with approval of Far East Command attached the 1st Provisional Marine Brigade to the 2nd Division and ordered a coordinated attack by all available elements of the division and the marines, with the mission of destroying the enemy east of the Naktong River and of restoring the river line. Accordingly, the marines, in the center, were to attack west the next morning at 08:00; the 9th Infantry, to which a company of the 72nd Tank Battalion and a battery of an anti-aircraft artillery battalion had been attached, would attack northwest above the marines and attempt to re-establish contact with the 23rd Infantry; remnants of the 1st Battalion, 9th Infantry, the 2nd Engineer Combat Battalion, and the 72nd Tank Battalion(−) would attack on the south of the marines to re-establish contact with the US

25th Division. Eighth Army then ordered a reserve unit, the US 24th Division headquarters and the 19th Infantry to move to Susanri area south of Masan. There they were to prepare to enter the future battle.[186]

The Marine attack started with the help of air strikes and artillery concentrations. The 1st Battalion south of the road pursued the retreating enemy force, and the 2nd Battalion north of the road had a harder time, encountering desperate enemy resistance. In this fight, the battalion knocked out 4 enemy tanks (T34). Meanwhile, the 3rd Battalion received orders to pass through the 2nd Battalion and continue the attack. Coordinating its attack with that of the marines, the US 9th Infantry advanced abreast of them on the southwest of Yongsan. On the morning of September 4, the 2nd Battalion of American marines quickly completed occupation of Hill 116, and the 1st Battalion occupied what appeared to be a command post of the NKPA 9th Division. The marine battalion captured two abandoned enemy tanks in excellent condition there.

In the meantime, in front of Ch'angnyong, the 1st Battalion of the US 23rd Infantry Regiment, which had tried to obstruct the enemy approach in the road of Kangjin ferry-Ch'angnyong, had been driven from the river positions and isolated. The battalion commander, determined to obstruct the enemy's advance, began 3-day stand as an island in a sea of enemy. The US 2nd Division did not leave that battalion in its isolated position. The division committed a battalion of the 38th Infantry to the battle to open the enemy-held road to the 1st Battalion. Eventually, the relief force broke through the enemy roadblock. Having succeeded in this action, General Haynes changed the boundary between the 38th and 23rd Infantry Regiments, giving the road sector to the former and the Pugok-Ch'angnyong defense sector to the latter.

An estimated enemy battalion launched an attack against the US 38th Regiment command post, and the regiment organized all officers and enlisted men present, including members of the mortar and tank companies and attached anti-aircraft artillery units, to clear its defense sector of enemy troops.

On the morning of September 5, in front of Yongsan, the American troops moved out in their third day of counterattack in a torrential rain. As the attack progressed, the American marines captured Obongri Ridge and the 9th Infantry approached Cloverleaf Hill. There, on the high ground ahead, they could see enemy troops digging in. In the afternoon that day, 300 enemy infantry led by tanks came from the village of Tugok, and struck the marine troops. The marines, however, did not give in; rather, they repelled the enemy, knocking down 4 enemy tanks. As the action nearly come to the finish, the Marines, on order from General Walker, were released effective as of 00:01 on September 5 from operational control of the US 2nd Division. They began to leave their lines at Obongri Ridge and headed for Pusan, to be prepared for the future landing operations on Inchon.[87]

The enemy attack tapered off with the coming of daylight that day, the 5th of September. However, during the predawn hours on September 8, the enemy 2nd Division, which had assembled in front of Ch'angnyong, resumed its attack against the US 23rd Infantry. Instantaneously it broke through the American defense line and advanced to Ponch'ori, the small village 5 km away from Ch'angnyong. All available men from Headquarters Company and special units were formed into squads and put into the fight at once to drive the enemy troops off. The Air Force gave invaluable aid to the ground troops at the most critical points. The battle lasted until the morning of the following day, but the enemy attack finally ceased shortly after noon that day. Even though its strength was largely spent by that day, the enemy 2nd Division continued to harass rear areas around Ch'angnyong with infiltrating groups as large as companies. In order to counter such enemy actions, the US 2nd Division also intensified its daily patrolling.

The enemy loss was heavy in this furious battle. The medical officer of the 17th Regiment, the NKPA 2nd Division, captured in that battle, said that the enemy division lost about 1,300 killed, and 2,500 wounded, thus losing almost all of its offensive strength. Likewise, the US 2nd Division, including the 1st Provisional Marine Brigade, suffered heavy losses; among them the US 23rd Infantry Regiment suffered most and had an estimated combat efficiency of only 38%.[188]

4. Offensive and Defensive near Haman-Masan

In late August 1950, the battle front near Masan was in a brief state of lull; increased enemy activities were sighted only in the rear areas. At this time, the US 25th Division was holding a front of almost 48 km, beginning in the north at the Namji bridge over the Naktong River and extending westward through Sibidangsan to the southern coastal road near Chindongri. The defense sector included Chinju-Masan railroad and highway, and the high mountain mass south of the road. General Kean, the division commander, placed the 35th Infantry in the low ground between Komanri and the Nam River, and the 24th Infantry in high around west of Haman up to and including Battle Mountain and P'ilbong. The 5th Regimental Combat Team held the southern spur of Sobuksan to the coastal road at Chindongri. He kept the 27th Infantry Regiment at Masan as a reserve unit.

The North Korean 6th Division, in the meantime, assembled in Chinju to prepare for the breakthrough effort, while the NKPA 7th Division was concentrated in the area northeast of Uiryong to attack north of Masan highway.[189] While most of the enemy force remained assembled in the rear areas, part of it moved out to build an underwater bridge across the Nam River, without being interfered with by the UN air strikes. The enemy plan of attack seemed to be for the 6th Division to push east along the main Chinju-Komanri-Masan road, and at the same time for the 7th Division to cut the Ch'irwon road south of the Nam River. These two avenues of approach formed the axes of the enemy main attack.

At 23:30 on August 31, two enemy divisions launched massive attacks in their respective zones of action. The NKPA 7th Division made a concerted crossing of the river to attack against the US 35th Infantry positions. The 2nd Battalion of the American infantry regiment, which had taken up positions on the river line, came under concentrated enemy attack. The American battalion, however, could repel this enemy attack with the help of proximity (VT) fuze fire of the 64th Field Artillery Battalion and the UN air strikes, inflicting heavy losses on the enemy. The North Koreans continued to cross the Nam River in the general area of the gap between the 1st and 2nd Battalions north of Komanri; thus a large number of North Koreans could approach villages such as Ch'irwon and Chungri in the rear area. The 2nd Battalion, even in a situation surrounded by enemy troops, performed greatly in close quarters on hills nearby. At this time, UN fighter planes, as if they were "flying bombs," rapidly delivered bombs on the enemy concentration in the rear area so that they could not move out.[190] The 1st Battalion which had been deployed on the high ground in front of Komanri repulsed the infiltrating enemy force; however, the position of B Company on Sibidang-san received hard blows from the enemy 13th Regiment(−), 6th Division. Sibidang-san just in front of Komanri was certain to figure prominently in the enemy's attack because it gave observation over all the surrounding country. It was therefore a key position in the American division line. In order to effectively counter the enemy armored attack, the American troops called in a Sherman tank and it knocked out an enemy tank. A 3.5-inch bazooka team destroyed an enemy self-propelled gun and several antitank guns.

The enemy 13th Regiment, which had secured a supply route and controlled rear areas, launched a frontal attack against the American troops. However, an antipersonnel mine field combined with barbed wire and booby traps which had been laid and installed in front of American defensive positions stopped the first enemy infantry assault. Others followed in quick succession. They were met and turned back with the fire of all weapons. B Company riflemen concentrated their resisting fire on enemy troops. After three furious engagements, the enemy attack subsided. On the slope below the American defensive position, a great amount of abandoned enemy equipment as well as the enemy dead were scattered. Among the dead lay the body of the commanding officer of the NKPA 13th Regiment, Han Il Nae.[91]

In the meantime, the 2nd Battalion of the US 24th Infantry Regiment which had taken up the center part of the American defense sector came under enemy attack. The main element of the NKPA 6th Division broke through the American battalion positions in front of Haman; most of the battalion members fled in disorder leaving the town open to direct enemy attack. The American division commander at once committed the 1st Battalion, 27th Regiment to the place. Artillery preparation preceded the battalion's counterattack, and the Air Force bombed, napalmed, rocketed and strafed Haman, making the town a sea of flames.

The American battalion moved out in the attack spearheaded by 8 tanks. But enemy fire destroyed one tank on a hill side west of Haman. The attacking infantry troops also suffered heavy casualties. All day air strikes had harassed the enemy and prevented him from consolidating his gains. However, on the morning of the following day, the North Koreans struck the American battalion in a counterattack. Instantaneously the infantry battalion repulsed the enemy force, with the help of air strikes; the American soldiers even pursued the enemy until they secured the former positions of the 2nd Battalion, 24th Infantry. The next day, the enemy attacked the 1st Battalion again. But American artillery, tank fire and air strikes met this attack. When the attack had been repulsed, hundreds of enemy dead lay about the battalion position. A prisoner said that the four North Korean battalions which had fought the American battalion lost about 1,000 men.[192]

In the afternoon on September 2, the 2nd Battalion of the US 27th Infantry Regiment was committed to the river line positions to rescue American soldiers who had remained isolated there. It took quite a long while for the battalion to drive the desperate enemy troops off the place; it reached the river line only in the afternoon the following day. There the American battalion, together with the remaining 2nd Battalion of the 35th Infantry, launched a concerted attack against enemy troops to regain the former positions. A combined effort of US infantry, armor, and artillery units was made in this attack.

As the enemy infiltrators attacked the 24th Infantry command post and several artillery positions at Chungri, the American division commander ordered the 27th Infantry to attack and destroy the enemy operating there. Accordingly, its 3rd Battalion attacked against enemy soldiers who had held the artillery positions and repelled them by the following morning. The 2nd Battalion launched its attack to seize and secure the high ground dominating the "Horseshoe," as the deep curve in the Masan road was called, east of Komamri and then relieve the pressure on the 24th Infantry rear. After the battalion advanced some distance, however, an enemy force counterattacked it and inflicted heavy casualties, which included 13 officers. Despite the losses in the morning, the battalion continued its attack and finally succeeded in taking the high ground in the afternoon that day, with the help of air force and armor units. The next morning, September 4, the battalion attacked straight ahead into the area between Komamri and Haman where enemy troops were operating, and with the help of numerous air strikes, it beat the enemy off. In this attack, the battalion counted more than 300 enemy dead.[193]

The 1st Battalion which had regained the Haman area turned its ridge positions over to the 1st Battalion of the US 24th Infantry Regiment at night on September 4. The next morning, however, being pressed by only a small group of North Koreans, the latter left its positions. Thus the 24th Infantry demonstrated once again its unstable nature in this fighting. Ever since its entrance into combat in the Sangju area in July, 1950, the regiment had given a poor performance. Aware of this fact, General Kean, the division commander, decided to recommend to General Walker the immediate removal of the 24th Infantry Regiment from combat.[194]

In the afternoon on September 4, the 2nd Battalion of the US 27th Infantry Regiment moved northward again as the river line positions of the 2nd Battalion, 35th Infantry, had been penetrated by the enemy. The battalion of the 27th Infantry was immediately in contact with enemy forces deployed on the roadside hills; North Korean machine guns fired on the American troops from three directions, thus blocking the battalion's advance. The North Koreans attacked the American battalion at the rear, trying to encircle it. As a result, both forces were locked in a furious battle. This time, torrential rains fell and observation became poor. To make the matters worse, by this time, the American battalion was running short of ammunition. However, the next morning, eight transport planes flew in with the air supply, and the battalion resumed its attack to the rear. Now the American battalion cleared the rear area of enemy soldiers.[195] Meanwhile, at about this time the US 35th Infantry also engaged enemy infiltrators in the rear area. These infiltrators came in platoon or company sized groups.

In this critical time, the US Fifth Air Force added its tremendous fire power to that of the division artillery in support of the ground force. General Kean, the US 25th Division Commander, speaking of the action during the past two days, said, "The close air support rendered by Fith Air Force again saved this division as they have many times before."[196]

In the meantime, in rear areas of the US 25th Division, guerrilla and espionage activities increased, with the most tragic single incident taking place
during the night of 3-4 September. That night a group of guerrillas attacked a
radio relay station at Ch'angwon near Masan. Even in Masan, at the peak of the
enemy offensive, the manager of the Masan branch of the Korean Press Association confessed that he was the chief of the South Korean Labor Party in Masan
and that he had funneled information to the enemy. The chief of guards of the
Masan prison turned out to be the head of a Communist cell and seven of his
guards were members. So the city appeared to be a nest of Communist sympathizers and agents. General Kean considered the situation so menacing that he
ordered Masan be evacuated of all people except a few necessary officials,
workers and their families. On 10 and 11 September alone the 25th Division
evacuated more than 12,000 people by LST from Masan.[197]

After September 5, the American troops were under much less enemy
pressure, and on the following day, the 1st Battalion of the US 27th Infantry
moved north to join the 2nd Battalion of the same regiment in cleaning up enemy troops below the Nam River. Sixteen different groups of the enemy reportedly were dispersed with heavy casualties during the day. The US 25th Division
buried more than 2,000 North Korean dead, killed between September 1
through 7 behind its lines. This number did not include those killed in front of
its positions.[198]

Even though the main element had collapsed, one remaining enemy
battalion held the crest of Battle Mountain. Thus the 3rd Battalion of the US
27th Infantry counterattacked up the mountain with the mission to retake the
peak. But the dug-in enemy repeatedly drove the American troops off and back
down the slope in three days of fighting.

The American regimental commander had two companies dig in on the
hill east of and lower than Battle Mountain to tempt the enemy troops, and sur-

rounded them with barbed wire, mine fields and registered artillery fires on all enemy approaches to the position. As had been expected, the North Koreans on the mountain attacked the lower American defensive position that night. But concentrated pre-planned fire of American troops not only drove the North Koreans off but helped pursue them until eventually retaking the mountain crest.[199] Meanwhile, after the 1st Battalion of the US 5th Regimental Combat Team had failed in its attempt for retaking Sobuk-san, reconnoitering skirmishes between the two forces continued quite a while in that regimental defense sector.

Most probably learning the limits of their offensive capability, North Koreans at this time turned to the defensive. On the other hand, the US 25th Division which had forced the enemy to fight a war of attrition by employing an offensive type of defense took the offensive and was prepared for a massive counterattack.

5. The Battle to Regain Yongch'on

On August 31, the enemy 8th and 15th Divisions, both of which belonged to the 4th Assault Grouping under the control of the NKPA II Corps, stood ready to attack two small towns of Sinnyong and Yongch'on. Opposing these enemy troops stood the ROK 6th and 8th Divisions on the defensive. The NKPA 8th Division built up its combat strength by receiving South Koreans conscripted in the area of Uisong and twenty-one tanks detached from the NKPA 17th Armored Brigade. The objective of the enemy division was Sinnyong, and to achieve it, the division first of all concentrated its main effort on breaking through the Chorim-san-Kap-ryong line. Meanwhile, the enemy 15th Division moved, on August 20, from the Tabudong area to Ipam northeast of Yongch'on, by way of Uisong. The NKPA 73rd Independent and 103rd Security Regiments were attached to the division. Also added were 166 artillery pieces of all kinds and twelve tanks.[200] The immediate objective of this division was Yongch'on which, if secured, would be used as a stepping stone for capturing Taegu.

At about this time, the ROK 6th Division formed a new main line of resistance at Sansong-Kap-ryong-Wha-san line astride the high grounds north of Sinnyong. The South Korean division placed its 2nd Regiment in the area of Unsandong in the axis of Kunwi-Sinnyong, the 19th Regiment on the Uisong-Sinnyong avenue of approach, south of Chorim-san, and one battalion of the 7th Regiment, together with the 15th Regiment which had been attached to the 6th Division, in Wha-san. The remaining 7th Regiment($-$) was kept as division reserve. In addition, three batteries (18 pieces of 105-mm.) of the 16th Artillery Battalion were to provide direct support for each infantry regiment.[201]

The ROK division Engineer Combat Battalion laid anti-tank and anti-personnel mines on all anticipated enemy approach or infiltration avenues in front of the division line. Four 3.5-inch rocket launchers were issued to the 1st Battalion of the ROK 19th Regiment in south of Chorim-san and one US tactical air control party was operating with the battalion.[202] The ROK 8th Division in north of Yonch'on placed its 21st Regiment on division left in the Noko-jae-Pohyon-san area, and the 16th Regiment on the right flank in the south of Ipam. These two regiments had been carrying out outpost actions since the end of August. Meanwhile, the 10th Regiment which had been attached to the ROK 3rd Division in P'ohang remained and was active there.

The town of Yongch'on was a junction point where roads from Sinnyong, Kusandong, and Ipam converged into it. The traversing road nets which ran from Yonch'on to Taegu, and to Kyongju had been well developed. It was also a railroad junction where the Central, Taegu, and Southeastern Coastal lines branched off. The town itself lay halfway from Taegu and Kyongju; 34km from the former and 28km from the latter. Therefore, should the enemy break through at Yongch'on, he would immediately threaten the safety of Taegu and Kyongju, cutting the east-west supply route. At the same time, he would have separated the ROK Corps in that area into two isolated units: the I and II Corps. In brief, Yongch'on was a point of strategic importance on the Naktong perimeter line.

When the North Koreans started the September offensive operations against the UN Forces, the NKPA 8th and 15th Divisions made a concerted attack, at night on September 2, against Sinnyong and Yongch'on. Right after the artillery preparation, the enemy 8th Division committed its armored element against the ROK army defensive positions. The 1st Battalion of the ROK 19th Regiment countered this enemy thrust successfully by a notable command achievement of the commander.

When unknown numbers of enemy tanks approached the ROK battalion front, the observation post immediately requested flares to light up the battle front. The ROK 16th Artillery Battalion and other organic weapons' fire concentrated on the infiltrating enemy troops. At once the the ROK 1st Battalion commander organized a special anti-tank team to be committed to the scene.

Accordingly, the special team led by 2nd Lt. Pyun Kyu Yong infiltrated into the enemy columns. They knocked out one enemy tank at the rear first, with 3.5-inch rockets, and then another, in turn, until they destroyed 7 tanks. They even captured 5 enemy tank crews. Only one enemy tank resisted not to be captured when the anti-tank team approached the enemy column. Five others had already been abandoned. All members of the special team were decorated, promoted to a higher rank, and as a team they received ₩ 500,000 for their distinguished works in that battle.[203]

Just before dawn, the ROK battalion also counted enemy dead equivalent to a company size unit near or on the battle ground, captured various weapons equivalent to two truckloads. At that time, UN airplanes, requested by the tactical air control party, flew over to another enemy concentration and assembled tanks in the area north of Kap-ryong to napalm and bomb them. The place was not far from the above mentioned battle ground.

Later, it was found that a total of 21 enemy tanks had been destroyed in that battle, including 8 knocked out by the anti-tank team of the 1st Battalion, ROK 19th Regiment. Thus the enemy 8th Division's plan for the breakthrough at the ROK army line was decisively defeated in a moment.[204] That day, the

Recapture of Yongch'on

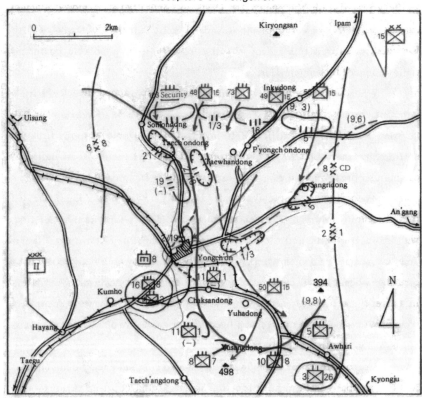

ROK 6th Division, while engaging the enemy in sporadic skirmishes, returned the 15th Regiment to its parent unit; in its place, it received the newly activated 8th Regiment of the ROK 7th Division.[205]

In the mean time, on the night of September 2, the ROK 8th Division came under attack by the NKPA 15th Division. As the 16th Regiment on its right flank had been penetrated, the ROK division withdrew to the area near Kiryong Mountain north of Yonch'on the next day. By the afternoon of September 4, the division realigned its defensive positions by placing the 21st Regiment on the left astride of lateral ridges, the 16th Regiment together with the 1st Battalion of the 3rd Regiment in the center, and the newly attached 5th Regiment on the right flank.

That day, the ROK Army Headquarters ordered the 8th Regiment of the 7th Division, which had been active at Sinnyong, to be attached to the ROK 8th Division in Yongch'on. The following day the headquarters' people also committed about 200 engineers of the 7th Division Engineer Combat Battalion to the Yongch'on front in an effort to reinforce the demoralized 8th Division.[206]

At about midnight on the 5th, the enemy 15th Division began to move down south in three different directions along the road between Ipam and Yongch'on. It was led by 5 tanks and supported also by all kinds of weapons fire. The ROK 16th Regiment and the 1st Battalion of the ROK 3rd Regiment in charge of the central sector were penetrated in depth by the main element of the attacking enemy forces in only a few hours. The ROK 21st and 5th Regiments on both flanks were not an exception; being pressed hard by the enemy, they were forced to withdraw to Sonjondong and Sangridong, respectively, all north of Yongch'on. That day, the ROK division, based on the Army headquarters' directives to set up a unitary command system in the Yongch'on battle front, was transferred to the ROK II Corps and continued the fight in Yongch'on under direct control of the corps commander.[207]

On the enemy side, on September 5, the NKPA high command relieved Park Song Ch'ol, the commanding officer of the 15th Division, of his post, calling him to account for delayed actions in capturing Yongch'on. It installed Cho Kwang Yol, the Assistant Commander of the division, in Park's place and pressed Cho hard for the breakthrough at Yongch'on. In the fierce fight which had lasted until late that night, the ROK 16th Regiment in the center sector was pushed back to the suburbs of Yongch'on.[208] Brig. Gen. Lee Song Ga, the Commander of the ROK 8th Division, at once ordered the anti-tank unit and the 8th Regiment of the 7th Division to launch a counterattack against the enemy. While the ROK 21st Regiment was holding the frontal line northeast of Yongch'on, the counterattacking troops drove the enemy off to Chokyodong in 5 hours. Thus the enemy's plan to exploit the initial gain fell through.

Prior to this battle, Brig. Gen. Yu Jae Hung, commanding the ROK II Corps, called an operational meeting to devise a countermove against the crisis at Yongch'on caused by the collapse of the ROK 8th Division line. The meeting was attended by Col. Kim Chong Oh, the 6th Division, Brig. Gen. Paik Sun Yup, the Commander of the 1st Division, Col. Lee Han Lim, the Chief of Staff of the II Corps, and Col. Lee Joo Il, G-3 of the II Corps.[209]

At the meeting, the attendants concluded that the enemy's objective had been Yongch'on, and the II Corps Commander decided to hold the town at all costs. He committed two more ROK regiments taken out of the 1st and 6th Divisions to the Yongch'on area. However, as the ROK divisions had been under continuous enemy threats at that time, it was risky and very difficult for them to despatch any troops on other missions.[210] Nevertheless, they did it. The II Corps commander, considering that he had to secure tank units to drive the enemy off, himself visited the headquarters of the US 1st Cavalry Division and the EUSA, to ask for support from them.

Starting at night on September 5, enemy artillery preparation fire began to land on downtown Yongch'on. At predawn hours the next day, main elements of the enemy troops, which had received replacements in the vicinity of Chokyodong, started moving toward the center of the town. Torrential rains fell at that time, but the enemy columns led by several tanks continued to move. Now, the surprised ROK 16th and 8th Regiments had no other choices but to withdraw to south of Yongch'on. Upon taking Yongch'on, the enemy lead elements proceeded toward Kyongju.[211]

The ROK division commander at once issued an order for the withdrawn regiments to rebuild their strength at the Osudong area, and at the same time requested the II Corps to send some reinforcements to him. At this time, the ROK 21st and 5th Regiments on both flanks were engaging enemy troops without knowing what was going on in Yongch'on because of communication failure. In the afternoon on September 6, the 45th Regiment of the NKPA 15th Division, which had engaged the ROK 21st Regiment on the left flank, moved down south to the Yongch'on area to join another NKPA unit which had been trying to exploit a success there. This enemy regiment had turned its former mission over to the 103rd Security and 73rd Independent Regiments.

During that morning, the ROK division Engineer Combat Battalion had launched a counterattack against Yongch'on with the help of an American armored platoon (5 tanks) which had newly arrived at the request of the ROK II Corps commander. The attacking combat engineers immediately defeated some North Korean soldiers who had been on guard duty at Yongch'on railroad station, and regained the town itself. In this battle, they captured about 40 enemy vehicles including more than 10 anti-tank guns. The South Korean engineers even proceeded to Wansandong with the help of American tanks; however, at the sunset that day, they moved back to their former positions for fear of the enemy's counterattack from the Chokyodong area.[212]

As soon as the reinforcements from the ROK II Corps arrived that after noon, the 11th Regiment(−) of the ROK 1st Division took up positions south of Yongch'on, and the 19th Regiment, the ROK 6th Division, advanced to Sinkidong on the right flank of the ROK 21st Regiment. Thus the ROK 8th Division now could strenthen its defensive positions in order to deny the enemy's effort for a breakthrough through the line towards Taegu. The division placed its 21st and 19th Regiments in the northeast of Yongch'on in that order, the Engineer Combat Battalion and part of the 5th Regiment in the town of Yongch'on, and in the south, the 11th Regiment took up positions. The 16th and part of the 3rd Regiments were kept as division reserve. In front of this ROK division, the NKPA 50th Regiment was operating just northeast of Yongch'on. This enemy unit, after it had penetrated into the ROK defense line there, was rapidly moving down south toward Imp'odong as if it would divide the friendly line into two. It was closely followed by another enemy regiment, and still another NKPA regiment was coming down south about 10 km from it. Meanwhile, the enemy 103rd and 73rd Regiments attacked the ROK 21st Regiment in an effort to exploit the breakthrough.

In the meantime, the ROK 6th Division in the Sinnyong area realigned its defensive positions by placing the 19th Regiment in Yongch'on, the 2nd Regiment on the left and right sides of Pongnimdong and Kap-ryong, and the 7th Regiment in the vicinity of Wha-san. Aware of the ROK troops' tactical aim, the enemy 8th Division, starting in the afternoon of the 5th of September, opened artillery fire on friendly positions, and at the same time concentrated its troops on the front line positions.

Being encouraged by taking Yongch'on, on the morning of September 6 the NKPA 8th Division rapidly overran Sinnyong. Thereupon, it launched a general attack against the ROK troops with its main effort on the Wha-san area in order to exploit the breakthrough at Yongch'on. The enemy division unexpectedly dared a daytime attack, probably miscalculating that there would be no air strikes because of the overcast weather. While the ROK 6th Division was scattering the enemy columns with artillery fire concentrated on them, combined flights of UN bombers and fighter bombers flew over to strike the enemy troops just short of the ROK defensive positions. The air strikes at this time lasted for about 30 minutes and the unprotected enemy troops suffered a heavy loss in the sea of flames.

Taking this opportunity, the 2nd Regiment of the ROK 6th Division decisively defeated the enemy 8th Division, and in effect, practically destroyed it. Of these battles around Wha-san an enemy diarist wrote, "On September 6, we underwent extremely desperate battles. With no place to hide or escape from the fierce enemy artillery bombardment and air strikes, our main force was wiped out."[213]

The enemy 8th Division was no longer active since that day. It never broke through the ROK army defensive positions in the Sinnyong area; rather, it suffered a heavy loss and only could remain within its own line. Mostly at night, the North Koreans carried out small unit actions by repeatedly sending out company sized units to make surprise attacks against the ROK army outposts.[214] Before and after the 9th of September, only small-scale skirmishes took place between both forces in the area of Kap-ryong and Wha-san. The number of surrenderers and deserters among the enemy soldiers was increasing every day. This resulted in the enemy's inaction and eventually he was forced to turn to the defensive.

On the other hand, the ROK 6th Division could easily frustrate the aim of the opposing enemy 8th Division, which had made a turning movement to attack against Yongch'on from the Sinnyong area. At that time, the assault of the ROK anti-tank team and the UN air strikes on the leading enemy tank columns contributed greatly to blocking the enemy's intention to break through the ROK defense line. Thus, the ROK troops secured a foothold for a future counteroffensive.

At predawn hours on September 7, the ROK 21st Regiment engaged the enemy 103rd Regiment and repelled it at several battle grounds. In this battle, the 6th Company of the South Korean regiment killed 300 and captured 98 enemy soldiers. In addition, they captured two truckload of small arms. Meanwhile, later that morning, the ROK 19th Regiment, locating enemy supply troops which had been moving southward, surprised them. They instantaneously knocked out about 30 vehicles and killed about 200 enemy soldiers. For their distinguished action there, the ROK 19th Regiment was awarded three million won. The Engineer Combat Battalion at this time attacked enemy troops which had blocked a road 8km southeast of Yongch'on, by killing about 200 enemy soldiers and driving the remnants off.[215] The ROK 11th Regiment immediately took the Wansandong area to cut off possible enemy followup units; however, it was driven back again by one enemy regiment of the 15th Division which had advanced to Chokyodong.

That day, the ROK Army Headquarters, receiving a report that the main body of an enemy unit had been moving toward Kyongju, ordered the 3rd Battalion of the ROK 26th Regiment which had been engaging enemy troops in the area of An'gang, to move to Awhari to counter the enemy there. The ROK 21st Regiment was attacked by the NKPA 73rd Independent Regiment on September 8; however, the South Korean soldiers repelled the enemy through intensive fire power concentrated on him. Meanwhile, the ROK 19th Regiment destroyed that enemy which had held Yongch'on and regained the town at 14:45 that day.[216] That night, this South Korean regiment proceeded southward to Chokyodong, where it launched a counterattack against one enemy regiment of the 15th Division which had encircled the ROK 11th Regiment. The ROK 11th Regiment, having been attacked by an enemy unit led by tanks at predawn hours, was rebuilding its strength at Chaksandong southeast of Yongch'on. In the meantime, the ROK 10th Regiment which had been attached to the ROK 3rd Division thus far was released and returned to its parent unit. The 10th Regiment, thereafter, proceeded to Awhari to take over the defensive mission from the 3rd Battalion of the ROK 26th Regiment. In close coordination with the ROK 8th and 5th Regiments on either side, it intercepted the enemy's further southward movement.

The prompt command action taken by the ROK Army Headquarters to obstruct the enemy's breakthrough of the Yongch'on line was not effective before he actually penetrated into it. Only after the line was broken through, were solid interlocking defensive positions formed around Yongch'on on September 8-9. This defensive line was in the shape of a fishhook which extended from north to south. It involved the ROK 21st Regimental positions in Sonch'on and those of the 5th Regiment in Awha, and lay along an enemy approach avenue centering around Yongch'on. This disposition seemed to be suitable for the defender to counterattack against the attacker by interdicting the latter in the rear and driving him into an encircled position.

The ROK II Corps launched a massive counterattack against the enemy on September 10. Under the control of the Corps, the 21st and 19th Regiments cut off the enemy's retreat in the north of Yongch'on, and in the south, four other regiments led by the 5th Regiment made a concerted counterattack.

With the help of US air strikes and artillery fire, the ROK 5th Regiment made a surprise attack against the enemy positioned in the vicinity of Impodong destroying 50 enemy vehicles and 10 pieces of artillery. Meanwhile, the ROK 10th, 8th, and 11th Regiments, with the support of American tanks, simultaneously advanced to Yusangdong and Yuhadong, driving away minor resistance from the enemy which had infiltrated into the south of the Taegu-Yongch'on-P'ohang road. Meanwhile, the ROK 16th Regiment which had suffered losses in the previous battles, advanced to Chaksandong immediately after it was rebuilt. There, it intercepted and pursued enemy soldiers who had been fleeing in confusion. Part of the regiment advanced as far as the eastern part of Taeuidong and captured about 300 small arms abandoned there.[217]

At predawn hours on September 10, the ROK 21st Regiment was ordered by the division commander to destroy enemy tanks which had been falling back along the road between Yongch'on and Jach'on. In the south of Jach'ondong, the 2nd Platoon, 5th Company, 2nd Battalion of the ROK regiment knocked out one enemy tank and captured 5 enemy soldiers. They also captured operational documents in which the NKPA 15th Division had requested their higher echelon to send reinforcements.[218]

As the ROK 11th Regiment on the right flank had returned to its parent unit, the 1st Division, the ROK 8th Regiment took over the additional mission. Nevertheless, the 8th Regiment moved northwest in close coordination with the 5th Regiment. The ROK 5th Regiment attacked against the headquarters of the NKPA 56 Regiment near Imp'odong and captured two enemy tanks and 6 mortars. Now the road between Yongch'on and Kyongju which had been blocked for 5 days opened up again.[219] The North Korean unit, in the process of being cut off, suffered a crushing defeat under the attack of the ROK troops. Only a few remnants were left to run in dispersion.

The ROK 10th Regiment which had pursued the retreating enemy in the south of Yongch'on was, on September 11, ordered by the ROK Corps commander to proceed to P'yongch'ondong by way of the Sinhungdong area, the unoccupied space between the ROK 21st and 19th Regimental zones. The 21st and 19th Regiments were also ordered to advance to Wolgokdong and Unch'ondong, respectively, to intercept retreating enemy troops. The following day the ROK 21st and 10th Regiments moved out to Jach'ondong-Inkudong line, and the ROK 8th Regiment reached so far as Samkidong, repulsing a counterattack by one enemy battalion. Meanwhile, the ROK 5th Regiment cut off the enemy's retreat toward Kigye and An'gang.[220] Eventually by September 12, the attack units successfully restored the initial main line of resistance of the ROK 8th Division, which had been set up just before the North Korean September offensive. On the other hand, the enemy 15th Division lost virtually all of its combat effectiveness.

The Yongch'on battle turned out to be a watershed which could affect the fate of both forces at the Naktong River battle. On September 5-6, when the safety of Taegu and Kyongju was in jeopardy, it was true that the enemy's breakthrough at Yongch'on aggravated the sense of crisis at the Naktong perimeter. The NKPA II Corps committed 5 regiments to the Yongch'on front attempting to advance to Kyongju after it overran the town of Yongch'on. Confronting this enemy, the ROK Army headquarters and Corps commanders committed two regiments of the ROK 1st and 6th Divisions, one regiment each, as well as the three regiments of the newly activated 7th Division, to the Yongch'on area. The ROK Army commanders' prompt judgement of the reinforcements needed to stem the North Korean attack in the area, and their rapid shifting of these reinforcements to the threatened sectors from other fronts, constitute a notable command achievement in the battle of the Naktong line.

In this battle, the ROK Army killed 3,799 enemy soldiers, captured 309 and destroyed 5 tanks. It also captured 2 armored vehicles, 85 trucks, and 2,327 small arms pieces. According to the North Korean commanders' review of the battle, the loss of Yongch'on had made defeat seem certain in the rest of the operations.[221]

6. Enemy's Seizure of An'gang-P'ohang

While the ROK II Corps was engaging the 4th assault group of the NKPA at Yongch'on, the ROK I Corps and the enemy 5th assault unit were locked along the axis of An'gang-P'ohang-Kyongju. Among the 5th assault group, the NKPA 12th Division which had held Kigye received some replacements, and it was supported by the NKPA 17th Armored Brigade. At about this time, the North Korean 5th Division which had assembled in the area of Hunghae, was also reorganizing itself by receiving some tanks and self-propelled guns. However, these North Korean divisions were low in food supply, weapons, and ammunition, and their men were in a state of lowered morale.

Nearest to the NKPA 12th Division was the ROK Capital Division under the control of the ROK I Corps. This South Korean division deployed the 18th, 17th (attached unit), and 1st Regiments in that order in the high hill mass south of Kigye. Meanwhile, the ROK 3rd Division placed the 10th (attached unit), 22nd, and 23rd Regiments in that order in the Hakch'ondong-Ch'onmasan area north of P'ohang. These South Korean divisions were supported by the US Air Force and naval fleets.

At about this time, with the war situation rapidly changing into an insecure state in the ROK division sector, General Walker, the EUSA Commander, dispatched Maj. Gen. John B. Coulter, newly appointed Deputy Commander, Eighth Army, to the ROK defense line, placing him in command of the friendly units there. Gen. Coulter immediately organized Task Force Jackson with the American and ROK units. Meanwhile, the ROK Army Headquarters appointed Brig. Gen. Kim Paik Il to the post of the ROK I Corps commander, Colonel Song Yo Ch'an to that of the Capital Division, and Colonel Lee Jong Ch'an to the 3rd Division commander post.[222]

At 03:00 on September 2, two enemy divisions under the 5th assault grouping launched a concerted attack against the UN forces. The NKPA 12th Division committed its main body spearheaded by 4 tanks to the axis of Kigye and An'gang, while placing its two supporting atttacks on either side of the ROK Capital Division line. Regiments of the South Korean division confronted this enemy in each defensive sector and only the ROK 17th Regiment, with the close support of US air strikes and 3.5-inch rockets, repelled the enemy which had attacked Hill 445 south of Kigye. The regiment knocked out all enemy tanks.

That night, however, part of the enemy 49th Regiment made a turning movement on the west side of the ROK 18th Regiment and penetrated into the rear after it overran Unju-san. At about midnight, the ROK regimental positions along the left flank of the ROK division finally collapsed. Taking advantage of the gap between the ROK 18th and 17th Regiments which resulted

Fall of An'gang-P'ohang

from its breakthrough, part of the enemy unit advanced to Orae-san northwest of An'gang, thus posing a threat to the western flank of the ROK Capital Division. The ROK I Corps Headquarters immediately committed the 26th Regiment which had been reorganizing to the Oksandong area in front of An'gang, to reinforce the ROK defensive positions there. At this time, the regiment was attached to the Capital Division.[223]

The ROK 3rd Division was also attacked by the enemy 5th Division that day. The 23rd Regiment of the South Korean division which had taken up positions on the east coast contended with this enemy unit for the control of Ch'onma-san (Hill 93); however, in the central sector, the ROK 22nd Regiment was thrown back to the Hyojadong-Tuhodong area, the outer wall of the P'ohang defense line.[224]

The commanding officer of the ROK 3rd Division ordered his regiments to launch a counterattack against the enemy infiltrators, thus to regain the initially established main line of resistance. He considered the line to be critical for defending P'ohang. Accordingly, the 22nd and 23rd Regiments, with the help of the 3rd Battalion of the US 21st Infantry Regiment which had been reinforced by a tank platoon, moved out to counterattack against enemy troops. But only the 3rd Battalion of the ROK 23rd Regiment secured the first step toward recovering its former positions.

The South Korean Battalion had formed a special group to be committed to either side of the enemy positions, while delivering a frontal attack against them. Thus they were successful in regaining the top of Ch'onma-san hill. Likewise, the ROK 22nd Regiment, which had failed repeated engagenmets thus far, succeeded, on September 3, in temporarily recapturing its former positions. However, the enemy seized it again. Thus the crisis in the P'ohang area continued.[225]

In the meantime, at predawn hours on September 4, the commander of the ROK Capital Division ordered his troops to withdraw to the line of Konje-bong-Homyongri line just south of An'gang as the division's left flank had been broken through. As a result, An'gang fell into enemy hands. By the time just before the sunset that day, the South Korean division completed its withdrawal and formed its new defensive positions by placing the 17th Regiment at Kapsanri south of An'gang, and the 1st Regiment in the area of Homyongri near An'gang. The 18th Regiment was to reorganize itself at Kyongju. Still, as the tension was increased in the area of An'gang, the ROK Army transferred the 3rd Regiment(−)[226] of the ROK 7th Division at Taegu to the control of the ROK I Corps, and committed it to the place. This time, the US 21st Infantry Regiment which had been under the command of Task Force Jackson was also ordered by Maj. Gen. Coulter to proceed from P'ohang to the area of Kyongju and was to counter the enemy's breakthrough there.

The NKPA 12th Division assembled in An'gang, with the aim of capturing Kyongju, that night, pushed southward part of its troops led by tanks. The ROK 1st Regiment which had been deployed in the areas of Homyongri and Nak-san located five enemy tanks approaching their positions and at once organized a special anti-tank group to destroy them. This special team immediately moved out to knock out 3 of them and repelled the rest.[227]

About this time, General Walker, in an effort to strengthen defensive capability in front of Kyongju, ordered the US 24th Division to move from its reserve position near Taegu to Kyongju. He redesignated Task Force Jackson as Task Force Church.[228] The ROK Army also ordered the ROK Independent Cavalry Regiment which had reorganized itself at Taegu to proceed to the Kyongju area. Meanwhile, Brig. Gen. Kim Paik Il, the ROK I Corps Commander, ordered the South Korean troops assembled in the area of Kyongju to be redeployed along Murung-san-Konje-bong hills near the city.[229]

In order to reinforce troops in that sector, the ROK Capital Division commander, in turn, moved the Cavalry and 3rd Regiments into the areas of Murung-san and Konje-bong, which were considered to be critical for covering lengthwise terrain on the west of the An'gang-Kyongju axis. The ROK 1st Regiment was to remain in Homyongri and the 18th Regiment was kept as a division reserve unit. In an effort to increase the in-depth defensive capability, the 3rd Battalion of the US 19th Infantry Regiment was placed in back of the South Korean troops. At the same time, the ROK 26th Regiment and the US 21st Regiment(−) proceeded to Kumi-san northwest of Kyongju to counter a possible enemy infiltration there.

In the early dawn on September 5, the ROK 3rd Division came under a heavy enemy attack. The ROK 22nd Regiment fought against heavy odds resisting enemy troops spearheaded by five self-propelled guns. In the very nick of time, however, five American tanks arrived at the scene from nearby airstrips. These tanks together with air strikes and artillery fire knocked out those enemy guns and repelled the enemy.[230]

Colonel Lee Jong Ch'an, the Commander of the ROK 3rd Division, immediately went on a scouting flight over the battle front. Since the adjacent Capital Division on the left had already withdrawn to the south of An'gang, he concluded the terrain feature there to be unfavorable to his troops for defending P'ohang. Thus he ordered his troops to move to form new defensive positions to the south of the Hyongsan River. As the level of water was as low as 80-90 cm at ordinary times, it was possible for troops to wade across the river; however, the 200-300 meter wide river with high embankment on either side could provide a bulwark for the defender.

The ROK division commander's defensive plan was, first of all, to hold the line east of the road between Chunghungdong and Kuryongp'o including Yongil Airfield with the help of the US naval gunfire and air strikes. In case the defensive positions had collapsed, he thought his troops would be able to withdraw south by sea on board one LST and 26 divisional supply boats which had been at anchor in the bay of Kuryongp'o. That day, the South Korean division, employing delaying tactics, crossed the Hyongsan, and took up new defensive positions on the southern bank of the river. It placed the 10th and 23rd Regiments on the river line positions and kept the 22nd Regiment and the 3rd Battalion of the 8th Regiment which had been attached to it as a division reserve.

At about this time, the NKPA 12th Division, most probably having considered that it would be impossible for them to advance to Kyonju without seizing Konje-bong hill, resumed its attack before daybreak of the 6th, September, massing against the area of Murung-san-Konje-bong. The ROK Capital Division line was broken within a few hours; in the center, the defensive positions of the ROK 3rd Regiment collapsed, and the Konje-bong positions which had been controlled by the ROK 17th Regiment were seized. Even the 3rd Battalion of the US 19th Infantry Regiment which had taken up positions in the rear was penetrated by one enemy battalion which had infiltrated into the friendly line with a turning movement.[231]

The ROK division commander immediately ordered the 3rd Battalion of the Cavalry Regiment to launch an audacious counterattack, and the battalion succeeded in regaining former positions of the ROK 3rd Regiment. The ROK 17th Regiment also made a counterattack against the infiltrated enemy troops. The main body of the US 19th Infantry, on order by General Church, repelled the enemy infiltrators. Thus the friendly forces got through the crisis for the moment.

However, fighting continued between the North Koreans and the ROK Capital Division on the hills for the possession of the crest of the Konje-bong which had been considered critical to both sides for future operations. As the North Koreans had massed their troops in the Konje-bong area since that day, there were no battles worth mentioning in other areas such as Murung-san and south of Nak-san.

Even after Konje-bong was taken by the enemy, the ROK 17th Regiment made a counterattack against him as many as 15 times but regained the hill only 7 times; it was a desperate war of attrition for the South Koreans. During these battles almost all ROK army officers including battalion commanders were killed or wounded; as occasion demanded, some were relieved. In the case of the 2nd Battalion, the commander was replaced twice. In an effort to fill up vacancies, the regimental commander commissioned NCOs within his unit on the spot to junior officers' grades and sent them to the front line.[232]

While the ROK Capital Division line was being penetrated by the enemy, the ROK 3rd Division faced a similar crisis on its front. Upon receiving an order from higher echelons that day to the effect that the 10th Regiment should be released to return to its parent unit, the ROK 8th Division, the 3rd Division commander, in turn, ordered his 22nd Regiment which had been in reserve position to relieve the 10th Regiment after sunset. However, the latter committed a serious tactical mistake.

The commander of the ROK 10th Regiment ordered his troops to start withdrawing even before completing the relief process. As a result, enemy troops of the NKPA 5th Division which had been in contact with the ROK regiment began to rapidly cross the river to infiltrate into the rear areas of the ROK defensive sector. When the lead element of the ROK 22nd Regiment reached the former positions of the ROK 10th Regiment, the enemy infiltrators began to fire upon them.

At that time, the ROK division commander thought that the most urgent thing to do was to stop the enemy rear party's crossing of the river. He ordered his 23rd Regiment to keep close watch on the left flank of the division line which was exposed to the approaching enemy troops. He also ordered the ROK 22nd Regiment to proceed to Oknyo-bong to check the enemy's southward advance.[233]

On September 8, taking advantage of drenching typhoon rains which had limited the UN air strikes, the North Korean 12th Division resumed its frontal attack against the ROK Capital Division, and took the Konje-bong position back again. Elements of the NKPA 5th Division, estimated to number about 1,600 men, who had infiltrated deeply into the gap between the ROK Capital and 3rd Divisions, reached the hills of Oknyo-bong and Unje-san.[234]

Meanwhile, upon receiving a report on the enemy infiltration there, Lt. Gen. Walker immediately ordered the US 24th Division to check any further advance of the enemy. Accordingly, Maj. Gen. Church and Brig. Gen. Kim Paik Il, the ROK I Corps commander, agreed that the US 24th Division would have to recapture Unje-san (Hill 482), and that the ROK troops would cut off the withdrawal route of the enemy and mop up the remnants of enemy forces.[235]

General Church ordered his assistant commander, Brig. Gen. Davidson, to form Task Force Davidson to recapture the Unje-san hill position. General Davidson now commanded the task force which was composed of a regimental size unit of various branch troops reinforced by a tank company. His troops arrived in the designated assembly area at Yongdokdong, 1.6 kilometers south of Yongil Airfield in the afternoon on September 10.[236] Meanwhile, General Kim Paik Il transfered the ROK 18th Regiment to Corps reserve position and placed it southwest of Unje-san so that it could check the enemy's advance to Kyongju. He ordered the 26th Regiment which had been attached to the ROK 8th Division to be released. The regiment at once returned to its parent unit, the ROK 3rd Division and thereafter was placed on the right side of Unje-san with a mission to obstruct the enemy's advance toward the airfield.[237]

In the mean time, the 22nd Regiment of the ROK 3rd Division launched its attack against the enemy positions in the area of Oknyo-bong, but it was immediately counterattacked and pushed back to the east of the hill by the enemy.

The division commander, worrying about the war situation in his sector which had been deteriorating by the hour, concluded that his troops could not even hold the Hyongsan River line positions. Accordingly, at about sunset on the 8th of September, he ordered his troops to take up new defensive positions in the areas of Songjongdong and Changdong so that he could secure a foothold for a future counterattack and at the same time protect Yongil Airfield. At about this time, a report on the enemy's capture of the Unje-san caused public unrest throughout the city of Kyongju. The ROK division commander had to stabilize the resulting chaos and restore social order by mobilizing both military and civilian police forces.

On September 10, the ROK I Corps commander committed the ROK 18th Regiment which had been kept as Corps reserve to the battle front. The 1st Battalion of the ROK regiment immediately overran Hill 197 north of Unje-san and the 2nd Battalion advanced to the high ground west of the Oknyo-bong which lay further north of Hill 197. Being encouraged by these successes, the 22nd Regiment of the ROK 3rd Division regained control of the top of Oknyo-bong.[238] As a result, the enemy troops on top of Unje-san became isolated. The next morning, September 11, Task Force Davidson, with the 1st Battalion of the US 19th Infantry Regiment leading, attacked against the surrounded enemy troops. North Koreans there held entrenched positions and their machine gun fire checked the American troops. On the morning of September 12, four Australian pilots struck the enemy positions with napalm, and then the US 2nd Battalion launched its attack passing through friendly lines. They secured the rough and towering hill, Unje-san, about noon.[239]

In the afternoon on September 12, the ROK 18th Regiment recaptured a low hill, Hyong-san, and restored part of its river line positions. A little later the ROK regiment sighted many enemy groups moving from Unje-san to the west of Hyong-san through an open field. The regiment immediately followed the withdrawing enemy troops in close coordination with the adjacent 1st Regiment of the Capital Division which had been operating in the area of Nak-san, on the left flank of the 18th Regiment. The two South Korean regiments concentrated machine gun and mortar fire on the retreating enemy columns and inflicted fatal damage on them. They further pursued enemy soldiers and mopped them up.[240] During the day, General Walker had visited the task force's command post to encourage both South Korean and American troops.

Now back on September 11, while Task Force Davidson was active in the ROK 3rd Division sector, the ROK Capital Division commander, in an effort to restore the divisional line, ordered his 17th Regiment to regain Konje-bong. At the beginning, the ROK regiment had a desperate battle faced with stubborn enemy resistance; so at once it organized a special attack unit to suppress the enemy machine gun positions, and then made a concerted attack against the hill. The following night, the South Korean regiment finally succeeded in recapturing the hill positions and thus could restore its main line of resistance south of An'gang. Regretfully, however, 12 men of the special attack unit had been killed by an accidental bombing by the friendly air force.[241] At about this time, in the area of Homyongri, the ROK 1st Regiment, even though isolated as the adjacent units on both flanks had been penetrated, had held Nak-san to the last, thus contributing to blocking the enemy's advance toward Kyongju.

At about this time, the offensive capability of the NKPA 5th Division was notably weakened. Taking advantage of this situation, the 23rd Regiment of the ROK 3rd Division attacked against enemy troops deployed on the river line positions on the right flank of the ROK division. A bloody battle lasted for two consecutive days, and another ROK special attack unit which had penetrated into the rear area eventually succeeded in surprising the enemy troops. The ROK troops charged the enemy from both sides, front and rear. Thus the ROK

23rd Regiment captured the small town of Yonil, and completely restored the main line of resistance along the Hyongsan River bank.[242] At about this time, the North Korean 5th and 12th Divisions under the command of the 5th assault grouping ceased their offensive actions, and changed to the defensive. They appeared to have reached the limit of their striking power. Aerial observers reported sighting survivors of the enemy troops moving north and east.[243]

This meant that the ROK Capital and 3rd Divisions under the control of the I Corps virtually destroyed two enemy divisions in the area along the Hyongsan River south of An'gang, and finally checked the enemy's advance toward Kyongju. In brief, the offensive and defensive operations on the east of the Naktong river line were dotted with a series of nip and tuck battles between both forces; an armageddon which would have decided whether the enemy forces broke through the line or the friendly forces checked the attacking enemy troops there. Anyway, a curtain of denouement on the Naktong front was finally lowered with the victory of the friendly forces.

7. Armageddon and the Turnover of the Initiative

As the writers stated in the above sections, the defensive operations at the Naktong line was a series of decisive battles. The friendly forces, especially the ROK forces, countered the massive North Korean attack to save the newly born country in dire extremity. Having been surprised by the North Korean People's Army at the very beginning of the war, the Republic of Korean Army was forced, over a period of 45 days, to move as far south as the Naktong river line. Despite the early participation of the United Nations Forces in the war, the demoralized ROK troops which had been inferior in numbers and equipment could not check the enemy's thrust, and as a result, about 90% of the South Korean territory was overrun by the North Koreans by August 1. Only part of north and south Kyongsang provinces centering around Taegu and Pusan was saved.

Accordingly, the ROK Army had no more ground to pull back to; not even space in which it could prepare for future counter-offensive operations. Practically, there were no more favorable terrain features left behind for it to take up than the Naktong River itself. Under such circumstances, the Naktong river line became a watershed for the South Koreans to keep their freedom and their adamant will to fight against Communism.

Therefore, the ROK Army swore to punish the North Korean Communist invaders at any cost to regain the lost territory by making a counterattack against them. Thus, with the help of UN Forces, it set up the last defensive positions, the so-called "Pusan Perimeter" line, along the Naktong river.

On the other hand, the North Korean Army which had attempted to communize the whole Korean peninsula certainly by August 15, 1950, the fifth anniversary of the Korean Liberation, mobilized all the resources of North Korea for breaking through the Naktong river line. In order to achieve this initial objective, the NKPA launched massive attacks separately in August and September. In its August offensive, the NKPA committed 11 out of 13 divisions to the Taegu-Pusan axis and pressed hard southward in various directions, while in September, it employed all of its 13 divisions except newly activated ones for the offensive operations. This time, they planned five major groupings of assault units and objectives and placed each unit on the front lines of Taegu, Youngch'on, Kyongju, Ch'angnyong, and Masan to defeat the UN troops one by one.

Thus on the western front, one NKPA assault group posed a threat on Haman-Yongsan-Ch'angnyong, and in front of Taegu, another enemy group reached an area 12 kilometers north of Taegu, availing itself of the gathered momentum after it captured Waegwan and Tabudong. Meanwhile, in the eastern front, still another assault group succeeded in seizing Yongch'on-An'gang-P'ohang. However, at about this time, the NKPA's combat effectiveness had been lowered to 53% of that of a regular combat unit, thus virtually losing its offensive capabilities.[244)

The ROK and UN forces held out in positions at Masan, Taegu, and Kyongju, all of which were critical for securing the Pusan Perimeter line. This perimeter turned out to be a stronghold from which the friendly troops could frustrate the enemy's war aim and take away the initiative from him. It, therefore, offered a major momentum for the United Nations forces to pass from the defensive to offensive operations on all battle fronts.

This dramatic reversion of the war situation was caused by various reasons : first of all, the heavy losses of the enemy at the battles which lasted for about 80 days since the beginning of the war notably weakened the NKPA's combat effectiveness. Secondly, the replacements who were forcibly conscripted from South Korea could not reinforce the enemy combat troops as might have been expected, because of the South Koreans' lack of will to fight. In addition, the enemy's extended communication routes, under the UN air supremacy and air strikes, could not function properly in supporting the front line attack units.

To make the matters worse, the North Korean Army miscalculated the possiblity of success through blitzkrieg, and may not have prepared for a protracted war. It certainly underestimated the South Korean people's and soldiers' emotion against Communism, with the illusion that most South Koreans would rise in revolt against their government in time with the North's southward invasion. The North Koreans also had no idea that a rapid and resolute collective UN security action would follow against them.

On the other hand, the predominant South Korean will to fight against the invaders overwhelmed that of the enemy's. When South Korea was at a very serious crisis, the President himself visited the Taegu front to express his adamant will to resist the enemy's invasion. He was followed by many South Korean field army commanders who took the initiative and set examples for their men on the battle fronts. Soldiers and policemen, officers and enlisted men, all united together to fight against the enemy. The general South Korean public was not an exception; they volunteered for various combat and combat support positions.

The Republic of Korean Army, taking advantage of the general war efforts, attempted to tactically economize its troops and secure reserve forces, and committed itself to the critical front lines. By so doing, not only could it resist the enemy's breakthrough, but also made effective counterattacks against him. As a necessary consequence, the ROK troops could effectively dissipate the enemy's combat effectiveness. In addition, the prompt action taken by the United Nations Security Council, as well as the support from the free world society led by the United States, greatly contributed to enhancing the morale of all the South Koreans. The participation of the UN froces in the war had not only convinced South Koreans of the ultimate victory of the free nations, but also encouraged the ROK soldiers to continue to fight against the Communists to the last.

Thus the ROK army, with relative supremacy in combat effectiveness, took the opportunity to move out from their defensive positions to launch a massive counterattack against the enemy. The naval and air supremacy offered by the United Nations forces over North Korean invaders played a decisive role in hamstringing the enemy's will to continue the fight by interdicting operations and strategic bombing in the enemy rear areas. In brief, the right moment arrived for the friendly forces to pass from the defensive to the offensive, from repeated withdrawals in the past to recovering counterattacks in the future.

Notes

1) Charles E. Heller & William A. Stofft, ed., *America's First Battle (1776-1965)*; Roy K. Flint, *T. F. Smith & the 24th Division: Delay and Withdrawal, 5-19 July 1950*(Univ. of Kansas Press: 1988), p. 296. The evolution of the Naktong defensive line could be traced back to a series of situational maps which had been drawn, since July 15, 1950, for General Baradley, in reports of introducing the daily Korean war situation to him. James F. Schnabel & Robert J. Watson, *The History of the Joint Chiefs of Staff and National Policy*, vol. 1 (Joint Chiefs of Staff: 1978), The War History Compilation Committee, ROK Ministry of National Defense, tr., *US JCS, History of the Korean War* 1990, p. 507.

2) BG. G.B. Barth, *Tropic Lightning and Taro Leaf in Korea*, vol. 6 (Library, Armed Forces Staff College, 1955), p. 11.

3) W.G. Robertson, *Counterattack on the Naktong 1950* (Combat Studies Institute, Leavenforth Papers, 1985), p. 10.

4) Ibid., p. 114.

5) WHCC, tr., *US JCS: the History of the Korean War*, vol. 1, p. 507; Japanese Society for Ground War Studies, *The Chosun War*, vol. 2; Research Dept. of Military History, ROK Army, tr., *The Korean War*, vol. 2(Myongsong Printing Co.: 1986), p. 66.

6) Division of Troop Information & Education, ROK Ministry of National Defense, *The First year of the Korean War: A Chronicle* (1951), pp. A 60-62.

7) ROK Army *Operational Order* 94 (03:00, August 2, 1950) was rewritten based on that of the Eighth US Army which had planned a general Korean war. The Defensive Lines X & Y included in the ROK Operational Order 119 represented only limited defensive fronts for the ROK troops. Accordingly, general beliefs that the Y-Line involved in the ROK Army Operational Order 94 would indicate the Tabudong-Pohyonsan line could be erroneous.

8) US 25th Infantry Division, *The Tropic Lightning in Korea-25 th Div.*(Atlanta, Georgia: Albert Love Enterprises, 1987), p. 13.

9) Roy E. Appleman, United States Army in the Korean War: *South to the Naktong, North to the Yalu* (Department of the Army, Washington,D.C.: GPO, 1961), pp. 242–247. Lt. Col. Check, the commanding officer of the 1st Battalion, US 27th Regiment, received a Distinguished Service Cross, as he distinguished himself by showing superb commandship in leading the combined Infantry, Armor, Artillery and Engineer patrol team.

10) ROK Army *Operational Orders* 91 (July 31, 1950), and 94 (03:00, August 2, 1950).

11) The ROK Army adjusted and curtailed its defensive sector by order 119 and on August 13, placed its troops on the Waegwan-northern Tabudong-Kunwi-Pohyunsan-southern Kanggu line. The ROK Army *Operational Order* 119(August 11, 1950); *Periodic Operations Reports,* Korean Army, No. 86.

12) ROK Army, tr., *The Korean War*, vol. 2, pp. 78–79; ATIS, *Interrogation Reports* on October 5, 1950,(Lt. Park Hung Sik, NKPA 102nd Regiment.) These documents are owned by the Korea Institute of Military History. The NKPA 102nd Regiment under the control of the NKPA Security Command in Occupied Areas was composed of mostly South Koreans; 90% of its members were South Koreans.

13) The NKPA urged its troops to fight more vigorously to capture Pusan by August 15, 1950. The NKPA *Supreme Commander's Order* 81(August 13, 1950), SNs 41 & 74; The NKPA's *propaganda leaflet* (August 6, 1950), SN 797.

14) Research Institute of History, North Korea, *Comprehensive History of Choson,* vol. 25: The War History of the Korean Liberation I (Scientific Encyclopedia Press, 1981), p. 231.

15) The NKPA concentrated green replacements and war supply items in Seoul, and thereupon, it sent them by rail down south to the battle fronts by way of Yongdungp'o station. ATIS, *Interrogation Reports* on August 23, 1950 (the espionage agent Cho Hee Sok, NKPA 3rd Div.), and on October 5, 1950 (2nd Lt. Whang Dok Ju, NKPA Replacement Regiment, I Corps).

16) That time, the UN Air and Naval forces were active at night; the airplanes making 4,635 sorties in July and 7,397 sorties in August. They continuously delivered bombs on enemy concentrations, vehicles and communication routes. As a result, the number of enemy artillery and mortars dwindled down to 1/3 of that they had had at the beginning of the war. Appleman, *South to the Naktong, North to the Yalu,* pp. 264 & 376.

17) Ibid., p. 264.

18) Ibid., p. 334.

19) Ibid., p. 264.

20) Ibid., pp. 292-303.

21) The Secretary of Defense, *The Test of War: History of the Office of the Secretary of Defense* (US G.P.O.: 1988), p. 52; WHCC, tr., *US JCS: History of the Korean War,* vol. 1, pp. 145-147.

22) Appleman, *South to the Naktong, North to the Yalu,* pp. 256-257.

23) HQs USAFFE & Eighth Army(Rear), *Logistics in the Korean Operations* (San Francisco: 1954), *Historical Manuscript* File, call No. 8-5, vol. 1, cp. 2, p. 5, p. 15.

24) Appleman, *South to the Naktong, North to the Yalu,* p. 260.

25) HQs USAFFE & Eighth Army, *Logistics in the Korean Operations,* vol. VI, p. 4, p. 21.

26) The War History Compilation Committee, the ROK MND, *The History of National Defense,* vol. 2 (1987), p. 31, p. 439.

27) Ibid., p. 111(*General Order* 40), p. 290.

28) Ibid., p. 292; ROK MND, *The First year of the Korean War: A chronicle,* (1951), p. C277.

29) WHCC, *The Battle of Tabudong* (1981), p. 41, p. 124.

30) WHCC, *The History of National Defense,* vol. 2, pp. 305 & 354. They had been mobilized based on the "Special Action Law on Requisition (July 26, 1950)," and working expenses for them were to be paid by the UN stationary troops, under the agreement between the ROK government and Eighth US Army.

31) Bradley J. Haldy, "*Korean Service Corps-Past and Present,*" Army Logistician (July-

August, 1987), pp. 22-23; The War History Compilation Commitee, *The History of Korean War*, vol. 3, 1970, p. 590; Early of August, 1950, 5,800 South Korean policemen together with about 10,000 combat police forces had been deployed at Taegu front. Yoo Kwan Chong, *The History of the ROK Police* (Library of Modern Police, 1982), p. 104.

32) Appleman, *South to the Naktong, North to the Yalu*, p. 386.

33) Ibid., pp. 251-252.

34) The MND, *The First year of the Korean War: A Chronicle*, p. C51.

35) Appleman, *South to the Naktong, North to the Yalu*, pp. 199 & 252; Department of Military History, KMA, *The History of Korean War* (Seoul: Ilsin Publishers Co., 1987), p. 310.

36) The MND., op. cit., pp. C57 & 61.

37) FEC G-2, *History of the North Korean Army*, 1952 (Document No. 856, Section 5, pp. 69-70. This document is owned by the Korea Institute of Military History.); The NKPA 10th Division arrived at Waegwan on August 8 by way of Sukch'on and Taejon on July 25.

38) Underwater bridge, also called underwater passage, was built with rocks, lumber, and gravel put in straw bags together with sand and mud. The North Koreans piled up these materials on the river bed in a pattern one above another until they reached a level of about 30 centimeters below the water surface; they continued piling up these materials across a river until they formed an underwater passage. Across this underwater bridge, they could pass vehicles and other heavy equipment. It was a Korean version of the Russian underwater passages which had been used in the German-Russian war.

39) *Periodic Operations Reports*, Korean Army, No. 73, SN. 1226; The War History Compilation Committee *The Battle of Tabudong*, pp. 73-75.

40) The ROK 15th Regiment was activated at Jungp'yong on July 15, 1950, by incorporating troops of the 13th Regiment; therefore, it was virtually the 13th Regiment organic to the parent ROK division. However, it was renamed as the 15th Regi-

ment for tactical reasons. (by the ROK division operational order 20 & 23).

41) *Periodic Operations Reports,* Korean Army, No. 76 (August 9, 1950).

42) The War History Compilation Commitee, *The Battle of Tabudong,* p. 113.

43) *Periodic Operations Reports,* Korean Army, No. 73 (August 8, 1950).

44) EUSAK *Periodic Intelligence Report,* Nos. 28 (September 9, 1950) & 29 (September 10, 1950); *Document* No. 1119, owned by the Korea Institute of Military History.

45) *After-action interview* with Lt. Col. Peter D. Clainos, Commander of the 1st Battalion, US 7th Cavalry Regiment; *Document* No. 1119 owned by the Korea Institute of Military History.

46) Appleman, *South to the Naktong, North to the Yalu,* p. 342; EUSAK *Periodic Operations Report,* Nos. 83-84(September 12, 1950); *Document* No. 1119, owned by the Korea Institute of Military History.

47) The ROK Army *Operational Order* 119 & the ROK II Corps *Order* 12 (August 12, 1950); This time, the defensive lines X & Y were different from those involved in the ROK Army *Operational Order* 94. The Line Y included Waegwan-P'onamdong-Suamsan-Yuhaksan-Sinjumak-Kunwi-Pohyonsan, while Line X indicated assembly areas in back of the former.

48) The War History Compilation Committee, *The Battle of Sinnyong & Yongch'on* (1984), pp. 17-19 & 79.

49) Ibid., pp. 21-22.

50) *Periodic Operations Reports,* Korean Army, No. 94(Aug. 15, 1950).

51) The 2nd Regiment of the ROK 6th Division captured the operational documents of the NKPA 8th Division and learned that the enemy's objective had been Taegu. The War History Compilation Commitee, *The Battle of Sinnyong & Yongch'on,* p. 87.

52) Ibid., pp. 30-36 & 91.

53) Ibid., pp. 97-100.

54) Appleman, *South to the Naktong, North to the Yalu,* pp. 342-345.

55) Ibid., pp. 345-347.

56) Ibid., pp. 351-353.

57) C Company of the 73rd Tank Battalion, two batteries of the 8th Field Artillery Battalion (105-mm), and two more batteries of the 37th Field Artillery Battalion (155-mm) were all attached to the US 27th Infantry Regiment.

58) MND, *The First year of the Korean War: A Chronicle*, p. B35; The War History Compilation Commitee, *The Battle of Tabudong*, p. 121.

59) Appleman, *South to the Naktong, North to the Yalu*, p. 354; *Periodic Reports*, Korean Army, No. 103 (Aug. 18, 1950).

60) The War History Compilation Commitee, *The Battle of Tabudong*, pp. 123-125.

61) *Periodic Operations Reports*, Korean Army, No. 109 (Aug. 20, 1950).

62) Appleman, *South to the Naktong, North to the Yalu*, p. 354; The War History Compilation Commitee, *The Battle of Tabudong*, p. 122. It was later known that, on August 20, 1950, the NKPA pulled out its 15th Division which had been deployed in the area of Yuhaksan, and transferred it to the area of Uisong so that it could prepare for an attack against Yongch'on.

63) Appleman, *South to the Naktong, North to the Yalu*, pp. 355-360.

64) ATIS *Interrogation Report*, No. 771 (Lt. Col. Chong Bong Uk, the 13th Artillery Regiment of the NKPA 13th Division, on August 26, 1950), *Document MF SN 267* owned by the Korea Institute of Military History; The War History Compilation Commitee, *The Battle of Tabudong*, p. 122.

65) *Periodic Operations Reports*, Korean Army, No. 115(Aug. 22, 1950).

66) MND, *The First year of the Korean War: A Chronicle*, p. B35.

67) The War History Compilation Commitee, *The Battle of Tabudong*, pp. 214-218; Appleman, *South to the Naktong, North to the Yalu*, p. 363.

68) Ibid., p. 293.

69) Ibid., pp. 293-298; Robertson, *Counterattack on the Naktong 1950*, pp. 22-32.

70) Robertson, *Counterattack on the Naktong 1950*, pp. 33-35.

71) Task Force Hyzer comprised the Reconnaissance Company of the US 24th Division, the 3rd Engineer Combat Battalion(−), and the 78th Tank Battalion(−).

72) Appleman, *South to the Naktong, North to the Yalu*, p. 298.

73) Robertson, *Counterattack on the Naktong 1950*, p. 49.

74) Ibid., p. 57; Appleman, *South to the Naktong, North to the Yalu*, pp. 301-302.

75) Appleman, *South to the Naktong, North to the Yalu*, p. 302.

76) The NKPA *Combat Diary* on August 13, 1950, SN 792. The NKPA ordered the 1st & 2nd Battalion of the 18th Regiment, 4th Division, which had executed a successful turning movement at Taejon, to cut off a road in the rear of friendly line.

77) Appleman, *South to the Naktong, North to the Yalu*, p. 303.

78) Ibid., pp. 306-307.

79) The enemy 29th Regiment, 10th Division, remained dug in on the hill mass near Hyonp'ung even at the most critical moment of the Naktong Bulge battle. Ibid., p. 309. The enemy 10th Division had been ordered to hold the Hyonp'ung assembly area until the NKPA II Corps could capture the city of Taegu.

80) Ibid., pp. 311-312.

81) Ibid., p. 313.

82) *Periodic Operations Reports*, the US 24th Div., No. 42, *Operations Instructions*, No. 26 (Aug. 17, 1950), *Document* No. 1041 owned by the Korea Institute of Military History; Appleman, *South to the Naktong, North to the Yalu*, pp. 313-315.

83) BG. G.B. Barth, *The Tropic Lightning in Korea-25th Infantry Division*, p. 13.

84) The US 27th Regiment stayed at Waegwan as Eighth Army reserve, and moved to Masan to be attached to the 24th Division. The Regiment was commited to the area of Chindongri near Masan, and together with the US 19th Infantry, it was patrolling over the Much'onri area.

85) FEC, *The History of North Korean Army*, p. 79.

86) *Perodic Operations Reports*, the US 25th Division, No. 55(18:00, Aug. 3, 1950), *Document* No. 1042 owned by the Korea Institute of Military History.

87) Appleman, *South to the Naktong, North to the Yalu*, p. 267; *Periodic Operations Reports*, HQs of the US 25th Div. No. 57(18:00, Aug. 4, 1950), *Document* No. 1042 owned by the Korea Institute of Military History.

88) Appleman, *South to the Naktong, North to the Yalu*, p. 269.

89) *Periodic Operations Reports*, HQs of the US 25th Div., Nos. 66(18:00, August 7, 1950) & 70(24:00, August 8, 1950), *Document* No. 1042, owned by the Korea Institute of Military History.

90) Appleman, *South to the Naktong, North to the Yalu*, p. 272; BG. G.B. Barth, *Tropic Lightning & Taro Leaf in Korea*, vol. 6(Library of Armed Forces Staff College, 1955), p. 16.

91) Appleman, *South to the Naktong, North to the Yalu*, p. 274.

92) ATIS, *Interrogation Reports* (Private Kim Kee Ju, the 83rd Motorized Regiment, NKPA 105th Armored Division, on August 18, 1950). The *Operations Order* 42 issued, on August 17, 1950, by the NKPA 6th Div. stated that should any subordinate unit be panic-stricken and withdraw in confusion again as they had done in Kosong, it would be punished severely. This statement clearly denoted the enemy's will of stubborn resistance. *Document* No. 796, owned by the Korea Institute of Military History.

93) BG. G.B. Barth, *Tropic Lightning and Taro Leaf in Korea*, vol. 6, p. 21.

94) Appleman, *South to the Naktong, North to the Yalu*, pp. 277-278.

95) Ibid., pp. 276-286; BG. G.B. Barth, *Tropic Lightning and Taro Leaf in Korea*, vol. 6, pp. 18-21.

96) FEC, *The History of North Korean Army*, pp. 64-66. The NKPA 7th Division was activated at Haeju, on July 3, 1950, incorporating the members of the 7th Border Constabulary Brigade. It comprised the 51st, 53rd, and 54th Regiments.

97) The Operations Order 42 issued, on August 17, 1950, by the NKPA 6th Division, *Document* No. 796 owned by Korea Institute of Military History.

98) BG. G.B. Barth, *Tropic Lightning and Taro Leaf in Korea*, vol. 6, p. 26.

99) The War History Compilation Committee, *The History of Korean War*, vol. 3, p. 285. The patrol team of the ROK police was attached to K Company of the US 3rd Battalion, and was operating near Battle Mountain.

100) BG. G.B. Barth, *Tropic Lightning and Taro Leaf in Korea*, vol. 6, p. 26.

101) Appleman, *South to the Naktong, North to the Yalu*, pp. 368-375.

102) Ibid., p. 375.

103) At about this time, UN airplanes supported in great force the US 25th Division. On August 27, 1950, the UN airplanes knocked out 20 trucks, 4 tanks, and 15 artillery pieces just in a single day's attack; *Periodic Operations Reports*, HQs of the US 25th Division, No. 127(24:00, August 27, 1950), *Document* No. 1042, owned by the Korea Institute of Military History.

104) FEC, *The History of North Korean Army*, pp. 64-66.

105) The War History Compilation Committee, *The History of Korean War*, vol. 3, pp. 288-295; Appleman, *South to the Naktong, North to the Yalu*, p. 366.

106) The 104th Regiment under the control of the NKPA Security Command in Occupied Areas was initially in charge of maintaining the public order in the Sach'on area; however, the worsening war situation brought the regiment into battle positions, lightly armed with machine guns and the like. ROK Army tr., *The Korean War*, vol. 2, p. 79.

107) The War History Compilation Committee, *The History of Korean War*, vol. 3, pp. 296-301.

108) On August 7, 1950, the ROK Army, calling him to account, relieved Brig. Gen. Kim Sok Won of his post as the commander of the Capital Division, and appointed Col. Paik In Yup in succession to him.

109) Appleman, *South to the Naktong, North to the Yalu*, p. 324.

110) Ibid., p. 324; The War History Compilation Committee, *the Battle of An'gang and P'ohang*, 1986, p. 95. The commanding officer of the ROK 22nd Regiment, Lt. Col. Kang Tae Min was court-martialed because of this serious mistake he had committed. Lt. Col. Kim Ung Cho was appointed as a successor to him.

111) *Periodic Operations Reports*, Korean Army, No. 82(Aug. 11, 1950).

112) Appleman, *South to the Naktong, North to the Yalu*, p. 325.

113) The ROK Army *Operations Order* 116(Aug. 10, 1950); *Periodic Operations Reports*, Korean Army, No. 81(Aug. 11, 1950). The ROK Combat Arms Command at P'ohang, also called Task Force P'ohang, was organized comprising the 25th,

17th, and 26th Regiments, the ROK Naval Combat Team in P'ohang, Independent 1st & 2nd anti-guerrilla Battalions under direct control of the ROK Army, and C Battery of the US 18th Field Artillery Battalion. As most of these element units, except the 17th Regiment and American artillery unit, had been newly activated incorporating student volunteers and members of the Korean Youth Society, their combat effectiveness was very low.

114) *Periodic Operations Reports,* Korean Army, No. 82(Aug. 11, 1950).

115) The War History Compilation Committee, *The Battle of Sinnyong & Yongch'on,* p. 200.

116) *Periodic Operations Reports,* Korean Army, Nos. 88(Aug. 13, 1950) & 91(Aug. 14, 1950).

117) Ibid., Nos. 95(Aug. 15, 1950), 100 & 101(Aug. 17, 1950).

118) The ROK Army *Operations Order* 134(14: 30, Aug. 15, 1950).

119) Appleman, *South to the Naktong, North to the Yalu,* p. 330.

120) Ibid., p. 331; GHQ FEC G-3, *Operations Reports,* Aug. 17, 1950.

121) *Periodic Operations Reports,* Korean Army, No. 101(Aug. 17, 1950)

122) The War History Compilation Committee, *The Battle of An'gang and P'ohang,* p. 118; Task Force Min, as of Aug. 19, 1950, was renamed as the 5th Regiment of the ROK 7th Division; reorganizing itself until August 26, it remained at Taegu, and it left for Sinnyong that day.

123) MND, *The First year of the Korean War: A Chronicle,* p. B34; The War History Compilation Committee, *The Battle of An'gang & P'ohang,* pp. 57-59.

124) Appleman, *South to the Naktong, North to the Yalu,* p. 332.

125) *Periodic Operations Reports,* Korean Army, No. 124(Aug. 25, 1950).

126) The War History Compilation Committee, *The Battle of An'gang and P'ohang,* pp. 167-168.

127) *Periodic Operations Reports,* Korean Army, No. 129(Aug. 27, 1950).

128) It had been customary that when the US Army organized a task force, they normally named it after its commander; however, in the case of Task Force Jackson,

the name Jackson was quoted from Stonewall Jackson, a nickname of General Thomas Jonathan Jackson, the well known hero of the Confederate Army in the Civil War.

129) Appleman, *South to the Naktong, North to the Yalu*, p. 398.

130) Research Institute of History, North Korea, *Comprehensive History of Choson*, vol. 25, p. 274.

131) Ibid., p. 272.

132) Ibid., p. 274.

133) Ibid.

134) FEC, *The History of North Korean Army*, section 5, pp. 64-70; The NKPA 9th Division had been on guard duty in Seoul from July 11 through August 12, 1950. Its 87th Regiment remained in the Seoul area to defend Inch'on, while two other regiments, the 85th and 86th, had left for Yongsan, South Kyongsang province.

135) Appleman, *South to the Naktong, North to the Yalu*, p. 395; ATIS, *Interrogation Reports*(Capt. Lee Jong Muk, the NKPA 5th Armored Brigade, on October 5, 1950); the recorded data on troop maneuver of the NKPA 17th Armored Brigade, MFSN, 59.

136) Research Institute of History, North Korea, *Comprehensive History of Choson*, vol. 25, p. 274(The NKPA *Supreme Commander's Order* on August 28, 1950).

137) ROK Army, tr., *The Korean War*, vol. 2, p. 76; The War History Compilation Committee, *The History of Korean War*, vol. 3, pp. 39-40; the NKPA 36th Division was later given the name of Royal Guards.

138) ATIS, *Interrogation Reports*(Private Chang Kee Wha, the NKPA 15th Division on September 20; Private Oh Sang Man, the NKPA 5th Div. on August 16; 2nd Lt. Kim Yong Ho, the NKPA 4th Div. on Oct. 3, 1950).

139) ATIS, *Interrogation Reports*(2nd Lt. Kim Yong Ho, the 45-mm. Anti Tank Artillery Battalion, the NKPA 4th Div. on Oct. 1950).

140) ATIS, *Interrogation Reports*(Private Cho Kyong Ok, the 13th Regiment, NKPA 6th Div. on Aug. 20; 1st Lt. Yoon Yong Song, the NKPA 6th Div. on Aug. 12; Pri-

vate Chung Hyong Tae, 1st Regiment, NKPA 6th Div. on Aug. 19; Private Oh Sang Man, the NKPA 5th Div. on Aug. 16; Private Whang Song Yil, the NKPA 13th Div. on Aug. 17, 1950).

141) Appleman, *South to the Naktong, North to the Yalu*, p. 264.

142) Ibid., 392.

143) Ibid., pp. 198–210; The ROK Joint Chiefs of Staff, *The History of Korean War*, p. 414; The War History Compilation Committee, *The History of Korean War*, vol. 3, pp. 307–319.

144) Appleman, *South to the Naktong, North to the Yalu*, p. 381.

145) The US I Corps was activated on August 2, 1950, and its headquarters arrived in Korea on September 6. The US IX Corps was also activated on August 10, the same year, but it came to Korea as late as September 23, because of a delayed organization of the supporting elements and staff members. The US X Corps was activated on August 26 mainly for the landing operations on Inch'on. The ROK Joint Chiefs of Staff, *The History of Korean War*, p. 424.

146) Ibid., 413; Appleman, *South to the Naktong, North to the Yalu*, p. 384.

147) The total strength of the JUSMAG-K as of August 1950 was 435 men including 175 officers. *Military Advisors in Korea*, USA, 1962, p. 161; The 3rd, 5th, and 8th Regiments of the ROK 7th Division were activated on August 20, 1950, by the MND's general order 49 and the 9th, 13th, and 20th Regiments of the ROK 11th Division were also activated on August 27, by the MND's general order 54. The War History Compilation Committee, *The History of National Defense*, vol. 2, p. 334.

148) Nam Sang Sun, *The Volunteer Student Forces* (Hyosung Publishers, 1975), pp. 63–70.

149) On September 6, 1950, under the command of the ROK 2nd Replacement Training Center, the Women Voluteers' Training Unit was activated. The War History Compilation Committee, *The History of National Defense*, vol. 2, p. 64; The ROK Office of Military Manpower Administration, *The History of Military Manpower*

Administration, vol. 1 (1985), p. 642.

150) USAF, FE & Eighth Army, *Logistics in the Korean Operations,* vol. 1, ch. 3, p. 25.

151) Appleman, *South to the Naktong, North to the Yalu,* p. 386; *Logistics in the Korean Operations,* vol. 1, cp. 3, p. 25; The War History Compilation Committee, *The History of National Defense,* vol. 2, pp. 351-352.

152) Appleman, *South to the Naktong, North to the Yalu,* p. 389.

153) Ibid., p. 388; USAF, FE & Eighth Army, *Logistics in the Korean Operations*(1954), vol. 1, cp. 3, pp. 11-14.

154) MND, *The First year of the Korean War: A Chronicle,* pp. C103 & C277; According to the logistics program of the US Far East Command, measures for refugee control and protection were also included in the program itself. Huston, *The Sinews of War,* p. 639.

155) USAF, FE & Eighth Army, *Logistics in the Korean Operations,* Vol. 2, cp. 4, p. 38, and 4. cp. 8, pp. 19 & 21.

156) The War History Compilation Committee, *The History of National Defense,* vol. 2, p. 363.

157) Ibid., p. 328; *Appleman, South to the Naktong, North to the Yalu,* p. 260; USAF, FE & Eighth Army, *Logistics in the Korean Operations,* vol. 2, cp. 4, pp. 67-69.

158) USAF, FE & Eighth Army, *Logistics in the Korean Operations*(1954), vol. 1, ch. 3, pp. 10-11.

159) Ibid., pp. 15-35. The US 3rd Logistical Command sent its advance party to In-ch'on, Korea on September 18, to operate a base command there.

160) Ibid., vol. 4, ch. 8, p. 17; Appleman, *South to the Naktong, North to the Yalu,* p. 261; Huston, *The Sinews of War,* p. 641. These equipment were produced under the re-build-up program of the US Far East Command.

161) USAF, FE & Eighth Army, *Logistics in the Korean Operations,* vol. 2, cp. 4, pp. 38-40 & 133. According to the US Army Field Manual, daily ration rate had been 20 rounds per 81-mm & 4.2-inch mortar, and 45 per 105-mm howitzer. However, the actual daily consumption during the month of August, 1950, had by far exceeded

that rate with 30, 25, and 75 rounds, respectively.

162) Appleman, *South to the Naktong, North to the Yalu,* pp. 260 & 380.

163) On August 18, 1950, enemy mortar shells landed on the downtown streets of Taegu, and the ROK Government ordered the citizens to evacuate the city. The government and National Assembly moved to Pusan that day. Troop Information & Education Department, the ROK MND, *The First year of the Korean War: A Chronicle,* pp. A37 & B33.

164) The Public Security Department of the ROK Ministry of Home Affairs, *The War History of the ROK Police* (1952), pp. 149-150.

165) WHCC, tr., *US JCS: History of the Korean War,* vol. 1, pp. 158 & 165.

166) Appleman, *South to the Naktong, North to the Yalu,* pp. 415-417.

167) Ibid., p. 417.

168) The official North Korean history stated that if their troops could not hold the Suamsan position, they would be forced back to recross the Naktong. This meant that the North Koreans had considered Suamsan was tactically important for them. Research Institute of History, North Korea, *Comprehensive History of Choson,* vol. 25, p. 262.

169) Appleman, *South to the Naktong, North to the Yalu,* pp. 411-412.

170) *Periodic Operations Reports,* Korean Army, Nos. 152 & 153(Sept. 3, 1950).

171) Appleman, *South to the Naktong, North to the Yalu,* p. 422; The War History Compilation Committee, *The Battle of Tabudong,* p. 295.

172) Ibid., p. 414.

173) Ibid., p. 419. Korean service laborers helped the withdrawing American troops by carrying supply items.

174) The ROK II Corps *Operations Orders* 31(Sept. 5, 1950) & 32(Sept. 6, 1950).

175) *Periodic Operations Reports,* Korean Army, No. 158(Sept. 5, 1950).

176) Appleman, *South to the Naktong, North to the Yalu,* p. 430; *Periodic Operations Reports,* Korean Army, No. 167(Sept. 8, 1950).

177) Appleman, *South to the Naktong, North to the Yalu,* p. 420.

178) Ibid., p. 421.

179) *Periodic Operations Reports,* Korean Army, No. 169(Sept. 9, 1950).

180) Appleman, *South to the Naktong,* North to the Yalu, pp. 432-435.

181) Ibid., p. 435; The ROK MND's *General Order*(Army) 70(Sept. 13, 1950); The ROK 1st Division captured about 800 enemy soldiers in the mountain areas of Ka-san and P'algong-san. The War History Compilation Committee, *The Battle of Tabudong,* p. 295.

182) FEC, *The History of North Korean Army,* pp. 67-69; The NKPA 9th Div.(−) was supported by one field artillery battalion, one AAA battalion two tank battalions of the 16th Armored Brigade, and one field artillery battalion of the 4th Div. The 3rd Regiment of the NKPA 9th Div. was placed in the area of Inch'on.

183) Appleman, *South to the Naktong, North to the Yalu,* p. 455.

184) Ibid., p. 470; The ROK Army, tr., *The Korean War,* vol. 2, p. 289.

185) Appleman, *South to the Naktong, North to the Yalu,* pp. 456-457.

186) Ibid., p. 462.

187) Ibid., pp. 465-467.

188) Ibid., p. 469; The captured medical officer stated that a daily average of 300 men of the NKPA 2nd Division had been evacuated to the North Korean MASH at Pugokri.

189) FEC, *History of the North Korean Army,* pp. 64-65.

190) BG, G.B. Barth, *Tropic Lightning and Taro Leaf in Korea,* vol. 6, pp. 28-29; Appleman, *South to the Naktong, North to the Yalu,* pp. 470-472.

191) Appleman, *South to the Naktong, North to the Yalu,* pp. 475-476; The enemy loss in this battle numbered 1,500 men including 480 dead. The casualties of the NKPA 35th Regiment alone totaled to 250 men. BG. G.B. Barth, *Tropic Lightning and Taro Leaf in Korea,* vol. 6, p. 29.

192) Appleman, *South to the Naktong, North to the Yalu,* pp. 479-483.

193) Ibid., pp. 473-475; BG. G. B. Barth, *Tropic Lightning and Taro Leaf in Korea,* vol. 6, p. 31.

194) Appleman, *South to the Naktong, North to the Yalu,* p. 486; On Sept. 6, 1950, an enemy sniper severely wounded Col. Champney of the US 24th Regiment while the latter was inspecting his front line positions west of Haman. He was evacuated at once, but died shortly. Lt. Col. Corley, commanding officer of the 3rd Battalion succeeded to the command of the regiment; BG. G.B. Barth, *Tropic Lightning & Taro Leaf in Korea,* vol. 6, p. 30.

195) Appleman, *South to the Naktong, North to the Yalu,* pp. 474-475.

196) Ibid., pp. 476-477.

197) Ibid., pp. 477-478.

198) BG. G.B. Barth, *Tropic Lightning & Taro Leaf in Korean,* vol. 6, p. 30; Appleman, *South to the Naktong, North to the Yalu,* p. 478.

199) *Periodic Operations Reports,* HQs of the US 25th Div., No. 19(18:00, Sept. 7, 1950), *Document* No. 1042 owned by the Korea Institute of Military History; Appleman, *South to the Naktong, North to the Yalu,* pp. 483-484.

200) The enemy 15th Div.(the combat order of the subordinate regiments varied from datum to datum, but in this writing, the authors described them as 48th, 49th, and 50th, in that order) started to leave, on about August 20, Tabudong and reached the area of Pohyon-san on the 25th. The ROK Army as well as the US Eighth Army had not known this enemy's whereabout thus far.

201) *Periodic Operations Reports,* Korean Army, No. 135(Aug. 28, 1950); The War History Compilation Committee, *The Battle of Sinnyong and Yongch'on,* p. 129.

202) Ibid., pp. 151-152 & 159.

203) The War History Compilation Committee, *The History of Korean War,* vol. 3, p. 547.

204) *Periodic Operations Reports,* Korean Army, No. 153(Sept. 3, 1950).

205) The ROK II Corps *Operations Order* 29(Sept. 3, 1950).

206) The War History Compilation Committee, *The Battle of Sinnyong and Yongch'on,* pp. 252-255.

207) *Periodic Operations Reports,* Korean Army, No. 158(Sept. 5, 1950).

208) The War History Compilation Committee, *The Battle of Sinnyong and Yongch'on,*

p. 258.

209) *Testimonies* of the ROK 6th Div. Commander, Col. Kim Chong Oh, and the G-3 of the ROK II Corps, Col. Lee Ju Yil. The War History Compilation Committee, *The History of Korean War*, vol. 3, pp. 584-585.

210) The ROK II Corps *Operations Orders* 31(Sept. 5, 1950) & 32(Sept. 6, 1950).

211) The War History Compilation Committee, *The Battle of Sinnyong and Yongch'on*, p. 269.

212) Ibid., pp. 269-271.

213) Ibid., p. 172.

214) *Periodic Operations Reports,* Korean Army, No.167(Sept. 8, 1950), 173(Sept. 10, 1950), and 176(Sept. 11, 1950).

215) *Periodic Operations Reports,* Korean Army, No. 164(Sept. 7, 1950); The War History Compilation Committee, *The Battle of Sinnyong and Yongch'on*, pp. 275-283.

216) *Periodic Operations Reports,* Korean Army, No. 167(Sept. 8, 1950).

217) Ibid., No. 169(Sept. 9, 1950).

218) *The testimonies* of Brig. Gen. Lee Song Ga, commander of the ROK 8th Div., and First Sergeant, Kim Jae Ui, platoon leader of the 2nd Battalion, 5th Company of the 8th Div. The War History Compilation Committee, *The History of Korean War*, vol. 3, p. 575; *The Battle of Sinnyong & Yongch'on*, p. 313.

219) *Periodic Operations Reports,* Korean Army, No.173(Sept. 10, 1950).

220) Ibid., Nos. 174(Sept. 10), 175(Sept. 11), 178(Sept. 12), and 181(Sept. 13, 1950).

221) The 3rd Annual Convention of the Central Committee of Chosun [North Korea] Labor Party held at Pyolch'onri, Manp'ojin, North Korea on Dec. 4, 1950. The War History Compilation Committee, *The History of Korean War*, vol. 3, p. 581.

222) Appleman, *South to the Naktong, North to the Yalu*, p. 398.

223) The War History Compilation Committee, *The Battle of An'gang and P'ohang*, pp. 150-163.

224) Ibid., pp. 164-165.

225) Ibid., pp. 165-168; Appleman, *South to the Naktong, North to the Yalu*, p. 401.

226) The ROK Army *Operations Order* 160(Sept. 3, 1950); The ROK 3rd Regiment was reactivated at Taegu on August 22, 1950, incorporating the Independent 1st Anti-Guerrilla Battalion by the ROK Army operations order 148. At that time the subordinate 1st Battalion had been attached to the 8th Division.

227) The War History Compilation Committee, *The Battle of An'gang and P'ohang*, pp. 161-162.

228) Appleman, *South to the Naktong, North to the Yalu*, p. 405.

229) The War History Compilation Committee, *The Battle of An'gang and P'ohang*, p. 173; The ROK Army *Operations Order* 163(Sept. 4, 1950)

230) Ibid., pp. 169-170; Appleman, *South to the Naktong, North to the Yalu*, p. 404.

231) The War History Compilation Committee, *The Battle of An'gang and P'ohang*, p. 178.

232) Ibid., pp. 176-182.

233) Ibid., pp. 182-185.

234) Ibid., p. 185; Appleman, *South to the Naktong, North to the Yalu*, p. 406.

235) On September 7, 1950, the ROK Army received a message from Eighth Army on the impending counter-offensive operations. In turn, the former ordered the ROK I & II Corps to clear enemy troops of the respective areas as early as possible, with a special emphasis on keeping the road between Kyongju and Yong-ch'on out of enemy artillery fire. The ROK *Army directive* 58(18:00, Sept. 7, 1950).

236) Task Force Davidson comprised the 19th Regiment(−), 3rd Battalion & Tank Company of the 9th Regiment, 13th Artillery Battalion, C Battery of the 15th Artillery Battalion, A Company of the 3rd Engineer Combat Battalion, and two batteries of M-16 Antiaircraft Machine gun Group; Appleman, *South to the Naktong, North to the Yalu*, p. 406.

237) The ROK I Corps *Operations Order* 89(Sept. 10, 1950).

238) The War History Compilation Committee, *The Battle of An'gang and P'ohang*, pp. 188-190.

239) Appleman, *South to the Naktong, North to the Yalu*, p. 407.

240) The War History Compilation Committee, *The Battle of An'gang and P'ohang*,

pp. 190-191.

241) Ibid., pp. 176-180.

242) Ibid., p. 192.

243) Appleman, *South to the Naktong, North to the Yalu,* p. 408.

244) Ibid., pp. 545-546.

Chapter Five   The Landing at Inch'on and Counter Offensive

I . The Landing Operations at Inch'on

1. The Plan of Landing Operations and Troop Organization

(1) The Development of the plan

As the authors already mentioned in the previous chapter, the ROK
Army which had been in dire extremity at the Naktong River front tided over
the national crisis with the great help of the United Nations Forces, particularly
the US forces. Both the ROK and UN forces, now having taken the initiative at
the Naktong river line, entered upon a new phase in which they could launch a
massive counterattack and at once effect a landing at Inch'on. With a strategic
aim of crushing the North Koreans in a single blow, UN forces had secretly
planned since the beginning of the war to make a turning movement and to land
at Inch'on.

At the order of General MacArthur, the landing at Inch'on had been
mulled over by the UN forces during the first week in July, 1950, with the Korean War little more than a week old. He told his chief of staff, General Edward
M. Almond, to begin considering plans for an amphibious operation designed
"to strike the enemy center of communications at Seoul, and to study the location for a landing to accomplish this."

These plans were undertaken by the Joint Strategic Plans and Operations Group (JSPOG), Far East Command, headed by Brigadier General Edwin

K. Wright, the Assistant Chief of Staff, G-3, of General MacArthur's UN Forces Command. The early plan for the amphibious operation received the code name "Bluehearts", and called for driving the North Koreans back across the 38th Parallel. The idea of this amphibious landing was that, while the US 24th and 25th Divisions launch a frontal counterattack against the enemy on the south line, the US 5th Marines and an infantry division, as an assult group, would simultaneously land at Inch'on behind the enemy's lines and proceed to Seoul for the enveloping counter blow.[1]

At the first operational meeting held at Far East Command headquarters on July 4, General MacArthur and other branch representatives discussed using a US Marine Combat Team which had already been assigned by the US Joint Chiefs of Staff, and the US 1st Cavalry Division in Japan as the ground attack units. Considering the preparation period needed for joint operations, they proposed July 22 as an approximate date for the amphibious operation. On July 7, on a US marine base, the US 1st Provisional Marine Brigade was activated, incorporating the 5th Marines which had been under the command of the 1st Marine Division. At the same time, the US 1st Cavalry Division began to train its troops in preparation for the amphibious operations. Thus the ground troops were almost ready. However, the operation plan, Bluehearts, was abandoned by July 10,[2] because of the inability of the ROK and US forces in Korea to hold the southward drive of the enemy. Holding the enemy and stabilizing the war situation at the frontline was more urgent than launching an amphibious operation; therefore, the US 1st Cavalry Division was committeed to the frontline.

Even though Bluehearts had been abandoned, General MacArthur never gave up his plan of an amphibious landing at Inch'on to win the Korean War. The more serious the war became, the more keenly he felt the necessity of landing in the rear of the enemy. He stressed the importance of Inch'on as one of the most feasible locations for the landing; however, he instructed his staff to study other possible locations.

Accordingly, the JSPOG went ahead with several plans studying Inch'on, Kunsan, Haeju, Chinnamp'o, and Chumunjin, all coastal cities and towns around the peninsula. On July 23, the JSPOG, upon MacArthur's instructions, circulated to the General Headquarters staff sections the outline of Operation Chromite, which called for an amphibious operation in September and postulated three plans: (1) Plan 100-B, landing at Inch'on on the west coast; (2) Plan 100-C, landing at Kunsan on the west coast; (3) Plan 100-D, landing near Chumunjin on the east coast. Plan 100-B, calling for a landing at Inch'on was favored the most.

According to Plan 100-B, the US 1st Provisional Marine Brigade which had already left for Korea and the US 2nd Infantry Division which had also been scheduled to proceed from the United States to Japan, were to be employed as landing attack troops. Simultaneously with the landing of these troops at Inch'on, other ground troops down south on the Naktong front were to pass from the defensive to a massive offensive.

This same day, July 23, General MacArthur informed the Department of the Army that he had scheduled for mid-September an amphibious landing behind the enemy's lines. However, the North Korean successes upset MacArthur's plans. As had been pointed out in the previous paragraphs, in early August, the two American units which had been designated as landing attack troops were committed to the Naktong front immediately after they arrived in Korea.

Being notified that the 1st US Marine Division would be available, the JSPOG group perfected Plan 100-B (landing at Inch'on) with a view to using this marine unit and the 7th Infantry Division, the sole reserve unit in Japan. On August 18, they distributed the plan to subordinate and other related units. This plan in terms of its fundamental concepts of operations was basically identical with those ones which had already been studied. The plan specifically named the Inch'on-Seoul area as the target that the 1st Marine Division would seize by amphibious assault, and postulated that the landing operation should be accomplished in close coordination with an attack by Eighth Army on the Naktong front. Nevertheless, the plan did not specifically point out follow-up troops; instead, it only stated a reserve unit of the US Far East Command should be used. The tentative date set for the operation was September 15, 1950. On August 15, General MacArthur established the headquarters group of the Special Planning Staff headed by Maj. Gen. Clark L. Ruffner to take charge of the projected amphibious operation. The mission of this group was to materialize Operation Chromite; it took full charge of drawing up directives of the GHQ FEC and distributing them to the sub-elements. The members of this group were later assigned to staff positions of the newly activated US X Corps.

(2) The Organization and Mission of the Landing Forces

Having decided the basic project for the amphibious operations, General MacArthur at once set to work organizing his landing troops. He decided to designate the X Corps as the landing force, and requested, on August 21, authority from the Department of the Army to activate Headquarters, X Corps. Upon receiving approval, he appointed, on the 26th, his Chief of Staff, Maj. Gen. Almond, as the commander of the Corps. Officers selelcted from the GHQ FEC filled up staff positions of the X Corps Command.

The X Corps comprised the US 1st Marine and 7th Infantry Divisions, the ROK 1st Marine and 17th Regiments, the US 2nd Engineer Special Brigade, and other support elements as shown in Table 1.

As the United States kept its standing army at a reduced level of strength in the summer of 1950, and, in addition, the war situation in Korea, particularly in July, had deteriorated, it was no easy matter for the US to assemble a landing unit in the Far East—at full strength—in the nick of time. In the case of the 1st Marine Division, the newly appointed commander, Maj. Gen. Oliver P. Smith, started to bring his division to war strength on July 25, the very day that he had assmumed command. But he had only 3,400 men in the divisional base as the 5th Marine Regiment which had been incorporated into the 1st Provisional Marine Brigade had already left for the Far East area.

Nevertheless, General Smith set to work building up his division by taking marines out from other bases of fleets, or receiving replacements, or even by recruting from called-up resources. It took him approximately two weeks to

⟨Table 1⟩ Table of Organization, the US X Corps[3]

Aug. 26, 1950

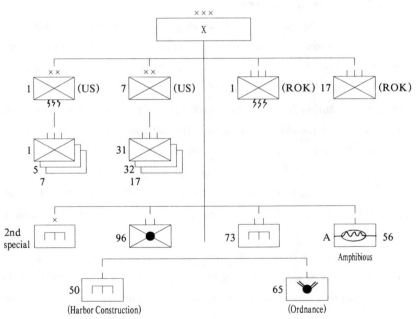

bring the 1st Marine Regiment and Headquarters units at full strength by August 10.[4] Even though it was difficult for him to obtain troops to fill the division, he later succeeded in forming the 7th Regiment. In this manner, after three times of repeated call ups, the American marine division perfected its organization consiting of the 5th, 1st, and 7th Regiments, and several support units. However, another difficulty had been waiting for General Smith: to assemble his troops in the combat area was not an easy matter. Thus the main body of the division, including the 1st Marine Regiment, could only arrive in Japan as late as September 6. That day the 5th Marine Regiment which had previously been committed to the Naktong river front returned to Pusan to join them. Meanwhile, the main elements of the 7th Regiment arrived at Pusan on September 9; however, the rest of the regiment could not join them until the time the amphibious operations were to be launched.

At that time, the US 7th Infantry Division which had remained in Japan as occupation forces was kept as a reserve unit under the Far East Command. The division comprised three infantry regiments: the 17th, 31st, and 32nd. Still, this division had also been understrength throughout the years. To make matters worse, during July, FEC had taken 140 officers and 1,500 noncoms and enlisted men from the division to augment the strength of the 24th and 25th Infantry and the 1st Cavalry Divisions as they in turn had moved to Korea. As of July 27, therefore, the division was at less than half strength. By September 4, however, FEC alloted to the American division 330 officers and 5,400 enlisted replacements plus 8,637 KATUSA[5] soldiers, so that the division was barely brought to war strength.

At about this time, the 1st ROK Marine Regiment was training about 3,000 recruits on Chejudo island. The regiment was shortly ordered to be incorporated into the landing forces by a coordination council of war held between the ROK and US Armies. On August 31, it was unexpectedly ordered to move out to Pusan. Accordingly, the regiment, led by Col. Shin Hyon Jun, the Commandant of the ROK Marine Corps, left Chejudo island and arrived at the sea near Pusan on September 6. There it underwent a special training for a short period jointly with the US 5th Marine Regiment: By September 11, they were prepared for moving out.

Finally, the ROK 17th Infantry Regiment which had been attached to the ROK Capital Division joined the landing forces. The regiment had been operating in the areas of An'gang and Kigye when it was selected. On September 15, it was relieved from the Capital Division, and on order it pulled out of the front line positions that day. Afterwards, it assembled at Kyongju to be transported to Pusan by train. There in Pusan, Col. Paik In Yup who had handed over the command of the Capital Division, assumed command of the regiment. As the regiment was at 2/3 less than full strength, he had to obtain troops to fill his regiment. Fortunately, however, he soon received replacements and combat equipment to bring his unit to war strength and his troops immediately underwent training for the impending amphibious operations.

The total strength of the UN landing force reached 70,000 men and its immediate objectives were as follows:[6]

- to gain and secure a beachhead at Inch'on;
- to rapidly advance to the inland area to regain and secure Kimp'o Airfield;
- to cross the Han River and recapture Seoul, the capital city of Korea;
- to take up positions in the vicinity of Seoul until the time when they could link up with troops of Eighth Army which were supposed to move up north from the Naktong front.

Accordingly, the concept of the maneuvering landing troops was to follow these objectives: first of all, they would neutralize enemy troops near anticipated landing sites with the help of the UN naval and air strikes, and then, the assault unit, the US 1st Marine Division, would move out to clear downtown streets of enemy troops. This action was considered necessary to secure the safety of the beachhead. After this, the marine division was to recapture Kimp'o Airfield, mopping up enemy remnants south of the Han River. Then would follow the crossing of the Han River and the drive on Seoul. Thereupon the American marines would advance to hill masses north of the city. Meanwhile, the US 7th Infantry Division would follow up the marine unit on its right flank by executing a turning movement in the south to retake hill masses south of Seoul. At the same time, the infantry division would take up the southern bank positions of the Han River. Still, part of the division would proceed toward Suwon to link up with troops of the Eighth Army.

(3) The Controversy on Landing and Fixing the Site

While the Joint Chiefs of Staff gave expressed approval to General MacArthur's proposal for an amphibious landing behind the enemy's battle lines, they never committed themselves to MacArthur's favored landing site of Inch'on.

The opposition to the Inch'on proposal came from General Collins, US Army Chief of Staff, Admiral Forrest P. Sherman, Chief of Naval Operations, and representatives of the US Marine Corps. Presenting other ideas, they opposed MacArthur's proposal from the beginning, or reserved their approval on it for various reasons.

The Navy's opposition to the Inch'on site centered largely on the difficult tidal conditions, narrow, twisting waterways, and low-lying shore lines. They pointed out that these things would probably limit the landing operations, and accordingly, they would not recommend Inch'on as a suitable landing site. The main approach by sea to the harbor was through a single narrow channel, so that it could not be used by large ships; they also feared the enemy's sowing of mines in this waterway, which might inflict heavy losses on the landing force. In addition, tides in the restricted waterways of the channel and the harbor have a maximum range of more than 10 meters; the greater part of the harbor becomes a mud flat at low tide which extends from 2 to 5 kilometers, leaving only a narrow dredged channel. Thus the resulting shallow water could not allow LST's (Landing Ship, Tank) or the like to come alongside the pier. As the tide reaches extreme range only two or three times a month, it would also be difficult for planners to set a date for action; there were no favorable landing sites, either. The artificial sea walls or waterbreaks that fronted the Inch'on landing sites might cause another problem. As they were as high as 5 meters above the mud flats, they could present a scaling problem except at extreme high tide. The landing force, therefore, would need ladders for its operations.

Since this opposition continued, the Joint Chiefs of Staff decided to send two of its members, the Army Chief of Staff and Naval Chief of Operations, to the Far East Command in Tokyo to discuss the matter with General MacArthur and his staff. They arrived at Tokyo on August 21. Upon arrival in Japan, Collins and Sherman engaged in private conversations with MacArthur and key members of his staff, including senior naval officers in the Far East. On the following day, they made an on-site inspection of the battle front in Korea, and in the afternoon on August 23, attended a full briefing on the subject which had been scheduled in the conference room in the Far East Command.[7]

Among those present, in addition to Generals MacArthur, Collins, and Admiral Sherman, were Vice Admirals Charles Turner Joy, Commander of the US Naval Forces, Far East, Arthur D. Struble, the 7th Fleet Commander, Generals Almond, Wright, some members of the latter's JSPOG group, and Rear Admiral James H. Doyle, Commander of Task Force 90, who was to head the landing force. Some members of Admiral Joy's staff who were to present the naval problems involved in a landing at Inch'on were also present. General Wright, the Operations Staff, briefed the group on the basic plan. Admiral Doyle then presented the naval considerations for about an hour. His general tone was pessimistic, and he concluded with the remark, "The operation is not impossible, but I do not recommend it."[8]

General Collins then proposed his idea of a landing at Kunsan, which Admiral Sherman had also favored. According to Collins, Inch'on was separated too far away from the Naktong front from which Eighth Army was to launch a counterattack, and as a result, a smooth link-up operations between the X Corps and Eighth Army could remain doubtful. In addition, as a probable landing site, Kunsan had more favorable natural conditions than Inch'on; there were no natural obstacles in the area of Kunsan harbor, and the port city itself was located closer to the enemy's communication route between Nonsan and Taejon.[9]

When the presentation ended, General MacArthur took the rostrum as the last speaker, and began to talk about the reasons why the landing should be made at Inch'on. He said that the enemy had neglected his rear and was dangling on a thin logistical rope that could be quickly cut in the Seoul area, that the enemy had committed practically all his forces against Eighth Army in the south and had no trained reserves and little power of recuperation.[10] He further stressed the strategical, political, and psychological reasons for the quick capture of Seoul. Pointing to the large map behind him, he added that the X Corps which would land at Inch'on could play a role of an anvil on which the hammer of Eighth Army from the south would crush the North Koreans.

Turning to a consideration of a landing at Kunsan, which General Collins had proposed, MacArthur responded saying, "a landing there would not result in severing the North Korean supply lines and destroying the North Korean Army." He added, "the amphibious landing at Inch'on is tactically the most powerful military device available to the United Nations Command, and the North Koreans consider a landing at Inch'on impossible because of the very difficulties involved, and because of this, the landing force will achieve surprise." Then, he concluded his long talk saying, "The Navy has never turned me down yet, and I know it will not now. It will save the lives of 100,000 men."[11]

The following day, Admiral Sherman, Chief of Naval Operations, met with Vice Admiral Joy, Commander of the US Naval Forces, Far East, Admiral Arthur W. Radford, Commander-in-Chief of the Pacific Theatre, Lt Gen. Lemuel C. Shepherd, Jr., USMC Commander-in-Chief of the US Fleet in the Pacific, Maj. Gen. Oliver P. Smith, Commander of the US 1st Marine Division, in a commanders' conference. They agreed that the P'osungmyon area, the shore line [recently a tide embankment has been constructed] at the bay of Asanman; 30 miles south of Inch'on could be a more favorable alternate landing site than any other locations because the shore there kept a constant level of deep water. On behalf of the participants, General Shepherd Jr. called on General MacArthur and asked him to change the landing site to this area without avail.[12]

Upon returning to Washington, Collins and Sherman informed Defense Secretary Louis Johnson and Preseident Truman of the result of their visit to Far East Command. Secretary of Defense Johnson himself firmly supported General MacArthur's Inch'on plan, and later he obtained the Presidental approval on it. On August 28, the Joint Chiefs of Staff eventually approved the projected Inch'on landing. Still, it attached conditions to it to the effect that General MacArthur should provide further details and information of the pending operation and concurrently prepare for an alternative plan for landing at Kunsan. However, MacArthur pressed ahead unswervingly and, on August 30, he issued his UNC operation order for the Inch'on landing.[13] Later, on the 6th of September, he finally confirmed his previous orders, and announced September 15 as D-day for the operation.

(4) Operational Plan of Joint Task Force Seven

In making preparations for the Inch'on landing, the missions the Navy would have to perform were just as important as those of the landing force. As the initial phase of the operation was to begin at sea by transporting the amphibious force to a beachhead, the Navy was responsible not only for the safe transportation, but also for securing a beachhead in the landing area.

The Commander of the US Naval Forces, Far East (NAVFE) took charge of making ready the Navy's part of the operation. According to the operation order issued, on August 30, by the NAVFE, the tasks of the Navy included the following: while maintaining naval blockade of the west coast of Korea south of latitude 39° 35′ north, conduct pre-D-day naval operations as the situation might require; on D-day, seize by amphibious assault, occupy, and defend a beachhead in the Inch'on area; transport, land, and support follow-up and strategic reserve troops, if directed, to the Inch'on area; and provide cover and support as required.[14]

In order to accomplish these objectives, the NAVFE organized Joint Task Force Seven and appointed the 7th Fleet Commander, Vice Admiral Struble to the post of the task force commander. It formed a total of seven subordinate parts to carry out its various missions such as Task Forces 90 and 92, which had detailed missions of attack and maneuvering, respectively.

The most important and specific mission of Task Force 90 was to transport landing troops to a beachhead and direct them until they could secure the beachhead. It was also to control and coordinate close naval and aerial support fire which would accompany the amphibious operation itself. Task Force 92, meanwhile, was composed mainly of landing units the US X Corps, and was to be commanded directly by the JTF-7 until the last element of the landing force could go ashore. Table 2 shows the organization of the task force.

〈Table 2〉   Organization of Joint Task Force-Seven

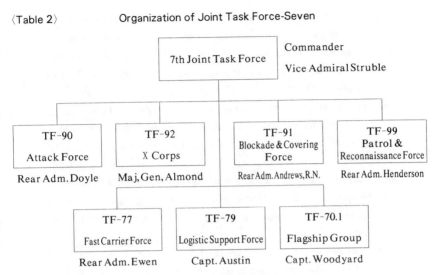

Source : Appleman, *South to the Naktong, North to the Yalu,* p. 497.

Joint Task Force-7 assigned to the operation a total of about 260 warships from Great Britain, Canada, Australia, New Zealand, France, and Netherland including the United States. Some ROK naval vessels such as four patrol ships (PC boats) and seven mine sweepers (YMS) also joined the task force. Among these, surface vessels were not allowed to operate within 12 miles of Soviet or Chinese territory nor aircraft within 20 miles of such territory.[15]

As the naval operation order had been issued as late as on August 30, the JTF-7's order, being pressed hard for time, was in turn issued hurriedly on September 3. It came out almost at the same time with the order of subordinate Task Force-90. Therefore, part of the operation order of the US 1st Marine Division's was readjusted. The gists of these orders were as follows.

Aircraft of the US marine division, US Air Force, and British Air Force, under the control of the flagship, USS Rochester, and taking off from respective aircraft carriers, would provide as much support as could be concentrated in and over the landing area. The objective area of the Joint Task Force would include an area 48 kilometers inland from the landing site. For the naval phases, the command post of the JTF-7 was to be located on the Rochester; that of Rear Admiral Doyle (Commander of TF-90: Attack Force) would be on the Mt. McKinley. Three landing beaches were selected: the north edge of Wolmido island, sea wall dock area of north Inch'on, and mud flat area at the south edge of the city. They were called Green, Red, and Blue Beaches respectively. The landings would be made on the early morning high tide at 06:30, September 15 (D-day, L-hour), and that afternoon at the next high tide, about 17:30 (D-day, H-hour). The assault landing parties would operate in the following order[6]:

- the 3rd Battalion Landing Team (BLT-3) of the US 5th Marine Regiment would land at Green Beach to gain a beachhead there and secure Wolmido on D-day, L-hour.
- the US 5th Marine Combat Team (less the BLT-3) was to land over Red Beach on D-day, H-hour to secure its objective O-A line; and maintain close contact with the US 1st Marine Combat Team in securing the Beachhead Line (BHL); then prepare to advance eastward.
- the US 1st Marine Combat Team was to land over Blue Beach simultaneously with the US 5th Marine Combat Team, by using its two battalions in a concerted attack; secure the immediate objective O-1 line; make continuous contact with the 5th Marines in securing the beachhead line and prepare for further advance eastward.
- the ROK 1st Marine Regiment was to be kept as the US 1st Marine Division's reserve force, and later, on order, land over Red Beach to mop up enemy troops in downtown streets of Inch'on in close coordination with the US 5th Marines.

As these landing operations were to be made by ground troops with an eleven-hour difference between the first and the last parties, some dangers for

Plan for Landing Operations

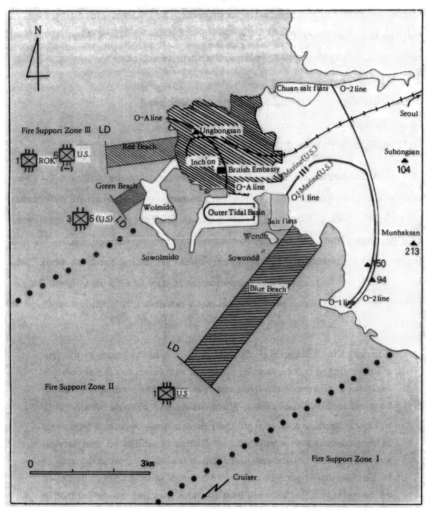

the lead elements were expected; they might be separated from the main body by an enemy interdiction. There was also a posibility of the enemy's reinforcements; however, the conditions and realities of tides and channels at Inch'on forced the JTF-7 to go ahead with its projects. They were decided to get out of these risks and dangers with the help of the naval gunfire and air strikes, as well as with a carefully thought-out plan and a surprise attack.

2. Landing Operation and Securing a Beachhead

(1) Intelligence Estimate on the Enemy in the Area of Seoul-Inch'on

According to an official intelligence estimate of the X Corps G-2 Section in the late August, the NKPA had committed almost all of its combat troops to the Naktong front to secure a Pusan bridgehead, and only small rear area garrisons, line of communications units, and newly formed, poorly trained troops were scattered throughout enemy's rear including Seoul. A book published by North Koreans, *The Comprehensive History of Choson,* volume 26, described the North Korean provision against a possible UN landing at Inch'on. It stated,

> Comrade Kim Il Sung made a public disclosure of the enemy's objective of attempting to make a landing operation with intent to cut our communications line between the front and rear areas. The landing sites would be at the Inch'on-Seoul area.... When the enemy's purpose turned out to be clear, Comrade Kim ordered the People's Army to form a west coast defense command to strengthen our defense capability on that area. It was to provide a unified commandship of the troops around the area of Inch'on-Seoul; the garrison and security forces which had been deployed on the west coast line between Inch'on and Kunsan were to be controlled by this command. The combat troops as well as war equipment would be concentrated on the Inch'on-Seoul area. He appointed Comarade Ch'oi Yong Gun to the post of the commander of the West Coast Defense Command.

In the meantime, about 400 North Korean soldiers, elements of the 3rd Battalion, 226th Independent Marine Regiment, and some artillery troops of the NKPA 918th Coastal Artillery Regiment had been active in Wolmido and the Inch'on area.[17] Starting from August 12, the 87th Regiment (Col. Kim T'ae Mo) of the newly activated NKPA 9th Division was operating in the downtown area of the city.[18]

A battalion of an unknown enemy brigade size unit (called unit 884) had been deployed on the coast line positions for about 5-6 kilometers, which extended from the causeway between Wolmido and Inch'on to the Chuan salt flats, northeast of the city.[19] Part of the defense operation order issued by the enemy 5th Battalion of Unit 884 on August 29 stated as follows:

① Having been hit hard by the Democratic People's Republic of Korea Army, the enemy [UN Forces] had been retreating in dispersion and confusion; however, despite defeat in the early stages of the war, the enemy now is making a military venture trying to land at Inch'on. Enemy troops further tried to proceed eastward to recapture Seoul, the capital city of Korea. For this purpose, the enemy concentrated his troops on board battle ships on and around the island areas of Dokjokdo, Yongyudo, and Yonghungdo. They are trying to make a surprise landing at Inch'on. In addition, enemy planes are continuously threatening against the city of Inch'on.

② Accordingly, the mission of our battalion… is to decisively defeat this enemy before he can set foot on the coastal area. The defense sector for the battalion covers the area that extends from the salt flats on the right to the causeway of Wolmido on the left.

Judging from the writers' analysis of this primary document, the enemy might have been aware of the UN landing operation and had anticipated it about two weeks before. However, they turned out to have been incapable of interfering with the landing. The estimated enemy strength in the Inch'on landing area was placed at about 2,000 men including those of the local garrison in the city.[20]

The enemy 9th Division (−) which had been on guard duty in the Seoul area moved, on August 12, to the Naktong river front,[21] and the 18th Division which had remained in Seoul also moved on toward the Naktong front in mid-September, just before the UN landing was made at Inch'on.[22] The remaining enemy strength in the Seoul area, therefore, was at that time estimated as about 5,500 troops including 500 men at Kimp'o Airfield. As of September 4, including an additional 2,500 soldiers reinforced there, the total enemy force active in the Inch'on-Seoul area was estimated at about 10,000 men.[23]

The possibility that the enemy might reinforce the Inch'on-Seoul area was also considered. He might take his combat troops committed against the EUSA in the south to the new front. If this were attempted, it appeared that the NKPA 3rd, 10th, and 13th Divisions, deployed on either side of the main Seoul-Pusan highway, could most rapidly reach the new Inch'on-Seoul front. The US Far East Command also estimated that North Korean naval elements were almost nonexistent and therefore, incapable of interfering with the landing. At this time, five fleets of small patrol-type vessels comprised the North Korean Navy; among these, only one was on the west coast at Chinnamp'o and the others at Wonsan on the east coast. Meanwhile, the North Korean Air Force which had had only 19 obsolescent Soviet-manufactured aircraft available[24] was not considered to be influential in the UN landing.

(2) Steaming toward Inch'on

As D-day for the landing at Inch'on drew close, Joint Task Force Seven began loading ships with the troops, equipment and supplies in early September at the ports of Pusan in Korea, Sasebo, Kobe, and Yokohama in Japan. Starting on September 10, the LSTs cleared the ports for Inch'on.

The US 1st Marine Division (−) and 7th Infantry Division left Kobe and Yokohama, respectively on September 11. On the way to Korea, they were to rendezvous at sea with the ROK 1st Marine and 17th Infantry Regiments which had departed Pusan, Korea. The next day Admiral Struble, Commander of JTF-7, left Sasebo for Inch'on on board the flagship Rochester. That night General MacArthur together with Maj. Gen. Almond, Commander of the X Corps, Brig. Gen. Wright, his G-3 Staff, and Lt. Gen. Shepherd of the US Marine Corps embarked on the Mt. Mckinley, the flagship of Task Force-90 commanded by Rear Admiral Doyle. They departed Sasebo for the landing area. Thus, by September 14, all of the warships assigned to the mission could assemble at the predesignated area at the central Yellow Sea near Dokjokdo island (Point California).

In the meantime, as a final means of carrying out the operation successfully, the US Far East Command continued checking on conditions in Inch'on harbor. At night on September 1, it sent US Navy Lt. Eugene F. Clark to Yonghungdo island near Inch'on. Accompanied by an interpreter, Lt. Clark infiltrated on to the island at the mouth of the ship channel of Inch'on harbor on board a ROK PC 703 (Commander Lee Sung Ho). On the island, Lt. Clark used friendly natives to gather the information needed. He organized an observation team and sent a few members on several trips to the Inch'on-Seoul area to measure water depths and the height of sea walls, to check on the mud flats, and to observe enemy strength including the numbers, locations of enemy batteries, troop movement and concentration points; he made them check even on enemy fortifications. Based on this intelligence officer's detailed reports, JTF-7 believed it could go safely ahead with its plans for landing at Inch'on. Other information gathering was done by ROK Army Colonel Kye In Ju and ROK Navy Commander Yon Chong who had belonged to a US military intelligence agency called Trudy Jackson. They also collected general information on Inch'on; Colonel Kye even employed 22 Korean agents to help him.

In order to work in concert with the vessels of the landing force steaming toward Inch'on, air attacks which had been coordinated by JTF began, on September 4, to neutralize possible landing areas and continued until the landing. US Marine air elements and other aircraft which had taken off from carriers struck Wolmido and nearby downtown Inch'on in a series of napalm attacks with the aim of isolating the landing sites. Starting from September 13, four UN aircraft carriers (two heavy and two light classes), 6 US destroyers, and 5 cruisers entered the approaches to Inch'on harbor and began the bombardment of Wolmido island. At this time, five enemy 75-mm guns returned the fire from covered emplacements; at once it resulted in an intense ship-shore battle which lasted quite a long while. After the fierce preliminary air and naval bombardment, Wolmido became tranquilized with only burning trees exposing skeletons; even downtown Inch'on appeared to be wrapped in black flames.

The sailing of the ships toward Inch'on and the preliminary bombardment of Joint Task Force Seven took place simultaneously in an effort to deceive the enemy of the UN landing plan itself, date and sites as well. The preparatory UN air strikes had been so evenly distributed throughout the possible landing sites on the west coast north from P'yongyang south to the Kunsan area including Inch'on, that the North Koreans might have been confused and, therefore, been able to determine not have spotted the exact UN landing site. The fierce UN air strikes on the port city Kunsan, which had been considered as one of the most feasible landing sites, might have further confused them. Even the full-scale UN naval gunfire which had been planned and delivered on Inch'on since September 13 was believed to achieve a surprise there by not allowing time or opportunity for the enemy force to be properly prepared to interfere with the landing.

Steaming for Inch'on Harbor

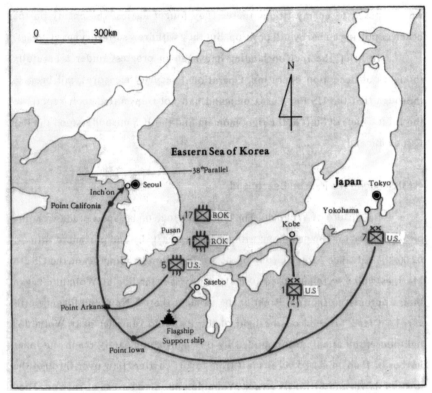

That was not all; at night on September 12, a combined force of the ROK, US, and British troops dared to make a feint amphibious operation at Kunsan, while on the east coast for two consecutive days, on September 14 and 15, UN aircrafts hit hard on the Samchok area, another possible landing area, to divert enemy's concern on the west. The student soldiers of the ROK 1st Independent Anti-Guerrilla Battalion (+) led by Capt. Lee Myong Hum (later renamed as Lee Chong Hun) even practically landed at the beach in Changsadong, south of Yongdok, at dawn on September 15. Unfortuately, however, as their

Landing Ship Dock (LSD) had run aground because of the typhoon Kezia, they were exposed to enemy troops there. They fought against the enemy on the beach capturing a nearby hill position. But they withdrew suffering heavy losses.

In brief, the Inch'on landing had been in progress under a carefully thought-out deception operation. Operational security measures had been so thorough that the US Far East Command had not transmitted their reports to the Joint Chiefs of Staff at the right moment and the JCS misunderstood the Far Esst Command.

(3) Securing the Inch'on Beachhead

Recapture of Wolmido: The landing at Inch'on began at predawn hours on September 15. The day came with a high overcast sky and portent of rain. At 02:00, the Advance Attack Group of the 3rd Battalion Landing Team, the US 5th Marines which were supposed to make an assault landing at Wolmido, began their approach to Inch'on. Right at the moment the US Navy intelligence officer, Lt. Clark[25] turned on the light of the P'almido [an islet near Wolmido] lighthouse; the attack group guided by this light could safely reach the inner harbor of Inch'on. At 05:00, aircraft from escort carriers flew over through the dusk of dawn, and furiously struck Wolmido and inland areas of Inch'on. They were immediately followed by naval gunfire from American destroyers. An intense rocket barrage of about 1,000 rounds was put down on enemy positions at Green Beach and the surrounding areas. The first wave of the advance attack group, on board 7 landing craft (LCVPs), crossed a line of departure which had already been established at sea.

As soon as the friendly rocket barrage was lifted at L-2 minutes, the LCVP's carrying the assault group moved toward the beach at full speed through the approach channel; at that time, US Marine Corsairs flew over the

ROKA training to fire 57mm anti-tank artillery

heads of attacking soldiers and delivered bombs and strafed the beach just in front of them. The first wave composed of a platoon of troops of the US marine G and H Companies reached the beach unopposed at 06:33, 3 minutes behind schedule. In two minutes, the Second wave also made the landing.

The troops of G Company ashore moved rapidly toward Hill 105, the crest of Wolmido, and H Company reached an outlet of the causeway leading to the inland Inch'on to interdict enemy troops there. While the two American assault companies were attacking their objectives, the third wave which was composed of 10 tanks arrived at the beach. Among these tanks ashore, six were M26 Pershing, two carried dozer blades, one mounted flame throwers, and the other was a tow tank. Just along behind these troops came the reserve unit, I Company.

At 06:50, Lt. Col. Robert D. Taplett, Commander of the assault battalion, who had landed at the beach prior to the reserve unit, received five minutes later a radio message from his G Company to the effect that the lead element, the 3rd Platoon, had reached the crest of the hill and raised the American flag on it. I Company, the battalion reserve, at that time was to move around H Company on its left flank and advance to the northern edge of Wolmido with a mission to clear the area of remnants of North Korean troops. While making the movement, I Company encountered a platoon sized enemy troops in foxholes. They were advised to surrender at the moment; however, enemy soldiers opposed stoutly, throwing hand grenades at American marines. Inevitably tanks were brought in, and a tank dozer together with an M26 Pershing and the accompanying marines sealed them in by filling their trenches and foxholes. A tank with flame throwers poured flames into their cave-like trenches. Only then did the North Koreans, paying dearly, come falteringly out of the trenches with their hands up. Still, more enemy troops in several cave positions around the island desperately resisted, refusing to surrender. But most of the surviving enemy soldiers, being demoralized, surrendered. Companies G and H which had been attacking Hill 105 and mopping up the enemy in the builtup areas close to the harbor, respectively, also encountered relatively light enemy resistance. Otherwise, all their actions went smoothly.

Eventually, the assault battalion completed its mop-up operations on the island by about noon after it had secured Wolmido at 08:00. In this battle of regaining Wolmido, the 3rd Battalion, US 5th Marines, suffered a relatively light loss; only 17 marines were wounded. On the other hand, it killed 108 enemy soldiers and captured 136. About 150 North Korean soldiers were estimated to have been sealed into their trench caves by tank dozers.

Securing the Beachhead: In the afternoon, when the tide was high again landing craft carrying the US 5th and 1st Marine Combat Teams which were supposed to make an assault landing, slowly moved in close to Red and Blue Beaches along the approach channel. Despite a rain which began to fall at that time, the US marine and naval air continued to range up and down inland roads which led to Seoul-Inch'on highway and over downtown streets of the city, isolating the port, the objective. The Naval Gunfire Support Group moved in closer to the inner harbor to cover the approach channel. Under these covering fires, assault troops of the US 5th and 1st Marines, together with the ROK 3rd Battalion of the 1st Marine Regiment, began leaving the transports and went on board the landing craft. At 16:45, the landing craft carrying the 5th Marine troops crossed the line of departure and moved in close to Red Beach, and simultaneously those carrying the 1st Marines moved toward Blue Beach after crossing the line.

At 17:33, the first wave of the US 5th Marines reached Red Beach, 3 minutes behind the pre-scheduled H-hour. A Company men of the 1st Battalion climbed over the sea wall with scaling ladders which they had prepared for the action; several boats put their soldiers ashore through holes in the wall made by the naval bombardment. The marines who had landed on the left flank (north) of the beach encountered enemy troops in communication trenches and a bunker just beyond the sea wall. They were immediately locked in an intense fight; as the American marines fought under unfavorable terrain conditions, they lost eight men killed and 28 wounded.

Twenty-two minutes after landing, A Company gained its immediate objective, Cemetery Hill. Meanwhile, the 2nd Battalion, the assault unit of the US 5th Marines, landing on the right flank (south) of Red Beach, encountered almost no resistance. It moved to the south of a railroad nearby, and thereupon proceeded to piers of inner harbor and a hill on which the British Consulate had run its office before the war. E Company landed on the beach at 17:40, and moved rapidly toward an inland hill, Ungbong-san.

Among the subordinate elements of the ROK 1st Marine Regiment, the 3rd Battalion attached to the US 5th Marines landed at Red Beach, following the assault landing units. Then the ROK marine regiment $(-)$ came ashore at about sunset, and assembled on the beach near Cemetery Hill to encamp in the open there.

On the left flank of the US 5th Marines, the 3rd Battalion secured the O-A phase line at 22:40, and on the right, the 2nd Battalion took up positions on the O-A line just past 24:00. Thus, the objective of the 5th marine on D-day, securing the O-A line, was achieved.

In the meantime, assault elements of the US 1st Marine Regiment began landing over Blue Beach at 17:32, 2 minutes behind the pre-scheduled H-hour. Most of them were forced to climb a high sea wall; some of them went astray and landed on the sea wall enclosing the salt flats (or salt farms) on the left of the beach. Fortunately, they encountered almost no resistance there; only minor losses were reported at that time. The 1st marine regiment gained its final D-day objectives, the O-1 line, by 01:30, the following day.

Thus the US 1st Marine Division secured took Wolmido just in time at the full tide early in the morning on D-day, and secured the assigned beachhead O-A and O-1 phase lines in time at the afternoon full tide that day. In its assault landing however, the division suffered 21 men killed, 1 missing in action, and 174 wounded. They captured about 300 North Korean soldiers.[26] The total UN strength that had landed on the beach on D-day reached about 13,000 men; also a large amount of equipment and supplies including 450 vehicles[27] were unloaded on the same beach.

On the morning of September 16, the US 5th and 1st Marine Regiments ashore established contact with each other by 07:30, and strengthened a solid defense line around Inch'on. The two regiments continued their eastward advances to secure the safety of the beachhead line.

Eight US marine aircraft, early in the morning that day, sighted six enemy tanks on a road 5 kilometers east of Inch'on approaching the city; at once, they hit the tanks with napalm and 500-pound bombs. Instantly, three of the enemy tanks were destroyed and the accompanying foot soldiers were scattered. In this air strike, however, a plane piloted by Marine Capt. William F. Simpson was hit by enemy fire. It crashed and exploded near a burning enemy tank. The pilot died a heroic death at the place. The marine Corsairs furiously continued their attack against the rest of the enemy tanks and destroyed them all.

The two US marine regiments, with the help of UN naval gunfire and air strikes, advanced rapidly to the inland areas, and by the evening of that day, had reached a point 10 kilometers from the landing area. There they gained critical covering terrain and thus concluded the US 1st Marine Division's 24-hour operations for securing the Inch'on beachhead. The division commander established his command post east of Inch'on and at 18:00, he took over the responsibility for operations ashore from the commander of the attack force, Task Force-90.

Mop-up Operations in Downtown Streets: The ROK 1st Marine Regiment took over mop-up work in downtown Inch'on. Early in the morning on September 16, the regiment placed its 3rd Battalion in the south of the Seoul-Inch'on railroad which passed through the downtown area of Inch'on, and the 1st Battalion north of the railway for the operation. The southern sector of the city was taken up by the 3rd Battalion which included the high ground surrounding Ungbong-san as well as the downtown itself. Even though most of the surviving North Korean soldiers appeared to have escaped from the city during the UN preliminary air and naval bombardment and assault landings, considerable numbers who had lost this opportunity were believed to have taken cover in the residential areas disguising themselves as civilians. Many of them were captured during the mop-up operation because patriotic citizens reported them to the ROK Marines. Some of them, demoralized, surrendered; still, some others resisted or tried to escape only to be killed.

Many Inch'on citizens who had not been able to flee for safety at the early stages of the war, and had hidden themselves in closets or the like, came out into the streets with haggard faces to meet the advancing ROK soldiers. They hugged soldiers for joy; most of them howled "hurrah" with tears in their eyes. Very soon waves of South Korean national flags spreaded all over the streets, and some patriots helped the marines in locating persons who had taken sides with the North Koreans. Thus the mop-up operations went smoothly. When the marines reached the Inch'on Police Station building they witnesssed there a horrible scene in a corner of the detention house. They shuddered at the North Koreans' atrocities: about 100 innocent South Korean people were found dead on false charges.

At 14:30 that day, after completing their missions, the 3rd Battalion of the ROK marines assembled at Towon Park near the Public Stadium to wait for orders from the US 5th Marines to which they had been attached and to be prepared for the future operations.

Meanwhile, the ROK marine 1st Battalion finished its relatively simple work. As most of the northern sector was scattered with small industrial factories and fewer residential districts compared to those in the southern sector, it could terminate the mop-up operation at about the same time as the adjacent 3rd Battalion had done its work. At 16:00, the ROK 1st Marine Regimental headquarters, together with the 1st Battalion, moved to the site of Inch'on Commercial Middle School, and at 17:30, the 3rd Battalion marched eastward from Towon Park to bivouac in the open in the Towhadong area.

The ROK marine regiment there controlled the main public offices and facilities. During the night, they intensified checking and patrolling critical points around the city. On the first day of the mop up operations, the regiment captured 181 North Korean soldiers.

3. Advance to the Han River

On September 16, the US 1st Marine Division which had secured the Inch'on beachhead began to move toward the Han River. The 5th Marine Regiment followed the main Seoul-Inch'on highway on the north, while the 1st Regiment advanced on the south of the road. The objective of the former was Kimp'o Airfield, and that of the latter was Yongdungp'o.

During that night, the two American marine regiments occupied a hill commanding the area of Pup'yung (Ascom City), and took up defensive positions there. The 2nd Battalion, the lead elements of the 5th Marine Regiment, took the high ground surrounding the Wont'ong pass west of the Pup'yung railroad station. F Company was placed on Hill 131 on the left flank of the Seoul-Inch'on railroad, and on the right of it was D Company. As the Seoul-Inch'on highway almost met with the railroad at an angle of 90 degrees near the Wont'ong pass, the acute angle curve offered a favorable terrain features for the D Company defense to fight against approaching enemy armored units. Aware of the vantage ground position, D Company placed its 2.36-inch rocket crew and the 2nd Platoon, which had been reinforced by machine guns, on Hill 89 in front of the curve point, using the platoon as outpost troops.

About 500 meters in depth along the road behind Hill 89, they placed 3.5-inch rockets of the battalion, 75-mm recoilless rifles of the regiment, and M26 Pershing tanks. These anti-tank weapons and crews were all deployed in pertinent depth.

At 05:45, just predawn hours on September 17, the 3rd day after the Inch'on landing, members of the advanced platoon of D Company saw the dim outlines of six tanks and accompanying infantry on the road east of Pup'yung, moving toward Inch'on. Closely watching the combined enemy armored force of six T-34 tanks and foot soldiers, the marine platoon members waited for an order from their leader.

At 06:00, when the enemy armored force moved past the hidden outpost of D Company, and the last tank was to pass the acute curve near the Wont'ong pass, the 2.36-inch rockets at a range of about 70 meters opened fire on the enemy tanks; other anti-tank weapons of the marine company and Pershing tanks immediately joined in the surprise attack. All six enemy tanks, being isolated and fired upon by the combined weapons of the American marine troops, were instantly destroyed. Enemy infantry soldiers who had accompanied the tanks fell in the confusion of the moment without even trying to return the marine fire. Two hundred of an estimated 250 enemy troops were killed, and the Wont'ong pass was flooded with blood. The American marines won the battle with only one man wounded.

After repelling this enemy counterattack at Pup'yung at dawn, the US 5th Marine Regiment began, at 09:00 that morning, action for recapturing Kimp'o Airfield. Its 2nd Battalion proceeded eastward about one kilometer along the Seoul-Inch'on highway and swung there to the north (left) to enter a narrow path to Kimp'o Airfield by way of an area east of Pup'yong. As their maps did not coincide with the terrain features there, however, the combined marine and tank force which had got through the town of Pup'yong lost much time in an open field of Kimp'o county trying to locate an exit toward the airport.

It was not until 14:00 that day when the American marine battalion was back on the right track for the airfield. This time, E Company led the battalion which had been reinforced by a tank company(−). The battalion rapidly advanced and by about 16:00, two hours later, captured its immediate objective, Hill 106, 5 kilometers south of Kimp'o Airfield almost unopposed. As its final operational objective for the day was to capture the airfiled, the battalion had to hurry its action. They had sufficient reasons for hurrying up their actions:

the importance of securing the airfield as early as possible and the desirability for taking the objective during the daylight hours.

Thus the battalion commander rapidly moved his companies toward the airport; E Company, together with a tank platoon, was ordered to attack against the east area of the runway, and D Company would attack against the west area. F Company, the battalion's reserve unit, would push in the center against the south of the runway. Meanwhile, A Company(−), the tank unit which had joined the battalion later, was to move more deeply into the enemy territory on the west than the foot soldiers.

The American marine battalion came for the first time under enemy fire from the southern edge of the runway. At once a combined marine and tank force suppressed two enemy automatic machine guns. The marines' charge against the enemy positions on the airfield was made about 18:00 that day. At this time, marine assault elements were under sporadic enemy small arms fire from all directions; howver, the enemy's resistance was ineffective. Even though 400-500 enemy soldiers had been deployed around the airfield, they appeared to have been surprised by the marines; the enemy had not even mined the runway, and fled hurriedly without even venturing any resistance. As the darkness of night settled over the place, the battalion could not seize covering terrain features nearby; however, it virtually secured important airport facilities such as the main office building and hangars on the airfield. At once, the marine companies took up defensive positions there.

In the meantime, the US 1st Marine Battalion which had followed up the 2nd Battalion from the town of Puch'on swung to the right at a point short of the airfield, and occupied Hill 71, 3 kilometers southeast of the airfield and 5 kilometers north of Puch'on(Sosa) at 19:00 on the 17th. It took up defensive positions there during the night. Their dispositions on the surrounding knobs and hills as well as on Hill 71 could command not only Kimp'o Airfield, but also the

main road between the towns of Kimp'o and Sosa. Taking advantage of the rela-
tive high ground positions, the battalion could maintain contact with the US 1st
Marine Regiment on the south and thus contribute to reinforcing the US X
Corps phase line there.

The 3rd Battalion, the reserve unit of the US 5th Marine Regiment, assembled at Samjongri, 4 kilometer west of the 1st Battalion, and the regimental
command post accordingly moved, at 16:30, to a point north of Pup'yong railroad station.

The rapid advance of the American marine troops forced the enemy at
the airfield positions to hastily withdraw with only ineffective, sporadic resistance. When the evening deepened, however, the enemy force which had reorganized their troops attempted to counterattack against the marines. Between
02:00 and dawn on the 18th of September, small enemy troops hit the perimeter
positions of marines at the airfield several times. The marines repulsed these
counterattacks, inflicting heavy casualties on them. Supporting tanks played
the leading role in these actions.

By the morning of September 18, the 5th Marine Regiment completely
secured the airfield by waging a searching and mop-up operation there.
Afterwards, the regiment brought its command post into the airfield. In this
action, the 2nd Battalion which had played the leading role, suffered 4 men
killed and 19 wounded. On the other hand, enemy casualties were counted as
about 100 men killed and 10 captured. The battalion also captured 3 enemy
planes including one Russian-built YAK. By the following day, the 5th Marines
captured such covering terrain features as Kaewha-san (131 meters) and Hill
118, all of which were near or on the Han River, and advanced to the river line
positions at the south bank of the river. At about this time, the ROK marines
which had turned over the responsibility for the security of Inch'on to the US
2nd Engineer Special Brigade moved up toward Kimp'o Airfield by way of Pup'-

yong, and captured, on September 18, Kyeyang-san on the west of the airfield. There it took over the responsibility for the security of the airfield, and at the same time, joined the American marines in preparing for the projected crossing of the Han River.

In the meantime, on September 17, the 3rd day of the Inch'on landing, the US 1st Marine Regiment, while the 5th Marine troops had passed through the Pup'yong area and swung thereupon to the left to enter a narrow path toward Kimp'o Airfield, began to move up toward the Han River along the Seoul-Inch'on highway. For this action, the regiment placed the 2nd Battalion on the north of the road, and the 1st Battalion on the south. It kept the 3rd Battalion in reserve. The 2nd Battalion attacked against Hill 208 astride the highway, and the 1st Battalion against Hill 176.

The two companies D and F of the 2nd Battalion were checked by an estimated company-size enemy force in the area near Hill 208, and E Company of the same battalion was also blocked by the enemy near a small village called Pugaedong(its old name was Mapunri)[28] situated in an open field, east of Pup'yong. However, the marine battalion, with the help of powerful artillery support fire, seized Hill 208 at around 12:00 that day. Meanwhile, the American marine regiment committed G Company of the 3rd Battalion reinforced by one tank platoon of the tank unit, B Company, to the area of Pugaedong to attack against the enemy positions there. The 3rd Battalion less G Company formed an armored unit which was comprised of landing vehicle tanks (LVTs), amphibious trucks(DUKWs), and the tank element B Company. It followed G Company along the highway.

The US marine troops saw an enemy T-34 tank among farmhouses at Pugaedong and opened preemptive surprise fire to destroy it; eventually they secured the town at about 16:00 that day. The 1st Marines continued their advance throughout the afternoon hours. The 3rd Batalion moved eastward along the highway, and on the south of the road, in an open field, the 2nd Battalion also advanced eastward astride the Seoul-Inch'on railway. The two battalions were to attack against a small village called Songnaech'on along the highway. Some subordinate elements of the North Korean 18th Division had taken up defensive positions near the town with about 10 emplaced anti-tank weapons alongside the road. The enemy appeared to have prepared for using considerable amount of artillery fire support there.

No sooner had American marines attacked against the town than the enemy opened up with surprise fire on them. Unexpectedly at that moment, the lead tank of the marine troops broke down. Marine soldiers at once spread out and marine tanks were locked in a fierce exchange of fire with the enemy. At that time, US Marine Corsairs which had been requested by the ground troops flew over the place to hit enemy positions in front of the town, with bombs, rockets, and strafing.

With the help of the air strikes, the 2nd Battalion on the extreme north flank first reached the edge of the high ground of the town. As the American marine tanks on the road followed up the advance party opening up with their 90-mm gun and machine gun fire, the enemy troops fled toward Sosa, a village halfway between Yongdungp'o and Inch'on. By about 18:30, the 1st Marine Regiment captured the town and cleared the remnant enemy troops of the place, and took up defensive positions during the night.

In this battle at Songnaech'on, the American marine troops destroyed 6 units of enemy anti-tank weapons, and killed or wounded quite a few enemy soldiers. On the other hand, three American marine tanks were destroyed in the battle. Meanwhile, American marines of the 1st Battalion which had been moving up to Sosa on the south of the marine regiment attacked against Hill 176 south of Hill 208 and seized it. They thereupon advanced to a southern ridge of Songju-san almost unopposed, and there they took up defensive positions in close coordination with an adjacent battalion.

Early in the morning on September 18, the 2nd Battalion together with the 3rd Battalion which had been reorganized as a mechanized unit, rushed the town of Sosa. At the entrance of the town, they were blocked by anti-tank obstacles and delayed for quite a while. But they quickly removed them and moved into the town, repelling a relatively light, sporadic enemy resistance there. Within that morning, they controled the whole town.

At around 12:00 that day, the 2nd Battalion under the cover of a tank company deployed alongside the Seoul-Inch'on highway, proceeded toward southeast of Sosa, and the 3rd Battalion advanced to a point northeast of the town and captured Hill 123 south of Wonmi-san.

On September 19, after taking the town of Sosa, the US 1st Marine Regiment continued its eastward movement. Although the heavily mined highway beyond Sosa forced the advance of the regiment to move slowly, they succeeded in reaching Kal-ch'on (currently Anyang-ch'on) just west of Yongdungp'o at about nightfall.

By September 19, with all assault landing units ashore, the US 1st Marine Division and the ROK 1st Marine Regiment successfully reached Kyeyang-san and Kaewha-san, and Kal-ch'on to secure the south bank of the Han River. There they prepared for the battle for Seoul.

The US 7th Infantry Division, the follow-up unit, had arrived that day to be deployed on the battle front, and joined other units in preparing for the attack against Seoul. The 32nd Infantry Regiment which had landed at Inch'on on the 18th moved up, the next day, toward the Han River to take over responsibility from the US 1st Marine Division for defending south of the Seoul-Inch'on highway. At that time the total effective strength of the 32nd Regiment was 5, 114 men. Among them 3,241 men were Americans and 1,873 were South Koreans (KATUSA). This ratio of about three to one in personnel organization of the unit apparently showed the important roles which KATUSA soldiers must have played in the Inch'on landing operations, let alone the participation of the ROK 1st Marine and 17th Infantry Regiments.

During the day (the 19th), the US 31st Infantry Regiment of the same division came ashore at Inch'on. A great mission of the US 7th Infantry Division was to take responsibility for the zone south of the Seoul-Inch'on highway, thus to check possible enemy reinforcement to the Seoul area from the south, and to link up with EUSA troops which had launched a massive counterattack northward at the Naktong River front.

In the meantime, the US Navy had supported the ground action thus far with effective naval gunfire. The USS Rochester and Toledo had been firing at ranges up to 27 kilometers (roughly to a line that extended from Kimp'o Airfield to Oryudong) in support of the US 1st Marine Division and the ROK marines on their left flank. On September 19, the USS Missouri arrived in Inch'on harbor from the east coast to join in delivering naval gunfire. The ship supported the US 7th Infantry Division on the right flank.

On the other hand, the North Korean Army had strengthened its defensive posture on the Seoul front by bringing in part of its troops from its rear areas in the north, and, at the same time, by withdrawing its 18th Division back to the Seoul-Inch'on area. This enemy division had initially headed for the Naktong River front.

II. The Recapture of Seoul

1. Strengthened Defensive Posture of the North Korean Army

As elements of the US X Corps rapidly advanced to the Han River front immediately after they landed at Inch'on, the NKPA frantically began to bring in miscellaneous troops which had been scattered around the Seoul area. As just mentioned in the previous section, in an effort to beef up its defensive strength in the Seoul area it even brought back troops which had been moving toward the Naktong front. For this purpose, North Korean Kim Il Sung personally ordered Marshal Ch'oi Yong Gun, commander of the west coast defense command, to act accordingly.[29]

In response to this order, the NKPA 18th Division, which had already left Seoul for the Naktong front prior to the UN Forces' Inch'on landing, hurriedly returned to the Seoul-Inch'on area and joined the NKPA 70th Regiment which had remained in the area of Suwon. At that time the enemy 42nd Tank Regiment which had been on the move southward from Sinuiju, a city on the northwestern tip of the Korean peninsula, arrived in Seoul early in September to join the 18th Division. Thus the enemy division had 18 T-34 tanks. According to statements of two captured enemy officers, a regimental sized enemy unit had already been committed to the Yongdungp'o area.[30]

The NKPA 107th Security Regiment which had been stationed in an area south of Kaesong also turned out to have placed its two battalions in the areas of Pup'yong-Kimp'o and Kangwha islet, respectively; it kept one battalion in reserve.[31] The US Air Force aerial observers had initially located the movement of unknown enemy troops in those areas on September 17, and later on the

18th, the numbers and titles of the units were identified by prisoners captured in the area of Kimp'o.

In other areas, after September 18, the US aerial observers reported large bodies of enemy troops moving toward Seoul from north and south of the city. However, they turned out to have been newly activated or local garrison forces as the NKPA's major combat troops had already been committed to the Naktong front. Thus the total enemy strength assembled in the Seoul area was, at the moment the US 1st Marine Division was preparing to cross the Han River, estimated at about 20,000 men.[32]

2. The Landing Units Prepare for the Recapture of Seoul

(1) The Han River Crossing and Advance to Sinch'on

The US 1st Marine Division, after its 5th Regiment secured Kimp'o Airfield on September 19, was preparing for the projected Han River crossing. On the division right, the 1st Marine Regiment was to begin the drive on Yongdungp'o after it had reached Kal-ch'on Creek. On September 18, the previous day, the division had been ordered by the X Corps to cross the Han River and to capture a hill position north of Seoul. The division, in turn, prepared its own orders for its subordinate elements. The order summed up the objectives of the division: on the 19th, it would first of all secure a crossing site near Haengju, cross the Han River on the 20th, capture Hill 125 (Dokyang-san; Haengjusansong, a mountain fortress), and advance to downtown Seoul.

Various combat elements had been attached to the US 5th Marine Regiment: the division Reconnaissance Company, A Company of the Tank Battalion and A Company of the 56th Amphibious Truck(DUKW) Battalion including the 1st Battalion of the ROK marines. The Division Engineer Combat Battalion, a

Coastal Battalion, and the Amphibious Truck Battalion(−) would directly support the marine regiment. In addition, the priority of the supporting fire was also given to the attacking regiment.[33]

On the 19th, the commander of the US 5th Marine Regiment formed a swimming party of fourteen men, mostly selected from the Reconnaissance Company, to locate a favorable crossing site on the opposite bank. At 20 : 40 that day, the party swam with the breaststroke across the river and safely landed at the Haengju ferry site at north side; they carried two small boats with them.

The party leader, Captain Kenneth J. Houghton immediately formed a patrol team comprised an officer and four enlisted men, and sent them out to reconnoiter the town of Haengju and Hill 125. It took them more than an hour to continue up the slope, but encountered no enemy force thus far. They hastily concluded that no enemy troops had been deployed there, and the leader, Captain Houghton signaled for the rest of the company to cross the river.

A moment later, when eight amphibious tractors carrying the Reconnaissance Company were halfway across the river, fierce enemy fire from Hill 125 suddenly struck among them. The patrol party had apparently made a mistake in searching for hidden enemy troops; they had most probably climbed up another hill instead of Hill 125, the objective of their patrol, and given a wrong signal for their company. Hit by enemy mortar and machine gun fire, a few tractors were stalled, and the rest were forced to turn around and made for the south bank.

When the deliberate river crossing at night failed, the commander of the US 5th Marine Regiment, out of sheer necessity, decided to prepare for an assault crossing of the river at daylight hours. At predawn hours on September 20, the regiment began a heavy artillery preparation against Hill 125. After this fire, at 06:45, I Company of the 3rd Battalion led the assault. Enemy fire from automatic weapons and small arms on Hill 125 inflicted rather heavy casualties on I Company; however, with the help of air strikes provided by American marine aircraft, the company secured the hill by about 09:45 after fighting a series of bloody fights. The 3rd Battalion less I Company, still riding amphibious tractors(LVTs), crossed the river encountering almost no resistance. At 08:30, it proceeded inland to Nungkok to the Seoul-Sinuiju railroad and a road parallel to it. Thereupon, they continued to move up southeastward for Seoul along the railroad track. The 2nd Battalion, which had crossed the river at 10:00 following the 3rd Battalion, passed through it and continued the advance. Thus, before nightfall the US 5th Marine Regiment with the 2nd Battalion of the ROK marines and the attached American tank company were across the river.

The ROK marines which had been relieved of the responsibility for the security of downtown Inch'on the previous day moved up to Kimp'o Airfield, and had joined the American marines in the river crossing during the morning. After crossing the river, they advanced to Hill 95 in the vicinity of Ch'angnung-ch'on.

That day, the American Engineer Combat Battalion began constructing a pontoon ferry at the Haengju crossing site. On the morning of September 21, the US 5th Marine Regiment, after repelling a company-sized enemy counterattack, advanced southeastward astride the railroad track and parallel road lines by way of Susaek, a small town in the outskirts of Seoul. Enemy resistance at first was light, but it steadily increased as the marines came near downtown Seoul. The 3rd Battalion captured Paeknyon-san (216 meters) north of Sinch'on, and the 1st Battalion seized Hill 68 southwest of the town. In the center, the 2nd Battalion of the ROK marines took Hill 104 due west of Sinch'on. Thus the combined ROK and US marine troops secured ridge line positions, which roughly linked hills Paeknyon-san, Hills 104, and 68 by the evening that day. There, they were ready for launching an attack against the heart of the capital city of Korea.

(2) The Recapture of Yongdungp'o

The US 1st Marine Regiment, which had advanced to Kal-ch'on as of September 19, was preparing for the attack against Yongdungp'o. The 1st Battalion, having taken over a hill mass including the highest Hill 118 near the confluence of Kal Creek and the Han River from the US 5th Marine Regiment, was in hasty defensive positions. The 2nd Battalion, meanwhile, prepared for the attack in its defensive positions near the Dok-gogae (pass) interdicting the Seoul-Inch'on highway. The 3rd Battalion, the reserve unit of the regiment, was to follow the 2nd Battalion. However, just before daylight on September 20, the two front-line battalions came under a preemptive enemy counterattack; the enemy troops which had fled to the Yongdungp'o area made a surprise attack against marine positions and both forces were locked in intense close combat. After having lost these hills to the 5th Marine Regiment the previous day, the NKPA placed powerful attack groups there to take them back. North Korean troops in front of the 1st Battalion crossed Kal-ch'on and arrived on Hills 80 and 85 to find them undefended. They continued on to Hill 118 where the 1st Battalion of American marines repulsed them. The marines there assaulted enemy troops again to recapture the hills and succeeded in taking back Hill 85, only after a bloody combat in which there were many marine casualties.

Elsewhere, on the Seoul-Inch'on highway, a battalion-size enemy force led by five T-34 tanks made a counterattack against the 2nd Battalion of American marines. At this time, however, the marines were in well-organized defensive positions astride the highway in the vicinity of the Dok-gogae. Taking advantage of favorable terrain features, they annihilated the enemy troops in a single blow. At dawn, American marines saw 300 dead enemy soldiers strewn about in the area of the pass. They also found two enemy tanks completely destroyed and one abandoned which appeared to have been operable. After this intense fight, the US 1st Marine Regiment advanced to the hill mass overlooking Yongdungp'o from the west side of Kal-ch'on. At 10:00, that morning, the US X Corps Commander General Almond visited the regiment, and authorized the regimental commander to shell Yongdungp'o. Holding its place on the high ground for the rest of the day, the American marine regiment prepared for the impending attack against Yongdungp'o, while overlooking the town wrapped with black flames which had been caused by the division artillery shells and the UN air strikes.

At dawn on September 21, after the artillery preparation against Yongdungp'o, the American marines resumed their attack at 06:30. The 1st Battalion crossed the rice paddies and Kal-ch'on near Hill 85 and moved toward downtown Yongdungp'o. This time, however, desperate enemy artillery fire caused many marine casualties. In an effort to delay the advance of American marines in this direction, North Koreans had concentrated troops there on the levees of rice paddies. Another fierce battle between both forces took place there at once.

In its part of the attack, the 2nd Battalion which had moved off from the southern end of the hill fought against heavy odds; enemy mortar and artillery fire from a hill on the battalion's exposed right flank[34] took a heavy toll in American marine casualties. Particularly when the battalion was crossing the rice paddies and Kal-ch'on, the enemy fire blocked its advance inflicting 85 casualties on the marine troops.

As the advance of the 2nd Battalion came to a standstill, the regimental commander, late in the afternoon that day, ordered the 3rd Battalion, the reserve element, to pass through the 2nd Battalion to continue the attack. While the two marine battalions were thus locked in heavy battles with enemy troops at northwestern and southwestern edges of Yongdungp'o, respectively, A Company of the 1st Battalion on the left flank crossed Kal-ch'on to reach the main part of the town by about noon that day, fortunately without encountering any enemy force.

A while later, A Company saw enemy reinforcements hurriedly proceeding from Seoul to Yongdungp'o. The marine company at once attacked these troops with surprise fire either destroying or dispersing them. The marines moved on eastward and went deep into the enemy rear. It reached the south bank of the Han River, and there the marines took up river line defensive positions.

At dusk that day, five enemy tanks, which had engaged American marine troops at the western edge of the town, attacked A Company apparently giving attention now to its (NKPA) rear. Marines' 2.36-inch bazookas instantaneously knocked out one, and damaged two of the tanks; the two undamaged tanks withdrew into the town of Yongdungp'o. During that night the enemy made five more separate attacks, but the American marine company repulsed them all. Dawn the following day disclosed about 275 enemy dead and 50 automatic weapons scattered on the levees and roadside. Aware of the fact that the northern edge of Yongdungp'o had already been seized by American marines, and they were also being pressed hard from the south, enemy troops, apparently for fear of being encircled, abandoned the town and retreated before daybreak. Eventually, on the morning of September 22, the US 1st Marine Regiment completely controlled the downtown streets of Yongdungp'o and occupied a hill near Noryangjin, where they could overlook the heavily damaged the Han River Bridge.

(3) Securing the Cities of Anyang and Suwon

On September 19, the 32nd Regiment of the US 7th Infantry Division, after taking over the responsibility for the security of the southern areas of the

Seoul-Inch'on highway from the 1st Regiment of the US 1st Marine Division, was stationed in the vicinity of Kal-ch'on 6 kilometers west of Yongdung-p'o. The objectives of the US 7th Infantry Division were to protect the right flank of the American marine division, to check or interdict enemy troops moving into Seoul from the south, and to provide support for friendly troops to recapture Seoul.

On September 20, the infantry regiment attacked west toward Anyang. But from the very beginning, it was delayed by an enemy mine field. Three tanks of A Company of the 73rd Tank Battalion, which had been attached to the infantry regiment, were damaged by exploding mines. The jeep of the regimental commander was also destroyed by a mine. After the engineer troops removed about 150 mines from the road, the infantry regiment moved on toward Doksan-ri and Anyang. On September 21, the following day, the regiment occupied the two towns.

At about this time, the Reconnaissance Company of the US 7th infantry division led by the Assistant G-2 of the division arrived at Anyang. There they received radio orders from the division to "turn south to Suwon and secure the airfield below the city." Accordingly, at around 16:00, spearheaded by a tank platoon, they left Anyang for Suwon. When they reached the entrance of the city of Suwon at around 18:00, they were joined by the division G-3 staff who had led a platoon of B Company, 18th Engineer Combat Battalion. The reinforced Reconnaissance Company then, together with the engineers, moved into the center of the city. At this point, they engaged in some street fighting with scattered groups of enemy soldiers, and captured 37 North Koreans including two enemy officers of the NKPA 105th Armored Division. Immediately after the engagement the American column moved on toward the airfield; however, as they had not carried maps with them, they unwittingly passed 5 kilometers south of the Suwon airfield.

At that point, they went into a perimeter defense astride the Seoul-Pusan highway to be prepared for a possible enemy counterattack. Unfortunately at that moment, they lost radio contact with their division. Therefore, the US 7th Division, in an effort to find the group, immediately formed Task Force Hannum and sent it toward Suwon.

This task force, headed by Lt. Col. Hannum, Commander of the 73rd Tank Battalion, consisted of a tank company, an infantry company, an artillery battery and a medical detachment; the 7th Division G-2 staff accompanied it.

That night, the Task Force hurried south in the full moonlight with all possible speed. On the way to Suwon, the division G-2 who had started in advance, reestablished radio contact with his assistant G-2, who had been with the Reconnaissance Company.

However, when Task Force Hannum reached the East Gate of Suwon, two enemy T-34 tanks hidden behind a building surprised the column destroying the leading American tank and killing the tank company commander who was inside it. The task force at once counterattacked the enemy T-34's and instantaneously knocked out one, but the other enemy tank escaped into the city to lurk somewhere. Considering the midnight situation, Commander Hannum decided to wait for daylight rather than to risk another enemy tank ambush in the darkness.

In the meantime, the Division G-3 and the Assistant G-2, who had been waiting for Hannum and his party at a point south of Suwon, decided to move up toward the city with several men from the Reconnaissance Company in four jeeps to meet Hannum's party. On the way northward, they saw four tanks approaching. The division G-3 flicked his lights to give a signal for what he thought were Task Force Hannum's tanks coming south from Anyang. The tanks stopped and suddenly their machine guns started firing. The men jumped from the halted jeeps and scrambled into the ditches. However, the the division

G-3 was killed and many were wounded.

The enemy tanks moved on south until they entered the Reconnaissance Company's defensive positions. At once American tanks made a surprise attack, and destroyed two of them. The other two T-34's turned to escape toward the city of Suwon.

At daybreak on September 22, the next day, Task Force Hannum reached Suwon airfield and secured it completely. Later that morning, the 31st Regiment of the US 7th Infantry Division arrived at the city and took over the responsiblity for the security of the airfield from Task Force Hannum. The Reconnaissance Company together with other reinforcing elements moved on south, reconnoitering the area south of Suwon, while Task Force Hannum returned to Anyang.

Thus in brief, as of September 21, the 5th Marine Regiment, 1st US Marine Division, which had secured a defensive line at Hills 216-104-68, was preparing for the attack against the heart of Seoul; on the 22nd, the 1st Marine Regiment occupied Yongdungp'o; and by that time, the US 7th Infantry Division occupied the small towns of Anyang and Suwon cutting off possible NKPA reinforcements from the south.

3. Operations for Recapturing Seoul

(1) Breaking Through the Enemy's Western Defensive Line

The leading role in recapturing downtown Seoul was played by the US 1st Marine Division. Concurrent with this, the US 7th Infantry Division occupied the cities of Anyang and Suwon, and thus organized a blocking position on the south bank of the Han River. On September 22, the 5th Marine Regiment, US 1st Marine Division, which had held Hills 216, 104 and 68, attacked together with the ROK 1st Marine Regiment, against enemy defensive positions at the western edge of Seoul. The intense fighting between both forces lasted four days.

At that time, the NKPA defense line was anchored on a ridgeline which extended from An-san (296 meters) to Hill 56 (Yonhee Hill), and on a cross compartment ridgeline comprising three hills, each 105 meters high, called as Uiryong Tunnel, Nogo-san, and Wau-san. In front of Hill 56 which was also called Yonhee hill was a 300-500-meters-wide, open field. The three 105-meter-high hills were also known as Hills 105 North, 105 Center and 105 South, respectively.

Taking advantage of the natural terrain features favorable to the defender there, NKPA troops had established a main line of resistance for the defense of Seoul. Thus they could control the main rail line and the road between Seoul and Sinuiju that passed through the area. The North Korean troops deployed in these areas were the 25th Brigade[35] and the 78th Independent Regiment.[36] The former had been formed a month earlier at Ch'orwon and was trained initially to be committed to the Naktong river front. But it moved to Seoul and was placed in that sector on September 19.

The enemy brigade was a special force with about 2,500 men and was composed of 2 infantry battalions, 4 heavy machine gun battalions, an engineer battalion, a 76-mm artillery battalion, a 120-mm. mortar battalion, and miscellaneous service troops. Most of the officers and NCOs of the brigade had had previous combat experience with the Chinese Communist Forces. The 78th Independent Regiment was also known as having elements similar to those of the 25th Brigade.

At 07:00 on September 22, the US 5th Marine Regiment launched an attack against those 105 meter high hills mass by placing the 1st Battalion of the ROK 1st Marine Regiment in the center, the 3rd and 1st American marine battalions on both flanks of it and its 2nd Battalion in reserve. In the center, the

ROK marine battalion was to take two knobs, its immediate objectives, Yonhee hill and Hill 88 just before reaching the main 105 meter high Ui-ryong Tunnel hill behind them.

The ROK marines set out to capture the Yonhee Hill less than 1 kilometer from the line of departure, Hill 104. Immediately, the enemy opened fire on them using all kinds of weapons including 120-mm mortars and heavy or light machine guns. The marine troops attempted to maneuver across the open field in front of the hill; friendly air strikes tried to destroy enemy positions on the opposite side, but they were of no avail. Immediately, the ROK marine 3rd Company was committed to the right flank of the battalion under the cover of American marine tanks. Still, they also failed in crossing the field because of heavy anti-tank weapons and machine gun fire from enemy positions on the Yonhee Hill. Inevitably, the ROK marine battalion pulled back to their initial line of departure under cover of darkness that night, only to be prepared for another try the next day. In that battle, the enemy fire killed 11 and wounded 45 men of the ROK marine battalion. Later, enemy prisoners said that the NKPA 25th Brigade had also suffered heavy losses. Meanwhile, at about 10:00 that day, the adjacent US marine 3rd Battalion on the left flank captured Hill 296. However, as they had secured only the crest of the hill, they could not control the ridges on the right flank of the hill where the enemy strength had been concentrated. Accordingly, the American marines could not help the adjacent ROK marine troops who had experienced such difficulty in its attack.

On the south, the 1st Battalion of American marines which had attacked the Wau-san was also blocked by intense enemy fire for quite a while; however, at 17:30, they succeeded in taking the hill only after concentrating all artillery and mortar fire available on enemy positions. The battalion suffered heavy losses in this battle.

The following day on the 23rd, the ROK marines resumed the battle for

capturing their immediate objective, the Yonhee Hill. This time, all three companies stood in the forefront. Enemy fire became frantic more than ever before
as if they had seen through the marines' effort to take the hill at all cost. The 1st
Company (Lt. Chung Man Jin) on the left flank attempted to cross the open field
by maneuvering part of its force to turn around the An-san; in the center, the
2nd Company (Capt. Kim Kwang Sik) tried directly to cross the field under cover
and concealment of the place; the 3rd Company(Capt. Lee Bong Chul) tried to
make a frontal attack against the Yonhee Hill. The 3rd Company, therefore, exposed itself to the more intense enemy fire than the other two companies did.
Still, it made a little gain there suffering continuing heavy casualties.

 As the ROK marine 1st Battalion had been blocked suffering about 150
casualties during the two days' battle, the commander of the US 5th Marine
Regiment ordered his 2nd Battalion which had been kept as a reserve unit to relieve the ROK marines.

 Accordingly, the American marine 2nd Battalion which had taken over
the attack passed, on September 23rd, through the ROK marine 1st Battalion,
and attacked against Hill 56 and the Yonhee Hill, their immediate objectives,
together with marine tanks. But they accomplished very little as they were
checked by an enemy artillery barrage. D Company which had led the attack
troops, after sustaining many casualties, failed in taking their objective. One
platoon of F Company suffered so many casualties that it only had seven men
left for duty that evening.

 After daybreak on the 24th, the American marine 2nd Battalion resumed its attack. D Company crossed the low ground under the cover of a dense
morning mist and reached the base of the Yonhee Hill. Instantaneously, they
came upon enemy troops in their trenches. Neither side saw the other because
of the fog and smoke until they were at close quarters. A tense moment lapsed
and a furious close fight between both forces followed, with many casualties

resulting from it.

In the afternoon that day, a total of 44 men of D Company moved out again in assault against the hill with the help of air strikes and ultimately secured the hill. The company commander was killed in the course, and only 26 marines reached the top.

The next day on the 25th, the US 5th Marine Regiment resumed its attack: the 2nd Battalion captured Hills 88 and 105 Center, Nogo-san; the 3rd Battalion on the left flank took another Hill 105 North, Ui-ryong Tunnel Hill, after it repulsed tenacious enemy counterattacks at Ansan. This concluded the ROK marine and US 5th Marine regiments' actions for capturing the critical western hill masses which had been held by the enemy, and which eventually collapsed his main defense line on the west of Seoul.

Both the ROK and US marines suffered a heavy loss in these battles; however, they made marked achievents at the cost of their lives. More than 1,200 dead enemy soldiers lay in and around trenches on ridges, and the American marines estimated the total number of enemy dead in the battle at 1,750.

In the meantime, the US 1st Marine Regiment began crossing the Han River in the area of Choldu-san (north of Dangsan rail line) at 08:00 on September 24, and advanced toward the action zone of the US 5th Marine Regiment. At that time, the latter, even though they had been engaging enemy troops at the area of Yonhee Hill, provided the former with good protection; the 1st Battalion of the 5th Marine Regiment had done this after it had captured Wau-san northwest of Youido. The 1st Marine Regiment took over the southern edge of northwestern hills of Seoul including the Nogo-san from the 1st Battalion, 5th Marines, and moved on toward Map'o on the south flank of the latter.

The US 7th Marine Regiment which had landed at Inch'on on September 21, crossed the Han River at Haengju ferry site on the 23rd and 24th, and advanced, on the 25th, to an area left of the 5th Marine Regiment. It's mission was to block the escape routes northward, by placing its troops on the line of withdrawal at hill masses north of Seoul.

On that day, the 25th, Kim's Troops (Kim Sung Eun) which had been in active in the area T'ongyong, a southeast coastal town, landed at Inch'on and joined the ROK marine regiment at Susaek to be redesignated as the 5th Battalion. Thereupon, the ROK marine regiment attached its 1st Battalion to the US 5th Marine Regiment, the 2nd Battalion to the 1st Regiment, and the 5th Battalion to the 7th Regiment. The 3rd Battalion of the ROK marines was kept as the US marine division reserve unit.

(2) Pressing the Enemy Hard from the Southeast

With the remaining two regiments having crossed the river by September 23rd and 24th, the 1st US Marine Division Commander had now all his regiments—including the 5th Regiment which had already been across the river—together north of the Han River. He concentrated his troops on the western front to break through the enemy defense line there as had been projected, and prepared to move on to the heart of Seoul. By this time, however, an important change had taken place in that plan. As the US 5th Marine Regiment and the 1st Battalion, ROK 1st Marine Regiment's efforts to penetrate into the enemy line west of Seoul had been blocked by the stubborn enemy defense, the marines had gained little for three days in the battle which had started on the 20th. Consequently, the US X Corps Commander grew impatient. He, therefore developed his own plan in which he would have to commit a fresh mobile force to the south of Seoul for an envelopment maneuver from south and north. By doing so, he thought he could hasten the recapture of the city of Seoul.

On September 23, the Corps commander visited the US 1st Marine Division Commander to explain his plan. They discussed the idea of committing the

US 1st Marine Regiment which had alrady retaken Yongdungp'o to the southern zone of Seoul. The division commander was, however, unwilling to act on the Corps Commander's suggestion, and on the contrary, the former wanted to have both 1st and 5th Marine Regiments break through into the western front as had been scheduled. So the Corps Commander gave him 24 hours longer to make headway, but if the division commander could not make it, the Corps commander would place the 32nd Infantry Regiment of the US 7th Division at the southern front for the envelopment. Accordingly, the marine division commander concentrated his troops on the 5th Marine Regiment zone by bringing the other two regiments, the 1st and 7th, into the battle; however, his troops could not penetrate into the enemy defense line by the 24th, the 24-hour limit.

On the morning of that day, the Corps commander arrived at 7th Division headquarters to tell the division commander (Maj. Gen. David G. Barr) he had decided that the 7th Division would attack across the Han River into Seoul the next morning. After returning to his command post, the Corps commander told the ROK 17th Infantry Regiment Commander that he expected to attach his regiment to the US 32nd Infantry Regiment for the attack on Seoul. At 14:00 that afternoon, at a commanders' conference held at Yongdungp'o, with the Commanders of the US 1st Marine and 7th Infantry Divisions present, the Corps Commander told the attendants that, "at 06:00 on the 25th, the 32nd Regiment, with the ROK 17th Regiment attached, will attack across the Han River into Seoul." For this purpose, he told his audience that he was changing the boundary between the two combat divisions. Thus from September 25, two different battle fronts were to be formed on the west and south of the city of Seoul.

At about this time, the 32nd Infantry, US 7th Division, was still engaging remnant enemy troops in the areas of Anyang, Kuryong-san (292 meters, CS2847), and Sinsari (currently Sinsadong, southern Seoul). On the 22nd, its 2nd Battalion advanced to a point 3 kilometers south of the railway and foot bridges over the Han River, and captured an unknown hill (180 meters, CS1850) near Sadangdong. The 1st Battalion of the American infantry regiment took Kuryong-san knob situated 5 kilometers from Sinsari on the 23rd. This lower hill, commanding a northward avenue to Seoul as well as the Han river bridges, was considered tactically important.

On the 24th of September, the 2nd Battalion surprised an NKPA regimental headquarters in the vicinity of Sinsari south of the Han River, and captured much enemy war equipment. It also destroyed elements of the enemy regiment which had been proceeding toward Seoul from a point south of the river. This cleared the south bank area of enemy remnants and thus made a great contribution to the river crossing that would follow the next day.

Meanwhile, the ROK 17th Regiment (commanded by Col. Paik In Yup), which had landed at Inch'on as a follow-up unit, advanced at 08:00 on the 24th, to the area of Huksokdong, just south of the river, by way of Pup'yong to be attached there to the 32nd Regiment of the US 7th Division. The mission of the US 32nd and ROK 17th Regiments was first to seize and secure the Nam-san (262 meters), then to secure Eung-bong (121 meters) east of Nam-san, and finally to seize Yongma-san (348 meters) dominating the Seoul-Ch'unch'on highway and Central Rail Line. That day, one battalion of the US 187th Airborne Regiment arrived at Kimp'o Airfield from Japan to take over the security mission there.

At 06:00 on September 25, after a 30 minute artillery preparation, the 2nd Battalion of the US 32nd Infantry Regiment made the assault crossing of the river at Sinsari ferry site toward Sobingo on the opposite bank. This time a ground fog obscured the river area providing the lead elements with a favorable protection from enemy observation. Without loss of personnel or equipment, the entire 2nd Battalion safely reached the north bank; thereupon, it moved on to the halfway slopes of the Nam-san. A while later, the ground fog was dispersed and intense UN air strikes came in on the hill and nearby Eung-bong. The 1st

Battalion immediately followed the 2nd across the river and moved east along the river bank toward Eung-bong. The 3rd Battalion which had crossed the river passed through the 1st and first captured the Eung-bong just afternoon that day.

At about 15:00, the 2nd Battalion reached the top of the Nam-san against moderate enemy resistance, and immediately dug in on a tight perimeter to be prepared for possible enemy counterattacks. About an hour later, the 1st Battalion took a position on a lower hill mass between the hills of Nam-san and Eung-bong. The river crossing of the US 7th Division might have surprised the enemy who had only lightly manned the areas of Nam-san and the crossing site.

Meanwhile, the ROK 17th Regiment which had crossed the river imme-diately behind the US 32nd Regiment at the Sinsari crossing site, reached Pokwangdong and Hannamdong at about 14:00. They rapidly moved east of the American regiment's line. The mission of the ROK regiment was to seize Yongma-san (348 meters) and then to advance to the Manguri area to interdict and block the Seoul-Ch'unch'on highway and the Central Rail Line. The regi-ment placed its 1st and 2nd Battalions on the forefront as assault units and kept the 3rd Battalin as reserve. They moved on over a pass between Hannam-dong and Changch'ungdan to occupy Muhak hill (93meters), and at 02:00 on the 26th, reached Chungnang Bridge overruning Hawangsibri. There they cleared the east area of Chungnang Creek of the remnant enemy force. At that time, the reg-imental headquarters and the 3rd Battalion, the regimental reserve unit, moved on to Whayangri.

At 04:30, in the predawn hours of the 26th, the NKPA troops counterat-tacked the 2nd Battalion, US 32nd Regiment, on top of the Nam-san. Just before daybreak, a furious battle took place between the two forces. The enemy force was estimated to number approximately 1,000 men. The American infantry po-sitions on the higher knob of Nam-san were secure, but the lower eastern hill was captured by the enemy. At once the 2nd Battalion Commander committed his reserve elements to the place, and finally repelled the enemy. The enemy attempted another counterattack that morning only to be driven back again. After the battle, the American battalion saw 384 enemy dead scattered in and around its defensive positions; they captured 174 North Korean prisoners.

(3) Street Fighting

On September 25, while the 32nd Regiment of the US 7th Infantry Division and the ROK 17th Regiment besieged the enemy in the south of the city of Seoul, the US 1st Marine Division and the ROK 1st Marine Regiment, which had mopped up enemy troops on the western front by that day, made a concerted attack against the heart of the city.

Prior to their attack, the American marine division had issued an operation order for its subordinate elements and the ROK marines elaborating respective zones of action and boundaries. According to the order, the 2nd Battalion (Maj. Kim Chong Ki, the commander) of the ROK marines, together with the US 1st Marine Regiment, was to occupy Miari, overruning downtown streets; the 1st Battalion (Maj. Koh Kil Hoon) was to seize the area of Central Government Office building with the US 5th Marine Regiment; the 5th Battalion (Lt. Col. Kim Dae Sik) together with the US 7th Marine Regiment would occupy the high hill mass around Pukak Mountain north of Seoul; and finally the 3rd Battalion was kept as a reserve unit for the American marine division.

In the meantime, just before dusk that day an air report claimed that enemy columns were streaming north out of the city. The US X Corps commander immediately ordered Corps artillery to place interdiction fire on the escape route in the areas of the Miari pass and Tongdaemun (East Gate)–Ch'ongyangri. He also ordered the 1st US Marine Division to pursue and attack the retreating enemy columns that night. In order to illuminate the attack roads, the Corps commander requested the US Air Force a flare mission and air strikes.

Maj. Gen. Smith, Commander of the US 1st Marine Division, however, did not want to attack through the city at night for these reasons: he could not see any sign of enemy retreat at least in front of his division's zone; he worried about difficulties of control and coordination between friendly troops in the complicated builtup area at night; the night attack might unnecessarily bring calamity upon friendly forces. But when he was told by the Corps chief of staff that the Corps commander had dictated the order and that it was to be executed without delay, he unavoidably telephoned commanders of the 1st and 5th Regiments at about 22:00 that night, and ordered them to launch an attack from the

Operation for Recapturing Seoul

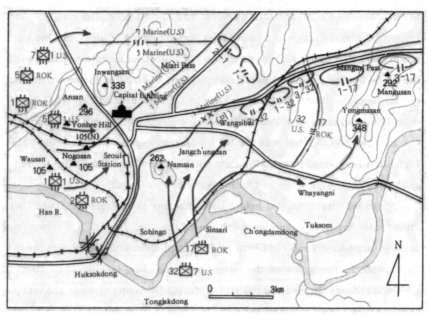

current line of contact.

The US 5th Marine Regimental commander immediately prepared for moving on by placing the 3rd Battalion, which had repelled an enemy counterattack in the west area of former Sodaemun jail building, in the forefront. However, at that very moment, an enemy force of approximately 200 men struck the battalion. Instantaneously an intense fighting took place between both forces, and by about 04:45 the following day, the American marines repulsed enemy troops there.

Likewise, the US 1st Marine Regiment, after a 15 minute artillery preparation at 01:30 on the 26th, prepared to attack with its 3rd Battalion moving along a streetcar track at Map'o. A patrol from the battalion moved out at the conclusion of the preparation and a short distance away encountered a large enemy force which appeared to have been prepared for a counterattack.

At 01:53, upon receiving the alarm message from the 3rd Battalion, the regimental commander requested fire support to be directed on the enemy. At once a friendly artillery barrage including mortar, tank, and automatic fire landed on the enemy force for about 15 minutes. The enemy force was estimated to number about 700 men supported by twelve tanks, two self-propelled guns, and 120-mm mortar fire.

The enemy's lead tank struck a mine they had laid, and was destroyed instantaneously; other tanks were also destroyed by bazookas and 75-mm anti-tank fire of the American marines. Buildings and private houses caught on fire, and the burning buildings illuminated the street scene in front of the American marine troops. Heavy artillery and small arms fire from both forces turned the night scene of the streets into that of the worst hell. The fighting continued until daylight. After daylight, the US 1st Marine Regiment counted about 250 enemy dead and captured four tanks and two self-propelled guns.

Because of the unexpected enemy counterattack during the night, the

US 1st and 5th Marine Regiments could not launch a night attack as had been ordered. Their lines were substantially the same as they had been the evening before. The enemy's desperate will to resist that night appeared to have originated in his commander's decision to delay the advance of the UN forces. After the collapse of the western defense line and the seizure of Nam-san by the UN forces, the North Korean commander in Seoul might have thought that the city was doomed, and decided to withdraw his major troops while leaving others to fight desperate delaying actions. The enemy's counterattacks against the ROK 17th and the US 32nd Regiments in the southern fronts of Seoul had apparently been carried out to execute this enemy commander's decision. The major enemy unit withdrawing at this time was known as the NKPA 18th Division which had pulled back from the Yongdungp'o area and assembled in Seoul. At nights on September 25 and 26, it retreated northward on the Uijongbu and headed for Ch'orwon.

After daybreak on the 26th, the American marine troops resumed their attack. The 1st Marine Regiment tried to move on through Map'o street only to gain less than 1.6 kilometers, being checked by enemy barricades at every strategic point and also by snipers who fired from houses along the way. The 5th Marine Regiment encountered even stronger opposition at a lower hill which stretched from An-san into Seoul, and made only slight gains.

Meanwhile, the US 7th Marine Regiment, after capturing a saddle ridge between high hill masses in northern Seoul, moved toward Miari Pass in the northeast of the city by way of Pukak-san. They were to cut the highway running northeast out of Seoul for Uijongbu, and part of the regiment turned down the Seoul-Sinuiju highway seeking to establish contact with the 5th Marines.

By September 26, the US X Corps troops held approximately half the city. But on the 27th, the next day, the battle of the barricades in Seoul continued. The barricades in the middle part of the city stretched across the streets

Seoul Street Fighting

from side to side and were placed at distances of 300–350 meters along the streets. Mostly they were chesthigh, and made of rice and fiber bags filled with earth; they were placed at almost all intersections. In front of them were emplaced antitank and machine guns. Enemy soldiers were also posted in adjacent buildings.

The American marine attack had to reduce these barricades one by one. While Navy and Marine planes would rocket and strafe them, and the infantry provided protection with mortar and small arms fire, the engineers eliminated the mines. At the same time, two or three Pershing tanks would advance to destroy the antitank guns and automatic weapons, and breach the barricades.

Occasionally, marine flame-throwing tanks overran stubbornly held enemy positions and helped reduce the barricades. Accompanying or following infantry gave the tanks protection, destroyed snipers, and cleared the area. A single barricade held up a battalion advance as much as an hour.

The 2nd Battalion of the US 1st Marine Division moved on from Map'o into the heart of the city, and at about 11:00 that day, captured the French Embassy. At 15:37 that afternoon, they captured the American Embassy and raised the American flag over it. Meanwhile, the 1st Battalion of the marine regiment captured the Seoul railroad station in the morning in heavy fighting. Driving up northward through Namdaemun (South Gate) boulevard, it encountered a series of strongly defended barricades there.

That day, the 5th US Marine Regiment, which had fought street fighting in the northwestern part of the city the previous day, advanced against relatively light resistance. On the regimental north flank, the 2nd Battalion entered Sodaemun (West Gate) Prison unopposed, and established contact with the 7th Marine Regiment which had been moving down from the north. Further south, the 3rd Battalion, the main axis of attack of the regiment, at 10:15, captured the Seoul Middle School (currently the site of Kyunghee palace) and Hill 79 just to the north of it. The battalion moved on toward the Central Government Building, its major objective. When it entered Kwangwhamun plaza and an intersection, the NKPA put up their last organized resistance. A marine flame-throwing tank drove up to an enemy barricade to spurt flame, and finally ended the stubborn enemy resistance.

After the marine tank's breakthrough through the enemy barricade at the Kwangwhamun intersection, G Company of the 3rd Battalion, US 5th Marine Regiment rapidly moved on toward the center of the city, the Central Government Building (until 1997 the National Museum). They finally occupied the building at 15:08 on the 27th, and the battalion commander established his command post in the building.

The 1st Battalion which had closely followed behind the 3rd Battalion turned off to the north after reaching the Seoul Middle School and attacked Inwang-san, a critical terrain feature, which dominated the surrounding Government House area and the Seoul-P'yongyang highway.

At about this time, the US 7th Marine Regiment, which had been active in the northern edge of Seoul, seized Hill 343 north of Songbukdong and one battalion of the regiment cleared Pukak-san (342 meters) of the enemy remnants.

In the meantime, the ROK marine battalions which had been attached to each American marine regiment were mostly engaged in mopping up enemy remnants and stragglers while carrying out combined operations with their respective American marine units. The 1st Battalion, ROK marines, which had been attached to the US 5th Marine Regiment, on the 27th cleared the areas of Sodaemun, Sinmunno, and Hyojadong of enemy remnants. Then closely following behind the 3rd Battalion of American marines, it occupied the Central Government Building. The 2nd Battalion which had been attached to the US 1st Marines mopped up enemy troops in the area of the Seoul railroad station, and helped American marines to secure such places and buildings as the Central Post Office, ROK Naval HQs (Hoehyondong), Home Affairs Ministry (currently the Korea Foreign Exchange Bank), Seoul City Hall, Doksoo Palace, and the American Embassy (currently the site opposite Hotel Lotte). At this time the ROK marine battalion established its command post at the Chosun Hotel. Finally, the ROK 5th Battalion attached to the US 7th Marines, after completing its interdicting mission at the high hill mass area north of Seoul, advanced to the Miari Pass with the American soldiers.[37]

At about this time, the 32nd Regiment of the US 7th Infantry Division and the ROK 17th Infantry Regiment had engaged enemy troops both in the southern and eastern streets of Seoul. At dawn on the 26th, the 2nd Battalion of the US 32nd Infantry Regiment, which had repelled the enemy counterattack at Nam-san, encountered another enemy force while moving eastward along the beltway near the hill. There it became locked in a fierce battle with the enemy, which lasted all that day.

The 3rd Battalion, meanwhile, had been moving on toward Yongma-san from Eung-bong, when L Company saw a large enemy column moving north-ward along the highway. The American company at once surprised this enemy force killing about 500, and destroying 5 tanks. It captured 40 vehicles, 3 artillery pieces, and 7 machine guns. It also destroyed or captured 2 ammunition dumps, much clothing and other products. It seized a large headquarters of corps size, which appeared to have been a command post of a principal enemy force in the defense of Seoul.

Meanwhile, the ROK 17th Infantry Regiment, which had cleared the area of Chungnang Creek by daybreak of the 26th, resumed its attack against its objective after daylight that day. With the 3rd Battalion in the axis of main attack and the 1st Battalion following behind, the regiment repulsed enemy troops in dispersed positions and captured the Yongma-san. Late that afternoon, the regiment took the Manguri Pass (292 meters) to block the Seoul-Ch'unch'on highway. The 1st Battalion proceeded to a point west of the Chungnang Bridge and Manguri Pass by passing through an area between the Chungnang Creek and Yongma-san. There it blocked the low ground that lay in the axis of Seoul-Uijongbu west of the Manguri Pass and east of the creek.[38] On the west of Chungnang Creek was the US 32nd Infantry Regiment to block the area.

That night, a reinforced battalion size enemy force approached the 1st Battalion, ROK 17th Regiment, from the direction of Taenung. The objective of this enemy may have been to open a path of retreat for North Korean troops leaving the city. Upon receiving an alarm message from its outpost guards, the South Korean battalion waited for the enemy troops to come closer to its line. Enemy soldiers continued to move up, apparently with little expectations to encounter UN troops. At about 23:00, at the very moment that the last enemy columns came within effective range of the battalion's fire, the battalion commander ordered his troops to fire. The fierce battle spread to adjacent units, the ROK 3rd Battalion and US 32nd Regiments; even American tanks rumbled into the fight, which lasted until 03:00 the following day. Enemy troops made several counterattacks; however, as they had been unexpectedly surprised by the friendly forces, many of them were killed or captured. Later at daybreak, American and South Korean soldiers found about 500 enemy dead scattered around the area of Manguri. Many of the enemy prisoners turned out to be 17 or 18 year old students who had been forcibly conscripted in Seoul to join the NKPA after they had received short-term, basic military training.

In the meantime, the 31st Regiment, US 7th Infantry Division, which had assumed responsibility for Suwon Airfield and held the high ground south of the airfield with an interdicting mission there, established, at 22:26 on September 26 at a point north of Osan, contact with Task Force Lynch of the 7th Cavalry Regiment, US 1st Marine Division, which had been under the command of the EUSA. This linking up operation was significant in that it was the first time that lead elements of the EUSA, which had been counterattackiing against enemy troops from the Naktong front, and the US X Corps, which had almost cleared the area of Seoul after it had landed on Inch'on, established contact.

On the 27th, 12 days after they had started the landing operation at Inch'on, the combined ROK and US forces now occupied most parts of downtown Seoul including the symbolic capital building, Central Government House. The defeated but still desperate and stubborn enemy troops withdrew from the city under cover of darkness. Thus the capital city of Korea was won back 91 days after it had been seized by the North Korean enemy in June 1950.

The combined ROK and US forces which had recovered the city strengthened their security mission there after retaking individual objectives and clearing respective areas of responsibilities of remnant enemy soldiers.

4. The Return of the ROK Government

By noon September 28, the ROK and US troops completed their mop-up operations in and around the capital city, and the city government opened its office to resume its work. The city police also started to recover its function by clearing the litter from destroyed buildings and, other public facilities, and thus rapidly restored the public order.

At about this time, the US X Corps began to distribute 50 tons of rice to the Korean people who had been pressed by hunger. Most of the rice and grain had been lifted from the United States for emergency use and part of it had been captured from the North Korean troops. Common citizens and some officials who had returned to the city ahead of others voluntarily joined in cleaning work in the downtown streets by using bulldozers; however, the city was crowded with many others who wandered from place to place seeking separated familiy members.

On September 29, the ceremony marking the historic return of the ROK Government to Seoul was held. General MacArthur and his party arrived at Kimp'o Airfield from Tokyo at about 10:00, and a little later, President Syngman Rhee arrived at the airport to meet the General and his party. They together proceeded to downtown Seoul.

Even though the wayside was dotted with scars of the battle, with buildings and houses destroyed and burnt down in the street fighting, wildly cheering throngs of South Koreans assembled and lined the streets to welcome the party, waving Taeguk flags, the ROK national flags, and the Stars and Stripes.

The Central Government House building, the site where the ceremony was to be held, was patrolled and guarded by troops from the ROK 17th Infantry and 1st Marine Regiments. Part of the US Marine units also provided securi-

ty there. American marines chiefly provided security along the route from the
Han River ponton bridge to the downtown streets including critical hills and regions surrounding the Government House building.

At 12:00 that day, the ceremony took place in the National Assembly
Hall.[39] The chamber was packed with selected South Korean officials and citizens and representatives of the combat units that had recaptured Seoul. President Rhee came into the chamber with General MacArthur and proceeded to
the dais and took their seats. At the beginning of the ceremony, President Rhee
decorated the General with the Order of Military Merit, T'ae guk.[40] Then General MacArthur delivered his address in a sonorous voice; he spoke of the
friendly forces that had liberated this ancient capital city of Korea under the
standard of that greatest hope and inspiration of mankind, the United Nations,
and of the seat of the South Korean government that from it President Rhee
might better fulfill his constitutional responsibilities. He also spoke of the 53
nations that had pledged their aid to the Republic of Korea in the righteous
wrath and indignation against Communism.[41]

Right after the General's speech, President Rhee who had been overcome with emotion rose to express the gratitude of the Republic of Korea for
the general's distinguished commandship and the pains of the United Nations
Forces in liberating its capital city. He then spoke comforting words to the fall-
en soldiers and their bereaved families. As the victorious, he did not forget to
express his generosity toward the North Korean people.

Even while the speeches were being delivered, roar of cannons were occasionally heard. Although it was not clear whether or not the sound of firing
shook the building, slivers of glass fell from the partially shattered glass paneled
roof; however, the two speakers gave them no heed. As there were no ceremonial
guards, nor bands, the ceremony itself might have appeared to be dull; on the
contrary, it was filled with emotion and profound in meaning. The short cere-

mony over, the ROK government opened its offices to resume its work in Seoul that afternoon. Other administrative agencies together with refugees hurriedly returned to Seoul.

Most of the people were unable to contain their joy; they expressed gratitude for the liberation, and the restoration of their soverign government. On the other hand, some of them would shift the responsibility for their having been occcupied by the communist army on to their government. Those people whose familiy members had been abducted to the north had mixed feelings of anger and absurdity; many others had remained bereaved or plundered by the communists. Those who had stayed home, as they could not have fled to other places for safety, had long been in adversity being pressed close by hunger and fear under the communist rule.

III. Massive Counterattack on the Naktong River Front

1. The UN Plan for the Counterattack

(1) The Enemy Situation

The United Nations Forces' massive counterattack began on September 16, the next day following the Inch'on landing. On the eve of Eighth Army's attack, a total of 13 NKPA divisions, with their frontline headquarters command at Kimch'on, were on line at western Masan-Namji-Yongsan-Ch'angnyong-Hyonp'ung-Waegwan-Tabudong-Yongch'on-An'gang-P'ohang. These enemy forces were supported by 1 armored division and 2 armored brigades; their total strength was estimated at about 100,000 men by the EUSA intelligence team.

Among them about 47,400 men of the NKPA 10th, 2nd, 4th, 9th, 7th, and 6th Divisions under direct control of I Corps were deployed at the west area of the Naktong, south of Waegwan. On the east of the river were about 54,400 men of the NKPA 3rd, 13th, 1st, 8th, 15th, 12th and 5th Divisions under the command of II Corps. These enemy organizations were estimated at an average of 75 percent strength in troops and equipment. The Eighth Army estimate credited the enemy with sufficient strength to be able to divert 3 divisions there to the Seoul-Inch'on area without endangering his ability to defend his positions around the Naktong front. This estimation also foresaw that the enemy was on the offensive and would retain this capability in all general sectors of the river front; neither did it expect that this capability would decline in the immediate future. But later, the estimate turned out to have been far too high; an examination of prisoner of war interrogations and captured documents revealed that the enemy's capability was far less than Eighth Army had thought. A fair estimate of enemy strength facing Eighth Army at the Naktong front was less than 70,000 men, and enemy equipment in heavy weapons and tanks was probably no more than 50% of the original equipment.[42]

Morale in the NKPA troops was also at a low point. Less than 30% of the original troops of the divisions remained; replacements had forcibly been conscripted in the South Korean cities and towns. Thus these unskilled soldiers were not only poor in the basic military training but also undernourished because of, what made matters worse, food shortages. Most of them were in a state of battle fatigue caused by repeated UN air strikes. A 35 year-old Major Son Dae Kwang, the medical officer of the 17th Regiment, NKPA 2nd Division, who had been captured at Ch'angnyong on September 17, stated, "we had only two meals a day, which consisted of rice balls; the lack of supplies in ammunition and war equipment were the worst situation. The only available means of transportation for us was horse or cow-drawn carriages."[43] Judging from these facts,

⟨Table 3⟩   The Combat Organization of the NKPA

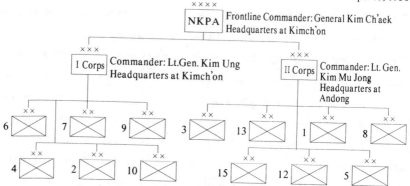

Sept. 15, 1950

the collapse of the NKPA force appeared only to be a matter of time. The combat organization of the NKPA on the eve of Eighth Army's counterattack is shown in ⟨Table 3⟩.

(2) Friendly Forces Situation

In mid-September, ground troops of the United Nations Forces, the main body of which was the EUSA, stood opposite the NKPA troops in the west of the Naktong river along a front which extended from Taegu to Masan. Meanwhile, the ROK Armies engaged the enemy along the eastern front which stretched from Taegu to the Hyongsan River in the vicinity of P'ohang. The US 1st Cavalry, ROK 1st, and US 24th Infantry Divisions, all under the direct control of the US I Corps, were responsible for defending the city of Taegu. South of them were the US 2nd Infantry Division in charge of the Ch'angnyong-Yongsan front, and the US 25th Division for the defense of Masan. The ROK II Corps commanding the 6th and 8th Infantry Divisions stood opposite the enemy at the Sinnyong-Yongch'on front, and the ROK I Corps with the 3rd and Capital Divisions took charge of the An'gang-Hyongsan River front.

The total strength of these friendly forces at that time was estimated at about 158,000 men; among them were 72,730 ROK troops including 60,000 men of six ROK divisions. The sub-total strength of Eighth Army numbered 84,478 men including 60,000 men of the main four American combat divisions. Also under the command of the Eighth US Army were 1,693 men of the British 27th Brigade.[44]

Since the beginning of the war, American battle casualties had totaled about 20,000 men including 4,280 killed, and others wounded, captured or missing. Thus some of the American rifle companies at this time had little more than 25% veteran soldiers. KATUSA recruits might have helped to ease the strength shortage situation; however, having virtually been untrained and not yet satisfactorily integrated, they were of little combat effectiveness at the time.

Even though the ROK Army appeared to have recovered its strength to pre-war levels—through replacement and reorganization during the war—it was still suffering from a low level of combat effectiveness because of the high casualty rate among the trained soldiers at the early stage of the war. However, the strength of the friendly forces favorably compared to that of the enemy force with a 2:1 ratio, and gave a considerable numerical superiority to the UN Forces. In the matter of supporting armor, artillery, heavy weapons and the availability of of ammunition for these weapons, friendly forces had even a greater superiority with a ratio of 6 to 1. In naval and air force combat capability, the United Nations Forces had no rival over the battle ground; they held both unchallenged naval and air superiorities. ⟨Table 4⟩ shows the combat organization of the EUSA as of September 15, 1950.

〈Table 4〉   The Eighth US Army Combat Organization

Sept. 15, 1950

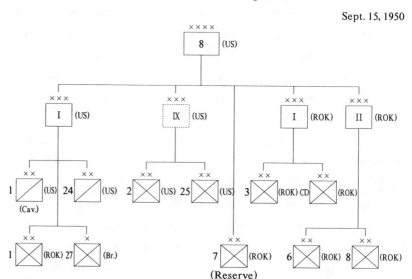

* The US I Corps:
  • August 2, 1950, activated at Fort Bragg, N.C., U.S.A.
  • August 13, 1950, Maj. Gen. John B. Coulter, the first commander
    (still unofficially appointed) arrived in Korea with his staff members.
  • September 11, 1950, Lt. Gen. Walker, the commander of Eighth Army, appointed Maj. Gen. Milburn who had arrived in Korea with the US IX Corps to the post of the I Corps commander.
  • September 11, 1950, the Corps became operational.
* The US IX Corps:
  • August 10, 1950, activated at Fort Sheridan, Ill., U.S.A.
  • September 5, 1950, Maj. Gen. Frank W. Milburn, the first commander
    (still unofficially appointed) arrived in Korea accompanied by a small group of his staff.
  • September 11, 1950, The Eighth US Army Commander appointed Major General Coulter (unofficial appointee to the I Corps) to the post of the IX Corps commander.
  • September 23, 1950, the Corps became operational.
* The ROK 7th Division was kept as a ROK Army reserve unit.
  (Sources : Appleman, *South to the Naktong, North to the Yalu,* pp. 544-547.)

(3) The Counterattack Plan

On September 6, the Eighth US Army made its attack plan which was coordinated with the US X Corps's Inch'on landing and sent it to the United Nations Command at Tokyo for approval. Later, Eighth Army revised part of the plan and published it as an operations directive to be distributed to the subordinate units.

The plan set the hour for attack by the friendly forces on the line of contact at 09:00 on September 16, one day after the Inch'on landing. The reason they had set the attack date one day after the landing operations was due to the Eighth Army's anticipation that the news of the Inch'on landing would have a demoralizing effect on the North Korean troops in front of it and an opposite effect on the spirit of its own troops.

According to the plan, the four American divisions with an American Corps under direct control of Eighth Army were to attack from the western and southwestern zones of the Naktong front, and the two ROK Corps in the eastern zone would launch a concerted counterattack against the enemy. The main effort would be made by the US I Corps in the center. The US I Corps was designated as the main attack unit because it had been deployed in the area most favorable to effect a junction with the US X Corps which had been making a turning movement, after its landing, to encircle enemy troops. It also had a good avenue, the Seoul-Pusan highway, which was considered favorable not only for maneuvering mechanized units but also for the smooth support services to combat troops. The gist of the attack plan was as follows:[45]

- The Eighth Army would attack from its present line of contact, at 09:00 on September 16, with its main effort directed along the Taegu-Taejon-Suwon axis to destroy the enemy forces on line of advance and to establish contact with the US X Corps.

- The US I Corps, the main attack unit, would make a frontal attack to seize a bridgehead over the Naktong River near Waegwan by using the US 5th Regimental Combat Team and the US 1st Cavalry Division. In order to facilitate the attack, the US 24th Infantry Division on the left flank and the ROK 1st Division on the right were to cross the river below Waegwan and above it, respectively.

- Upon securing the bridgehead the US 24th Division would drive on Kimch'on and Taejon, followed by the 1st Cavalry Division which would patrol its rear and lines of communications.

- Each of the US 2nd and 25th Divisions, and the ROK I and II Corps would make a frontal attack and fix the enemy troops in their zones and exploit any local breakthrough to make the main effort easy. Especially, the US 2nd Division would strive to cross the river so that it could support the US I Corps troops' mission of establishing a bridgehead across the Naktong. After the breakthrough is completed, Eighth Army would rapidly try to achieve a junction with the US X Corps and at the same time, together with the latter, drive on to the 38th Parallel pursuing the enemy troops until they could annihilate them all below the line. For this purpose, Eighth Army elaborates its directions and objectives of the pursuing operations as follows:

- The US I Corps would make the pursuit in the axis of Waegwan-Kimch'on-Taejon to rapidly establish a contact with the X Corps and to interdict the retreat path of the enemy I Corps troops. If events warrant it, the American units could use the Taegu-Tabudong-Sangju axis. The latter corridor traverses the former axis near Sangju so that from Sangju, the American troops could turn west toward the Kum River north of Taejon or bypass Taejon for a more direct route to the Suwon-Seoul area.

- The US 2nd and 25th Divisions would pursue enemy troops by way of the Chiri Mountain area and move on toward a phase line at the lower reaches of the Kum River.

- The ROK II Corps would pursue the enemy by way of Andong and

Wonju toward Ch'unch'on, and the ROK I Corps would drive straight
up the coastal road toward the 38th Parallel line.

2. The Penetration Operations at the Naktong River Front

(1) The UN Forces' Breakthrough in front of Taegu

The historic United Nations Forces' massive counterattack at the Naktong front was launched at 09:00 on September 16, 1950, as had been scheduled.
The US I Corps which had won its battle at Taegu by the skin of their teeth now
were to change from the defense to the offensive. It was to break through the enemy line there, and to drive on northward in the direction of Waegwan-Kimch'on-Taejon-Suwon, to eventually establish contact with the US X Corps.

At this time, the US 1st Cavalry Division of the Corps stood opposite
the NKPA 3rd and 13th Divisions in the area 12 kilometers north of Taegu,
while the ROK 1st Division was engaging the enemy 1st Division and part of the
enemy 13th Division at the Ka-san Fortress and P'algong-san areas. As a Corps
reserve unit, the US 24th Division assembled at Kyongsan. In addition, the
newly joined British 27th Brigade was preparing for a future attack mission in
the area of Chukokdong-Sindangdong southwest of Taegu, where the two rivers
Kumho and Naktong flowed together. It also provided for the security of the
western flank of the corps.

The US I Corps commander had a plan for maneuvering the 1st Caval-
ry Division (to which the US 5th RCT was attached) in the area north of Taegu.
There, the Cavalry Division would first penetrate into the enemy line to seize
Waegwan securing a bridgehead, then it would be followed behind by the US
24th Division, the Corps reserve. Then maintaining its attack momentum, the
Cavalry Division would drive on toward Kimch'on. Meanwhile, the ROK 1st

Division, according to the corps commander's concept, would attack against the enemy on the right flank of the Cavaly Division to support the American cavalry troops' crossing of the Naktong. For this purpose, the South Korean division was to cross the river at a point near Naktongri and move on toward Sangju.

Regardless of the cancellation of the scheduled air strikes because of heavy rain on the morning of September 16, the 5th and 8th Cavalries of the US 1st Cavalry Division attacked against Waegwan and Tabudong, respectively. The attached 5th RCT moved up the riverside road in the area of Hasandong northwest of Taegu. The cavalry division commander's plan was to beleaguer and annihilate enemy troops in his division zone by placing the 5th Cavalry in the center to fix the enemy force, and maneuvering other units for flanking attacks. For this purpose, the 5th RCT was to attack against Waegwan with its eastern (right) flank covered by the 5th Cavalry; the 8th Cavalry would penetrate into Tabudong line from Ch'ilgok, and the 7th Cavalry, the division reserve, would on order rapidly drive on toward enemy's western flank along the Taegu-Waegwan-Tabudong route.

The ROK 15th Regiment (to which the 1st Battalion of the 11th Regiment was attached) of the 1st Division was to attack against Ka-san, on the left flank of the division, while the 11th Regiment (−) and 12th Regiment was ready to move against the center and Ch'angp'yongdong on the eastern (right) flank of the division, respectively.

The ROK division commander tried to hold the enemy in check in the Ka-san area by using part of his 15th Regiment which had been engaging enemy troops there; by so doing, he thought that the main body of his division in the center could move rapidly northwestward through a ravine approach and a road which led to Kunwi on the eastern flank and cut the routes from Tabudong to Kunwi and Sangju. Then, he thought, he could cut off the enemy's retreat path not only in his division zone but in the Corps's action zone. It was considered a highly ambitious plan.

Since the weather conditions in the action zones improved, the UN air force became active again starting from September 18; that day 42 B-29 bombers flew over and bombed west of Waegwan across the Naktong. However, the US 1st Cavalry Division, the main attack unit, gained little. Its 5th Cavalry could not break through the enemy's main defensive positions in the area of Hills 253 and 371 five kilometers southwest of Waegwan. Nor could the 8th Cavalry advance as they encountered die-in-place North Koreans at a point 5 kilometers south of Tabudong. Only the US 5th RCT on the left flank could reach Kummu-bong (268 meters) 4 kilometers south of Waegwan where it was ready to attack the hill. This hill was considered as one of the most critical terrain features in that area because it dominated the Taegu-Waegwan road and the town Waegwan as well.

In the meantime, the 15th and 11th Regiments of the ROK 1st Division, which had on the previous day moved up to and through the compartment ridges (Hills 583 and 655) on the east of the Walled City of Ka-san (Ka-san Fortress), secured a stepping-stone for a future attack. The ROK 12th Regiment on the eastern flank made a search for an approach avenue in its axis for advance, and spotted an unmanned ravine in the boundary between the two enemy divisions, the 1st and the 8th; the Regiment rapidly moved on through it. Thus, having fixed the enemy at Ka-san on the 18th, the ROK 15th Regiment made a turning movement to the right flank to capture a dominating high ground position (Hill 558) in the division center. Also the ROK 11th Regiment (−) bypassed the hill to proceed to the Maekogdong area halfway in the ravine approach and destroyed uncovered enemy troops there. The ROK 12th Regiment managed to gain 10 kilometers for two consecutive days and took hold of Kalmoe, a junction point on the road between Tabudong and Kunwi. As a result, the enemy's retreat eastward was cut off. The NKPA 1st, 3rd, and 13th Division which had been committed to the area north of Taegu, and enemy troops in the Ka-san Fortress as well in front of the ROK 1st Division, were all to be intercepted.

Now utterly disorganized enemy troops were forced to evacuate their positions. As a result, the US 1st Cavalry Division which had been held in check in the south of Tabudong was able to resume its attack.

In contrast to the impressive progress of the ROK 1st Division, the US 1st Cavalry Division made very slow progress. In particular, the 8th Cavalry Regiment was so slow that the Eighth Army commander, that day, expressed his displeasure on this matter to the American I Corps and Cavalry Division commanders. The latter two commanders also believed the 8th Cavalry Regiment was not pushing hard. The cavalry division commander attached two battalions from the division reserve unit to the frontline regiments, one to each regiment. He then told the 8th Cavalry Regiment commander that the regiment must break through the enemy line during the day of September 19.

Prior to this, the I Corps commander altered his plan of maneuvering troops to find a way out of the trouble caused by the slowness of the US 1st Cavalry Division. He committed the US 24th Division to the western flank of the corps, and reverted the US 5th RCT to the 24th Division, and ordered both divisions rapidly break out of the Taegu perimeter and drive on toward Kimch'on.

The US 24th Division commander planned a nighttime, instead of daytime, crossings of the Naktong River to escape unnecessary disasters. Early in the morning on the 18th, his troops moved to designated assembly areas for the crossing. After dark, the 21st Regiment was to cross the river at Kumnamdong and Hasandong ferry sites, where the 5th RCT had cleared the ground. Once landed on the other side, the regiment, side by side with the 5th RCT, would attack north along the west bank of the river to a point opposite Waegwan. The US 19th Regiment and the Division Reconnaissance Company were to cross at the same time and block the roads between Taegu and Songju to be prepared for

Penetration Operation at the Naktong Front (Sept. 16)

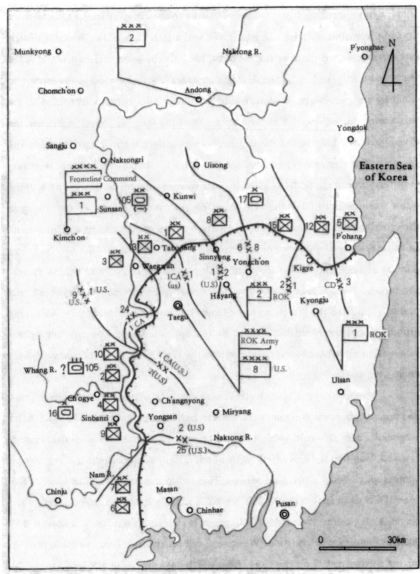

a possible enemy threat.

In proceeding from its assembly area to the crossing sites, the American division had first to cross the Kumho River, a tributary of the Naktong. But a setback developed there at the moment; the I Corps engineers had not bridged the Kumho as planned. So the division engineer troops hurried to the stream to sandbag an underwater bridge. While the bridge was being constructed, there was a long line of vehicles backed up south of the Kumho. Being impatient, the division commander urged the engineers to overnight hurry in sandbagging and repairing the underwater bridge that the 5th RCT had already used. A makeshift ferry constructed from assault boats moved the troops across the Kumho but it was not until 05:30 the next morning, the 19th, that they all moved up to the crossing site. As there was no indication of the enemy on the opposite bank in the murky fog of dawn, boats of the first wave pushed off into the Naktong. Almost at once enemy fire from the high ground on the opposite bank caught the troops. Even under heavy fire, the crossing continued. At daybreak airplanes supported the attacking troops and thus, by sunset of that day, American ground troops captured hill masses on the opposite bank. The crossing operation was hazardous; however, once across the river, they encountered only light enemy resistance.

Meanwhile, the US 5th RCT, with the help of air strikes, attacked that day against Kummu-bong near the eastern bank of the Naktong. The NKPA 7th Regiment, 3rd Division, which had dug into hill positions and desperately resisted, was finally driven off with about 250 dead including the regimental commander's body remaining behind. This led to the collapse of the North Korean II Corps in its left flank. The 5th RCT rapidly drove on north and at 14:15 on the 19th entered the town of Waegwan. It moved on to attack Jako-san (Hill 303), an important hill north of Waegwan, and recaptured it on the 20th, thus securing a crossing site on the bank. It was 18th days since the US 1st Cavalry Division had lost it to the enemy. Thus starting from that evening, the 5th RCT, which had destroyed the main body of the NKPA 3rd Division, was able to cross the Naktong at a point 1.6 kilometers north of the railway bridge over the river and began to construct the Waegwan bridgehead. Meanwhile, immediately after the newly attached British 27th Brigade had relieved the US 19th Regiment of the mission for blocking the road to Songju, the regiments of the US 24th Division which had already completed the river crossing moved north in columns along the riverside road on the 20th, and captured Hill 170 on the opposite of Waegwan and other hill masses north of it. Eventually, the 24th American division and 5th RCT secured a bridgehead from which they could attack west toward Kimch'on.

At about this time, in the ROK 1st Division's zone of action on the eastern flank of the US Corps, enemy troops on the Ka-san Fortress began to withdraw toward Kumi and Kunwi as if they were giving up their positions on the hill. Part of the ROK 15th Regiment which had been engaging these enemy forces there attacked the Ka-san Fortress. Meanwhile, taking advantage of a ravine in the center of the division's zone the main elements advanced to Puldong and Hapandong on the road between Tabudong and Kunwi. On the way, the main force of the ROK 15th Regiment encountered relatively light enemy resistance, and turned south to advance toward Tabudong. In the center, the ROK 11th Regiment proceeded from Maegokdong to Hap'yong destroying a stubborn enemy resistance there; it further advanced to Sangjangdong on the road between Tabudong and Sangju, and intercepted the enemy's path of retreat toward Sangju. On the right flank of the Corps, the ROK 12th Regiment at Kalmoe attacked against western hill masses (Hills 272 and 392) and secured them. These dominated the Tabudong-Kunwi road and, as a result, could be used by enemy troops as a covering position for their retreating columns. Now the ROK 1st Division created a favorable condition for annihilating the main body of the NKPA II Corps within the action zone by intercepting both paths of enemy retreat.

While friendly troops on both flanks of the Corps had been securing stepping stones for future offensive actions, the US 1st Cavalry Division, which had been designated as the main attack unit for the initial breakout in the center, decisively broke through the enemy line on the 19th with the two frontline regiments to which two battalions from the reserve unit, one to each regiment, had been attached. Among the two regiments, the 5th Cavalry engaged in very heavy fighting with fanatical, die-in-place enemy troops on Hills 253 and 300, and captured them all. For the first time, a barrier gate to Waegwan fell into hands of the UN forces, and it unquestionably helped the 5th RCT to capture Waegwan that day. But in this battle the 1st Battalion suffered tremendous battle casualties of 207 men, and the resulting battalion's combat effectiveness stood at only 30%. As soon as an approach to Waegwan was secured, the 7th Cavalry, the reserve unit, moved to the west of the division as scheduled on the 20th. It passed through Waegwan opening up a new route on the east side of the road to reach a village, Togae, by that evening, which was halfway between Waegwan and Tabudong. Upon hitting tough terrain, the regimental commander, apparently fearing that the enemy should have manned the area, decided to make a daylight attack the next day and to encamp there.

Upon receiving the report on the 7th Cavalry's halt for the night, the division commander was angered. He had been waiting for the 7th Cavalry to create a condition for enclosing enemy troops within the division zone by rapidly attacking against the enemy rear at Tabudong and by completing its breakthrough to help the 8th Cavalry to move out. Even facing the enemy, he unexpectedly and resolutely replaced the 7th Cavalry regimental commander that evening. Instead, he put in command of the regiment Lt. Col. William A. Harris, commanding officer of the 77th Field Artillery Battalion.

Lt. Col. Harris issued orders about midnight in an emergency action conference to subordinate unit commanders. To execute the orders, on the 21st one battalion of the regiment reached Tabudong and there it turned south to make contact with the 8th Cavalry at Samhandong. Another battalion established defensive positions astride a road north of Tabudong. Thus the US 1st Cavalry succeeded both in the linking-up operation and capturing Tabudong as initially scheduled; however, its long-deferred actions could not stand out as having contributed to the Corps' encircling movement and other actions.

On September 21, combat supporting elements of the US 24th Division continued to cross the river at Waegwan, and on the 22nd, an M2 pontoon float treadway bridge was completed across the 230-meter-wide and 2.5-meter-deep stream at Waegwan. Now with the heavy equipment and vehicles west of the river, the 24th Division was ready to lead the attack west toward Kimch'on. Meanwhile, for the ROK 1st Division, the 15th Regiment controlled the Ka-san Fortress area by completely clearing the place of enemy remnants. It also established a contact with the US 1st Cavalry Division at Tabudong. The ROK 11th Regiment captured Ch'onsaeng-san, a critical terrain feature north of Yuhak-san and advanced to Okgol on a road which led to Sangju from Taegu. The ROK 12th Regiment also advanced to Sangnim on the Taegu–Tabudong–Sangju road. Thus the ROK 1st Division was ready to drive on toward Sangju after it had destroyed the enemy 1st Division and part of the 13th Division within its action zone. Meanwhile, the US 1st Cavalry Division which had secured Tabudong reorganized itself to get ready for its march northward. Eventually, the US I Corps succeeded in breaking through the enemy defense line, annihilating the NKPA 1st, 3rd, and 13th Divisions within its action zone by an enveloping movement, six days after it had launched the massive counterattack on the Naktong front. Now the Corps was completely ready for a northward march to link up with the Inch'on landing troops.

The success of the US I Corps in its breakout had caused the collapse of enemy units. The statement of Senior Col. Lee Hak Ku, chief of staff of the NKPA 13th Division, who had surrendered on September 21 to the 1st US Cavalry Division, confirmed the well-nigh disorganized NKPA situation. According to him, his division line had already collapsed with his unit's extremely lowered combat effectiveness.

He further said that his division was no longer an effective fighting unit; regiments had lost communication with the division headquarters. Strengthwise, the 19th Regiment had 200 men, the 21st Regiment 330, the 23rd about 300, and thus the total 13th Division's strength stood at no more than 1,500 men; among them from 70 to 80 percent were South Korean conscripts. All tanks that had been attached to the division were destroyed, and 9 howitzers and 5 120-mm mortars remained. Only 30 trucks were operational. Rations were down one-half of those they had had a month ago and even ammunition supplies for small arms were not enough because of poor means of transportation. Therefore, according to him, the enemy division was practically disintegrated, and its survivors had begun to flee toward Sangju the night before.

Mr. Choo Yong Bok, who had served as the NKPA II Corps Engineer Chief at that time, confirmed the NKPA 13 Division's situation in the vicinity of Tabudong described by Col. Lee. Attesting to the truth of the defector's statement, and his motive of defection, Mr. Choo said,[46]

The [NKPA 13th] division commander had victimized so many subordinates mercilessly in an effort to faithfully follow words of Kim Il Sung. Lee Hak Ku repeatedly complained of the numerous dead of his soldiers. Ch'oi Yong Jin, division commander, had insisted that if we [North Koreans] had been united to push hard [against the UN forces] a little more, with one decisive assault against it, Taegu might fall into our [their] hands; that was it. Despite worsening situation with hundreds of wounded soldiers covered everywhere and thus the situation called inevitably for evacuation and withdrawal of the troops, there was no order from the division commander. Lee Hak Ku as well as the division commander had not heard of the UN forces' Inch'on landing. Lee Hak Ku once told the division commander, "Now we can't attack, neither can we sit idle like this; we would rather pull back." The division commander replied, "I'll kill you." Then the former responded saying, "You kill me? I'll rather kill you to save thousands of other soldiers' lives." [Instantaneously] Lee Hak Ku shot the commander Ch'oi in his arm. The latter fell crying, "Oh! That hurts!" Running out of the office room, Lee shouted to regimental commanders to withdraw, and he himself defected to the South, accidentally to an American unit.

Lee Hak Ku's personal reports and Mr. Choo's witness all confirmed that numerous so-called "South Korean volunteer conscripts" as well as North Korean soldiers had sacrificed their lives at the Naktong front, being compelled by the reckless North Korean Kim Il Sung and military leaders. Their words and testimonies clearly demonstrated that the internal discord within the NKPA leaders' circle had been on the verge of eruption. This situation might inevitably have accelerated the collapse of their defense at the Naktong front.

(2) The UN Breakout from the Southwestern Front

The UN forces' counterattacks on the southwestern Naktong river front south of Waegwan were made by the US 2nd and 25th Divisions. Under direct control of Eighth Army, the two American divisions broke through the enemy line in each division zone. Afterwards, for their pursuit battles they were attached to the newly activated US IX Corps as of September 23.[47]

Penetration Operation at Ch'angnyong-Yongsan: The US 2nd Division (commander, Maj. Gen. Lawrence B. Keiser) which had held the enemy's massive

September offensive in check at the Ch'angnyong-Yongsan front confronted the NKPA 2nd, 4th, 9th, and part of the 10th Divisions there. The combat effectiveness of both forces had notably been lowered due to heavy losses in the battles thus far. Fortunately, however, American soldiers there were full of fighting spirit as their division had passed from defensive to offensive as of 09:00 on September 16.

With a mission to drive enemy troops back across the Naktong, the American division launched a 3-regiment attack with the 38th Regiment at Hyonp'ung, the 23rd at Ch'angnyong, and the 9th at Yongsan, all making a complete turn from the old defensive now to the offensive in each zone.

As that morning dawned with murky skies and heavy rain, the American ground troops' attack was launched without support from the air force or artillery fire. Immediately, the stubborn enemy resistance caused many American casualties. But the weather had cleared in the afternoon and numerous air strikes helped the ground troops in reducing enemy strongpoints. In late afternoon that day, the North Koreans began to vacate their positions and flee across the Naktong. That night the enemy's 2nd Division command post withdrew across the river, followed by three infantry regiments, the division artillery regiment and other elements. Their crossings and flight toward the west of the river continued into the next day.

As the weather was improved on the 17th, the US Air Force fighter planes dropped 260 110-gallon tanks of napalm on the enemy in the vicinity of the Naktong west of Ch'annyong and strafed the fleeing enemy troops across the river. As a result, enemy soldiers abandoned large quantities of heavy equipment. That evening, Eighth Army chief of staff made a report to the United Nations Command in Tokyo that an oportunity for breaking through the Naktong line was ripe. On the morning of September 18, with enemy troops withdrawn from its sector, patrol parties of the US 38th Regiment crossed the river near

Pugokri and found the west side of the river clear of enemy troops. At 16:00 that day, the main body of the American regiment which had been ready to cross it made an assault crossing of the 100-meter-wide and 4-meter deep river. Against only light resistance, they captured Hill 308 which dominated nearby roads and secured a bridgehead there. In this battle, the US 38th Regiment captured 132 prisoners including a major. It also captured about 125 tons of ammunition and new rifles still packed in cosmoline, all had been buried in the sand near the crossing site. Thus the US 2nd Division drove the enemy troops in its sector back across the river and regained control of the ground east of the river, except those on high ground positions on its southern and northern boundaries.

Upon receiving the report on successful crossings of the river, the Eighth Army commander complimented the US 2nd Division commander on his performance saying, "the most spectacular success on the 3rd day of our counterattack." The following day, the US 38th Regiment(−) completed its crossing of the river with some tanks and other heavy equipment over a floating bridge hastily constructed by the US 2nd Engineer Combat Battalion down-stream from the destroyed old Ch'angnyong-Pugok bridge.

On the 20th, the 3rd Battalion of the US 23rd Regiment, the 2nd wave of the river crossing, slipped across it in assault boats at a site north of Pugok, where Sinban Creek enters the Naktong. The battalion achieved surprise so complete that without opposition it captured Hill 227 dominating the Sinbanri town and an NKPA lieutenant colonel and his staff asleep in a trench. From a map captured at this time, the battalion learned the locations of the enemy 2nd, 4th, and 9th Divisions in the Sinbanri area. Meanwhile, the 1st Battalion, the US 23rd Regiment, which had crossed the Naktong that afternoon, encountered the Sinban Creek. As none of the American troops knew that there was a creek in the battalion's axis of advance, the creek caused several hours of delay. How-ever, the 1st Battalion, 23rd Regiment managed to cross it and captured its initial objectives, Hill 208 north of Hill 227.

On the 21st, the US 38th Regiment moved on north toward Hapch'on and advanced to a point near Ch'ogye, while the 23rd Regiment which had been attacking south toward Sinbanri suffered heavy losses while facing strong enemy resistance. That morning, the 3rd Battalion of the latter was eating breakfast under cover of a rainstorm when enemy troops surprised one American platoon and inflicted 26 casualties.

The US 2nd Division continued its attack against the enemy; on the 22nd, the 2nd Battalion of the 38th Regiment entered the town of Ch'ogye, and the 23rd Regiment attacked up the road toward Sinbanri. But an estimated two battalions of enemy troops held the American regiment in check in front of the village. These enemy troops turned out to be a covering force for their divisions which were to assemble in Sinbanri to be reorganized for an efficient withdrawal action, and therefore they desperately tried to resist and delay attacking American troops. However, the US 2nd Division with its two regiments having already completed the river crossings and secured a bridgehead for the pursuit operation, now was ready to attack northwest.

Breakout from the West of Masan: The US 25th Division in Masan, the extreme southwest of the Naktong front, had stood against the NKPA 6th and 7th Divisions. According to the Eighth Army's counterattack plan, the American division was, at 09:00 on September 16, to attack against Chinju, its immediate objective, with the 24th Regiment in the areas of P'il-bong and Battle Mountain in the center, the 27th Regiment in the south, and the 35th Regiment in the north. But the divison could not advance toward Chinju because its 24th Regiment in the center was still engaging enemy forces behind its line at P'il-bong and Battle Mountain. The experience of Task Force Kean in early August, when the concealed enemy had closed in behind it from the mountains, was still fresh in the minds of the commander and his staff.

Therefore, in order first to clear the division front of the enemy before it could attack against Chinju, the division commander organized a composite task force under command of Maj. Robert L. Woolfolk, commander of the 3rd Battalion of the 35th Regiment and ordered it to attack against the heights of P'il-bong and Battle Mountain. For two days on the 17th and 18th, the task force attacked these heights, heavily supported by artillery fire and air strikes, but was driven back with heavy casualties. On the 19th, the next day, the task force was dissolved. Fortunately, however, the US 24th Regiment discovered that the enemy had abandoned their positions on the mountain top that morning, and moved up and occupied it without bloodshed.

It was clear that enemy troops which had stubbornly resisted there for three consecutive days had started their withdrawal the night of the 18th. Among them the NKPA 7th Division withdrew to the north of the Nam River, covered by the 6th Division. Then the latter withdrew from its positions on Sobuk-san south of P'il-bong. Still, stragglers made frequent appearances in the mountain areas.

The US 35th Regiment which had moved up the road between Masan and Chinju on the 19th captured Chungamri after driving off enemy troops there in a heavy fighting. It drove on to the ridge line running to the Nam River southeast of Chinju, and, on September 21, past the town of Much'onri to the high ground at Chinju Pass.

The US 24th and 27th Regiments which had begun moving forward toward Chinju in the center and along a road in the south respectively made slow advances because of the rugged terrain they had to traverse. Near Tundok west of P'il-bong, at daybreak on September 22, the bivouac area of A Company of the 24th Regiment was surprised by enemy infiltrators and suffered minor casualties. A little later enemy mortar fire fell on an operation meeting at 1st Battalion headquarters, and wounded the battalion executive officer and other staff officers.

A fierce offensive and defensive battle took place in the area of the Chinju Pass–Tundok between lead elements of the US 25th Division which had tried to break through the enemy line and the enemy 6th Division which had tried to cover the withdrawal of their main body to Chinju and northward across the Nam River.

(3) Breakout Operations in the Eastern Front

As of September 15, on the eastern front the ROK I Corps (commander, Brig. Gen. Kim Paik Il) confronted the NKPA 12th and 5th Divisions at the An'gang Plain and the Hyongsan River. With its Capital Division in the south of An'gang and the 3rd Division in the south of P'ohang, the ROK I Corps was getting ready to pass into the offensive after it had blocked enemy troops which had tried to penetrate into the Kyongju area. On operation order 180 (September 13, 1950) from the ROK Army, the corps was first to occupy the Ch'ongsong (Tokch'ondong)–Yongdok line, its immediate objective, and in turn, established its intermediate phase line at the Top'yongdong (2 kilometers south of Injidong)–Ch'ongha line.[48]

Breakout from the Hyongsan River (P'ohang) Line: The ROK 3rd Division (commander, Col. Lee Jong Ch'an) had held the NKPA 5th Division in check at the Hyongsan River line with its 23rd, 22nd, and 26th Regiments in that order deployed on the southern bank from west to east.

At that time, the Hyongsan River was swollen with rain; so it could not be forded particularly at a point near the bridge where the river was about 200 meters wide. The only bridge over the river had been bombed and destroyed in early September, but soldiers in a line could walk over a span that had been saved.

The South Korean division planned first to cross the river with its two regiments, the 23rd and 26th, at the upper and lower streams while the 22nd Regiment in the center was to cover the crossings of the two lead elements; then the latter would cross it following behind them.

On September 16, the ROK 23rd and 26th Regiments formed a platoon-size special patrol party and sent it out to reconnoiter the northern bank area. The patrol party infiltrated into a point 500 meters north of the Hyongsan, but it was driven back by a stubborn enemy resistance. The following day, under naval gun support from East Sea, the South Korean division rushed to cross the river as planned despite the heavy rain. However, enemy troops deployed along the opposite dike blocked this effort by concentrating their fire upon the assault crossing South Korean soldiers. Another attempt was made by the ROK troops that afternoon and part of them landed on the opposite dike; however, enemy heavy machine gunners cut them down. On the 18th, the ROK 23rd Regiment for the first time succeeded in crossing the river with the help of naval gunfire and air strikes. The ROK division commander himself acted as a leader of the crossing troops. The 26th Regiment gained a foothold across the bridge at heavy cost; platoons while rushing for the northern end of the bridge one after another suffered considerable losses; in a final desperate step, 31 ROK soldiers volunteered for a suicide corps to cross it, and of the thirty-one who charged, 19 fell on the bridge. Others barely reached the dike north of the river. Other ROK troops quickly reinforced the handful of men and dislodged the enemy from his dike positions. Fighter planes helped the suicide corps by making dummy strafing passes against the enemy positions. Second Lt. Kim P'an San, leader of the 3rd Platoon, 5th Company of the 26th Regiment, who led the lead element, later stated that he saw two enemy gunners whose feet had been tied to their water-cooled machine gun in a trench north of the river; one was dead and the other was seriously wounded without consciousness.[49]

Other elements of the South Korean division crossed the river following behind the lead units which had been moving on northward across the river against heavy enemy resistance. On the 20th, the ROK 26th Regiment recaptured P'ohang. By that time, main elements of the enemy 5th Division had already withdrawn from the city; only part of it desperately resisted in an effort to help cover the withdrawal of the main body.

The enemy 5th Division occupied a delaying position in the vicinity of Toksun-san hill 5 kilometers west of P'ohang to stubbornly resist the advance of the ROK troops; therefore on September 21, the ROK division made a turning movement there, and its 22nd Regiment regained Hunghae by the following morning and advanced to Ch'ongha, its intermediate objective. The main body of the enemy division, which was also virtually destroyed in the 5-6 day period since the ROK troops launched a counterattack, continued to withdraw along Coastal Road 7 toward Uljin. Part of it slipped into Pihak-san northwest of Hunghae.

Penetration into An'gang: While holding the NKPA 12th Division and 10th Regiment, 5th Division, in check, the ROK Capital Division (commander, Col. Song Yo Ch'an) near An'gang was getting ready for its counterattack against the enemy, with all its three regiments, the 1st, 1st Cavalry, and 18th. The Capital Division had planned to drive toward its immediate objective Ch'ongsong (Tokch'ondong)-Kiran (Ch'onjidong); however, it had first of all to secure An'-gang and Kigye in order to advance to the Top'yongdong (south of Injidong)-Taejondong area, its intermediate objective. The town of An'gang was considered as critical for both sides in terms of strategy and transportation. It was a junction point which dominated roads horizontally from Yongch'on to P'ohang and vertically from Kigye to Kyongju. It had also a large plain developed along the downstream of the Hyongsan River.

The Capital Division tried to recapture An'gang by committing all three regiments to the frontal attack; it placed the 18th Regiment on the west, the 1st Regiment on the east for a pincer movement and in the center, the 1st Cavalry Regiment would make a rapid frontal attack against the town.

On September 16, the division moved out as planned; the 1st Regiment attacked northeast of An'gang from Homyongri and Yangdong, while the 18th Regiment proceded westward from Kapsanri to the high ground north of Munung-san. There, the latter captured unnamed high hill masses from which they could control the An'gang plains. Thus the 18th Regiment not only gained a stepping-stone from which it could drive on toward northwest of An'-gang, but also cut off enemy troops committed to the Munung-san area. Main elements of the enemy 12th Division had been placed in the Munung-san positions which dominated the areas south of An'gang and Kyongju. By threatening enemy troops to abandon their positions at Munung-san, the ROK 18th Regiment helped the adjacent 1st Cavalry Regiment in approaching the hill smoothly. The following day, the two South Korean regiments tried to encircle the isolated enemy units at the hill positions and annihilate them. Then the ROK troops would be ready for northward attack. Being pressed hard from southwest of An'gang by the ROK 18th and 1st Cavalry Regiments—at the same time the northeast area of the town was taken by the ROK 1st Regiment—the enemy, apparently for fear of being enveloped, abandoned his defense at An'gang and withdrew northward to an area near Nodangch'i.

That day the 8th Regiment (commander, Lt. Col. Kim Yong Joo) of the ROK 7th Division (commander, Col. Shin Sang Ch'ol), advancing from the west to Todok-san, established contact with elements of the Capital Division and closed the gap between the ROK I and II Corps.

On September 18, the third day of the offensive operations, the ROK

18th Regiment resumed its attack from the west across the An'gang Plain in which rice plants had turned yellow, and the 1st Regiment moved out from the east toward Kigye. From the center, the 1st Cavalry Regiment attacked frontally and entered the town of An'gang. The 1st Cavalry drove on north toward Kigye to join the division operation in regaining Kigye. At that time the enemy 12th Division which had withdrawn from An'gang desperately resisted in their dug-in positions at cross compartment ridges south of Kigye, and the enemy 10th Regiment, 5th Division, was also stubborn in holding the area of Tanguri in the east. Therefore, it was only on September 21 that the ROK 18th Regiment on the left flank could reach and secure those ridges and advance to Todok-san (12 kilometers northwest of An'gang). That day the ROK 1st Regiment took the high hill masses south of Tanguri, and the 1st Cavalry Regiment in the center moved up a ridge north of Nodangri to capture Kigye with the help of UN artillery fire and air strikes.

Finally, the ROK Division succeeded in breaking through the Naktong front. The NKPA 12th Division had fled northwest without even evacuating wounded soldiers, and part of the enemy 5th Division had disappeared in the direction of Pihak-san north of Kigye. Luckily, the clear weather helped their combined ground and air actions, and the ROK Capital Division's success on that day coincided with the commander Col. Song's, promotion to brigadier general.

Prior to this, on the previous day of the 19th when the division drove on toward Kigye after it overran the town of An'gang, the ROK Defense Minister Shin Song Mo, accompanied by the ROK Corps commander Kim Paik Il, visited the division command post at Kyongju to encourage the South Korean soldiers. In his imprompt speech, he said,

I would like to express my heart-felt gratitude to all of you who have courageously fought delaying actions thus far, and moved out on the general offensive with deficient and inadequate war equipment. Friendly forces have reached the outskirt areas of Seoul; however, that does not warrant any optimism. We must continue to fight until we can annihilate the last North Korean Communist. By winning over the Communists, we can not only reunify our nation but also contribute to keeping a peaceful world.[50]

(4) Penetration Operations in the Mid-Eastern Front

On September 15, the ROK II Corps on the mid-eastern flank was also getting ready for its part in the UN counterattack with its 6th and 8th Divisions in Sinnyong and Yongch'on, respectively. These divisions had checked advances of the enemy 8th and 15th Divisions in each division sector. According to the ROK Army operation order, the corps was to frontally break through enemy defensive positions and capture the Hamch'ang-Yech'on-Andong line, its immediate objective. For this purpose, the corps designated the Towondong-Kusandong-Uisong line as its interim phase line.

Breakout from Sinnyong: The ROK 6th Division in Sinnyong was ordered to seize its immediate objective at the Yech'on-Hamch'ang line, and Towondong was also set as its intermediate objective. The division, under command of Brig. Gen. Kim Chong Oh, had thus far desperately resisted the advance of the enemy 8th Division to defend Sinnyong. It was then preparing in the high ground of Kap-ryong-Wha-san basin north of Sinnyong for the impending massive counterattack.

For the attack, the division planned to use its two regiments, the 2nd (commander, Col. Ham Pyong Sun) and the 7th (commander, Col. Lim Pu T'aek) as assault units. The former was initially deployed in the west of Kap-ryong, and the latter was in the Wha-san basin area east of Kap-ryong. The division reserve, the 19th Regiment (commander, Col. Kim Ik Yol), was first to occupy Chorim-san (638 meters) which, along with Kagsok-san (572 meters) on its east flank, had been considered as critical obstacles in the division zone, blocking its mobility.

The ROK division moved out as had been scheduled on September 16. At 08:00, its 2nd Regiment, which had repelled the enemy attack from his Chorim-san positions the previous day, counterattacked against it. After fighting a seesaw battle, the regiment recaptured Hills 349 and 332 south of Chorim-san at about 17:30 that day. At 21:40, the 7th Regiment advanced to Togch'on east of Chorim-san. At that time, one regiment of the NKPA 8th Division dug in on Chorim-san and was stubbornly resisting the ROK troops.

The South Korean division attacked Chorim-san positions again on the 17th, the following day, but the attack was in vain. What made matters worse, on the 18th, a prisoner revealed that a regiment size force had reinforced the enemy from north of Chorim-san. The division commander immediately ordered his 19th Regiment to make a turning movement to the northwest of Chorim-san in an effort to cut off enemy reinforcement there. He wanted to annihilate the enemy in a double envelopment through a pincer movement by maneuvering his 7th and 19th Regiments from both flanks and the 2nd Regiment in front of Chorim-san. However, enemy troops dug in to hill positions were so hard to deal with that the South Korean division had little gain there.

Under this circumstance, the ROK division commander, reconsidering the topographical features and stubborn enemy resistance there, changed his attack plan. According to his new plan, the ROK 2nd Regiment would make a frontal attack, while the 19th Regiment on the left and the 7th Regiment on the right were to cover the attacking unit with fire in each regimental zone. Concurrently, the latter two regiments were also to protect the right flank of the 2nd

Regiment against a possible enemy penetration into the gap. Prior to this attack, the division Reconnaissance Company infiltrated deep into the enemy positions to reconnoiter the enemy rear, gather information, harass the rear guard, and interdict retreat paths.

However, on September 21, the ROK 2nd Regiment failed again to secure the Chorim-san. As already implied above, sheer cliffs of Chorim-san provided the enemy with a natural protection, which reinforced the die-in-place enemy resistance. The commander of the ROK 2nd Regiment himself concluded that he could not gain his object by traditional means of attack; the more he tried to use it, the more he would suffer. Therefore, he tried to form a new scheme.

That night the regimental commander assembled 170 vehicles available under his command for a deception operation. He organized a convoy for a diversionary activity. Cadres of the regiment got in the foremost and hindmost cars, and from north of Sinnyong, the motor march began to move northward with all the headlights on and soldiers loudly singing military songs. This column drove up a little distance, and then moved back down silently with all the headlights and tail lights off. They repeated this back and forth demonstration motor march three times that night. It was designed to deceive the enemy into thinking that a large group of UN troops had been brought in to reinforce the attack against Chorim-san. At this time, the ROK 19th and 7th Regiments on either flanks tried to hold the enemy in check in each regimental zone so that no enemy troops could move out to reinforce the enemy in Chorim-san positions.

After this demonstration motor march, the ROK 2nd Regiment commanded by Col. Ham Pyong Sun resumed, at daybreak of the 22nd, its attack against Chorim-san. It was captured without bloodshed because the once desperate enemy had already departed. The commander's uncommon idea for the motorcade ruse had apparently threatened the enemy to withdraw the previous night. As a result, the ROK regiment could snatch the critical hill north of Sinnyong out of the enemy's hands.[51]

Thus the ROK division, which had only gained 2 or 3 kilometers during six days of counterattacks against the enemy, penetrated into the main enemy defense and eliminated one of the most difficult stumbling blocks in the axis of its advance.

Penetration into Kusandong: In order to accomplish the ROK II Corps's counterattack plan, the ROK 8th Division (commanded by Brg. Gen. Lee Song Ga) was to seize Andong, its immediate objective. This was the same division which earlier had recaptured Yonch'on. Its interim phase line was set at Kusandong–Uisong. But the division had first to take the Kiryong-san (961 meters) and Pohyon-san (1,124 meters) area east of its axis of advance. In these high hill masses, where fierce battles between both forces had taken place in August and early September, the enemy 15th Division had been deployed.

On September 16, the division launched a counterattack against the Kiryong-san and Nogo-ryong pass (west of Pohyon-san). Its 10th Regiment attacked along a high hill mass south of Kiryong-san, the 21st Regiment along the road from Yongch'on to Kusandong, and a division reserve, the 16th Regiment, was in the rear. But the pouring rainstorm at that time delayed the attacking units which had had to move up the mountaineous action zone. Therefore, the division gained very little by the following day.

At about this time, a patrol party from the 6th Company, 21st Regiment infiltrated into the area of Hasongdong in the predawn hours of the 17th. The party, while gathering information in the enemy rear, surprised an enemy 1/4-ton jeep which had been rushing toward the Nogo-ryong pass. They captured a wounded enemy captain at the place, and at once evacuated him to their battalion aid station. Cutting open the prisoner's uniform to give him first-aid treatment, they found a document there.

It was a letter published by the enemy 73rd Regiment to be sent to its higher echelon, the NKPA 15th Division headquarters. The letter read, "We have been suffering for lack of strength, equipment and ammunition; we cannot hold the current defense line any longer, so we request your approval for our withdrawal."[52]

After making a comparative analysis of the letter and gathering information on the enemy situation, the ROK division concluded it was a most appropriate moment for the annihilation of enemy troops in its zone of action. Immediately, the division ordered its frontline regiments to resume the attack and seize assigned objectives within 48 hours. At the same time, it assigned the mission of capturing Pohyon-san northwest of Kiryong-san to its reserve unit, the 16th Regiment. The division committed the 16th Regiment to the gap between the two frontline regiments for that purpose.

Thus on September 18, all three regiments of the division resumed their attack: the 10th regiment against Kiryong-san, the 16th against Pohyon-san, and the 21st against Nogo-ryong. The 10th Regiment on the east, however, could not break through the enemy line even after it fought hand-to-hand with desperate enemy troops who had dug in at Kiryong-san. The following day, the 1st Battalion commander, who had been in charge of capturing the crest of Kiryong-san, changed his battalion's maneuvering plan. According to the new plan, his two frontline companies were to remain as they had been the previous day in each zone to fix the main enemy force on the southern ridge of Kiryong-san, while the reserved company turned towards and infiltrated into the west where the enemy's defense was considered to be loose. The attempt proved to be effective and at about noon that day the battalion occupied the top of the hill. Eventually, other enemy troops were forced to withdraw by that afternoon, and the 2nd and 3rd Battalions of the ROK 10th Regiment on both flanks easily took their assigned objectives.

Meanwhile, the ROK 21st Regiment which had attacked on the west flank of the division against Nogo-ryong made little gain as it was threatened by the enemy 73rd Regiment deployed to its right in the Pohyon-san positions. The main body of the South Korean regiment, seizing an opportunity from the weakened enemy's resistance caused by the commitment of the ROK divisional reserve unit, fixed a large enemy force in front of the hill. Its 1st Battalion (commanded by Capt. Ch'ae Myong Sin) then made a turning movement to the right to surprise the enemy. It succeeded in its surprise and on the morning of the 19th it captured the regimental objective.

As the division reserve the ROK 16th Regiment, having captured Hill 818 south of Pohyon-san by the 20th, advanced to Pohyon-san on the next day, the 21st. Enemy units which had occupied Pohyon-san positions in advance withdrew northward, apparently for fear of being cut off at the news that Nogo-ryong had been taken by the ROK forces.

Nogo-ryong was considered as the last stronghold of the NKPA 15th Division. But now the ROK 21st Regiment which had taken the hill completely cleared the surrounding area of enemy remnants, and was active in eliminating any enemy threat to the main supply route. When adjacent ROK troops advanced to Pohyon-san, the regiment resumed its attack and seized Kusandong on the morning of the 22nd.

The ROK 8th Division completed its mission by capturing the tactical points, Kiryong-san and Pohyon-san north of Yongch'on, and Kusandong within its interim phase line. Thus the division secured a stepping-stone for future actions of pursuit.

3. Pursuit of the Enemy toward the 38th Parallel

Both ROK and UN forces had succeeded in penetrating the enemy defense line at the Naktong River a week after they began their counteroffensive. Even after the UN Inch'on landing, the NKPA Frontline Command was apparently lost in wild fancies that it could occupy Taegu or Pusan, and thus continued its stubborn resistance at the Naktong front. However, in the north, on September 18, as Kimp'o Airfield fell to the hands of the UN landing troops, a bridgehead was set up in the south on the west bank of the Naktong River by the UN troops, and as UN forces broke through the western flank of Tabudong, a notable symptom of collapse seemed to appear everywhere in the enemy's defenses. Now they entered into a serious phase in which they had to decide whether or not they should hold the current defense line.

As a last resort, Kim Il Sung, with a view to maintaining the main force for future operations, instructed the NKPA to form a new defense along the Kum River and Sobaek Mountain Range with troops withdrawn successively from the Naktong front. At the same time, he stressed the importance of securing reserve units for connecting troops in the Seoul-Inch'on and Naktong areas. Accordingly, the commander of the NKPA Frontline Command attempted to keep his reserve forces at Taejon and Kimch'on, designated as frontline and western front reserve units, respectively. While the NKPA II Corps was stubbornly to defend Kimch'on, and at the same time to hold the ROK and the UN forces in check in the east coastal front, the enemy I Corps together with other troops on the western front would first be converted to take the role of the reserve forces. For this purpose, from September 19th, the frontline commander began to pull his main forces back.

But as Waegwan fell to the friendly forces which had penetrated to points behind enemy lines, and the ROK forces entered P'ohang the following day, the enemy II Corps' defense line rapidly collapsed. On the 21st when the news on the UN landing at Inch'on reached them, the extremely demoralized North Korean soldiers seemed to care nothing for what their high command had urged them to fight. From the 22nd the North Korean defense line collapsed everywhere around the Naktong front. Only then did Kim Il Sung come to his senses, and give up his idea of forming a new defense line elsewhere; on September 23, he ordered the NKPA Frontline Command to withdraw all its troops northward.[33]

Meanwhile, the EUSA commander who had seen through the enemy's mind and confirmed his full swing retrogade movement by inteligence reports and prisoners' statements, decided on September 22 to launch the pursuit phase of the breakout operation. He issued his order for the "pursuit" that day. Gists of this order were as follows:

- Enemy resistance has deteriorated along the whole front making possible the general offensive of friendly forces. All efforts must be directed toward the destruction of the enemy by effecting deep penetrations, fully exploiting enemy weaknesses; through the conduct of enveloping movements friendly forces will get astride enemy lines of withdrawal to cut his attempted retreat and destroy him.
- The US I Corps will make the main effort along Taegu-Kimch'on-Suwon axis and to effect a junction with X Corps; the US 2nd Division will launch an unlimited objective attack along Hapch'on-Koch'-ang-Anui-Chonju-Kanggyong axis.
- The US 25th Division on the army's southern flank will capture Chinju and be ready to attack west or northwest on army order. The ROK Army in its zone will destroy the enemy by deep penetrations and encircling maneuvers.

This order especially made a considerable point that "commanders will feel free to advance where necessary without regard to lateral security." That day, Eighth Army issued orders making the US IX Corps (under Maj. Gen. John B. Coulter), operational as of the following day. The IX Corps would control the US 2nd and 25th Divisions attached to it, and carry out the missions previously assigned to the two divisions.

In the meantime, on that day, the ROK Army also issued, in close coordination with Eighth Army, its operation order 191, which stated,

- The ROK I Corps will launch an unlimited objective attack with the main effort on Ch'ongha-Yongdok-P'yonghae axis and the supporting effort in the axis of Injidong-Ch'onjidong-Ch'unyang. Then it will be prepared to drive on to the north or northwest on order.
- The main effort of the ROK II Corps will be placed in the axis of Towondong-Hamch'ang-Ch'ungju, while the corps' supporting attack will be made in the Uisong-Andong-Yongju axis. The corps will also attack against unlimited objectives, and then be prepared to move on to the north or northwest on order.

For more efficient command of the attacking troops, the ROK and Eighth Armies moved their headquarters from Pusan back to Taegu, respectively reopening there on September 23, the following day.

(1) Link-up with Inch'on Landing Troops

The mission of the US I Corps, the main attack unit of the friendly counteroffensive, was to rapidly drive and link up with the US X Corps which had landed at Inch'on, and thus to envelope the NKPA I Corps troops committed to the western front of the Naktong river. By so doing, the American corps could isolate enemy ground troops in both east and west zones, and smash them one by one. For this purpose, the American corps plans initially required the US 1st Cavalry Division to seize Waegwan to gain and secure a bridgehead there, and follow the US 24th Infantry Division toward Kimch'on and Taejon. As the breakout action progressed, however, the US I Corps changed the plan so that the US 24th Division (to which the US 5th RCT and British 27th Brigade were attached) which had first secured a bridgehead at Waegwan could pursue a course toward Kimch'on-Taejon, and the US 1st Cavalry Division would attack toward Sangju-Poun-Ch'ongju-Ch'onan-Osan, a course east of and generally parallel to that of the 24th Division. And at the same time, the ROK 1st Division would be kept as the corps reserve and follow behind the American cavalry division.

The US 1st Cavalry Division commander, who had broken through the Tabudong line and had been ordered to pursue the enemy force on the 22nd, made a plan for his 7th Cavalry regiment to lead the pursuit movement. Accordingly, the 7th Cavalry commander, with a 2-battalion regiment, the 1st and 3rd, and other attached tank and artillery elements, organized Task Force 777 for the effort.[54] Among this task force, the 7th Cavalry commander assigned Lt. Col. James H. Lynch's 3rd Battalion as the lead unit, calling it Task Force Lynch. This extraordinary task force included, in addition to the 3rd Battalion, two platoons of C Company, 70th Tank Battalion; the 77th Field Artillery Battalion(-); the 3rd Platoon, Heavy Mortar Company; B Company, 8th Engineer Combat Battalion;[55] the regimental Intelligence & Reconnaissance Platoon, and a tactical air control party.

At 08:00 on September 22, spearheaded by Task Force Lynch, the US 1st Cavalry Division started to move northward from Tabudong. Led by tanks, Task Force Lynch, brushing aside small scattered enemy groups, moved forward and reached the Sonsan ferry, the initial objective, at 15:45. Just prior to this, when the task force was still short of its objective, a liasion plane flew over and dropped a message ordering it to continue north to a river crossing site at

Naktongri. Therefore, the task force commander reported back to his division commander for confirmation and at 18:00 the former received it from the latter.

The task force resumed its move forward under a bright moon, and arrived at the bluff overlooking the river crossing site at Naktongri at about 22:30. At that time, men in the lead tank saw an antitank gun and fired on it. The round struck a concealed enemy ammunition truck, and shells in the truck exploded causing a great conflagration. The resulting illumination caused by the chance hit lighted the surrounding area. There the American tank crew saw abandoned enemy tanks, trucks, and other vehicles littered the scene; they also saw hundreds of enemy soldiers in the water walking through the underwater bridge across the river.

Task Force Lynch at once fired into them, killing an estimated 200 in

〈Table 5〉   The Organization of Task Force Lynch

Sept. 22, 1950

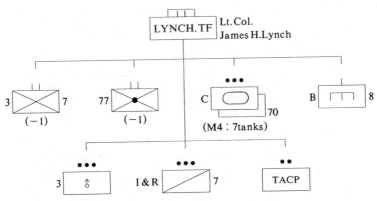

Sources : • Appleman, *South to the Naktong, North to the Yalu*, pp. 590–591.
        • ROK MND, *The History of Korean War*, vol. 4, p. 209.
        • Task Force Lynch was named after Lt. Col. Lynch, the commander of the 3rd Battalion, US 7th Cavalry Rgt.

the water. It captured a large amount of enemy equipment at the crossing site including two abandoned and operable T-34 tanks, 50 trucks, and ten artillery pieces. According to prisoners taken at the time, this enemy force consisted principally of the NKPA 3rd Division, but it included also some men from the NKPA 1st and 13th Divisions.

At dawn on September 23, Task Force Lynch waded the waist-deep river through the Naktongri ford, and secured a bridgehead at the far bank without being resisted. Thus in the 22 hours since leaving Tabudong, the task force captured 5 enemy tanks, 50 trucks, 20 artillery pieces, and 6 mortorcycles. It also killed or captured an estimated 500 enemy soldiers. That day, the 1st Battalion of the American task force pursued the enemy force across the river and drove on to Sangju, which it found abandoned by the enemy.

On September 24, the American cavalry division engineer battalion began to improve the old North Korean underwater bridge with the help of 400 South Korean laborers so that it could be used for transporting tanks and other vehicles through the Naktongri crossing site. By the afternoon that day, American tanks crossed the river through the bridge.

As soon as American tanks joined his unit, Lt. Col. Harris, commander of the US 7th Cavalry Regiment, sent Task Force Lynch up the road to Poun. On September 24-25, while its lead unit, Task Force 777, stayed at the town of Poun, the US 1st Cavalry Division concentrated other elements of the division in the area of Sangju and Naktongri. As the division commander had received a radio message from the corps commander forbidding him to advance his division any farther at about dark on the 25th, the former wanted to protest it. But he was unable to establish radio communication with the corps. So he sent a message to Eighth Army headquarters by liaison plane requesting authority to continue a hot pursuit and join X Corps in the vicinity of Suwon. Eighth Army granted authority for him to go on the forced march day and night. The division commander issued orders that at noon on September 26 the division would resume its moving day and night until it could join the X Corps near Suwon. His order stated,

> Task Force 777 would resume its pursuit along the Poun-Ch'ongju-Ch'-onan-Osan road, and division headquarters together with the artillery would follow. The 8th Cavalry Regiment would move on Ansong by way of Koesan. The 5th Cavalry Regiment would form the division rear guard to drive on Ch'onan via Choch'iwon; on the way, it would defeat retreating enemy troops in the south and west; then it would wait for further orders.

Task Force Lynch, the lead element of Task Force 777, placed the regimental Intelligence and Reconnaissance Platoon, and the 3rd Platoon of C Company, 70th Tank Battalion, at the head of it. At that time, Lt. Baker, leader of the 3rd Platoon, of tanks, was ordered by Lt. Col. Lynch to move at maximum tank speed and not to fire unless fired upon. The lieutenant moved out from Poun at 11:30, 30 minutes earlier than he was to start, and drove on at full speed unopposed. South Korean villagers only gave cheers watching the column go past.

Baker's tanks ran past Ch'ongju that afternoon, and at 18:00 stopped near a road junction at Saamri southwest of Chinch'on, North Ch'ungch'ong Province, because they had run out of gasoline. They had to refuel three of the six tanks from gasoline cans collected in the column. A moment later, three enemy trucks approached them in the near dark. However, when the North Korean truck drivers realized that they had come upon an American tank clolumn, they immediately abandoned their trucks. On the trucks, American soldiers found enough gasoline to refuel the other three tanks.

The regimental commander Harris ordered Lt. Col. Lynch to drive on, at the latter's discretion, in the darkness with vehicular lights on. The task force commander at this time made Baker's platoon of tanks lead the column rather than the I&R Platoon, and placed other tank platoons in the rear. At 20:00 the column proceeded northward, and at about 20:30 it reached the Seoul-Pusan highway junction point at Ch'onan. A ridiculous situation happened at the moment; not knowing which way to turn at a street intersection, Baker stopped and asked a North Korean soldier on guard pointing, "Osan?" Apparently resigning themselves to their fate, groups of enemy soldiers who had been chasing through Ch'onan just stood around without opposition, and watched the American column go through the town. Beyond Ch'onan, Baker's tanks marched north catching up with an estimated company of enemy soldiers and firing on them with tank machine guns. Rushing toward Osan, they passed enemy vehicles on the road, enemy soldiers on guard at bridges, and other small groups. When the lead element outdistanced the rest of the column, the task force commander Lynch tried to reach them by radio to slow them. But he was unable to communicate with them. In this situation, he formed a new point with an infantry platoon and a 3.5-inch bazooka team riding trucks. Actions against small enemy groups began to increase both in scale and in number. When they reached a point 16 kilometers south of Osan, they heard from up ahead the sound of tank and artillery fire. Lt. Col. Lynch ordered the column to turn off its lights.

Meanwhile, Baker's three tanks, without receiving any message from the task force commander, entered Osan at full speed. As they passed through the town and stopped just north of it, they thought vehicles of the task force were following behind them. But they were out of radio communication with the latter. At a point (near Chungmi-ryong) 5 or 6 kilometers north of Osan, Baker's tanks suddenly encountered enemy fire. Right at the moment his tanks ran through it, Baker saw American M26 tank tracks.

At this point fire against his tanks increased. An antitank round sheared off the mount of the machine gun on the third tank, and killed one of its crew members. Baker's tanks had been approaching the lines of the friendly forces, the US X Corps, and now the former were receiving small arms and 75-mm. recoilless rife fire from the latter. The US X Corps troops on the line held their fire because the excessive speed of the approaching tanks, the sound of their motors, and their headlights caused them think that they were not enemy. One tank commander let the first of Baker's tanks pass through, intending to fire on the second, when a white phosphorous grenade lit up the white star (the symbol of American Armed Forces) on one of the tanks and identified them in time to avoid a tragedy. Finally, Baker had established contact with the 31st Regiment of the 7th Infantry Division, the US X Corps. The time at this dramatic and impressive moment was 22:26, September 26,[36] 11 hours after they started at Poun and drove 170 kilometers.

American soldiers from both units hugged each other with tears in their eyes. The Eighth US Army's 1st Cavalry Division succeeded in linking up with the X Corps five days after it had started driving up from Tabudong on the Naktong front.

That Baker's tanks ever got through and established the contact with the Inch'on landing unit was a matter of great good luck. At that time a new defense line of the NKPA was being organized north of Osan which was not far from American frontline positions at Chungmi-ryong. 1st Lt. Baker had run through a strong enemy tank force south of Osan, then through the NKPA lines north of the town and finally into Chungmi-ryong. Apparently, the enemy was unable to identify Baker's tanks in the dark and thought the latter were some of his own. That was not all; just before Baker's tanks arrived, American antitank weapons and antipersonnel mines on the road in front of the US 31st Regimental position at Chungmi-ryong had been removed for the regiment to launch a preemptive attack against enemy troops north of Osan. In addition, the US X Corps had in advance received a radio message warning that elements of coun-

The U.S. 1st Cav. Division Established Contact with the Inch'on Landing Troops

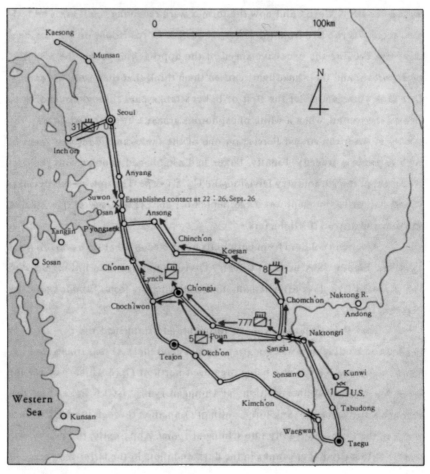

terattacking troops might appear at any time in the X Corps zone of action for
the link-up. Therefore, the defending X Corps troops had been taking every
precaution to identify approaching troops. Although there had been no direct
correspondence between both forces, Eighth Army commander who had flown

from Taegu and landed at Suwon that afternoon conferred with members of the US 31st Regiment staffs. In that meeting, General Walker said that elements of his troops would probably meet the regiment within 36 hours.

In the meantime, the main body of Task Force Lynch, which had been marching at far behind Baker with the vehicular lights off, encountered enemy tanks at a point short of Osan at about noon on September 26. It destroyed them all in a fierce tank battle, and entered Osan at 08:00 the following day. A little later at 08:26, at a small bridge north of Osan, a man of L Company of the 7th Cavalry Regiment, US 1st Cavalry Division, met elements of H Company, 31st Regiment, US 7th Division. Before noon that day, the US 1st Cavalry Division commander arrived at Osan and met the commanding officer of the 31st Infantry, US 7th Division. This concluded the US 1st Cavalry Division's mission for the link-up with the Inch'on landing troops, and for cutting off the retreat path of the NKPA I Corps in the southwestern area of South Korea. Afterwards, the American cavalry division mopped up enemy troops in the Suwon–Ch'ongju–Koesan–Sangju area, while protecting a friendly communication route there.

(2) Recapturing Taejon

The US 24th Division, the main attack unit of the US I Corps which together with the attached US 5th RCT had secured a bridgehead at Waegwan, launched a pursuit on September 23. The American division began to move from Waegwan northwest toward Kimch'on along the Seoul–Pusan highway, with its three regiments echeloned in depth. This formation was to maintain impetus in the attack by making a fresh regiment take the lead at short intervals. This time the 21st Regiment took the lead.

The enemy 105th Armored Division blocked the way with dug-in camouflaged tanks, antitank guns, and extensive mine fields.

That day, the British 27th Brigade, attached to the US 24th Division for the pursuit, was to move against Songju. On a high ground short of the town, they were locked in a fierce battle with enemy troops, and suffered a heavy loss of about 60 casualties by a mistaken friendly air attack. But the British brigade drove on toward Songju the next day.

At dawn on September 24, the 1st Battalion of the 19th Infantry, US 24th Division, attacked south from a junction point at Pusang on Waegwan-Kimch'on highway and recaptured Songju. From there it moved to link up with the British 27th Brigade below the town. There the US 19th Regiment and British brigade mopped up enemy remnants by the next day, the 25th. Then the British brigade was released from attachment to the US 24th Division, and reverted to the US I Corps control. An enemy surgeon captured that day estimated that the NKPA I Corps in the Songju area had been suffering from lack of ammunition and fuel, and fled after burying its artillery. He further stated that an enemy division had about 25% of its original strength, and the NKPA I Corps commander (Lt. Gen. Kim Ung) ordered all its subordinate units to retreat northward.

Meanwhile, at dawn on the 24th, the US 5th Regimental Combat Team (RCT) passed through the US 21st Infantry Regiment to take the lead driving north toward Kimch'on. It encountered enemy troops in positions on Hill 140 at Wolch'ondong in the suburb of Kimch'on. At that time withdrawing enemy troops were concentrating in Kimch'on, the city where the NKPA Frontline Command and I Corps headquarters had been situated. Attempting to fight a major delaying action there to permit those retreating units to escape, the enemy placed the 9th Division, remaining tanks of the 105 Armored Division, and the 849th Independent Anti-Tank Regiment in the front. As a result, a fierce battle erupted between both forces.

In this battle, the US 24th Division lost 6 M46 Medium Patton tanks

while destroying 8 enemy T-34s. The NKPA 849th regiment was practically destroyed by American tank fire and air strikes. The US 5th RCT also lost approximately 100 men killed or wounded.

On September 25, the US 21st Regiment moved into the downtown
street of Kimch'on to join the 5th RCT in a pincer attack on the town. In the
evening, the 21st Regiment continued its attack westward along the highway.

With the fall of Kimch'on, the enemy resistance was gone and enemy
troops were apparently intent only on escaping. The following day the US 19th
Infantry, which had acted as the rear guard of the division, took the lead and
entered Yongdong unopposed. It moved on and at predawn hours of the 27th, it
reached Okch'on. A while later at dawn that day, when the American regiment
resumed its move toward Taejon, the lead tank hit an enemy antitank mine and
was destroyed. The regiment encountered a strong enemy position on the
heights west of Okch'on, which were considered as the threshold to Taejon.
Right there, as they had done in the south of Kimch'on, enemy troops attempted
to delay approaching American forces to permit time and space for their retreating fellow soldiers so they could safely escape to Taejon. As expected,
Taejon was an assembly point for retreating enemy units south and west of
Waegwan, the areas called by Koreans as Yongnam and Honam, respectively.
Therefore, the city was crowded with enemy soldiers and war equipment from
various units all intending to escape. In a battle southeast of Taejon that day
the American division took approximately 300 prisoners from seven NKPA divisions and destroyed reportedly 13 or 20 enemy tanks.

At 16:30 on September 28, the day that the capital city of Seoul had
been restored, scouts of the 2nd Battalion, US 19th Regiment and C Company of
the US 3rd Engineer Combat Battalion, reached the outskirts of Taejon. An
hour later the main elements of the 19th Regiment entered downtown streets of
the city after engineers had cleared mines. Both units, the engineers and the

19th regiment, were among the last to leave the city on July 20, about 10 weeks earlier, when the US 24th Division suffered a disastrous defeat there even losing its commander. Now what a sweet revenge and joy it was for them to reenter the city!

With the recapture of Taejon, the US 24th Division accomplished its mission in the pursuit. By the end of September, the division captured many North Korean prisoners and much enemy equipment.

However, there was bitterness too. Far from being joyful, American soldiers shuddered at the North Korean atrocities to discover scenes of tragedy. During mopping up streets, they witnessed a horrible scene of one of the greatest mass killings: about 500 South Korean soldiers had been buried dead in a place near Taejon Airfield, with all their hands tied behind their backs. For about a week from September 28, within the city, they discovered an estimated 5,000 or 7,000 South Korean civilian dead, 17 bodies of the ROK and approximately 40 of American soldiers buried.[57]

The Communist North Koreans, when they had captured the city on July 20, sent many patriotic civilians whom they had classified and called as South Korean "reactionaries," officials, and celebrities to mass internment camps temporarily established at the Taejon jail and various Catholic Church buildings. However, from September 21, when the first UN troops had crossed the Naktong river, and their defeat seemed certain, enemy troops began executing these innocent people before they themselves retreated in the face of the UN advance. The Communists took them out in groups of 100 and 200, bound them to each other and tied their hands behind them. They led these South Korean people to previously dug trenches, and shot and buried them all. On September 26, when UN forces had approached so close to Taejon, the North Korean Security Police knew the impending danger, and hurried to liquidate those held in jails. Among the victims, six people including two American soldiers, one ROK soldier, and three South Korean civilians, miraculously survived the massacre to provide eyewitness evidences to North Korean atrocities.

According to their testimonies, they had been shot, but feigned death to be buried alive with their wounds under a thin layer of loose soil. Among them the two American soldiers were able to breathe through a draft of air. One of the two punched a hole to the surface with his lead pencil to breathe sufficiently to stay alive. They were rescued when parts of the bodies were being uncovered by friendly soldiers.

After completely securing Taejon, the US 24th Division had the task of protecting the army's line of communications which extended 161 kilometers from Taejon back to the Naktong river. Its 19th Regiment held the Taejon area up to the Kum River, the 21st Infantry extended from Taejon to Yongdong, the 5th RCT was in the Kimch'on area, and the division Reconnaissance Company secured the Waegwan bridge.

Mopping up the Rear Area: The ROK 1st Division which had been kept as the US I Corps reserve during the pursuit crossed the Naktong River at Naktongri on September 25, and on order from the corps, it drove up north in the Sonsan-Sangju axis[58] to join the attacking units.

The division closely followed behind the US 1st Cavalry Division to advance to Miwon via Sonsan-Sangju-Poun. During the pursuit northward, it interdicted and mopped up remnants and stragglers from the NKPA 2nd, 3rd, 4th, 7th, and 9th Divisions,[59] who had been attempting to escape to the north from the Naktong front along the rough mountain range of Sobaek. Then it further advanced to Chungp'yong, Koesan, Chinch'on, and Umsong to clear the areas of enemy remnants. After this the ROK division concentrated at Ch'ongju to be prepared for future operations. During these series of pursuit actions, the division killed 4,543 enemy soldiers, captured 5,211 prisoners and 36 pieces of various guns and artillery. It suffered 355 killed, 1,023 wounded, and 77 missing.[60]

(3) Cut Off at the Kum River Line

The UN pursuit operations from the southwestern sector of the Naktong River was launched by the US IX Corps. The Corps had planned to attack the enemy from a foothold secured in the southern bank of the Nam River and from a bridgehead also secured by the US 2nd and 25th Divisions at the western bank of the Naktong River. The corps first attempted to attack and secure Kanggyong to secure the Kum river front, and then would try to cut off the enemy retreat route in the western zone of the Seoul-Pusan highway. By so doing, the corps would be able to destroy the isolated and beleaguered enemy troops one by one within its zone of action.

By September 22, the day on which the pursuit order had been issued by the corps, the US 2nd Division was engaging enemy troops at Ch'ogye and in the outskirts of Sinbanri, while the 25th Division contended with the enemy for Chinju.

The Capture of Kanggyong: The objective of the US 2nd Division in its pursuit operation was to take Kanggyong by way of Hapch'on-Koch'ang-Anui-Chonju. On September 23, its 23rd Regiment captured Sinbanri, and the 38th Regiment which had seized Ch'ogye the previous day moved on toward Hapch'-on. The 38th Infantry had hard fighting before overcoming enemy delaying forces. At that time, parts of the NKPA 2nd, 4th, and 9th Divisions which had resisted in the area of Sinbanri passed through Hapch'on, while the rest were building up in the town.

The following day, the American division committed its 23rd Regiment which had occupied Sinbanri to the southwest of Hapch'on to attack against the town in a double envelopment movement with the 38th Regiment. While the latter interdicted and destroyed enemy troops still in the town by blocking the Hapch'on-Kimch'on road, the former entered Hapch'on during the day of the 25th. That day, UN Air Force hit hard at enemy troops fleeing in utter disorder, flying 53 sorties in the area. The 38th Infantry killed an estimated 300 enemy soldiers at its roadblock and entered the town at night.

At daybreak the next day, the US 38th Regiment started for Koch'ang. On the road in front of the regiment, were many vehicles and heavy equipment abandoned by the fleeing enemy 2nd Division, commanded by Maj. Gen. Ch'oe Hyon. The hard-pressed enemy remnants numbered about 2,500 men. The Ameircan regiment captured 14 antitank guns, 4 artillery pieces, and numerous other equipment; it also captured 450 enemy soldiers there. The regiment continued its pursuit and advanced almost 47 kilometers during that day reaching the outskirts of Koch'ang.[61]

At 08:00 on September 26, the US 38th Infantry Regiment entered the town, and a little later the US 23rd Regiment joined it there. There in Koch'ang, the former captured a North Korean field hospital containing 45 enemy wounded. Prisoners disclosed that elements of the NKPA 2nd, 4th, 9th, and 10th Divisions were to have assembled at the town, but the swift advance of the US 2nd Division had frustrated the plan.[62] That evening the US 23rd Infantry continued the advance to Anui without being opposed. As the area was a maze of flooded paddies, the regiment inevitably moved into the village streets to bivouac there. At dawn the next morning, one enemy group which remained in the vicinity fired an artillery and mortar barrage on the American troops, hitting the 3rd Battalion command post. Six American soldiers including the battalion executive officer and other staff members were killed, and 25, including the battalion commander, were wounded on the spot.

At dawn on September 28, the US 38th Regiment left Koch'ang for Anui via the town, and advanced across the Sobaek Mountains to Chonju. Meeting only light resistance, the forced regimental motor march covered as many as 117 kilometers in 9 and a half hours to enter the city at 13:15. At Chonju, the American regiment killed about 100 and captured 170 among an estimated 300 enemy soldiers of the NKPA 102nd and 104th Security Regiments. At that time, the US 38th Regiment suffered from lack of fuel for its vehicles. Fortunately, a liaison plane flew over the town and the pilot learned the situation. He reported it to the division and corps which rushed gasoline forward.

On September 29, the American regiment departed Chonju for Kanggyong, and reached the town at 03:00 the following day via Nonsan. Thus the US 2nd Division had accomplished its mission. Now that the division had secured strategic terrain on the Kum River line, it could launch a frontal attack against the NKPA I Corps, already encircled by the UN link-up operations. By penetrating into the enemy line in the center the American division was able to defeat enemy troops one by one.

At the end of September, the US 2nd Division redeployed its three regiments along the Kum River for mopping up enemy remnants and protecting the UN communications route in the rear area. The 38th Regiment was in the Chonju-Kanggyong area, the 23rd in the Anui area, and the 9th in the Koryong-Samga area.

During its pursuit operations, the 2nd Division killed about 360 enemy soldiers and captured 757. It also captured 23 artillery pieces, 32 antitank guns, 1 self-propelled gun, 22 mortars, 10 motorcycles, 17 trucks and 425 tons of ammunition. On the other hand, it suffered numerous casualties including 32 men killed.[63]

The Capture of Kunsan: The US 25th Division was to recapture Chinju and there, on order, to move west or northwest. Accordingly, the division planned first to attack and rapidly capture Chinju. In an effort first to meet the newly appointed corps commander's operational directives, the division commander tried to close the gap between his division and the adjacent US 2nd Division which had been driving toward Sinbanri. At the same time, on September 23, in order to break the stalemate at the Chinju pass, the division commander adjusted part of the maneuver plan for his units. He placed the 27th Infantry, which had been moving from south toward Chinju, in the division's north at Chungamri, and committed Task Force Torman, the nucleus of which was the division Reconnaissance Company,[64] to Paedunri to which the 27th Infantry had advanced. The division commander tried to lay siege to and occupy Chinju through a pincer attack made by the 27th Infantry and the Reconnaissance Company, while the 35th Infantry Regiment in the center attempted to make a frontal attack.

The division drove forward with its newly adjusted plan, and by the afternoon of the 25th, the 35th Regiment seized Chinju supported by the Reconnaissance Company and cleared the city of enemy remnants. As the Nam River bridge had remained damaged at that time, all three elements of the division had first to construct an underwater sandbag ford. This work caused much delay and the 27th Regiment crossed the river only on the 26th to attack and secure Uiryong.

On the 24th, when the US 25th Division was engaging the enemy, the Eighth US Army altered its earlier operational order and directed the US IX Corps to "execute unlimited objective attacks to seize Chonju and Kanggyong."[65] To carry out his part of the order, the 25th Division commander organized two main task forces with armored support centered about the 24th and 35th Regiments. Of the two, Task Force Matthews from the 24th Regiment[66] was to proceed, on the division left, westward from Chinju toward Hadong-Kurye-Namwon-Sunch'ang-Kimje-Iri and Kunsan. On the division right (north side),

Task Force Dolvin of the 35th Regiment[67] was to advance to the Kum River line by way of Chinju-Hamyang-Namwon-Chonju-Iri-Kanggyong. Thus the division, spearheaded by the two task forces which were to start their drives from Chinju, planned to bypass Chiri-san both in the south and the north to reach Namwon and then to advance to the Kum River line.

Task Force Dolvin comprised two tank-infantry teams, each of which had a tank company and an infantry company. At 06:00 on September 26, the task force with the infantry riding the rear decks of the tanks moved out of Chinju. On its pursuit west toward Namwon, the task force encountered mine fields and blown bridges. So it had to halt several hours while engineers and Korean laborers constructed bypasses. Sometimes it had to crush enemy resistance with the help of air strikes. It moved on west pursuing the NKPA 6th Division, and bypassed Chiri-san on the north. By the afternoon on the 28th, the task force entered Namwon via Hamyang, and found that Task Force Matthews was already there.

Blown bridges over the Nam River west of Chinju delayed the departure of Task Force Matthews by a day. It left Chinju for Kurye via Hadong on the road south of Chiri-san. On its pursuit, the column was repeatedly told by Korean civilians and captured NKPA prisoners that a group of American prisoners had been taken to the northwest, so that it sped up the attack, and rescued 11 American prisoners at a point 16 kilometers north of Hadong. Meanwhile, just past noon of the 28th, when the column was to enter Namwon, it found the town was full of enemy troops. However, as the enemy's attention was apparently centered on F-84 jet planes striking the town at that time, enemy soldiers were unaware that pursuing ground troops were so close. As a result, the North Koreans were surprised and panicked by the task force. Right in the town, the task force liberated 86 more American prisoners who had been kept by the enemy.[68]

On September 29, Task Force Dolvin resumed its pursuit operation passing through Chonju, which had been occupied by the 38th Infantry, US 2nd Division, and advanced to the Kum River line via Iri. Prior to this, on September 28, while Task Force Matthews remained in Namwon, the 3rd Battalion(also called Task Force Blair) of the US 24th Regiment, which had closely followed behind, the next day led the pursuing columns in reaching the Kum River line, overrunning Chongup and Iri. The 1st Battalion of the US 24th Infantry captured Kunsan, its pursuit objective, without bloodshed.

Thus in crossing southwest Korea from Chinju, Task Force Dolvin of the US 25th Division had advanced 222 kilometers while Task Force Matthews traveled 354 kilometers. After recapturing Kunsan, the American division took charge of security of the supply road in the rear; its 24th Regiment maintained security in the Kunsan area, 35th Infantry in the area of Iri, and the 27th Regiment in the area of Chinju-Hamyang-Namwon.

The 2nd and 25th Divisions under the US IX Corps, which had launched the counteroffensive on the southwestern zone of the Naktong front starting from September 16, now completely secured the Kum River line by rapidly pursuing enemy troops and exploiting results. They had practically destroyed the five enemy divisions under the NKPA I Corps: the 2nd, 6th, 4th, 9th, and 7th. The lightening speed of the American troops at that time did not allow any time for regrouping of enemy units. The former virtually numbed the chain of command of the latter, and encircled and destroyed enemy troops one by one. However, many of the interdicted enemy troops, in groups or individually, had sneaked into the rough terrain of Chiri-san, and later acted as enemy guerillas turning the mountain into their bases.

(4) Pursuit Operations in the East

In the mountainous eastern area of Korea, the pursuit and exploitation was made by the ROK I Corps. The corps, which had broken through the enemy line by September 22, advanced to the Kigye-Ch'ongha line, and there it received the ROK Army order that "the corps would make an unlimited objective attack toward the line of Ch'unyang-P'yonghae, and, on order, get ready to move north or northwest."

Accordingly, the ROK corps commander designated the 3rd Division, which had already occupied Hunghae and had been driving toward Ch'ongha, as the main attack unit, and the Capital Division which had secured Kigye as the supporting effort. He tried to cut off a retreat path for enemy troops in his zone of action, by rapidly advancing along the axis of the coastal road and and mountain routes with the Taebaek Mountain Range in between. He wanted to destroy enemy troops one by one within his zone, and his troops moved out for the pursuit on September 23.

Pursuit Operations in Hunghae-Inguri: The commander of the ROK 3rd Division which had secured Hunghae on the east coast, in turn, issued his own order, based on the ROK Army order, that the division would attack with its main effort on coastal highway 7. Gists of his pursuit order were as follows:

> The division will place the 26th Regiment in the lead and the 22nd Regiment will follow up. The two regiments will rapidly pursue enemy troops along the road between Ch'ongha and Uljin. The 23rd Regiment will attack and destroy the enemy 5th Division headquarters and the main body of his 10th Regiment concentrated in the area of T'osongdong west of Hunghae. After completing its mission there, the 23rd Regiment would assemble in Hunghae and remain as the division reserve.[9]

Meanwhile, the NKPA 5th Division, which had faced the ROK 3rd Division and had been practically destroyed by the ROK troops in the week after the latter launched their successful breakout operation, moved northward with its main elements, and part of it sneaked into Pihak-san west of Hunghae.

At 05:30 on September 23, the ROK division resumed its attack with the 26th Regiment in the lead, the 22nd following behind, and the 23rd in division reserve, and recaptured Ch'ongha. The 26th Regiment drove on and advanced to a point near Kanggu by the 24th, and on the 25th, it retook Yongdok. When the South Korean regiment entered the town, they found most of the town on fire with a huge cloud of black smoke hanging overhead. Apparently surprised by the ROK troops, the enemy abandoned large amounts of weapons and equipment and fled in great haste. Some of the abandoned enemy trucks were found with motors still running, and artillery pieces were still in position with ammunition at hand. Horse-drawn carts (used for communication purposes) were found with limping Mongolian ponies hitched and tied to nearby trees. At that time, the remnants of the NKPA 5th Division were estimated at no more than a regular regiment, and they, instead of taking roads northward, turned inland for escape into the mountains.[70] Impressed by the gains made by the ROK units that day, General Walker, commander of the Eighth US Army, remarked, "Too little has been said in praise of the South Korean Army which has performed so magnificiently in helping turn this war from the defensive to the offensive."

In the meantime, in Yongdok, through the good offices of a KMAG adviser, the ROK division secured twenty-five 2.5-ton trucks, which greatly increased its mobility. The 26th Regiment which had recaptured Yongdok started to move up northward, and proceeded toward Uljin via Yonghae, while the 22nd and 23rd Regiments advanced to the Yonghae line by way of Yongdok. At that time, the division attached engineer companies, one to each infantry regiment, for clearing the road of mines and repairing the road for the attacking units. The division at the same time put its artillery battalion in an advanced position. That day, the ROK I Corps headquarters moved from Kyongju to Kigye.

On September 26, the ROK 22nd and 23rd Regiments passed through the 26th Regiment to seize P'yonghae, their pursuit objective, and moved up the coastal road. The following day, the former two regiments in close coordination entered Uljin against negligible enemy resistance. At that time, the town was on fire, having been napalmed and bombed by F-51 fighter planes. The ROK 3rd Division headquarters moved to Susanri in Uljin, and the division artillery battalion rapidly switched its position and moved up to provide close fire support for the attacking units.

Upon securing the division's pursuit objective, the commander, with an idea to rapidly attack toward Kangnung, issued a new operational order. According to this order, in an effort to cut off retreating enemy troops and annihilate them within the division zone of action, the 22nd Regiment was to rapidly move up to Kangnung. At the same time a battalion of the 23rd Regiment would protect the division's rear in the area of Uljin and Chukpyon, and the main body of the regiment would also advance to Kangnung. The 26th Regiment was to assemble in Uljin to remain as division reserve. In order to execute its part of this order, on September 28, the 22nd Regiment $(-)$ penetrated into enemy defensive positions at Uljin-Chukpyon, and continued on toward Samch'ok to reach a point south of it at sunset that day. At that time, the 3rd Battalion of the regiment was driving toward Ch'ongsong.

The 23rd Regiment $(-)$ proceeded from Uljin to Imwonjin, while its 1st Battalion remained in Chukpyon providing security for the town and reorganizing itself there. The division reserve, the 26th Regiment, was moving toward Imwonjin at that time.

Encouraged by the impressive gains by the 3rd Division and also by the

South Korean troops as a whole, the ROK Army issued, on September 29, operation order 199 (dated September 30, 1950) calling that all units must be reorganized for future "March North" operations in the designated areas south of the
38th Parallel.

The detailed mission for the 3rd Division was "to advance to Chumunjin along the Samch'ok-Kangnung axis, and stay there for maintenance and
reorganization. Then, on order, get ready for future operations." In turn, the division commander in his order emphasized that "troops in the pursuit should
move up north regardless of negligible enemy resistance."

The 22nd Regiment of the 3rd Division took the lead in attacking
against Samch'ok, and secured it on the morning of the 29th. There the regiment
continued its northward movement to occupy Mukho, and by sunset that day, it
reached an area south of Kangnung. It was followed by the 23rd Regiment, the
main element of which was concentrating on Mukho via Samch'ok. The main
body of the 26th Regiment, the division reserve, also advanced to Imwonjin.

The 1st and 2nd Battalions of the 22nd Regiment, which had led the attacking columns all the way up from Uljin, encountered light enemy resistance
at Aninjin on the 29th. At 08:00 on September 30, the two lead battalions
advanced to Unsanri six kilometers south of Kangnung. From there in Unsanni,
the 22nd Regiment, in close coordination with the reinforced 2nd and 3rd Battalions of the 23rd Regiment, attacked against Kangnung at 15:30 and succeeded
in retaking the city. The artillery battalion in Aninjin helped them greatly. At
about this time the 1st Regiment of the ROK Capital Division also advanced to
Kangnung driving across the Taegwal-ryong pass.

Meanwhile, the 3rd Battalion (commanded by Maj. Chung Soon Min) of
the 22nd Regiment, which had proceeded inland from Yongdok toward Ch'ongsong, turned back seaward again via Ch'ongsong-Chinbo-Ch'ongri-Yongyang-
Ch'oram to join the main body of the regiment at Kangnung on the 30th, 5 days

after it had acted alone.

The 3rd Battalion commander later recounted that "in narrow mountain trails my battalion pursued approximately 3,000 or 4,000 enemy remnants, and took many of them as prisoners. We also captured about 50 ponies which had been used for carrying enemy mortars and other heavy equipment. We formed a cavalry reconnaissance team with those ponies, which were very useful for our actions."[71]

While the 22nd Regiment cleared Kangnung of enemy remnants, main elements of the 23rd Regiment drove on north. At about 20:00 that night, they encountered about 300 enemy troops in an area 4 kilometers north of Chumunjin. In this relatively brief engagement which lasted until 23:00, the ROK 23rd Regiment defeated and repelled most of the enemy soldiers achieving brilliant results. The regiment continued on toward the 38th Parallel, and reached Inguri just south of the parallel line. An advanced company of the 3rd Battalion, 23rd Regiment, even crossed the line to reach a point near Yangyang. It was the first unit to reach the 38th Parallel among all units of the United Nations Command and the ROK Army.

In brief, by September 30, during the 15 days since it started the counteroffensive on September 16, the ROK 3rd Division, with the help of US naval gunfire and air strikes, had traveled 260 kilometers from P'ohang to the 38th Parallel. The marvelous speed it had demonstrated in this pursuit operation was an average of 17.3 kilometers per day. The NKPA 5th Division which had opposed the ROK 3rd Division in the eastern coastal area was once a formidable organization, originally composed largely of Korean veterans of the Chinese Communist Army. However, it suffered a complete debacle in the face of the undaunted pursuit of the ROK 3rd Division. Terrified enemy soldiers had sneaked into the T'aebaek Mountain Range or fled across the 38th Parallel to Yanyang. In this pursuit operation, the division killed 1,351 enemy soldiers and captured 230 prisoners. It also captured about 700 rifles of various types, 230 pieces of heavy weapons, 2 enemy tanks, and a large amount of ammunition, equipment and other war supply items. The division lost 71 men killed, 477 wounded, and 2 missing.

Pursuit Operation in Kigye-Seorim: The ROK Capital Division, which had recaptured Kigye, was ordered on September 22, "to make an unlimited objective attack in its zone along the axis of Injidong-Ch'onjidong-Ch'unyang as a supporting effort in the pursuit of the corps."[72]

In order to execute its part of the order, the division made its own maneuvering plan: the 1st Regiment would make a turning movement toward Kusandong on the division's west flank to cut off a path for retreating enemy troops near Top'yongdong, and the 18th and 1st Cavalry Regiments would, from present positions, press hard against the enemy troops.[73]

Starting from September 23, the 18th and 1st Cavalry Regiments moved out of Kigye and proceeded toward Top'yongdong-Ch'ongsong. The 1st Regiment, which had reached Kusandong the previous day, began its attack from the northwest against Top'yongdong. By using combined tactics of a turning movement and a frontal pursuing attack, the division tried to interdict and annihilate the retreating enemy force in a single blow.

On the same day, in the provisional capital city of Pusan, President Syngman Rhee in his statement on a pressing question declared, "No longer does the 38th Parallel as such exsist. We have thus far contained our passions considering international relations; however, we shall not recognize the existence of the 38th Parallel line."[74] This statement was significant in that he not only contradicted the existing 38th line but also he publicly expressed his will to march to the north across the line. His statement was welcomed by most of the South Korean people, particulary by the ROK soldiers who considered it as

a signal for approving their desire to "March North." The words of the aged
president Syngman Rhee at that time were, as it were, an expression of the long
cherished Korean national desire for reunification of the South and North. It
greatly raised the morale of all the South Korean troops.

Inspired by the sweeping dash and a series of victories made by his regiments, Brig. Gen. Song Yo Ch'an, commander of the ROK Capital Division,
decided, on September 24, to change his strategy in the pursuit. He thought he
would lay aside tactics for attacking enemy troops at small hill positions or
local areas; instead, he would let the main elements of his division rapidly
break through the enemy's strong points along the axis of advance and reach
the 38th Parallel as early as possible. Accordingly, exploitation and mopping up
operations after successful penetration were to be handed over to the rear
guards or follow-up troops.

The ROK 18th Regiment (commanded by Col. Lim Ch'ung Sik) advanced
to Taejondong after overrunning To'pyongdong. In the face of rapidly advancing
ROK troops, the main body of the NKPA 12th Division which had stood opposite the ROK Capital Division fled north in great haste, leaving behind 10
horse-drawn carts fully loaded with supplies and 10 military horses. Enemy
remnants who had missed the chance for withdrawal put up individual
resistance and sneaked into the T'aebaek Mountain Range. The ROK 1st Cavalry Regiment (commander: Col. Paik Nam Kwon) advanced to Ibam-Top'yongdong
that day, and continued its pursuit exploiting the gaps developed by lead elements. At that time in Top'yongdong, Lt. Col. Han Shin, commander of the ROK
1st Regiment, urged speedy pursuit telling the commanders of companies and
above, "We have to move up faster than the enemy did pushing down south in
the past."

The 18th Regiment seized Ch'ongsong on September 25, and the 1st
Cavalry Regiment which had closely followed behind it also entered the town.

The division and regiments assembled in the town, and each of them immediately set up command post there. The division commander at that time awarded a citation and 500,000 won to each regiment, the 1st and the 18th, complimenting brilliant results they had achieved thus far.

In the meantime, the ROK 3rd Division, the adjacent unit on the right, captured Yongdok that day, and the ROK 8th Division on the left seized Andong. The command post of the ROK I Corps moved to Kigye north of An'gang on that same day.

On September 26, the Capital Division continued its pursuit with the 18th and 1st Cavalry Regiments in the lead, and the 1st Regiment in reserve. The 18th Regiment proceeded from Ch'ongsong to Toch'onri southwest of Ch'unyang via Yongyang, the 1st Cavalry Regiment advanced to Togyedong north of Yongyang, and the 1st Regiment reached Yongyang. The 1st Regiment mopped up enemy remnants frequented there in the vicinity of the town. The pursuit operation progressed so fast that it elongated the supply route, and as a result, the ROK troops had to secure mobilized means to meet the demand on the frontline.

On September 27, the 18th Regiment proceeded from Toch'onri to Ch'unyang via Pongsong defeating minor enemy resistance. The 1st Cavalry Regiment moved out of Togyedong and advanced to Ch'unyang, and the 1st Regiment drove to Ch'unyang from Yongyang. Thus the ROK Capital Division accomplished its mission in the pursuit. Three regimental command posts were established in Ch'unyang, and those of the division, and the corps moved to the same town. Thus the ROK commanders from higher and lower echelons could, for the first time since their couteroffensive started, get together in one place. At this meeting, they talked and seriously discussed future pursuit operations anticipating their actions north of the 38th Parallel. They also talked about supply problems and measures to solve them.

At about this time, hard pressed and confused enemy troops of the NKPA 12th Division and part of the NKPA 5th Division fled into Odae-san by way of Yongwol-Taewha; some of them sneaked into mountainous area northeast of Yongwol, where they slipped down into the mountain valley to plunder private houses for food and clothing.

On September 28, the very day when Inch'on landing troops recaptured the capital city of Seoul, the motorized troops of the ROK 18th Regiment left Ch'unyang, its assembly area, for Yongwol early that morning. They soon entered Yongwol, and after a brief stop in the town for troop maintenance, they continued the motor march and reached P'yongchang very shortly. Meanwhile, the 1st Cavalry Regiment proceeded from Ch'unyang to Yongwol. On the way to Yongwol, it captured 67 prisoners, 45 rifles, and 2 motorcycles.

As the pursuit operation progressed at an accelerating pace everywhere the ROK Army issued Operational Directive 78, additional guidelines for the pursuit operations, to make them perfect. The essential points are as follows:

> Direct all efforts on the decisive points so that enemy troops can not afford to reorganize themselves and resist. Cut off the enemy's retreat paths to envelope and annihilate him. For this purpose, press enemy troops hard through frontal attacks and turning movements. At night, keep close coordination between friendly troops so that no enemy force can break away, and proceed with thorough pursuit.

Another directive came out on that same day. Gists of Directive 79 entitled "on the Presidential award for troops which first reach the 38th Parallel" are as follows:

> When the UN Forces made the successful surprise landing at Inch'on, they gained momentum as they passed from the defense to the offense. They also succeeded in the link-up operation between ground forces

from the south and north within 10 days. Now the opportunity for them to break through the 38th Parallel was at hand. Concerning this matter, the President instructed that he would decorate and award citation for the unit which first reached the 38th line. Commanders and leaders of all echelons were requested to inform their soldiers the meaning of this purpose, and be ready to win this honor so that their brilliant achievement could be recorded in their unit history.[75]

On September 29, main elements of the NKPA 12th and 5th Division, which had continuously been in flight, crossed the Seoul-Kangnug highway in the Taewha-Kangnung area to retreat northward across the 38th Parallel via the Odae Mountain. Remnants who had broken away from the retreating columns were moving toward Inje by way of Ch'angch'on-Hyonri due north of Taewha.

At about this time, the Capital Division received the ROK Army operation order 199 which stated that the division would "move on to Taewha-Ch'angch'on-Hup'yong, and halt in the Yongp'o area for reorganization; then on order get ready for future operations." Accordingly, the 1st Battalion (commanded by Lt. Col. Chang Ch'un Kwon) of the 18th Regiment, Capital Division, stopped in a mountain valley on the axis of advance toward P'yongch'ang-Taewha to have a meal and rest. Right at the moment, a surprising event took place that might have turned a misfortune into a blessing.

The Division commander Brig. Gen. Song Yo Ch'an arrived there to personally grasp the frontline situation. When the general asked the battalion commander about the location of the advance party, the latter replied in his bewilderment that it might have advanced to Taewha, 5 or 6 kilometers north of the place they were. But in reality, the advance party was far from Taewha at that time. The battalion commander did not imagine that the general would venture to visit the forefront troops. However, the division commander, upon receiving the battalion commander's report, rushed toward Taewha. The general didn't know that an unexpected situation was waiting for him and his party there. A little later, they encountered a company-sized enemy force on the road short of Taewha.

The general mistook enemy soldiers for his own troops and came closer to them. But what a surprise! He found that they were enemy soldiers in various tattered uniforms. At that time even the ROK soldiers wore uniforms of all kinds, so that they might have appeared very similar to those enemy soldiers. At once the general turned back and the escorting ROK MP's on their jeeps opened up with machine gun fire against the enemy soldiers. Momentarily, the enemy soldiers were taken aback much more than the general and his party. At this unexpected surprise attack, the enemy soldiers surrendered with their hands up, and the main body of the ROK battalion rapidly drove up to the place to capture them all.[76]

Under such circumstances, the ROK Capital Division continued its attack on the 30th, the following day. The 18th Regiment advanced to Seorim just south below the 38th Parallel via Ch'angch'on north of Changp'yong, and its lead elements which had passed through the town of Seorim broke through the 38th Parallel. There they launched patrol and searching operations.

The 1st Cavalry Regiment proceeded from Soksari to Kwangwonri south of Seorim, while the 1st Regiment which had moved to Soksari from P'yongch'ang via Taewha was getting ready for further pursuit toward Taegwal-ryong-Kangnung.

During the 15 days of pursuit operation from September 16 to 30, the the ROK Capital Division had made a remarkable advance with irresistible force from An'gang through Ch'ongsong, Yongyang, P'yongch'ang and Seorim. It had moved toward the 38th Parallel through rugged mountain paths and defiles in the stiff Odae-san and T'aebaek Mountain Range.

The NKPA 12th and 5th Division, which had initially attempted to co-unterattack against the ROK troops from their positions in the area of An'gang-Kigye, began to run away when their defensive line collapsed. On the other hand, the ROK Capital Division had made a forced march all the way in some instances traveling more than 40 kilometers a day in an effort to closely pursue fleeing enemy troops. As a result, supply routes were elongated for the ROK troops, and their rear guard units experienced great difficulty in transporting supplies to the attacking units.

(5) Pursuit Operations in the Mid-Eastern Zones

The pursuit operations in the mid-eastern areas of Korea were made by the ROK II Corps which broke through the enemy line in its sector on the Naktong River front. According to the ROK Army operation order 191 issued on September 22, the corps was to pass immediately onto the offensive and to launch an unlimited objective attack in the pursuit. It was first to attack and se-cure Ch'ungju and Yongju, then on order to get ready to move north or north-west.

In order to execute its part, the corps moved out, on September 23, for the pursuit with its 6th Division in Sinnyong as the main attack unit, and the 8th Division in Kusandong as supporting effort.

Pursuit Operation from Sinnyong to Ch'unch'on: The ROK 6th Division in Sinnyong was ordered, on September 22, the day when it had recaptured Chorim-san hill, that as the main attack unit for the corps it would pursue ene-my troops along the axis of Towondong-Hamch'ang-Ch'ungju.

Meanwhile, the NKPA 8th Division (commanded by Maj. Gen. Oh Paik Ryong) which had confronted the ROK 6th Division, began a general retreat after it was defeated in the Chorim-san battle. Main elements of the enemy division slipped out of their positions in the direction of Andong-Yongju-Tanyang like a falling tide.

Judging that the situation had turned favorable to him, the ROK division commander ordered his troops to go on the pursuit. On the 25th, the ROK 2nd Regiment advanced to Uihong north of Chorim-san, the 19th Regiment to Ch'ongnodong north of Uihong, and the 7th Regiment to T'apdong north of Ch'-ongnodong. Thus the three regiments of the ROK 6th Division could, along the road 28 from Sinnyong to Uisong, keep pace with other friendly troops in the pursuit operations toward the 38th Parallel.

All three regiments of the ROK 6th Division reached and assembled in Toriwon(also called Towondong 10 kilometers southwest of Uisong) the following day. On the 25th, each of them left Toriwon to reach Ssangodong and Naksan-dong, small towns at the Naktong riverside. There the regiments crossed the river that night, and advanced to Hamch'ang. The next day all three regiments again assembled in Chomch'on.

On the 27th, the 2nd Regiment proceeded to Poun and Koesan, and the 19th Regiment moved to Yugokri north of Chomch'on. There the 19th Regiment engaged two enemy battalions in a fierce fight, and destroyed them all. The 7th Regiment at that time advanced to Munkyong, and the division command post moved up to Chomch'on. The next day the 7th and 19th Regiments drove to-ward Ch'ungju across the Ewha-ryong pass northwest of Munkyong. The division command post also moved up north. Thus the whole division made a re-markable advance with a crushing force as shown by its capture of Chorim Mountain back.

At about this time, the ROK division received the Army order 199 which was considered as a preliminary order for future penetration into the 38th Parallel. The order called for the division to continue on to Ch'unch'on along the Chech'on-Chup'ori-Wonju axis, and on order to get ready for furture operations.[77]

The division commander placed the 2nd, 7th, and 19th Regiments, in that order, on the axis of Wonju-Ch'unch'on for the pursuit operation.

On September 30, the 2nd Regiment moved out of Ch'ungju in the lead, and entered Wonju against enemy resistance. At about 16:00 the 3rd Battalion (commanded by Maj. Song Tae Hoo) of the 2nd Regiment reached Hoengsong.

On Octerber 1, the 2nd Regiment proceeded from Wonju to Hongch'on, and its lead unit, the 3rd Battalion, drove north toward Ch'unch'on via Hoengsong and Hongch'on. When the battalion reached the Wonch'ang Pass 10 kilometers south of Ch'unch'on, an organized company sized enemy struck the battalion with savage fury. But the battalion immediately repelled them, and chased fleeing enemy soldiers to enter the city of Ch'unch'on.

In the meantime, the 7th and 19th Regiments which had closely followed behind the 2nd Regiment advanced to Wonju that day. In the areas of Yangp'yong and Munmak, however, the 19th Regiment encountered two battalion sized enemy remnants. In a fierce fight, the ROK 19th Regiment smashed them.

At about that time, approximately 2,000 North Korean soldiers, remnants of the NKPA II Corps, who had been chased by the ROK 8th Division but had become isolated and bypassed in the Sinnim Pass between Chech'on and Wonju, attempted to escape northward by attacking the frontline command posts of the ROK 6th Division and the II Corps located at Wonju. This enemy force killed many ROK soldiers including 5 American officers who had been attached to the ROK corps. The North Koreans ran amok in Wonju, killing an estimated 1,000 to 2,000 local civilians.[78]

Anyhow, the ROK 6th Division recaptured the city of Wonju at the end of September via Hamch'ang-Munkyong-Ch'ungju in 15 days after it broke out at Sinnyong on September 16. By October 2, the division entered Ch'unch'on, and prepared for future operations there. It was a great joy and coincidence that the division, which had staged delaying actions in Ch'unch'on at the beginning of the war and had been pushed back far down to the Naktong river line, now came back to the city twice as fast as it had been in the withdrawal.

Pursuit Operations from Uisong to Tongduch'on: On September 22, the day when the ROK 8th Division carried Pohyon-san and occupied Kusandong, it was ordered to "launch an unlimited objective attack along the Uisong–Andong–Yongju axis as the supporting effort for the ROK II Corps; immediately after securing Yongju," the order called for the division to "get ready to move north or northwest on order."

The first and foremost mission for the division, therefore, was to recapture Uisong. To accomplish the mission, the division committed, on September 23, its 21st Regiment which had occupied Kusandong to a frontal attack, while maneuvering the 10th Regiment to the north of the town, so that the division could cut off enemy troops in the town. Taking Uisong, the division would attempt to lay siege to Andong and attack against it.

Although they had suffered a crushing defeat in the area of Kusandong, part of the desperate enemy troops had taken up a hill position south of Uisong in an effort to delay the advance of the ROK troops. On September 24, the ROK 21st Regiment attacked this enemy force with all its elements in an assault formation to break through the enemy position from the front. The regiment concentrated all its fire power and thick smoke from the resulting battle covered the area.

At that time, the ROK 10th Regiment made a turning movement from the east of Uisong to capture the high ground north of the town and intercepted the retreating enemy. Then the two South Korean regiments, the 21st and the 10th, pulled tight their encircling net against the enemy both from the front and rear. As the enemy attempted to break out making repeated counterattacks, fierce hand-to-hand fighting took place between both forces. After the battle, the ROK division completely controlled the town, and moved its advanced command post to it from Yongch'on. Enemy prisoners stated that the headquarters of the NKPA II Corps had been located at Uisong, and the corps commander, Gen. Kim Mu Chong, had slipped out of the place. According to them, with his pistol drawn, and with his face turned ashy pale, he had ruthlessly urged his soldiers to fight vigorously several hours before they fled in disorder.[79]

In this battle, the ROK division captured more than a 100-tons of rice and other war materiel, and supplies that might have equipped a division size troop.

After Uisong, the division continued on toward Andong, and reached an area near Andong bridge over the upper stream of the Naktong River on September 25. Five spans in the middle of the 35-span bridge had been destroyed by the enemy the previous day, which delayed the advance of the ROK troops there. Enemy troops had also laid mines in ford areas near the bridge anticipating the ROK troops to wade the river. The enemy attempted to allow the maximum time for his echelons by delaying the attacking ROK force there.

To conquer the difficulties, the ROK division commander immediately requested air strikes on concentrated enemy troops, while his artillery neutralized extensive enemy mine fields. Thus the division succeeded in clearing the river bank of the enemy and securing crossing sites. The first assault wave, the 10th Regiment, rapidly started wading the waist-deep water against sporadic enemy artillery and machine gun fire, and reached the opposite bank. However, they encountered another mine field there. Supporting engineer elements were at once called in to clear the passage, and eventually the regiment secured a bridgehead. The 21st and the 16th Regiments in that order followed the advance elements to wade the river and entered the town of Andong. In the town, they found about 10 enemy tanks destroyed by the friendly air strikes and other numerous vehicles abandoned by enemy troops. Enemy remnants on the run sometimes resisted the attacking columns.

By September 27, the division cleared the outskirts of Andong of enemy stragglers and remnants. Being informed that the NKPA 8th Division which had suffered approximately 4,000 casualties was retreating on toward Yech'on, the ROK division made its 21st Regiment abruptly turn to the right toward Yongju-Tanyang, and take the Chuk-ryong pass so that it could interdict and annihilate the enemy there.

Meanwhile, the ROK 10th and 16th Regiments which had resumed their pursuit that night advanced to reach Yongju by 09:00 the next day. By way of P'unggi, they moved on to reach the Chuk-ryong pass and join the 21st Regiment which had arrived there the previous day.

On September 29, the 10th Regiment took the lead in the division's pursuit to Tanyang and smashed a company sized enemy maneuvering there. Then it stayed there in the town taking all around security, offering protection for the follow-up units, the 21st and 16th Regiments, and at the same time reorganizing itself. At about this time, the division received the ROK Army operation order 199, which called for the division to drive on toward Uijongbu along the axis of Ch'ungju-Wonju-Hoengsong-Yongduri-Yangp'yong-Yangsuri-Suyuri. The Army order, which was a defacto prelimiary attack order for crossing the 38th Parallel, further stated that the division halt at Uijongbu for troop maintenance and reorganization, and on order get ready for future operations.

The division commander planned to move out with his two regiments, the 21st and 10th, as attacking elements and the 16th as the reserve unit. On September 30, the division left Tanyang and reached an area near Silim south of Wonju via Chech'on. The next day it continued on toward Wonju along a rough mountain pass paying particular attention to high ground on either side. When the 21st Regiment reached the ridge of the Silim Pass (also called as the Ch'iac Pass) which was a gateway to Wonju, it encountered a regiment sized enemy force. As the ROK 6th Division, adjacent to the left of the ROK 8th Division, had already entered the city, this enemy force was isolated there attempting to break out. Enemy soldiers desperately resisted to secure time for escaping northward under cover of darkness.

The ROK 8th Division commander, Brig. Gen. Lee Song Ga, reported the situation to the ROK II Corps commander, Maj. Gen. Yu Jae Hung, and suggested a pincer attack against this enemy by the two divisions, his and the 6th from the south and north. However, as his suggestion was ignored, the division commander advanced his division artillery to a point just short of the Silim Pass ridge to provide for a direct fire support for the 21st Regiment which had reached the ridge. There the regiment captured 30 enemy trucks facing north in columns of twos on the mountain road. Together with the 10th Regiment which had closely followed behind, the 21st regiment continued on toward Wonju thoroughly guarding against high grounds on either side of the mountain pass.

Meanwhile, the enemy force which had been pressed hard by the ROK 8th Division even surprised the headquarters of the ROK 6th Division and the II Corps in Wonju on their flight northward.[80]

The ROK 8th Division commander, Brig. Gen. Lee Song Ga, visited the II Corps commander, Maj. Gen. Yu Jae Hung, in his office to tell him the results of the battle of the previous day and to receive an order for future operations. At this time, an argument developed between them on the failure to closely co-ordinate between the ROK 6th and 8th Divisions; particulary on the failure to destroy approximately 2,000 enemy troops which had been in a desperate position at the Silim Pass. The ROK troops had on the contrary been surprised by the enemy at that time. General Lee Song Ga later stated on the dispute as follows:[81]

As the Corps Chief of Staff, Brig. Gen. Lee Han Rim, asked me, 'What caused the delay of the 8th Division at that time?,' I simply retorted, 'Who do you think did not want to make a haste in such a situation? Enemy remnants concentrated in the area of Silim-Wonju had been so desperate. Then who in the world could make a rapid advance against them?' I added asking him, 'We had reported the enemy situation by a radio and requested a pincer attack from south and north at that time. Who did receive that radio message?' The Chief of Staff replied, 'Upon receiving them, we had at once ordered the 6th Division commander, Brig. Gen. Kim Chong Oh, to committ troops to the south of the ridge of the Silim Pass.' But it was later known that the 6th Division had deployed its troops in the high grounds on either side of the pass. They should have placed their troops along the side of the pass or in the open field to easily locate the enemy force, as it was dark at that time. As a result, enemy troops, taking advantage of such a blind spot, could break out of the place and fled northward via Wonju making surprise attacks on both headquarters of the ROK troops.

Even without a moment of rest, on October 2, the ROK 8th Division proceeded from Wonju to Yangp'yong, and overran Yangsuri-Tonong-Miari the following day. Right in Miari, each element of the division took its own assembly area to have a rest and to be reorganized. Then on October 6, the division resumed its pursuit and advanced to Tongduch'on via Uijongbu. There the division was given a passionate welcome by local citizens who had been oppressed for about 100 days under the Communist control. Learning that several anti-Communist guerrilla groups organized by local patriotic youths including a few South Korean stragglers had been active in the town, the division formed a special guerrilla force by recruiting them.[82] Among the self-organized local guerrilla groups, the so-called "Mach'a-san Guerrilla" was well known by the local South Koreans, which had fought in isolation against North Koreans.

During the 15 days of the pursuit operations from September 16 to 30, The ROK 8th Division in full fighting spirit drove up north from Pohyon-san Kusandong, Uisong, Andong, Yongju and Chech'on, defeating and repelling the NKPA 8th Division and the main force of the enemy II Corps. Enemy remnants had escaped northward to the north of Chech'on.

At dawn on October 1, the ROK 8th division entered Wonju, and two days later on October 3, it reached Miari of the capital city, Seoul. By October 16, the division occupied Tongduch'on, a small town just short of the 38th Parallel.

In the meantime, the ROK 7th Division, which had been assembled in Kyongju as a reserve unit for the ROK Army, moved up north toward Munkyong following behind the 6th and 8th Divisions at the end of September. At about this time, the division was released from the ROK Army to be attached to the ROK II Corps(as of September 29) by the Army order 199. Then the division continued on toward Seoul via Suanbo-Ch'ungju-Changhowon. It entered Seoul on October 7, and proceeded to P'och'on the following day to get ready for future operations.

Thus by the end of September, the ROK and the US Army had virtually restored the pre-war situation by recapturing Seoul and driving off enemy troops from South Korean territory below the 38th Parallel after they had made the historic landing at Inch'on and the massive counteroffensive from the Naktong River front.

In the blitzkrieg that had been launched on September 15, and lasted for about two weeks, the North Korean People's Army had practically collapsed through a series of tactics of encirclement and penetration by the ROK and UN Forces. Therefore, the North Korean government by itself was no longer capable of carrying out the war. The NKPA frontline commander and his staff had fled from Kimch'on to the area of socalled "Iron-triangle," and the

NKPA I Corps command had dissolved itself at Choch'iwon. Enemy commanders and part of their staff had slipped into the T'aebaek Mountains. The NKPA II Corps command had escaped to Kimwha above the 38th Parallel, and enemy divisions which had been also liquidated fled northward in dispersion.

Among those committed to the frontline battles, an estimated 25,000 or 30,000 enemy soldiers had broken out the friendly forces' encircling net and escaped to the north across the 38th Parallel. Since the beginning of the war, including 9,294 men captured by the counterattacking troops, a total of 12,777 enemy soldiers had been captured, and the rest who had survived sneaked into the Chiri-san or T'aebaek-san. Enemy troops had abandoned almost all of their vehicles because they had not only been cut off but also had no fuel left to run those vehicles.

Thus the enemy loss in personnel and equipment far outnumbered and was more serious than that which the ROK Army had suffered from the North Korean surprise attack at the beginning of the war. The North Korean Navy and Air Force were also thoroughly destroyed in terms of equipment and base facilities.

Thus far the friendly forces owed their victory over the NKPA to a combination of the following factors: the war leaders' impeccable estimate of the situation and planning, absolute naval and air superiority and the superior mobility of the US Army in the ground battles. The excellent performance of the ROK Army was the more remarkable because it, unlike the US Army, was not mobilized and its soldiers moved on foot through high rugged mountain areas such as the T'aebaek Range and its branches. Despite the shortage of motor vehicles, ROK troops rapidly drove north day and night keeping pace with the Eighth Army. Sometimes they achieved surprises, cut off retreating enemy units, and even encircled and destroyed enemy troops. They had outdistanced the motorized UN forces to reach the 38th Parallel.

In brief, the ROK and UN Forces' Inch'on landing and the counteroffensive from the Naktong front had been, in a manner of speaking, a perfect victory gained by a combined strategy and tactics which had not only practically destroyed the enemy troops but also deprived the enemy of his will to fight. The victory was, in other words, the result of uniformly applied principles of war: surprise, mobility, offensive, objective, mass or concentration, and unified command plus intelligence, creativeness, and morale.

Notes

1) Appleman, *South to the Naktong, North to the Yalu,* p. 488.

2) Ibid., p. 489.

3) The War History Compilation Committee, *Landing Operations at Inch'on,* 1983, pp. 50-53.

4) As of August 1950, the US marine strength stood as follows: Among a total of 74, 279 marines on duty, 27,703 men were with the fleets, 11,087 were on garrison duty, and 1,574 were on board ships. Among the 11,853 fleet marines in the Pacific, 7,779 men belonged to the US 1st Marine Division, and 3,733 were in the 1st Marine Air Wing. Meanwhile, the strength of the US marine fleet in the Atlantic stood at 15, 803 men, and among them 8,973 were on the US 2nd Marine Division, while 5,297 men were with the 2nd Marine Air Wing. The US Marine Corps Headquarters, *The Inch'on-Seoul Operation*(1950-1953), 1955, pp. 20-21.

5) This marked the beginning of the KATUSA system, the Korean Augmentation Troops to the US Army.

6) The War History Compilation Committee, *Landing Operations at Inch'on,* p. 77; Lee Kuk Song, *An Account of the ROK 17th Regimental Role in Recapturing Seoul on September 28,* April 30, 1995.

7) WHCC, tr., *US JCS: History of the Korean War,* vol. 1, 1990, p. 162.

8) Ibid., p. 162.

9) Ibid., p. 163.

10) Appleman, *South to the Naktong, North to the Yalu,* p. 493.

11) The War History Compilation Committee, tr., *US JCS: History of the Korean War,* p. 163.

12) Ibid., pp. 163-164.

13) Ibid., p. 165.

14) Appleman, *South to the Naktong, North to the Yalu,* p. 497.

15) The War History Compilation Committee, *Landing Operations at Inch'on,* p. 107.

16) Ibid., pp. 80-83.

17) Appleman, *South to the Naktong, North to the Yalu,* p. 506.

18) Far East Command Intelligence Department, *The History of the North Korean Army,* 1952, p. 146.

19) *Operation order* of the 5th Battalion, NKPA Unit 884 (August 29, 1950), owned by the Korea Institute of Military History.

20) Appleman, *South to the Naktong, North to the Yalu,* p. 508.

21) FEC, *The History of North Korean Army,* p. 146.

22) The War History Compilation Committe, *The History of Korean War,* vol.3, p. 618.

23) Appleman, *South to the Naktong, North to the Yalu,* p. 500.

24) Ibid., p. 500.

25) Lt. Eugene F. Clark belonged to the US Far East Command. He was sent to Yonghungdo, an islet at the mouth of the ship channel off Inch'on harbor, togather information needed for the Inch'on landing operation. He used friendly natives there, and transmitted reports by radio to friendly vessels in Korean waters from September 1 to 14. At midnight on September 14, he turned on the light at the lighthouse to guide friendly vessels there.

26) WHCC, *Landing Operations at Inch'on,* pp. 165-167.

27) Ibid., pp. 165-167.

28) According to the ROK administrative division, this small village had initially been called Mabunri, Punae-myon, Puch'on county. But on the then current map and literature, it was described as Mahangri because of apparently erroneous pronunciation of the Chinese character "bun" as "hang." The War History Compilation Committee, *Landing Operations at Inch'on,* p. 199.

29) After scientifically analyzing the situation in which the enemy's [the UN Forces] combat capability had been increasing, Comrade Kim Il Sung ordered the West Coast Defense Command to strengthen its defense capability in the Inch'on-Seoul

area…. Accordingly, part of the NKPA troops which had been committed to the Naktong river front, tank units in the areas of Namp'o, Munch'on, and Haeju, the NKPA reserve units which had been deployed in depth in the rear, and combined NKPA forces in the Ch'orwon and Kumch'on area were all mobilized to be dispatched to Seoul. Research Institute of History, N.K., *Comprehensive History of Choson,* vol.25, (North Korean Encyclopedia Publishing Company, 1981), p. 26.

30) The War History Compilation Committe, *Landing Operations at Inch'on,* p. 220.

31) Ibid., p. 219; A captured NKPA *military map* (September 21, 1950). This map owned by the Korea Institute of Military History reveals the NKPA 107th Security unit's plan for the defense at Kimp'o. The 3rd Battalion of the ROK marine corps had captured this map on September 21, 1950 when it surprised the command post of the enemy 107th Regiment at Kimpo, and the then battalion commander presented it to the War History Compilation Committee on October 31, 1980.

32) WHCC, *Landing Operations at Inch'on,* p. 220.

33) Ibid., p. 211.

34) The reasons that the battalion's right flank was exposed to the enemy could be summarized as follows: the US 7th Infantry Division which had been in charge of the southern area of the Seoul-Inch'on highway made a delayed attack at that time after marines started their advance; the division made its attack in the axis of Inch'on-Anyang which leaned to the south; as a result, they could not make a coordinated attack against the enemy. The War History Compilation Committee, *Landing Operations at Inch'on,* pp. 250-259.

35) The US Far East Command Intelligence Department, *The Order of Battle of the North Korean Army,* October 15, 1950, p. 157; The War History Compilation Committee, *The History of Korean War,* vol. 3, p. 745.

36) The US Far East Command Intelligence Department, *The Order of Battle of the North Korean Army.* The regimental commander was Col. Park Han Rin, and the regimental organization and strength were very similar to those of the enemy 25th Brigade.

37) The War History Compilation Committee, *Landing Operations at Inch'on*, pp. 325-326.

38) Ibid., pp. 315-317.

39) The ROK National Assembly opened its office in the Central Government building on May 31, 1948 and remained there until Jun. 27, 1950. The Research Institute for Korean Culture and Mind, *Encyclopedia of Korean Culture*, vol. 3, 1989, p. 779.

40) Franchesca's Memoir, "The Korean War and President Syngman Rhee," The JoongAng Ilbo, August 8, 1988; The War History Compilation Committee, *Landing Operations at Inch'on*, p. 335.

41) Appleman, *South to the Naktong, North to the Yalu*, p. 537.

42) Ibid., pp. 545-546.

43) The US Far East Command, *Interrogation Report* on Maj. Son Tae Kwang, September 19, 1950.

44) Appleman, *South to the Naktong, North to the Yalu*, p. 547.

45) Eighth US Army *Operation Order* 10 (September 11, 1950). This document is owned by the Korea Institute of Military History; The War History Compilation Committee, *The History of Korean War*, vol. 4, pp. 22-23.

46) Korea Broadcasting System, a *documentary paper, entitled, "Korean War"* I, 1991, pp. 288-291. Lee Hak Ku surrendered, on September 21, 1950, to the US 1st Cavalry Division. He was sent to Japan to be interrogated, and then impounded in the Koje prisoner's camp. He was the ranking North Korean prisoner at the time and remained so throughout the war. But he was not treated as a defector; later he became a notorious leader of the Communist prisoners, leading the prisoners' riots in the camp. After the war, he was repatriated to North Korea only to be purged by the Communists.

47) Appleman, *South to the Naktong, North to the Yalu*, p. 545.

48) ROK Army *Operation Order* 180 (September 30, 1950).

49) The War History Compilation Committee, *The History of Korean War*, vol. 4, p. 54.

50) Ibid., p. 82.

51) *A Written Testimony* by Ham Pyong Sun (Seoul: Overseas Development Corporations of Korea, 1968), owned by the Korea Institute of Military History.

52) The War History Compilation Committee, *Sinnyong-Yongch'on Battle*, p. 339; the NKPA 73rd Regiment was not organic to the 15th Division; it was rather believed to have been attached to the division as a newly activated, independent unit. The US Far East Command Intelligence Department, *the Order of Battle of the North Korean Army*, as of October 15, 1950.

53) Research Institute of History, North Korea, *Comprehensive History of Choson*, vol. 26, p. 44; Appleman, *South to the Naktong, North to the Yalu*, p. 572; the War History Compilation Committee, *The History of Korean War*, vol. 4, pp. 10-11.

54) Appleman, *South to the Naktong, North to the Yalu*, pp. 590-591; the War History Compilation Committee, *The History of Korean War*, vol. 4, p. 209.

55) Task Force 777 was actually a regimental combat team. Each digit of the number represented one of the three principal elements of the force: the 7th Cavalry Regiment, and its two attached units, the 77th Field Artillery, and the 70th Tank Battalions. But Task Force Lynch was named after the 3rd Battalion commander, Lt. Col. Lynch.

56) Appleman, *South to the Naktong, North to the Yalu*, p. 595.

57) Ibid., p.887.

58) The War History Compilation Committee, *The History of Korean War*, vol. 4, p. 158.

59) Ibid., p. 159.

60) Ibid., p. 166.

61) Appleman, *South to the Naktong, North to the Yalu*, p. 580.

62) Ibid., p. 580.

63) The War History Compilation Committee, *The History of Korean War*, vol. 4, p. 242.

64) Appleman, *South to the Naktong, North to the Yalu*, p. 574; This unit was called Task Force Torman after Capt. Charles J. Torman, commander of the division Reconnaissance Company.

65) Appleman, *South to the Naktong, North to the Yalu*, p. 575.

66) Ibid., p. 576; Task Force Matthews was under command of Capt. Charles M. Matthews, commander of A Company of the US 79th Tank Battalion. It comprised an engineer platoon, a medical section, and a tactical air control party, all centered about the Tank and division Reconnaissance Companies. Matthews replaced Torman in command of the latter's task force after Torman had been wounded and evacuated.

67) Appleman, *South to the Naktong, North to the Yalu,* p. 578; Task Force Dolvin, under command of Lt. Col. Dolvin, commander of the US 89th Tank Battalion, consisted of two tank companies, two infantry companies, a heavy mortar platoon, an engineer platoon, a medical detachment, and Task Force trains.

68) Appleman, *South to the Naktong, North to the Yalu,* pp. 576-577.

69) The War History Compilation Committee, *The History of Korean War,* vol. 4, pp. 57-58.

70) Appleman, *South to the Naktong, North to the Yalu,* p. 599.

71) The War History Compilation Committee, *The History of Korean War,* vol. 4, p. 65.

72) The ROK Army *Operation Order* 191(September 22, 1950).

73) The War History Compilation Committee, *The History of Korean War,* vol. 4, p. 86.

74) Ibid., p. 87.

75) Ibid., p. 89.

76) Ibid., p. 90.

77) The ROK Army *Operation Order* 199 (September 30, 1950). This was a preliminary order for breaking through the 38th Parallel.

78) Appleman, *South to the Naktong, North to the Yalu,* p. 599.

79) The War History Compilation Committee, *The History of Korean War,* vol. 4, p. 104.

80) Ibid., p. 135.

81) *Testimony* by Gen. Lee Song Ga, March 3, 1965, the Korea Institute of Military History.

82) The War History Compilation Committee, *The History of Korean War,* vol. 4, p. 116.

Chapter Six   March North for the Reunification

I. Controversy on Crossing the 38th Parallel and the United Nations' Resolution

1. The Military Strategic Decision on the Crossing of the Line

As soon as the ROK and UN Forces, which had succeeded in recapturing Seoul after the Inch'on landing and in breaking out from the Naktong front, approached the 38th Parallel, the question whether they should cross the line became a most difficult policy issue.

In other words, outstanding questions at high levels at that time centered on whether the ROK and UN Forces should be allowed to cross the line to annihilate the retreating North Korean Armed Forces, and, if they succeeded, what about the reunification of Korea? The question of crossing the line became the more difficult one as it could cause a possible Chinese or Soviet intervention. Therefore, the decision that would be made on these questions was to be directly related to the destiny of not only the war but also the Korean nation as a whole.

The ROK and US Governments had begun to discuss this matter from mid July, when such political issues could not be at stake as, at that time, the ROK and UN Forces were staging delaying actions in the withdrawal to Taejon. Upon President Truman's demand "to present strategic alternatives to be executed in case the North Koreans withdrew north across the 38th Parallel," the US National Security Council had begun to review the questions. Meanwhile,

President Syngman Rhee expressed his adamant will to cross the line in his letter to President Truman, dated July 19. In this letter, he wrote, "Now that the North Korean government which had been established by the Soviets unlawfully invaded the South across the line by force, there is no reason that we should respect such line as the 38th Parallel. Accordingly, we would never tolerate only pre-war conditions to be restored."[1]

Based on the instructions and requests from the presidents of both nations, revised political directives for the UN Forces in Korea were prepared and made public on August 18 by Warren R. Austin, the US ambassador to the United Nations. In his speech, Ambassador Austin told diplomatic circles, in effect, that the UN Security Council had decided to finally terminate hostilities and maintain peace on the Korean peninsula as its utmost goal, and this goal should be pursued such a way that the UN would never tolerate any attempt for aggression in the future.[2] He further mentioned that even though the North Korean government had rejected the UN resolution on the establishment of a unified Korean government through a fair and free election, the resolution still remained valid.[3] His speech was, as it were, a suggestive expression of a policy that the US government would support the UN resolution with conditions attached that North Koreans should admit their defeat, and at the same time, cease hostile activities.

Later, on September 1, President Truman clarified this position in his political statement referring to the Korean question. He mentioned he firmly believed that the Korean people held their right to be as free and independent as they cherished, and likewise held the right to reunify their country. He added that the United States would do her share in this effort to help the Koreans to enjoy their rights under the United Nations' guidance. In a press conference, he also mentioned that the decision to cross the 38th Parallel with UN Forces rested with the UN.[4] His words could be interpreted as having suggested a new

American policy direction in solving the Korean question, specifically that the UN Forces' crossing of the 38th Parallel and subsequent reunification of Korea was within the prerogatives of the United Nations. At the beginning of the war, the United States had initially set the goal at restoring the pre-war conditions.

At about this time, the UN Forces enjoyed bright prospects from the Inch'on landing and the general counteroffensive at the Naktong front. These had succeeded in repelling the NKPA's massive offensive at the river front and, at the same time, had secured relative superiority over the enemy in terms of combat capability. Supported by the statements and speeches of leaders and ranking officials of the ROK and US, the war situation raised the pros and cons on the UN Forces' crossing of the 38th Parallel in the United States and other democracies as well. The Communist camp, however, stoutly opposed it. Supporters in the friendly camp insisted that should the ROK and UN Forces discontinue their pursuit at the 38th Parallel, the dismantled NKPA would reorganize itself to reinvade the South. Then, the hostililties on the peninsula would be repeated, which would require a long-term stay of the UN Forces there. They also argued that stopping at the 38th line would not only run counter to the spirit of the universally admitted rights for the pursuit, but also be unreasonable if they were restricted to only ground attacks while air strikes were still going on in the North Korean zone. Others who did not agree on these arguments pointed out that the crossing of the 38th Parallel might invite the Chinese and Soviet intervention which would, in turn, lead to another world war.

The official United States position on these questions—that the UN Forces should continue its military activites beyond the 38th Parallel so that a unified, independent Korean government could be established on the peninsula, thus respecting the spirit of the UN resolution—was explicitly stated by Dean G. Acheson, the State Secretary on September 20, in his keynote address at the UN General Assembly.[5] Thus the opinion of the friendly camp began to converge into a supporting argument.

Meanwhile, On the opportunity of the speech delivered by US ambassador to the UN Warren R. Austin, the Chinese Communists who had thus far focused on the Taiwan question, took a new attitude toward the Korean War. Chou En-lai, the Chinese Communist Foreign Minister, sent a radio message to the UN on August 20 requesting the attendance of Chinese representatives at the meeting to discuss the Korean question.[6] Later, on September 25, a proxy of the Chief of Staff, Chinese Communist Forces, directly warned K.M. Panikkar, India's Ambassador to Communist China, that "Chinese people will not tolerate the US Forces' crossing of the 38th Parallel."[7]

Prior to this, on August 1, taking a pessimistic view of the war which had not progressed as they had planned, the Soviet representative, Jacob A. Malik, insisted that the Korean War be concluded as early as possible because it was a civil war between the North and South. At that time, he had returned to the UN Security Council after a long absence. Warning, on August 22, that if the war continued for long, it would inevitably escalate,[8] he attempted to throttle discussion on the UN Forces' crossing of the 38th Parallel in advance. Later, on September 21, Soviet Foreign Minister Andrei Y. Vyshinsky proposed in the UN General Assembly a so-called "declaration of peace"[9] with the purpose of establishing a ceasefire on the 38th Parallel. It was also construed as the Communist side's attempt to block the UN crossing of the line.

In the meantime, as the war situation took a favorable turn, the ROK Government, which had in mid-July intimated to President Truman that it intended to cross the line, declared its intent to the world. Upon receiving the news of the UN landing at Inch'on on September 15, the South Korean people held a national rally in Pusan, the provisional capital city of the ROK, to expedite the reunification of Korea. At this rally they adopted a resolution to be sent to the General Secretary of the United Nations expressing their long cherished wish for a unified Korea, which had yet to be realized despite the endeavours both the Republic of Korea and United Nations. At the same time, the South Korean people argued that a peaceful reunification was thwarted by the Communists' invasion of the South. Thus, on behalf of all 30 million Koreans, they earnestly requested the UN Forces to rapidly cross the line to realize their wish.[10]

On September 20, South Korean President Syngman Rhee justifiably reiterated his conviction on the need for the reunification by crossing the 38th Parallel. In his speech, delivered at a mass rally on September 20, to celebrate the UN Inch'on landing, he said:

> We know that there have been so many men with so much talk in the world about the 38th Parallel; I think, however, theirs' are idle thoughts. Our fundamental policy goal has lain in reunifying both the South and the North, and will remain so in the future ⋯. The Soviets' interference with the Korean question, and their support for the North Koreans' invasion into the democratic government in the South have been intended to subjugate the democratic society to their rule. To hold this sinister design in check, the United Nations Forces came to Korea and has been fighting against the Communist forces in close coordination with our Army. Therefore, I think we should neither halt at the 38th Parallel, nor cease this fighting. We should continue this fight against Communists pressing them hard across the line until we could mop them up at the Yalu and Tumen River line. By so doing, we will shatter the so-called "Iron Curtain."[11]

Thus the sharply divided opinions between the parties concerned persisted, while the United States concluded in her policy draft(NSC 81) that the June 28 UN resolution had provided for a legal basis for military operations beyond the 38th Parallel to repel or destroy the North Korean Armed Forces. This policy plan had been mapped out on September 1, the day when President Truman delivered an administrative policy speech. According to this policy plan, the United States should authorize the UN Forces Commander to conduct military operations for that purpose north of the 38th Parallel, provided that there was no major Soviet or Chinese Communist Forces entry into North Korea, or announced intention to enter, in order to counter UN military operations there. If he were placed in such circumstances—the intervention of Chinese or Soviet Forces—General MacArthur would halt his troops at the 38th Parallel and wait for the UN Security Council's reaction to the matter.[2] In brief, the US government had decided to direct "march north" operations in order for executing the legitimate June 28 UN resolution.

This policy draft went through a consultation process with the US State and Defense Departments, chiefly with the Joint Chiefs of Staff, and was finally approved by President Truman on September 11. It was then settled as the policy for the UN Forces' military operations(NSC 81/1). Pursuant to this policy, the US JCS, on September 15, sent to General MacArthur a comprehensive directive to govern his future actions: the commander of the United Nations Forces possesses a legal right for military operations north of the 38th Parallel, but he should avoid involvement with the Soviet or Chinese Communist Forces.[3] The JCS, at the same time, began to prepare details for its directives and obtained the presidential approval for them. Thus the military operational directives, related to the UN Forces' crossing of the 38th Parallel and military operations north of the line, later known as the "September 27 Directives," were finalized. The purport of the directives were as follows:

> Your military objective is the destruction of the North Korean Armed Forces. In attaining this objective you are authorized to conduct military operations, including amphibious and airborne landings or ground oper-

ations north of the 38th Parallel in Korea, provided that at the time of such operation there has been no entry into North Korea by major Soviet or Chinese Communist Forces, no announcement of intended entry, nor a threat to counter our operations militarily in North Korea. Under no circumstances, however, will your forces cross the Manchurian or USSR borders of Korea and, as a matter of policy, no non-Korean Ground Forces will be used in the northeast provinces bordering the Soviet Union or in the area along the Manchurian border. Furthermore, support of your operations north or south of the 38th Parallel will not include Air or Naval action against Manchuria or against USSR territory.

In the event of the open or covert employment of major Soviet units south of the 38th Parallel, you will assume the defense, make no move to aggravate the situation and report to Washington. You should take the same action in the event your forces are operating north of the 38th Parallel, and major Soviet units are openly employed.···

In the event of the open or covert employment of major Chinese Communist units south of the 38th Parallel, you should continue the action as long as action by your forces offers a reasonable chance of successful resistance···

When organized armed resistance by North Korean forces has been brought subtantially to an end, you should direct the ROK forces to take the lead in disarming remaining North Korean units and enforcing the terms of surrender.···

Although the Government of the Republic of Korea has been generally recognized (except by the Soviet bloc) as the only legal government in Korea, its sovereignty north of the 38th Parallel has not been generally recognized. The Republic of Korea and its Armed Forces should be expected to cooperate in such military operations and military occupation as are conducted by United Nations forces north of the 38th Parallel, but political questions such as the formal extension of sovereignty over North Korea should await action by the United Nations to complete the unification of the country.[4]

The "Directives of September 27" clearly provided the UN Forces with an operational guideline, by permitting it to cross the 38th Parallel, but strictly restricting its mission to the destruction of the North Korean Armed Forces, that is, to the military target. The directives especially cautioned the UN Forces against possible engagement with Soviet or Chinese Communist forces. The process through which the directives had been mapped out clearly revealed the reorientation of US policy and military strategy on the Korean question, and it appeared clear that such changes had been made by the war situation on the Korean peninsula at that time.

General MacArthur, while making his own plan to proceed north of the 38th Parallel based on the directives, put his demand on the air on October 1 to the effect that the Commander in Chief of the North Korean forces should surrender. In this radio message, he called upon the North Koreans to lay down their arms and cease hostilities to prevent unnecessary bloodshed and destruction of property. He said:

It may be inevitable that your armed forces and its potential combat capability will soon completely be defeated and destroyed. Since the UN resolution might be carried out with a minimum of further loss of life and destruction of property ···, I demand that you and the armed forces under your command lay down arms and cease hostilities under such military supervision as I might direct in whatever part of Korea they may be located. I also demand that you immediately liberate all of the UN prisoners of war and non-combatant internees under your command ··· to be transported to the places I might designate. North Korean people including prisoners of war will be continuously protected by the UN Forces command, but will be liberated as early as possible ··· to be repatriated.

I hereby harbor expectations ··· that you would decide on these matters as quickly as possible in order that you prevent unnecessary bloodshed and destruction of property in the future.[15]

2. The October 7 UN Resolution on the Reunification of Korea

Closely watching the development of the war situation, the United States had with utmost secrecy prepared the "September 27 Directives" and "March North" operations. At the same time, concluding that the UN Forces' occupation of North Korea and the resulting matter of reunifying the country would require a political solution, the United States tried to isolate such political questions from its military strategic goal and work out the problem within the limit of the UN For this purpose, if North Korean armed forces crumbled and the Soviet and Chinese Communist forces did not enter the war, the United States planned to let General MacArthur occupy North Korea in the name of the United Nations. The US would also let the ROK troops and those from other Asian member nations of the UN occupy important areas of North Korea. Thus the United States would minimize its intervention in the war and pull its troops back as early as possible. The United States prepared a draft recommendation to be presented to the UN after consultation with South Korea and other friendly nations. This recommendation would establish United Nations organizations to deal with such matters as relief, rehabilitation, reunification, and the security of Korea,[16] all of which would be confronted with after the UN occupation of North Korea.

On September 30, this draft was introduced by the British delegate on the agenda of the 5th UN General Assembly. It was presented on the joint motion of eight nations[17] including the Philippines, but the United States was not included at that time. Since the Korea-related draft resolution which had once been prepared and presented to the UN Security Council at the instance of the United States had been rejected by a Russian veto, this time it was laid before the General Assembly. Even though the British Government had endorsed the

Chinese Communist Government, it took sides with the UN Forces on the crossing of the 38th Parallel and participated in the joint motion of the eight nations.

Opposing this proposal, on October 2, the Soviet Foreign Minister Vyshinsky made a counterproposal calling for an immediate cease fire in Korea, the withdrawal of all foreign troops, a general election for the Korean National Assembly, and establishment of a South and North Joint Administrative Committee which consisted of equivalent numbers of delegates.[18] That day, the Chinese Communist Foreign Minister, Chou En-lai definitely told K.M. Panikkar, India's Ambassador to Peking, that China would enter the war if the UN Forces crossed the Parallel, but would not intervene if ROK Forces only attacked across the line.[19] Thus, prior to the balloting at the UN General Assembly on the resolution which was to influence the future of Korea, opposition and backlash from the Communist camp reached a climax.

At that time, South Korea had neither a deputation, nor a voice in the matter as it was a non-member nation. Nevertheless, it sent a diplomatic mission consisting of Lim Pyong Jik, Foreign Minister, Chang Myon, ROK Ambassador to the US, and other officials to the United Nations. This mission was actively engaged in persuading international delegates to support President Syngman Rhee's diplomatic goals at the UN: (1) The UN Forces should cross the Parallel; (2) The Republic of Korea is the only legitimate government on the Korean Peninsula; (3) A general election should be enforced after the UN Forces' crossing of the Parallel under UN supervision; (4) The ROK is strongly opposed to placing the area north of the Parallel under a UN trusteeship; (5) The ROK has no objection to the UN Forces' provisional stationing in Korea. When the UN draft resolution was laid before the UN General Assembly, the ROK diplomatic mission was especially active in persuading delegates from UN member nations. It asserted that so long as the UN resolution, which had been adopted in 1947, had set the goal of establishing a unified, independent

Korean government, it was time for the UN to carry out its original objective. Numerous nations gave approval to it.[20]

After a week-long deliberation on drafts presented by the British and the Soviet delegates, only the one proposed by the former was put to a vote at the UN General Assembly. On October 7, the bill was passed by a vote of 47 to 5, with 7 abstentions and 1 absence. In this resolution, the UN General Assembly reminded the international society of its fundamental objective for establishing a unified, and independent democratic government on the Korean peninsula. For this purpose, it encouraged the following programs and procedures:

General Assembly
1. Recommends that
    (a) All appropriate steps be taken to ensure conditions of stability throughout Korea.
    (b) All constituent acts be taken, including the holding of elections, under the auspices of the United Nations for the establishment of a unified, independent and democratic Government in the sovereign State of Korea,
    (c) All sections and representative bodies of the population of Korea, South and North, be invited to co-operate with the organs of the United Nations in the restoration of peace, in the holding of elections and in the establishment of a unified Government,
    (d) United Nations forces should not remain in any part of Korea otherwise than so far as necessary for achieving the objectives specified at (a) and (b) above,
    (e) All necessary measures be taken to accomplish the economic rehabilitation of Korea;
2. Resolves that
    (a) A Commission consisting of Australia, Chile, Netherlands, Pakistan, Philippines, Thailand and Turkey, to be known as the United Nations Commission for the Unification and Rehabilitation of

Korea be established to (i) assume the functions hitherto exercised by the present United Nations Commission in Koera, (ii) represent the United Nations in bringing about the establishment of a unified, independent and democratic Government of all Korea, (iii) exercise such responsibilities in connexion with relief and rehabilitation in Korea as may be determined by the General Assembly after receiving the recommendations of the Economic and Social Council...

3. Requests the Economic and Social Council, in consultation with the specialized agencies, to develop plans for relief and rehabilitation on the termination of hostilities and to report to the General Assembly within three weeks of the adoption of this resolution by the General Assembly;

4. Also recommends the Economic and Social Counicl to expedite the study of long-term measures to promote the economic development and social progress of Korea and meanwhile to draw the attention of the authorities which decide requests for technical assistance to the urgent and special necessity of affording such assistance to Korea;

The above is the gist of the later "October 7 Resolution on the Korean Unification." This UN resolution appeared to reflect, like the "September 27 Directives," the logic of a situation at that time in which the North Korean combat capability had virtually been destroyed. The UN Forces were almost sure to clinch the final victory over the NKPA. The October 7 UN resolution was, therefore, significant in that the United Nations, together with the United States, had drawn up a determined policy plan to realize the Korean dream of reunification under its initiative and in line with its military victory.[22]

However, the ROK Government raised an objection to the "October 7 Resolution" through Foreign Minister Lim Pyong Jik. It took the position that it partly welcomed the idea of enforcing the general election in North Korea, but strongly opposed enforcing a new election in the South.[23] According to them, the ROK Government, which had been established through the general election under supervision of the UN, and acknowledged by the international organization as the only legitimate government, would not repeat the identical process again.

Anyway, the US Joint Chiefs of Staff, informing General MacArthur of the "October 7 UN Resolution," added that the United States Government considered it as a support for military operations north of the Parallel.

Thus the UN Forces could secure both the military objective and political aim in Korea: the destruction of the North Korean Armed Forces north of the Parallel and the policy decision reflected in the UN resolution on the Korean unification.

Although the UN Forces could proceed north of the 38th Parallel based on the "September 27 Directives," it had been withholding military actions until the passage of the additional UN action, the "October 7 Resolution." The apparent reason for this was to allow the United States to obtain legal authority for the "September 27 Directives," and, to be more exact, to provide the United States a political safety valve—i.e. it was trying to accomplish the mission enjoined by the UN resolution and not to pursue its own interest in a unified Korea —which could be used in the possible contingency of intervention of Soviet or Chinese Communist Forces.

On October 9, the Commander of the UN Forces addressed and dropped leaflets with the gist of the "October 7 UN Resolution," to the Commander in Chief of the North Korean forces. At the same time, the former issued an ultimatum calling upon the North Koreans to lay down their arms and cease hostilities. This completed the required tactical and strategic procedures and preparations for the UN Forces to proceed north of the 38th Parallel.

3. Decision on the Crossing of the 38th Parallel by the ROK

By the end of September, the UN Forces had covertly prepared for the crossing of the Parallel based on the "September 27 Directives," while it overtly forwarded a scheme for the passage of the October UN resolution. By that time, however, the ROK Government and its forces had neither been notified of the "September 27 Directives," nor received any order for the "march north" operations. They became impatient. It was later known that General MacArthur and US Ambassador to the ROK John J. Muccio, who had been very cautious not to stimulate the Soviet and Chinese Communists, did not inform President Syngman Rhee of the facts and planned to carry out covert military operations north of the Parallel.[24]

After attending the ceremony held at the Central Government House at noon on September 29 in celebration of the returning of the Government to Seoul, President Syngman Rhee met with General MacArthur to talk about the work in hand. At this meeting, the former assumed a grave look and insisted upon his favorite subject, the "march north without delay." The latter immediately declared himself against it on the ground that the United Nations had not authorized him to do that. The President reassuringly responded to him asking, "You may wait until the UN decides on this matter, but who do you think can hold the ROK forces in check in case it crosses the 38th Parallel?" The President added, "This country is theirs. Even if I did not order them to do, they may cross the border and proceed toward the north."[25]

President Syngman Rhee tried to resolutely communicate his will to the General that his forces would independently push northward across the parallel if no action should immediately be taken by the UN Forces. The President apparently thought that this was the way to meet the wishes of his people for reunifying their country at that time. For this purpose, not only the President himself, but also his government and the ROK National Assembly had already affirmed this idea before the world several times. He had been positive that the right to make the decision on the crossing of the Parallel belonged to the authority of the only legitimate Republic of Korea.

On that day, however, it was reported that General Walker had informed reporters of his plan that the Eighth Army would halt at the Parallel to wait for further orders(to cross the line), and at the same time, to reorganize itself.[26] It enraged the President, and to be more exact, it disheartened both the soldiers and people of South Korea.

While the matter of crossing the Parallel had bred discord in terms of political tactics between the enemy and friendly camps, and even between the ROK and the US, on the frontline, ROK troops continued their pursuit operations. The ROK 3rd Division proceeded to Kangnung on September 29, and the ROK Capital Division advanced to Taewha that day. In the meantime, the ROK 6th and 8th Divisions recaptured Ch'ungju and Tanyang, respectively. Thus they all reached points a day's distance from the 38th Parallel.

President Rhee concluded that the political matter should not delay the ROK forces, and visited the ROK Army Headquarters at Taegu at two o'clock that day afternoon. As the president of an independent country, and at the same time, as the Supreme Commander of the ROK Armed Forces, he wanted to exercise his sovereign power and the prerogative of supreme command. He convened an urgent meeting of the ranking military officials there.[27] General Chung Il Kwon, the Joint Army, Naval, and Air Force Commander and other ranking staff officers attended the meeting. The President asked a rhetorical question to them, "Who do you think is the Commander in Chief of the ROK Armed Forces? General MacArthur or the President of this nation?" Then he added, "I think the UN Forces should not hold the ROK forces from crossing the 38th Parallel and check our efforts to reunify the country. I therefore would like for our forces to proceed north of the Parallel. What do you think?" In response to his question, General Chung said, "It's a complicated matter. The right of command and operational control for the ROK forces had already been transferred to the Commander of the UN Forces effective as of the date you signed the documents in the past. If you should order us to cross the Parallel, I fear that it would lead to confusion. Concerning the UN Forces' crossing of the Parallel, we should rather wait for the UN decision which will be made in time. But I am talking about the matter related only to the channel of command; if you make a firm resolution looking upon it from international politics or grand national strategies, and order us to do so, we are ready to comply with it." As the other staff officers agreed with their commanding officer, the President took out a written order from his bosom pocket and handed it over to General Chung saying, "proceed." The order read, "I am the Commander in Chief [of the ROK Armed Forces], so I order you to procced northward." It carried his signature of "(man)," which was part of his first name, "Syngman" in Chinese character, on the bottom.

As things were getting serious, General Chung Il Kwon, determined to proceed north of the Parallel, tried to discuss the matter with the Commander of the 8th US Army. In order first to request the authority for him to cross the Parallel, General Chung thought that he should secure well-grounded reasons. So he maintained radio contact with Brig. Gen. Kim Paik Il, commander of the ROK I Corps which had already advanced to Kangnung, and asked if the latter had had in mind a critical terrain north of the Parallel, which would threaten the advance of his troops should it not be captured in advance. After a while, General Chung received a telegraphic reply from the Corps commander to the effect that the latter had been concerned about an area, Kisamunri, just north of the Parallel and in front of his 3rd Division.

Upon receiving the report, General Chung at once visited the Eighth Army Commander to tell him that the ROK 3rd Division would suffer serious losses by fierce enemy fire from a position just north of the Parallel, and in order to eliminate the enemy threat, he would inevitably make his troops to attack and secure the position. He stated a reason that there was neither a clear-cut geometrical line drawn, nor a barrier set up along the 38th Parallel; so he would brave it out. General Walker readily consented to it.

Thus on September 30, General Chung Il Kwon visited the ROK I Corps Headquarters at Kangnung and made an inspection tour of the frontline positions of the 23rd Regiment, the ROK 3rd Division. He verbally ordered the I Corps Commander to proceed north of the Parallel. This verbal order was later issued in a written form entitled as the ROK I Corps operation order 103, and in turn the ROK 3rd Division operation order 44.[28] This was the first of its kind, and the ROK troops were to make the historic crossing of the Parallel accordingly, on October 1, 1950.

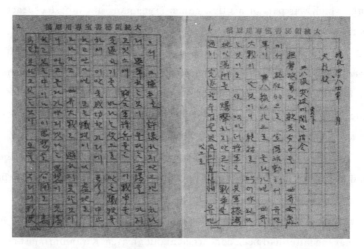

President Syngman Rhee's Handwritten Order for Crossing the 38th Parallel

Thus the decision on the crossing of the 38th Parallel on October 1 had been initiated by President Syngman Rhee's determination and his order, and General Chung Il Kwon, Commander of the ROK Armed Forces, dealt with the complicated matter properly. Gen. Chung had removed possible friction between the ROK and US through a well-timed coordination, leading the ROK troops to first cross the Parallel. The ROK forces' crossing of the line was immediately backed up by the United Nations Command Operations Order 2, which was issued the following day. The UN troops rushed into "march north" operations only after the October 7 UN Resolution was announced.

II. The Capture of Wonsan-P'yongyang

1. Operation Plans of Both Forces

(1) The NKPA's Defensive Plan at the 38th Parallel

After the ROK and UN Forces' Inch'on landing and recapture of Seoul, and the Eighth US Army's successful breakout from the Naktong River front, the North Korean army continuously took to flight. By the end of September, about 25,000-30,000 extremely exhausted North Korean soldiers fled north across the Parallel without any combat potential, and another 30,000 men, having been intercepted their retreat, sneaked into the high mountain ranges of Chiri-san, Sobaek-san, and T'aebaek-san. These enemy remnants waged guerilla warfare or attempted to escape to the north across the Parallel.

In order to establish a new defensive line along the 38th Parallel, the NKPA High Command divided the line into two parts, the western and the eastern sectors. The defensive sectors were assigned to Choi Yong Gun(Defense Minister) and Kim Chaek(Vice Premier and Minister of Industry), respectively.

The NKPA West Coast Defense Command comprised newly organized infantry divisions such as the 19th, 27th, and 43rd, and one armored division, the 17th. They were all deployed along the area of Paech'on-Kaesong-Korangp'o -Samich'on,[29] and their missions were to check the advance of the UN troops and at the same time protect NKPA stragglers and remnants retreating northward from the western front, with all available means.

Likewise, in the eastern sector which extended from Sami-ch'on to the east coast, the NKPA troops under the Frontline Commander Kim Chaek took defensive positions along the 38th Parallel. These enemy troops included the NKPA 5th, 12th, and 15th Divisions which had withdrawn from the Naktong River front[30] and other reserve units in the enemy rear. A North Korean book entitled 'Comprehensive History of Choson' described the NKPA defensive measures at that time as follows: [31]

> The West Coast Defense Command concentrated all available troops such as coast guards, tank units, garrisons, security units and reserve units which had already been deployed along the 38th Parallel on the axis of Kaesong-Namch'on(P'yongsan). They took charge of the defense that included the land area from the estuary of the Yesong River to Sami-ch'on(Changp'ung and Yonch'on), and the west coastal area from Namp'o to the mouth of the Yesong. The Frontline Command consisted of Seoul garrison units which had moved to the 38th border line, reserve units which had been deployed on the eastern front, and part of the divisions which had maneuvered back to the north from the Naktong River front. These troops were all enjoined to defend the eastern sector with special emphasis on the roads between Uijongbu and Ch'orwon, P'och'on and Kimwha, and Ch'unch'on and Whach'on.

However, these remnant NKPA troops had been torn asunder and were left without even the will to fight. As all their supply lines had generally been cut, there seemed no hope of success in their effort to defend the Parallel unless they secure support from other countries.

(2) The "March North" Plan of the ROK and UN Forces

Based on the "September 27 Directives," General MacArthur had authority from the US Joint Chiefs of Staff to cross the 38th Parallel for the destruction of the North Korean Armed Forces. On October 2, he issued an order to advance into North Korea, which reflected plans he had formulated in his mind for the next phase of Korean operations. Followings are the gists of the United Nations Command Operations Order 2: [32]

① As the main attack effort, the 8th US Army will cross the 38th Parallel, and attack northward along the axis of Kaesong-Sariwon-P'yongyang.

② The US X Corps will land at Wonsan, port city on the east coast, within a week after the main attack troops launched their attack. The X Corps will secure a beachhead there and to proceed northwest along the axis of Wonsan-P'yongyang to link up with Eighth Army, and thus to interdict and encircle enemy troops.

③ The UN Forces will halt at a line along Chongju-Kunuri-Yongwon-Hamhung-Hungnam, and the ROK troops will assume full responsibility of military operations north of that line.

The initial United Nations Command's operations plan had not placed the X Corps under Eighth Army command. It proposed that while Eighth Army crossed the 38th Parallel on the west to capture P'yongyang, the US X Corps would move from the west to east by water for an amphibious landing at Wonsan. Then the two commands would form a joint front in and along the most narrow P'yongyang-Wonsan corridor in North Korea to cut off the retreating NKPA troops there. They would move on north until they would reach the so-called "MacArthur Line" which connected Chongju with Hamhung. They were to halt at this line, and the ROK forces were to take charge of further operations beyond that line toward the Manchurian and Soviet borders. The MacArthur Line which set limits to the further advance of the UN troops lay laterally 90-170 kilometers south of the Yalu River along 39° 40′-50′ North Latitude.

　　　Although General Walker, commander of the Eighth US Army, felt that the X Corps should become part of Eighth Army and that all UN Forces in Korea should operate under a unified field command, General MacArthur de-

〈Table 1〉　Organization of the UN Forces for Operations North of the 38th Parallel

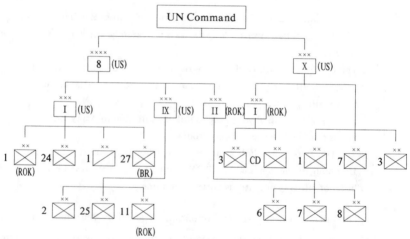

* The ROK 11th Division was under operational control of the US IX Corps as of October 5, 1950.
* The ROK I Corps was under operational control of the Eighth US Army as of October 20, 1950, and after that day, the former was placed under operational control of the US X Corps.

cided on two separate commands in Korea for the following reasons:

① The T'aebaek-san Range rises to rugged heights in the east part of the peninsula in a generally north-south direction, forming another mountain range called Nangnim north of it. This rugged terrain would cause problems for lateral operational coordinations, wire and transport communications between troops separated by it.

② In terms of logistical support, he could not supply both Eighth Army and X Corps from Pusan or Inch'on for a quick continuation of the pursuit northward. So he reasoned that a landing at Wonsan, northeast coast, might be inevitable to support troops operating in those areas. By so doing, he believed that two separate forces could operate in Korea without impairing the effectiveness of either.

Based on General MacArthur's United Nations Command Operations Order 2, dated October 2, Eighth Army Commander the next day issued an operations order to implement its part in the plan for the attack into North Korea. The order called for,

① the US I Corps(the US 1st Cavalry and 24th Divisions, British 27th Brigade) will execute the followings:
- to rapidly seize critical positions west of the Imjin River with not less than a division, and to protect the rest of the corps to be prepared for the future attack.
- to rapidly hand over the current security mission in the rear to the US IX Corps, and prepare for attack against P'yongyang by concentrating the main element of the corps in an assembly area north of Seoul.
- to conduct operations on A-day(date for crossing the Parallel) with the US Cavalry Division as the main effort along the Seoul-Sinuiju highway. At the same time, make the US 24th and ROK 1st Divisions protect the corps flanks and form a reserve with part of them.

- A-day will be given later.

② The US IX Corps(the US 2nd and 25th Divisions) will relieve the US I Corps' responsiblity for the security of the communication route between Seoul and Pusan, and mop up enemy remnants and guerilla forces in South Korea in close coordination with the ROK police. The newly activated ROK 11th Division will be attached to the corps at Namwon on October 5.

③ The ROK Army will prepare for the advance into North Korea by concentrating its I Corps in the area of Chumunjin-Younp'o, and the II Corps in the Ch'unch'on-Uijongbu area, respectively. The ROK Army will also attach its 11th Division to the US IX Corps by October 5 to help the corps' operations in the southwest area of Korea.

Thus the US X Corps, which had in the outskirts of Seoul handed over its responsibility for actions in the Seoul-Inch'on area to the EUSA during the period of October 2-7, began to prepare for the landing at Wonsan. Eighth Army, in the mean time, having relieved the US X Corps in the Seoul-Inch'on area, deployed its troops along the 38th Parallel, and on October 10, made a concerted attack across the Parallel.

However, this military campaign in North Korea encountered most difficult logistical problems. The transport and communication capability was inevitably limited because of restricted port facilities, and destroyed roads and bridges. The EUSA could not satisfactorily meet the logistical demand of its troops which quickly continued the pursuit northward. In order to provide logistical support to troops operating north of the 38th Parallel, Eighth Army had two alternatives: (1) to transport supply items using trucks from Pusan or Inch'on to the frontline troops via Seoul, or (2) to airlift those items from Japan or Kimpo' Airport to the frontline supply points.

Initially, the daily supply requirement for the attacking US I Corps was estimated at 3,000-tons while the daily quantity of supply goods transported through the Inch'on harbor was approximately 4,000-5,000-tons. Therefore, it was considered that they could meet the supply demand of Eighth Army should they use the maximum available facilities at the Inch'on harbor.

At that time, however, the harbor facilities were devoted exclusively (from October 6 through 16) to outloading the US 1st Cavalry Division which was to land at Wonsan. Consequently it set aside the Eighth Army's unloading at Inch'on. The alternative means of airlifting could process only several tons per day so that they could not depend on it except for transporting urgent supply items. As a result, the only other alternative was to use Pusan harbor which had 10,000-tons of daily unloading capability. However, nearly all the Seoul-Pusan rail lines and road bridges had already been destroyed by UN aerial action, together with enemy demolitions, at the beginning of the war and during the UN defensive operations at the Naktong front. It was virtually impossible for Eighth Army to transport supply items through them. Accordingly, weeks of concentrated work by Engineer troops would be required to repair them. Thus the repair work became an important factor for Eighth Army in making the decision on the departure time.

To rebuild these bridges, Eighth Army marshaled all available troops and equipment; the US Railroad Engineer Corps, the 8th Construction Engineer Corps and the US I Corps engineer troops, aided by the ROK engineer troops and local Korean laborers, worked together to restore the highway bridges northward by the end of September. They completed the repair work for the railroad from Waegwan to Yongdungp'o by October 10. It was not until that time that Eighth Army could secure full scale logistical support. The daily supply requirement for Eighth Army was estimated at about 4,000 tons, and to meet this demand they had to set out 6 and 1/2 trains every day from Pusan.[33]

2. Operations for Capturing Wonsan

(1) Advance from the 38th Parallel to Outskirts of Wonsan

The northward march to capture Wonsan had already been in progress when the ROK 3rd and Capital Divisions, I Corps, crossed the 38th Parallel on October 1. At the end of September, the ROK Government had decided that it would independently cross the Parallel, even before written orders were issued through channels from the United Nations Command and Eighth Army.

On September 30, Brig. Gen. Kim Paik Il, commander of the ROK I Corps, who had received the order to cross the 38th Parallel from the supreme commander of the ROK Armed Forces, planned to maneuver part of his troops to facilitate succeeding operations north of the Parallel. For this purpose, he ordered the 3rd Division to continue its pursuit toward Yangyang to capture and secure it, and at the same time, to help the Capital Division's advance. He also ordered the Capital Division to immediately concentrate its subordinate units and proceed along the axis of P'yongch'ang-Kwangwonri-Sorim, and there to prepare for future operations.

Pursuant to this order, the ROK 3rd Division, spearheaded by its 23rd Regiment, crossed the 38th Parallel in the north of Inguri at 05:00 on October 1, and continued on toward Yangyang. It was on a clear autumn morning that ROK troops made the historic crossing of the 38th Parallel for the first time. Col. Kim Chong Soon, regimental commander at the time, reminisced, "It was overwhelming; I thought that that damned line which had separated our people and the country so long was about to crumble, and we would be reunified; we were all so excited that we practically ran across the 38th Parallel." In order to commemorate the historic event, the ROK Government designated this day of October 1 as the ROK Armed Forces Day.

ROKA 11th Division marching north across the 38th parallel

At 14:00 that day, the ROK 23rd Regiment entered Yangyang 20 kilometers north of the Parallel along the east coastal road against relatively light enemy resistance. At that time, the bulk of the NKPA 5th Division was defending the area. Right at that moment, the ROK Capital Division, headed by its 18th Regiment, also crossed the 38th Parallel from north of Sorim and reached Yangyang.

That day, the ROK corps commander, Brig. Gen. Kim Paik Il, encouraged the soldiers by saying, "through each division's expeditious pursuit, we finally broke through the 38th Parallel which had separated our nation and the people, and were able to take a giant step toward recovering the lost territory. From now on we will free fellow North Korean brethren who have been suffering under the Communist oppression for a long time; for this purpose, we will carry out the much-anticipated advance to our objective, the Tumen River. I expect all of you to further exert yourselves and offer your lives for the honorable victory of our country."

On October 3, the ROK 26th Regiment of the 3rd Division, passing through the 23rd Regiment, launched an attack against Kansong and seized it. Then the 23rd Regiment took the lead again to advance to Kojinri north of Kansong against sporadic enemy resistance. There the 22nd Regiment which had followed behind as the division reserve led the attacking troops. Meanwhile, the ROK Capital Division, led by the 18th Regiment which had advanced to Kansong, drove on northward along the east coastal route.

That day, the ROK corps commander met with General Walker, commander of the EUSA, who flew to his headquarters and discussed matters on the future operations.

At about this time, the enemy, having failed in defending Kansong, attempted to launch a series of counterattacks against friendly troops along the axis of Kosong-T'ongch'on-Kojo. Part of the enemy troops sneaked into the Odae and Sorak Mountain areas to prepare for guerrilla warfare and to cut off the rear supply routes.

Leading the attack, the ROK 22nd Regiment of the 3rd Division captured Kosong on October 4 against light enemy resistance, and on the 5th, it entered Changjon after fighting a fierce battle. In this battle, the regiment captured a company-sized enemy force and killed many who had attempted to flee to the East Sea. It also captured enemy tanks and 76-mm guns. In the meantime, the ROK 18th Regiment which had followed behind the ROK 3rd Division changed its initial axis of advance from Kansong toward the Chinpu-ryong Pass on the 4th, and moved on toward the Wont'ong-Yanggu area on the 5th. Elsewhere, other regiments of the Capital Division continued on toward the East Sea. This change of avenue was made by the ROK Corps which had attempted to minimize the vulnerability of crowding 6 regiments of the two divisions into the narrow east coastal route, and at the same time, to mop up enemy remnants who had been active to the east of T'aebaek Range.

On October 5, in accordance with the US Eighth Army's operations order(October 3), the ROK Army issued operations order 205 in an effort to capture Wonsan and to advance to the Iron Triangle area. Gists of this order read as follows:

> **The ROK I Corps**: the 3rd Division will attack against Wonsan, the ultimate objective, and capture it after overrunning T'ongch'on and Kugyeri; the Capital Division will pass through Whach'on and Anbyon to attack against and secure Wonsan in cooperation with the 3rd Division.
>
> **The ROK II Corps**: the 6th Division will first seize Whach'on-Kimwha-Ch'angdori, and then continue to attack Hoeyang, Yongjiwonri, and Chikyongri; the 7th Division, in close cooperation with the 6th Division, will first take Kimwha and then immediately be released from the II Corps' control to be placed under dirct control of the ROK Army; the 8th Division will first seize Ch'orwon and P'yonggang, and then capture Yongjiwonri in close coordination with the 6th Division.

Pursuant to this order, the ROK I Corps in turn issued operations order 113(dated October 6) to the effect that the 3rd and Capital Divisions would attack against Wonsan. Accordingly, the ROK 22nd Regiment of the 3rd Division left Changjon on October 6, and seized T'ongch'on after defeating strong enemy resistance several times. At that time, the 23rd and 26th Regiments closely followed behind the former. In the meantime, with the exception of the ROK 18th Regiment which advanced to Yanggu and continued on toward Hoeyang through the valley of Mundungri, the other two regiments(the 1st Cavalry and 1st Regiments) of the Capital Division drove on northward, closely following behind the ROK 3rd Division. This resulting concentration of five regiments along Route 7 on the east coast was a weakness dangerously exposed. In order to make up this vulnerability and at the same time, to clear the area of enemy remnants, the ROK corps ordered the Capital Division to proceed to the axis of Hoeyang-Singgosan-Wonsan.[34] Accordingly, the Capital Division left T'ong-ch'on to cross inland from the T'aebaek Range and to head for Whach'on. This was the second measure taken by the ROK Army to prevent the over-concentration of troops, and also to mop up enemy remnants and stragglers escaping northward through the T'aebaek Range.

The leading 1st Cavalry Regiment of the ROK Capital Division advanced to Whach'on by crossing over the Ch'uji-ryong Pass in the T'aebaek Range. At that time, the 1st Regiment, which had closely followed behind the cavalry regiment, also reached the ridge of the Ch'uji-ryong Pass and located an estimated 400 men enemy force which had been moving north through the mountain range from Inner-Kumkang. The ROK regiment captured them all after a brief fight. That day(October 7), the ROK 18th Regiment of the Capital Division, which had proceeded inland from Yanggu to Whach'on, reached Malwhiri. The following day, the 1st Regiment of the same division captured Hoeyang. Meanwhile, on October 7, the 23rd Regiment of the ROK 3rd Division, passing through the 22nd Regiment at T'ongch'on, occupied Kojo and reached Songjonri by pressing hard against the retreating enemy.

When the bulk of the ROK Capital Division had crossed over the T'aebaek Range and advanced to the Whach'on area northeast of Kumkang-san the previous day, the division ordered the 1st Battalion of the 1st Cavalry Regiment to proceed toward Wonsan along the axis of Whach'on-Tonapri-Anbyon, so that the battalion could protect the division right flank. Meanwhile, the main body of the division moved toward Singgosan, a strategic point on the Seoul-Wonsan railway, by making a turning movement at Whach'on deep into the inland areas. There, however, was an obstacle they had to overcome, the Ch'ol-ryong Pass.

The Ch'ol-ryong Pass, a mountain ridge of 685 meters above the sea, situated between Hoeyang and Singosan, had 88 dangerous bends. In addition, an unidentified enemy unit was stubbornly holding the natural fortress. The ROK 1st Regiment of the Capital Division attempted in vain to break through enemy positions at the pass during the day time, and was forced to withdraw. The 2nd Battalion of the 18th Regiment freshly attacked against this enemy at night(19:00) again, but failed. Under such circumstances, the regimental commander, Col. Lim Ch'ung Sik, ordered the 1st Battalion commander, Maj. Chang Ch'un Kwon, to break through the enemy defensive line at the pass during the night and advanced to Singosan.

While racking his brains and talking with his staff officers to find a way to successfully penetrate the enemy line, the battalion commander hit upon a prisoner's statement that "NKPA troops get extremely terrified and run away when they see American tank units." Hence, he decided to employ deceptive tactics by using 5 captured Russian-built Zis trucks.[35]

He removed the mufflers from the trucks to make their engines sound like tanks; shortly, at 22:00 that night, the 1st Battalion made its assault against the enemy, led by the 5 Zis trucks with about 40 vehicles following with all their headlights on. This tactic apparently gave the enemy an illusion that a mechanized force reinforced by tanks was approaching the enemy positions. The tactic worked and the demoralized enemy started to escape toward Singosan, giving up his defensive positions. Eventually, the ROK battalion crossed over the Ch'ol-ryong Pass and seized the town of Singosan by the morning of October 9.

In the meantime, on the east coast, the ROK 23rd Regiment commanded by Col. Kim Chong Soon captured Wolp'ori. In the predawn hours of that day, the regiment left Songjon via Chasan-Ssangumri to resume its attack against the village surrounded by knobs and hillocks up to 200 meters above sea level. The town of Wolp'ori dominated the nearby area, so that the ROK soldiers there could have an entire view of Wonsan's streets across the the Namdae-ch'on.

Advance from the 38th Parallel to Wonsan

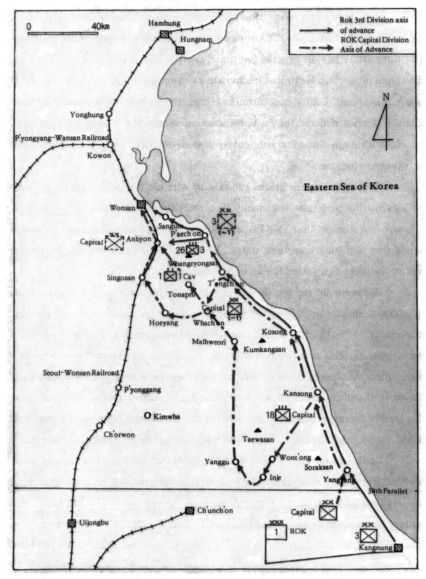

Meanwhile, the ROK 22nd Regiment, the 3rd Division reserve unit followed the 23rd Regiment to drive north toward T'ongch'on, and the 26th Regiment diverted its axis of advance at Koewhari short of Chasan toward the inland areas, and continued on toward Anbyon by way of P'aech'onri and the Piun-ryong Pass.

On October 9, the ROK Capital Division, which had advanced to Singosan after the overnight fighting at the Ch'ol-ryong Pass, cut off the Seoul-Wonsan railway and began searching the area. During this searching operation, the ROK division captured a large amount of war materiel and equipment which could have supported an enemy division. They captured about 3,000 burp guns abandoned and still packed in cosmoline, a flat train which had apparently headed for Wonsan from Ch'orwon loaded with 6 tanks, 4 artillery pieces, 11 82-mm. mortars, 30 heavy machine guns, 500 light machine guns, 5,000 rifles, and another car full of medical supplies.

Despite extreme fatigue from the night before, breaking through enemy positions at the Ch'ol-ryong Pass, soldiers of the 1st Battalion, the advance unit of the ROK 18th Regiment, Capital Division, resumed march by motor on that morning toward Wonsan. This was to get their lead in the pursuit operations from the ROK 3rd Division which was about 20 kilometers ahead of them on their east flank.

The ROK battalion defeated one enemy battalion of the 2nd Brigade, the NKPA Wonsan Garrison, at Namsanri northwest of Anbyon, and at around 16:00 that day broke through enemy's Wonsan perimeter positions built at Pangwhari. The battalion continued on toward Wonsan and in the vicinity of Paewhari, a junction point 12 kilometers south of Wonsan, surprised an enemy artillery battalion from its rear capturing a battalion size unit of artillery pieces. At about this time, the 1st Battalion(commanded by Maj. Chung Se Jin) of the ROK 1st Cavalry Regiment, which had been separated at Whach'on and fol-

lowed its own axis of advance, reached Anbyon via Tonamri as scheduled. The
ROK 1st Cavalry Regiment(−1), which had closely followed behind the 18th
Regiment over the Ch'ol-ryong Pass, itself reached Singosan. There it carried
out mop up operations killing approximately 200 enemy soldiers and capturing
1,500 small arms, 2 million rounds of ammunition, and 3 truckloads of grain. At
that time, the ROK 1st Regiment, which had followed behind the cavalry regiment, also entered the town of Singosan exploiting and executing mop up operations. At the same time, the 1st Regiment performed troop maintenance in preparation for the attack upon Wonsan.

Meanwhile, the ROK 3rd Division on the east coast was ready for the
attack against Wonsan by securing favorable positions. On October 9, its 23rd
Regiment crossed the Namdae-ch'on and secured a vantage point from which it
could attack against the Wonsan Airstrip situated on the small Kalma Peninsula, eastern tip of Wonsan City, and downtown streets on the west of the airfield
as well. The 22nd Regiment, which had followed behind it as division reserve,
passed through Sangumri that afternoon and reached a hill which dominates
the Namdae-ch'on. There the regiment prepared to attack Wonsan the following
day on the left flank of the 23rd Regiment. In the meantime, the 26th Regiment,
which had crossed over the Piun-ryong Pass and moved north along the inland
bypass route, captured Anbyon.

In brief, as of late afternoon of October 9, four of the six regiments of
the ROK Ⅰ Corps, except for two reserve regiments, were only 4 kilometers
away from Wonsan, and readily positioned to attack against the port city along
their respective axis of advance. In addition, the advance command post of
each division moved up to the front line areas; that of the 3rd Division moved
from Kojo to Sangumri, while the Capital Division's advance command post
moved to Singosan from Hoeyang. This concluded the first-phase operations for
the attack against Wonsan.

(2) Operations for Capturing Wonsan

Situated on the east coast of the Korean Peninsula, the city of Wonsan was known not only as the center of politics, economics, culture, and transportation of North Korea, but also a port of strategic importance. The NKPA had already fortified the city and was still building up strong defensive positions in the outskirts by assembling remnants who had escaped from other areas. Due to the fact that Wonsan is the terminus of the Seoul-Wonsan, P'yongyang-Wonsan, and Najin-Wonsan railways, and especially being the starting point of the P'yongyang-Wonsan highway, the collapse of this strategic city would simultaneously cause the destruction of the NKPA's lateral defensive line along the Seoul-Wonsan railway, and separate its troops in the eastern and western fronts. If this were to happen, the North Korean capital city of P'yongyang would apparently be pressured by friendly forces from the east. In addition, situated at the southwest side of the large Yonghung Bay surrounded by the Hodo Peninsula, Wonsan is the principal, natural port on the east coast of Korea. Thus Wonsan harbor receives various military equipment, supplies and other war materiel from the USSR.[36] The Wonsan Airfield is only 20-30 minutes away by air from P'yongyang, so that it could function as a crucial base for dominating air superiority of the whole North Korean area.

For the necessity of the defense of Wonsan, the North Korean official publication, the *Comprehensive History of Choson*(vol. 26) stated as follows:

> [The NKPA Supreme Command] enjoined its Naval Command(East Coast Defense Command) to concentrate and deploy all available combat troops and equipment under its control to the area from the left bank of the Kwang-gyo-ch'on (T'ongch'ongun) to Wonsan, and annihilate enemy troops invading from the inland and the sea. Accordingly, the [East Coast Defense Command] set up its primary

defense phase line at a point 25-30 kilometers southeast of Wonsan, and a secondary line of defense at 10-15 kilometers, respectively.[37] In addition, in the outskirts of the city, it dug in to circular defensive positions.[38]

In mid-September when the UN Forces landed at Inch'on, the NKPA 588th Infantry Regiment had initially been in charge of the defense of Wonsan. Thus the regiment planned to place its headquarters unit and the 3rd Battalion in downtown streets of the city, and the 1st and 2nd Battalions in the Wonsan Airfield on the Kalma Peninsula, and Hungnam respectively.[39] Later, however, increased number of stragglers and remnants, and also of available units in the area enhanced the NKPA's defensive capability, and made it reorganize defensive units and positions:

① Activation of the Wonsan Defense Command consisted of the NKPA 249th Brigade.

② Activation of the NKPA 42nd Division with approximately 8,000 men from the 588th and 599th Infantry Regiments, and the 590th Coastal Defense Regiment. 28 pieces of guns were added to the division.

③ Reorganization of the NKPA 12th Division centered around part of the 5th Division troops and the 101st Regiment.

④ Reorganization of approximately 3,000 remnants assembled in an area near the Sokwangsa Temple(These enemy remnants had initially belonged to the NKPA 1st, 2nd, 3rd, 4th, 5th, 7th, 8th, and 15th Divisions which had escaped and arrived there from areas of Ch'orwon, Kimwha, and Ch'unch'on).

⑤ Reinforcing NKPA units arrived in Wonsan from the Hamhung area.

⑥ Other troops including 2,000 men from the NKPA Independent Kangnung Brigade, 1,000 from the Independent Battalion, a battalion under direct control of the NKPA Naval Force Command, and a company under direct control of the NKPA Air Force joined the Wonsan Defense Command.

Thus the reorganized NKPA troops at the Wonsan area was estimated at a minimum of 20,000 men equipped with 12 tanks, 8 120-mm mortars, 1 82-mm mortar, and 76 76-mm guns. Three artillery battalions equipped with 122-mm and 76-mm howitzers supported them.[40]

At dawn on October 10, the ROK I Corps initiated its attack against Wonsan. In order to seize and secure the city, the corps had first to take the two hill masses which dominated the downtown streets of Wonsan. One of them on the eastern edge of the city comprised Hills 189, 136, and 73, and the other was a ridgeline that stretched from Yowang-san(355 meters) to Pukmang-san(143 meters) and sloped down almost to downtown streets from the west of the city. The 4 kilometer-long city of Wonsan was narrow at its center due to the Yonghung Bay on the sea side and the Yowang-san mountain ridge on the opposite side, and was well developed along both the east and west ends. The eastern industrial area of the city had the Wonsan Switchyard, Petroleum Refinery, and the Airfield, while the west side had important administrative offices such as the city hall, Wonsan Railroad Station, and the harbor facilities.

Considering the characteristic terrain feature and the high grounds dominating streets of the city, Brig. Gen. Kim Paik Il, the ROK corps commander, assigned the eastern high hill mass area to the 3rd Division on the right flank, and the western Yowang-san area to the Capital Division as their immediate objectives. Once the divisions succeeded in capturing these objectives, they were to make a pincer attack against the center of the city.

However, during the attack, the two divisions were plunged into confusion when they entered the city because of unclarified boundaries and the rivalries to be the first to take the objective. Thus each division crossed each other's combat zone twice.

At 05:30 that day, the ROK 23rd Regiment, lead element of the 3rd Division on the eastern side of the city, launched its attack with the help of various artillery, mortar, and 76-mm self-propelled gunfire. The regiment defeated the desperate enemy resistance and broke through his defensive positions set up along the Wonsan Switchyard-Hill 73-Airfield line. At about 07:00, the regiment reached downtown streets to engage the enemy there. Right at that moment, the cavalry regiment of the ROK Capital Division, which had left Paewha near Singosan early that morning, approached the 3rd Division zone. The cavalry regiment had to cross the latter's zone of action to reach its objective, the airfield on the Kalma Peninsula.

At that time, however, the ROK Cavalry Regiment fell into the enemy's ambush at the orchards in the vicinity of Hills 189 and 136 and was no longer able to advance; three enemy tanks and other guns held the regiment in check. But in the nick of time, the ROK 22nd Regiment of the 3rd Division, which had been attacking the city from the other direction, located the enemy firing positions and inflitrated into them by hiding under sheafs of rice. Once the enemy was within the effective range of M-1 rifles, the ROK regiment concentrated its fire and suppressed him. With this help of the 22nd Regiment, the ROK Cavalries resumed their advance, and, when the commanding officers of both regiments, Cols. Paik Nam Kwon of the latter and Kim Chong Soon of the former, came across at the entrance of the city of Wonsan, they rejoiced over the success and encouraged each other.

From there, the 1st Battalion(commanded by Maj. Chung Se Jin) of the ROK 1st Cavalry Regiment, Capital Division, which had thus far overrun enemy positions with Japanese Toyota trucks disguised as a motorized task force, proceeded to the Wonsan Airfield. The cavalry regiment($-$) at the same time followed behind the 23rd Regiment of the ROK 3rd Division and seized the eastern half of Wonsan after having won a street fight.

In the meantime, the ROK 26th Regiment, the left flank unit of the 3rd Division which had made a turning movement inland toward Anbyon, continued on toward the Yowang-san area for which the Capital Division was responsible. At that time, the ROK 18th Regiment which had advanced to Paewha, the outskirts of Wonsan, the previous day, as the lead element of the Capital Division, was also driving toward Yowang-san. Brig. Gen. Song Yo Ch'an, commander of the Capital Divison, and Col. Lee Ch'ee Up, commanding officer of the 26th Regiment, met each other at the foot of the mountain, and argued with each other over their action zones contrasting overlays drawn not on a military map but on an ordinary map. After this brief bickering between them, it was decided that the 18th Regiment of the Capital Division would continue on toward Yowang-san, and the 26th Regiment would move toward Sojae-bong (297 meters) 3 kilometers on the left of Yowang-san via Ch'unsanri and Changhungri to cut off the southwestern part of the city of Wonsan.

The ROK 18th Regiment, despite commiting all of its three battalions to the Yowang-san area with the help of the 10th Artillery Battalion positioned at the Paewha Girls Middle School, failed to advance due to the stubborn enemy resistance. At that time, however, the US marine F-4u's led by a Mosquito Polygon which had been supporting the ROK Capital Division flew in to strike the area and enabled the 18th Regiment to capture Yowang-san. Part of the regiment reached the edge of the city of Wonsan shortly after 10:00 that day. Meanwhile, the ROK 1st Regiment, the Capital Division reserve, had left Singosan that morning and advanced to an area near Paewha, the outskirts of Wonsan.

After such a confused battle, each of the two ROK divisions which had entered the center of the city almost at the same time, claimed that it had reached it ahead of the other. In support of their positions, each of them presented check marks of the time made by its leading reconnaissance element with chalks, or pointed out the dominating topographical crest it had captured first. This covering terrain feature could have been crucial in seizing the city.

In an effort to settle rival claims as to which division entered the city first, the ROK corps commander, Brig. Gen. Kim Paik Il, decreed that both divisions launched the attacks simultaneously at 05:00 and that both secured it at 10:00

In actuality, however, the city was not secured then. Col. Emmerich, KMAG senior advisor with the 3rd Division, entered the city with the front line troops of the ROK 23rd Regiment at around 13:30 that afternoon. Until almost noon, the NKPA troops had maintained a heavy artillery fire from various parts of the city. Then, after withdrawing most of their guns from Wonsan, they fired into the city all afternoon from its northwest sector and the hills behind it to obstruct friendly mop-up operations there.

The two ROK divisions' mop-up operations were still under way after sunset, but at around 22:00 that night, an enemy armored unit led by ten 76-mm self-propelled antitank guns counnterattacked the ROK troops. Commanders of the ROK 3rd and Capital Divisions immediately ordered their troops to temporarily withdraw to nearby high ground. Three enemy self-propelled guns broke through the defensive line of the 1st Battalion, ROK Cavalry Regiment, and returned to the airfield. They destroyed most of the buildings and hangars there, and retreated.

Once the enemy armored troops retreated, the ROK 3rd Division resumed its attack at 03:00 the following day(the 11th), and fought through the center part of the city against heavy enemy artillery, mortar, and small arms fire. By that evening, the division advanced to the bank of Chokjon-ch'on north of the Wonsan Railroad Station. Meanwhile, the ROK Capital Division cleared the downtown streets of enemy remnants and at the same time, strengthened its defense of the airfield. That day, Lt. Gen. Walker, commander of the US Eighth Army, and Maj. Gen. Earl E. Partridge, commander of the US Fifth Air Force, flew into Wonsan Airfield. Finding it in good condition, the latter had 22 planes of the Combat Cargo Command fly in 131 tons of supplies for the ROK I Corps troops the next day.

ROKA 6th Division marching toward the Yalu River, 1950

Once the ROK troops were in the city, they saw dozens of bodies of innocent people that had been slaughtered scattered around the harbor, about 300 in an air-raid shelter in Sinp'ungri at the foot of Yowanng-san, and also about 230 at Wonsan beach, totaling about 600 bodies. This heinous act done to the same race by the NKPA was unspeakable.

Minister Han Joon Myong, who had been confined to the Wonsan People's Enlightenment Center(a prison) as a political offender and then miraculously survived the butchery at the Sinp'ungri air-raid shelter later testified the circumstances as follows: [41]

I thought that they [North Korean Communists] were going to evacuate us when they tied us in a group of four, and took us into the bomb shelter at Sinp'ungri from the prison. But once we were inside the shelter, I felt by instinct that they were going to slaughter us. We saw piled up bodies slaughtered at the far end of the dark shelter shaped like the letter "T." Instantaneously, with sounds of gunfire, I had collapsed with my friends tied together on the pile. But with the blessing of heaven I survived and was trapped in there for two days because the entrance was blown shut. When the ROK soldiers came in, I was miraculously rescued.

This Wonsan massacre victims' exhumation was filmed by military documentary film reporters and shown to the public. About 9,000 remaining Wonsan citizens had gone through an enormous ordeal such as slaughter, abduction, and so on, but still waited for the ROK troops to enter the city. Once the ROK troops entered the city, the citizens welcomed them with great enthusiasm.

3. The Crossing of the 38th Parallel in the Central Front

The crossing of the 38th Parallel from the central front had fallen under the responsibility of the ROK II Corps. According to the ROK Army Operations Order 205 (October 5), the 6th Division of the corps was to advance in the axis of Whach'on-Hoeyang-Chikyongri (the outskirts of Wonsan), the 8th Division in the axis of Ch'orwon-P'yonggang-Yongjiwonri (north of Singosan), and the 7th Division was to follow behind as the corps reserve after capturing Kimwha in cooperation with the 6th Division.

Thus the three ROK divisions under control of the II Corps reached the 38th Parallel between October 3 and 8. The 6th Division, the right wing of the corps, first reached the Parallel in an area south of the Mojinkyo bridge (also called the 38th Parallel bridge) on the 3rd, while on the 7th, the 8th Division, the left wing, advanced to Ch'osongri north of Tongduch'on and 2 kilometers south of the Parallel. The 7th Division, the corps reserve, advanced to Yangmunri north of P'och'on and situated on the 38th Parallel.

Upon receiving the "March North" order, the ROK II Corps (commanded by Maj. Gen. Yu Jae Hung) crossed the 38th Parallel between October 6 and 8 and continued on northward. On the right flank, the 6th Division (commanded by Brig. Gen. Kim Chong Oh) started first to cross the Parallel at the Mojinkyo bridge on the 6th and defeated two enemy regiments of the NKPA 9th Division in the area. Then it captured Whach'on in the late afternoon of the 8th. It continued on northward and by October 10, it occupied Kimwha.

On October 8, the ROK 10th Regiment, the lead unit of the 8th Division (commanded by Brig. Gen. Lee Song Ga) on the left, crossed the 38th Parallel from the north of Ch'osongri repelling part of the NKPA 27th Brigade. The regiment immediately crossed the Hant'an River and advanced to Chonkok. Having secured the town, the ROK division resumed its pursuit with the 10th and 21st Regiments on the front and the 16th Regiment in the rear. The division captured Yonch'on and Ch'orwon on the 9th and 10th, respectively, and continued to press hard against the fleeing enemy columns toward P'yonggang.

Meanwhile, the ROK 7th Division (commanded by Brig. Gen. Shin Sang Ch'ol), the corps reserve, belatedly crossed the 38th Parallel at Yangmunri on October 9 and advanced to Chikyongri near Kimwha the next day.

As the ROK II Corps smoothly made gains north of the 38th Parallel, the ROK Army issued Operations Order 211 on the morning(11:00) of October 8. It was to maneuver the II Corps to Wonsan to relieve the ROK I Corps there, and at the same time, to have the latter attack west toward P'yongyang and link up with the US I Corps. However, this order was revised to Operations Order 212 at 20:00 that night, which was to have the ROK I Corps secure the Wonsan area and the II Corps continue on toward P'yongyang via Wonsan. The ROK Army had initially tried to avoid disorder that might result from relieving the two ROK corps, but only created some confusion in their operations.

Eventually on October 10, when the ROK I Corps captured Wonsan, the ROK Army, in close coordination with the US Eighth Army, clarified the two ROK corps' mission for the future operations by issuing Operations Order 212(revised) as the following:

> The I **Corps**: In order to secure the Wonsan Harbor until the US X Corps will arrive there, it will first secure the Yonghung Bay area by taking up positions along Anbyon Yongp'ori, Yongt'anri and the estuary of the Yongtan River. Then it will cut off the enemy's supply route and proceed north along the axis of Munch'on, Yonghung, Chongp'yong, Hamhung, P'ach'unjang and Hun-gnam to annihilate the enemy.
>
> The II **Corps**: It will rapidly move on toward Wonsan. From there, it will continue on toward P'yongyang along the axis of Yangdok-Changnimri-Kangtongri in its zone to establish contact with the US I Corps. During this process, it will cut off and annihilate enemy troops moving north and south in the area.

As a result, the ROK I Corps, which had secured Wonsan north of the Ch'ugaryong Trough and Ch'orwon south of it by October 10, became operable on the northeastern front, while the ROK II Corps continued to proceed north from the central front after it joined the operations at P'yongyang.

4. Operations for Capturing P'yongyang

(1) Maneuvering Plan of Friendly Forces

On October 3, the US I Corps (commanded by Maj. Gen. Frank W. Milburn), which had been designated as the main attack unit by Eighth Army and was to attack against and capture P'yongyang, the North Korean capital city, across the 38th Parallel, had decided to rapidly move on toward its objective before the retreating NKPA troops could reorganize their troops and defensive positions as well. For this purpose, the corps planned to alternatively commit its two divisions equipped with superior fire power and mobility to the axis of Kaesong-P'yongyang. The corps commander had estimated that the advance to P'yongyang would relatively be easy once the enemy's defense positions north of Kaesong along the 38th Parallel were broken through. An estimated enemy force of four divisions, the bulk of the remaining North Korean Army, was known to have been deployed there. Therefore, rather than confronting the enemy directly, he decided to make a turning movement to encircle him by taking advantage of mighty shock power and mobility of mechanized American troops. He at once issued the corps operations order[42] as follows:

① The US 1st Cavalry Division(to which the British 27th Brigade was attached), the main attack unit, will break through the the 38th Parallel in front of Kaesong to envelope and destroy enemy troops in the area of Kumch'on. Then it will drive on north along the axis of Namch'onjom-Sariwon-Whangju-P'yongyang.

② The US 24th Division will protect the corps left flank with part of its force, and be prepared to pass through the 1st Cavalry Division at any time.

③ The ROK 1st Division, the right wing of the corps, will cross the 38th Parallel in front of Korangp'o, and then cover the right flank of the corps while proceeding north along the axis of Sibyonri-Sinkye-P'yongyang.

On October 4, in an effort to expedite operations north of the 38th Parallel, the US I Corps commander turned over each division's mission in the rear to the US IX Corps. At the same time, he had the US 1st Cavalry Division advance to the Kaesong area to protect the corps assembly area. He also enjoined the US 24th and ROK 1st Divisions to proceed and assemble to the west bank of the Imjin River and to the Korangp'o area, its northern bank respectively.

Pursuant to the corps orders, the US 1st Cavalry Division, which had started to advance north on October 5, crossed the Imjin River at Munsanri. It reached the area of Kaesong by October 8 and occupied the corps assembly area.

At about this time, the ROK 1st Division, which had been clearing the Poun area of North Ch'ungch'ong Province as the corps reserve unit, moved out on October 7 to advance north. On October 10, it reached Korangp'o on the northern bank of the Imjin by way of Ansong-Seoul. The US 24th Division, meanwhile, moved from the Ch'onan-Taejon area to the Seoul-Pongilch'on area on the 8th.

On October 7, the US Eighth Army, which had received a message from the United Nations Command to the effect that it could attack immediately when ready, set October 9 for D-day. Accordingly, the US I Corps crossed the 38th Parallel that day and proceeded toward its objective, P'yongyang.

(2) Pursuit Operations from the 38th Parallel to P'yongyang

The US 1st Cavalry Division, the main effort of the US I Corps, was to take Highway 1, the most favorable avenue between Kaesong and P'yongyang. Ready for the attack, the American cavalry division commander deployed three regiments side by side on the 38th Parallel and kept the attached British 27th Brigade in reserve. In the center, the US 8th Cavalry Regiment (led by Col. Raymond D. Palmer) was to attack frontally against Kumch'on 24 kilometers north of the 38th Parallel along the main highway(Route 1) axis from Kaesong to Kumch'on; on its right, the 5th Cavalry Regiment (commander: Col. Marcel B. Crombez) was to swing eastward in a circular flanking movement designed to attack Kumch'on from the rear. Meanwhile, on the division left, the US 7th Cavalry Regiment(commanded by Col. William A. Harris) faced the task of crossing the

Yesong River to get on the road running north from Paekch'on to Hanp'ori, 10 kilometers north of Kumch'on, where the main Kaesong-P'yongyang road crossed the Yesong River. At Hanp'ori, the 7th Cavalry Regiment was to establish a blocking position to trap the enemy forces, and the 8th and 5th Cavalry Regiments were to drive northward in a formation of double envelopment. These were the maneuvers involved in the cavalry division commander's operational concept. At 09:00 on October 9, the division commander issued his orders and the regiments moved up along the designated axis fighting their way northward.

Based on the previous day's reconnaissance report that the railway bridge had been left partially intact and was usable for foot troops, the 7th Cavalry Regiment on the left decided to make a quick crossing of the Yesong River through the bridge. As had been expected, however, the enemy opened and concentrated fire on the possible crossing sites. After the regiment's delivering three hours of preparatory artillery fire against enemy positions that afternoon starting from noon, C Company of the 1st Battalion, 7th Cavalry, started first to cross the bridge. As a platoon of the company rushed across the bridge using railings as shields, the enemy 43rd Division opened a barrage fire on it as if they had been waiting. Suffering a few casualties from that small arms fire, the platoon succeeded in crossing the bridge and seizing the immediate approaches on the far side. Following this platoon, B Company, 8th Engineer Combat Battalion, went on the bridge to repair holes on the bridge. Simultaneously, the rest of C Company reached the far side across the bridge and occupied the hill on the south of the bridge. In this manner, the 1st Battalion completed the river crossing around sunset; however, enemy mortars continued to fire heavy concentrations on the bridge and nearby battalion areas. The Cavalry Regiment also countered the enemy mortar fire, utilizing all available weapons.

Once the 1st Battalion crossed to the other side, the supporting artillery barrage had to be lifted from the immediate environs of the bridge. The enemy, who had watched for an opportunity, concentrated his mortar fire on the 1st Battalion positions inflicting heavy loss upon the battalion. In this crossing attack, the battalion had 78 casualties, mostly from C Company.

After dark the NKPA troops launched a counterattack against the 1st Battalion. To reinforce the battalion, the regimental commander promptly ordered his 2nd Battalion to cross the bridge and to seize the southern sector of the 1st Battalion positions. This concluded the 7th Cavalry Regiment's successful crossing of the Yesong River.

In the meantime, the US 8th Cavalry Regiment, which had launched a frontal attack in the center along the main Kaesong-Kumch'on highway, at 12:00 on October 9, made a very slow advance. The armored spearhead repeatedly came to a halt because the highway had been heavily mined. Engineer troops were brought in to remove the mines, but it took considerable time. As a result, the regiment gained very little only capturing Songak-san 3.5 kilometers north of Kaesong.

On the division right the 5th Cavalry Regiment, which had swung from Changdan northeastward attempting to envelop enemy forces, barely made it to the 38th Parallel at 19:30 on October 9. There the cavalry regiment discontinued its drive, and bivouacked overnight to prepare for the following day's attack. Meanwhile, at 02:00 the next day (October 10), the 2nd Battalion of the 7th Cavalry Regiment, which had crossed the Yesong River the previous day, resumed its attack westward along the Paech'on road. This attack progressed only a short distance when a heavy enemy counterattack struck the flank of the attack columns. The enemy counterattacked the American columns three more times with superior fire power injuring the American battalion commander Lt. Col. Gilmon A. Huff. The commander refused to be evacuated and remained with his battalion throughout the battle. He showed superb leadership in this night battle and eventually repelled the enemy. At daybreak the battalion resumed its

Advance from the 38th Parallel to P'yongyang

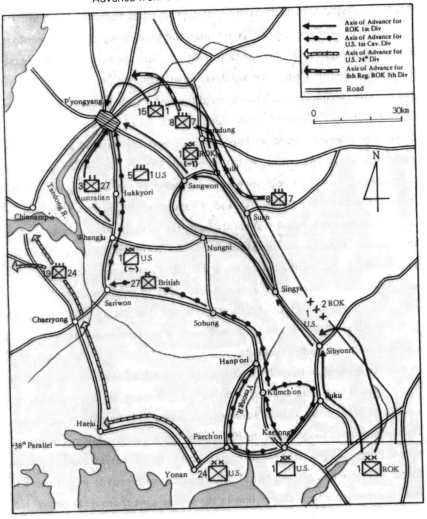

attack against Paech'on and seized the town and high ground north of it.

In the division center the 8th Cavalry Regiment made a very slow advance waiting for Engineer troops to remove enemy antitank mines as it had done the previous day. Only its 3rd Battalion snatched Pongmyong-san hill(411 meters) from the enemy 19th Division which had built strong defensive positions astride main highway 1. With the help of artillery fire, the battalion repelled the enemy counterattack upon the hill during that night. On the division right the 5th Cavalry Regiment, which had crossed the 38th Parallel from an area north-east of Kaesong, advanced north along the 5th route between Kaesong and Puku. The regiment seized an important hill near the Parallel almost unop-posed. Initially, it had estimated that the enemy 27th Division which had held a long ridge with several knobs, such as Kuksa-bong(764 meters), Ch'onma-san(560 meters), Kuknak-bong(471 meters), and Whajang-san(560 meters), all of which dominated Route 5, would stubbornly resist the advance of the regiment; but the enemy resistance was unexpectedly weak. Against this enemy's sporadic resis-tance, the regiment advanced to a point 10 kilometers north of Whajang-san. As it became dark, the regiment halted there to organize hasty defensive positions. On October 11, the 7th Cavalry Regiment on the division left turned to the north at Paech'on, and continued on toward Hanp'ori all night without encountering any enemy resistance.

In contrast to this advance on the right, the 8th Cavalry in the division center gained less than 2 kilometers that day checked by desperate enemy resistance. What made matters worse was the powerful enemy fire power. When the regiment tried to approach the high-rising Tusok-san, five kilometers north-west of Pongmyong-san, the enemy barrage was so fierce that it looked as if both forces had been in a pitched battle. Thus together with heavily mined route 1, the concentrated enemy disposition in the center zone thoroughly obstructed the advance of friendly forces toward P'yongyang.

In the meantime, on the division right the 5th Cavalry Regiment re-sumed its attack that day from the north of Whajang-san. Removing mines layed in the area of Komisong, the regiment captured the long ridge consisting of Hills 174, 175 and 179. Near the town of Puku dominated by the hill positions, enemy fire stopped the 1st Battalion. The stranded battalion was forced to bivouc there that night waiting for the 3rd Battalion to join it. That day(October 11), the Cavalry Division commander(Maj. Gen. Hobart R. Gay) ordered the 27th British Commonwealth Brigade to attack against the right flank of Kumch'on by maneuvering through a gap between the regiment which was advancing slowly in the center and that on the division right.

On that very day(October 11), the ROK 1st Division which had advanced toward P'yongyang side by side with the US 1st Cavalry Division on its east flank, crossed the 38th Parallel. The ROK division had reached Korangp'o late on the previous night and assembled there. Right at that time, on its left the adjacent US 1st Cavalry Division, which had already crossed the Parallel, was moving for a close-in envelopment of Kumch'on.

General Paik Sun Yup, the ROK division commander, who was worried over the belated departure of his troops, ordered the 1st Battalion of the 15th Regiment which had reached the Parallel at 15:00 on October 9, ahead of the others, to check the enemy defensive situation at the 38th Parallel. He hoped to have that intelligence report before the bulk of his division could cross the Parallel, so that the division could attack immediately after it arrived and assembled there. The battalion led by Maj. Yu Jae Sung left Korangp'o and moved northwestward unopposed. It captured Majonri 3 kilometers north of the Parallel. But it was officially recorded that the main body of the ROK 1st Division crossed the Parallel on October 11, two days later than the US 1st Cavalry Division. Even though their division was late, the soldiers were full of fighting spirit and determined to reach P'yongyang, their objective, ahead of the others.

The ROK division's immediate objective was the important road junction Sibyonri, which was situated farther north than Kumch'on, the immediate objective of the adjacent US 1st Cavalry Division. It was about 32 kilometers north from the 38th Parallel. For the attack northward, the ROK division placed its 15th Regiment on the right flank and the 11th Regiment on the left. The 12th Regiment was kept as division reserve, and was to follow behind the 11th Regiment through the valley of the Sami-ch'on. On October 11, main elements of the ROK division crossed the 38th Parallel simultaneously and launched a massive attack northward along the preplanned axis of advance. On the division right the 1st Battalion of the 15th Regiment, which had made a turning movement along the Imjin River, captured Sangnyong 25 kilometers north of the 38th Parallel by noon that day. There the battalion continued on north toward T'osan 13 kilometers north of Sangnyong. On its way to the town, it engaged an estimated battalion force of the NKPA 27th Division. The ROK battalion made a night attack against this enemy and captured T'osan. Meanwhile, the main body of the ROK 15th Regiment advanced unopposed to Ch'ongjongri on the Sami-ch'on about 2.5 kilometers north of the 38th Parallel after it had crossed the Parallel from the north of Korangp'o.

On the division left, the ROK 11th Regiment launched its attack at predawn hours that day. However, strong enemy defensive positions at Tugok with an estimated battalion force delayed the advance of the ROK regiment. Therefore, it was not until around 23:00 that day that the regiment reached Sodujong-jang 4 kilometers north of the 38th Parallel. This delay was partly caused by the unexpectedly stubborn enemy resistance and the mines as well, but most importantly, the ROK regiment could not make an audacious attack because captured enemy documents had indicated the mine fields were layed and weapons emplaced along its axis of advance. The ROK regiment, therefore, cautiously moved on destroying those weapons emplacements one by one. However, ROK soldiers found almost all those emplacements were empty when they captured them; it was obvious that extremely demoralized North Korean green replacements had abandoned their brand new weapons and positions altogether and escaped, or retreated even before the ROK troops attacked against them.[43]

That day, except for the 1st Battalion of the ROK 15th Regiment which had turned and moved toward Sangnyong, the ROK division made a very slow advance; the 15th Regiment($-$) on the division right and the 11th Regiment on the left gained only 2.5 and 4 kilometers, respectively.

Aware of the slow advance, the ROK division commander Brig. Gen. Paik Sun Yup became worried that he might not reach P'yongyang ahead of US troops, which he had promised Maj. Gen. Milburn, the US I Corps commander. At that time, Col. Henning, commander of the US 10th Anti-aircraft Artillery Group, who had been supporting the ROK division since the time of the Tabudong Battle, suggested a combined operation of infantry, tank, and artillery to break through enemy positions. He meant that once friendly tanks covered by infantry troops, with the help of the artillery fire and air strikes, broke through enemy positions, motorized main elements would rapidly follow up to exploit it. For this purpose, he promised to provide 50 ammunition trucks of his artillery group.

The ROK division commander, after conferring with his staff officers and advisors, accepted the suggestion as being effective. Thus the ROK 12th Regiment, the division reserve unit, led the combined operations with the help of tanks of C Company (21 M46 Pattons) of the US 6th Tank Battalion, US 10th AAA Group,[44] and C Battery of the ROK 17th Artillery Battalion.

Meanwhile, on the morning of October 12, the 3rd Battalion, US 7th Cavalry Regiment, on the left flank of the ROK division, advanced to Hanp'ori 9 kilometers north of Kumch'on and cut off the enemy escape route there.

At that time, the NKPA 19th and 27th Divisions had been stubbornly resisting the advance of the US 8th and 5th Cavalry Regiments in the Kumch'on area. Therefore, cutting off the thousands of enemy troops' path to retreat there had been a major achievement of the US 7th Cavalry Regiment. The regiment established an interdicting position in that area and waited for the enemy's retreat.

During the night, the retreating enemy columns, driven by the US 8th and 5th Cavalry Regiments, swarmed in to the US 7th Cavalry Regiment roadblock from Kumch'on, the southeast area of the blockade. With the their lights on, 11 NKPA trucks rushed into the ambushed area off guard, where a platoon of US L Company was waiting. The platoon waited until the enemy vehicles came within the effective shooting range, and then opened a barrage fire upon them. They destroyed 4 trucks loaded with ammunition, captured 6 others, killed about 50 enemy soldiers, and captured an equal number.

Among the latter was a mortally wounded NKPA officer who had in his possession a document indicating that two NKPA divisions(the 19th and 27th) intended to break out of Kumch'on the night of October 14 and to withdraw to Namch'onjom. The enemy officer said part of the enemy force in the Kumch'on area had been ordered to withdraw to Namch'onjom 24 kilometers north of Kumch'on.

The long-distance drive of the US 7th Cavalry Regiment northward to Hanp'ori after crossing the Yesong River could not have taken place without one of the most successful logistical supply operations of the Korean War. In the discussions before the 7th Cavalry Regiment attack at the Yesong River bridge, the US 1st Cavalry Division G-4 had told the regimental commander that he could not provide the gasoline, rations, and certain types of ammunition for the drive north from Paech'on even if the river crossing attempt was successful. However, due to the effort of the regimental commander Col. William A. Harris and the S-3, Capt. James B. Webel, 13 LCV's carried the needed logistical support from Inch'on to the crossing site at the Yesong River.

In the early morning battle of October 12, the leading 1st Battalion of the US 5th Cavalry Regiment was blocked at a narrow path which led to Puku near Hill 175 by an estimated enemy battalion force supported by about 10 self-propelled guns. The cavalry regiment committed its 2nd Battalion to the battle ground, and barely drove off the North Koreans and secured the area that afternoon. Right at the moment, the regiment made contact with the ROK 1st Division which had arrived there at Puku from the southeastern town of Ku-whari. They left for Kumch'on.

Meanwhile, the 27th British Commonwealth Brigade which had followed behind the US 5th Cavalry Regiment advanced to Hongwhari, 7 kilometers west of Puku. There the brigade tried to find a proper avenue that would lead to Kumch'on via the northern slope of Kuksa-bong hill. However, due to the wrong report of the cavalry division's aerial observer, the brigade erroneously entered into the 8th Cavalry's zone; thus the British troops never got into the fight for Kumch'on.

October 13th promised to be a critical day for the US 1st Cavalry Division to close the Kumch'on area. With the 7th Cavalry Regiment blocking the exit road from Kumch'on, the decisive action now rested with the 5th and 8th Cavalry Regiments which were trying to compress the enemy pocket from the east and south. Attacking from the east, the 5th Cavalry encountered an almost continuous mine field in its approach to Kumch'on, and it also had to fight and disperse an enemy force estimated to number 300 men at a point 13 kilometers west of Puku. As a result, the regiment was delayed; however, overcoming these difficulties, it pressed ahead and reached the outskirts of Kumch'on by the evening of that day.

Meanwhile, the US 8th Cavalry Regiment which had been driving north along the Seoul-Sinuiju highway was confronted by strong opposition in the area of Tusok-san. At once the regiment called for fire support, and on the morning of the 13th, an artillery preparation blanketed enemy positions there

in the mountain area. Because of the closeness of the American troops to the enemy, a planned B-26 bomber strike was canceled. But a new flight of fighter
planes continued to bomb the enemy positions every thirty minutes. However,
the NKPA troops resisted stubbornly with counterattacks using tanks, artillery, mortars, and various automatic firearms. In one of the counterattacks,
enemy tanks rumbled out of the early morning mist to strike an outpost of B
Company, the US 70th Tank Battalion. Immediately, both forces were locked in
a fierce tank battle. In the day's series of attacks and counterattacks, the UN
Air Force and B Company, 70th Tank Battalion, both supporting the 8th Cavalry Regiment, destroyed a total of 8 enemy T-34 tanks without loss to themselves.

While the bulk of the NKPA 19th Division fought desperately in the
Tusok-san area south of Kumch'on to prevent the US 8th Cavalry Regiment
from closing in on the town, a large enemy column of trucks and carts with an
estimated 1,000 soldiers moved northward out of Kumch'on on route 1. The enemy troops apparently did not know about the roadblock set up at Han-
p'ori by the US 7th Cavalry, and ran into it. In the ensuing action, the 7th Cavalry, aided by air strikes, killed an estimated 500 and captured 201 of this enemy
force.

The leading 2nd Battalion, US 5th Cavalry Regiment, which had been
attacking against Kumch'on, resumed its attack on the town at midnight that
day, and entered and seized the northern part of it after dispersing an enemy
force in the outskirts of the town. The 3rd Battalion following behind seized the
southern part. On the 14th, the next day, the 2nd Battalion turned north toward
the US 7th Cavalry at Hanp'ori and the 3rd Battalion south to meet the 8th Cavalry which had been moving north. The 1st Battalion remained behind to clear
the town and secure it.

Advancing northwest, the 2nd Battalion of the 5th Cavalry Regiment
successfully joined elements of the 7th Cavalry above Hanp'ori at about noon.

An enemy force, estimated to number 2,400 men, which had been attacking the 7th Cavalry roadblock position at Hanp'ori, escaped into the nearby hills when the 2nd Battalion approached from the south. Meanwhile, attacking south from Kumch'on, the 3rd Battalion established contact with Task Force Walton of the 8th Cavalry Regiment at a point 6.5 kilometers south of Kumch'on at around noon that day. This concluded the US 1st Cavalry Division envelopment and capture of Kumch'on which had been carried out in five days.

Once Kumch'on and the 38th Parallel defensive line fell to the US 1st Cavalry Division, North Korean Premier Kim Il Sung was embarassed and outraged, and commanded, "Do not retreat one step farther. Now we have no space in which to fall back." He directed that unit commanders organize a special group, which he termed the "Supervising Army."

In the meantime, the ROK 12th Regiment(commanded by Lt. Col. Kim Chom Kon), which had been kept as the ROK 1st Division reserve and at the same time designated as the coordinated infantry-tank-artillery unit, was ordered by the division to advance toward Kuwhari 14 kilometers north of Korangp'o. At that time, the regiment enjoined its 1st Battalion(led by Maj. Han Soon Wha) to board tanks of C Company, US 6th Tank Battalion, which had been attached to the ROK Regiment.

On October 12, led by the ROK division commander who was on board the 2nd tank, the combined forces rapidly advanced to Kuwhari along the dike of Sami-ch'on. At the beginning, the combined troops had difficulties due to inadequate communications and lack of experience; however, from that afternoon everything went well. Once the ROK 12th Regiment captured Ku-whari, by sunset it continued to proceed to an area near Puku, 10 kilometers northwest, availing itself of the gathering momentum. That area was the ROK 1st Division zone of action, and it included a strategic road junction which led north to Sibyonri and west to Kumch'on. However, as had been described above, in a conference on the spot, the US 5th Cavalry Regiment took precedence on the road until it captured Puku and turned west toward Kumch'on, and the ROK 12th Regiment of the 1st Division moved on toward Sibyonri via Puku.

The leading 2nd Battalion, the ROK 11th Regiment on the division left, had advanced farthest to Sodujongjang the day before. Taking advantage of the weak enemy resistance at 01:00, the battalion advanced further gaining eight more kilometers to Komisong. There it cut off the enemy's path of retreat. Meanwhile, the regiment(−) on the right proceeded to Tugokri via Kuwhari.

At 01:00 on October 13, the leading 1st Battalion of the ROK 15th Regiment continued making turning movements from T'osanri toward Sibyonri and captured the east edge of Sibyonri at 07:30. Early that morning the 15th Regiment(−) left Sangnyong, and at 14:00, its 2nd Battalion drove to Kusongri west of Sibyonri blocking the enemy's path of retreat there. Meanwhile, the 3rd Battalion advanced to Sibyonri at 15:00. The ROK 12th Regiment, which had passed through the 11th Regiment in the vicinity of Wich'onri at dawn that day, crossed over the Whanggyech'i Pass of the Masik-ryong Range and continued on toward Sibyonri. However, the regiment was delayed while removing enemy mines after it crossed the ridge of the pass. Leading the combined infantry-tank-artillery forces, the regiment gained 25 kilometers during the morning and arrived at Sibyonri in the early afternoon. There the regiment rejoined the ROK 15th Regiment and together they moved to the outskirts of the town to block its northern edge. There they took up hasty defensive positions for the night. The 11th Regiment, which had followed behind the 12th Regiment as the division reserve, also arrived at Sibyonri around sunset.

Thus the ROK 1st Division succeeded in controlling the important road junction town of Sibyonri and at the same time cut off the enemy's path of retreat. The enemy troops began to surrender in groups after their retreat path was blocked. As many as 225 North Korean soldiers surrendered during that day almost causing problems of accomodation and evacuation. The following day, the ROK division had its 12th Regiment whose troops were on board American M-46 Patton tanks in the front lead off, and let the 11th Regiment closely follow behind the 12th Regiment. The 15th Regiment, the division reserve, was kept in the rear.

The ROK division continued to pursue the enemy force which had started to retreat toward Singye and Koksan. In the area of Miudong northwest of Sibyonri, the division defeated an estimated enemy regiment which was supported by various guns and artillery including 6 T-34 tanks, and advanced rapidly to Singye by that night.

In the meantime, the ROK II Corps, which had been moving north through the rugged mountain areas of the central front on the east(right) of the US I Corps, received an operations order dated October 10 from the ROK Army. The order stated that the corps would continue on toward Wonsan as fast as possible and once the corps reached Wonsan, it would move toward P'yongyang along the Yangdok-Changnimri-Kangdongri axis in an effort to join the US I Corps.[45] In order to accomplish his mission, Maj. Gen. Yu Jae Hung, commander of the ROK II Corps, revised the Army order and issued his own operations order enjoining his divisions to take part in the attack toward P'yongyang.

Pursuant to this order, the ROK 2nd Regiment, the leading element of the 6th Division, left Singosan on the night of October 13 along the Wonsan-P'yongyang highway via Wonsan, and by the next day advanced to Tokwon, 5 kilometers west of Wonsan. On the corps left the ROK 8th Division, which had resumed its drive north from P'yonggang, captured Yich'on on the upper stream of the Imjin River the night of the 13th. On the next day, the division slowly moved west toward Singye after it crossed over the Masik-ryong Range. At that time, the ROK corps commander directed the 8th Division to turn toward

Koksan and move toward the northeast of P'yongyang to avoid disturbing the ROK 1st Division's zone of action.

In the meantime, the ROK Army reserve, the 7th Division, which had entered P'yonggang on October 12 via P'och'on-Chikyongri and cleared the area, was reattached on October 14 by ROK Army Operations Order 215 to the ROK II Corps. Its measure was to attack toward P'yongyang.

The enemy's three known lines of defense at the 38th Parallel now had been crushed by the US I Corps' envelopment of Kumch'on and Sibyonri and the ROK II Corps's pressure against P'yongyang along the Singye-Ich'on-Tokwon axis during the 6 days from October 9 until the 14th. Consequently, the friendly operations to attack against P'yongyang could be progressed more vigorously. The next step for US I Corps operations was to advance toward the Whangju-Yulri line about 60 kilometers from the present line(Hanp'ori-Singye). On the corps right the ROK 1st Division was to advance to Suan via Singye situated on the upper stream of the Yesong River. In the corps center the leading US 7th Cavalry Regiment, 1st Cavalry Division, was to attack toward Sohung after it crossed over the Myolak Range from Namch'onjom; the remaining two US cavalry regiments and the 27th British Commonwealth Brigade were to follow behind the 7th Cavalry from the Namch'onjom-Kumch'on line. On the corps left, the US 24th Division enjoined its 21st Regiment to prepare to attack toward Haeju via Paech'on and its two other regiments, the main attack units, to assemble in the area of Kaesong.

In accordance with the corps operations plan, Maj. Gen. Gay, commander of the US 1st Cavalry Division, devised his own plan for maneuvering his troops to capture Sariwon, the strategic road junction town on the 38th Parallel-P'yongyang axis:

H-hour will be at 07:00, October 15. Once the leading 7th Cavalry Regiment, which had been driving north along the axis of Namch'onjom-Sohung, captured Sohung, the 27th British Commonwealth Brigade which had been following behind the regiment will pass through it and frontally attack Sariwon. Then the US 7th Cavalry Regiment will swing to Sindangri from Sohung to advance to Whangju, 18 kilometers north of Sariwon. By so doing, the cavalry regiment will cut off the enemy's path of retreat and attack the city of Sariwon from the north using part of its troops. The 5th Cavalry Regiment will turn to the west and attack against Sariwon from the axis of Namch'onjom-Ch'ongsokduri-Sinwon-Sariwon.

General Gay attempted to make a pincer attack against the town from three sides as he had estimated that his advance would be easy since there was no mountainous terrain available to the enemy to cover him.

On the morning of October 15, the 2nd Battalion of the US 7th Cavalry Regiment attacked Namch'onjom from Hanp'ori. UN air strikes which preceded the attack bombed and strafed Namch'onjom, using napalam bombs, rocket and machine gun fire, which made the town a sheet of flames from the early morning hours. Because of the unexpectedly stubborn enemy resistance, the battalion entered Namch'onjom at around noon suffering about 40 casaulties in the battle. North Korean prisoners at that time said that the UN strafing attacks had destroyed the NKPA 19th Division command post and killed the division chief of staff.

However, despite their continued defeat from the Kumch'on battle, the NKPA troops, under supervision and coercion, still resisted with well-organzied delaying actions. In addition, the drizzle that had started since early that afternoon turned into torrential rains, which in turn turned the dusty roads into a sea of mud. These all interfered with the US 5th Cavalry Regiment's maneuver plan to move from Namch'onjom to the west to cut off the retreating enemy from Haeju. Accordingly, the advance of the US 1st Cavalry Division was delayed far behind the initially planned schedule. Reflecting General Walker's impatience with the US I Corps' slow advance, the corps commander, Maj. Gen. Milburn, that day decided to make an all-out pincer attack against Sariwon and capture it using all available troops. He ordered the US 24th Division Commander(Maj. Gen. John H. Church) to move north on the left of the 1st Cavalry Division to seize Sariwon, and then attack north toward P'yongyang. On the same day, the 1st Cavalry Division commander Maj. Gen. Gay ordered the 27th British Commonwealth Brigade to closely follow behind the US 7th Cavalry Regiment and be prepared to pass through it to seize Sariwon, once the 7th Regiment had captured Sohung. Thus the commanders were pressing hard for the early capture of P'yongyang, but their troops were totally tired and nervous at that time.

The US 3rd Battalion(commanded by Lt. Col. James H. Lynch), 7th Cavalry Regiment, which had resumed its attack from Namch'onjom on the early morning of October 16, seized Sohung overruning Sinmak at around noon that day. The 1st Battalion of the same cavalry regiment, which had closely followed behind the 3rd Battalion, turned north at Sohung and advanced to Sindangri along a narrow local road on Changch'on Creek. Meanwhile, the US 21st Regiment(commanded by Col. Richard W. Stephen) of the 24th Division left Paech'on and advanced to the outskirts of Haeju via Yonan as initially planned. Both the US 5th Cavalry Regiment and the US 19th Regiment, 24th Division, turned west toward Nuch'onri at Namch'onjom and drove on toward Ch'ongsokduri with the latter trailing the former. If they seized the town, the 19th Regiment would turn west toward Sinwonri and continue on toward Jaeryong and Sariwon, while the 5th Cavalry would turn northeast to advance toward Sohung.

As a result, on that day a bad traffic jam developed on the road between Kumch'on and Namch'onjom where the motorized columns of the 7th

Cavalry, the 27th British Commonwealth Brigade, the 5th Cavalry, and the 19th Regiment were all on the road. In the midst of this confusion word came that the corps commander Maj. Gen. Milburn had told the commanders of the 1st Cavalry and the 24th Divisions that whichever division reached Sariwon first would thereby win the right to lead the corps attack on into P'yongyang. The competitive spirit was high among the soldiers of the two divisions. A dominant characteristic of all units in the advance at this time was the strong rivalry prevailing between divisions, and even between regiments within a division to be the first to reach P'yongyang.

Under such circumstances, on the 17th, the US 7th Cavalry Regiment, led by its 1st Battalion at Sindangri, slowly moved west following the narrow "cow-path" road in the valley of the Whangju-ch'on. They then continued on toward Whangju, 26 kilometers north of Sariwon, following a circuitous route. Also that morning, the 27th British Commonwealth Brigade passed through the lines of the US 7th Cavalry Regiment at Sohung and took up the advance along the main highway toward Sariwon. The brigade drove north in a column formation with the Argyll British Battalion in the front, the Australian 3rd Battalion in the middle, and the Middlesex Battalion in the rear. The Argyll 1st Battalion advanced to a point 6 kilometers south of Sariwon unopposed, but beyond that point, the battalion came under heavy enemy fire. On hills on either side of the circuitous road bend, the enemy, heavily armed with antitank guns and automatic weapons, had been waiting for the battalion's approach. Maj. David Wilson, A Company commander, who had controlled his company at a point about 100 meters behind the point tank, located the enemy troops which had started to fire on the leading 1st Platoon's tank column from a hillside apple orchard on the left. At once he deployed his men on both sides of the road and directed all available fire power and antitank guns of his company to the orchard. They killed about 40 and captured others including equipment in this brief action.

Afterwards, the 27th British Commonwealth Brigade continued to advance encountering no further enemy resistance, and entered Sariwon at 16:00 that day.
They found the large town had been almost devastated by the continued UN air
strikes and bombing.

At 17:00 that day, the Australian 3rd Battalion left Sariwon upon receiving the Brigade Commander, Brig. Gen. Basil A. Coad's, order to pass through the
Argylls in the town and to advance 8 kilometers north of it toward Whangju to
cut off the Sariwon-P'yongyang highway. From there they were to prepare for
future attacks. There the Australians went into a perimeter defensive position
in front of a range of hills strongly held by the enemy, and prepared to attack
the next morning.

In the meantime, on the division right the US 7th Cavalry Regiment,
which had swung to the northeast from Sohung on the morning of October 17
and advanced along the Sindangri-Whangju axis, continued on toward
Whangju 26 kilometers north of Sariwon with Lt. Col. Peter D. Clainos' 1st Battalion in the lead. At around 16:00 in the afternoon when the regiment advanced
to a point 5 kilometers southeast of Whangju and was to strike the Seoul-
Sinuiju main highway again, it received a message the division commander
dropped from a light plane. The message said that the roads between Sariwon
and Whangju were crowded with hundreds of enemy soldiers. It directed the
regimental commander to have the bulk of his troops capture Whangju, and at
the same time, to have one battalion turn south to defeat the enemy soldiers and
meet the Australian Battalion in the north of Sariwon.

Accordingly, the 2nd and 3rd Battalions of the US 7th Cavalry Regiment continued their advance northward, while the 1st Battalion headed south
toward Sariwon. Soon after turning south on the Sariwon-P'yongyang highway,
the 1st Battalion captured an enemy cavalry detachment which comprised 37
horses. According to the prisoners' statement, a North Korean Battalion was

dug into the high ground positions on either side of the Sariwon-Whangju high-way and was prepared to counter the UN troops. The 1st Battalion proceeded south cautiously in a combat-ready formation; as was anticipated, it came under fire from the enemy on the east side before its lead element gained 3 or 4 kilometers. Shortly, both forces were locked in a fierce fire fight.

Right at that moment, the tactful battalion commander Lt. Col. Clainos had his South Korean interpreter reach the enemy forward position and yell out that "the column you [North Koreans] were fighting was Russian." Then a platoon size enemy troops came up to a point where Lt. Col. Clainos was near, and was quickly disarmed by the US troops who had been in ambush duty near-by. Finding that they had been tricked, some of the enemy tried to resist, but after one of them was shot down, the rest surrendered. Other NKPA soldiers who had observed this progress in the nearby hills began pouring in to surren-der. Almost all enemy soldiers from the eastern side of the position surrenderd, and many on the western side also came out to surrender. Thus until dark that day, approximately 1,700 enemy soldiers and 13 female nurses surrendered to the 1st Battalion.

At 18:00 that day, the battalion commander sent a radio message to the Australian 3rd Battalion Commander Lt. Col. Charles H. Green, who was hold-ing north of Sariwon, that the motorized column of the 1st Battalion of the US 7th Cavalry Regiment was coming south with vehicle lights on. At 22:30, the American battalion reached the Australian perimeter.

Thus, ahead of the US 24th Division, the US 1st Cavalry Division had captured Sariwon first against stubborn enemy resistance, and as the corps com-mander had promised, it became the leading unit for the P'yongyang attack. On this same day, the US 21st Regiment, US 24th Division on the corps left, seized Haeju, and the 19th Regiment reached a point 10 kilometers off Sariwon on the axis of Ch'ongsokduri-Sinwonri-Jaeryong. However, as the town had already been seized by the 27th British Commonwealth Brigade which had been attached to the US 1st Cavalry Division, the corps commander ordered the US 24th Division to discontinue its advance toward Sariwon. Therefore, the US 24th Division turned toward Chinnamp'o the next day and drove on.

Meanwhile, on October 14 when the ROK 1st Division captured Singye, the division commander called for an operational meeting that night to discuss an action plan for capturing Sangwon and Yulri. It was decided in that meeting that on the division right the 12th Regiment would advance north along the axis of Singye-Suan-Yulri, the 11th Regiment on the left would drive on the axis of Singye-Nungri-Sangwon, and as the division reserve the 15th Regiment together with the division headquarters unit would follow behind the 12th Regiment.

On the morning of October 15, the ROK division started its advance as planned. The 12th Regiment left a road junction 2 kilometers west of Singye and moved north along the Singye-Suan road. Headed by a combined infantry-tank-artillery element, the regiment gained about 30 kilometers to reach Hayuri south of Suan before sunset.

On the division left the ROK 11th Regiment also left Singye to move north along the axis of Taep'yongri-Doari-Nungri. Without encountering enemy resistance, it gained 21 kilometers and reached Kwangsuri by sunset. In the meantime, the 15th Regiment together with the division headquarters unit moved to Singyri from Sibyonri.

The following day (October 16), the ROK 12th Regiment left Hayuri to move northwest toward Suan. According to the division Reconnaissance Company's report, an estimated NKPA battalion had dug into Hill 445(Chang-san) southeast of Suan, and another in Yodong-san north of the hill. Therefore, the regimental commander planned to attack against a knob behind Changhung-dong and Yodong-san via Suan by placing his 2nd Battalion on the right, and the 3rd Battalion on the left, respectively. Accordingly, the 2nd Battalion, with the help of the attached American tanks, reached the knob(373 meters) behind Changhungdong at 12:30, and there it provided fire support for the 3rd Battalion's effort to capture Yodong-san. Thus the ROK regiment accomplished its mission to seize Yodong-san and the village Suan on the west of the mountain. Meanwhile, by sunset that day, the the 11th Regiment reached Nungri which was close to the boundary between the regiment and adjacent US 1st Cavalry Division.

On the morning of October 17, the 12th Regiment, leading unit of the ROK division, left Suan for Yulri. The regimental commander enjoined his 1st Battalion, the reserve unit, to pass through the 2nd and 3rd Battalions, on board the American tanks which had been attached to the regiment. When the 1st Battalion reached a point 1.3 kilometers south of Yulri and entered a valley with high rising cliffs on both sides, it came under fire from an estimated two enemy battalions on the hill barrier ahead; enemy troops with two guns and four mortars had been deployed on a dominating hill, Yondae-bong(350 meters), that lay obliquely on the left, and on a steep ridge(200 meters) on the right front. The battalion halted and called for immediate air support while awaiting the 3rd Battalion to rejoin it. In about 15 minutes, when the latter reached the scene, the 1st Battalion launched its attack against Yondae-bong, and the 3rd Battalion attacked the left front ridge. When both battalions approached the enemy positions (around 17:00), the 2nd Battalion, which had advanced to Sanghamri as the regimental reserve unit, reinforced the 1st Battalion in capturing Yondae-bong and Yulri. Once they seized Yulri, the 2nd Battalion continued on toward Sangwon 17 kilometers west of Yulri on board about 10 American tanks. They drove west in a combined infantry-tank-artillery formation to meet the 11th Regiment on the left.

In the meantime, on the division left the 11th Regiment left Nungri at 05:00 on the 17th and marched northwest toward Sangwon on foot. When its leading 2nd Battalion reached enemy lines at the Kakdae-bong peak southwest of Sangwon and its extended edge, Hill 190, a battalion size enemy force stopped it. The ROK battalion (commanded by Maj. Cha Kap Joon) dared to attack this enemy with the help of B Battery, the 17th Artillery Battalion. At 16:30, when the battalion came near the enemy position, apparently demoraled enemy troops abandoned their positions and escaped toward P'yongyang. The ROK 11th Regiment entered Sangwon at 18:00 that evening. At about 21:00 that night, when the 2nd Battalion, 12th Regiment, arrived at the town, the two regiments rejoined there. The 11th Regiment then advanced to Ch'okwidong 7.5 kilometers north of Sangwon along the Sangwon-P'yongyang road, and took up an all-round defensive position there by about 23:00.

Thus, on October 17, the ROK 1st Division had reached the Sangwon-Yulri line, 26 kilometers southeast of P'yongyang, with a remarkable single day's gain of 42 kilometers since it crossed the 38th Parallel. Despite its inferior mobility, and delayed crossing of the Parallel by two days, the division came closer to P'yongyang than of any the US 1st 1st Cavalry Division units which had reached Whangju on the same day. Anyway, by reaching the Whangju-Sangwon line the US I Corps soldiers thus far had broken through the enemy's P'yongyang perimeter, and almost had the North Korean capital city before their eyes.

At about this time, the ROK division commander Brig. Gen. Paik Sun Yup who anticipated the stronger enemy defense in the outskirts of the capital city, estimated that he might need an additional tank company to break through it. He requested assistance from the corps commander, General Milburn, and the latter attached D Company of the US 6th Tank Battalion, 24th Division to the ROK Division. As a result, about 50 American tanks from two tank companies assembled at Sangwon and were busy preparing to attack against P'yongyang the following day.

(3) Entering Into P'yongyang

As of October 17, the US I Corps, which had advanced to the Whangju-Yulri line, the P'yongyang perimeter, was only 40 kilometers off the North Korean capital city. At about this time, the ROK 6th Division, II Corps, which had slowly moved west along the Wonsan-P'yongyang lateral road, reached Tongyang. The ROK 8th Division advanced to a point 17 kilometers south of Yangdok from P'yonggang along Route 3. The ROK 7th Division which had followed behind the 8th Division crossed the Masik-ryong Range and advanced to Kogsan on the upper stream of the Yesong River. The 8th Regiment of the 7th Division advanced to Yulri in the late afternoon of the 17th. Thus P'yongyang was being enveloped from three sides—south, southeast, and east. On that day, South Korean President Syngman Rhee instructed the ROK Army Chief of Staff, Maj. Gen. Chung Il Kwon, that ROK troops should first capture P'yongyang in defiance of all difficulties.

The President's instruction might have come out because there was a greater chance that the mechanized US 1st Cavalry Division, the main attack unit of the US I Corps, might capture P'yongyang first.

Upon receiving the President's order, General Chung visited the headquarters of the ROK II Corps (at Kogsan), and relayed the President's intent to the corps commander, Maj. Gen. Yu Jae Hung. The corps commander then hurried to the headquarters of the ROK 7th Division (at Chongbongri), and together with the division commander (Brig. Gen. Sin Sang Ch'ol) went to visit the ROK 8th Regiment (commanded by Col. Kim Yong Joo) at Yulri, the closest town to P'yongyang. There the corps commander ordered the regimental commander in person to capture P'yongyang before the US troops.

In the mean time, the ROK Army, after conferring with the US Eighth Army, issued Operations Order 218 at 18:00 that day (October 17) for the ROK II

Corps. Gists of the order were as follows:

① The II Corps will use all available roads and paths to move its entire troops, including headquarters unit, to the west of Kangdong within the shortest time possible.

② In close coordination with the US I Corps, the ROK II Corps will swing and attack to the east and northeast of P'yongyang.

③ The 6th Division of the ROK II Corps will attack against Anju via Songch'on and Sunch'on.

④ The II Corps will prepare to move northward.

Thus, among the three divisions of the ROK II Corps, only two divisions, the 7th and 8th, were to take part in the operations for capturing P'yongyang.

At about this time, the NKPA activated the P'yongyang Garrison Command (Commander: Maj. Gen. Ch'oi In) in an effort to hold the advance of the ROK and UN forces. However, as its P'yongyang perimeter, the Whangju-Yulri defensive line set up in the Myolak Range, had already been penetrated, the NKPA instead tried to build strong defensive positions along the Taedong River and in the Eastern P'yongyang area. It was estimated that the enemy would undertake a token defense of the city by delaying the advance of friendly force, so that North Korean government organizations could have time to withdraw north and, at the same time, protect retreating NKPA troops. At that time, the US Eighth Army G-2 estimated that less than 8,000 effectives of the NKPA 17th and 32nd Divisions were available for the defense of P'yongyang.

The US 1st Cavalry and ROK 1st Divisions, and the ROK II Corps led the attack into P'yongyang on October 18. The US 1st Cavalry Division was to attack toward southern P'yongyang by leaving Whangju and moving north along the relatively favorable main Seoul-Sinuiju highway and the railroad. The division launched its attack against P'yongyang with the 7th Cavalry Regiment in the lead.

At daylight on the 18th, the US 7th Cavalry led by its 3rd Battalion, crossed the ford in Whangju and began the advance. Resistance was light until the leading elements arrived near Hukkyori, 12 kilometers south of P'yongyang.

However, when the leading battalion approached closer to Hukkyori, it came under fire from enemy with antitank guns and 120-mm. mortars. The enemy in the front was estimated to be a reinforced battalion which held prepared defensive positions in the south of the town. Twenty tanks of C Company, US 70th Tank Battalion, supported the cavalry battalion. But the battalion attacks failed because of stubborn enemy resistance with three or four dug-in tanks and a mined roadway. In the midst of the fierce fighting, enemy small arms fire shot down an F-51 fighter plane which was providing close air support.

Dissatisfied with the 3rd Battalion's progress, at sunset that day the cavalry division commander ordered the 1st and 2nd Battalions of the same regiment to start flanking movements against the enemy positions. Pursuant to this order, the two battalions moved off toward the enemy flanks in a night-long movement, and attacked the enemy positions early on the morning of the 19th. But they only found the enemy positions abandoned.

As a way to remedy the state of slow advance and at the same time to maintain the momentum of the attack, the US 5th Cavalry Regiment was committed to the Hukkyori position. Spearheaded by F Company (commanded by 1st Lt. James H. Bell), and reinforced with five tanks, a platoon of engineers, and a section of heavy machine guns, the 5th Cavalry passed through the 7th Cavalry at Hukkyori and moved toward P'yongyang. F Company moved on against minor resistance, while UN fighter planes supported the attacking column in close coordination with artillery elements. When F Company reached the 20-meter-wide Mujin-ch'on, a tributary of the Taedong River at the southern edge of P'yongyang, enemy troops behind the opposite embankment tried to thwart the company's crossing of the creek with three antitank guns. F Company suppressed the North Korean antitank gun fire with its mortar fire in about half an hour, and then crossed the Mujin-ch'on and entered the southwestern edge of the North Korean capital city, East P'yongyang, at 11:02.

Meanwhile, on the corps right the ROK 1st Division resumed its attack toward the eastern flank of P'yongyang from Ch'okwidong north of Yulri. The division had a good chance of entering P'yongyang first only if it could successfully cross 8 kilometers of rugged mountains and advance to the Nangnang Plain. However, the aerial picture presented by the US I Corps showed that the NKPA troops had taken up triple in-depth defensive positions along the avenue from Sangwon to P'yongyang.

The first phase defensive line was set up in the area of Kwanum-san and Panyong-san hills on each side of the road near Taedongri; the second phase defensive position was at Jaeryong-san hill along the Sangwon stream, 4 kilometers northwest of Taedongri; and the last one was located on the lower hills in the midpoint of the plain area which led to East P'yongyang.

Considering such an enemy situation, the ROK 12th Regiment, the main effort of the 1st Division, planned to leave Sangwon in a combined infantry tank column to pass through the ROK 11th Regiment and advance toward the Taedong river bridge along the axis of Taedongri–Sonkyori; the ROK 15th Regiment, the supporting unit, would swing to the northeast of P'yongyang along the Samdung–Kangdong axis; the ROK 11th Regiment at Ch'okwidong would first support the 12th Regiment during the latter's passing through, and then assemble at Munsanri to remain as division reserve.[46]

On the morning of October 18, the ROK 1st Division resumed its final attack against P'yongyang. Its 12th Regiment together with the two attached tank companies of the US 6th Tank Battalion passed through the 11th Regiment at Ch'okwidong, and advanced toward Taedongri. When the regiment just began to pass through a defile between Kwanum-san and Panyong-san hills short of Taedongri, it came under fire from an estimated two-battalion-sized enemy force.

Since the enemy situation in the area had already been analyzed by aerial photographs, the regimental commander at once committed his 2nd and 3rd Battalions to the Kwanum-san and Panyong-san areas on each side of the road, and enjoined the US 6th Tank Battalion(−), covered by the ROK 1st Battalion, to penetrate frontally into the enemy position. Eventually, the ROK regiment captured Taedongri.

The regiment continued to pursue retreating enemy troops from Taedongri, and, when it reached a point one kilometer north of Taedongri, an estimated regimental size enemy force desperately resisted it. With 16 guns and various howitzers emplaced on the opposite bank of the Sangwon stream, the enemy concentrated its fire upon the leading tanks of the friendly forces. Heavily mined roads and the stream which functioned as a natural barrier stopped the regiment's forward advance.

In the midst of a fierce battle between both forces, the ROK division commander, Brig. Gen. Paik Sun Yup, called for an urgent operational meeting that night to discuss alternative measures. A night attack by a combined infantry and tank column was favored at the meeting; at around 23:00, under cover of the dark, the regiment crossed the ford of Sangwon and neared the foot of the ridge of the hill positions with its 1st and 2nd Battalions in the lead; however, it was unable to break through the enemy line until daybreak next morning.

In the meantime, the ROK 15th Regiment, which had left Yulri at night on October 17 and swung to Samnung, moved west to cross the Taedong River in the early morning of the 18th. By about 22:00, the regiment completely controlled the southern bank area near Ssanggangp'o, the upper stream where the Taedong and the Nam Rivers join each other, about 11 kilometers away from the Taedong Bridge. There the regiment was busy reconnoitering and locating proper wading points or ferry sites — preparing for the river crossing the following day (October 19).

At dawn on October 19, the ROK 12th Regiment, the main attack unit of the division, made an assault upon enemy positions and seized its objective with the help of various artillery and tank fire; unexpectedly however, soldiers found the dug-in positions, from which the enemy had stubbornly resisted the previous day, had already been abandoned.

The ROK 12th Regiment thus overran two of the three enemy defensive lines that had been built in the outskirts of P'yongyang, and moved on toward the Nangnang Plain in a column of the 1st, 2nd, and the 3rd Battalions in that order. At that time, the 1st Battalion had each platoon board 4 of the attached American tanks and they drove through the dry hilly country of corn and millet fields at speeds of 50 km/hr.

When the lead elements of the regiment reached Oryuri short of East P'yongyang,[47] an estimated two-battalion enemy force opened fire to stop them. This was considered the third and the last of the NKPA's line of resistance.

Tanks of C Company, the US 6th Tank Battalion, immediately spread out to attack against both flanks of the enemy position, and under cover from foot soldiers, three tanks in the center rushed frontally into the enemy center positions. Right at that moment, other tanks also rapidly rumbled into the enemy flanks under covering fire from infantry and engineer soldiers. Thus they succeeded in breaking through the enemy's last P'yongyang perimeter line, inflicting about 300 casualties upon the enemy. At that time, the division engineer company, which had been attached to the ROK 12th Regiment, removed 72 antitank mines there in the battle area, but additional enemy antipersonnel and antitank mines delayed the advance of the ROK regiment.

Anyway, the ROK 12th Regiment proceeded smoothly to East P'yongyang and reached the Sonkyori traffic circle about 100 meters east of the Taedong bridge by 11:00 that day, and thus became the first unit of UN Forces to enter the city.

Meanwhile, on the right flank of the 12th Regiment, the adjacent ROK 11th Regiment almost made a double time march in advancing toward the Mirim and Munsuri Airfields(also called P'yongyang Airfields). However, the regiment was an hour and half behind the headquaters unit of the ROK 15th Regiment (11:00) and arrived at the Mirim Airstrip at 12:35. It continued on toward the Munsuri Airfield and occupied the day's final objective at 14:40. While approaching the city, the ROK 11th Regiment had much difficulty in the Ch'uulmi area, where the North Korean Defense Minister and the NKPA High Command were located, because of the 3,000 enemy troops which they intercepted surrendered to it. Among the prisoners, 1/3 were later identified to have belonged to the so-called "volunteer forces," who had forcibly been conscripted from the South Korean areas. Arrangements were made to send these people home after a brief interrogation process.

The ROK 15th Regiment, which had swung to the northeast of P'yongyang, reached the upper stream of the Taedong River late in the afternoon of the previous day, and each battalion of it secured a ford to cross the river. At 05:00 on that day (October 19), the 3rd Battalion completed its river crossing at Masanri ahead of others, and was followed by the 2nd and 1st Battalions which crossed the river at Ich'onri (2nd Battalion) at 08:30, and at Samsandong (1st Battalion) at 10:30, against minor resistance. They continued on toward the main part of P'yongyang where the Moran-bong and Kim Il Sung University were situated.[48]

In the meantime, the commander of F Company of the 2nd Battalion, US 5th Cavalry Regiment, who had entered East P'yongyang shortly after 11:00 that day, advanced to the Yanggak Island in the Taedong River by passing over

a span of the railroad bridge. He had been ordered to secure the Taedong Railroad Bridges and a bridgehead on the north bank of the river. After a hasty examination of the eastern bridge he found that only one span of each of the two
railroad bridges was intact. At that time, the North Koreans on the opposite
bank blew up the span north of the island. As a result, the company was unable
to reach the northern bank of the river and became trapped on the is land. Only
after the 3rd Battalion which had followed behind relieved the company could
it withdraw back to East P'yongyang.

While F Company was on the Yanggak Island, the rest of the 2nd Battalion crossed the Mujin-ch'on, and turned right toward the main highway
Bridge, the Taedong Bridge. It was the only bridge still intact; however, when
the leading elements of the 2nd Battalion neared the bridge, the NKPA troops
on the northern bridgehead blew up the center span. Now all of the main highway and railroad bridges over the Taedong were cut off. Right at that moment,
the 2nd Battalion of the US 5th Cavalry Regiment met with the elements of the
ROK 12th Regiment, ROK 1st Division, which had arrived a little earlier at the
Sonkyori traffic circle about 100 meters east of the Taedong Bridge trying to locate favorable fording sites. Both troops shared the joy of capturing the enemy
capital while the commanders of the corps and the two divisions met to discuss
future operations there.

Meanwhile, the 3rd Battalion of the ROK 15th Regiment, which had
continued on toward the Moran-bong, seized it at around 14:50. At that time, a
company-sized enemy force had desperately resisted from a number of trenches
and natural caves; having been struck by the ROK regiment, however, enemy
soldiers lost their will to fight and fled. The ROK regiment then advanced to the
main part of P'yongyang, and occupied important North Korean administrative
buildings. At the same time, it cut off the enemy's paths of retreat and began to
clear the city of enemy remnants. The 3rd Battalion entered the North Korean

cabinet building located at Mansudae, Moran-bong, the 2nd Battalion on the left flank drove south toward the North Korean Government offices at the hillock of Mansudae along the western bank of the Taedong, and the 1st Battalion moved west toward the West P'yongyang Railroad Station to intercept enemy troops retreating northward.

As mentioned above, the regimental headquarters unit (training center) captured the Munsuri Airfield at 14:10 after it overran the smaller Mirim Airstrip, and then turned it over to the ROK 11th Regiment which had arrived there shortly after. Then at 16:45, the unit crossed the Taedong River at a ferry site 1 kilometer north of the airfield and arrived at the Moran-bong which had already been secured by friendly forces. Thus the ROK 1st Division had the honor of capturing P'yongyang first, by having the 11th and 12th Regiments in East P'yongyang and the 15th Regiment in the main part of the city.

In the meantime, the ROK 8th Regiment (commanded by Col. Kim Yong Ju) of the 7th Division, ROK II Corps, which followed behind the 15th Regiment and drove toward P'yongyang pursuant to the ROK Army Operations Order 218, finally entered main P'yongyang. The 8th Regiment had left Yulri on the morning of October 18, and arrived Samdung at about 21:00 that day. However, the 15th Regiment, ROK 1st Division, which had left the same village the night before for Samdung, had reached the upper stream of the Taedong by about 22:00 via Hwach'on, Sunghori, and Samjongri, and was reconnoitering crossing sites.

On the morning of October 19, the ROK 8th Regiment belatedly left Samdung and followed the same avenue through which the 15th Regiment had already passed. Soldiers of the regiment waded across the river water at Samsanri with their rifles over heads, and advanced to Nosanri, northwest of the ford on the far side, shortly after 13:00. This village town was situated on a turn in the road between P'yongyang and Kangdong, and the ROK 15th Regiment had also passed through it that morning.

By sunset of that day, the 8th Regiment had advanced west to Kim Il Sung University unopposed, but it only trod in the foot steps of the 3rd Battalion, 15th Regiment. There the 8th Regiment moved on toward the Moran-bong and reached the Moran-bong-Kirimri (West P'yongyang) line at about 20:00. It then entered deep into the city again only to find the major buildings had been occupied by friendly forces. The regiment returned back to the Moran-bong.

In the meantime, on October 19, the ROK 8th Division captured Songch'on and advanced to Kangdong the following day. But since P'yongyang had already been captured by friendly forces, the division turned to the north to attack against Tokch'on.

Colonel Crombez, the commander of the US 5th Cavalry Regiment which had entered Sonkyori in East P'yongyang ahead of other UN troops was amazed by the ROK 1st Division's performance. When he found that the latter had already crossed the river and beat him there, he asked Brig. Gen. Paik how his troops found the ford so quickly. Paik answered smiling, "I am a native of P'yongyang. I know the fords."

At daybreak on October 20, the ROK 11th and 12th Regiments in East P'yongyang crossed the Taedong River using M-2 assault boats and pontoon bridges connecting the Taedong Bridge and Panwoldo, all provided and constructed by American engineer troops the night before. Across the river, the two regiments rejoined the ROK 15th Regiment which had entered the main part of the city the previous day.

By 10:00 that day (October 20), the ROK 1st Division secured the entire city, and the streets were full of people waving T'aeguk (national) flags to welcome the ROK troops.

The US 1st Cavalry Division also crossed the Taedong River. The leading 5th Cavalry Regiment crossed the river using assault boats and floating bridges, and advanced to the main part of the city from East P'yongyang. The bulk of the cavalry division followed behind the 5th Regiment and moved across the river. Then the 5th Cavalry Regiment was deployed in the southern outskirts of the city, the 8th Cavalry Regiment in the northern outskirts, and the 7th Cavalry Regiment at Chinnamp'o. The 7th Cavalry made a forced night movement from the city and entered Chinnamp'o in the dead of night. The division commander, General Gay, established his command post in the buildings of the North Korean Military Academy, and was responsible for the internal security and public order of the city in compliance with the corps' order.

The ROK 1st Division, in the meantime, was to guard the northern part of the city above the Taedong Bridge adjacent to the US 1st Cavalry Division boundary that extended from east to west. The ROK division established its command post at the North Korean cabinet building.

The US Eighth Army commander established his advance headquarters at the gray brick building (next to the P'yongyang City People's Committee Office building) which had been the headquarters of Kim Il Sung (October 24). On October 21, General MacArthur had flown into P'yongyang and reviewed F Company, 5th Cavalry Regiment, which had been the first American unit to enter the city. He asked all men in the company who had been with it in Korea since the beginning of the war to step forward. Only five men stepped forward; three of them had been wounded. About 96 days earlier when the company had landed in Korea, it numbered nearly 200 men, but now so many young men's lives had been taken away by the cruelty of war.

On October 16, when it appeared probable that P'yongyang would fall in the near future, the US Eighth Army had organized a special task force known as "Task Force Indianhead." Its name derived from the shoulder patch of the US 2nd Infantry Division. This task force was to enter East P'yongyang with the advance units of the US 1st Cavalry Division, and with the ROK 1st Division's approval, it entered the main part of the city.

The mission of the task force was to secure and protect specially selected government buildings and foreign compounds until they could be searched for enemy intelligence materials. Commanded by Lt. Col. Ralph L. Foster, Assistant Chief of Staff for G-2, US 2nd Division, the task force comprised K Company of the 38th Infantry Regiment, US 2nd Division, 6 tanks of C Company, US 72nd Medium Tank Battalion, and included Engineer demolition troops, a detachment of the US 82nd Anti-Aircraft Artillery Battalion, and counterintelligence troops. By October 20, the task force had secured most of its assigned objectives in the city, and obtained a considerable amount of intelligence material. It transported both miitary and political material to Tokyo on October 22.

In brief, the US I Corps' operations for capturing P'yongyang was completed on October 19, 11 days after it crossed the 38th Parallel on October 9. As of October 19, the 11th and 12th Regiments of the ROK 1st Division, and the 5th Cavalry of the US 1st Cavalry Division had secured East P'yongyang; the 15th Regiment of the ROK 1st Division and the 8th Regiment, ROK 7th Division, which had closely followed behind, had seized the main part of the city. The next day, the ROK 1st Division and the bulk of the US 1st Cavalry Division entered the main part of P'yongyang to clear the city of enemy remnants. Ten days after, on October 30, a huge welcoming ceremony was held at the City Hall (formerly the City People's Committee Hall) attended by President Syngman Rhee.[49] The President delivered his speech in an excited tone at that soul-stirring moment:

> My dear fellow citizens!
> After 39 years of absence suffering all sorts of hardships abroad, I returned to my home country, and arrived here at P'yongyang for the first time across the Taedong River to meet you all. As I stand before you, my lovely fellow citizens, I am choked with so much emotion that I cannot express all that I have in my mind. When we recall back about 40

U.S. 7th Division approaching Hae-San-Jin, 1950

years of hellish lives under the torturous Japanese rule, we are full with
tears of remorse ...

From now on, whether male or female, whether in the south or in the north, we should firmly be resolute to build a new nation and begin a brand new life ⋯

As we have hitherto fought the bloody fight to establish a free and an independent nation ⋯ we should never forget that traditionally we have been a unified nation with valiant will and spirit. So, from now on, we should throw away the selfish partisan prejudices based on regional groupings like south or north, and instead, we should be united with a determined will to live together and die together without allowing any further intrusion of the Communists ⋯

My dear fellow North Korean brethren! Let us make up our mind and declare to the international society that we would never allow any foothold for the Communists, and that if they, whether Soviets or Chinese, reinvade our territory, then we would fight against them and drive them off to the last ⋯

The presidential speech touched deep into the hearts of the people who had suffered under both the Japanese and Communist rules. They might have thought that a truely free, peaceful, and unified nation would soon be realized. That day, the ROK 1st Division, which had entered the city first of all the ROK troops, was decorated with awards and prizes.

III. Up to the Yalu River

1. The NKPA's Last-ditch Resistance

While the ROK and UN troops were racing each other in advancing toward Hukkyori with P'yongyang before their eyes, the NKPA P'yongyang Garrison Command joined other enemy troops which had been retreating from the areas of Sariwon, Ch'orwon, and P'yonggang. Leaving only one regiment at the city, the bulk of the enemy garrison command withdrew to the north of the Ch'ongch'on River.[50]

The North Korean Government also moved to Sinuiju from its capital city of P'yongyang, and later moved again to Kanggye in the mountains, a natural fortress.[51] While demanding soldiers on the frontline to fight desperately, the NKPA Supreme Command assembled its mechanized troops in the Chongju area north of the Ch'ongch'on River, and the bulk of its infantry troops in the Kanggye area. The enemy high command at the same time massed and deployed all of its troops along the river line setting up three defensive phase lines as follows: [52]

- The 1st defensive line: the Anju-Kaech'on-Tokch'on line.
- The 2nd defensive line: the Huich'on line.
- The 3rd defensive line: the Kanggye line.

At that time, the NKPA troops which had retreated north from the area of P'yongyang across the Ch'ongch'on River to the Anju-Kaech'on line numbered approximately 40,000 men, while those which took up positions at the 2nd defensive line were estimated at about 20,000 men who had retreated from the Iron Triangle (Ch'orwon-P'yonggang-Kimwha) area.

At about this time, North Korean Premier Kim Il Sung decided to intensify guerrilla activities in the rear of friendly forces as a measure for retrieving the war situation. Thus, based on the theories of guerrilla warfare, he strengthened the organization of the People's Guerrilla and the 2nd Front units. The North Korean official publication, The *Comprehensive History of Choson* [North Korea] described Kim's strategy as follows: [53]

It was to form a 2nd Front in the enemy rear by using a combined NKPA unit, and at the same time, to organize People's Guerrilla forces by recruiting patriotic people to harass the enemy rear area and to ceaselessly weaken the enemy strength ⋯. For this purpose, they were to actively cut off enemy reinforcements, and, should friendly [NKPA] forces on the frontline pass into the counteroffensive, they were to help the regular forces by hitting hard the enemy [ROK or UN forces] from his rear.

Thus the North Korean 2nd Front unit became active from October 16. Its major objective was to destroy the ROK or UN transportation units, trains, supply points, and traffic or communication facilities. Friendly forces suffered severe loss by this enemy. As a result, the US IX Corps was forced to stay in the rear area to protect supply routes and at the same time, to suppress this enemy's activities. The ROK III Corps which had been activated at that time was also committed to mopping up this enemy.[54]

Prior to this, on October 14, the NKPA Supreme Command held a meeting for the so-called "self-criticism" and admitted that their defeat was due to their negligence in the enveloping operations and failure to effectively resist the ROK and UN counteroffensive. At this meeting, they decided to impose seven stricter regulations on their troops such as putting deserters to summary decisions, operating supervising units, and so on. This decision was issued in the form of an order signed by the NKPA Supreme Commander Kim Il Sung and Park Hun Yong, the General Director of the North Korean Political Bureau.[55]

In terms of strength and equipment, the NKPA was then inferior to the ROK and UN forces, and, as the war situation had turned critical, the NKPA High Command demanded "do-or-die" resistance from its soldiers who were extremely demoralized. They organized many supervising units in a worthless attempt to tightly control their own soldiers.

2. The UN Plan for Exploitation

On October 15, when the US Eighth Army crossed the 38th Parallel and was continuing on toward the north, General MacArthur met President Truman on Wake Island for a strategic conference. At that time, the former was optimistic about the UN victory and told the President that he expected formal enemy resistance to end by Thanksgiving Day. He further said that the continuing enemy resistance was only to save face, and there were only about 100,000 troops left without training, equipment or systematic command chain.

The General also said that the chances of the Chinese Communist Forces intervention were very slight, and the Chinese had already missed the favorable opportunity to effectively enter the war. He added that as the UN forces had air superiority, the Chinese would suffer a major loss if they tried to get down to P'yongyang.[56]

Under the assumption that the war would soon end, as he had stated at the Wake Island conference, General MacArthur issued UNC Operations Order 4 (October 17, 1950) which would apply after the capture of P'yongyang.

In this order, General MacArthur lifted the previous restriction called the MacArthur Line, a line below which all UN ground forces could operate, and authorized a new line which allowed his forces to advance northward. This new line extended in an arc from Sonch'on on the west coast to Songjin on the east coast. Accordingly, the US Eighth Army on the left was to advance northward along the axis of Sonch'on - Ch'ongsanjangsi - Hoemokdong - Koindong - P'yongwon-Toksilri, and on the Eighth Army right, the US X Corps would advance north toward the Toksilri-P'ungsan-Songjin route. This order was to be effective as of October 20. The new line was about 30 miles north of the previous Chongju-Hamhung line, and was generally 48-64 kilometers below the Manchurian-North Korean border. Only the ROK troops were allowed to operate north of this line.[77]

Prior to this, on October 16, the General had ordered the US X Corps to operate independently as the UNC reserve unit and to control the ROK and US troops operating in the northeastern front. Accordingly, as of October 20, the operational control for the ROK I Corps was transferred to the US X Corps from the US Eighth Army. He also notified Eighth Army commander that the US 187 Airborne Regimental Combat Team would be airdropped to the areas near Sukch'on and Sunch'on.

In response to this UNC plan, the ROK Army issued its own Operations Order 221 with an objective to occupy the Hoemokdong-Toksilri line and clear the area below that line of enemy remnants. Following is the gist of this order:

> The I Corps: will be released from the ROK Army control as of 12:00, October 20, 1950 and be attached to the US X Corps. From that time on, the Corps would be under command of the X Corps for future operations.
>
> The II Corps: ① will immediately assemble its 7th Division in Samdung and release it from the corps control so that the division can be under command of the ROK Army as Army reserve;
> ② will capture and secure the objective "A" line[58] in its zone, and prepare for future operations.
>
> The III Corps: will mop up enemy remnants within its zone in coordination with the police force.

The ROK III Corps had been activated on October 16 with the newly activated ROK 5th Division (October 8, 1950) and the 11th Division activated on August 7, 1950. Its primary misssion was to protect the rear area extended from Inje-Yangyang in the north to Seoul-Ch'unch'on in the south, and at the same time, to provide support for the frontline units.

Pursuant to the orders issued in series, the US airborne unit air-dropped over the Sukch'on-Sunch'on area on October 20, and on the 21st the US Eighth Army continued to attack northward on the west, and the US X Corps advanced north toward the MacArthur Line drawn at the Sonch'on-Songjin area.

3. Securing the Ch'ongch'on River Line

(1) Airborne Attack upon the Sukch'on-Sunch'on area

When ground forces of the US Eighth Army were driving north toward P'yongyang, the US 187 Airborne Regimental Combat Team(commanded by Col. Frank S. Bowen, Jr.), the US Far East Command strategic reserve, was waiting for its operations order at Kimp'o Airfield.

General MacArthur planned to employ the airborne troops which had not been used since the beginning of the Korean War in a drop north of P'yongyang in an effort to cut off the bulk of enemy troops, reinforcements, rear supply routes, and North Korean officials, and at the same time, to rescue hundreds of American prisoners of war who would be evacuated northward at that time.

The D-day for the airdrop was set on the day when P'yongyang would be completely secured by friendly forces, and Sukch'on (principal drop zone) approximately 56 kilometers north of P'yongyang and Sunch'on about 17 kilometers east of Sukch'on were selected as drop zones. These areas were considered critical in terms of military strategy and transportation because not only did the main Seoul-Sinuiju and Manp'o railroads pass through them from P'yongyang but also well developed highways ran parallel to the railroads which led to the Manchurian border.

At 02:30 on October 20, the airborne combat team turned out in a heavy rain for reveille, and waited at the airfield for the weather to improve. Shortly before noon the rain let up and the sky began to clear. The regimental combat team loaded into 113 C-47 and C-119 planes of the US 314th and 21st Troop Carrier Squadrons.[59] The first plane, carrying the regimental commander Col. Bowen, was airborne at noon, and the rest joined it to fly in formation over the Han River estuary. They then headed to the north of P'yongyang along the west coast of Korea.

As the troop carriers approached Sukch'on, the principal drop zone, American fighter planes preceded them rocketing and strafing the ground. At about 14:00 troops began dropping from the lead planes over Sukch'on. There was no enemy antiaircraft fire and only sporadic fire by resisting force came into the drop zone. The 1st and 3rd Battalions together with the regimental Headquarters and Headquarters Company landed first, and after the troop drop came that of about 74 tons of heavy equipment including 105-mm howitzers, 90-mm antitank guns, ammunition, and other vehicles. This was the first time heavy equipment had been dropped in combat zones, and C-119 cargo planes had been used in a combat parachute operation.

Upon jumping in the drop zone, the regiment captured dominating hills northeast of Sukch'on, cleared the town itself, and set up a roadblock north of it. By 17:00 that day, the regiment captured all of its objectives and completed its tactical mission of establishing roadblocks. Meanwhile, the 2nd Battalion began dropping onto the area southwest of Sunch'on at 14:20 as planned, and secured its objective by that night. Two companies of the battalion established roadblocks south and west of Sunch'on, and another established contact with elements of the ROK 6th Division which had been moving north toward the Ch'ongch'on River from southeast of Sunch'on.

On October 21, the day following its airdrop, the 3rd Battalion encountered 2,500 enemy troops of the NKPA 239th Regiment which had retreated from P'yongyang and taken up defensive positions at Op'ari and Yongyu 12 kilometers south of Sukch'on. The airborne battalion surprised this enemy from his rear.

Right at that time, the 27th British Commonwealth Brigade, the lead element of the US 24th Division, which had been driving north toward the Ch'ongch'on River from P'yongyang, reached Yongyu and engaged this enemy from the south. As a result, from south and north the British and the American airborne troops were able to launch a pincer attack against this enemy. In this battle, they took many prisoners and established contact at 11:00 the next day.

On the 21st, upon receiving a civilian report that about 200 American prisoners had been massacred inside a tunnel 9 kilometers north of Sunch'on, the 2nd Battalion of the airborne regiment in the town set out to search, and rescued 23 survivors and discovered 66 dead. Afterwards, at 09:00, the battalion established contact with the task force which consisted of the 1st Battalion of the US 8th Cavalry Regiment, 1st Cavalry Division, and a tank company of the US 70th Tank Battalion. This task force had advanced northward from P'yongyang.

By the time the American airborne regiment met the elements of ground forces on October 22, it killed 2,000 enemy soldiers, and captured 3,818; however, it suffered about 100 casualties-46 men during the airdrop and 65 others during ground battles.[60]

In brief, the result of the airborne operation in the area of Sukch'on and Sunch'on was far below its initial objectives to block the path of enemy retreat and to rescue American prisoners. At that time, General MacArthur had expected to trap about 25,000 of the 30,000 enemy remaining troops, but the actual number of enemy soldiers captured was not even close. According to the towns-people, North Korean officials and the main elements of the NKPA troops had already fled evacuating American prisoners northward around October 12, long before the fall of P'yongyang.

(2) Advance to the Ch'ongch'on River

The ROK II Corps had been driving northwest day and night to join in the P'yongyang battle; however, it could not keep pace with the US I Corps which had driven so fast toward P'yongyang. Only the 8th Regiment of the ROK corps had been able to join the P'yongyang operation. Nonetheless, because of that, the ROK corps was able to advance to the Ch'ongch'on River before the US I Corps.

On October 19, the day P'yongyang was captured, the 6th Division of the ROK corps seized Songch'on 50 kilometers northeast of P'yongyang, and on the 20th, its 7th Regiment took the lead to enter Sunch'on where the elements of the US 187 Airborne Regimental Combat Team had airdropped six hours before. There the ROK regiment established contact with the American airborne troops at 20:00 that day, and from then on, it advanced northward ahead of the other troops of the US Eighth Army. To accomplish its own part of the ROK Army Operations Order 221, the ROK corps issued its own operations order that day. Gists of this order were as follows:

- The objective of the corps will be Huich'on.
- The 6th Division will first capture Kaech'on and then proceed toward Huich'on.
- The 8th Division will seize Tokch'on and proceed to Huich'on via Kujang-dong.

Pursuant to this order, the ROK 6th Division, the lead element of the Eighth Army, left Sunch'on at 06:00, October 21, and advanced to Kaech'on on the Ch'ongch'on river. The leading 7th Regiment had the 2nd Battalion(commanded by Lt. Col. Kim Chong Soo) in the front driving toward Kaechon 30 kilometers north, and its 3rd Battalion was prepared to pass through the former at any moment necessary.

The two battalions had been motorized so that they could achieve the effect of a surprise attack. Most of the trucks used(approximately 150) were those which enemy troops had abandoned when the ROK 7th Regiment attacked them at Whach'on after crossing the 38th Parallel. By utilizing these trucks the regiment was able to keep the lead.

At about this time, the ROK 2nd and 19th Regiments of the same division were advancing northward on foot from Songch'on, 35 kilometers south. As a result, it was impossible for them to keep contact with the leading troops. The risk from lack of communications continued as the leading 7th Regiment continued its independent motor march against sporadic enemy resistance. Fortunately however, at that time the NKPA troops were fleeing northward leaving behind not only the wounded and stragglers, but also their vehicles and major equipment still operable on the roads. Enemy troops hastily fled even leaving their prepared meals behind. Wall posters which had urgently demanded enemy troops to reassemble in Kanggye apparently attested to the enemy situation at that time. Women and children who were thought to have been family members of ranking North Korean officials were crying and begging for their lives in roadside millet fields.

In the meantime, the ROK troops were high in spirit due to the pride of being the advance unit and at the same time, the expectation that they were getting closer to the border area. Even though they were in old flimsy summer uniforms and tattered sneakers with worn-off bottoms, and despite the forced marches day and night, they were still indefatigable and volunteerd to lead the attack.

However, there were internal problems. Due to the lack of logistical support, the ROK troops had to live off the country to solve their food and fuel problems. Platoon leaders and company commanders were out of military maps; so they just followed the roads. Especially, the artillery units almost ran out of ammunition and had to borrow 400 shells from the 2nd Battalion of the US 187th Airborne Regimental Combat Team.

At about 13:00, when the advance party of the ROK 2nd Battalion entered the P'ungkwang-san gully 15 kilometers southeast of Kaech'on, it came under surprise fire from an estimated enemy company. The battalion would not be able to advance forward unless it defeated this enemy because of the high mountains on either side of the defile. The battalion fought against the enemy for over an hour utilizing all available strength and firepower, but it was not able to break through the enemy line.

Upon receiving the report on the situation in his command post, the ROK regimental commander, Col. Lim Pu Taek, at once enjoined his 3rd Battalion which had closely followed behind to pass through the 2nd Battalion, and to capture Kaech'on by that day. Kaech'on was about 30 kilometers away from Sunch'on and it takes an hour by car. The 3rd Battalion immediately left Sunch'on, and passed through the 2nd Battalion at the Changsong Pass. When it reached a junction point 8 kilometers southeast of Kaech'on, it encountered two company sized enemy troops heading north in two columns.

Right at the moment they saw the reinforcing vehicles of the ROK 3rd Battalion, the enemy troops began to flee in all directions. Under such circumstances, the battalion commander, Lt. Col. In Song Kwan, decided to take his chance and ordered his men to rapidly drive directly through the retreating enemy columns toward Kaech'on. He thought that he did not have enough time left to engage the enemy if he were to capture his objective during that day. He also ordered his men not to fire unless fired upon.

The motorized ROK battalion rushed through the middle of the road with the lights on, and ROK soldiers yelled, "the war is over; drop your guns and go back to your homes." Most of the confused enemy soldiers abandoned their weapons and escaped in all directions; some sneaked into nearby forest areas with only individual rifles. After this, the ROK soldiers slowed down their speed chanting military songs on the way toward their objective and captured Kaech'on without shooting and even without shedding a single drop of blood.

The ROK battalion was followed by the regimental Reconnaissance Company(−), and the 2nd Battalion which had also followed behind. They bivouacked for the night at Mosigol of Old Kaech'on just southeast of Kaech'on. Thus the ROK 7th Regiment secured and completely controlled the town which was an important road junction on the Ch'ongch'on River. The 3rd Battalion now in Kaech'on was welcomed by the towns-people, and was provided with food. Some of the people also gave the ROK battalion valuable information that a division size enemy force had escaped north toward Huich'on early on the morning of October 21.

At 21:00 that night, unexpectedly a train was heard heading northward from the west of the town. Without knowing that the town had been captured by the ROK troops, the train was coming up to the Kaech'on station from Sinanju. The ROK soldiers momentarily panicked, but the battalion commander at once ordered his Heavy Weapons Company commander to have the machine guns and mortars ready to fire upon the Kaech'on railroad bridge, and at the same time, he alerted all the cadres of the battalion including his staff officers to take up positions on the eastern bank of the Kaech'on creek. Then he ordered the rifle companies which had been in separated areas to go into alert status and guard the outskirts of the town. He had the Reconnaissance Company(−) only deploy together with the battalion headquarters unit on the northern bank of the creek.

Unconscious of the situation, the enemy train approached the railroad bridge just before the ROK battalion's disposition was completed. But the battalion opened a concerted surprise fire upon the train, signaled by a caliber 50 heavy machine gun fire. When an 81-mm mortar shell struck the locomotive engine, the train came to a sudden stop, and the engineman together with a platoon size escort force jumped out of it to escape. The ROK battalion commander captured the engineman and interrogated him. The train turned out to be a supply train with 10 cars loaded with various firearms and military uniforms. The battalion captured them all including 8 T-34 tanks loaded on the flat cars. It was a major military achievement for the battalion.

The ROK battalion waited for the daybreak doing nothing except for guarding the area since it was dark and too much captured equipment to be properly handled. At that time, the battalion heard another train heading north from the identical direction. This second train halted itself as the train ahead blocked the railroad. As soon as the former came under concentrated fire from the ROK battalion, the train crew together with also a platoon sized convoy troops hastily fled into the darkness. Eventually, the battalion captured another six cars loaded full of enemy supply materiel without much effort.

Around daybreak, most of the ROK soldiers changed into new NKPA uniforms, sneakers and even magazine belts, making it impossible to distinguish them from real enemy troops. However, no one could really say anything against those soldiers' extraordinary behavior because their own flimsy summer uniforms had been so dirty, tattered and worn out. Similar things happened to ROK troops which later arrived there, putting a rumor in circulation that the ROK 6th Division got its supply from the NKPA.

Men of the ROK 3rd Battalion, 7th Regiment, finally had a chance to relax that morning from the previous night's tension and excitement caused by the enemy supply trains. But it was not long before ROK troops located a regimental size enemy force in two columns approaching them from Anju.

The ROK battalion commander at once deployed his troops in Majan-gri, southeast of Kaech'on, in an attempt to surprise the enemy columns which were superior in number. Right at the moment when the enemy advance party reached the Kaech'on bridgehead, he ordered his troops to open all available fire upon it. The unprepared NKPA troops either fell down or ran away. Surprisingly enough, ROK soldiers saw a coordinated infantry-tank force appear from the enemy rear firing upon them with tank and machine guns. This unit was turned out to be Task Force Elephant of the US I Corps and consisted of soldiers from the ROK 1st Division and C Company, US 6th Tank Battalion with the mission to block the railroad between Kaech'on and Kujangdong. It had been on its way to Kaech'on via Anju and encountered this same enemy unit. At 08:00 on the 22nd, the unit contacted the ROK 3rd Battalion, 7th Regiment.

The task force was delayed in reaching Kaech'on because it had engaged in a battle at Yongyu with the enemy and managed to pass through Sukch'on during the predawn hours that day. The task force was supposed to seize Kaech'on to cut off the enemy's retreat ahead of other friendly units; however, the 3rd Battalion of the ROK 7th Regiment captured the town a day earlier and successfully completed the task force's mission there.

At dawn on October 22, immediately after the disconnected communication was reopened, the ROK 7th Regimental commander Col. Lim Pu T'aek was notified of the previous night's achievement by his 3rd Battalion commander and complimented the men of the battalion. At once the former ordered the battalion to remain at Kaech'on as regimental reserve, and then ordered the 1st Battalion to pass through the 3rd Battalion and capture Huich'on.

Pursuant to this order, the 1st Battalion left Sunch'on at 06:00 that day and at a nearby junction town, Kunuri (Kaech'on on some maps), advanced northeast toward Huich'on after it passed through the 3rd Battalion. The battalion saw Task Force Elephant was engaged in a battle with unidentified numbers of enemy forces 4 kilometers north of Kunuri. They passed through the task force to help defeat the enemy. Then the ROK battalion moved on toward Kujangdong via Wonri. When it reached Chajak 8 kilometers north of Wonri, soldiers found an enemy supply train with 50 cars scattered around the railroad. Leaving the booty with follow-up units, the battalion continued on toward its objective against minor resistance. It captured about 20 enemy sodiers on the way and seized the town of Kujangdong without suffering any casualties.

Kujangdong was a critical road junction through which the Manpo railroad (P'yongyang-Manp'ojin), and P'yongtok line (P'yongyang-Tokch'on-Kujangdong) passed. In addition, mountain trails and narrow paths in the area all led to Kujandong. Therefore, the battalion had anticipated a major enemy resistance there; however, they found the town was empty. The battalion moved on, and on its way to Huich'on, ROK soldiers recovered the bodies of 28 American prisoners slaughtered by NKPA troops inside a tunnel 7 kilometers north of Kujangdong and rescued 3 Americans still alive, who had narrowly survived the massacre.

One of the survivors said that the NKPA troops had been taking about 30 American prisoners northward. On the morning of the 22nd, realizing that they were pressed hard by ROK troops, they pushed the prisoners into the tunnel and wildly shot them down. He added that it had only been 5 or 6 hours since the last elements of the NKPA passed through the place.

Shortly after, the battalion reached a ford on the Ch'ongch'on River. This was Wonch'am, where there used to be a bridge over the river which later had been bombed and destroyed. The battalion attempted to wade across the shallow lower stream, but they couldn't. ROK soldiers found that destroyed NKPA vehicles together with cars of the high ranking North Korean officials, which had apparently tried to cross the river at that point, had been struck by UN air planes and had been piled up in the water. A total of 22 expensive sedans and about 100 Japanese or American-built military trucks had been deserted either on the river bank or in the water; some were found intact attesting to the hasty situation the North Koreans had faced at that time. Some North Korean officials or high ranking soldiers, who were being pressed hard by the ROK 7th Regiment, were thought to have attempted to drive across the shallow water, but they were forced to abandon their cars because the water unexpectedly got deeper. Among the captured vehicles were some very rare and expensive ones.[61]

The ROK battalion shoved several of the vehicles out of the way and waded across the river. There it continued on toward Huich'on. While moving on with its 1st Company in the lead, the battalion captured 13 NKPA officers who had been eating their meal on the roadside north of Whap'yongch'am. At the entrance of the town, the battalion engaged in a brief battle with about 500 enemy troops, and captured most of them after it shot down several who resisted.

This brief engagement in which a company-sized ROK force defeated battalion size enemy troops without blood shed indicated that the NKPA troops had lost their will to fight and, as a result, the war was approaching the end. However, the increased number of the NKPA prisoners was a new problem. Since the ROK battalion had been active independently, it did not have sufficient strength or time to either accomodate or evacuate the prisoners it frequently captured. In an attempt to ease the problem, the battalion selected those who had been wounded lightly, looked too young or obedient, and sent them back home; the ROK battalion took only the cadres and the extremists in custody.

Meanwhile, the ROK regimental commander ordered the battalion which had been separated from the bulk of the regiment by about 40 kilometers to halt at an area 25 kilometers south of Huich'on and north of Whap'yongdong for the night bivouac, and to resume the attack at daybreak on the 23rd. At that time, he worried about the darkness and the risky situation under which the battalion was to move independently. He also notified the battalion that the main body of the regiment would follow behind it for the pursuit toward Huich'on the following day.

At 06:00 on October 23, the leading 1st Battalion, ROK 7th Regiment, left Whap'yongch'am for Huich'on. When the motorized battalion gained about 9 kilometers and reached a road junction at Hahaengdong, it came under concerted fire from an estimated enemy battalion. At once the ROK soldiers got off their vehicles to engage the enemy for about half an hour; they suppressed the enemy and continued on toward their objective. At around 14:30, the battalion reached Yujungch'am where the streets of Huich'on were in sight. While the soldiers had a mingled feeling of joy and tension with their objective before their eyes, an enemy 122-mm shell suddenly zipped through the air and landed on the town. It was soon followed by machine gun bullets fired from a military crest of Hill 490 northeast of Huich'on. The NKPA troops began to desperately resist with howitzer and machine gun fire from their dug-in positions on the hill. Immediately a fierce fire fighting between both forces shook the area for about an hour. At around 16:00, the main elements of the enemy force withdrew northward apparently giving up their defense at Huich'on and part of the remnants surrendered. The enemy troops fled toward Kanggye so hastily that they left behind the wounded as well as bodies of their comrades.

According to the prisoners' statement, the enemy force was part of the NKPA 18th Division, and the bulk of the division had been deployed in the high ground near the Kuhyon-ryong pass which was situated 25 kilometers north of Huich'on. The pass was considered tactically important because the town of Kanggye was situated over it. At this Huich'on battle the ROK battalion captured 20 T-34 tanks, and a 6-boxcar train loaded with medicine and other supply items.

The ROK battalion remained at Huich'on strengthening its guard for the night based on the regimental order that the battalion would wait for further orders once it seized Huich'on. At about this time, the 2nd Battalion of the ROK 7th Regiment was at Hahaengdong 16 kilometers southwest, and the 3rd Battalion together with the regimental command post were located at Kujangdong further south of Hahaengdong.

In the meantime, the ROK 2nd Regiment, the division reserve, was ordered to capture Onjongri. For this purpose, it planned to quickly advance to Chajak south of Kujangdong and there it would cross the Ch'ongch'on River; then it would continue on toward Onjongri on foot. The 19th Regiment(−), after relieving the 2nd Regiment, remained at Kunuri as division reserve, and its 3rd Battalion which had seized Yongbyon the previous day awaited further orders there.

On the corps right the ROK 8th Division (commanded by Brig. Gen. Lee Song Ga) started to move toward Huich'on via Kach'ang, Pukch'ang and Tokch'on after it assembled at Sonch'on on October 21 following behind the leading ROK 6th Division.

The 10th Regiment, the lead elements of the ROK 8th Division, captured Maengsan east of Kaech'on on the same day that the 6th Division took Huich'on, and continued toward Yongwon north of Maengsan. The 16th Regiment of the same division captured Tokch'on, the division objective, at 13:00 after it passed through Maengsan.

The 8th Division had planned to move toward Huich'on through rugged mountain areas. As expected, the division made a very slow advance and was behind other friendly units 40-50 kilometers south of Huich'on. Despite its belated start and geographical restrictions, the division had proceeded to Tok-ch'on, its immediate objective, over exceedingly mountainous country which no troops might ever have ventured to pass.

When the 1st Battalion of the 16th Regiment, 8th Division, was about to enter Tokch'on, approximately two company-sized enemy troops deployed on nearby Hill 273 resisted, and both forces exchanged gunfire. After defeating the enemy troops there in about half an hour, the ROK battalion secured the P'yongtok railroad line, which invigorated the whole division activities.

Meanwhile, the division headquarters and the 21st Regiment, the division reserve, took up the advance to Pukch'ang, and eventually established contact with the ROK 6th Division which had entered Kaech'on the previous day. Now, the two ROK divisions were able to closely cooperate with each other and resume balanced, well-coordinated operations under control of the corps.

At that time, the US I Corps, which had already captured P'yongyang, started to move toward the Ch'ongch'on River on October 21 to keep pace with the ROK II Corps accomplishing UNC Operations Order 4.

The US I Corps was to advance to the western sector of the MacArthur line with the US 24th Division (attached: the 27th British Common-wealth Brigade) on its left, the ROK 1st Division on its right flank, and the US 1st Cavalry Division as reserve. The US cavalry division was responsible for the security of the P'yongyang area.

Accordingly, from October 21, advance elements of each division left P'yongyang. The ROK 1st Division, spearheaded by its 12th Regiment to which D Company of the US 6th Tank Battalion was attached, led the attacking columns.

Full of fighting spirit, the ROK 1st Division soldiers who had had the honor of being the first to enter P'yongyang reached Kaech'on on the 22nd via Sunch'on. Its 12th Regiment led the division and the 11th and 15th(−) Regiments arrived at Sunch'on following behind it.

At 07:00, October 23, the 12th and 15th Regiments of the ROK 1st Division continued on toward Anju. From Kaech'on, the former advanced westward along the southern bank of the Ch'ongch'on River, while the latter moved northward along the northwestern route from Sunch'on. The 11th Regiment(−), the division reserve, followed behind the 15th Regiment leaving the battalion which had been attached to the US 1st Cavalry Division in P'yongyang.

Anju situated on the southern bank of the Ch'ongch'on had been a strategic town throughout Korean history, where Korean ancestors fought against continental powers who had repeatedly attempted to invade their country. When the coordinated infantry-tank point elements of the ROK 12th Regiment were about to enter the town, they saw two NKPA tanks and two self-propelled guns. The combined unit quickly knocked them out and entered the town capturing another T-34 intact.

Afterwards, the friendly infantry-tank unit drove up to Sinanju, and checked the enemy situation in the nearby areas. The main body of the regiment which had closely followed behind seized Anju and patrolled the town to locate favorable crossing sites on the Ch'ongch'on River. They found the bridge that connected Sinanju and Maengjungri had already been destroyed and the wooden bridge over the river in front of Puksongri six kilometers north of Anju had also been half-destroyed.

Repair of the Anju Bridge began at once and continued through the night with the help of the US corps of engineers. By 09:00 the following day, wheeled traffic, including 2 1/2-ton trucks, could cross on it. The regiment also found a tank ford 5 kilometers east of the bridge, which allowed the American tanks to cross the river there. At about this time, the ROK 15th and 11th(−) Regiments entered Anju and prepared to continue their northward advance.

On the left of the US I Corps the US 24th Division, which had assembled in P'yongyang on October 22, prepared for the northward advance. After establishing contact with the US 187th Airborne Regimental Combat Team at Yongyu, that afternoon the division drove northward along the Seoul-Sinuiju highway with the attached 27th British Brigade in the lead. The British brigade arrived at Sinanju at 15:00 on the 23rd reaching the Ch'ongch'on River. It was 4 hours later than the ROK 1st Division's arrival at Anju, and 46 hours after the ROK 6th Division captured Kaech'on.

However, the bulk of the US 24th Division had fallen further behind other friendly units because of its delayed start at P'yongyang. By that time, the American division only reached Sunan. In addition, another problem for the division was finding a way to cross the Ch'ongch'on River as the water was more than 4 meters deep and the bridge over it had been destroyed. On the following day, the 1st Battalion of the brigade crossed the river using assault boats. The main body of the brigade together with tanks and other vehicles crossed the river at a point near the Anju bridge in the ROK 1st Division's zone. After crossing the river, the brigade swung toward Maengjungri north of Sinanju. By that night the motorized 5th Regimental Combat Team arrived at Sinanju, and the 21st Regiment which had followed behind it drove up to Sukch'on. This concluded the US Eighth Army's advance to the Ch'ongch'on River front. The 6th Division of the ROK II Corps was the first to reach the line, and it was followed by the ROK 8th Division, ROK 1st Division attached to the US I Corps, and the US 24th Division in that order.

4. Advance to the Yalu River

(1) The United Nations Command's Order for Massive Attack

On October 24, General MacArthur instructed commanders of the US

Eighth Army and the X Corps to press forward to the northern limits of Korea as rapidly as they could by utilizing all available forces. At that time, the main elements of Eighth Army had been crossing the Ch'ongch'on River on the west, while on the east, the X Corps prepared for its landing operations at Wonsan. General MacArthur, who had restrained, a week before on October 17, UN ground forces other than ROK troops from operating north of the initial objective line, lifted this restriction by saying that the line was to be valid only if the enemy had surrendered. Under such circumstances as the North Koreans attempting to continue their resistances, it would be meaningless for him to respect the line.[62] An argument and bickering developed between the general and the US Joint Chiefs of Staff over this matter because the latter stated that General MacArthur's order was not in accord with the directive of September 27. However, he justified lifting the restriction as a matter of military necessity. He said that the ROK forces could not handle the situation by themselves, and in order to end the war as early as possible, he insisted, all available ground forces should be committed to the effort. Then he added that should the UN forces once reach the border, they would be relieved by the ROK forces.[63]

Based on General MacArthur's instruction, General Walker, commander of the US Eighth Army, removed all restrictions and ordered his troops to make a concerted attack on the 24th. At the same time, he advised the commander of the US I Corps, Maj. Gen. Frank W. Milburn, to utilize the ROK 1st and 7th Divisions for operations in the border areas if possible. For this purpose, the former ordered the ROK 7th Division to be attached to the I Corps as of 24:00 on October 23.[64]

Maj. Gen. Yu Jae Hung, commander of the ROK II Corps, immediately issued an operational brief for his troops which were to drive on toward the northern border of North Korea. It stated,[65]

- The II Corps will advance to the border area between Chungkangjin and Pyoktong with the 8th Division on the right and the 6th Division on the left.
- The 6th Division will proceed northwest on the axis of Huich'on-Onjongri and capture Ch'osan and Pyoktong.
- The 8th Division will proceed northeast on the axis of Huich'on-Kanggye and capture Manp'ojin and Chungkangjin.

Meanwhile, Maj. Gen. Milburn, commander of the US I Corps, ordered the ROK 1st Division on his right flank to drive northeast toward the Sup'ung Reservoir along the axis of Anju-Unsan, and the US 24th Division on the left to proceed toward Sinuiju via Sonch'on across the Ch'ongch'on River.[4]

(2) The Pursuit Operations toward Ch'osan and Chungkangjin

Upon receiving the order from the ROK II Corps, Brig. Gen. Kim Chong Oh, commander of the ROK 6th Division, formed his own plan and issued a verbal order to accomplish his part of the mission. In this plan he placed the 7th Regiment on the right and the 2nd Regiment on the left. The 19th Regiment was kept as division reserve. He ordered the 7th Regiment to capture Ch'osan, and the 2nd Regiment to seize Pyoktong by way of Onjongri.

Accordingly, at 07:00 of the 24th, the ROK 7th Regiment moved out to take its immediate objective, Hoemokdong, which was considered as a stepping stone to capture Ch'osan. Its 1st Battalion, which had already overrun Huich'on, and the 2nd Battalion stationed at Hahaengdong, took a short-cut through mountain trails to attack Hoemokdong. The 3rd Battalion left Kujangdong, and moved along a road toward the same objective via Hawolim.

As the commanders' major concern at that time was to reach the Yalu or Tumen River on the Manchurian border ahead of others, the advance of their troops was not to be closely coordinated; each column was free to advance, in those unlimited objective attacks, as fast as possible through passes without respect to gains made by others on either west or east flank.

The 7th Regiment, ROK 6th Division, left Huich'on and moved through the Kugsong-ryong Pass 35 kilometers north of the town. The Kugsong-ryong pass, a branch of the Chokyu-ryong Mountain Range, was only 654 meters above the sea level; however, it was a critical terrain, in reality, a watershed in that area neighboring Ch'osankun county, through narrow short-cut trails of which one could reach the town of Ch'osan. Nevertheless, no enemy troops were found to have been deployed in that mountain pass. By that time, the NKPA had apparently been under an illusion that the motorized ROK or UN forces would travel up only along the highway. What made the matters worse for the enemy was that they had not enough troops left to be deployed along the rough mountain pass. The ROK 7th Regiment(−) crossed the pass and reached Hoemok-dong on the morning of October 25.

The 1st Battalion of the ROK 7th Regiment discovered an ominous situation developing in the area through interrogating a captured prisoner: a division size Chinese Communist Force had been standing ready in the Tongnim-san area east of the road between Onjong and Pukchin. The battalion immediately informed its regimental commander of the new development.

Being frightened by the information that CCF had infiltrated into his rear area, the regimental commander at once called the division headquarters to ascertain whether it was true. However, the division commander, at that time apparently ignoring the presence of the CCF, ordered his regimental commander to press the enemy hard until he could capture his objective.

At about this time, the top-level commanders had apparently estimated that it might have been too late for the CCF to intervene, and even if that happened, the CCF could not check the advance of the ROK and UN troops which had already reached points within a day's distance to the Manchurian border. At that time, the soldiers of the ROK 7th Regiment were in such high spirits that they could have smashed the CCF, or any the mightier forces.

The 7th Regiment, the lead element of the ROK 6th Division, left Hoemokdong and moved on toward Kojang. Meeting battalion-size enemy opposition on the way just south of Kojang, it captured the town itself at 18:30 that day. The regiment was less than 30 kilometers away from the border.

At 07:00 on October 26, the next day, the 7th Regiment launched the final attack toward the Yalu driving the enemy to the last ditch. The motorized 1st Battalion of the regiment rushed toward Ch'osan through the road and nearby hills covered with the first snow of the year.

At about this time, a regimental size enemy force was concentrating in the area of Ch'osan. Maj. Gen. Oh Paik Ryong, who had commanded the NKPA 8th Division at the Naktong River front, was bringing enemy remnants together there.

At a narrow mountain path 6 kilometers south of Ch'osan, the ROK battalion came under enemy fire. The ROK troops at once dismounted from their vehicles to counter the enemy, and opened up with all available fire. Both forces were locked in a fierce battle which lasted over an hour and half. Being driven to the last ditch, enemy soldiers were desperate, but at last they began to flee.

Meeting no further opposition, the ROK battalion rapidly entered the town of Ch'osan. Contrary to their expectations, however, the ROK soldiers found the town empty, and could not see the Yalu River. The river was in reality 6 kilometers away from the town. Therefore, the battalion hurriedly moved on toward the border. When soldiers reached the head of a mountain pass at Sintojang(also called Angt'odong), the blue wave of the Yalu attracted their eyes. "We finally arrived at the Yalu River!" They shouted for joy with vociferous cheers. It was 14:15 on October 24 that soldiers of the ROK 6th Division first reached the river to realize their long cherished dreams.

Soldiers were busy with reporting their arrival at the Yalu to the higher echelon commands through wire or wireless communication channels. The advance platoon drove a flagpole into the river bank and hoisted the Korean national flag. Soldiers filled their canteens with the river water in commemoration of the occasion.

Officers and men of the battalion were buoyed up by their self-important and proud achievement in that they had been the first unit to reach the northern border of North Korea among the ROK and UN units. As the spearhead of the pursuing troops, they had reached there in 41 days since they broke out at the Naktong River front on September 16. Finding a floating footbridge that connected Sindojang, North Korea, with T'ongch'ongu, Manchuria, the battalion destroyed it with 57-mm recoilless rifle. Then the battalion placed its 1st Company in the town of Sindojang with a mission to secure and patrol the riverfront, and pulled its main body back to the town of Ch'osan.

A day earlier, on October 25, when the 7th Regiment was marching toward Kojang, the ROK 2nd Regiment at Onjongri left for Pyoktong on the Yalu. On its way to Pukchin, the immediate objective, the 2nd Regiment encountered an enemy force and fought hard at the foot of Tongrim-san. The ROK troops thought that it was a small force of North Koreans, but it immediately turned out to be part of the Chinese Communist Forces. The CCF destroyed and dispersed the ROK 3rd Battalion, the lead unit of the 2nd Regiment. The 2nd Battalion of the same regiment moved out to support it; however, it suffered the same fate that had overtaken the 3rd Battalion. A Chinese prisoner captured that afternoon said that Chinese forces had been waiting around Pukchin since October 17. Having been cut off from Onjongri by the CCF, the ROK 2nd Regiment escaped southward to T'aep'yong.

At about this time, the ROK 8th Division was operating on the east (right) flank of the 6th Division. On October 24, Brig. Gen. Lee Song Ga, commander of the 8th Division had been ordered by Maj. Gen. Yu Jae Hung, Corps commander, to capture Manp'ojin and Chungkangjin by proceeding on the axis of Huich'on-Kanggye. The town of Kanggye was an important objective since it was known as the place where the North Korean governmental officials and high military commanders had assembled. To accomplish his mission, the 8th Division Commander considered that he had first to advance to Huich'on, which had been under control of friendly forces. However, in this effort he had to overcome rugged mountain ranges which formed a natural barrier to his advance. To approach Huich'on from Tokch'on where the main body of the division was stationed, and from Yongwon where his 10th Regiment stayed, he thought he had only two alternatives which were to bypass Myohyang-san (1,365 meters) on either right or left side of it. Accordingly, he planned to maneuver the 10th Regiment through a narrow mountain trail on the east(right) of Myohyang-san and cross the O-ryong pass to Huich'on, while the 16th Regiment would take a narrow passage on the west(left) of Myohayang-san to reach Huich'on via Kujangdong from Tokch'on. The division reserve, the 21st Regiment, and the division headquarters unit would follow behind the 16th Regiment to advance to Kujangdong.

On the morning of the 24th, the 10th Regiment started toward a small town, Tuamri. At the ridge of the mountain village, it captured about 30 enemy soldiers. Unexpectedly, the prisoners turned out to have belonged to the NKPA 15th Division which had fought at Yongch'on on the Naktong river front. Prisoners said that a mixed NKPA troops of approximately 5,000 soldiers assembled in the area of Ch'orwon had been moving north toward Kanggye. At 16:00 of the 24th, the ROK 10th Regiment passed Songp'yongdong north of Yongwon, and arrived at Huich'on at 13:00 of the 26th ahead of other units of the 8th Division. There in Huich'on, which had been occupied by the 7th Regiment of the

ROK 6th Division three days before, the 10th Regiment joined the 19th Regiment, the reserve unit of the ROK 6th Division.

In the meantime, the 16th Regiment, which had left Tokch'on on the morning of the 24th, captured about 250 enemy soldiers on the way to its objective. These enemy soldiers, who had scattered and slipped into nearby mountain ranges when the ROK 6th Division captured Kujangdong, surrendered to the 16th Regiment after the pincer attack launched by the ROK 8th Division. At 15:00 of the 25th, the regiment entered Kujangdong followed by the 21st Regiment, the division reserve unit. There, the Division Commander placed the 16th Regiment on the division reserve, and the 21st Regiment on the left to lead the division toward Huich'on.

At 14:00 of the 26th, when the 21st Regiment reached Sinhungdong, it received a rush order from the ROK II Corps to the effect that the 8th Division would discontinue its operations and assemble at Kujangdong to wait for further order, and at the same time, let its 10th Regiment advance to Onjongri to support the 2nd Regiment, 6th Division. Right at that time, the 2nd Regiment had been was withdrawing south in dispersion after having been struck by an organized CCF force.

The ROK II Corps' emergency order was to cope with a newly developed situation, the open intervention of the CCF, and at the same time to rescue the 2nd Regiment and recover the abandoned equipment. For this purpose the Corps commander decided to commit two regiments in Huich'on to Onjongri: the 19th Regiment, the 6th Division reserve, and the 10th Regiment of the 8th Division. But these two regiments were heavily defeated suffering the same fate that had overtaken the 2nd Regiment.

These startling developments in Onjongri brought to the commander of the 6th Division a grave concern on the fate of the 7th Regiment which had advanced to Ch'osan. Worrying over the CCF's possible cut off, on October 27 the division commander, approved by the Corps commander, ordered the 7th Regiment to withdraw south and rejoin the division as the 2nd Regiment had been defeated and scattered.

To the 7th Regiment which had been patroling the northern border in the area of Ch'osan and the Yalu River front, this order was like a bolt out of the blue sky. The regiment started south; however, having already been cut off, it had to go through a thorny path in an effort to make its way south. Large numbers of soldiers scattered into the hills so that the regiment was virtually disorganized.

Since the three regiments of the ROK 6th Division and one regiment of the 8th Division had been driven into a corner, the ROK II Corps commander attempted to bring the withdrawing soldiers together by deploying the remaining two regiments of the 8th Division in the north of Kujangdong. On the 29th, the US Eighth Army ordered the ROK 7th Division, which had been kept as the US I Corps reserve, to be released from its control to revert to the ROK II Corps. On November 1, the ROK 7th Division was to be committed to the area of Kujangdong-Tokch'on with a mission to protect the east(right) flank of Eighth Army. However, the CCF, which had already infiltrated into the area, made it impossible. Eventually, the ROK II Corps withdrew to the Kaech'on-Wonri area.

(3) The Pursuit Operations toward Sinuiju and Sup'ung

The ROK 1st Division, which had been ordered to proceed to Sup'ungri (Sup'ung) by the US I Corps, started to cross the Ch'ongch'on River at Anju at 11:00 on October 24, and moved toward Unsan. On the division right, the 15th Regiment drove toward Yongbyon in an effort to attack the eastern flank of Unsan from the east of Kuryong River, and on the division left, the 12th Regiment was to make a frontal attack against Unsan after it took Yongsandong by driving from the west of the Kuryong River. The 11th Regiment(−), the division reserve, was to wait at Anju, and advance to Yongsandong in case the 12th Regiment secured it. There they would wait for further orders from the division.

At 15:00 that day, the 15th Regiment reached Yongbyon, where it linked up with the 3rd Battalion of the 19th Regiment, ROK 6th Division. The 3rd Battalion had entered Yongbyon two days earlier to secure the town. The motorized 3rd Battalion troops left for Huich'on to rejoin their regiment, and the 15th Regiment took over the town.

The advance company of the 12th Regiment on the division left, however, encountered strong enemy resistance at a point one kilometer south of Yongsandong and was driven back briefly. Yongsandong, the road junction between Pakch'on and Unsan, and also between T'aech'on and Yongbyon, was considered a strategic point, and therefore, the enemy had deployed a battalion size force reinforced by tanks around the junction area to stubbornly check the advance of the friendly force.

Col. Kim Chom Kon, commander of the ROK 12th Regiment, attacked against this enemy force with his two battalions on both right and left flanks. At once heavy fighting raged between the two forces. The enemy showed no signs of stepping back. Right at that moment, from the east of Yongsandong a tank platoon of the ROK 15th Regiment rumbled into the rear of the town to destroy enemy tanks. But it was not until the ROK regiment's pincer attack that the enemy force began to escape. Eventually, the ROK 12th Regiment seized Yongsandong, which completed part of the ROK 1st Division's mission for securing its immediate objectives, Yongbyon and Yongsandong.

On the morning of October 25, the ROK 1st Division launched its attack against Unsan. Its 15th Regiment left Yongbyon and drove along the east bank of the Kuryong River to attack the east flank of Unsan, and the 12th Regiment moved out at Yongsandong and continued on along the road to attack the southern flank of Uusan. At about 11:00 that day, they entered the downtown of Unsan against minor enemy resistance. But they located no enemy soldiers there. Now, the two ROK regiments decided to move on toward the Sup'ung Dam (hydroelectric dam built at Sup'ung on the Yalu River), their final objective. They continued first on toward Ch'ongsanjangsi, their intermediate objective.

Ch'ongsanjangsi was a town dotted on the "MacArthur Line." At around 11:00 that day, when the ROK 15th Regiment reached it, it suddenly engaged the enemy force there. Half an hour later, the ROK regiment identified the enemy as part of the CCF, and immediately reported it to the division. A little later, at 11:44, it captured the first CCF soldier taken prisoner in the Korean War. The prisoner said there were 10,000 Chinese Communist troops near Unsan, and another 10,000 in the vicinity of Huich'on. The following day, three prisoners including this Chinese captive were brought into the US Eighth Army advance command post in P'yongyang. The ROK 1st Division committed all its available troops including even its reserve, the 11th Regiment, to Unsan, to open up some more advance avenue, but to no avail.

Meanwhile, complying with the US I Corps' order to capture Sinuiju, the US 24th Division drove toward Pakch'on at dawn of the 24th spearheaded by the 27th British Commonwealth Brigade which had bivouacked at Maengjungri, north of Sinanju the previous night. At 10:00 that day, the 1st British Battalion entered the town of Pakch'on only to find empty streets.

The British brigade had first to cross the Taeryong River in order to capture Chongju 30 kilometers west of Pakch'on. Although it was a tributary to the Ch'ongch'on, the Taeryong was a great river with width and depth next only to the Ch'ongch'on. The US 24th Division requested the construction of a bridge, and immediately received an airlifted 15-ton floating bridge set with 15 soldiers from the Corps Engineer Floating Bridge Company.

At about this time, the US Eighth Army Headquaters, having confirmed that most of the NKPA's mechanized units including the 18th Armored Division had withdrawn toward Sinuiju, hoped for a rapid advance of friendly tank units across the river.

Under such circumstances, two battalions of the 27th British Brigade crossed the river utilizing nearby ferries, and the remainder were waiting for the completion of the floating bridge. At 18:00 of the 26th, the brigade came under enemy surprise attack. Immediately, it requested the tactical air control party for air strikes, which suppressed the enemy with strafing and napalm bombs. The bridge was completed in the meanwhile, and the remaining 2nd Battalion together with a tank company crossed the river that night. Thus the British Brigade completed the crossing of the Taeryong.

On October 27, the brigade left Pakch'on and continued on toward Chongju. But at around noon, when it gained approximately 10 kilometers, suddenly it met strong enemy opposition near the Hyosong-ryong Pass.

The brigade was held in check by the concerted enemy fire; from their defiladed positions, and supported by tank and self-propelled gun fire, enemy soldiers directed all their weapons fire toward the brigade. Requested by the British Brigade, a formation of the UN air force fighter bombers flew over and napalmed and bombed enemy positions around the Hyosong-ryong Pass with 1,000-ton bombs. At the same time, combined tank and infantry forces of the brigade made an assult to knock out ten enemy T-34 tanks and two self-propelled guns. The enemy was driven off and the brigade resumed its advance. At about 15:00 the following day, when it reached the valley at Hasori east of Chongju, it located a company-size force of enemy troops accompanied by two tanks. The brigade immediately destroyed the tanks and dispersed the enemy soldiers. On the morning of October 29, the Australian 3rd Battalion, 27th British Brigade, took the lead to attack toward Chongju. Aerial observers reported that four enemy tanks with foot soldiers blocked the road ahead in the vicinity of Sangsori.

Friendly air force fighter bombers flew over again to destroy four tanks, and the battalion rapidly advanced to gain the pass and adjacent ridge lines. That evening the enemy, led by tanks and self-propelled guns, counterattacked the Australian battalion there. Until 21:00 that night when the battalion reached Talch'on River east of Chongju, it was locked with the enemy in a severe battle. In the course of it, the Australian battalion destroyed three enemy tanks with the help of an American tank company.

On the morning of the 30th, the 2nd Battalion of the British Brigade passed through the Austrailian 3rd Battalion to enter the town of Chongju, and cleared the streets of enemy remnants. The commander of the British Brigade asked Maj. Gen. Church, commander of the US 24th Division, to relieve his British troops since he believed they were very tired after the several battles that they had fought. Acceding at once, the division commander ordered the US 21st Infantry Regiment to take over the mission of the 27th British Brigade and to lead the pursuit on the axis of Sinuiju.

The lead unit of the division, the US 21st Regiment, commanded by Col. Stephens, passed through the 27th British Brigade at Chongju and headed north toward Kwaksan. When the regiment passed through a small town, Hadandong, the men could hear the rumble of withdrawing enemy tanks. The regiment speeded up for the night attack pressing hard against the enemy. It was September 20 by the lunar calendar and the silvery moon grew brighter as the night advanced. After midnight at 2 o'clock, in the predawn hours of October 31, when the 2nd Battalion commanded by Lt. Col. Perez reached a point near Solmaegol west of Kwaksan, North Korean troops opened fire to stubbornly resist the attacking column. The enemy had attempted to ambush the advance unit of the US 21st Regiment by placing seven tanks and 500 troops in the valley of Honamri. His concerted surprise fire with tank cannons and machine guns at

300 meters' range held the American battalion in check.

Since the enemy had revealed his positions, American tanks immediately returned fire at the enemy gun flashes. Commanders of the American regiment and battalion consistently directed the battle through their radio communication nets. In this nighttime tank battle, the US 21st Regiment destroyed 5 enemy tanks, 1 self-propelled gun, and 7 antitank guns. The North Koreans escaped toward Kwaksan, leaving behind about 50 dead. After this night of battle, the NKPA's resistance sharply decreased, and the American regiment encountered almost no resistance while it advanced to Wondong via Sonch'on.

At about this time, the US 1st Cavalry Division, the US I Corps reserve, was committed to the area of Unsan, and the 8th Cavalry Regiment relieved the ROK 12th Regiment on October 31. There the two ROK and US divisions tried to defeat the enemy and pursue him northward; however, the situation only turned for the worse.

On November 1, upon relieving the 2nd Battalion, the 1st Battalion of the US 21st Infantry Regiment took the lead in driving toward the North Korean border city, Sinuiju. The battalion traveled about 20 kilometers to reach Chonggodong without opposition; the town was only about 33 kilometers away from Sinuiju on the border. So, if it could move on at the same speed as it did the previous day, it meant that the battalion would reach the North Korean border the following day.

But the soldiers' hopeful dream of ending the war momentarily vanished when they were ordered to halt, consolidate their position, and be prepared to defend in depth. The order from the 24th Division commander hit the 1st battalion, US 21st Regiment, "like a bolt out of the blue."

There, acting on orders from the division, the regimental commander ordered the 1st Battalion to stop and pass from the offense to the defense. This order apparently disappointed and strained the men of the battalion who had reached the northern most point of North Korea ahead of the other UN soldiers on the western zone of action. By a strange coincidence, the advance unit which had reached a point short of the Yalu was Lt. Col. Smith's 1st Battalion, 21st Infantry Regiment, part of which had fought the first American ground battle (Task Force Smith) at the Chukmi-ryong Pass north of Osan nearly four months earlier, at the beginning of the Korean War. The battalion commander was the identical person: Lt. Col. Charles B. Smith. Thus Lt. Col. Smith was to be recorded as the battalion commander who had fought the first battle and at the same time, the northernmost action in Korea.

That night (November 1) the 1st Battalion, US 21st Regiment, which had stood on the defensive at Chonggodong together with one tank company of the US 6th Medium Tank Battalion, came under enemy attack. Seven enemy tanks and an estimated 500 infantry made a surprise attack upon them. Capt. Jack G. Moss, commanding the tank company, reacted quickly to lead his tanks out to destroy the enemy armor. In a blazing tank and infantry battle that lasted half an hour, they drove off the enemy. In the course of it, they knocked out all seven enemy tanks and killed an estimated 100 men. This battle was the last one fought by a unit of the US Eighth Army in the first offensive action north of the 38th Parallel.

Meanwhile, the 5th Regimental Combat Team (RCT), the US 24th Division, continued on toward T'aech'on and Kusong on the east flank of the US 21st Regiment and the 27th British Brigade which had been operating on the Seoul-Sinuiju axis. The T'aech'on-Kusong axis was to follow a rugged mountainous approach which led to Sup'ung at a halfway point between Chongju and Unsan.

The US 5th RCT left Pakch'on on the morning of October 28 without knowing the enemy situation ahead. Right at the moment when its lead elements, the 2nd Battalion and one tank company, US 6th Medium Tank Battalion, were to cross over the tortuous pass called Kokok-ryong, they engaged an estimate 300 NKPA troops in a heavy fight which lasted until 13:00 the next day, when the 5th RCT controlled T'aech'on. In this heavy battle, the US 5th RCT distinguished itself by killing about 100 men, capturing 89 prisoners, and destroying 9 tanks and 4 self-propelled guns.

From T'aech'on, the RCT turned northwest toward Kusong. When it was to reach Tokwhadong southeast of Kusong by way of T'oeum-ryong on the northwest, it engaged another large NKPA force. This enemy was estimated to number 5,000 to 6,000 men, supported by tanks and self-propelled guns. But the 5th RCT, strongly supported by tactical air, broke through the enemy positions at Tokwhadong and captured Kusong at about 12:00 on the 31st. While pursuing the enemy until Paegundong, north of Kusong, the regimental combat team killed an estimated 300 enemy soldiers and captured 2 self-propelled guns, 6 antitank guns.

The town Kusong was known as a famous historical site, where Gen. Kang Kam Ch'an of the Koryo dynasty had smashed an estimated 10,000 Koran (a Manchurian Kingdom) force. Anyway, the American soldiers' rapture over their recent series of victories could not last long when, on November 1, a liaison plane came over to drop a message in which their division commander ordered the regiment to stop and hold in place.

That day, the US I Corps commander visited the headquarters of the ROK II Corps to review the combat situation there. With his ROK counterpart, he discussed measures to hold the Anju-Kaech'on line. Upon returning to his office, the I Corps commander called for a division commanders' meeting that night. At 23:00, he ordered the participants to withdraw south to the line of Pakch'on-Yongsandong-Yongbyon-Unhungri. The divisions, accordingly, began to withdraw from the midnight of November 1.

Since no corps reserve units had been available at that time, the US

"March North" (up to the Yalu) Operation (Western Front)

Eighth Army committed its own reserve forces to the direction of Kaech'on in an effort to protect withdrawing friendly troops, and at the same time, to counter any possible enemy breakthrough. Now the UN general offensive on the western front stood at a standstill after a week of operations toward the Manchurian border in which they had suffered considerable losses.

Since the ROK forces had encountered the Chinese Communist Forces at Unsan and Onjongri for the first time on October 25, and captured CCF prisoners there, the UN general offensive on the western front, based on General MacArthur's order, had begun to face a grave situation. However, the US Eighth Army, which had interrogated CCF prisoners, had apparently hesitated to acknowledge the fact that it had engaged part of an orgarized CCF at Unsan and Onjongri. Instead, they tried to interprete it as a sign of the Chinese Communists' effort to reinforce the NKPA by dispatching Korean-Chinese to the battle front. They maintained that the US Eighth Army had located no signs of an open intervention of the Chinese Communists in the war. The United Nations Command had, in its reports on the estimate of the situation during October 16 through 30, also erroneously concluded that no organized Chinese Communist units entered Korea.[67]

Ⅳ. Pursuit Toward the Tumen River

1. Securing the Wonsan Beachhead

(1) The Plan and Order for Securing the Beachhead

Initially, the Wonsan beachhead was to be secured by the US Ⅹ Corps within a week after the main elements of the US Eighth Army crossed the 38th Parallel. However, this plan had to be inevitably changed because the ROK I Corps had already captured the city on October 10, even before the US X Corps completed its loading for the landing at Wonsan. Accordingly, the ROK I Corps was to take charge of the security for the beachhead, and the US X Corps was later to make an administrative landing at the port city. Then the two ROK and US Corps together were to continue pursuit opeations north of the 38th Parallel in the northeast area of the Nangnim Mountain Range.

Pursuant to the readjusted plan, the ROK I Corps was ordered by the ROK Army Headquarters to secure Wonsan harbor for the safe landing of the US X Corps. For this purpose, the ROK I Corps would first secure Yonghung by holding Anbyon, Yongp'ori, Yongt'anri, and the mouth of the Yongt'an River as its main line of resistance, and then advance northward on the axes of Yonghung-Chongp'yong-Hamhung, and P'ach'unjang-Hungnam.

In an effort to first secure the Wonsan beachhead and to delimit the zones of action along the Yonghung line between the ROK Capital and 3rd Divisions, the ROK I Corps commander, in turn, issued his order on October 15. In this order, he called upon the 3rd Division to give protection for the city of Wonsan and its vicinity and at the same time to help support the US X Corps's landing at the harbor. He ordered the Capital Division to annihilate the enemy by advancing northward on the axes of Yonghung-Chongp'yong-Hamhung, and P'ach'unjang-Hungnam.[68]

On October 17, when the city and the beachhead at the Tonghanman bay area were about to be secured by the friendly control of Hamhung and Hungnam, the MacArthur Line, which had been set by the General as the northern phase line, was extended northward to the Sonch'on-Songjin line. In addition, from the 20th, the ROK I Corps was put under operational control of the US X Corps, and was ordered to advance to the North Korean border the same day. Thus the ROK I Corps could be active in the "March North" operations utilizing the Wonsan beachhead as a strong foothold.

(2) The Pursuit Operations on the Axis of Yonghung-Hamhung-Songjin

After the ROK Capital Division (commanded by Brig. Gen. Song Yo Ch'an) together with the ROK 3rd Division captured and secured the port city of Wonsan, the 18th Regiment, Capital Division, continued on toward Yowangsan-Munch'on-Kowon-Yonghung. On October 15, they reached the Kumjin River, roughly a halfway point between Yonghung and Chongp'yong. Meanwhile, the 1st Regiment, Capital Division, left Togwon to successively capture Machonri-Sinch'angri-Ch'onnaeri, and then advanced to Yonghung. The motorized 1st Cavalry Regiment of the same ROK division, which had been on guard at Wonsan and handed the mission over to the ROK 3rd Division, drove to Yonghung on the 15th to rejoin the 1st and 18th Regiments there. Thus the ROK Capital Division was ready to continue to proceed from Yonghung to Hamhung and Hungnam, and further north beyond that point.

Upon receiving an order from the Corps commander "to proceed to Hamhung and Hungnam" that day, the ROK Capital Division commander moved his advance command post from Wonsan to Yonghung to be prepared for the attack against the industrial city of South Hamkyong Province, Hamhung, and Hungnam, the port city of the same province. For the attack, the division commander issued the following orders:

> The enemy troops including the 42nd Division and 249th Brigade
> began to retreat from their defensive positions at around Wonsan to-
> ward Hamhung by way of Munch'on, Kowon, and Chongp'yong. They
> are concentrating on Hamhung, and an unidentified enemy artillery
> unit has apparently emplaced and dug in in the vicinity of the city of
> Hamhung.

- The division will attack against Hamhung and Hungnam; the H-hour is set at 13:00 on October 17.
- The 1st Regiment will attack against Hungnam, and the 18th Regiment will attack against Hamhung. The 1st Cavalry Regiment will be kept as division reserve.[69]

In order to accomplish his part of the mission, that is, to attack and capture Hamhung, Col. Lim Ch'ung Sik, commander of the ROK 18th Regiment, began his operations a day earlier, trying to first capture Chongp'yong where, he believed, enemy covering forces might have dug in. His regiment advanced to Chongp'yong at around noon almost unopposed, and by 16:00, reached Hungsangmyon, small town village 10 kilometers southwest of Hamhung.

Lt. Col. Han Shin, commanding officer of the ROK 1st Regiment, left the town of Yonghung, and advanced to Unnamri, short of Hungnam, at 17:00 via Chongp'yong and Sinhungri. The two attacking regiments bivouacked that night in each place just before their objectives.

At 05:00 on October 17, the 18th Regiment attacked against Hamhung from the northern flank, while the 1st Regiment launched its attack against Hungnam from the south at 06:00 that morning. The division reserve, the 1st Cavalry Regiment, closely followed behind the 18th Regiment.

The 2nd Battalion of the 18th Regiment engaged the enemy at an entrance of the city of Hamhung, and defeated him in heavy fighting which lasted about an hour. It entered downtown streets at 11:30. Meanwhile, the 1st Battalion defeated a platoon sized enemy force on its way to the city, and captured a hill north of Yudungri, Hamhung, at 16:00. There the battalion mounted guard that night.

In the mean time, the ROK 1st Regiment left Unnamri and crossed the Songch'on River at 10:00 closely keeping pace with the advance of the adjacent 18th Regiment. It entered Hungnam, and by 12:00 it completely controlled the city. During that afternoon, it gained 10 more kilometers north toward Hamhung to link up with the 18th Regiment, and returned to Hungnam. The 1st Cavalry Regiment advanced to Jikyongri 5 kilometers south of Hamhung to guard against roving enemy remnants in the northeastern areas.

When the ROK forces entered the city of Hamhung, some anti-Communist citizens rose up against the North Korean troops and helped the ROK soldiers' crossing the Songch'on River so that the ROK troops could easily control the whole city.

At 15:00 on October 18, an impressive welcoming ceremony to comemorate the triumphal entry of the ROK forces into the city was held with a large attendance of the citizens and commanders of the ROK troops including Maj. Gen. Kim Paik Il, commander of the ROK I Corps, and Brig. Gen. Song Yo Ch'an, commander of the Capital Division. Most of the people seemed to have been impelled by a strong sense of gratitude as they were liberated at last from the tyrannical Communist government, but some were apparently filled with deep sadness being unable to know the safety of their parents, brothers and sisters.

Approximately 12,000 citizens were known to have been slaughtered by the retreating Communist NKPA troops in the city alone. All kinds of abominable cruelty was displayed by the NKPA in the massacre; North Korean Communist soldiers beat innocent people to death with clubs or pieces of firewood. They pushed some people from behind into well waters to crush them to death. They tied hands of others behind their backs to bury them in the sea with heavy rocks tied behind their backs, still others were confined in air-raid shelters or cellars to be blasted. They even buried some people alive in a hole dug in the ground, sinning against God and man.[70]

The numbers of civilian people who had been abducted or missing were not included in the above statistics. This meant that much more innocent North

Korean people had apparently been slaughtered by Communist North Koreans who had tried to vent their spite after being defeated in the fratricidal war. This atrocity committed by the North Korean Communist Government would leave an indelible stain on its own history.

At about this time, approximately 6,000 men of the NKPA 249th Brigade together with the 588th Artillery Battalion, who had thus far defended Hamhung and Hungnam, withdrew northwest toward Changjin (Chosin) Reservoir via Onori northwest of Hamhung, with all their artillery pieces and tanks. Part of the NKPA 588th Regiment and about 6,000 men from the Mari Training Center were believed to have left Onori to withdraw toward P'ungsan by way of Sinhung. Meanwhile, the NKPA 598th Regiment which had been deployed in the area northeast of Hungnam was believed to withdraw toward Nanam via Hongwon, and the 10th Brigade which had been stationed at Hongwon was removed north toward Kapsan.

Under such circumstances, the ROK Capital Division commander ordered his 18th Regiment to proceed toward Sinhung and Changjin northwest of Hamhung, and the 1st Infantry and 1st Cavalry Regiments northeast toward Hongwon from Hungnam. Conforming to this order, that day, the 18th Regiment advanced first to Onori which was considered a critical road junction 5 kilometers north of Hamhung, and the 1st Regiment proceeded from Hungnam to Hongwon. The 1st Cavalry Regiment, the division reserve, moved from Chikyongri to Hamhung.

On the morning of October 19, the 1st Battalion of the 18th Regiment occupied Onori, and continued on northwest toward the Changjin Reservoir. Main elements of the regiment($-$), except for the 1st Battalion, advanced northeast toward Sinhung and the Pujon Reservoir. Meanwhile, the ROK 1st Regiment, which had moved up along the east coastal route, reached a point near Hongwon that day.

At about this time, enemy troops were escaping northward in dispersion in three directions: from north of Hamhung toward Reservoirs Changjin and Pujon, from Pukch'ong toward the Whangsuwon Reservoir-P'ungsan, and from Pukch'ong toward Tanch'on-Songjin along the east coastal road.

The ROK Capital Division commander immediately ordered the 18th Regiment to press hard against the enemy toward the Changjin and Pujon Reservoirs, the 1st Regiment to first seize Hongwon and then move on northwest toward P'ungsan via Pukch'ong, and the 1st Cavalry Regiment to drive toward Tanch'on-Songjin along the east coastal road.

On October 20, the ROK 18th Regiment in the north captured Sinhung, while the 1st Regiment in the east seized Hongwon and Sinp'o.

On the 21st, the next day, General Almond visited the headquarters of the ROK Capital Division (at Hamhung) which had been on the move north ward, and had a talk about future operations.

On October 22, the ROK 1st Regiment defeated approximately 600 enemy troops (two battalion-sized units) at a point 12 kilometers south of Pukch'ong, and captured the town. There the regiment turned due north and continued on toward the Whangsuwon Reservoir and P'ungsan. The 1st ROK Cavalry Regiment, in the meantime, engaged unknown numbers of enemy troops on its way to Pukch'ong, and repelled most of them capturing 13 prisoners. As the 1st Regiment, which had pursued the enemy side by side with the cavalry regiment along the coastal road, changed its axis of advance at that point, the 1st Cavalry Regiment single-handedly moved on north along the road. At that time, the temperature dropped to sub-zero in their zone of action in Hamkyong Province. As a result, freezing temperatures at the beginning of the winter together with rugged mountain terrain hindered the smooth operations of the friendly forces.

Meanwhile, retreating enemy troops waged delaying actions on the axes of the Changjin Reservoir and Kapsan-Hyesanjin. Particularly in the direction of the Reservoir, approximately 11,200 enemy soldiers centered around the NKPA 2nd Division with about 8,000 men were desperate in checking the advance of the ROK 18th Regiment there. In the northeastern zone, a regimental size enemy force which had been defeated at Hamhung was driven off by the ROK 1st Regiment, which had seized Pukch'ong. This enemy force of about 2,500 men escaped toward P'ungsan, Kapsan and Hyesanjin.

On October 24, the day when the UN operations order for the general pursuit was issued, the ROK 1st Cavalry Regiment left Sinpukch'ong to capture Iwon, and seized Tanch'on as well on the next day, the 25th. The 1st Battalion of the 18th Regiment, after relieving the 26th Regiment, ROK 3rd Division, at Majonri, moved northeast to Sinp'ungri via Onori. At Kyonghungri, the 2nd Battalion, 18th Regiment, was preparing for the attack toward the Pujon Reservoir, while the 3rd Battalion of the same regiment advanced to a point 4 kilometers north of Sinp'ungri.

The ROK 1st Regiment, which had turned toward P'ungsan since October 22, captured the ridge of the Huch'i-ryong Pass on the 27th after a heavy fight which lasted for three days. The 2nd Battalion of the regiment advanced to Whangsuwon. Meanwhile, on the 26th, the 3rd Battalion of the ROK 18th Regiment attacked against Whajopch'i,[71] an impasse between Sinhungri and Whangsuwon. On its west flank, the 2nd Battalion of the 18th Regiment drove toward the Pujon Reservoir, and captured both the Reservoir and nearby Paegam-san.

The 1st Cavalry Regiment, in the mean time, proceeded from Tanch'on toward Songjin on the east coastal route. On the way, the regiment encountered a reinforced regimental size enemy force at the Mach'on-ryong Pass at a point halfway in between, but by the 27th, it finally took the ridge of the pass after a fierce battle which lasted for about five hours. This enabled the regiment to secure a favorable high ground position overlooking the downtown streets of the city of Songjin.

On October 28, the ROK 1st Regiment, which had controlled Whang-suwon, seized P'ungsan, and the 1st Cavalry Regiment captured Songjin. The 18th Regiment, meanwhile, took up defensive positions at Paegam-san to engage a stubborn enemy force in the areas north of the Pujon-ryong pass and at Susangri, east of the pass.

On the whole, by the end of October, troops from the ROK Capital Division had the Manchurian border under their eyes. The 1st Regiment had already passed over the Hamkyong Mountains, the 18th Regiment had reached the Kaema Highlands, and the 1st Cavalry Regiment had taken the ridge of the Mach'onryong Mountains. At that time, despite the cold weather in the beginning of the winter, most of the South Korean soldiers were still shabbily dressed in summer uniforms. However, they were full of fighting spirit as they were inspired by the prospect of soon realizing their long cherished wishes, the reunification of the country.

At about this time, advance patrolling parties reported back to ROK troops that approximately three regimental size enemy units, including two Chinese Communist regiments, were concentrated for a counteroffensive at the southern tip of the Pujon Reservoir, to the north of the ROK 18th Regimental zone of action. To the east of the Reservoir, however, the NKPA remnants in front of the ROK 1st Regiment escaped northward from P'ungsan toward Samsu, and those enemy forces on the east coastal route were believed to be withdrawing toward Kilju-Ch'ongjin, leaving only part of it at high hill masses north of Songjin to delay the advance of friendly forces.

(3) Operations for Pacifying in Wonsan-Hamhung Corridor

After securing the port city, Wonsan, the ROK 3rd Division cleared its zone of the enemy remnants and took over the security mission there. For this purpose, its 22nd Regiment took up positions in the high ground in the vicinity of the city, and nearby Anbyon and Kojo, the 23rd Regiment in Munp'yong and the Masik-ryong Pass, and the 26th Regiment in Kowon and on the Chot'an River bank. That day, ordered by the ROK corps commander to tightly protect Wonsan and its outskirts, the ROK division commander, in turn, issued an order for the redeployment of his troops by adjusting regimental boundaries.

Accordingly, the 22nd Regiment took up positions in the southern part of Wonsan and redeployed its troops heavily at the Kalma Airfield-Kojo-Anbyon line. The 23rd Regiment also deployed along the outskirts of the port city which extended from Sudalri-Hodo peninsula along the northern shore line of the Yonghung Bay to Majonri on the P'yongyang-Wonsan highway. Adjacent to the north of the 23rd Regiment, the 26th Regiment took charge of the high ground along Munch'on-Kowon-Yonghung, so that it could establish contact with the adjacent ROK Capital Division.

On October 17, the ROK 23rd Regiment searched the bay area thoroughly and killed six enemy soldiers capturing one 200-ton enemy boat, and ten rifles including two coast artillery guns. This had apparently prevented the enemy from launching a surprise attack against anticipated friendly mine-sweeping operations at the Yonghung Bay. On that day in Wonsan, President Syngman Rhee felicitated the soldiers of the ROK I Corps on their successes, and awarded the men of the corps the honor of being promoted to a higher rank in appreciation of their services.[72]

In the meantime, on October 24, the ROK 23rd Regiment engaged unknown numbers of enemy force in the vicinity of Kowon, and killed 105 men and captured 15 tanks, 5 machine guns, 8 locomotives, and 1 freight car including 3 enemy soldiers.

On October 25, the ROK 26th Regiment relieved the 18th Regiment of the ROK Capital Division at Sangt'ongri about 12 kilometers toward the Changjin Reservoir from Hamhung, and confronted an enemy force deployed in the direction of the reservoir. The ROK 23rd Regiment also moved to Hamhung. Only the 22nd Regiment was left in the city of Wonsan waiting for the landing of the US X Corps there.

That day, the ROK 26th Regiment reached a point near the 1st and 2nd hydroelectric power plants south of the Changjin Reservoir, and captured an enemy prisoner there, who was later identified as a Chinese Communist soldier. The Chinese captive stated in cipher that he had belonged to the 5th Regiment of the CCF 8th Army, and 4,000-5,000 CCF had been deployed in the vicinity. Anyway, he was the first Chinese prisoner captured in the eastern zone of action, and coincidently on that very day, the ROK 1st Division on the western front captured another Chinese Communist soldier as has already been described.

On October 26, the ROK 3rd Division handed its security mission at Wonsan over to the US X Corps immediately after the latter landed at the port city. Now the ROK division, with its rejoined 22nd Regiment from Wonsan, could devote itself entirely to clearing and pacifying the area of Hamhung.

On October 29, the ROK 26th Regiment, which had been deployed on the north of Hamhung, engaged an enemy force of about 1,000 men in fierce close combat in the vicinity of the 2nd hydroelectric power plant one kilometer north of Sudong, short of Hakaluri(Changjin). Although the regiment was supported by a friendly artillery battalion(−), it was stranded in its position from that afternoon and was shelled by an enemy reinforced with mortars. Still, in this battle the regiment captured 16 Chinese Communist and about 60 North Korean soldiers. The ROK I Corps commander himself identified the Chinese captives, and notified the US I Corps commander of the fact. The latter visited the headquarters of the ROK I Corps the following day to interrogate the Chinese prisoners. At that time, the prisoners stated that most of them had initially belonged to Chiang Kai-shek's Chinese Nationalist Army a year earlier, but had become members of the Chinese Communist Forces as their division had surrendered to the Communists when the mainland China was communized in 1949. They further stated that on October 16(later corrected that it was October 14), they had crossed the Yalu River to advance south toward Changjin via Manp'ojin as members of the 370th Regiment, 124th Division of the CCF 42nd Army. They added that the headquarters of their division and regiment were situated at Hakaluri, at the southern edge of the Changjin Reservoir, and the attack they had made there upon the ROK forces was the first offensive action since the CCF's intervention into the war. This clearly showed that the CCF had openly intervened in the war, and the NKPA forces apparently tried to delay the advance of the friendly forces to support the deployment of the CCF in Korea.

For about 20 days from October 16 to November 3, the ROK 3rd Division mopped up enemy remnants in the areas of Wonsan and Hamhung, and held the line of Sudongri-Majonri-Kojo. By so doing, the division secured the beachhead at the Yonghung bay in and around the Wonsan-Hungnam area, which facilitated the landing operations of the US X Corps and at the same time, provided support for the ROK Capital Division's continued advance northward.

2. Landing Operations at Wonsan and Consolidation of Battle Fronts

(1) The Landing at Wonsan

The US X Corps' (the US 1st Marine and 7th Infantry Divisions) landing operations at Wonsan was not made until October 26, far behind schedule, after the ROK I Corps secured the beachheads at Wonsan and the Yonghung Bay

Landing at Wonsan & Phase Line for the U.N. Advance

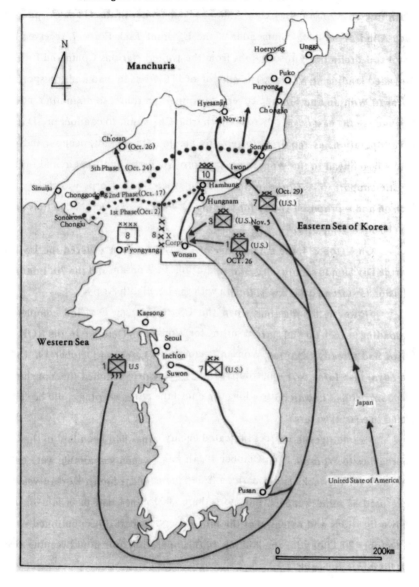

areas. About the time the ROK I Corps crossed the 38th Parallel and started north toward Wonsan, Maj. Gen. Almond, Commander of the US X Corps, and Vice Admiral Struble, Commander of the US Joint Task Force-7, received on October 1 preliminary instructions from the United Nations Command for the projected landing at Wonsan. The mission of JTF-7 was to load and transport X Corps to Wonsan and provide cover and support en route; to maintain a naval blockade of the east coast of Korea south from Ch'ongjin; to conduct pre-D-day naval operations as required; to seize by amphibious assault, occupy, and secure a beachhead in the Wonsan area; to provide naval gunfire, air, and initial logistic support to X Corps in the Wonsan area. The X Corps was to load at Inch'on and a proposed D-day for landing at Wonsan was October 15 (this date later changed to the 20th).[73]

On October 4, the commander of the US X Corps ordered the US 1st Marine Division to secure a base for operations in Wonsan, and the 7th Infantry Division to start an attack west to join with the US Eighth Army.

However, by the time when the US 1st Marine Division completed outloading at Inch'on and started sailing for Wonsan on October 16, the ROK I Corps had already captured Wonsan (October 10). Later, on October 19, when the naval task force carrying troops of the US X Corps reached the Yonghung Bay curve, it had to wait quite a long time until the minesweeping could be completed in coastal waters.

As intelligence sources indicated enemy mines had been laid in the sea approaches to Wonsan, from October 10, all minesweepers available were concentrated for the task. Ten American, 8 Japanese, and 1 South Korean vessels were used as minesweepers. But more than 3,000 mines had been laid in unknown locations and extent, that the minesweeping operations continued even on October 20, D-day for the landing. In this operation four minesweeping vessels hit mines and sank.[74]

Meanwhile, on October 20 as planned, the commander of the US X Corps flew from the USS Missouri by helicopter to the Wonsan Airfield to assume command of troops in the X Corps area, including the ROK I Corps. As of 12:00 that day, he took over the control and responsibility for military operations in the northeastern zone of the Korean Peninsula at the corps' forward command post. The total strength he was to command at that time numbered approximately 90,000 men from tactical organizations of the ROK Capital, 3rd, US 1st Marine and US 7th Infantry Divisions and from other supporting elements.

However, after arriving off the objective area, the flotilla carrying the US X Corps steamed slowly back and forth(the restless marines called it Operation Yo-yo) for almost a week in the East Sea of Korea just outside the Wonsan channel, waiting for the completion of the minesweeping operations. On October 25, 21 transports and 15 LST's came into the harbor and dropped anchor off Wonsan, and the corps began landing on the 26th, the following day. As it was a quiet, administrative landing after about 10 days of afloat, it was a great relief to everyone of the US 1st Marine Division.

In the meantime, the US 7th Infantry Division, which had left Pusan on October 19, remained idly afloat off the Pusan harbor for ten days because of the minesweeping operations at Wonsan. Finally, on the 27th it received orders from the US X Corps to directly proceed northward to Iwon and to unload there. Iwon was not an initially projected landing site, and the reason for this abrupt change was due to the changed order dated October 19 from the United Nations Command. The UNC, considering the belated landing of the X Corps which occurred much later after the capture of P'yongyang by other friendly troops, had called upon the X Corps to land as close as possible to its axis of advance inland toward North Korea's northern border.

(2) The Consolidation of the Battle Fronts

At about the end of October when the US X Corps landed at Wonsan, the Capital Division of the ROK I Corps was driving toward Sinhungri north of Hamhung and northeast toward P'ungsan and Songjin. The ROK 3rd Division was also on guard in the rear area in the vicinity of Wonsan and Hamhung, providing support for the landing operations of the US X Corps, and at the same time, confronting elements of the CCF near Sudong. Maj. Gen. Almond, commander of the US X Corps, called an operations meeting on October 26, and at this meeting, based on General MacArthur's order for a general offensive on October 20 and estimates of the battle front situation, he issued new orders for his plan of operation.[75] The gist of his orders was as follows:

- The Corps will attack northeast toward the Manchurian border. The ROK I Corps will continue its advance along the coastal and Musan routes, capture the northeast border east of Paektu Mountain, and clear its zone of enemy remnants. The ROK Corps will also deploy part of its troops in the areas of the Changjin and Pujon Reservoirs and P'ungjon, and press hard against the enemy until the US 1st Marine and 7th Infantry Divisions re-ach the area. The ROK 3rd Division, which were responsible for the security of the Wonsan area, will hand the mission over to the US 1st Marine Division and follow up behind the ROK Capital Division.
- The US 1st Marine Division will capture the Changjin Resevoir area and move on toward the Manchurian border; it will have the responsibility of securing the Wonsan–Hamhung area until the US 3rd Infantry Division arrives at Wonsan.
- The US 7th Infantry Division will advance to Hyesanjin west of · Paektu Mountain via P'ungsan and the Changjin Reservoir immediately after landing at Iwon.

- The US 3rd Division will secure the Wonsan-Hamhung area, protect the corps rear from guerrilla interference, and at the same time, keep open the corps lines of communication.

In order to accomplish his part of the mission, Maj. Gen. Oliver P. Smith, commander of the US 1st Marine Division, issued orders for his plan of operation: [76)]

The commander of the 1st Marine Regiment to relieve ROK Ⅰ Corps elements in the Kojo and Majonri areas south and west of Wonsan and secure the responsible areas; the 5th Marine Regiment to secure the Wonsan area, the Yonp'o Airfield south of Hungnam, and the west flank of the Ⅹ Corps; and finally, the 7th Marines to relieve the ROK 3rd Division along the Hamhung-Changjin Reservoir corridor, secure the power installations of the Changjin and Pujon Reservoirs, and to move on northward.

Acting upon this order, on October 28, the US 1st Marine Regiment, which had protected the Ⅹ Corps supply installations at Kojo south of Wonsan for two days, advanced to Majonri via Wonsan. There on the 29th the regiment relieved the 22nd Regiment of the ROK 3rd Division, and took up defensive positions. While the US 5th Marines protected the Ⅹ Corps west flank in the area near Yonp'o Airfield between Wonsan and Hungnam, the motorized US 7th Marines left Wonsan that morning for a point near Sudong south of the Changjin Reservoir by way of Hamhung. There the regiment relieved the 26th Regiment of the ROK 3rd Divison on November 2.

In the meantime, on October 27, the ROK 1st Marine Regiment, minus the 2nd Battalion, landed at Wonsan to join the US 1st Marine Division for the defense of the Wonsan-Hamhung area. This combined force of ROK and US marines concentrated on Kosong at the beginning of November to cut off the enemy's line of retreat through the T'aebaeksan Range, and to mop up enemy remnants in the area of Kansong-Majonri.

At about this time, Maj. Gen. David G. Barr, commander of the US 7th Infantry Division, ordered his 17th Regiment to come ashore at Iwon and move north on the axis of Pukch'ong-P'ungsan-Hyesanjin. He ordered the US 31st Regiment to proceed from Iwon toward the Pujon Reservoir-Sinkalp'ajin along the Pukch'ong-Hamhung-Onori-Sinhung route. The US 32nd Regiment was kept as reserve and was ordered to protect the division rear.

On October 29, lead elements of the 17th Regiment, the regimental headquarters and the 1st Battalion, landed at Iwon and immediately moved from the beachhead to Ch'ori together with the 49th Field Artillery Battalion and A Company of the 13th Combat Engineer Battalion via Sinpukch'ong-Pukch'ong-Changhungri. The 2nd and 3rd Battalions were to follow behind.

By the evening of the next day, the lead elements of the regiment reached P'ungsan across the 1,335 meter high Huch'i-ryong Pass. Right at that time, the 1st Regiment of the ROK Capital Division engaged a stubborn enemy force just north of P'ungsan. The US 17th Regiment(−2) helped the ROK regiment repulse the enemy attack. On November 2, when the battle was over, the ROK 1st Regiment handed over its positions to the American regiment, and moved to Songjin, the east coastal city, to closely follow behind the ROK 1st Cavalry Regiment.

On November 3, the 31st Regiment of the US 7th Division, which had landed at Iwon, moved to the Pujon Reservoir along the road of Iwon-P'ungsan, apart from its initially planned axis of advance. There the regiment relieved the 18th Regiment of the ROK Capital Division. The ROK 18th Regiment, in turn, assembled in Soyangri north of Hamhung and moved toward Songjin.[77] Meanwhile, the US 32nd Regiment, which began unloading on November 4 and came ashore at Iwon, moved to Hamhung and there turned northeast to Tamp'ungri in preparation for its part in the operation.

Thus the ROK I Corps which had handed most of its mission west of the Mach'on-ryong Range (South Hamkyong Province) over to the US X Corps took full responsibility for operations east of the Range (North Hamkyong Province). The ROK 3rd Division, which had been relieved by the US 1st Marine Division, could move on north along the east coastal road, and the ROK Capital Division relieved by the US 7th Division committed its 1st and 18th Regiments to the Kilju-Ch'ongjin route where the 1st Cavalry Regiment alone had been marching north.

3. Advance to the Changjin Reservoir and Hyesanjin

(1) Pursuit Operations toward Sudong and the Changjin Reservoir

The US 1st Marine Division, which had advanced toward the Changjin Reservoir after it relieved the ROK 3rd Division, began to encounter organized CCF resistance from October 29. Immediately after its 7th Marine Regiment arrived at Sudong on November 2 and relieved the ROK 26th Regiment in its position, the marine regiment confirmed that Chinese troops opposed it. During the day engagement, American marines captured 3 CCF prisoners who stated that they had belonged to the 370th Regiment of the CCF 124th Division. The fighting was close that night, and in this overnight battle the American marine regiment killed about 700 enemy soldiers. The American marines also suffered heavy losses; however, they succeeded in repelling the CCF troops at this first engagement.

With the help of marine aircraft, the US 7th Marines continued on toward the north. They passed Sudong and Chinhungri, crossed over the ridge of the Whangch'o-ryong Pass, and finally captured Kot'ori by the 10th. According to the statement of Chinese prisoners captured on the 6th, other CCF Divisions such as 125th and 126th had assembled in the vicinity of the Changjin Reservoir. However, those enemy troops which had attacked the American regiment at Sudong began apparently withdrawing north toward the reservoir, while engaging the American marines.

On November 9, the 26th Regiment of the ROK 3rd Division was attached to the American marine division, and the former proceeded from Hongwon to Chikyongri via Hamhung. There the South Korean regiment was committed to the high-ground area of Madung-ryong-Chunch'ang-ryong to protect the west flank of the American marine troops.

At about this time, in the snow-laden zone of action the temperature dropped 20 degrees centigrade to 25 below zero. This must have been threateningly painful-particularly at night-to the American soldiers who had apparently been unaccustomed to such cold Korean weather.

Despite the characteristic subzero temperatures in their zone of action, the US 7th Marine troops on the battle front moved on smoothly, while the US 3rd Infantry Division started landing at Wonsan. This made possible the turning over of Marines responsibility in the rear area. The US marine division commander then issued orders for his plan of operation on the 13th:

Up to the Changjin Reservoir

① The division will continue its attack toward the Manchurian border via the Changjin Reservoir.

② The 1st Regiment will capture Huksuri and then protect the left flank of the division.

③ The 5th Regiment will keep open the main supply route between Kot'ori and Chinhungri.

④ The 7th Regiment will capture Hagaluri, and then be prepared to attack against Yudamri on division order.

Pursuant to the order, that day the US 5th Marines closely followed behind the 7th Regiment to secure the main supply road between Kot'ori and Chinhungri, and the 1st Regiment, after handing over the security mission at Wonsan to the US 3rd Infantry Division, assembled at Chikyongri.

In the meantime, the US 7th Marines, the lead element, captured Kot'ori and Hagaluri south of the Changjin Reservoir on November 10, and 16, respectively. Finally on the 24th, it seized Yudamri on the west of the reservoir. The American marine regiment captured two CCF prisoners during its attack against Yudamri, who stated that they belonged to the 267th Regiment of the CCF 89th Division, and crossed the Yalu River 10 days earlier. The prisoners' statements testified that they had belonged to a CCF unit other than the one to which three CCF prisoners captured about two weeks before had belonged. It meant that several other CCF units had apparently been committed to the area in the vicinity of the Changjin Reservoir, and a few more to the area north of the reservoir.

(2) Pursuit Operations toward Iwon and Hyesanjin

The US 7th Infantry Division, which had been ordered to move toward Hyesanjin, engaged the enemy in heavy fighting immediately after it relieved the ROK Capital Division in the latter's position. The US 17th Regiment, which had relieved the 1st Regiment of the ROK Capital Division at P'ungsan on November 2, defeated two regimental size enemy units and pursued enemy remnants. The US 31st Regiment, which had relieved the 18th Regiment, ROK Capital Division, in the latter's positions near the Pujon Resevoir, engaged in a battle with an estimated enemy battalion on the eastern slopes of Paeksan on November 18. This defeated enemy was later identified as part of the CCF 376th Regiment, 126th Division of the 42nd Army. The Chinese force withdrew with at least 50 killed. The appearance of the CCF in the Pujon Reservoir area together with that in the Changjin Reservoir made the American division tense, and the whole X Corps became more apprehensive. Meanwhile, on this same day a patrol of the American regiment met an American marine patrol in the south of the Pujon Reservoir, thus establishing the first contact between the two American divisions since the UN Inch'on landing. At that time, the US 32nd Regiment was carrying out its mission of securing the supply route in the area between P'ungsan and Ch'ori.

Based upon a comprehensive review of the enemy situation at that time, the commander of the US X Corps, who had flown into P'ungsan on November 12, ordered the US 7th Division commander to continue the advance northward. The division commander, who had discreetly believed the enemy that had confronted him at the eastern edge of the Pujon Reservoir was part of an organized Chinese force, in turn ordered his 17th Regiment to seize Kapsan and then go to Hyesanjin, the border city on the Yalu. He also ordered the 31st Regiment to proceed north to Singalp'ajin on the Yalu along the Pujon River, and the 32nd Regiment to protect the supply route in the rear between Iwon and P'ungsan.

On November 15, the US 17th Regiment crossed the Ungi River 20 kilometers north of P'ungsan against desperate enemy resistance, and on the 19th, seized Kapsan after a coordinated infantry, tank, and artillery attack. Meanwhile, to the southwest in the mountainous waste, the US 31st Regiment steadily advanced utilizing ox-drawn carts or sleds to transport supplies and evacuate the wounded. On November 16, the regiment continued on northwest toward Handaeri, at the northern end of the Pujon Reservoir, along the route of Susangri and the eastern shore of the reservoir. Near the Pujon hydroelctric power plant at Handaeri, it encountered about 200 CCF soldiers and drove them away after a brief fight to capture the power plant. Beyond that point, however, as the narrow, snow-covered mountain defiles were almost impassable except for ox or horse-drawn carts, the regiment could not advance.

Accordingly, on November 20, the American division commander began moving the bulk of the 31st and 32nd Regiments to the P'ungsan and Kapsan areas. Since the 31st Regiment was forced to halt due to the lack of a favorable roadnet, the division commander ordered the 32nd Regiment which had concentrated at Kapsan to proceed to Singalp'ajin via Samsu and take up defensive positions on the west flank of the 17th Regiment. That day the 17th Regiment continued on toward Hyesanjin and on the following morning, entered the border city unopposed. Thus the regiment secured and completely controlled town streets and its suburbs on the Yalu River, but it found the city was empty with houses and buildings destroyed by marine Corsairs. It stood guard on the northern edge of the city there.

The Yalu which runs through the northern part of Hyesanjin is not a great river; 45-70 meters wide when it is filled to the brim, but it remained only 2 meters wide when the American regiment first stood on its banks. The bridge across the stream at Hyesanjin had been destoyed before the 17th Regiment arrived there, and about 300 meters north across the river in Manchuria there was a Chinese village Changbaek. There American soldiers saw CCF sentries walk their rounds and their officers come and go.

Thus the US 17th Infantry Regiment was the second to reach the North

Chinese Red Army crossing the Yalu River, 1950

Korean-Manchurian border and the Yalu after the ROK 7th Regiment, 6th Division, and the first among the United Nations Forces.

In the meantime, the US 3rd Infantry Division[7b](commanded by Maj. Gen. Robert H. Soule), which had been attached to the US X Corps to reinforce friendly troops on the eastern front, was greatly under-strength. Except for its 65th Regiment which had landed at Pusan in mid-September, the division, including the headquarters, 7th, and 15th Regiments, had an actual strength of only 7,494 men at that time. So it was scheduled to receive 8,500 KATUSA soldiers after its arrival in Japan as a reserve unit for the US Far East Command. Through October the 3rd Division received Korean draftees, and as a result, squads of the division often consisted of two American enlisted men and eight Koreans.

The US 65th Regiment which had already come ashore on Pusan landed at Wonsan on November 5, and the main body of the division, the 7th and 15th Regiments, left Japan for Korean waters at the beginning of November and finished its landing at Wonsan on November 17.

Advance to Hyesanjin From Iwon

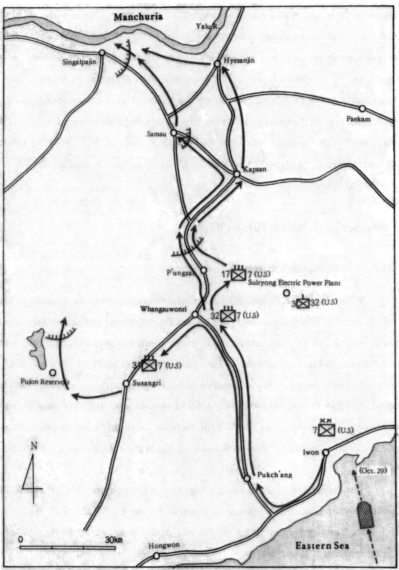

The US 3rd Division's primary mission was to relieve all 1st Marine Division troops in the Wonsan area and south of Hamhung. There it was to block the main roads in the corps rear zone against guerrillas and bypassed NKPA soldiers, and to protect the Wonsan-Hamhung coastal strip. The division zone of responsibility(measured 144 by 56 kilometers) was so large as to make centralized division control impracticable; therefore the division commander decided to establish four regimental combat teams and to assign sectors and missions to each. For this purpose, he used the ROK 26th Regiment, 3rd Division, which had been released from the US 1st Marine Division to be attached to the US 3rd Division for operations.

4. Advance toward the Tumen River

(1) Pursuit Operations toward Kilju-Ch'ongjin

When the ROK Capital Division, after handing over its mission in the Pujon Reservoir-P'ungsan area to the US 7th Division, was preparing for the attack against Kilju by concentrating its main elements on Songjin on the east coastal route, unknown numbers of Chinese Communist soldiers were spotted in the area of the Changjin-Pujon Reservoirs making friendly troops tense. In the north of Songjin at that time the NKPA 41st Division and 507th Brigade desperately resisted the advance of the UN forces from their defensive positions built for a series of delaying actions at Kilju, and Myongch'on-Orang-ch'on north of the town.

On November 1, Brig. Gen. Song Yo Ch'an, commander of the ROK Capital Division, launched his attack toward the town of Kilju with a plan to use his 1st Cavalry Regiment for the frontal attack and the 1st Regiment for a turning movement to the east.

The two South Korean regiments which had left Songjin moved on north until the 1st Cavalry Regiment reached Ilsindong 12 kilometers south of Kilju the following day, and the 1st Regiment advanced Wahyondong at the mouth of the Whadae-ch'on southeast of Kilju. Both of them were in a position to get into a double envelopment of the town. On November 3, the ROK 1st Cavalry Regiment advanced along the road that ran along the small Namdae-ch'on and reached an open field short of Kilju. At that time, the enemy on Hill 552 southeast of Kilju opened fire upon the ROK troops, which immediately made an emergency request for air and artillery strikes back upon the enemy positions. The ROK attack thus developed into a hard battle against the enemy-held hill positions which controlled the Namdae-ch'on, and the open field on both banks including the town of Kilju. Accordingly, flanks of the frontal attacking ROK 1st Cavalry Regiment were completely exposed to the enemy fire.

At about this time, the ROK 1st Regiment, which had been driving along the Whadae-ch'on southeast of Kilju, passed the rearward slopes of Hill 552 and continued on toward Houidong 4 kilometers east of the hill. On November 5, the ROK 1st Cavalry Regiment, with the help of friendly air and artillery support, attacked against the desperate enemy and broke through his defensive positions to capture Kilju. The ROK 1st Regiment at that time made a turning movement to the east of Kilju threatening to encircle enemy troops in Kilju from their rear. It moved on toward Whanggokdong and Myongch'on via Houidong pursuing enemy remnants and stragglers.

Defeated at Kilju by the ROK troops, the main body of enemy troops retreated north toward the Orang-ch'on north of Myongch'on. At that time, fresh enemy troops were moving south along the coastal road from the Ch'ongjin-Nanam area toward the Orang-ch'on, to apparently prepare for defensive actions there utilizing the rugged terrain along the creek as natural barriers.

To counter this enemy threat, the ROK Capital Division planned to deploy its 1st Cavalry Regiment in the direction of Hapsu, and the 1st Regiment to attack against Myongch'on moving north along the east coastal road. At the same time, the division enjoined its 18th Regiment, which had been moving up from Hamhung, to pass through the 1st Regiment to attack against Ponggang and the Orang-ch'on. From the 7th, the ROK 1st Regiment started to attack against Myongch'on and repulsed resisting enemy remnants from the NKPA 507th Brigade and approximately 400 other soldiers from the NKPA 893rd Coast Guard Battalion. On the 10th, the South Korean regiment advanced to Yongdong north of Sinmyongch'on to prepare against possible enemy counter-attacks there.

On November 8, the ROK 18th Regiment arrived at Myongch'on by train, and the next day, launched an attack against enemy positions in the area of the Orang-ch'on-Ponggang. At 06:00 that day, the 1st Battalion (commanded by Maj. Lee Byong Hyong) led the division in the movement to contact the enemy, and at 14:30 via Yongamri-Chomak-san, advanced to Hill 104 at an entrance to Ponggang. At that time, on a low hill along the far bank of the Orang-ch'on two battalion-size enemy units were waiting, dug in to strong defensive positions.

The ROK battalion commander planned to cross the Orang-ch'on from Hill 104 and reach Hill 100 north of the creek. There he tried to attack against enemy positions on Hill 132. However, the heavy enemy fire from the opposite bank delayed the battalion's crossing. It suceeded in crossing the creek against the enemy fire only that afternoon with the help of friendly heavy weapon and artillery fire upon enemy positions; it captured the area around the northern bank of the creek.

On the 10th, the following day, the ROK battalion engaged enemy troops in heavy fighting near the high hill masses northwest of Ponggang, Hills 104, 132, and 90. The battalion fought against heavy odds as the desperate enemy was reinforced continuously at that time.

Advance to Ch'ongjin from Kilju

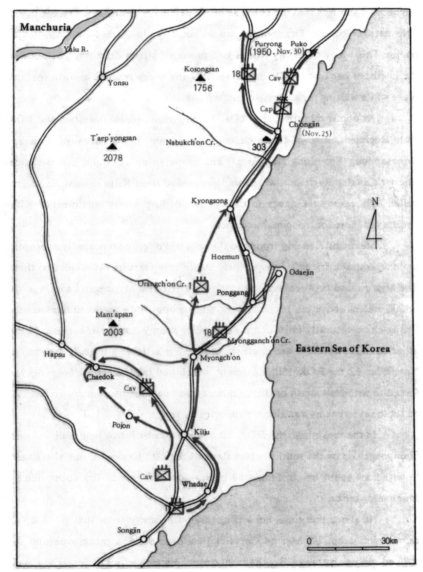

Defeated at Songjin, Kilju and Myongch'on in that order, the enemy might have thought that the collapse of his defensive positions along the favorable natural barrier Orang-ch'on would directly threaten the safety of Ch'-ongjin. This was why enemy troops had prepared strong defensive positions on the northern bank of the Orang-ch'on, utilizing every possible terrain features there while waiting for a decisive battle.

At about this time, the ROK 1st Regiment, to southwest of the ROK 18th Regiment, dug in-depth defensive positions in the area of Yongan-Yongsandong-Yongdong-Hap'yongri and prepared an all-round defense there. The 1st Cavalry Regiment, which had proceeded from Kilju toward Hapsu, repelled light enemy resistance in the vicinity of Kapsangok northwest of Kilju and stayed there for troop maintenance.

Meanwhile, enemy troops in the area of Ponggang repeatedly attempted to counterattack friendly troops, using the terrain features favorabled to them. The high ground between the creeks, Orang-ch'on and Myonggan-ch'on was 100 or 200 meters above sea level, and the steep slope of the northern bank on the Orang-ch'on naturally provided the defending enemy with fortifications; on the other hand, however, it was a great obstacle for attacking friendly troops. On November 12, the ROK 18th Regiment, which had tried to seize Ponggang, was forced to withdraw south of the stream and was counterattacked by an estimated six to seven enemy battalions supported by tanks.

In the meantime, the ROK 1st Regiment, which had held Hill 197 near Sinmyongch'on on the southwestern flank of the 18th Regiment, was also forced to withdraw south by concentrated enemy gun and mortar fire supported by four enemy tanks.

At about this time, notwithstanding the heavy snow that piled up 15 centimeters deep, US Marine Corsairs flew over the Ponggang area and destroyed two enemy tanks. But the stubborn enemy moved out to revert to a massive counterattack. The ROK 18th Regiment in front of the Ponggang area was cornered, and the regimental commander, Col. Lim Ch'ung Sik, for the time being, decided to withdraw to adapt himself to new circumstances.

The ROK regiment withdrew south to another high ground, Yondae-bong and Hill 175, south of the Myonggan-ch'on, and took up defensive positions there. On the morning of the 14th, however, an estimated two companies of enemy force resumed their attack against the hill across the creek.

The 18th Regiment concentrated all available fire including artillery and mortars upon this enemy to repulse him. The 10th Artillery Battalion which had been attached to the regiment was credited with defeating the penetrated enemy troops and thus reverting the situation to the offensive again. The 2nd Battalion of the ROK Regiment, which had held Yondae-bong, crossed the Myonggan-ch'on to drive off two other enemy companies which had threatened to attack Yondae-bong. Thus the battle between both forces developed into a day-long advance and retreat over the small stream.

Subsequently at 02:00 on the 15, approximately two battalion size enemy units tried to dislodge the 1st Battalion of the ROK 18th Regiment from Hill 175 situated on the bulge area on the southern bank of the Myonggan-ch'on. As a result, a fierce close-in fight took place between both forces. The ROK battalion moved back to a ridge south of Hill 175 to resume its attack during the daylight hours. Together with the reinforced 2nd Battalion troops, the 1st Battalion launched an assault against enemy positions at daybreak. Supporting artillery and Heavy Weapons Company concentrated their fire upon the enemy at that time and broke the brunt of the enemy's attack. Taking advantage of the moment, ROK troops reached the crest of the hill at around 11:00 and completely controlled it. Enemy troops started to wade back across the stream to escape northward.

On November 16, the ROK 18th Regiment attacked across the Myonggan-ch'on against the enemy main line of resistance formed at the high hill masses between Yongan and Kukdong north of the creek. The regiment broke through the line after a fierce fight that lasted 5 hours, and captured a high hill beyond it. There the ROK regiment took up defensive positions for the night.

At about this time, the ROK 1st Regiment drove north to Hill 468 (EB412713) south of the Orang-ch'on and northwest of Yongan to keep pace with the 18th Regiment on the east.

However, as the ROK Capital Division had generally made little gains in the area of the Orang-ch'on, the ROK corps ordered the Capital Division commander to consolidate his command and resume the attack against the assigned objective by making the latter's 1st Cavalry Regiment hand over its mission to the ROK 3rd Division and drive north along the east coastal road.[79]

Pursuant to this order, the 1st and 18th Regiments of the ROK Capital Division, which had advanced to a point north of the Myongch'on, by the 18th, secured defensive positions along the southern bank of the Orang-ch'on centered on Ponggang; the 1st Cavalry Regiment, after handing over its zone of action to the 3rd Division, proceeded to Yongdong north of the Myongch'on via Kilju. There the Cavalry regiment as the division reserve prepared to reinforce the 18th Regiment. Thus all the ROK Capital Division troops now were prepared to resume their attack against the Orang-ch'on within a week after they withdrew from the Ponggang area.

At about this time, reinforcing elements of the NKPA 41st Division and the 507th Brigade, which had escaped from the battle at Kilju, desperately tried to counterattack advancing friendly troops for 5 consecutive days. However, being pressed hard by the ROK Capital Division in a series of penetrations and encirclements, the fatally smashed enemy force retreated to the northern bank of the stream and tried to reassemble its strength in the low hill area near Ponggang.

On November 19, the ROK 18th Regiment crossed the Orang-ch'on from the southern edge of Ponggang and defeated the enemy on the northern bank of the creek to capture his positions there. Meanwhile, the ROK 1st Regiment on the west of the 18th Regiment also crossed the stream and moved north. It seized Hill 355, continued on northward, and surprised an estimated one battalion enemy force which had attempted to counter attack from the Yongam area. This concluded the 10 day-long battle of advance and retreat between both forces with the final victory to the ROK Capital Division.

Enenmy troops which had suffered a deathblow at the Orang-ch'on battle withdrew north toward Chool and Ch'ongjin by way of Hoemun. Still, on their retreat, they tried to check the advance of the ROK Capital Division by digging in defensive positions to wage a series of delaying actions. The 1st Battalion of the ROK 18th Regiment, however, continued on northward and captured Hoemun Airstrip by the afternoon the next day, and then Hill 188 west of it to completely control the town of Hoemun. The ROK Capital Division moved on north along the east coastal road, seized Chool on the 21st, Kyongsong on the 23rd, and finally on the morning of the 24th it entered the town of Nanam unopposed.

At about this time, the enemy dug in on the high hill masses near the Nabuk-ch'on at Ch'ongjin and Hill 303 on the far side bank of the creek and concentrated all his available strength there. At 11:00 that day, the 1st Battalion of the ROK 18th Regiment attacked against Hill 303 but gained little because of the open field and the creek in front of the hill. The battalion commander at that time decided to make it a night attack despite numerous disadvantages it might present to him. He made a daring night attack and seized Hill 303 at 21:00.

As a result, dislodged from their stronghold(Hill 303) in the south-western outskirts of Ch'ongjin, which dominated the downtown streets of the city, the bulk of the enemy troops started to escape north and east toward Hoeryong and Unggi, leaving part of them as covering force to delay the pursuit of ROK troops. On November 25, the 18th Regiment, ROK Capital Division, resumed its attack during the predawn hours and advanced to Songjondong northwest of Ch'ongjin, and the 1st Regiment at that time seized Songdong(Pine Valley) northwest of Susong just short of downtown Ch'ongjin, where it could virtually control the city.

(2) Pursuit Operations toward Kilju and Hapsu

After handing over its responsibility for the security of the Wonsan-Hamhung area to the US 1st Marine Division, all the troops of the ROK 3rd Division moved to the Hongwon-Sinp'o-Sinbukch'ong area by November 8 and protected the corps rear there. But the 26th Regiment(commanded by Lt. Col. Suh Jong Ch'ol) was attached to the American marine division as of the 9th and proceeded from Hongwon to Chikyongri Meanwhile, enemy units which had started to withdraw north toward the Songjin-Kilju-Ch'ongjin area tried desperately to delay the advance of friendly forces in an effort to secure time for reinforcing strength and equipment. But the enemy had been off his balance and begun to flee since October 26 when troops of the US X Corps equipped with mighty fire power started to land at Wonsan. Enemy troops at that time had begun to withdraw north in two directions: from Kilju to Ch'ongjin and from Kilju to Hapsu north of it. In the area of Hapsu approximately 1,000 enemy soldiers had already dug in, and just north of it, in Paekam, another 4,500 men from the newly activated NKPA Laborer's Brigade were believed to have assembled. In addition, special forces and guerrillas frequently surprised or intercepted friendly troops and their supply routes in the rear area.

On November 13, when the corps headquarters moved from Hongwon east of Hungnam to Songjin, the 22nd and part of the 23rd Regiments of the

ROK 3rd Division followed behind it to Songjin. As the corps reserve unit, the division protected the corps rear, and at the same time trained its soldiers as occasion called. In this manner, the division strengthened its combat effectiveness preparing for future actions.

On November 16, the division received operations order 120 from the Corps commander, Maj. Gen. Kim Paik Il. Gists of this order was as follows:

- The 3rd Division would move its headquarters unit and the 23rd Regiment along two routes to attack and secure Hapsu: one column from Immyong-dong to Hapsu, and the other from Kilju to Hapsu.
- The division anti-tank battalion would stay at Tanch'on, and one company of it would move out to attack against the Sul-ryong power plant and secure it.
- The 22nd Regiment under direct command of the corps would place one of its battalion at Songjin, and its main body would move back to Kilju to rejoin the parent unit.
- The Capital Division commander would pull back his 1st Cavalry Regiment from Hapsu after it was relieved by elements of the 3rd Division, and then attack and secure his assigned objective on the east coastal road with the integrated division force.

The ROK 3rd Division's combat zone on the axis of Kilju-Hapsu (Paekam) and Hyesanjin was considered critical as it ran from the Yalu across both South and North Hamkyong Province to the East Sea, along the rugged Mach'on-ryong Range which stretched south from Mt. Paektu, the highest mountain in Korea. Thus the highland area formed a plateau with the altitude of more than 1,500 meters above the sea, and the temperature in the zone already had dropped from 20 to 30 degrees centigrade day or night. What made matters worse in that particular winter was that the division zone of action had been covered with several meters deep snow, which afflicted both attacking and defending forces there.

Upon receiving the corps order, the ROK 3rd Division commander enjoined his 23rd Regiment to advance north on the axis of Songjin-Immyong-dong-Hapsu, and the 22nd Regiment to move on north along the road between Kilju and Hapsu. Thus the two regiments were to make a double envelopment on the Hapsu area and capture the town.

Pursuant to the division order, the ROK 23rd Regiment, spearheaded by the 1st Battalion which had already advanced to Immyongdong, moved on toward Hapsu on the 20th. At Taesinri 30 kilometers south of Hapsu, the regiment relieved the 1st Cavalry Regiment, ROK Capital Division. Subsequently, the 23rd Regiment encountered a strong enemy resistance at a point southeast of Hapsu; however, with the help of the US Air Force, it continued on toward Hapsu and finally seized the town by the 22nd.

Meanwhile, the ROK 22nd Regiment, led by its 2nd Battalion which had left Kilju first toward Chaedok, started to move along the Chaedok-Hapsu route. The regiment reached Hapsu a day late behind the 23rd Regiment.

The 23rd Regiment moved on northwest from Hapsu, and on the 25th, it took Paekam capturing four abandoned locomotive engines there. The next day, the 22nd Regiment(the 1st Battalion) arrived at Paekam to relieve the 23rd Regiment and took over the mission for the security of the Paekam-Hapsu area.

In the mean time, the ROK 26th Regiment which had been attached to the US 7th Division was active in its assigned area, and the antitank battalion detached one of its companies on the security mission at the Sul-ryong Pass as of the 22nd. This antitank company took over the mission of protecting the power plant there from a company of the US 32nd Infantry Regiment, 7th Division.

In brief, the ROK 3rd Division completed its mission for capturing Hapsu by committing its two regiments to the hill mass area for four days from November 19 to 22, and reached Paekam 5 kilometers north of Hapsu.

V. A Switchover to a New War

1. The Final Offensive Made by the UN Forces

The ROK and UN soldiers on both east and west fronts had thus far been so excited and high spirited when the Yalu and Tumen Rivers were under their nose. They had launched the general offensive to take the ultimate objectives based on the "UN Commander's order on October 24," and subsequently on October 26, the US X Corps had landed at Wonsan.

On the western front, lead elements of ROK troops had captured Ch'osan the border town on the Yalu River, and part of the US troops had advanced to Chonggodong just south of Sinuiju. Unexpectedly, however, at that time they had encountered a fresh enemy force, the organized CCF, and were in danger of being encircled by it. The attacking columns had narrowly escaped from the changing situation, and by early November, secured instead a bridgehead at the Ch'ongch'on River between Sinanju and Wonri. The US Eighth Army commander had to bring the US IX Corps, the Army reserve, into the center of the defense line to counter the changed situation. By so doing, he could reinforce his troops along the bridgehead and at the same prepared for resumption of the offensive there.

On the other hand, on the eastern front, the US 1st Marine Division had advanced to Yudamri in spite of the confirmation of the CCF's open intervention in the battle near the Changjin hydroelectric power plant at the identical period of time. Elsewhere in the northeastern zone of Korea, friendly troops had defeated resistance of the remaining NKPA units, and moved on north exploiting and pursuing the enemy. By late November, the US 7th Infantry Division had reached Hyesanjin on the North Korea-Manchurian border to the west of Mt. Paektu, the ROK 3rd Division had advanced to Hapsu and Paekam, and the ROK Capital Division to Ch'ongjin. Thus the advance of the friendly units on the eastern front had been impressive and sharply contrasted with that on the western front.

During this period, at the ROK and US high command and at Army head-quarters, ranking officials and commanders tried to make estimates of the recent CCF intervention in the war and discussed alternative strategies for the changing situation. However, intelligence organizations of either nation failed not only to correctly estimate the objective of the CCF intervention but also to estimate strategic or tactical scales the enemy might employ. Even the military intelligence parties on the battle fronts had underestimated the changed situation due to the lack of information except for that obtained by interrogating the enemy captives. Inaccurate and unreliable information further misled or confused war leaders and military commanders of both nations so that they could not agree on a single military strategy. Thus none of them might have anticipated that their uncertainty and the resulting confusion could bring an irrevocable calamity upon the ROK and the UN Forces.

In the mean time, with the objective of obliterating the enemy's combat capability in Korea by cutting off additional enemy reinforcements and supplies streaming into Korea from Manchuria across the Yalu, the United Nations Command, launched from November 7 a large scale strategic bombardment upon bridges over the river and other supply routes, including major factories and communication facilities, along the North Korean border. This massive bombing operation lasted for two weeks.

At about this time, General MacArthur was optimistic and overestimated the friendly situation. He was impressed by the fact that his troops on the west had prepared for a massive attack, and on the east the advance of friendly forces had been equally impressive. He believed the strategic bombing on and around the Yalu had isolated the battle from Manchuria. Although he was aware that organized units of CCF had been and were being used against UN Forces,[80] he never believed that the Chinese would intervene in full force. He said optimistically that should they do so, his air power would destroy them.[81] Based on this calculation, he decided to launch his so-called, "the final offensive."

General MacArthur's ultimate offensive started at 09:00 on November 24. He made it public that should he succeed in this offensive operation, the fighting would be over by Christmas and he would get all UN troops back to their homes.[82] So the attack was later called by American soldiers the "final offensive," or "Christmas offensive." At that time, the United Nations Command estimated the enemy strength at 82,799 North Koreans and 40,000 or 70,935 Chinese; [83] however, the actual strength of the CCF units committed to the battle ground numbered 300,000 men.

For this last offensive, the US Eighth Army, along the Ch'ongch'on River bridgehead, deployed the US I Corps(US 24th and ROK 1st Divisions, and the reserved British 27th Brigade) on the west, the US IX Corps(US 25th and 2nd Divisions, and the reserved Turkish Brigade) in the center, and the ROK II Corps (ROK 7th and 8th Divisions, and 6th Division as the reserve) on the east. The objective of Eighth Army was an anticipated enemy concentration in the Kanggye–Huich'on area.

The first day, it seemed as if all went well as scheduled. However, on the second day, when the US I Corps on the left wing was approaching Chongju, the ROK II Corps on the right was struck hard by a Chinese Communist force at the Tokch'on-Yongwon area. The right flank of the line was immediately crushed by the CCF and the UN offensive was abruptly forced to pass into the defensive.

In the meantime, with an objective to close gaps between Eighth Army and the US X Corps, the latter launched its offensive operations on November 27, 3 days after the former started to attack. For this purpose, the X Corps had partly changed its initial plan for moving north, and instead, enjoined the US 1st Marine Division to proceed from the Changjin Reservoir to Mup'yongni. The American marines were first to curtail the enemy supply route from Manp'ojin through Kanggye and to Huich'on, and then advance to Manp'ojin, the border city. Part of the US 7th Division moved to the east flank of the reservoir to continue on toward Huch'angkangku, the direction in which the American marine division initially had planned to attack. The US 3rd Infantry Division was to establish contact with the Eighth Army.

The ROK I Corps planned to move its 3rd Division toward Musan on the Tumen River, and the division in turn enjoined its 26th Regiment to attack against Hyesanjin. The ROK corps at the same time enjoined the ROK Capital Division to advance toward Hoeryong and Unggi, the northern most towns of North Korea.

At about this time, the NKPA Labor Division which had confronted the ROK I Corps moved from Paekam to Hyesanjin and Musan, and the bulk of the NKPA 41st Division, 507th Brigade, and unidentified coastal garrison forces assembled in the area of Musan-Hoeryong. An enemy covering force was also active in the areas of Puryong 30 kilometers north of Ch'ongjin and Puko to form a line of resistance there.

The ROK 23rd Regiment of the 3rd Division which had seized Hapsu moved to Nanam and attacked against Musan there. Meanwhile, the ROK 26th Regiment, which had been attached to the US 7th Division, moved to the area of Tanch'on-Honggun-P'ungsan and took over the mission of the US 31st Regiment which was to move to the north of the Changjin Reservoir.[84] The ROK regiment there advanced toward Kapsan-Samsu, and the 1st Battalion of the regiment reached Hyesanjin on the 29th. The main elements of the ROK 22nd Regiment guarded the Hapsu-Paekam area, while its 3rd Company entered Hyesanjin on the 30th. The 18th Regiment of the ROK Capital Division which had secured Ch'ongjin continued on toward Hoeryong, and its Cavalry Regiment pursued the enemy toward Unggi. On November 30, this cavalry regiment reached Puryong and a point south of Puko against relatively light enemy resistance. Thus the regiment was only 40 kilometers away from Hoeryong on the North Korean-Manchurian border, and 50 kilometers away from Unggi on the North Korean-Russian border.

The US 7th Division which had seized Hyesanjin prepared to strike northwest through Samsu to Singalp'ajin approximately 30 kilometers west of Hyesanjin. Task Force Kingston led the US 32nd Regiment of the division and started for Samsu. At that time, enemy forces fought effective delaying actions north of Samsu; even a small-scale enemy unit in the Hyesanjin-Singalp'ajin area stubbornly resisted friendly troops by blowing bridges or establishing road craters. As a result, the US 17th Regiment, which had been to provide a lateral support for the task force, was immobilized. Task Force Kingston was inevitably delayed so that not until November 28 did it reach Singalp'ajin.

In the mean time, unlike the situation on the northeastern zone of action, the US 1st Marine Division, which had started for Mup'yonri from the Changjin Reservoir, was blocked from the very first day by a strong Chinese force there. What made the matters worse, that night the only one division communication route between Hamhung and the reservoir was intercepted by the enemy force and the attacking US marines were virtually encircled. The enemy was later turned out to be eight CCF divisions.

As the American division on the eastern front was stranded following the worsening situation on the western front, General MacArthur on the night of November 28 called Generals Walker and Almond to an operational meeting at Tokyo, where he decided to withdraw all the UN Forces. Accordingly, friendly troops on the eastern front started to move south on November 30, following the US Eighth Army which had already started to withdraw south from its positions on the west two days earlier.

In conclusion, the final UN offensive operations which had been launched in the hope of ending the war—despite the intense cold with sub-zero temperatures of 20 degrees to 30 centigrade, and rugged terrain formed by 6 great mountain ranges including the Chogyu-ryong Range—was terminated 60 days after the UN crossing of the 38th Parallel and the confirmation of the CCF's intervention in the war in full force.

2. A Turnover to a Totally New War

As the Chinese Communist Forces' open intervention in the Korean War was made clear when the UN Forces launched their last offensive operations, the war entered into a new phase. Pursuant to an operational instruction, which North Korean Kim Il Sung had designed in conspiracy with the Soviet leader Stalin to carry out a preemptive strike against South Korea, the North Korean People's Army initially had made a surprise attack against the South on June 25, 1950. Thus it had started as a hostility between the NKPA and ROK forces. At the very beginning of the hostility, the ROK forces, with only half of the NKPA strength, could not absorb the North Korean surprise attack. Thus with its capital city, Seoul, having been snatched away within three days, the ROK forces in the confusion of the moment crossed the Han River without even using proper means of river crossing to hurriedly form a defensive line on the southern bank of the river. It had tried to fight delaying actions to pass into the immediate counteroffensive there.

At about that time, part of the United Nations Forces had arrived in

South Korea to form a combined defensive front with the ROK forces. The UN Froces had been dispatched, according to the UN collective security measures as specified on the charter, to help the ROK government to repel the North Korean aggressors, and to restore security and peace on the Korean peninsula. As of July 14, South Korean President Syngman Rhee had transferred his right for operational control of the ROK Forces to the UNC commander, considering that the UN Forces would better make a coordinated effort for helping his country under the unified leadership of the UNC commander. Now the ROK forces, although not legally considered part of the UN Forces, had practically fought the war as if it had been part of the UN Forces. Thus the war had developed into a hostility between the NKPA and the UN Forces, a brand new character.

In the early phase of the war, the ROK and UN Forces had fought delaying actions to resume their combat capability until they reached part of the Pusan perimeter: the Naktong River front. There they had engaged in a life-and-death battle to repulse the North Koreans and had taken away the initiative from the enemy. Meanwhile, the enemy had initially planned to communize South Korea by August 15, using blitz tactics; however, he was soon countered by the determined resistance of the anti-Communist and free-loving South Korean people. The UN forces' participation in the war had deprived him of relative superiority of power, and the inadequate support from his rear, in terms of strength and war materiel, had also reduced his combat effectiveness. In his memoir, former Soviet leader Khrushchev stated that the Pusan Perimeter had never been an impregnable fortress; Kim Il Sung had been in want of strength and war materiel in the final phase of his attack; he had suffered heavy losses particularly in tanks; should he have had one additional tank corps, he could have broken through the perimeter line and won the final victory ···. Soviet military advisors had not provided sufficient support for him because they had not comprehensively reviewed all possible factors in the process of planning; in this respect, Stalin deserves severe criticism; Kim Il Sung had neither requested additional support even though the Soviet could have provided him with one more corps of tanks. Khrushchev pointed out an erroneous estimation in the process of planning, and debilitated combat effectiveness of the NKPA as factors of contributing to its defeat.[85]

　　　Both ROK and UN forces had passed from the defensive to the offensive as of September 15, when the UN forces successfully landed at Inch'on. By the end of the month, 97 days after the war had broken out, they had recaptured almost all lost grounds and virtually restored the pre-war conditions. At that time, the NKPA, which had suffered heavier loss than that of the ROK forces at the early stage of the war, had been dismantled and hurridely escaped northward. Part of its troops which had been encircled by friendly forces had sneaked into the rugged mountain areas of the T'aebaek and Sobaek Ranges to become guerrillas. In the mean time, many innocent Korean people who could not evacuate during the NKPA's occupation had been harassed by the Communists' brainwash, abduction, and forcible recruitment into the Communist army or support service units. Some patriotic, anti-Communist people had stubbornly resisted the Communist rule to their death. Thus the inhumane aspect of ideological war had presented gruesome sights too miserable to look at, and as a result, Communism apparently could not be deeply rooted again in this country.

　　　When friendly forces had reached the 38th Parallel, South Korean President Rhee had ordered his own troops to cross the Parallel; he thought that the 38th Parallel had crumbled at the moment the NKPA crossed it to attack against the South, so that it should not be considered as an obstacle; instead, he had to cross it to reunify the South and North Korea. The US Government had also concluded that military operations north of the Parallel should be lawful in the light of the UN Resolution on June 28 for the destruction of the North Korean Armed Forces, and instructed the UN forces to operate there. At the same time, anticipating political unification of Korea after the military victory, the US Government had drafted the October 7 UN Resolution on a unified Korea. The Chinese Communist government had opposed it assuming a threatening attitude that it would intervene into the war, should UN troops cross the Parallel, and the Soviet Communists had also opposed the draft resolution on October 7 calling for an immediate ceasefire and withdrawal of all foreign troops from Korea.

On October 1, the historic UN "March North" operations had started spearheaded by ROK troops. At that time, friendly forces had crossed the Parallel adventurously without having closely analyzed the possibilities of the Chinese Communists or Soviet intervention in the war. The ROK and UN forces had broken through enemy defensive lines, capturing P'yongyang on October 19, and advanced to the Ch'ongch'on River line. At that time, North Korean leader Kim Il Sung had stated in despair, "no place to escape; Americans would sure continue on northward to occupy whole North Korea."[86] He had moved his headquarters to Kanggye, tripling his defensive lines at the Ch'ongch'on River, Huich'on, and Kanggye, and had been fully determined to resist to the last by employing guerrilla warfare.

On October 24, UN forces which had thus far secured the Ch'ongch'on River line, launched the massive offensive toward the North Korean-Manchurian border. Lifting the UN restrictions that only ROK troops should operate near the Manchurian border, General MacArthur at that time ordered all friendly units to advance toward the Yalu and Tumen Rivers on that border.

Pursuant to this order, advance elements of the ROK forces had once entered the border town of Ch'osan on the Yalu, but they unexpectedly engaged an organized Chinese Communist force there. Since that time on, the UN forces on the western front had been forced to withdraw south to the Ch'ongch'on River line. On the eastern front, however, the ROK troops had approached Ch'-

ongjin and advance elements of American troops had continuously pursued the enemy toward the border, thus seizing Hyesanjin. Despite the appearance of organized Chinese forces there, General MacArthur, who erroneously underestimated the situation and had neither seen through the CCF's objective or its intent as well, ordered his troops to launch the last offensive on November 24 soon after the US Eighth Army prepared to resume its attack. However, the UN troops had been countered by a massive CCF counteroffensive at that time, and were generally forced to withdraw south on November 30.

As a result, a new battle front was formed along Chongju-Yongwon-the Changjin Reservoir-Hyesanjin-Hapsu-Ch'ongjin. The UN forces, which had comprised troops from 12 nations,[57] confronted a fresh enemy only within a foot from the North Korean-Manchurian border. But it was a frustrating and tragic moment that shattered the long-cherished Korean dream of reunification.

Thus the Korean War was escalated to a new phase of hostility: the combined NKPA and CCF vs. the ROK and UN Forces, or the Communist forces vs. the UN forces, or virtually a war between the CCF and UN Forces. When military support of the Communist nations including the Soviet Union for the North Korean government was considered, the war eventually developed into a conflict between the Communist and free Democratic camps under the cold war structure at that time.

As the authors had mentioned above, the Korean War was steadily transformed into an uncanny showdown between the CCF and the UN Forces, changing almost all the peninsula from the Naktong to Yalu into a battle ground during the initial 6 months of the war. Accordingly, the character of the war bore different meanings if described as a Korean civil, ideological conflict or international war. Thus the Korean War was, as it were, about to stand at the crossroads that could lead to another world war or remain as a limited local war. Therefore, the war was entering on a new phase that no one could control or anticipate. The final results would shape the fate of the Korean nation.

Notes

1) Han P'yo Wook, *The Infancy of the ROK-US Diplomcy*(Seoul: 1984), pp. 94-95. Warren Austin, US Ambassador to the UN, told the UN Security Council on June 30 that the objective of the US military actions in Korea was to restore the prewar conditions on the peninsula.

2) The War History Compilation Committee, tr., *The Chinese Communist Forces Cross the Yalu*(Seoul: 1989), p. 109.

3) The War History Compilation Committee, tr., *The History of the Joint Chiefs of Staff and National Policy: The Korean War*, vol. 1., 1990, p. 173.

4) The War History Compilation Committee, *The History of the Korean War*, vol. 4, p. 275.

5) Han P'yo Wook, *The Infancy of the ROK-US Diplomacy*, pp. 98-99.

6) The War History Compilation Committee, tr., *The CCF Cross the Yalu*, p. 98.

7) The War History Compilation Committee, *The History of the Korean War*, vol. 4, p. 275.

8) The War History Compilation Committee, tr., *The CCF Cross the Yalu*, p. 98.

9) Ibid., p. 279.

10) Ibid., p. 277.

11) ROK Ministry of Public Information, *A Collected Speeches of Dr. Syngman Rhee* (Seoul: 1953), pp. 39-40.

12) The War History Compilation Committee, tr., *The History of JCS & National Policy: Korean War*, vol. 1, p. 174.

13) Ibid., p. 177.

14) Ibid., p. 179; Schunabel, *Policy and Direction*, p. 183.

15) The War History Compilation Committee, *A Collection of National Defense Treaties* (Seoul), p. 638.

16) Schunabel, *Policy and Direction*, pp. 193-194.

17) The Eight nations that drafted the joint proposal were Britain, Australia, the Philippines, Netherland, Denmark, Brazil, Cuba, and Pakistan.

18) The War History Compilation Committee, tr., *The CCF Cross the Yalu*, p. 154.

19) Schunabel, *Policy and Direction*, p. 197.

20) Han P'yo Wook, *The Infancy of the ROK-US Diplomacy*, p. 91, p. 98.

21) Chung Il Hyong, *The United Nations and the Korean Questions* (Seoul: 1961), pp. 25-26.

22) *UN Resolutions* 112 on November 14, 1947, 195 on December 12, 1948, and 293 on October 21, 1949.

23) Department of Troop Information & Education, ROK Ministry of National Defense, *The First hear of the Korean War: A Chronicle*, pp. A 18-A 19.

24) Han P'yo Wook, *The Infancy of the ROK-US Diplomacy*, p. 102.

25) Franchesca's Memoir, "*The Korean War and President Syngman Rhee*," The JoongAng Ilbo, July, 1983.

26) Schunabel, *Policy and Direction*, p. 183; WHCC, tr., *The History of the JCS & National Policy: Korean War*, vol. 1, p. 186; According to this source book, the reports on General Walker's statement were not confirmed. The US Government was also embarassed at the reports and notified the UNC Commander that Washington's intent was to make sure that he should feel free in terms of strategy and tactics north of the 38th Parallel. Washington rather hoped that he had desired to do so.

27) The War History Compilation Committee, *The History of the Korean War*, vol. 4, p. 287.

28) The ROK I Corps *Operations Order* 103(September 30, 1950); the ROK 3rd Division *Operations Order* 44(October 1, 1950).

29) The ROK Joint Chiefs of Staff, *The History of Korean War* (Seoul: 1984), pp. 448-450.

30) The War History Compilation Committee, *The History of the Korean War*, vol. 4, p. 326.

31) Research Institute of History, North Korea, *Comprehensive History of Choson*, vol. 26(Scientific Encyclopedia Press, 1981), pp. 63-64.

32) The ROK Joint Chiefs of Staff, *The History of Korean* War, p. 444.

33) Appleman, *South to the Naktong, North to the Yalu*, pp. 638-640; (1) a train of nine cars to Taejon for the 25th Division, (2) a ration train of 20 cars(200,000 rations) to Yongdungp'o, (3) two ammunition trains of 20 cars each, (4) one hospital train, (5) one POL train of 30 cars, and (6) one train of 20 cars every other day in support of ROK troops based in the Seoul area.

34) The ROK Army *Operations Order* 205 (October 5, 1950).

35) The War History Compilation Committee, *Operations for Capturing P'yongyang* (Seoul: 1986), p. 44.

36) The War History Compilation Committee, *The History of the Korean War*, vol. 4, pp. 325-326.

37) The 2nd 10-15 kilometer defensive line was known as the NKPA's general guard area (general observation posts) which the NKPA division commanders were to designate. For this particular defensive operation, the enemy had set the line at Sangumri-Anbyon-Namsanri in the outskirts of Wonsan. Meanwhile, the 1st defensive line of 25-30 kilometers was set at Kojo-Hoeyang-Singosan. (source: the ROK Army Staff College, *Tactical References*, 1982).

38) Research Institute of History, North Korea, *Comprehensive History of Choson*, vol. 26, pp. 63-73.

39) The NKPA 588th Unit, A *Sketch Map* on Combat Disposition of NKPA Troops at Yonghung Bay Area, drawn by its commander Kim Chun T'aek (September 15, 1950), on a scale of 1 to 200,000.

40) The War History Compilation Committee, *The History of the Korean War*, vol. 4, pp. 325-326.

41) Ibid., pp. 336-337.

42) The War History Compilation Committee, *Operations for Capturing P'yongyang*, p. 62.

43) *Testimony* of then Col. Kim Tong Bin, the ROK 11th Regiment, the Korea Institute of Military History.

44) The US 10th AAA Group had 155-mm. howitzers and 90-mm. AAAs as well.

45) The ROK Army *Operations Order* 212 revised as of 20:00, October 10, 1950.

46) The War History Compilation Committee, *Operations for Capturing P'yongyang*, p. 137.

47) The city of P'yongyang is situated astride the Taedong River, one of the larger streams of Korea, meandering through the city in a letter "S." Its population at the outbreak of the war was approximately 500,000 with the important public buildings on the west side of the river, called Main P'yongyang. A large, relatively new industrial suburb sprawled on the east side, called East P'yongyang. Toward the Yangkag islet on the south side of the city, there were two railroad bridges of the Seoul-Sinuiju railroad over the river. Two and half kilometers north of the railroad bridges, there was the Taedong bridge, the main highway bridge 618 meters long. The Taedong at P'yongyang averages about 400-500 meters in width. As the current is swift, it constitutes a major military obstacle making it unable to wade in the west side of the river where it joins the smaller Namkang River about 10 kilometers upstream of the Taedong.

48) The War History Compilation Committee, *The History of the Korean War*, vol. 4, p. 453; also *Operations for Capturing P'yongyang*, p. 147.

49) The Department of TI & E, the ROK MND, *The First year of the Korean war: A chronicle*, pp. B-60 & C-20-21; Franchesca's Memoir, "*The Korean War and President Syngman Rhee*," The JoongAng Ilbo, July, 1983.

50) The War History Compilation Committee, *The History of Korean War*, vol. 4, p. 15.

51) WHCC, tr., *The History of the US JCS and National Policy: Korean War*, vol. I, p. 208.

52) The War History Compilation Committee, *The History of Korean War*, vol. 4, p. 16.

53) Ibid., pp. 16-17; Research Instititute of History, North Korea, *Comprehensive History of Choson*, vol. 26, pp. 101-102.

54) The War History Compilation Committee, *The History of Korean War*, vol. 4, p. 17.

55) The NKPA *Commander-in-Chiefs' Order* on October 14, 1950, owned by the Korea Institute of Military History.

56) The ROK Army, tr., *The Policy and Direction* (Seoul: 1974), pp. 275-278.

57) WHCC, tr., *The History of the US JCS and National Policy: Korean War*, vol. I, p. 208; Schunabel, *Policy and Direction*, p. 216.

58) The "A" line was also called MacArthur Line, which had been set up roughly at a point 35 miles south of the Yalu River to restrict the UN ground operations north of the line. Only the ROK forces were allowed to operate north of it.

59) Appleman, *South to the Naktong, North to the Yalu*, p. 654.

60) Ibid., p. 661.

61) The War History Compilation Committee, *The Battle at the Ch'ong-ch'on River* (Seoul: 1985), p. 34.

62) The ROK Army, tr., *Policy and Direction*, p. 285; Appleman, *South to the Naktong, North to the Yalu*, p. 670.

63) WHCC, tr., *The History of the US JCS and National Policy: Korean War*, vol. I, pp. 209-210.

64) The War History Compilation Committee, *The Battle at the Ch'ong-ch'on River*, p. 49.

65) Ibid., p. 50.

66) Ibid., pp. 50 & 71.

67) WHCC, tr., *The History of the US JCS and National Policy: Korean War*, vol. I, p. 215.

68) The ROK I Corps *Operations Order* 115(October 15, 1950).

69) The ROK Capital Division *Operations Order* 106(October 15, 1950).

70) The War History Compilation Committee, *The History of the Korean War*, vol. 4, p. 499; A breakdown of North Korean atrocities included: about 700 men killed in North Korean jails, estimated 200 men in the basement of the Memorial Tower, about 300 men in the basement of the North Korean Security Police Bureau office building, approximately 6,000 men in a nickel mine at Tok-san, and about 1,200 men in a 4 kilometer-long air-raid shelter at Panyong-san. Thus a total of about 8,400 innocent people were killed.

71) The narrow pass situated on the high ground boundary between the two counties
of Pukch'ong and P'ungsan, South Hamkyong Province. It is also called "The Red
Ants Pass," the only mountain trail which leads north to Susangri and Whangsuwon from Sinp'ungri. The plateau passage is a 25 kilometer-long, zigzagging
mountain path with the altitude of 1,000-1,500 meters above sea level. In general,
both North and South Hamkyong Province are well known as mountainous high
ground terrain covered with many high, long, narrow, rugged mountain trails, and
this defile, Whajopch'i, is one of them. Currently, the place is situated on the
boundary of Yangkang and South Hamkyong Provinces. The War History Compilation Committee, *The History of the Korean War*, vol. 4, p. 516.

72) The ROK 3rd Division, *The History of the 'Bones and Skeleton' Division*(Seoul: 1980),
p. 214; The War History Compilation Committee, *The History of the Korean War*,
vol. 4, p. 505.

73) Ibid., pp. 582-583.

74) Appleman, *South to the Naktong, North to the Yalu*, pp. 633-637; The ROK Army, tr.,
Policy and Direction, p. 273.

75) The War History Compilation Committee, *The History of Korean War*, vol. 4, p. 599.

76) Ibid., p. 586.

77) The ROK Capital Division *Operations Order* 110(November 5, 1950).

78) The US 65th Infantry Regiment, 3rd Division (commanded by Maj. Gen. Robert
N. Soule) had landed at Pusan on September 22 to reinforce the US X Corps. The
American regiment sailed from Puerto Rico, an eastern island in the west Indies
on August 25, and came ashore at Pusan via the Panama Cannal. The US7th and
15th Regiments together with the division headquarters departed San Francisco
on August 30, and arrived at Moji, Japan on September 16.

79) The ROK I Corps *Operations Order* 120(November 16, 1950).

80) WHCC, tr., *The History of the US JCS and National Policy: Korean War*, vol. I, p. 238.

81) Appleman, *South to the Naktong, North to the Yalu*, p. 765.

82) WHCC, tr., *The History of the US JCS and National Policy: Korean War*, vol. I, p. 265.

83) Schunabel, *Policy and Direction*, p. 273.

84) Billy C. Mossman, *Ebb and Flow* (CMH, USA.: 1990), p. 86.

85) *Khrushcheov Remembers* (Little Brown & Company, 1990), p. 146.

86) Ibid., p. 147.

87) Initially, 12 nations including the United States took part in the Korean War: Britain, Australia, the Netherlands, New Zealand, Canada, France, the Philippines, Turkey, Thailand, South African Republic, and Greece. Later, four other nations joined them and dispatched combat troops to Korea, which increased the number of nations to 16.

APPENDIX 1

CHRONOLOGY

Date	Event
13 August 1945	Soviet ground forces landed at Ch'ongjin.
15th	Japan surrendered and Korea was liberated.
	The US drew up and distrilbuted General Order No. 1 to the Allied Nations.
24th	Soviet forces entered P'yongyang.
2 September 1945	General MacArthur issued General Order No. 1.
	Japan formally signed the instrument of surrender.
8th	US Forces landed at Inch'on and entered Seoul.
9th	Japanese governor Abbe Nobuyuki signed the instrument of surrender.
14 October 1945	A welcoming ceremony for Kim Il Sung was held at P'yongyang.
16th	Syngman Rhee returned to Seoul, Korea.
21st	North Korean Constabulary Force (parent body of the North Korean People's Army) was activated.
24th	The United Nations was founded.
11 November 1945	A Coast Guard was organized in the South.
13th	Office of the Director of National Defense was established in the South.
18th	Kim Il Sung took office as the First Secretary of the North Korean Communist Party.
23rd	Kim Ku and other core cabinet members of the Provisionary Korean Government returned to Seoul, Korea.
27 December 1945	The trilateral foreign ministers meeting at Moscow issued a plan for placing the Korean peninsula under a five-year U.N. trusteeship.
11 January 1946	The North Korean Railroad Constabulary Force was activated.
15th	The South Korean Defense Constabulary Force (the 1st Regiment) was activated.

Date	Event
8 February 1946	North Korea organized the Provisionary People's Committee (chaired by Kim Il Sung).
20 March 1946	The 1st US-Soviet Joint Committee meeting was held.
29th	The Office of the Director of National Defense was renamed as the Ministry of National Defense(MND).
8 May 1946	The 1st US-Soviet Joint Committee meeting ended in a rupture.
15 June 1946	The MND was renamed as the Department of Internal Security and was called "T'ongwibu."
12 September 1946	Yu Tong Yol took office as the Chief Department of Internal Security (The first bureau chief of T'ongwibu).
1 October 1946	An armed riot broke out in Taegu.
17 February 1947	The North Korean People's Committee chaired by Kim Il Sung was organized.
21 May 1947	The US-Soviet Joint Committee opened its 2nd-round meeting.
30 August 1947	The South Korean Coast Guard assumed the guard mission.
17 September 1947	The Korean question was presented to the UN General Assembly.
21 October 1947	The 2nd-round meeting of the US-Soviet Joint Committee ended in a rupture.
14 November 1947	The UN General Assembly adopted a resolution on the establishment of the UN Temporary Commission on Korea & the enforcement of the general election in Korea.
8 February 1948	North Korea announced the activation of the North Korean People's Army.
3 April 1948	The April 3rd Riot Incidents broke out on Cheju Island.

Date	Event
10 May 1948	South Korea held the general election under the supervision of the UN Temporary Commission on Korea.
15th	Department of Internal Security (T'ongwibu) activated an Aviation unit.
15 August 1948	The Republic of Korea Government was established.
16th	South Korean Defense Constabulary Force and Coast Guards were integrated into the ROK Armed Forces.
24th	The ROK-US Military Security Agreement was signed.
9 September 1948	The Democratic People's Republic of Korea(North Korean) Government was established.
19 October 1948	The Yosu-Sunch'on Rebellion broke out.
2 November 1948	The Taegu Rebellion broke out.
10 December 1948	North Korea, the USSR, and Communist China held a strategic meeting at Moscow.
12th	The U.N. General Assembly approved the ROK Government and at the same time, adopted a resolution on the withdrawal of all foreign troops from Korea.
26th	The Soviet troops completed withdrawal from North Korea leaving military advisors(to each infantry battalion and higher echelon).
5 March 1949	Kim Il Sung and Stalin held a summit meeting.
17 March 1949	North Korean-Soviet Military, Economic, and Cultural Agreement was signed.
28 April 1949	Kim Il and Mao Tse-tung held a conference.
5 May 1949	Two battalions of the ROK 8th Regiment defected to North Korea.
29 June 1949	The US troops completed their withdrawal from South Korea; North Korea organized a "Democratic Front for Unified Fatherland."
1 July 1949	The US Military Advisory Group In Korea was established.

Date	Event
15th	North Korea formed a supporters' organization for its armed forces.
1 October 1949	The ROK Armed Forces was subdivided into Army, Navy, and Air Force; The People's Republic of China (Communist government) was formally established.
16 December 1949	Mao Tse-tung and Stalin held conferences which lasted until February 16, the next year.
12 January 1950	The US State Secretary Dean G. Acheson delivered a speech on the US Pacific defensive perimeter.
26th	The ROK-US Mutual Defense Aid Agreement was signed.
15 March 1950	10 training aircrafts (T-6, named "Konkuk" by South Koreans) were inrtoduced to the ROK.
April 1950	Kim Il Sung and Stalin met together.(3. 30-4. 25)
10 April 1950	One Patrol Vessel(PC) arrived at Chinhae harbor.
27 April 1950	ROK troops were put on alert status.
13 May 1950	Kim Il Sung met Mao Tse-tung.(5. 13-5. 16)
29th	North Korea set up plans for a preemptive attack against the South.
30th	South Korea held a general election.
7 June 1950	North Korea launched a false peace offensive against the South.
10th	Important commanders and staff officers of the ROK Armed Forces faced a sweeping personnel shake-up; The North Korean Defense Ministry secretly convened a commanders' meeting.
12th	NKPA combat units moved to and assembled along the 38th Parallel.
17th	US Presidential advisor John F. Dulles visited South Korea.
18th	The NKPA Supreme Command issued reconnaissance orders to its subordinate combat units.

Date	Event
22nd	The NKPA divisions in turn issued combat orders.
23rd	The ROK Armed Forces all cleared the alert status; The NKPA finishied Forward Deployment of the Attacking unit.
25th	The NKPA troops unlawfully crossed the 38th Parallel to attack the South; The ROK Government immediately called on the United States and the U.N. for military aid.
26th	The ROK National Assembly passed a resolution on sending messages to the US Congress and the President; The UN Security Council adopted a resolution on the immediate halt of hostile activities and withdrawal of all NKPA troops from the South; South Korean town of Uijongbu was captured by the NKPA; US F-80 fighter planes for the first time encontered Russian-built Yaks, and shot down 3 of them.
27th	The ROK Government evacuated to Taejon; The US Government decided to provide naval and air support for the ROK, and to blockade the Taiwan Strait with the US 7th Fleet; Advance command and liasion party of the US Far East Command was dispatched to Suwon, Korea.
28th	The UN Security Council passed a resolution on military aid to the ROK; The ROK army blasted the highway bridge over the Han River; Seoul was captured by the NKPA; The ROK Sihung Combat Command organized the Han River defensive positions.
29th	The US Navy and Air Force extended their zone of action to north of the 38th Parallel; General MacArthur made an on-site inspection of the Han River defensive positions.

Date	Event
30th	Washington decided to commit US ground troops to the Korean War; Major General Chung Il Kwon was appointed the Commander-in-Chief of the ROK Armed Forces and concurrently the Army Chief of Staff; The Republic of China (Taiwan) suggested the dispatch of a 33,000 man ground force to help South Korea.
1 July 1950	Advance party of US ground troops landed at Pusan; The ROK-US military leaders(Chung Il Kwon and Church) met to coordinate the combined operations of both forces.
2nd	The ROK Air Force received 10 F-51 fighter planes.
3rd	North Korean tanks crossed the Han River; the ROK Army Headquarters evacuated to Suwon.
4th	The ROK Army Headquarters moved to P'yongt'aek; the ROK Army issued orders for consolidation and reorganization of its defensive fronts; General Mac-Arthur established the US Army Forces in Korea at Taejon and the Pusan Base Command.
5th	Task Force Smith for the first time engaged North Korean troops at Osan (Chukmi-ryong); The ROK Army reorganized its troops for the first time and activated the I Corps; The ROK and US forces formed a combined defensive front with the former assuming the mid-eastern front and the latter the western flank.
6th	The US 24th Infantry Division took up defensive positions in the vicinity of P'yongt'aek along the 37th Parallel.
7th	The U.N. Security Council resolved to activate a Unified United Nations Command, and Washington appointed General MacArthur the Commander of the UNC; Australian and British naval and air forces joined the ROK and US forces in the war.

Date	Event
8th	The ROK Government placed South Korea(except for South and North Cholla Provinces) under martial law.
9th	The US Eighth Army had its Headquarters at Taegu.
10th	The US 25th Infantry Division landed at Pusan; the US Fifth Air Force moved to South Korea.
12th	The ROK and US signed the Taejon Agreement on the status of US Forces in Korea.
13th	Lt. Gen. Walker, commander of the US Eighth Army, took charge of all American ground forces in Korea for operational control; the UNC opened the Logistical Command at Pusan.
14th	The Authority for operational command of the ROK forces was transferred to the UNC Commander; The ROK Army Headquarters moved to Taegu; The UN General Secretary advised member nations to dispatch ground forces to Korea.
15th	The ROK II Corps was activated at Hamch'ang.
16th	The ROK Government moved to Taegu from Taejon.
18th	The US 1st Cavalry Division landed at P'ohang.
19th	The New Zealand Navy took part in the Korean War; President Truman aired a special message on Korean matters(conscription would be imposed, reserve forces would be reenlisted, and four National Guards would be mobilized into regular divisions)
20th	Taejon fell to enemy hands and Maj. Gen. Dean, commander of the US 24th Division, went missing; The US 24th Division first destroyed enemy tanks with 3.5inch bazookas; Kim Il Sung, at the NKPA frontline headquarters at Suanbo, urged his soldiers to capture Pusan by August 15.
21st	The ROK Government placed South and North Cholla Provinces under martial law.

Date	Event
24th	The ROK Army reorganized its troops the 2nd time, with changes in its chain of command. The United Nations Command became operational at Tokyo.
28th	The Canadian Air Force participated in the war.
29th	General Walker ordered his troops to defend their positions to the last.(Issued "Stand or Die" Order)
30th	The Canadian Navy also joined the UN Forces.
31st	The US 2nd Infantry Division(-) arrived at Pusan; General MacArthur visited Taiwan to meet Generalissimo Chiang Kai-shek.
1 August 1950	The ROK and US troops organized a defensive line along the Naktong River; The Soviet delegation returned to the UN Security Council meeting.
2nd	The US 5th Marine Brigade landed at Pusan and moved to Masan.
3rd	The NKPA launched its August Offensive and part of it crossed the Naktong River.
13th	The ROK Army adjusted its defensive sector at the Naktong front and took up positions south of the Waegwan-Tabudong-Kunwi-Pohyon-san-Kanggu line.
14th	The ROK Army 1st Training Center was activated.
15th	Kim Il Sung urged the North Korean people to concentrate their war effort upon the battle fronts.
16th	98 B-29s carpet-bombed an area near Waegwan northern bank of the Naktong; The KATUSA system was introduced and part of these Korean soldiers joined the US 7th Division as replacements.
18th	The ROK Government moved to Pusan from Taegu.
19th	General MacArthur and Collins and Admiral Sherman had operational conferences at Tokyo.

Date	Event
20th	The ROK Army set up a plan for activating 10 infantry divisions during the period of August 20 – November 11; The ROK 7th Division was reactivated on this date.
22nd	A conscription system was enforced for all eligible status.
28th	The British 27th Brigade arrived at Pusan.
31st	The NKPA launched its September offensive.
1 September 1950	The US Government drafted its Korean Policy NSC 81 in an effort to furnish legal basis for the U.N. ground forces' crossing of the 38th Parallel.
5th	The Headquarters of the ROK Army and the US Eighth Army evacuated to Pusan.
6th	The ROK 8th Division started to counterattack against Yongch'on.
11th	The US Government drafted the Korean Policy NSC 81-1 to allow U.N. operations north of the 38th Parallel.
15th	The US X Corps made a historic landing at Inch'on.
16th	The US 7th Infantry Division arrived at Inch'on; The US Eighth Army launched a massive counterattack at the Naktong front.
17th	The US 5th Marines, 1st Marine Division, recaptured Kimp'o Airport.
18th	Kim Il Sung ordered a phased withdrawal of the NKPA units.
19th	Philippino ground forces arrived in Korea.
22nd	The US Eighth Army commander issued orders for the pursuit of the enemy; The ROK Army Headquarters returned to Taegu.
23rd	Kim Il Sung ordered a general retreat of the NKPA troops; A Swedish hospital ship arrived in Korean waters.

Date	Event
26th	Task Force Lynch of the US 1st Cavalry Division established contact with the US 31st Regiment, 7th Division of the US X Corps, at a point north of Osan.
27th	The US Joint Chiefs of Staff issued the "September 27 Instruction"; The combined ROK and US forces recaptured Seoul, the capital city of Korea.
28th	General MacArthur made a summary report to US JCS on his plan of crossing of the 38th Parallel; The U.S 24th Division recaptured Taejon; Australian ground forces arrived in Korea.
29th	A ceremony commemorating the return of the ROK Government to Seoul was held at the Capitol building; Washington approved the UN operations north of the 38th Parallel; The US 25th Division recaptured Kunsan.
1 October 1950	The UNC Commander demanded Kim Il Sung surrender; The ROK 3rd and Capital Divisions crossed the 38th Parallel; The NKPA took up defensive positions along the 38th Parallel.
2nd	The United Nations Command ordered its troops to cross the 38th Parallel.
3rd	The Chinese Communist Foreign Minister Chou En-lai warned of the Chinese Communist Forces' intervention in the war.
4th	The Air Force of the South African Republic participated in the war.
7th	The UN General Assembly passed a resolution on the establishment of the UN Commission for Unification and Rehabilitation of Korea(UNCURK).
9th	The UNC Commander again demanded the unconditional surrender of the North Korean Armed Forces; The UN Forces started military operations north of the 38th Parallel.

Date	Event
10th	The ROK Capital and 3rd Divisions captured Wonsan.
11th	Kim Il Sung ordered his troops to make a last-ditch, desperate resistance.
12th	The UN Interim Committee on Korean Affairs voted for a resolution on administrative measures in the occupied area.
15th	Wake Island Conference.
16th	President Syngman Rhee issued a written protest against the UN Interim Committee's resolution dated October 12.
17th	The ROK Capital Division captured Hamhung and Hungnam; The MacArther line which restricted UN operations was extended to include the Sonch'on-Songjin line; Turkish ground forces arrived in Korea.
19th	The UN Forces captured P'yongyang; Chinese Communist Forces intervened into the war.
20th	The US 187th Airborne Regiment dropped over the Sukch'on-Sunch'on area.
21st	The US I Corps imposed military rule on P'yongyang.
24th	The restriction on UN operations beyond the MacArthur Line was lifted. UN Forces launched the tolal Offensive.
25th	UN Forces for the first time encountered CCF soldiers at Unsan, Onjongri, and the Changjin Reservoir; The CCF launched its first October offensive.
26th	The ROK 7th Regiment, 6th Division, reached Ch'osan on the Yalu River; The US 1st Marine Division made an administrative landing at Wonsan.
27th	The ROK government agencies returned to Seoul.
29th	The US 7th Division landed at Iwon.

Date	Event
30th	President Rhee issued statements on the cooperation with the UNCURK on the matters of unification and the military administration in the occupied areas; A welcoming ceremony for the ROK and UN Forces was held at P'yongyang.
5 November 1950	The US 3rd Division made an administrative landing at Wonsan.
7th	Thai ground forces arrived in Korea.
10th	Thai Naval forces joined the UN forces in Korea.
20th	India's Mobile Army Surgical Hospital arrived in Korea.
21st	The US 7th Division occupied Hyesanjin.
24th	General MacArthur issued orders for the final offensive in an effort to end the war; Netherland's ground forces arrived in Korea.
25th	On the eastern front, the ROK Capital and 3rd Divisions advanced to Ch'ongjin and Hapsu, respectively; The CCF launched its 2nd(November) offensive; The Greek Air Force joined the UN Forces in Korea.
28th	The US 7th Division occupied Shingalp'ajin; Military conferences were held at Tokyo.
29th	The ROK 26th Regiment advanced to Hyesanjin; French ground troops arrived in Korea.
30th	The 3rd Company of the ROK 22nd Regiment, 3rd Division advanced to Hyesanjin; the ROK Capital Division reached the area of Puryong-Puko north of Ch'ongjin; The ROK and UN Forces started an all-out retreat.

APPENDIX 2

BIBLIOGRAPHY

(1) Primary Sources

▩ Domestic Documents & Official Publications

ROK Ministry of National Defense, *A File of MND Special Orders,* 1949-1950.

ROK MND, the War History Compilation Committee, *Testimonial Documents* Related to the Korean War.

ROK Army HQs, Office of Military History Studies, *A Historical Journal of ROK Army* (1), 1945-1950.

ROK MND, *General Orders* 3(July 5, 1950), 5(July 7), 35(August 2), & 20(July 24, 1950).

ROK MND, *General Orders* 49(August 20, 1950), 54(August 27, 1950).

ROK MND, *General Order* (Army) 70(September 13, 1950).

ROK Army, *Special Order* 11(July 7, 1950).

ROK Army, *Urgent Order* 8(July 21, 1950).

ROK Army, *Instruction* 58(September 7, 1950).

ROK Army, *General Order* (Army) 43(June 1, 1950).

ROK Army, *Operation Order* 38(Army Defense Plan, March 25, 1950).

ROK Army, *Operation Orders* 47(April 21, 1950), 67(May 8), 78(June 11), 83(June 25).

ROK Army, *Operation Orders* 19(July 3, 1950), 20(July 5), 55(July 19), 57(July 20), 70(July 25, 1950).

ROK Army, *Operation Orders* 91(July 31, 1950), 94(August 2), 116(August 10), 119 (August 11), 134(August 15), 160(September 3), 163(September 4, 1950).

ROK Army, *Operation Orders* 180 (on the counteroffensive at Pusan and South Kyongsang Province, September 30, 1950), 191(September 22), 199(September 30), 205(October 5), 212(20:00, October 10, 1950).

ROK I Corps, *Operation Orders* 1(July 5, 1950), 40(July 31), 89(September 10), 103(September 30), 120(November 6, 1950).

ROK II Corps, *Operation Orders* 12(August 12, 1950), 31(September 5), 32(September 6), 115(October 15, 1950).

ROK Capital Division, *Operation Order* 110(November 5, 1950).

ROK 3rd Division, *Operation Orders* 44(October 1, 1950).

ROK 8th Division, *Operation Orders* 14(July 9, 1950), 16(July 11, 1950).

ROK Marine Corps, *Operations Order* 1(July 14, 1950).

The Library of the ROK National Assembly, *Reports on the UN Commission on Korea* (1949, 1950), 1965.

Yu Song Ch'ol, "*My Testimony*," The Hankook Ilbo, November, 1990.

Lee Sang Jo, "*Personal Witness*," The Hankook Ilbo, 1989.

Franchesca, "*The Korean War and the President Syngman Rhee*," The JoongAng Ilbo, 1983.

North Korean Documents & Official Publications

North Korean People's Army, *Leaflets* (August 6, 1950).

NKPA *Commander-in-Chief's Order.*

NKPA 6th Division, *Operations Order* 42(August 17, 1950).

NKPA, *Combat Journal.*

NKPA II Corps, *Operations Instruction*(July 11, 1950).

NKPA 588th Unit, *A sketch map* of defensive deployment at the Yonghung Bay area(scale: 1 to 200,000, September 15, 1950).

NKPA Supreme Command, NKPA *Commander-in-Chief's Order*(October 14, 1950).

NKPA 5th Battalion, 884th Unit, Battalion *Combat Order* (August 29, 1950).

NKPA 107th Security Regiment, *Defensive Plan at Kimp'o* (captured on September 21, 1950, by the 3rd Battalion, ROK 1st Marine Regiment)

NKPA, A *Route Map for the Preemptive Strike Plan*, released by Kortkonov August 29 1992.

NKPA, *Reconnaissance Order* 1(June 18, 1950, Russian and English versions).

NKPA 2nd Division, *Combat Order* 001(June 22, 1950).

NKPA 4th Division, *Combat Order* 001(June 22, 1950).

▨ Foreign Documents & Official Publications

Korean Army, *Periodic Operations Reports*, 1950.

BG. G.B. Barth, *Tropic Lightening and Taro Leaf in Korea*, vol. 6, Library of the US Armed Forces & Staff College, 1955.

GHQ ATIS, *Interrogation Reports*, 1950-1951.

HFEC G-2, *History of the North Korean Army*, 1952.

8086th AU(AFFE) Military History Detachment, *Evacuation of Refugees and Civilians from Seoul*, 1956.

Headquarters United States Army Forces, Far East & Eighth US Army(Rear), *Logistics in the Korean Operations* (San Francisco, 1954), *Historical Manuscript File*, call No. 8-5.

Foreign Service of the USA., *Tiger Kim vs. the Press*, May 12, 1951.

EUSAK, *Periodic Intelligence Reports*, 1950.

Commanding Officer, 1st Battalion, 7th Cavalry Regiment, *After action interview with Lt. Col. Peter D. Clainos*, 1950.

24th Division, *Periodic Operations Report*, 1950.

25th Division, *Periodic Operations Report*, 1950.

US Department of State, *Foreign Relations of the United States*, 1943-1950.

War Department Intelligence Division, *Intelligence Review*, 1946.

US Department of State, *Department of State Bulletin*(September 28, 1947).

US Department of State, *The Conflict in Korea*, 1951.

UN Official Record; *Third Session, Supply No. 9*, 1948.

UN, *Year Book of the UN*, 1948-1949.

The Reporter, *How Russia Built the North Korean Army*, September 26, 1950.

FEC G-2, *Order of Battle Information, North Korean Army*, 1952.

FEC G-2, *Order of Battle Information, the CCF in North Korea*, 1952.

EUSAK, *Eighth Army Operation Plan* No. 10(September 11, 1950.

Korea Institute of Military History, *Russian documents on the Korean War*(April 1993).

ROK Foreign Ministry, *Secret Russian diplomatic documents related to the Korean War*, vols. 1-4(1994).

(2) Secondary Sources

Domestic Publications

Troop Information & Education Bureau, ROK MND, *The First year of the Korean war: A Chronicle*, 1951.

Legislation Committee, ROK MND, *A Complete Collection of Laws and Regulations* I, 1960.

War History Compilation Committee, ROK MND, *The History of Korean War*, Vol. 1(an old edition), 1967.

War History Compilation Committee, ROK MND, *The History of Korean War*, Vols. 1, 2, 3, and 4(1967-1980).

War History Compilation Committee, ROK MND, *A Summary of Korean War* (Seoul: Kyohaksa Publishers, 1986).

War History Compilation Committee, ROK MND, *The History of the Ministry of*

National Defense, 1954.

War History Compilation Committee, ROK MND, *The History of National Defense*, vols. 1 & 2(1984 & 1987).

War History Compilation Committee, ROK MND, *A Collection of Defense Treaties*, vol. 1, 1988.

War History Compilation Committee, ROK MND, *Battle at Tabudong*, 1981.

War History Compilation Committee, ROK MND, Early Battle at the 38th Parallel(Mid-Eastern Front), 1981.

War History Compilation Committee, ROK MND, *U.N. Landing Operations at Inch'on*, 1983.

War History Compilation Committee, ROK MND, *Battle at Sinnyong-Yongch'on*, 1984.

War History Compilation Committee, ROK MND, *Early Battle at the 38th Parallel* (Western Front),1985.

War History Compilation Committee, ROK MND, *Battle at the Ch'ongch'on River*, 1985.

War History Compilation Committee, ROK MND, *Battle at An'gang-P'ohang*, 1986.

War History Compilation Committee, ROK MND, *Operation for Capturing P'yongyang*, 1986.

War History Compilation Committee, ROK MND, *Battle at Tanyang-Uisong*, 1987.

War History Compilation Committee, ROK MND, *Battle at Chinch'on-Wharyongjang*, 1991.

War History Compilation Committee, ROK MND, *The History of Counter-irregular Warfares*, 1988.

Korea Institute of Military History, *Battle at Ch'ungju-Chomch'on*, 1992.

Office of Military History Chief, ROK Army, *The History of War in the Rear Areas (Logistics & Personnel)*, 1953.

ROK Army Headquarters, *History of the ROK Army Development,* vol. 1, 1970.

ROK Army Headquarters, *History of the ROK Army in The Korean War,* vols. 1 & 2, 1952 & 1953.

ROK Army Headquarters, *Early Days of the ROK Armed Forces, Studies on Military Science,* vol. 11, 1980.

ROK Army Intelligence, *Analysis on the North Korean Invasion in 1950,* 1970.

ROK Army, tr., *Policy and Direction,* 1974.

ROK Joint Chiefs of Staff, *The History of Korean War,* 1984.

ROK Marine Corps, *History of Marine Combat,* vol. 1, 1962.

Korea Military Academy, *History of Korean War* (Seoul: Ilsinsa Publishers, 1988).

Korea Military Academy, *Thirty Years of ROK Military Academy,* 1978.

ROK Office of Military Manpower Administration, *History of Military Manpower Administration,* vol. 1, 1985.

ROK Army Security Command, *Thirty Years of Counter-Communist Activities,* 1978.

ROK 3rd Division, *History of the 'Bones & Skull' Division,* 1980.

War Memorial Service, Korea, *History of Korean War,* vols. 1,2, 3, & 6, 1993.

War Memorial Service, Korea, *The Contemporary ROK Armed Forces* (Seoul: Tae-kyong Publishing Co., 1990).

Institute of Foreign Studies, ROK Foreign Affairs Ministry, *Twenty Years of ROK Diplomcy, Appendices,* 1966.

ROK Foreign Affairs Ministry, *Thirty Years of the ROK Diplomacy,* 1979.

Police Bureau, ROK Home Affairs Ministry, *History of Police at War,* 1952.

ROK Unification Board, *Studies on the Background of Korean War,* 1972.

ROK Culture & Information Ministry, *Korean War Documentaries,* 1990.

ROK Office of Public Information, *A Collection of President Syngman Rhee's Speeches,* 1953.

ROK Office of Public Information, *A Handbook of ROK Statistics,* 1953.

Ch'ae Kun Sik, *An Undisclosed History of Armed Independence Movement* (Seoul: Office of Public Information, 1978).

Criminal Investigation Department, Supreme Public Prosecutors Office, *A Collection of Incidents Related to Leftist Activities*, vols. 1-11, 1956-1975.

ROK Public Relations Association, *The Korean War*, 1973.

Korea Institute of Cultural Studies, *Encyclopedia of Korean Nation*, 1991.

ROK Research Institute of Communist Societies, *General Survey on the North Korean Society*: 45-68, 1968.

The Choongang Il-bo, *Witnesses of the Korean Nation*, vol. 1, 1973.

The Seoul Sinmun, *Thirty Years of American Forces in Korea*, 1979.

Han P'yo Wook, *The Infancy Period of ROK-US Diplomacy*(Seoul: the Choongang Il-bo, 1984).

Korean Broadcast System, *The Documentary Korean War* I, 1991.

The Chosun Il-bo, *Syngman Rhee and the Establishment of ROK Government*, 1995.

Chung Il Kwon, *The Korean War and Ceasefire* (Seoul: The DongA Ilbo, 1985).

Paik Sun Yup, *The ROK Army & Me as a Soldier* (Seoul: Taeryuk Research Institute, 1989).

Park Kyong Sok, *Five-Star General Kim Hong Il* (Seoul: Somundang Printing Co., 1984).

Lee Ung Joon, *Reminiscences for 90 Years*: 1890-1981(Seoul: 1982).

Kang Song Jae, *General Lee Jong Ch'an, the True Soldier* (The DongA Ilbo, 1988).

Yu Kwan Jong, *The History of the ROK Police at War* (Seoul: Modern Police Library, 1982).

Nam Sang Son, *The Student Volunteer Forces* (Seoul: Hyosong Publishers, 1975).

Yo Jong, *The Bloody Taedong River* (Seoul: The DongA Ilbo, 1991).

Park Kap Tong, *The Korean War and Kim Il Sung* (Seoul: Wind & Waves Printing Co., 1992).

Na Chong Il, *The Witnesses on the Korean War* (Seoul: Yejin Publishers, 1991).

Han Yong Won, *The Birth of the ROK Armed Forces* (Seoul: Pakyongsa Publishers, 1985).

Chung Il Hyong, *The United Nations & Korean Question* (Seoul: Sinmyong Publishers, 1961).

Kim Ch'ang Soon, *Fifteen Years of North Korea* (Seoul: Chimunkak Printing Co., 1961).

Chang Joon Ik, *The History of North Korean Armed Forces* (Seoul: Somun-dang Publishers, 1991).

War History Compilation Committee, ROK MND, tr., *The History of the US JCS and National Policy: Korean War*, vol. 1, 1990.

War History Compilation Committee, ROK MND, tr., *The CCF Crosses the Yalu River* (Seoul: 1989).

ROK Army Headquarters, tr., *The History of the US Navy in the Korean War* (Seoul: 1985).

MacArthur's Memoirs (Seoul: Sint'aeyangsa Publishers, 1964).

Korea Research Institute of International Strategies, tr., Dmitri Volkogonov, *Stalin*(Seoul: Sekyongsa Publishers, 1993).

Chung Hong Jin, tr., *Khrushcheov Remembers* (Seoul: Hannim Publishers, 1971).

North Korean Books & Publications

Research Institute of History, North Korea, *Comprehensive History of Choson*, vols. 24, 25, and 26 (P'yongyang: Scientific Encyclopedia Press, 1981).

Hur Chong Ho, *The Choson People's History of Justice War for the Fatherland Liberation* vol. 1 (P'yongyang: Social Science Publishers, 1983).

North Korean Cultural Sciences Co., *A Selected Reading on Kim Il Sung* (P'yongyang: Cultural Sciences Co., 1967).

Choson Central News Agency, *Choson Central Yearbook*: 49-53(1949-1954).

▨ Foreign Books and Publications

Roy E. Appleman, *United States Army in the Korean War: South to the Naktong, North to the Yalu.* Department of the Army, 1961.

The Secretary of Defense, *The Test of War: History of the Office of the Secretary of Defense,* 1988.

James F. Schnabel, *Policy and Direction: The First Year,* OCMH, US Department of Army, 1972.

Robert K. Sawyer, *Military Advisors in Korea-KMAG in Peace and War,* OCMH, US Army, 1962.

James A. Field Jr., *History of United States Naval Operations in Korea,* 1963.

USAFIK, *History of USAFIK,* 1982.

US Marine Corps, *US Marine Operations in Korea* 1950-1953, 1954-1972.

Robert F. Futrell, *The United States Air Force in Korea* 1950-1953, Department of the Air Force, 1983.

Strobe Talbott, *Khrushcheov Remembers, The Glasnost Tapes,* Little Brown and Company, 1990.

Charles E. Heller and William A. Stofft, ed. *America's First Battle*(1776-1965).

Roy K. Flint, *T.F. Smith and the 24th Division: Delay and Withdrawal,* July 5-19, 1950, Univ. Press of Kansas, 1988.

Mark W. Clark, *From the Danube to the Yalu,* New York: Harper & Brothers, 1954.

James A. Huston, *The Sinews of War: Army Logistics* 1775-1953, Office of the Chief of Military History, 1966.

Draft Field Manual, The Logistical Command, C & GSC, 1950.

Tamara Moser Melia, *Damn the Torpedoes-A Short History of US Naval Mine Countermeasures*(1777-1991), Naval Historical Center, Department of the Navy, Washington, D.C., 1991.

W.G. Robertson, *Counterattack on the Naktong 1950* (Combat Studies Institute

Leavenworth Papers), 1985.

US 25th Infantry Division, *The Tropic Lightening in Korea, 25th Infantry Division* (Georgia: Albert Love Enterprises).

Bradley J. Haldy, *Korean Service Corps: Past and Present,* Army Logistician, 1987.

James P. Finley, *The US Military Experience in Korea* 1871-1982, HQ USFK/ EUSA, 1983.

US Navy, *History of United States Naval Operations — Korea*, 1971.

Montross and Canzona, *Inch'on-Seoul Operation* (1950-1953), 1955.

Billy C. Mossman, *Ebb and Flow*: November 1950-July 1951, Center of Military History U.S. Army, Washington, D.C., 1990.

James F. Schnabel, Robert J. Watson, *The History of the Joint Chiefs of Staff, vol* III, *The Korean War,* Joint Chiefs of Staff, 1978.

Song Yong Bok, *The NKPA's Invasion into the South and Its Debacle*, The Japan Journal of Korea Review Co., 1979.

Japanese Science Academy of Historical Researches, *The Choson People's History of Justice War for the Fatherland Liberation*, vol. 1, 1961.

Morita Yoshio, *Records of the Korean War*, Annando Publishers, 1964.

Ground Battle Research and Distribution Society of Japan, *The Korean War*, vols. 1-10, Harashiobo Printing Co., Shiowa 41.

Sasaki Harataka, *The Korean War: South Korea*, vols. I, II & III, Harashiobo Printing Co., Shiowa 51.

Editorial Staff (Korean Version)

Editor in Chief   Chae Han Kook   Chief Researcher
Editor   Chung Suk Kyun   Senior Researcher
Editor   Yang Yong Cho   Junior Researcher

Translated into English by

Professor, Korea Military Academy   Yang Hee Wan
Professor, Korea Military Academy   Lim Won Hyok

Revised by

US Army Colonel(ret.) Thomas Lee Sims
Former Chief Researcher   Kim Chong Ku
Chief Researcher   Chae Han Kook